D0026306

PHILOSOPHY
Theory
and Practice

JACQUES P. THIROUX
BAKERSFIELD COLLEGE

PHILOSOPHY
Theory and Practice

MACMILLAN PUBLISHING COMPANY
NEW YORK

Collier Macmillan Publishers
LONDON

Copyright © 1985, Macmillan Publishing Company, a division of Macmillan, Inc.

Printed in the United States of America

All rights reserved. No part of this book may be reproduced or transmitted in any form or by any means, electronic or mechanical, including photocopying, recording, or any information storage and retrieval system, without permission in writing from the Publisher.

Macmillan Publishing Company
866 Third Avenue, New York, New York 10022

Collier Macmillan Canada, Inc.

Library of Congress Cataloging in Publication Data

Thiroux, Jacques P.
  Philosophy : theory and practice.

  Bibliography: p.
  Includes index.
  1. Philosophy. 2. Religion. 3. Religions. I. Title.
BD21.T46 1985   100   83-20302
ISBN 0-02-419910-9

Printing: 1 2 3 4 5 6 7 8   Year: 5 6 7 8 9 0 1 2 3

ISBN   0-02-419910-9

This book is dedicated to all my children and grandchildren:
to my sons, Paul, Stephen, Mark, and Jason;
to my daughters, Julie and Abigale;
to my granddaughter, Isabel;
and to my grandson, Edward;
and especially to the memory of my granddaughter, Danielle.

Preface

This book is intended to combine philosophical theory and applications of it to students' everyday lives. For this reason, at the end of every chapter, with two exceptions, there are "Situations" that will encourage students to apply their philosophy to their relationships with others, to school, or to work. The two exceptions are Chapter 8, which has ethical cases scattered throughout the text, and the last chapter, which has a personal philosophy paper assignment. In addition, there are "Additional Questions and Activities for Study and Discussion" sections at the end of each chapter except the last.

Chapter 2, "Learning How to Philosophize," is relatively different from most introduction to philosophy texts in that it suggests how to read and write philosophy and take tests in it at the original source, secondary source, or personal view levels. This is in addition to discussing briefly what logical reasoning entails and how to spot and avoid the more common logical fallacies.

I have tried also to expand on what I feel are the more interesting and applicable areas of philosophy to students. There are three chapters on the nature of a human being; three on ethics; four on philosophy of religion, including brief, but fairly intense surveys on Western and Eastern religions and also nonreligious views; and three on knowledge, truth, belief, and perception.

I have included a final short chapter that encourages students to start establishing their own personal philosophy and world view and have given them detailed instructions on how to do this in a systematic and organized way. Most introduction texts have no such chapter.

I intend this book to be as flexible as possible for use by both the instructor and the student. Except for the first two chapters, which should be taught first and then used for reference when covering the various other areas, each part is fairly self-contained so that any one part could be taught before or after the others without too much difficulty. I do, however, liberally refer to other parts of the book (especially Part I) when dealing with any chapter so that students can see relationships, for example, between the existence of an Ultimate Reality (philosophy of religion) and how we can know this (epistemology).

I wish to thank the many students I have taught for helping me to solidify and organize the ideas and approaches to teaching philosophy in this book; also Lynne Radeleff, for doing most of the typing under lots of pressure, and everyone around me who had to put up with my labor pains while I was writing it.

J. P. T.

Contents

CHAPTER 8

PART 4

Philosophy of Religion

CHAPTER 9

CHAPTER 10

CHAPTER 11

CHAPTER 12

Contents

PART 1

Introduction:
What Philosophy Is
and How to Do It

CHAPTER 1

What Philosophy Is and Does

Philosophy Is Abstract and Theoretical— Some Misconceptions

What is philosophy? Most people, if they have heard about philosophy at all, either get it confused with psychology or think of it as a highly abstract and theoretical activity practiced by a few college or university professors who have a lot of idle time and, of course, have nothing better to do. This view is characterized by the views of two contemporary comedians: Robin Williams, who made a record album entitled, "Reality—What a Concept!," and Bill Cosby, who described philosophers as people who go around asking such questions as, "Why is there air?" Cosby goes on to say that every physical education major knows why there is air—to blow up volley balls, basketballs, and footballs. A third comedian, Steve Martin, whose comedy routines are based on the absurdities of life, says he got most of his ideas from studying existentialism, a twentieth-century philosophy that states, among other things, that reality is absurd and has no meaning unless human beings give it meaning.

SOME FURTHER MISCONCEPTIONS

If people have heard anything about philosophy or philosophers at all, they generally feel that

1. Philosophers are human beings who isolate themselves on mountain tops or in "ivory towers" and deign not to mingle with real people or the real world.

2. Philosophy is something one can do only if one is idle and highly intellectual.
3. Being philosophical means that one never gets excited or involved but always remains cool and detached, never complaining about setbacks or tragedies in life.
4. Philosophy is not a part of "real" life, and what philosophers used to do has largely been taken over by other fields, such as the physical and natural sciences, the social sciences, and mathematics.

Before specifically attempting to dispel some of these misconceptions, it would be beneficial to look at some historical background to reveal how, when, and where philosophy got started.

HISTORICAL BACKGROUND: HOW DID PHILOSOPHY BEGIN?

ART AND RELIGION. Formal and systematic philosophy did not come first in history because its greatest tools are oral and written language, and the origin of language is lost somewhere back in the mists of early time. What seem to have emerged first, however, are art—painting, sculpture, music—and religious practices, usually intertwined and intermixed. What have been found earliest, through archeology and other sciences, are things like cave paintings, sculptures of gods and goddesses, and ritualistic burial sites and graves. These, of course, were not evidences of early philosophy in any systematic sense, but they do indicate that human beings were attempting to cope with questions of life, survival, and death, as well as trying to understand their environment and what lay behind it.

THE GREAT ORAL TRADITIONS. Most ancient cultures evolved from great oral traditions. While written documents or books were not available until quite late in history, there is abundant evidence that the Egyptian, Greek, and Hebrew cultures flourished long before anything much was written down. It's hard to know how these traditions were passed on from generation to generation, but there is some evidence, given how the written down parts of these traditions (for example, *The Iliad, The Odyssey,* the Old Testament of the Bible) are composed, that they were maintained in stories, myths, legends, and fables that could be easily transmitted at ceremonies and gatherings by word of mouth. They could also be acted out in pageants, rituals, and, later, in dramas.[1] Even though these works did not systematically philosophize, they did attempt to answer human questions about the nature of the world and human beings, to prescribe codes of behavior and conduct, and to teach the customs and mores of a particular group of people.

For example, if the *Iliad* and *Odyssey* are studied carefully, one can find an untold number of references on how to treat strangers hospitably and what constituted the important values and proper conduct of the Greeks of the time. There are also references to gods and goddesses that were attempts to explain various events in nature. For instance, Achilles' great strength and bravery—greater than most men of the time—was explained by saying that Achilles was actually half divine and half human, the product of a "mixed marriage" between divine and human persons. So it can be seen that even before formal philosophy as such, human beings were philosophizing, that is, asking questions about themselves and the world around them and seeking and proposing answers to those questions.

THE BEGINNINGS OF PHILOSOPHY—THE PRE-SOCRATICS.   Formal philosophy is thought to have begun with Thales in the late sixth century B.C., and it is quite interesting to note that the early philosophers up to Socrates were really rudimentary scientists, for they were concerned with the world around them and with nature, and they put forth theories concerning the building blocks of the world and themselves. Some of them thought that one or more of the four elements—air, earth, fire, water—were the basic building blocks; others thought that there were special unseen "substances" that provided the basis for everything in "reality." For example, Democritus, who was actually later than the pre-Socratics, was an atomist; that is, he believed that reality was composed of atoms (from the Greek *atomon,* meaning "indivisible")—small unseen but indivisible units that were in constant motion—and the space or void in which they could move. To think that merely from observing the world around them and reasoning from their observations without the benefit of any technology whatsoever that philosophers could come up with theories that are still valid today is astounding. Many people, I'm sure, feel that the atomic theory began with the great physicists and mathematicians of the twentieth century, but, as one can see, it began with the early philosophers of Greece.

THE TURNING POINT—SOCRATES AND PLATO.   A great turning point in philosophy's development came with the advent of Socrates (470–399 B.C.) and his most famous pupil, Plato (428 or 427 to 348 or 347 B.C.). Socrates, who never wrote anything, so far as anyone knows, emphasized the inner life of the human being rather than the external world around him. His greatest concern was not with what the building blocks of nature were, but what constituted truth, beauty, justice, and goodness. In other words, he was concerned with a human being's awareness of himself, his life, his values, and his reasoning and attainment of wisdom, not with those things outside of him. Plato, who wrote many dialogues, using his teacher as the major character, dealt with ethics, politics, psychology, sociology, mathematics, and science (to some extent). With Plato, actually, the first great philosophical system or complete world view was presented. In his famous *Republic,* Plato not only attempted to show how the individual human being should develop himself or herself, but also he attempted to show how to set up the perfect social and political society through reasoning. To do this, he presented a view of an ultimate reality beyond the natural world, integrated it with human psychology and sociology, and put forth a world view in which the individual and society were connected so intimately that society, to Plato, was merely the "individual writ large."[2] Even as the individual, to Plato, should be controlled and governed by his reasoning mind, so society should be governed by its "mind," the philosopher-king or wise ruler.

ARISTOTLE—THE SYNTHESIS.   Aristotle (384–322 B.C.), Plato's star pupil, followed in his teacher's footsteps, but also brought a concern for the external world and nature back into the picture, blending it with the philosophy that dealt with the nature of a human being. As a matter of fact, Aristotle was history's first great marine biologist and research scientist. He also was concerned with creating a complete world view—writing of nature, the supernatural, and poetics (the meaning of literature) as well as ethics and politics—again emphasizing the philosophical concern with developing the "perfect" or "ideal" human being who would "reason well for a complete life."[3]

Therefore, as we look at the earliest history of philosophy and philosophers, we find that although these men thought deeply and abstractly, they also applied their thoughts to real life and real-life situations, thereby blending the theoretical and abstract with the practical and the applicable. This trend does not stop with the Greeks, but continues down through the ages to the present. For example, Marcus Aurelius (121–180 A.D.) was a Roman emperor and statesman in addition to being an important Stoic philosopher; Thomas Aquinas (1225–1274) was a priest, teacher, writer, and theologian; René Descartes (1596–1650) was a mathematician, music theorist, and optician; John Locke (1632–1704) was involved with chemistry, physics, and eventually became a physician; David Hume (1711–1776) was an historian, librarian, and politician; and Bertrand Russell (1872–1970) and Alfred North Whitehead (1861–1947) were mathematicians.

It should be obvious, then, that philosophy is not out of the mainstream of life at all or reserved for rich, idle intellectuals, but rather the activity of vital, active men and women who are involved in life to the fullest. Therefore, I propose at the outset that philosophy and philosophizing are not merely abstract and unrelated to life but, at their best, are a significant and meaningful blend of both theoretical reasoning and its application to life, which is why I have entitled this book *Philosophy: Theory and Practice.* I hope to prove this assumption as I continue this chapter and also as I approach specific issues and problems in each of the following chapters.

What Philosophy Is—Speculation and Analysis

SPECULATION

Philosophy begins in wonderment, in curiosity, in questioning—everything—and in speculating about answers to these questions. The word *speculation,* when used philosophically, means to consider a subject or an idea and to contemplate it profoundly. I suspect that this particular aspect of philosophy is the main reason that most people are attracted to philosophy or become philosophers in the first place. Since human beings are often curious—asking the what, why, how, where, and when questions—speculation is the most exciting and "fun" part of philosophy. One gets to ask all those "great questions" about the universe and oneself and to speculate about the answers.

In addition, at least part of the nature of some human beings has been the desire to transcend (to go beyond, to exceed) themselves and even their world. That is, even though human beings may function from day to day without concerning themselves with the underlying nature of the universe, religious questions, and other abstract concerns, they often have a desire to "stretch" themselves and their thoughts beyond everyday existence—they want to question and they want answers whenever they can get them. Anyone can speculate and everyone probably does from time to time. This is the easiest part of philosophy because all one needs is some imagination and the desire to raise questions about anything; however, there is a knack to selecting significant and meaningful questions, as we shall see later.

This part of philosophy is imaginative and creative, and we can just let our minds wander freely in thinking about everything, sort of brainstorming with ourselves or others about our speculations. This is the easier part of philosophizing, and, as I have stated, almost anyone can do it; however, often the difference between a superficial "dime-store" philosopher and the more serious and systematic philosopher is another aspect of philosophy called *analysis.*

ANALYSIS

Most philosophers are not content merely to wonder or speculate about things but feel that they must also subject their imaginings, wonderings, and speculations to rigorous analysis. It is not enough to ask questions about the universe and speculate about the answers; philosophers must also ask questions *about* their questions and about their answers, subjecting them to a process of analysis through logical reasoning. This is probably the major difference between just anyone's philosophizing and that of a more serious philosopher; the former is content to speculate about the universe and perhaps hold a belief that is untested, whereas the latter is not. For example, even though Socrates was perhaps one of the greatest speculative philosophers of all time, he was never merely content to hold a belief unquestioningly or without testing it through rigorous analysis. Again and again in Plato's dialogues, Socrates forces students and other would-be philosophers to question such easy and unquestioned beliefs as "justice" means "doing good to your friends and bad to your enemies" or that it means "might makes right" by forcing them to analyze carefully what such beliefs really mean and entail.[4]

Analysis involves taking a question, answer, belief, or theory and subjecting it to careful scrutiny, breaking it down into its parts, using would-be philosophers to question such easy and unquestioned beliefs as "justice" means "doing good to your friends and bad to your enemies" or that it means "might makes right" by forcing them to analyze carefully what such beliefs really mean and entail.[4]

Analysis involves taking a question, answer, belief, or theory and subjecting it to careful scrutiny, breaking it down into its parts, using physical evidence wherever it is available and also applying a rigorous form of reasoning, called *logic*. For example, many religious people hold the belief that if human beings do not believe in a supernatural being or follow one religion or another, there can be no meaning in their lives. They believe this no doubt because they feel that their lives were less meaningful before they became religious than after. There may be a difficulty, of course, in defining the word "meaningful" when used in this context, but even if we use the term broadly, we will find that these people are guilty of generalizing their own particular feelings about religion into "how everyone else must feel." An examination of the lives of various nonreligious people will probably reveal no more "meaning" or lack of it than will an examination of those who are religious. At the very least, such an examination will reveal one must be careful anytime he applies a particular assumption to *all* human beings. The real point is, however, that one should not hold such a belief without first examining evidence to support or refute it and without subjecting it to careful logical reasoning and analysis.

SPECULATION AND ANALYSIS—A SYNTHESIS

It seems obvious, then, that philosophy at its best and fullest is comprised of both speculation and analysis. People need to allow their minds to consider anything and everything without being hampered by strictures of any kind—they need a free flow of ideas and a full play of the imagination about anything they want to consider. They must, however, subject any conclusions, beliefs, or speculations they may end up with to whatever evidence supports their speculations and to a careful analysis through logic and reasoning. Specifics about how to philosophize, that is, how to speculate and analyze will be presented in some detail in Chapter 2.

What Does Philosophy Emphasize?

So far we have discussed the fact that philosophy begins in wonderment and speculation and ends in analysis; that it is abstract and theoretical and yet can be practical and applicable; and that it began in early Greece and involves questioning about the nature of the world and human beings. The word *philosophy* comes from two Greek words: *philein,* meaning "love of" or "friendship for," and *sophia,* meaning "wisdom." Therefore, the common understanding of the activity of philosophy is that it is a "love of wisdom" or a love of truth. Some have described philosophy as a "search for *the* Truth" as if there were one great and unalterable "Truth" that, once known, would provide answers to all the questions in our lives. I prefer to think of philosophy as a search for truths wherever we can find them about those things in life that have some importance to us.

I think that we also ought to see the distinction between "knowledge" and "wisdom." We can know many things, but we cannot always be wise; that is, we can know how to develop atomic power, but do we know how or when to use or not use it? The knowledge about atomic energy does not *necessarily* include the wisdom of how to use it. Wisdom requires more than just knowledge. Perhaps that is why philosophy is more properly called "the love of wisdom" rather than "the love of knowledge" because philosophy involves more than just gaining knowledge for its own sake; it also involves understanding the implications of that knowledge and its uses for oneself and others with some purpose of value in mind. Maybe this is the reason there always seems to be some urgency to the philosopher's questioning and why Socrates expanded on the *philein* aspect of philosophy to call himself an *erastos,* a lover in a passionate, almost erotic sense. That is, he believed that the philosopher should search for truths and wisdom in an intense, almost passionate, way, as if his life depended on it, and according to Socrates, it really does, as characterized in his most famous statement, "The unexamined life is not worth living." Philosophy, then, to Socrates and the philosophers before and after him, is serious business, in fact, perhaps the most serious of all of humanity's endeavors. After all, what can be more important to human beings than knowing as much as they can about themselves and their world and then being able to use that knowledge wisely enough to live a life "worth living"?

AREAS OF STUDY IN PHILOSOPHY

What does philosophy study? What does it emphasize? On what does it concentrate? Traditionally, there are three major areas of emphasis from which all other concerns branch out: metaphysics (the study of reality and what is real), ethics (the study of morality), and epistemology (the study of knowledge).

METAPHYSICS.   The word *physics* in Greek means "nature," and the word *meta* means "beyond." So literally, *metaphysics* means "beyond nature." But even though the area of philosophy called metaphysics deals with anything that may or may not exist, it is not merely a concern with what is "beyond nature"—the occult, supernatural, or ghostly. As a matter of fact, the term came about somewhat by accident. In Aristotle's lecture notes, the section on metaphysics was called so merely because it followed (was after or "beyond") the section on physics.[5] Metaphysics *can* certainly be concerned with the supernatural, whether it exists or not, and what it is like, but it is also concerned with *anything* that is real or that exists and its nature. For example, it concerns itself with the nature of physical objects and asks questions about whether or not there are also mental "objects" (thoughts, ideas, imaginings). Questions about whether there is or isn't a supernatural existence, or a soul, or a human mind, or a self are also a part of metaphysics. Notice that these questions are not narrow and specific as in biology, which might ask what is the nature of a plant or animal cell, or physics, which might ask what is the nature of atoms or molecules, but rather general and more all encompassing such as, What kinds of objects exist in reality (for example, physical and mental)? What are their natures? And how do they relate to one another, if at all? Questions other than these that are asked in this kind of study are, Is there really cause and effect in reality, or are they really only mental constructions of human beings? If there is causation, then what is its nature and how does it work? What is the nature of a human being—body, mind, emotions, self, soul, animal, a combination, or what? Is there really any such thing as freedom, or is everything predetermined? Is the physical world really out there the way we perceive it, or is it quite different from what we perceive? Is reality really separate from us, or do we create reality with our brains or minds? You might say that metaphysics is concerned with "things" (any "things"), their existence and their nature.

ETHICS.   From philosophy's earliest beginnings and especially with Socrates and after, ethics, or the study of morality, has been a major concern. In Plato's great scheme for a society, *The Republic,* the whole point of knowledge was to arrive at "knowledge of the Good," and Aristotole, even though he was interested in the sciences, metaphysics, and knowledge, created one of the most elegant systems of ethics in history and was definitely concerned with how human beings could be good and act rightly. Most philosophers, no matter what their special interests or emphases in philosophy might be, are and have always been concerned with human behavior and conduct and the difference between right and wrong and good and bad. I could have been more general here and said that it's really *axiology* (the study of values) that is the third philosophic emphasis, but I believe that the part of axiology called ethics, dealing with the moral behavior and conduct of human beings, is the major area of concern along with metaphysics and epistemology. Ethics is often a difficult area to work with because it does not deal solely with factual judgments, such as that truth and falsity apply to propositions or there are both physical and mental objects in reality. It deals, rather, with value judgments, such as human beings *should* not harm other human beings, or Socrates was a moral man. To come to conclusions is often difficult in ethics, and yet it is this area, more than any other in philosophy, that often characterizes the difference between knowledge and wisdom.

For example, we obviously have the knowledge to create and use advanced technology so powerful that we can destroy the world and ourselves, but whether we *should* use it and when or where we *ought* to use it for the "good" of humanity are ethical, not factual, questions, and they involve more than just gaining knowledge for its own sake. Some ethical questions are, What constitutes any person or action being good, bad, right, or wrong, and how do we know? What part do self-interest, or the interests of others, play in making moral decisions and judgments? What theories of conduct are valid or invalid and why? Should we use principles or rules or laws, or should we let each situation decide our morality? Are killing, lying, cheating, stealing, and sexual acts right or wrong? Difficult to work with or not, what is more important to human beings than learning how to have meaning and value in their lives and how to relate to each other in creative and good, rather than destructive and bad ways? Ethics, then, is not concerned with "things," as in metaphysics, but rather with values and value judgments concerning human conduct and behavior.

EPISTEMOLOGY.   Since it is quite obvious that philosophy is concerned with a search for knowledge, truths, and wisdom, then the whole area of thinking and knowledge has to be one of its major concerns. Philosophers must know what the limits of human knowledge are and what knowledge is, and they must be aware of the sources of human knowledge and their reliability. Logic, which is considered by many philosophers to be an entirely separate area of study, I feel, is a part or branch of epistemology. It provides the tools and the methods by which we gain knowledge and truth and, therefore, is closely related to and indeed a part of the study of knowledge. Perception is another area of epistemology that is important, for much of our knowledge is based on what we perceive through our five senses (seeing, hearing, touching, tasting, and feeling). One can see, therefore, that the aforementioned metaphysical question concerning the nature of the physical world and our perception of it must also be considered, at least in part, an epistemological question. Other epistemological questions are: What are truth and falsity and to what do they apply? What is knowledge and what is required for one to *know* something? What is the nature of perception and how reliable is it? How do we know when we are being logical or illogical and when our reasoning is sound or faulty? And what is the difference and relationship between truth and belief? In other words, epistemology is concerned with thinking and its processes and sources, not with things or values.

OTHER PHILOSOPHICAL CONCERNS.   These three areas, then, constitute the major areas of emphasis for philosophy, but philosophy can also be applied to almost any other area of the sciences or arts. For example, a second part of axiology is aesthetics or the study of beauty, ugliness, and the arts and what they mean (painting, sculpture, music, literature, and so forth). There can also be courses in the philosophy of religion, law, science, social science, and mathematics that study *about* these fields, not in them. It is possible, as evidenced by the course catalogues of most four-year colleges and universities, to develop a philosophy course on almost any specialized area of human interest: economics, government, sociology, engineering, medicine, and even veterinary medicine.[6] Philosophy, then, being broad in scope and general and fundamental in approach, can be successfully applied to any area of interest and will yield a good deal in the way of discovering what lies behind such specialized areas and fields as those just listed. For example, have you ever stopped to think that the type of government employed by nations and their leaders or people is often determined by a particular view of the nature of human beings? For instance, if one's philosophy of human nature is that it is basically good, then government may be less restrictive and controlling. On the other hand, if human nature is considered to be basically bad or brutish, then a more restrictive government may be used to control and "civilize" human beings. Therefore, one can ask about almost any human activity or study, "What assumptions or ideas or beliefs lie behind this (science, law, or politics, for example), and what effect do these assumptions have on how these activities or studies are carried out?"

Views of Philosophy

There are also various views of what philosophy is and does, all of which contribute something to the understanding of its meaning.

ONE'S PHILOSOPHY OF LIFE

Questions such as, "What is your philosophy of life?" "Do you believe in God or not?" "What do you think is or are the most important thing or things in life?" and "Do you think we're doing the right thing about. . . . ?" all deal with a "philosophy of life," which usually means a set of beliefs that someone has acquired or developed. This view of philosophy implies that it is important to know "where you stand" on certain matters or issues. Unfortunately, these beliefs or stands are often held uncritically, without having been tested either by evidence or logic; however, this view also implies the personal involvement aspect of philosophy, which states that people should really have some beliefs and not just function in life as if they did not.

Another aspect of this view, which involves a misconception about philosophy and philosophers, is that of "being philosophical." Many believe that "being philosophical" means that one takes life as it comes, cooly and calmly, without ever getting excited, angry, or intense about anything. I once had an administrator express surprise that I had gotten visibly (and vocally) upset at a certain situation over which I had expressed displeasure intensely and forcefully. He looked at me and said, "I thought philosophers were supposed to sit back quietly, stroke their beards, and not get angry and excited." Philosophers are certainly contemplative and meditative at times, but inactivity is not a very common aspect of philosophy as characterized by Socrates dubbing himself an *erastos,* as I described earlier. Socrates was himself in the center of controversy in Athens where he was brought to trial for "corrupting" the youth by teaching them to question everything. And

Bertrand Russell was hardly inactive when, in the 1960s, he was in the forefront of protests in London against the war and nuclear weapons; in fact, he was jailed several times for his activities.

PHILOSOPHY AS A DISCUSSION OF PROBLEMS AND ISSUES

Philosophy can also be understood as a discussion of various problems and issues. Such questions as, "What is the nature of a human being?" "What is a physical object?" "Is there a purpose for the universe and human beings?" "Is there a God and an afterlife?" "How should people behave or act toward one another?" "How can one tell truth from falsity?" are all questions that lead to general and specific discussions in philosophy in the areas of metaphysics, ethics, and epistemology. In fact the approach used in this book will be, in Chapters 3 and beyond, what might be called a problems and issues approach. That is, we will not proceed historically through philosophy but rather will take up specific problems and issues that affect every human being at one time or another and in one sense or another. In this way, we can first discover what our basic problems are and then probe and question the assumptions that lie behind them. Then we can try to come to some conclusions about them by applying our experience and reasoning, thereby using philosophy to deal with serious and fundamental issues that affect us and our world.

PHILOSOPHY AS ANALYTICAL AND CRITICAL

As stated earlier in the discussion about philosophy as being both speculative and analytical, philosophy can be seen to be questioning, analytical, critical, and evaluative. This means that, ideally, the philosopher questions everything—every belief, statement, theory, hypothesis—presented to him or her, without exception, and analyzes and evaluates what is questioned as critically and fully as possible. This view places the emphasis on inquiry and analysis rather than on the formation of personal philosophy or developing ethical systems or world views. In fact, during the early part of the twentieth century, a major group of philosophers decided that this should be *the* major thrust of philosophy and stressed logic and analysis, attempting to eliminate such other philosophic concerns as aesthetics, ethics, and metaphysics from the realm of philosophy. Their feeling was that the sciences—natural, physical, and social—had taken over subject areas that were formerly a concern of philosophers and that the philosopher's job was now to question the findings, theories, language, and reasoning in these fields through logic and analysis. In other words, philosophers' new and complete tasks were to be as logicians and analysts, dealing with the language and logic used by various scientists, religionists, and artists as well as those used by "ordinary" people, but not concerning themselves with the content, as such, of any field.

PHILOSOPHY AS INTEGRATIVE

A view of philosophy harking back to the original emphasis on speculation is that of philosophy as an integrative activity or one that provides a synthesis of various elements or parts into a combined, coherent whole, as opposed to analysis, which means a breaking down or separating of something into its various parts. Many philosophers' systems of thought were "synthetic," that is, meant to be world views composed of smaller, coherent parts. For example, Plato, Aristotle, Kant, and Descartes, among others, attempted to establish a coherent view of human beings in the world, which included epistemology, metaphysics, ethics, aesthetics, politics, science, and many other areas. In a more practical sense, perhaps, one can see philosophy as an activity that, by the nature of its broad and generalized approach, can help human beings and societies integrate their science, economics, politics, religion, and psychology, so that clear relationships, where they exist, are noted and recognized, enabling human beings to live more meaningfully and vitally and in a more unified manner, rather than fragmented and unrelated and isolated from one another and even from themselves. Since philosophy is not *of* any of these areas but can be *about* any or all of them, it can provide the perfect means of developing a unified world view, connecting all the aspects of human beings, nature, and any supernature together.

AN EVALUATION OF THESE VIEWS

The "one's philosophy of life" view emphasizes the personal involvement that is important to philosophy because philosophy should be personal and should involve people in important life questons. It is significant also because it stresses the intensity of that involvement, suggesting that philosophic concerns are indeed important concerns and that human beings should take them seriously. The drawback of this view, if carried too far, is that it can stress the emotional aspect of one's beliefs and allow them to go untested or unqestioned, which may cause them to be false or unreliable.

The "philosophy as a study of life problems and issues" view is also important because it applies philosophy to specific situations and problems affecting human beings and takes philosophy out of the strictly theoretical and abstract realms of wondering and speculating. However, one of its drawbacks can also be that without analysis, one can become too subjectively involved with these problems and avoid stepping back and objectively appraising them. Further, without integration, one can make the mistake of seeing reality as a series of fragmented and unrelated problems and issues rather than as an interrelated, interconnected whole.

The "philosophy as critical and analytical" view, of course, provides the antidote to oversubjectivizing philosophy in that it requires philosophers to examine and analyze their philosophies of life and life issues and problems carefully and critically, guarding against strictly emotional interpretations and applying logic, reasoning, and evidence to question, clarify, support or reject conclusions arrived at through speculation and wondering. Its drawback is that it can become so calculating, detached, and objective that life issues and problems may become mechanical, theoretical, and abstract and lose their vibrancy and personal relevance.

The "philosophy as integrative" view is important because it tries to be all encompassing, tends to try to develop the total human being, not just the fragmented specialist, and tends to unite all aspects of life and the world into a unified whole. Its drawback is that in striving for this all-encompassing unity, one may try to fit things together that do not fit, that is, to integrate by force those aspects of life that will not integrate. Also when one has established a "world view," anything that does not fit into it may tend to be rejected even though it may be important or true. An example of this danger occurred in Galileo's time when it was thought that the earth was the center of the universe instead of the sun. Everything in religion and society at the time was based on this assumption, and when Galileo proposed his scientifically correct theory that the sun, not the earth, was the center of the universe, his views were rejected and he was ostracized. Had the state and church leaders of the time been willing to question and analyze their world view in relation to this change in theories, they would not have continued to rest it on false assumptions.

A SYNTHESIS

It seems obvious, then, that the best approach to philosophy is to combine or "synthesize" these views wherever possible, allowing the disadvantages of one to be corrected by the advantages of another. The best approach to philosophy and philosophizing, then, would be to personalize philosophizing as much as possible yet temper it with careful questioning, analysis, and evaluation—to involve oneself intensely in one's philosophizing but also to remain objective and detached enough to be willing to correct wrong assumptions without becoming so detached that one's humanity is calculated right out of the picture. Further, one needs to approach problems and issues analytically and rationally, tearing them apart and seeing how each part works, but one also needs to put the parts back together and to see their relationship to the whole. For example, any investigation of the relationship of brain, mind, and body would be interesting in itself, but it would seem that the questions, "What does this mean to me and humanity as a whole?" and "How does what I've learned here apply to society or culture and its view of humanity in the areas of science, the social sciences and religion?" would be extremely important in making philosophy more purposeful and applicable. In my opinion, then, philosophy at its best is personal and intense; questioning, critical, and logical; and at the same time analytic and synthetic.

Is Philosophy Practical or Impractical, Useful or Useless, Applicable or Inapplicable?

WHY DO WE NEED PHILOSOPHY?

Probably the most common criticism of philosophy is that it is impractical, useless, or inapplicable to everyday living and that we can certainly do without it; in fact, we can do *better* without it. Who needs philosophy to function in a job, raise a family, earn a living, or enjoy leisure time? Aren't there other fields, such as the sciences and religion, to help us here? Also, doesn't philosophy ask rather vague questions for which there are really quite simple and functional answers attained without all the probing and questioning that philosophers seem to think is necessary?

For example, in answer to the question, "What is knowledge?" isn't the answer quite simply that it is the information I've gained from experience and stored in my brain? As for the question, "What is reality?" isn't the answer that reality is merely what I perceive it to be through my five senses? Furthermore, who cares if the universe has a purpose? It is just there, it works, and I exist in it—is there anything else I need to know? As for human purpose, societies and individuals can decide this—for example, if I want to be an engineer, then my purpose in life is to build bridges, aqueducts, or roads. The point is, Who needs to bother asking a lot of questions about such abstract things? What good does it do? What purpose does it serve? I can live until I die without all that impractical and useless questioning and wondering, can't I?

It is quite true that people can get by, living their lives from day to day, without philosophizing at all or at least doing it very little, but if you examine this assumption, don't you find out (heaven forbid!) that it rests on a philosophical assumption concerning human purpose and capability, a value system that states what is or is not important in human life—in short, is this not, too, a philosophy of life and subject to the same "philosophical" questioning as any other? The first question one who holds this viewpoint needs to ask is, "Is all human life merely centered in functioning, producing, and consuming, or are there other considerations, such as being moral, having deep human feelings, and having rights and obligations, that transcend functioning?" Besides, even just plain "functioning" (if there really is anything as simple as this) in a world as complex and pluralistic as ours cannot be done so well if one just goes from day to day without any plan. Doesn't one need some system or "philosophy" with which to approach or deal with the confusions and difficulties of daily living?

For example, if you're a customer in a store and someone gives you too much change back, shouldn't you have some value system established that tells you what you should do, or should you decide each situation as it occurs? Wouldn't this moment-to-moment decision making based on whim be at best inconsistent and at worst chaotic? Also, if people do not question themselves and others and various beliefs and theories, then how can they know where they are or where they are going or what they are doing? How can people make the best decisions in their lives about anything if they have no clear basis for them because they have not questioned but merely acted? Further, living life daily is difficult enough, but the unexpected often happens, and if we merely function from day to day without a system or plan, then how can we cope with what we haven't planned for? For example, if a young woman has built her daily living around being a wife to her husband and a mother to her children, what happens to her if any these people die? What value system or approach to or plan for life will help her to continue living meaningfully despite the awful tragedy that has struck her?

In Arthur Miller's play, *Death of a Salesman,* the main character, Willy Loman, goes through his entire life thinking that all there is to life is selling, telling jokes, and putting up a phony for-he's-a-jolly-good-fellow front for buyers and other salespersons. When he comes into his sixties, his whole life crumbles about him when he discovers he has had the wrong value system all his life and that there is more to life than what he has always thought. At least part of his problem is that he "bought" without questioning a philosophy of life that had never really suited him, that had never really related well to his innermost thoughts, desires, or feelings. It is true that this is a play and that it takes place on the stage, but how many people have come to the ends of their lives or entered their retirement years and suddenly realized that they have not really done what they wanted to do or lived the way they really wanted to live? If people have systematic plans for their lives that encompass an understanding of themselves and human beings in general, the world around them, society and its institutions, and a value system from which to make decisions about what's right or wrong or good or bad in their lives and in their actions, then it would seem that they have at least a better chance not to end up like Willy Loman. People's lives may still not end up exactly as they wanted them to, but at least they will have tried and, I feel, will have succeeded more than if they had not questioned or planned at all.

WHAT CAN PHILOSOPHY DO FOR HUMAN BEINGS?

PHILOSOPHY CAN MAKE PEOPLE THINK AND BE MORE AWARE. Whatever else philosophers agree or disagree about, all philosophers believe that human beings should question—everything. Nothing—not even the very basis for philosophy itself, one's strongest and most long-held beliefs, or one's most cherished feelings or opinions—is exempt from this questioning. No unquestioned belief or theory is worth holding, and it's risky to do so—that's one of the major tenets of most philosophers. If people question and think about every idea, feeling, or theory they come into contact with, how can they help but become more aware of themselves, others, and the world around them? Students have often told me, "I never thought of that" or "I have never thought about that in such detail or depth." In becoming more thoughtful and aware, people can grow more, enlarging their spheres of observation and contemplation and learning how to think and act more creatively.

For example, for people who have been brought up narrowly in one religion, studying philosophy can enlarge their views and attitudes about religion in general by learning what problems there are in arguing for or proving any religion, by discovering that other religions are also held with great intensity by their followers, and by seeing that there's more to religion than worshipping. This will give them a chance to break out of their narrowness without necessarily having to give up their religious beliefs and to understand and be aware of the implications of holding or not holding a religious belief. They will also discover the impact of their beliefs on science, history, and philosophy, and vice versa. In other words, they will gain a deeper understanding of their religious beliefs in light of their philosophical studies.

IT CAN HELP PEOPLE BECOME MORE TOLERANT. In enlarging their points of view and learning to question every theory and belief, including and especially their own, people, it is hoped, will become more aware of the difficulties with and complexities of dealing with life's problems. They may also gain a greater respect for and tolerance of other people's methods of doing so, as well as for the beliefs and theories on which their methods rest. Most problems are so complex that sometimes one theory or belief will not give a complete answer, and therefore one will find that others' theories and beliefs have something to offer them even if they cannot embrace them wholeheartedly. For example, a woman may find it difficult to accept the Roman Catholic church's strong position against abortion, but in examining its beliefs and its theories, she may gain respect for and agree with its general concern for the preservation of all human life, especially unborn human life. It's certain that people cannot become tolerant of others if they have not questioned their own beliefs or examined beliefs that oppose theirs. It is always my hope that one of the things students will gain from studying philosophy is a greater appreciation for the complexity of human problems and a tolerance for the many ways others try and have tried to deal with and solve them.

PHILOSOPHY CAN PROVIDE SYSTEMATIC METHODS TO SOLVE PROBLEMS.   As was said earlier, anyone can speculate, wonder, ask questions, and provide some kind of answer, but true philosophers differ from just "anyone" who philosophizes because they try to be systematic in approaching and engaging in these activities. Philosophy tries to provide some ground rules and some methods for approaching these life problems and issues systematically. As I have already pointed out, philosophers, when speculating on a problem, begin to analyze the problem and break it down into its parts. They question, yes, but systematically, not just haphazardly. Philosophy teaches us how to look for fallacies in logical reasoning in any arguments, ours included, and it teaches us how to check ours and others' hypotheses and theories for lack of evidential support and for invalid arguments. In short, it attempts to teach us to think deeply and to reason logically and well. Who can deny the importance of these last two? At any rate I intend to spend a good deal of time in the next chapter elucidating the methods and means of philosophizing so that students can apply them to the following chapters.

PHILOSOPHY CAN PROVIDE CONSISTENCY IN LIFE.   If people question deeply and analyze and evaluate everything carefully, then they have a good chance to become more consistent in living their lives. Consistency that is overly rigid and inflexible, of course, would not be desirable (as a matter of fact, it is really antiphilosophical); after all, life is not itself rigid and inflexible, but vital and even, at times, spontaneous. However, philosophy attempts to avoid carelessness and chaos in human living. The purpose or end of all the questioning, analyzing, and evaluating is to strive for enough consistency so that one approaches life and its problems rationally and in an orderly fashion. If people go along from day to day merely reacting to each situation or event that confronts them without having thought through any fundamental principles that might guide them, then life can be harder to deal with than for the person who has established a workable system to deal with any problems he or she might face.

For example, if a woman has studied and analyzed the moral problem of abortion, then if and when she has an unwanted pregnancy, she will have already considered the principles behind aborting or not aborting, the evidence and logic of both sides of the question, and the ramifications of having or not having an abortion. Her decision will still be a difficult one to make, but she will have at least some significant and reasoned basis from which to make it. She won't be so completely in a quandary as the woman might be who had not given the matter some thought and had not already considered the pro's and con's of the abortion question. One thing we have all learned with each difficult experience we have had to confront is that it is easier to theorize and philosophize about such problems as abortion when they are not happening to you or members of your family, but this is all the more reason why philosophy should be applied as well as theoretical. It is not enough to talk about principles such as the value of life and individual freedom (in the case of abortion, freedom for women) and their conflicts; one must also take up the specific situations in which these principles are applied and try to resolve the conflicts within actual situations. Philosophy, then, can provide some basis or background to enable people to make decisions and live their lives with order and consistency.

PHILOSOPHY—THE MOST PRACTICAL OF SUBJECTS

It is true that speech, English composition, mathematics, and such specific skills as accounting, typing, welding, drafting, and learning how to give injections are extremely important subjects to study. It is very important to have mathematics skills for everyday use; it is also important to know how to type or do accounting if one is in business; to know how to weld and use drafting skills if one is a tradesperson or an engineer; and to know how to give injections if one is a nurse or a doctor. No one would question the importance of learning these "practical" subjects, and learning them well, depending on one's career.

What, however, could be more immediately practical to all people, regardless of vocation or profession, than to discover what and how they know anything, how to tell truth from falsity, how to distinguish between knowledge and belief, and how to know and be able to make the right moral decision in a specific situation? After all, despite our vocations or professions, aren't we all human beings first? Put another way, should we allow ourselves to become merely engineering or medical machines, or should we be human beings who are also engineers and doctors? To be fully human as doctors or engineers, we must come to grips with the whole process of being human (knowing, believing, feeling, thinking, reasoning), and this and a study of the relationship between human beings and everything else are the concerns of philosophy in all of its aspects and at all levels.

PHILOSOPHY CAN BE A RISKY BUSINESS

Before closing this introductory chapter on what philosophy is and does, it is important that to point out that even though philosophy can be very stimulating and creative, it can also be disturbing and risky. Unfortunately, most cultures—and perhaps our modern culture more than others—do not encourage speculative and analytic thinking either at all or unless it fits into a prescribed set of limits established by tradition or the power structure in that culture; therefore, if some people question and analyze everything and anything, they are likely to upset other people, institutions, and organizations, many of whom or which may mean a great deal to those who are philosophizing. When people question freely, traditions, customs, and established value systems come under close and critical scrutiny. When this happens, conflicts are bound to arise.

For example, when children have been raised at home and in their culture to accept certain values and traditions and after seriously questioning them find problems with them and even reject them, there are bound to be conflicts—it is always disturbing to have what you believe in challenged, especially by young people. Therefore, it often takes a great deal of courage for questioners and critics to "stick to their guns" or to refuse to give up questioning and acting on what their questioning reveals. One needs courage, honesty, and a great deal of tolerance to do this kind of questioning. Indeed, one must often decide whether striving for the truth and what one believes is right, based on sound reasoning, is worth pursuing in the face of upsetting or disturbing others and even being rejected by them. I can only say that many philosophers and other people who have thought deeply and become critical of their cultures have always believed that the search for truths and wisdom was worth the risk and that if one did not strive for these and what was good and right, then life indeed was "not worth living." Socrates refused to agree to stop questioning and teaching and was executed for them; Mahatma Gandhi was thrown into prison for his nonviolent protesting of colonialization and oppressive rule; Jesus of Nazareth was condemned to death for his beliefs; and Martin Luther King, Jr., the Kennedys, and many others were assassinated because they believed in certain ideals and would not give up their beliefs or the right to question the status quo of their times.

Not all these people were philosophers in the professional sense, but it is quite obvious that they had philosophized a great deal to arrive at their beliefs and value systems and that they strove hard to have them applied for what they reasoned was the good of humanity. No one can make the decision to take such risks except you, yourselves, but if you proceed with honesty, concern for others, and tolerance, then it seems to me the risk is worth taking because philosophy cannot help but enrich your lives by deepening your thinking and feeling and helping you to become more aware and more creative in living your lives.

Conclusions

Introductory chapters, especially those for philosophy, are extremely difficult to write, but I hope I have given you at least a feel for what philosophy is and does. I have tried to show you that although abstract and theoretical at times, it is also applicable, practical, and useful in a most humanly immediate sense. I have also tried to show you that from its conception it stands behind and at the beginning of many human activities and concerns—it is no accident that it has been referred to as the "queen of the sciences" and at times as the "mother" of all learning. I have attempted to indicate, further, that at its best it combines human wonder and curiosity, which have initiated all of humanity's greatest accomplishments, with analysis and careful reasoning; that it consists of the pursuit of truths and wisdom, a most noble human endeavor; that it combines personal involvement and a discussion of problems and issues with analysis and criticism, and attempts to integrate all of these into a world view; and that it attempts to make people think and be more aware, creates tolerance, provides a systematic method to solve human problems, and gives people consistency in their lives.

In the next chapter, I will go more deeply into how to philosophize or how to "do" philosophy, and in the following chapters we will take up specific problems and issues. In the meantime, however, I have set up several situations to get you to begin to think philosophically. These situations and the questions I will ask you about them should enable you to begin your own search for truths you can discover about yourself, others, and the world around you.

Applying Philosophy—
Situations for Thought and Discussion

In learning how to philosophize and in applying philosophy to specific life problems, deal with any or all of the following situations or circumstances.

SITUATION 1

Deciding One's Career. Very often we may decide on a career because it is what our parents have done before us, or because they have wanted us to become a . . . (doctor, lawyer, teacher, business man or woman), or because it pays well. To what extent are any or all of the following questions important in deciding on a career, and to what extent are they philosophical questions (as you understand the word "philosophical" now) and not really questions in and of the particular vocations or professions you are considering?

1. To what extent are any of the foregoing reasons valid for deciding on a career and why?
2. To what extent are any questions concerning your purpose in life or that of humanity in general important in making these decisions?
3. How important are the following in choosing a career and why? Comment in detail on each one:
   a. Your happiness
   b. Your parents' happiness
   c. Your spouse and children's happiness
   d. Financial security
   e. Financial luxury
   f. Fame, prestige, or power
   g. Contributing something to society
   h. Helping those in need
   i. Meaningfulness of career and job satisfaction regardless of monetary gain
   j. How will any career fit in with your life-style (for example, can you work at a job all of your life merely to enjoy yourself when not working?).

4. In choosing or in having chosen your career, to what extent did you consider all of the preceding factors? Do you feel that it is important that you should or did consider these? Why or why not?

SITUATION 2

Making a Moral Decision. You are in need of money because of excessive and unexpected bills this month. You have just purchased $2.50 worth of groceries and give the clerk a $5.00 bill. She has given you back change for a $10.00 bill. Should you give it back or keep it? In making your decision, how important are the following questions (answer each one in detail)?

1. How important is your own self-interest, the interests of the clerk and the store owner, or the interests of everyone in deciding what to do? In what priority would you place these, and why?
2. If you believe that there is a certain rule, law, or principle that you should follow in this situation (for example, never steal or cheat), then why do you believe it? To what extent do your needs in this particular situation allow for an exception?
3. To what extent does "not being caught" have something to do with your decision, and why?
4. Does it make any difference to your decision if you discover the mistake while you're at the store or in the parking lot or whether you don't discover it until you get home? Why or why not?
5. How important to your decision is the belief that most people would keep the money and think you a fool for not doing the same?
6. How important is it to your decision that a good friend whose opinion you usually trust says either "Keep the money; don't be a fool" or "It's unethical to keep the money; you must give it back"?
7. What if you were out of work and your family was barely surviving at the poverty level? Would your decision be any different?
8. List all the reasons why and how you can justify keeping the money and all the reasons why and how you can't? Extract from your reasons and justifications on both sides of the issue what your main values are in dealing with other people in matters such as these.

SITUATION 3

Questioning a Theory of Human Nature. Some scientists and social scientists theorize that human beings are merely animals who have expanded animal capabilities; their opponents suggest that humans either are completely different from animals or that they have something more to them that makes them different from animals (mind, consciousness, soul, spirit, self, and so on). How would you go about deciding how you stand on this issue, and how *do* you stand on it? Deal with the following in detail.

1. Observe as many animals as you can, using your past experiences of having observed them also. What similarities and differences do you discover when comparing them with yourself and other humans?
2. A difference that is often cited (in Western religion, basically) is that humans have a soul or spiritual being. Can you prove the existence of such an entity and further prove conclusively that animals have no such thing? How? What difficulties and problems occur as you try to prove its existence in humans or its nonexistence in animals?
3. Other differences sometimes cited are that humans have minds, not just brains, and that they have a self, which animals do not have. Some scientists and social scientists say that there is no direct or indirect evidence for the existence of either of these. Humans have only brains and bodies, just like animals, and tests with rats, pigeons, and dogs prove this. Humans react to external stimuli in the same basic fashion as animals—they are conditioned by external stimuli and their environments, and they merely react to these stimuli as animals do. Can you find any evidence for mind or self or are we just basically brain and body, like any other animal? In examining your own living processes, do you believe that you react to external stimuli as animals do? Why or why not?
4. What have you discovered in trying to define human nature even from this aspect alone (humans as merely animals)? What difficulties and problems arise in trying to define what a human being is? Do the physical, natural, and social sciences define human beings adequately, or is some other area of study and emphasis needed? Why or why not?

Chapter Summary

I. Philosophy is abstract and theoretical—some misconceptions.
   A. Misconceptions.
      1. Philosophers are isolated and in ivory towers, not in the mainstream of life at all.
      2. To be a philosopher, one has to be idle and intellectual.
      3. Philosophers never get involved, intense, or excited, but always remain cool and detached.
      4. Philosophy is not a part of real life, and what it used to be and do has now been replaced by the sciences and mathematics.
   B. Historical background.
      1. Art and religion came first, but even with these, human beings were trying to cope with life, survival, and death.
      2. The great oral traditions came next, before any evidence of written language, but human beings were still trying to philosophize through poetry, music, ritual, and pageantry.
      3. The beginnings of philosophy—the pre-Socratics. These philosophers were rudimentary scientists who tried to discover what the basic elements of all reality were.
      4. The turning point—Socrates and Plato. These two philosophers changed philosophy from outward to inward with such concerns as what the good life for human beings and society in general was.
      5. Aristotle presented a synthesis between the pre-Socratics and Plato and Socrates.
      6. Most philosophers were practical and involved as well as theoretical and abstract, and they attempted to apply and live their philosophies; therefore, philosophy has historically been of the mainstream of life, not out of it.

II. What philosophy is—speculation and analysis.
   A. Speculation. Philosophy begins in wonderment and curiosity and in questioning everything.
      1. This is the most exciting part of philosophy.
      2. It helps human beings to transcend themselves and their world.
   B. Analysis. Subjects speculation to a breaking down into parts, careful scrutiny, and the application of logical argument and reasoning.
   C. Speculation and analysis—a synthesis. Philosophy at its best is composed of both speculation and analysis.

III. What does philosophy emphasize?
   A. "Philosophy" means literally "love of wisdom."
      1. This concerns the search for truths.
      2. There is also a distinction between knowledge and wisdom.
         a. Knowledge involves gathering information and facts.
         b. Wisdom involves knowing how to use and apply that knowledge.
         c. There is an urgency about philosophizing as exemplified by Socrates calling himself an *erastos* (a lover of truth and wisdom in an almost passionate sense).
   B. Areas of study.
      1. Metaphysics. A study of "things" and existence involving reality questions—questions about what exists and its nature.
      2. Ethics. A study of values involving human behavior and conduct—value and judgment questions pertaining to human behavior, conduct, and relations.
      3. Epistemology. A study of thinking—knowledge questions which examine how and what we can know about the other two areas of philosophy.
      4. Other philosophical areas of study are
         a. Aesthetics. Value questions dealing with beauty and art.
         b. Philosophy of religion, politics, law, science, mathematics. These studies are *about* these fields not of or in them.
IV. Views of philosophy.
   A. Philosophy of life. A set of beliefs or values often untested and held uncritically.
   B. Philosophy as a discussion of problems and issues.
   C. Philosophy as analytical and critical.
   D. Philosophy as integrative.
   E. Evaluation of these views.
      1. The philosophy of life view indicates the personal quality and personal involvement so important to philosophizing but is often superficial and uncritical.
      2. Philosophy as a discussion of problems and issues is good because it involves philosophy in life problems, but it can also create too much subjectivity and fragmentation in dealing with such problems.
      3. Philosophy as analytical and critical is a good antidote for oversubjectivizing in philosophy, but it has the danger of being too detached, cool, and calculating in the process.

4. The philosophy as integrative view is good because it tries to synthesize rather than analyze (put together rather than break into parts), but its danger is that once a world view is established, one may become too rigid and inflexible and reject something that doesn't fit in but that may be important or true.

5. The best approach is to synthesize these views, trying to correct the disadvantages of one with the advantages of the other.

V. Is philosophy practical or impractical, useful or useless, applicable or inapplicable?

    A. Why is philosophy needed? Can't supposed philosophical questions be answered simply, and even if they can't, can't we live our lives without either the questions or answers—do we really need philosophy to function well?

       1. Is the glorification of functioning all there is to life, or does it also involve creativity, morality, rights and obligations, love and friendship, and meaning and purpose?

    B. What can philosophy do for human beings?

       1. It can make people think and be more aware.

          a. It encourages questioning.

          b. It breaks down narrowness.

       2. It can create tolerance.

       3. It provides systematic methods to solve human problems.

       4. Philosophy, then, is the most immediately practical activity for human beings.

    C. Philosophy can be a risky business.

       1. It is very stimulating, creative, and nonstagnating.

       2. However, it can also be upsetting and disturbing because questioning of traditional systems and values is often a threat to those who have always supported them without question.

       3. One needs courage, honesty, and tolerance to question, analyze, and evaluate, and one often needs to decide whether or not such questioning is worth the risks.

       4. It might help to know that another common ground among philosophers is that they have *always* believed that the search for truths and wisdom was worth the risk and that the unexamined life is *truly* not worth living.

Additional Questions and Activities for Study and Discussion

1. Have you ever wondered or speculated on anything important, such as the purpose of your life, the existence of God, and the meaning of death? Without limiting yourself to these questions, describe as well as you can the process of your speculations, and the conclusions you came to.

2. Spend some time observing and listening to people around you. To what extent do you feel they have a well-thought-out, workable philosophy of life? Do most people have such a basis from which to live their lives or not? Answer in detail giving examples and illustrations.

3. Ask someone or several people to present their "philosophy(ies) of life" as fully as they can (for example, your parents, brothers or sisters, close friends, your boss). Do their beliefs as presented to you belong to metaphysics, ethics, or epistemology? See if you can determine (for yourself) if they have been critical and analytical in establishing their beliefs.

4. Have you ever questioned the way in which things were done traditionally or have you felt that people were doing wrong and you were attacked or in some way punished for your questioning? Describe as fully as you can what happened, the issue you were questioning, the arguments of your "opponents," and the results of your having questioned. After the experience was over, what were your reactions? Do you feel that it took courage on your part to question as you did? Would or will you do it again if you think something is wrong? Why or why not?

5. Define "metaphysics," "ethics," and "epistemology" in your own words as fully as you can, and describe and present one problem or issue from each that relates to you and your experiences, that is, that you have thought about or experienced (for example, "How much freedom do I really have?" "What is truth to me, and how do I know when I have discovered it?" and "What do "good" and "bad" mean to me—What do I mean when I say that a person is bad or good or when I say an action is right or wrong?") Also attempt to resolve or solve the problems or issues as well as you can.

6. Write a clear, coherent essay on Socrates' statement, "The unexamined life is not worth living." Do you really believe this is so? Why or why not? Is it true that a life that is not examined is really not worth living, or do you feel that statement is too strong? De-

fine what you think an "examined life" or an "unexamined life" means and describe what each would be like.

7. Define what you mean by "knowledge" and "wisdom." How would you distinguish the difference between these two? Answer in detail and give clear, concrete examples of both.

8. Select one of Plato's dialogues with your professor's help and analyze it carefully. Which area of study in philosophy is he discussing (metaphysics, epistemology, ethics)? If he discusses more than one in the dialogue, then distinguish this. Describe his approach to teaching and philosophizing—what are his methods and how does he deal with problems and issues? Do you think his methods are upsetting to his students and would be to authorities? Why or why not?

9. Read the play by Arthur Miller, *Death of a Salesman,* and determine the philosophies of Willy, Linda, Biff, Happy, and Ben Loman as well as those of Charley and Bernard (the Lomans' next-door neighbors). Describe them in detail. Are any of these characters really aware of what they are doing and why? Have any of them really analyzed or been critical of their beliefs? What are the problems that Willy and Biff are having with each other and with their lives? Answer in detail.

10. Read the story, "The Death of Ivan Ilych," by Leo Tolstoy. Does Ivan's philosophy of life change in the story? From what to what and why? None of us wants to die or is looking forward to it, but why is Ivan in such agony over his dying? Ivan philosophizes a great deal as he realizes he is dying and seems to have a lot of regrets about his life. Why? Could any of these regrets have been prevented? How? What are the implications of waiting until you discover you are dying before philosophizing? To what extent does Ivan use speculation and to what extent does he use analysis? Be specific and give examples. Show how he deals with the problems and issues of metaphysics, ethics, and epistemology by giving specific examples of each.

Footnotes

1. See Eric A. Havelock, *Preface to Plato* (New York: Grosset and Dunlap, 1967), esp. Chaps. 3, 4, 5, and 7.

2. Frederick Copleston, S.J., *A History of Philosophy* (Garden City, N.Y.: Image Books, 1962), Vol. I, Part I, p. 250.

3. Copleston, Vol. I, Part II, pp. 90–91.

4. Francis M. Cornford, trans., *The Republic of Plato* (New York: Oxford University Press, 1945), pp. 14–29.

5. Copleston, Vol. I, Part II, p. 16.
6. See Anne C. Roark, "Do Animals Reason? A Philosopher Brings Ethics to a Veterinary School," *The Chronicle of Higher Education* (Washington, D.C.), March 16, 1981, pp. 3–5.

Bibliography

Adler, Mortimer J. *The Conditions of Philosophy*. New York: Dell, 1967.

Bontempo, Charles I. and S. Jack O'Dell, eds. *The Owl of Minerva*. New York: McGraw-Hill, 1975.

Commins, Saxe, and Robert N. Linscott. *The World's Greatest Thinkers*. Buffalo, New York: Washington Square Press, 1954.

Cornford, Francis M. *From Religion to Philosophy: A Study in the Origins of Western Speculation*. New York: Harper, 1958.

Durant, Will. *The Story of Philosophy*. New York: Pocket Books, 1953.

Hospers, John. *An Introduction to Philosophical Analysis*. 2nd ed. Englewood Cliffs, N. J.: Prentice-Hall, 1967.

Hyland, Drew. *The Origins of Philosopy*. New York: Putnam, 1973.

Scriven, Michael. *Primary Philosophy*. New York: McGraw-Hill, 1966.

Troxell, Eugene A., and William S. Snyder. *Making Sense of Things*. New York: St. Martin's, 1976.

CHAPTER 2

Learning How to Philosophize

Developing a Philosophical Attitude

This chapter contains considerable introductory material. It is in no way intended to replace a course in logic or in composition, and I would definitely recommend that all students take courses in both. However, this chapter is designed to introduce you to some tools, methods, and ideas that will help you to begin to philosophize. These will include learning how to read and write philosophy as well as learning how to reason and discuss philosophy intelligently and how to avoid the more common logical fallacies in your reasoning. Since there is so much information in this chapter that is relevant to you in your ongoing involvement with your philosophy course and philosophizing, I suggest that you consider the chapter as a small, and brief, set of guidelines to which you are encouraged to refer whenever needed. With this clarification of purpose, I would now like to indicate what you can do to develop a philosophic attitude.

TRY TO EXPAND YOUR THINKING

We are mostly taught to think in simple and rather superficial ways. The process of thinking, of course, is never really very simple; rather, it is always somewhat involved and complex. However, we are generally not taught to think abstractly or deeply about too many things. We seem to be encouraged instead to use our intelligence to follow directions and orders and to function from day to day usually without questioning or being too critical. This type of thinking is promoted very early in life when we tell our children after they ask "Why?" "Never mind asking why; just do as I say or follow my instructions."

To "do" philosophy, however, it is important that you try to expand your thinking, to open your mind to new and different ideas without rejecting them out of hand because they seem too strange or too abstract for immediate use in everyday life. As I have said, most of our thinking is quite narrow and either limited to our immediate experience or to instructions we have received from others. In philosophy, that type of thinking is just not good enough; we must instead develop our minds to allow ideas to enter them and "stay awhile," as it were, rather than to be rejected or not considered because they do not fit in with some preconceived notion about what is important or worthy of consideration. No idea or theory should be rejected as being unworthy until it has been considered in a careful and critical way. Actually when we begin to do this, we find very few ideas or theories that are not worthy of at least some examination. Therefore, I urge you to give yourself time while taking this philosophy course to investigate philosophy as fully and as fairly as you can in the short time that you have. I guarantee that if you apply yourselves, you will learn some things about yourselves, your minds, and the world around you that you can apply to your own life, to many other courses you will take, and to other activities you will engage in from day to day.

SKEPTICISM

As I have indicated in the first chapter, questioning everything is one thing that most philosophers agree on, and to question, one has to develop a skeptical outlook; that is, one has to doubt everything for which there is no conclusive evidence.

TOTAL SKEPTICISM.   Some people have claimed that human beings must be skeptical about everything to the point that they have to say that they cannot really know anything for certain and that belief is the only thing they can have. They argue that to know anything, they would have to know everything, and this is impossible; therefore, they cannot know anything. This is an absurd statement. First, the criteria for knowing something, in this strong skeptical sense, are impossible—it is quite true that if we had to know everything to know even one thing, then we could never have certain knowledge; however, why, for example, would we have to know whether there is life on other planets to know that we are now reading a book? Knowledge is certainly interconnected, but one need not know everything to know one particular thing. Second, the skeptic cannot even make the statement that he and the rest of humanity really know nothing—how can he *know* this if he cannot know anything? The point is that this type of skepticism, which a few new philosophy students are fond of espousing, is philosophically destructive and self-defeating. We certainly must be aware of our ignorance and the difficulty of gaining knowledge, especially certain knowledge, but we need not accept the self-defeating assumption that we can never know anything. Absolutely no one can live his or her life based on this assumption.

PARTIAL, CREATIVE SKEPTICISM.   Neither, on the other hand, should we say we know anything if we do not have the proper evidence to say it. What I am suggesting is a middle ground in which we have a creatively healthy, constructive skepticism, one that allows us to question in the hope that we can attain knowledge at least about some things. To do this, we must, of course, believe that some knowledge is attainable. We need not, with this creative skepticism, even give up our most cherished beliefs or theories, but we should be able to "set them aside" temporarily, without rejecting them until we have had a chance to examine the evidence and reasoning to support them.

René Descartes established this kind of skepticism or creative doubting when he started his philosophizing and search for certain knowledge with the idea that he would

> accept nothing as true which I did not clearly recognize to be so; that is to say, carefully to avoid precipitation and prejudice in judgments, and to accept in them nothing more than what was presented to my mind so clearly, and distinctly that I could have no occasion to doubt it.[1]

Edmund Husserl (1859–1938), the philosopher who developed a method called phenomenology, elaborated on Descartes' basic approach to creative skepticism by saying that philosophers should put aside their beliefs, opinions, theories, and claimed knowledge "in brackets" [–], not rejecting them, but creatively doubting whether there was enough evidence for their acceptance as certain knowledge. In this way, Husserl felt that philosophers could examine everything without rejecting anything by just setting things aside for the time being and then bringing them out of brackets once knowledge of them had been truly established. This, then, is creative skepticism, which is necessary for developing a philosophic attitude.

CONSIDERATION OF OTHER VIEWS

The second attribute necessary in developing a philosophic attitude is to really listen to others and to read others' views thoughtfully and carefully. In this way, your mind will be open to learning information or ideas and theories that you may not have considered before. You also need to try to understand the basis for others' opinions, stands, and beliefs to see why they believe as they do. To understand, you must try to suspend your own judgments and opinions temporarily (using "brackets" again) until you've heard other views completely. You also must avoid being dogmatic (arrogantly rigid in your assertions) or overbearing while stating your own beliefs, opinions, and criticisms. It is better to use "I believe," "I think," "I feel," and "It seems to me" when you are unsure of your facts or arguments or when they are indeed basically your own opinions or beliefs. Also, you should not preach or pontificate; rather, you should discuss and exchange ideas.

You need further to try to approach each discussion or reading of someone else's views with tolerance and charity. To give their arguments full consideration, you should examine them in the most favorable context possible. For example, in approaching Bishop George Berkeley's (1685–1753) statement that no physical world or physical objects exist outside of a human being's sense experiences, instead of reacting with anger or rejecting his statement without further investigation, you should "bracket" your own assumptions about the external world and be willing to read and consider without prejudice Berkeley's arguments. You should assume that Berkeley is a serious philosopher and, therefore, give his arguments serious consideration. At the very least, you will be exposed to a different theory, which might shake loose any narrowness of thinking you might have developed; at best, you will become aware of the complexity and limitations of *any* human being's sense experiences and the difficulties of knowing anything about the unobserved external world. If an argument is convincing, you will learn something new; if it isn't, you will come to the point at which you can *intelligently* reject it after fair examination.

CRITICAL ANALYSIS

Using Sense Experience.   At the same time that you are trying to expand your thinking and consideration of other views, you should develop a critical eye and turn your creative skepticism on every major statement you hear, read, or make. You should examine every statement made in the light of your own experience. This is partly what Husserl meant by the phenomenological method. It involves using your five senses to verify those statements that can be verified in this way and your "internal" senses to verify statements made about human feelings, awarenesses, and so on. Second, you should examine all theories and hypotheses, especially those about human nature, in light of your own experiences in general from the past, present, and future.

You must, of course, be as conscientious, careful, and accurate in performing these examinations as you can.

For example, there are scientific theories that state that seeing an object is caused by light waves and that hearing something is caused by sound waves, and some scientists have gone so far as to state that human beings are really in fact seeing light waves and hearing sound waves. If, however, you examine your own sense experiences, as I have examined mine, you will probably have to state that you have never, ever seen a light wave or heard a sound wave. Instead, you see a red shirt or hear a bell ringing. Further, when you see and hear things in your dreams, where are the light and sound waves? These analyses in no way dispute the theories that there are light and sound waves, or that they cause us to see and hear, but they certainly raise questions about trying to reduce sense experiences merely to physical occurrences outside of human beings. They also raise questions about what human beings actually do experience when they perceive something with one or more of their senses.

USING REASONING AND LOGIC

You must also examine all arguments and statements, including your own, using good methods of logic and reasoning and being careful to spot common logical fallacies in reasoning and arguments and also being careful to avoid them yourself. Methods of logic and reasoning and various common fallacies will be described later in the chapter under philosophical methods.

To summarize, then, the basic ways of developing a philosophic attitude are (1) keep an open, yet skeptical mind; (2) be tolerant, charitable, and fair toward other people and their opinions; and (3) be critical of positions, theories, and arguments, using your own and others' sense experiences and proper methods of logic and reasoning.

How to Read Philosophy

READING PHILOSOPHY—SOME GENERAL SUGGESTIONS

Since most students taking an introductory course in philosophy have never read any philosophy before because philosophy courses are not offered below the college level, it's important to realize that reading philosophy is quite different from reading any other subject. First, it contains a presentation not only of facts, ideas, and theories but also arguments and discussions of a philosophical nature. Further, all these are about concerns that most people have not considered or have not been involved in any sort of formal or systematic way, such as its areas of study (metaphysics, ethics, and epistemology). With these differences in mind, you should give yourselves more time and the best conditions possible to read philosophy.

You should try to give yourself at least an hour to an hour and a half free from distraction. You should also plan to read your philosophy assignment at least two times—three times would be the best, if you can arrange it. The first time, read through the assignment without stopping, noting any words you might need to look up or passages that are especially difficult to comprehend. You should mark both in some way for future reference as you read. You should make full use of an ordinary dictionary and any glossary provided. Also a good dictionary of philosophy terms would be of great assistance. You can usually find one at any library or you can purchase one in paperback edition. Philosophy majors must have one of these.

You should look up difficult words and then read through your assignment a second time more slowly, underlining key ideas or outlining the main points of the assignment on a separate sheet of paper. During this period, you should reread difficult passages and try to understand them more fully. Next, read over your outline and definitions for sense, and then reread the entire assignment without stopping, but trying harder this time to grasp the ideas being presented and the reasoning behind them.

As was described in the section on developing a philosophic attitude, be sure to read as much as possible with an open mind and be willing to receive the ideas being presented, no matter how strange they may appear to you. In other words, give them and their author a chance. Try not to reject ideas or theories as you read, but finish the assignment, and don't consider counterarguments or attacks or rejection until after the second or third reading. At this time write down your own reactions to and criticisms of what you have read. With this careful approach to reading philosophy in general, you should not only be able to understand what you have read, but also you should be prepared to begin to discuss or write about your assignment critically.

READING INTRODUCTION TO PHILOSOPHY TEXTBOOKS

In reading an introduction to philosophy or just general philosophy textbooks like this one, follow the suggestions just listed, and use any devices that are made available by the authors who have designed the texts and the material presented with students in mind. For example, notice and make use of chapter and section headings printed in bold-face type or italics. Also note the first and last sentences of each paragraph and each section within chapters. In reading, look out for listings of key items, which are numbered or lettered within the textual material, such as "There are three areas that philosophy studies: (1) metaphysics, (2) ethics, and (3) epistemology."

Further, make full use of any additional and specialized aids, such as chapter summaries like the ones provided in this book. These summaries can be of great assistance if you refer to them after the first and even the second readings of the chapter and may actually take the place of having to make an outline of the chapter (although making an outline of your own in your own words can still be a great aid to your comprehension). You should also try to answer study questions at the end of chapters that are designed to cover text material, such as "Define 'metaphysics,' 'ethics,' and 'epistemology' in your own words, and give examples of each." Answering such questions can aid you greatly in seeing if you have really grasped the material presented. For example, if your mind goes blank when you read the word "metaphysics," then you know that you didn't understand it well at all and need to look it up again. Finally, make full use of any glossaries and indexes presented in the text because they can give you special insights into the meanings of words, concepts, and theories that you cannot ordinarily acquire from regular dictionaries. Whether such a book is assigned for reading in your class or not, you should know that it can give you a good, introductory background in philosophy and its problems and issues. Often such a book is accompanied by original readings in philosophy or an anthology of original readings, which we will examine next.

READING PRIMARY OR ORIGINAL PHILOSOPHICAL WRITINGS

Primary or original philosophical writings, such as Plato's *Republic,* Aristotle's *Nichomachean Ethics,* Immanuel Kant's *Critique of Pure Reason,* and Jean-Paul Sartre's *Being and Nothingness,* are difficult enough reading merely because they are philosophical in nature, but they are often made more complicated by the fact that they are translations from a foreign language (Greek, Latin, German, French) and also written in another time when even English was used somewhat differently from its usage today. Therefore, approaching the reading of this type of philosophy will require more patience and attention than will reading introductory texts. You will need to seek background material from either historical and biographical readings or your professor's lectures to discover what the times were like when the philosopher was writing; what biographical information about him can help you to understand his writings; and what are the special ways in which he defines words or uses language that can help you to understand what he is saying. For example, to read and understand Plato, it is important to know something about his and Socrates' struggle to change the thinking processes of the Greeks, the use of the dialogue form, and the dialectical method of reasoning invented by the two philosophers (I will describe this method later in the chapter).

Second, you must understand what the philosopher is actually discussing in the particular text you are reading. For example, he might be trying to define a particular word or concept like "justice"; arguing that humans can't have ideas without sense experiences; or trying to prove that being ethical means always acting in one's own self-interest. It is important that you understand his main ideas, his definitions of terms, the major points of his arguments, and the examples or illustrations he uses to support his arguments. You should seek help here from your professor or from any additional explanatory reading material he has assigned to aid you in understanding what you're reading.

Only after you are fairly sure you understand what the philosopher is saying should you then attempt to analyze and critically evaluate his arguments. At this point, again, you should follow your professor's instructions, but you may also consider using the following questions as guidelines:

1. Has the philosopher defined key terms according to the way they are understood by nonphilosophers as well as philosophers? You should check his definitions against an ordinary dictionary and also against your experience of how the term or concept is usually used in ordinary language. If his definition is different, then how is it different? Is his definition close to or far from the word's ordinary use? Is his definition a valid one?
2. If he supports his arguments with evidence based on sense experience, is his description of what is perceived accurate? Does it square with your own sense experiences and perceptions and those that other people have reported to you?
3. Does he use inductive and deductive reasoning accurately and according to the rules of logic?
4. Has he avoided logical fallacies?
5. Is the whole point of his arguments—his conclusions—supported by factors outlined in questions 2, 3, and 4?

READING SECONDARY SOURCES

Secondary sources are commentaries, analyses, and critical evaluations of what a philosopher has presented in an original or primary work. They are usually written by another philosopher who is often attacking the first philosopher's arguments and theories. In such works, in addition to the guidelines listed for reading in general and for reading primary sources, you should consider the following:

1. Be sure you have read and understood the primary or original writing first. How else can you understand the point of the second philosopher's discussion or analysis?
2. In addition to using all of the aforementioned techniques to understand this author, ask these questions:
   a. Is the second philosopher using the same definitions as the first or has he changed them in some way? If so, how, and what difference does it make?
   b. What are the main points of *his* arguments, and what conclusions does *he* draw?
   c. How well does he support or justify his main points and his conclusions?
   d. Is he being fair in his evaluation, analysis, and criticism of the first author?

In conclusion, secondary sources can be quite valuable in understanding what the original philosopher is getting at and in seeing where he has "gone right or wrong" in his assumptions or reasoning. They must, however, be approached as critically and carefully as any primary author's writings.

Learning How to Philosophize

SPECULATION

"Speculation" has already been defined (in the first chapter), and as we have seen, philosophers can merely let their minds wander over a range of thoughts, feelings, and ideas until something catches their interest. They also may be stimulated to speculate by some other person's (philosopher or otherwise) observation or view of an issue that they find interesting or important. Basically, therefore, in some way or another, philosophers become aware of a problem or an issue and then attempt to find out about and deal with it.

For example, if one reads an article against abortion by a right-to-life advocate and then an argument for abortion by a pro-choice advocate, one begins to see that some important questions surrounding the whole issue of abortion are, When does human life begin? When should it be given value? And what rights do women and unborn fetuses have? Philosophers can, of course, select any problem or issue to deal with, and sometimes it may be valuable not to be too hasty in selecting one, but rather to think more speculatively about a lot of things before deciding on just one issue or problem. Of course, if a problem or issue calls for an immediately decision or action, then one might have to be immediately selective. For example, if a man and his wife or daughter are confronting the abortion issue in the family, then what they should do specifically in *this* situation is of paramount concern. If there is no such pressure, however, it might be best if people considered the whole problem of abortion when they have time to speculate and let their minds range over the entire problem *before* it has to be confronted in actuality. That way, some ethical and logical groundwork can be laid to help people make the most appropriate decisions in the event they become involved in such a situation.

I would consider that how important or crucial the problem or issue is to the lives, well-being, and growth of human beings (to you, your family, and others) as the first and most important criteria for selection of a topic for speculation and analysis. Other criteria that can be used for such selection are

1. How important is it to a better and fuller understanding of you, others, and the world around you?
2. How useful will it be to deal with and resolve it?
3. How intellectually interesting is it to you? The awareness of an issue or problem and its selection, then, is the first stage in philosophizing.

ANALYSIS

After one has selected the topic to be dealt with, he or she should continue speculating about it, but also apply the following seven steps in philosophizing to approach the issue or problem systematically and analytically and attempt to resolve it.[2]

1. Define the issue or problem clearly and carefully. For example, in contemplating the abortion issue, as described, you might decide that you need to zero in on the problem of when human life begins. It is important in the process of taking this first step to define clearly all key terms, such as "zygote," "embryo," "fetus," "gestation," and so on.
2. The second step is to gather all the data you can that are relevant to the problem or issue.
   a. Using sense observation and experiences—yours and others—gather all the sense evidence you can that is applicable to the problem. For example, you should do some research in biology and genetics to discover what happens from conception onward to the fertilized ovum of the female.

b. Using your intellect, you should also examine arguments, theories, and ideas about when human life begins from a religious, psychological, sociological, anthropological, and philosophical point of view.

3. Next, you should analyze, organize, and classify these data. For example, you might use three major categories for classification of evidence and reasoning: (1) the strong pro-life position, (2) the strong pro-choice position, and (3) the moderate in-between positions of all other theories.

4. At this point, you may formulate hypotheses, tentative solutions that have occurred to you during step 3, based on your own reasoning. For example, you might begin to hypothesize that if people want to take the safest moral position, they should accept the strong pro-life approach; on the other hand, if they are concerned about the rights and individual freedom of women over their bodies and lives, then they should consider the pro-choice position.

5. The fifth step is to see what deductions you can draw from your hypotheses about what else will be true if your hypotheses are correct. For example, you might deduce from your hypotheses that if abortion is encouraged or allowed, then a lack of respect for human life in other areas (mercy killing, war, infanticide) may result.

6. You then have to verify your deductions in some way. For example, you might gather data from around the world as to whether or not making abortion laws more permissive has resulted in a decline in the respect for human life overall, and if you find little or no evidence to support this contention, then you can dismiss it as invalid.

7. The last step in the process is to ask what the implications of the philosophizing you have done for yourself and others and the world are, and also what relationship they have to other important issues and problems. For example, what are the implications of abortion or nonabortion positions for welfare, child abuse, or the future lives of individual women who become pregnant? This last step is very important because it not only applies theories and analyses to real-life situations but it also can lead beyond knowledge to wisdom, the distinction between which was described in Chapter 1.

These steps, then, can be used to philosophize about any problem or issue and also comprise, at least to some extent, a way of dealing with problems and issues in other areas such as the sciences and social sciences. So far, throughout Chapter 1 and also this entire chapter, we have been talking about reasoning, logic, and fallacies; at this point, in learning how to philosophize, it is appropriate that some introductory information on logic and reasoning be presented.

TYPES OF REASONING

INDUCTIVE REASONING.   Inductive reasoning is based heavily on sense observations or experiences, and it moves from particular cases observed to general conclusions that can only be considered probable. In other words, general conclusions are "led into" (the literal meaning of "induction") from particular instances. An example of inductive reasoning would be, "Every crow I have ever seen is black; therefore, all crows are *probably* black." The reason why the conclusion is probable is that to say for certain "all crows are black," one would have to have observed all crows that have ever existed, that exist now, and that will exist in the future. This, of course, would seem to be quite impossible. One might ask, then, what is the significance of knowledge arrived at through induction, and the answer lies in its degree of probability. The knowledge gained from induction in which the probability is very strong and supported by a good number of clearly observed, closely related, and well-substantiated cases certainly would have a high level of reliability.

For example, one inductive conclusion we all adhere to is that if we drop something, it will fall to the ground. Our common experience tells us this, and it has occurred so frequently that it has even been established as a "law" of nature, the law of gravity. In this situation, the probability that the next time we drop something it will fall is so high that we can even predict on the basis of past occurrences that it will happen again and will continue to happen in the future. We still must, however, recognize that being able to say, "I know for certain that everytime something is dropped it will always and forever fall to the ground," would require more evidence than induction can give us.

An example of weak probability would be, "President Kennedy was assassinated when he went to Dallas; therefore, any famous public figure who goes to Dallas will be assassinated." Obviously, more evidence would have to be forthcoming to draw such a conclusion. The probability of that conclusion being true is very, very weak. This is one of the problems with inductive reasoning—that in some cases there are not enough examples to justify the general conclusion arrived at. The question arises as to how many occurrences or examples would have to occur for there to be strong probability, and the answer is that it would depend on the type of situation. Generally speaking, however, the greater the number and similarity of examples and occurrences, the greater and stronger the probability that the conclusion is true and will continue to be so.

Another problem is that one must be careful that too great a conclusion is not drawn from inductive reasoning for the particular cases to support. For example, in using the Kennedy assassination example to conclude that, because President Kennedy was killed there, all people of Dallas are violent or Dallas is a more violent city than most U.S. cities would be too great for the example given. Even if several killings of famous people had occurred there, one could not draw either one of these conclusions without more evidence and comparative studies with other cities in the United States.

If we are careful to avoid either one of these problems, however, inductive reasoning yields us a great deal of information and a great many operating truths. A good deal of scientific experimentation and resultant hypotheses and theories are based on induction as well as a number of things in our lives we call "facts."

DEDUCTIVE REASONING.   Deductive reasoning is not based as heavily on sense experiences; rather, it "deduces" or derives particular statements or conclusions from general statements. That is, particular statements are "led from" (the literal meaning of "deduction") general ones. Some examples are

1. The syllogism: Its symbolic form:
   All men are mortal   All X's are Y's
   Socrates is a man   Z is an X
   Therefore, Socrates is mortal.   Therefore, Z is a Y.
2. The either-or form: Its symbolic form:
   It will either be a boy or a girl.   Either B or G.
   It's not a boy.   Not B.
   Therefore, it must be a girl.   Therefore, G.
3. The "and" or "both-and"   Its symbolic form:
   form:
   Both John and Irene went to   Both J and I.
     the hospital.
   Therefore, John went to the   Therefore, J.
     hospital.
4. The "if-then" form: Its symbolic form:
   If the car starts, then the bat-   If S, then G.
     tery is good.
   The car started.   S
   Therefore, the battery is good.   Therefore, G.

A deductive argument, unlike inductive arguments, can yield a certain truth, *if* two things occur in the process of the argument. (1) The premises of the argument must be true (All men are mortal; Socrates is a man). And (2) the argument must be *valid;* that is, the conclusion (Therefore, Socrates is mortal) must follow from the two premises.

An example of deductive argument that does not yield a true conclusion because its premises are false is

1A. All cows are green.
     Nixon is a cow.
     Therefore, Nixon is green.

Notice that the foregoing argument is as *valid* as argument 1 concerning Socrates but that its premises and, therefore, its conclusion are all false (cows are *not* green; Nixon is *not* a cow; and Nixon is *not* green).

A deductive argument that does not yield a true conclusion because it is an invalid argument is

4A. If the car starts, then the   If S, then G.
     battery is good.
     The battery is good.   G.
     Therefore, the car must   Therefore, S.
     start.

Note that this is a reversal of the correct form of argument 4 basically in the second premise and the conclusion. It is easy to see that even if the battery is good, the car may not start; it may, for example, have a broken starter motor, or all its plugs may be disconnected. Naturally for a more complete study of the arguments and forms of arguments that are invalid, one would need a much fuller course in logic than I can present in part of one chapter in an introductory philosophy text, but you can at least, I hope, see what the two major types of logical arguments are and be aware of their problems in general.

ARGUMENT FROM ANALOGY.   Another type of argument sometimes found in philosophy, as well as in other fields of study, is called argument from analogy. When people argue in this fashion, they compare one thing with another to clarify complex and confusing issues and to get readers to see the similarities between two things. We see and hear analogies all the time. For example, when we hear people say, "A is like B, in that . . ." we are expecting an analogy. In the next chapter, we will see several analogies being set up concerning the human mind, that it is like a "blank slate," a theater, or a computer. Analogical arguments can be very helpful, provided that the similarities described really are similar and that the argument squares with our experiences.

One of the most interesting analogies in philosophic literature is Plato's "Allegory of the Cave" in his *Republic* in which Socrates compares an ordinary human being to someone chained in a dark cave, who can only observe the flickering shadows of things projected on the wall, but who not knowing any better, thinks these shadows are the real things. Not until people can unchain themselves and walk out to observe these things in the bright sunlight of ultimate reality can the real truth be known.[3]

Another famous analogy is used in the *argument from design,* which tries to prove that the universe must have had an intelligent designer by comparing the complexity of the universe to that of a watch. The argument states that we know that nothing as complicated as a watch could have just happened; in fact, we can even observe watchmakers design and make watches. Since the universe is at least as complicated as a watch, then it must have been designed by some intelligent being.

One can immediately spot problems with this argument. First, how really like the universe is a watch? A watch is a mechanical object made up of interconnected moving parts that is meant to tell time. It has gears, springs, jewels, and other metal pieces all fitted and bolted together. Where are the springs, gears, and jewels of the universe, and does the universe tell time? Does it even have as clear a purpose as a watch (that is, clear to us)? Furthermore, we can observe a watchmaker design and make a watch, but has anyone ever seen anyone or anything design and make a universe? This example points out the main problems with an argument from analogy. To be effective, the two objects of the analogy really must be similar in a number of respects— the more similarities, the better, obviously. Also, we really must be able to compare them. In the God-watch analogy, part of the proof of the analogy is hidden from us in that we never have seen a universe designed.

DIALECTICAL REASONING.   One last form of reasoning I feel I must present is called dialectical reasoning, which was invented by Socrates and Plato. I've already stated that Plato wrote his philosophical works in dialogue form in which Socrates and his students enter into a give-and-take discussion or "dialogue" to arrive at various truths. The words "dialogue" and "dialectic" are derived pretty much from the same root. *Dialogue* means a conversation, discussion, or debate between two people, and *dialectic* means a dialogue or "conversation" between two ideas. Dialectical reasoning is composed of three parts: (1) thesis, (2) antithesis, (3) and synthesis. A thesis or idea or theory is presented for discussion and analysis; it is confronted by an opposing theory or antithesis; out of this confrontation or conflict, the first thesis is shown to be lacking in some way or even to be false, but usually out of this conflict arises a new thesis (a *syn*-thesis) that often combines the best parts of both thesis and antithesis and drops the weak or defective parts of both. Sometimes the thesis is merely shown to be defective by its antithesis, and a new and different thesis is presented. However, by this process of dialoguic confrontation, one learns, according to Socrates and Plato, how to winnow out the truth from falsehood. Many examples can be found in most Platonic dialogues, but I would recommend the three arguments concerning what justice is in the opening book and chapters of the *Republic*.[4]

Logical Fallacies

Fallacies are really nothing more than poor ways of arguing and fall into two major categories, which I will call *fallacies of oversimplification* and *fallacies of deception*.[5]

FALLACIES OF OVERSIMPLIFICATION

Fallacies of this type tend to oversimplify major issues and also to ignore or neglect significant facts; six of these will be discussed.

MERE ASSERTION. People often feel that all they need to do is to assert something in fairly strong or definite terms, and their argument will be convincing. For example, the famous (or infamous) bumper sticker that states, "God said it; I believe it; and that's the end of it" proves nothing at all. It is merely an assertion of belief. The first rule in arguing philosophically is that one must substantiate or support any argument that he or she presents with evidence or logic. Merely asserting an idea, belief, or theory and expecting people to accept it as a bonafide argument is a fallacy.

FALSE DILEMMA. Another type of oversimplification is a fallacy called false dilemma or the "black-white," "either-or" fallacy. Very few things in life are either one thing or the other without other alternatives being possible. One of these is pregnancy—a woman is either pregnant or she's not; she can't be only partially pregnant or just a little bit pregnant. Sometimes, however, people will set up a false dilemma, saying that it's either A or B, when C, D, and E are also possible. For an example from religion, some Christians will argue that Jesus was either God or a madman, trying to convince their listeners that those are the only two possibilities. Of course, arguing against Jesus and calling him a madman when one might not think he's divine but still admire his teachings is supposed to force the listener to choose the former—that he must be divine because he can't be a madman. However, this false dilemma, like all false dilemmas, ignores the possibility of other alternatives. For example, maybe his followers made up the stories that he said he was God, or that maybe they misunderstood him when he said it, or maybe he was in such pain and agony from his crucifixion that he was not mad, but delusionary. I am not really trying to refute the theory that Jesus was divine, but only to indicate that this particular argument is fallacious for the reasons stated.

IRRELEVANT ARGUMENT.   In this type of fallacy the arguer tries to set up an attack on a position that is irrelevant to the major argument and tends to draw the reader or listener's attention away from the main issue being presented. For example, when arguing against any kind of gun control, proponents will often say that more people are killed each year in traffic accidents by automobiles than are killed by guns. This is an irrelevant argument—what have automobiles and automobile accidents really to do with the proliferation of handguns? People die from all sorts of causes every year, but what has that to do with whether or not guns ought to be controlled? The issue is whether or not there should be gun control, not whether more people are killed in other ways.

CIRCULAR REASONING.   Sometimes called "begging the question," this type of fallacy occurs because its user argues "in a circle" proving nothing. For example, when people say that God exists because the Bible says so and then when someone asks how they know the Bible is true, the answer is that God inspired it, these people are arguing in a circle. It may indeed be true that God exists and inspired the Bible, but it can't be proved by this argument. The way this argument is presented, it cannot be presumed that the Bible proves God's existence without *already* assuming that God exists (to inspire the Bible and make it true).

APPEAL TO IGNORANCE.   This fallacy tries to shift the necessity for proof to the fact that something is *not* the case rather than that something is. It is generally assumed that when people are trying to prove something is the case, the burden of proof is on them. They cannot argue that, because there is no proof that something is *not* the case, it then must be true that it is. For example, if a newspaper or magazine says that Senator X is a drunk and a womanizer, and the senator makes no reply, and if the publication attempts to state that because the senator did not deny the allegation, it must be true, then the publication is arguing from ignorance. The senator may not wish to dignify such an accusation with a reply; certainly because he does not reply does not mean that the accusation is true. The burden of proof is still on the publication, not the senator, and more proof than just the allegation itself or rumors about the senator is necessary.

STEREOTYPING.   This fallacy occurs when people tend to judge one member of a class of things or people from a false or too great a generalization about that class. For example, if one assumes that all women are emotional, weak, and weepy, then, of course, Betty will not be able to function in a job that calls for a "man's logic, strength, and coolness" (another stereotyping). Always be wary of the use of "all" when referring to human beings and also be wary of such sentences as "She's a *typical* woman." Avoid stereotyping by not thinking of anything or anyone as merely a member of a class, but rather as woman 1, woman 2, or better yet as Betty or Helen. Certainly you must avoid making statements such as, "all Mexicans are lazy," "all orientals are inscrutable," and "all Southerners are bigoted."

FALLACIES OF DECEPTION

Fallacies of this kind tend to throw up a "smokescreen" to win an argument; they appeal to things that are usually not pertinent or relevant to the truth or to an argument.

PERSONAL ATTACK.   This fallacy is called in traditional logic the *ad hominem* ("to" or "at the man") argument. Instead of arguing against people's theories or contentions, one argues against the people personally. Recently, a Republican senator attacked the Senate majority leader (a Democrat), who is quite heavyset, as very large and fat and as both a physical as well as a political "obstruction" to the Republican administration's getting its bills through Congress. That the majority leader may be obstructive in a political sense is one thing, but using his physical stature as a way of proving or enforcing the senator's argument is unfair and an attack on the man, not on his politics. You should always attack your opponents' arguments, theories, or opinions, not the people themselves.

EVERYBODY DOES IT.   We have all probably used this argument and have committed this fallacy at some time or another. We may argue that it is all right to take home supplies from the businesses where we work because "everybody does it, and we all know that's true." One of the first things we will learn in the chapter on ethics (Chapter 6) is that this is no argument at all for what people ought to do or what's right or wrong. Simply because everyone or even most people do something is no conclusive argument for doing it, nor does majority practice make any fact true or any argument valid. Prior to 1492, *most* people believed that the earth was flat, but this had nothing to do with the truth. Another form this fallacy often takes is the statement, "Everybody knows that is true." For example, "Everyone knows that all atheists are communists" or "Everyone knows that all Republicans are fascists" are arguments that may have a majority appeal, but they are not true on those grounds. Even if it were true that most people believe these two statements to be true, their beliefs or the number of people who believe them would not make the statements true. The appeal here is to people who want to be included in the majority or who want to be allowed to climb on the "bandwagon," but the listener or reader must guard against such an appeal.

APPEAL TO PITY.   This argument brings in some element of pity or sentimentality that is intended to cloud an argument and steer the reader or listener away from any relevant facts. For example, when the Watergate scandal nearly caused the impeachment of President Richard Nixon and did cause his resignation from office, he and many of his supporters tried to appeal to pity by citing what he had been through during the scandal. That he had been through a lot is not in doubt; however, that he caused most of his own troubles and also lied and cheated causing serious corruption that was detrimental to the government and the American people should not be clouded by the fact that he had some bad times in the process. Appealing to the effects on him did not change the facts of what he and his administration, with his encouragement and blessing, had done to the government and its people.

APPEAL TO VANITY.   People should not be led away from the facts or overlook the validity of any argument because it contains an appeal to their vanity. For example, any editorial or article in a magazine that leads off with something on the order of "We know, of course, that the readers of this magazine are the most intelligent in America . . ." is obviously appealing to its readers' vanity and hopes to win them over to its argument by flattery. And when the editorial or article goes on to say that "all intelligent people know that Republicans are really interested in keeping the poor in poverty and making the rich richer," readers had better be careful that they are not drawn into accepting the argument in order to be considered intelligent.

CHANGING MEANINGS.   The last fallacy to be mentioned under the heading of deception is that of changing meanings of key terms in the process of an argument. For example, to say that since Jesus said, "Love one another even as I love you" he then condoned any type of heterosexual or homosexual activity in or outside of marriage is to shift definitions of "love." Jesus was probably using the term in the sense of spirituality, friendship, and caring. This meaning is, of course, not necessarily absent from the use of the term in matters of sexuality, but

51

neither does it follow that he condoned illicit heterosexual or homosexual relationships or activities because he told human beings to love one another. To argue that he did is to change the meaning of "love" as it is used in one situation to another situation entirely.

REDUCTIONISM AND EXPANSIONISM

Two other problems in examining arguments should be mentioned before leaving the problem of fallacies: reductionism and expansionism.

REDUCTIONISM.   It is a good rule of logic that one should strive for the simplest meaning of an argument or the simplest view of reality rather than make things unnecessarily complex. For example, anyone who has studied fractions in mathematics knows that one should reduce fractions to their "lowest common denominator." One should apply the same approach to theories of reality as well as arguments *provided that* things can be reduced with nothing left over. This is often easy in mathematics, but what about reality? At one time ancients viewing the planet that we now call Venus thought they were looking at two separate stars, the morning star and the evening star. When it was discovered that there really was only one star, the two names were dropped in favor of one. It would be silly to call the same thing by two names—this involves unnecessary complexity. Another example can be found in discussions about the essence of a human being. Some philosophers use the terms "self," "soul," "mind," and "spirit" interchangeably, but if they all mean the same thing, then why use four terms to account for one thing? Therefore, one should settle on one term and define it carefully; this would simplify the whole problem and eliminate the proliferation of terms.

In using reductionism, however, people must be careful not to reduce two or more things to one when they really won't reduce—that is, when they are really two things and not one. For example, we will see that one of the discussions in the chapter on the mind versus the brain is that materialism that says there is only brain and no mind is attacked by the dualist (one who believes in both brain and mind) as a reductionist argument. The dualist claims that the materialist tries to reduce the mind down to the brain and that the mind is really quite different from the brain. What the materialist is guilty of, according to the dualist, is unnecessary reductionism.

EXPANSIONISM.   Expansionism is the opposite of reductionism and, therefore, has the same advantages and problems only in reverse. Sometimes a temporary expansionism can be useful. For example, in the next chapter, I purposely expand views of human nature to include several of the major ones held throughout the history of the world, even though the biggest discussion in philosophy has always been between the views of mind versus brain and body. This expansionism opens the whole area of human nature up as widely as possible to analyze it in depth. However, reductionist critics might say that I have overcomplicated the definition of human nature by including as separate aspects soul, spirit, emotions, and will. They argue that everything is really reducible to mind and body or even to body only or mind only. The advantage of using expansionism, however, is that one is able to distinguish between or among different parts or aspects of whatever is being examined; its disadvantage or difficulty is that it may overcomplicate things by creating more distinctions or parts than are really necessary. For example, if finding out what caused nature and the universe is difficult and complicated; then why add to the difficulty by saying that their cause came from something supernatural, especially when the supernatural is even harder to explain or account for than the natural? This is one of the objections presented by the naturalists against the supernaturalist or religionist argument that there is a supernatural being and that it caused nature and the universe to exist.

CONCLUSION

There are of course many more fallacies than I have presented, but this is not a book on logic, so I suggest that all students take an introductory course in logic in which they will learn much more about reasoning, logical fallacies, and other aspects of critical thinking. I have listed several very fine books on logic and critical thinking in the bibliography at the end of this chapter.

Taking Tests and Writing Papers in Philosophy

OBJECTIVE TESTS

Objective tests in philosophy will be like those in most other subject areas; that is, they should call for you to identify material in readings and lectures and not call for opinions. They may differ, however, in that

1. They may call for you to grasp distinctions, for example, "(true-False) Deductive reasoning yields certainty, whereas inductive reasoning yields only probability."
2. Also, they may call for you to understand facts that are more abstract or conceptual in nature than are other subjects. For example,

"(true-false)   It is never right to expand what could be simplified in examining human nature."

If, however, you apply good reading and study techniques like those described earlier in this chapter, you should have no difficulty once you catch on to how philosophy differs from other subjects. Two additional suggestions are

1. Take full advantage of any study guides or questions given to you by your professor or any texts you are using (for example, chapter summaries and study questions at the end of each chapter in this book).
2. Don't leave your studying for last-minute cramming and don't presume that you can pass any objective examination in philosophy without studying—the material is usually too new, too conceptual, and therefore too difficult when compared with other subjects for you to take such a chance.

WRITING PHILOSOPHY

Writing philosophy can be similar to other writing, such as reportive writing, straight research, or expository writing, but most writing in philosophy also involves analysis, criticism, and argument. These often require special techniques and strategies.

GENERAL SUGGESTIONS.   Many techniques for any type of good writing are the same for philosophy:

1. Always organize *before* you write, whether you are writing in class (essay examination questions) or outside of class (a critical or personal philosophy type paper).
2. Define key terms clearly.
3. State and clarify main ideas.
4. Develop these ideas fairly fully by giving examples and illustrations to bring out their meaning.
5. Write a first draft and proofread and correct carefully; then, rewrite it. *Never* turn in a first draft!
6. Use appropriate English grammar, usage, sentence structure, and paragraph writing. Some students feel they need not adhere to proper English requirements because this is a philosophy and not an English course, but good college-level English should be considered a *minimum* requirement and will be expected by any philosophy professor. Also, do not use pompous or ornate language; rather, be as direct and precise as you can.
7. Get help from your English professor or from anyone else who is

proficient in English if you need it to help you straighten out any problems you may have in English.

ADDITIONAL SUGGESTIONS FOR PHILOSOPHICAL WRITING.   In addition to these general suggestions, the following are specific suggestions to point out and deal with the basic differences between philosophic writing and writing in other subject areas. You may, as needed, be required to

1. Analyze and critically evaluate the ideas, theories, and arguments of others as well as specific problems and issues (for example, ethical relativism versus ethical absolutism, the pro's and con's of materialism as a theory, God's existence versus His nonexistence).
2. Present your own personal philosophical views of various philosophical issues in metaphysics, ethics, and epistemology.
3. Learn how to incorporate sense evidence with logical reasoning and argument (both inductive and deductive) and how to spot and avoid logical fallacies in doing 1 and 2.

STRATEGIES FOR ANALYZING A PHILOSOPHER'S ARGUMENTS.   Suggestions for writing an analysis and critical evaluation of another philosopher's theory or arguments are

1. Describe and carefully present philosophers' positions, clarifying any of their special definitions of terms and listing the main points of their arguments without any criticism or evaluation. Be careful not to misrepresent anything they say.
2. Analyze and critically evaluate their positions or theories (you may defend or attack them) in an organized, systematic fashion. Often a point-by-point support or refutation is the best strategy here, building up to an overall evaluation of their positions.
3. Support and justify with evidence and reasons all your contentions about their theories as fully as you can. If you are to compare, contrast, and critically evaluate two philosophers' arguments on the same problem or issue, then double up on the foregoing strategies.

STRATEGIES FOR ANALYZING AN ISSUE OR PROBLEM.   On being assigned the task of analyzing and critically evaluating a specific philosophical issue or problem (for example, the mind-body issue), you should do the following:

1. State the issue or problem carefully and clearly, being sure to define key terms.
2. Present the strongest arguments on either side of the issue and the basis and reasoning behind these arguments.
3. Analyze and critically evaluate each side's contentions, showing lack of evidence and fallacies in either side's reasoning and arguments.

4. If you are required to, present your own view and the reasons therefor (see the following section for strategies on how to do this); then substantiate and justify it as fully as you can.

STRATEGIES FOR WRITING PERSONAL PHILOSOPHICAL VIEWS.   If you are asked to write your own personal philosophical views on some issue or issues,

1. Be sure you understand what your professor expects from you.
2. Review the seven steps under the section of this chapter listed as "How to Philosophize," which means that you should know the pro and con arguments of the issue.
3. Describe and present the problem or issue clearly.
4. Present and discuss, as fully and as clearly as possible, your position on the issue.
5. Be sure to marshal as much evidence as you can to support your position, and be sure to check for logical fallacies and weaknesses in your own arguments and reasoning.
6. Give as many examples and illustrations as you can to clarify your main points.
7. Incorporate other philosophers' views on the issue in your writing where needed, being sure to give proper source credit (footnotes and bibliographic entries). Don't accept or present their views unquestioningly.

CONCLUSION

From all the preceding suggestions, you may think that you will be required to be absolutely original in presenting your philosophy or philosophical arguments and to be able to match, in your thinking or writing, the great philosophers; on the contrary, there are not many issues or problems that have not already been discussed and argued by many fine thinkers of the past. Naturally, then, most of what you will do will not be new or original; however, you will learn how to philosophize from the experience of trying to reiterate, clarify, analyze, and evaluate other philosophers who have dealt with these issues. The important thing to remember is that what you are trying to do in philosophy and in using philosophical methods is to expand, develop, and deepen your own thinking processes so that you will live your lives becoming more aware of yourselves, others, and the world around you. With this in mind, then, I hope that this particular chapter will provide a basis for starting to philosophize and a helpful reference for you as you begin to encounter the philosophical issues and problems presented in the remaining chapters of this book.

Applying Philosophy—
Situations for Thought and Study

SITUATION 1

Take a controversial topic about which you have strong feelings and write a short essay supporting the completely opposing point of view as strongly as you can.

1. Suggested topics: mercy killing, capital punishment, gun control, belief or nonbelief in God, abortion, women's rights, premarital sex, adultery, homosexuality, pornography.
2. Try very hard to "bracket" or set aside your own views temporarily.
3. Do any research for this that you can, and try diligently to argue for the opposite side using all the sense evidence, reasoning, and logic you can muster.
4. What did you get out of this assignment?
   a. Can you see the other side's viewpoint any better than you did before, and do you understand it any better now?
   b. Did writing this paper have any effect on your original position? If so, what? If not, why not?
   c. Has your original position changed at all from what it was? Why? Has it been strengthened or weakened by having to do this paper? Why? How?

SITUATION 2

Take an article from a newspaper, magazine, or other source that deals with any of the controversial issues listed in Situation 1 or any other controversial issue and analyze it for lack of sense evidence and poor reasoning and logic. Use the following questions as guidelines in doing a complete analysis:

1. Does all sense evidence presented square with yours and other people's sense experiences about which you have information?
2. If inductive reasoning is used, are enough similar and related examples given to justify the probability of any conclusions drawn?
3. If deductive reasoning is used, are the premises true, and does the conclusion follow from the premises?

4. If analogy is used, are the things that are compared truly similar in all respects? Are both parts of the analogy observable?
5. Has the writer committed any of the logical fallacies described in this chapter?
6. Is the writer guilty either of overreductionism or overexpansionism?

SITUATION 3

Write a short paper (three to five well-developed paragraphs) using an expanded form of any or all of the following on any topic of your choice that lends itself to the type of argument or reasoning you choose:

1. Deductive reasoning and argument
2. Inductive reasoning and argument
3. Analogy
4. Dialectical reasoning
5. Reductionism
6. Expansionism

Chapter Summary

I. Developing a philosophical attitude.
   A. Try to expand your thinking.
   B. Skepticism means doubting, and you should be skeptical.
      1. Total skepticism is destructive and self-defeating.
      2. Partial, creative skepticism is where you question everything, no matter how cherished. You need not reject any belief or theory, but merely put it in "brackets" or set it aside until it can be proved true.
   C. Be willing to consider other views.
      1. Again "bracket" your own thoughts and feelings.
      2. Give the best possible consideration of others' agruments, and try to see them in their best light.
   D. Critical analysis should be applied at this point checking the philosophers' theories and arguments against sense experience, reasoning, and logic.
II. How to read philosophy.
   A. Reading philosophy in general—suggestions.
      1. Give yourself an hour to an hour and a half free from distraction.

2. Read the assignment two or three times, making full use of ordinary dictionaries, dictionaries of philosophy, and glossaries.
3. Underline key points and outline the chapter or article.
4. Apply the philosophical attitudes listed earlier.

B. Reading introduction to philosophy textbooks. Follow the general suggestions listed and in addition, use any devices or aids provided by the authors, such as summaries of chapters, boldface type and italics, numerical listings within the chapter, and exercises.

C. Reading primary or original philosophical writings.
   1. Seek historical and biographical background material.
   2. Know about language difficulties and special uses of definitions.
   3. Understand what the philosopher is actually discussing, which means that you must understand his main ideas, definitions of terms, the major points of his arguments, and his examples or illustrations.
   4. After doing this, you may analyze and critically evaluate the arguments with instructions from your professor, but you may also follow these guideline questions:
      a. Has the philosopher defined his or her terms appropriately in accordance with ordinary language?
      b. If he uses sense evidence as support, does it square with your own and others' sense experiences?
      c. Does he use inductive and deductive reasoning according to rules?
      d. Has he avoided logical fallacies?
      e. Are his conclusions supported by guidelines a–d?

D. Reading secondary sources.
   1. Be sure that you have read and understood the primary source first.
   2. In addition to general suggestions and those for reading primary sources, ask the following questions:
      a. Is the second philosopher using the same definitions as the first, or has he changed them in some way?
      b. What are the main points of his arguments and what conclusions are drawn about the primary author?
      c. How well does the second philosopher support or justify his main points and conclusions?
      d. Is the evaluation, analysis, and criticism of the primary author fair?

III. Learning how to philosophize.
   A. Speculation is the way in which you become aware of an issue or a problem. How an issue or problem is selected should be based on the following:
      1. How important or crucial is it to the lives, well-being, and growth of human beings?
      2. How important is it to a better and fuller understanding of you, others, and the world around you?
      3. How intellectually interesting is it to you?
   B. Analysis—a seven-step process:
      1. Define the issue or problem carefully.
      2. Gather all the relevant data you can.
      3. Analyze, organize, and classify these data.
      4. Formulate hypotheses or tentative solutions.
      5. See what deductions you can draw from these hypotheses.
      6. Verify and accept or reject deductions.
      7. Discover what the implications of your philosophizing are.
   C. Types of reasoning.
      1. Inductive reasoning goes from particular cases to general conclusions and is based heavily on sense observations.
         a. This type of reasoning yields only probable truths, but the probability can be either weak or strong.
         b. You must be sure that there are enough relevant particular cases to yield a reliable conclusion with strong probability, and also that the conclusion you draw is not too great for the particular cases you have cited to support that conclusion.
      2. Deductive reasoning is not based heavily on sense experience and derives a particular truth from a general statement. Four examples of deductive arguments are presented:
         a. The syllogism.
         b. "Either-or" form.
         c. "And or both-and" form.
         d. "If-then" form.
         e. Unlike inductive arguments, deductive arguments can yield certain truths provided that the premises of the argument are true and that the argument is valid (that is, the conclusion follows from the premises).
      3. Argument from analogy involves a comparison of one thing with another to clarify complex issues and to see similarities between two like things.
         a. The two things being compared should be truly similar in as many respects as possible.

60

      b. You must really be able to compare them—both things in the comparison must be observable or otherwise available for comparison.

    4. Dialectical reasoning began with Socrates and Plato and consists of three parts:

      a. Thesis—an idea or theory is presented for discussion and analysis.

      b. Antithesis—it is confronted by an opposing theory or idea.

      c. Synthesis—either a new thesis arises that combines the best and eliminates the worst of the first two ideas, or the original thesis is disproved and a new thesis is posited for discussion. At this point the whole process can begin again.

IV. Logical fallacies.

  A. Fallacies of oversimplification

    1. Mere assertion—does not prove anything but simply asserts, usually strongly, a belief or an opinion.

    2. False dilemma—sets up a black-or-white, either-or situation ignoring any other alternatives that may exist.

    3. Irrelevant argument—argues irrelevantly not on a major issue but on an unimportant side issue or an unrelated issue to the main one.

    4. Circular reasoning—attempts to prove itself by arguing in a circle, which of course can prove nothing (sometimes called "begging the question").

    5. Appeal to ignorance—since the burden of proving that something is true is always on the proponent, the burden cannot be shifted by saying that since we can't prove, something is *not* true; therefore, it must *be* true.

    6. Stereotyping—makes a judgment about one member of a class from a false or too great a generalization about that class.

  B. Fallacies of deception.

    1. Personal attack *(ad hominem)*—attacks, usually personally and unfairly, the person and not his or her arguments.

    2. Everybody does it—appeals to majority rule and the desire of most people to be members of the in-group.

    3. Appeal to pity—brings in elements of pity or sentimentality that are irrelevant to the argument to win listeners over.

    4. Appeal to vanity—appeals to the vanity of the listeners by flattery and attempts to coerce them into accepting an argument on this basis.

    5. Changing meanings—involves changing the meanings of key

words in order to win an argument or set up a false analogy.

C. Reductionism and expansionism are two other problems.

    1. Reductionism means to reduce statements, arguments, or views of reality to their simplest forms. It's a good practice provided that everything is reducible; otherwise, theories become oversimplified.

    2. Expansionism means to expand theories out into many parts or to present several different views of reality. The advantage is that if there are really complexities that cannot be explained simply, then expansionism helps to explain them. The disadvantage is that a fairly simple view or idea may be overcomplicated by presenting too many aspects or theories.

V. Taking tests and writing papers in philosophy.

A. Objective tests will be like those in other subject areas except that they may call for you to grasp distinctions and also to understand facts which are more abstract and conceptual in nature than other subjects. Suggestions are

    1. Apply good reading and study techniques.

    2. Take full advantage of study questions and summaries.

    3. Don't leave studying for last-minute cramming.

B. Writing philosophy—general suggestions:

    1. Organize before you write.

    2. Define key terms clearly.

    3. State and clarify main ideas.

    4. Develop ideas fully through examples or illustrations.

    5. Write a first draft, correct it, and write a final draft.

    6. Use appropriate English composition methods, getting help if you need it from someone proficient in English.

C. Writing philosophy—additional suggestions:

    1. Analyze and critically evaluate ideas and theories of others as well as specific problems and issues.

    2. Learn how to incorporate sense evidence and logical reasoning and how to spot logical fallacies.

    3. Present your own philosophical views.

D. Strategies for analyzing a philosopher's arguments:

    1. Describe and carefully present philosophers' positions.

    2. Analyze and critically evaluate these positions.

    3. Support and justify your contentions with sense evidence and reasoning.

E. Strategies for analyzing an issue or a problem:

    1. State the issue or problem carefully and clearly.

2. Present the strongest arguments and their bases you can find on both sides of the issue.
3. Analyze and critically evaluate each side's contention.
4. If required, present your own view and the reasons therefor.

F. Strategies for writing personal philosophical views:
   1. Be sure you understand what your professor expects.
   2. Go through the seven steps of how to philosophize.
   3. Describe and present each issue clearly.
   4. Present and discuss as fully and as clearly as possible your position on the issue.
   5. Marshal as much evidence as possible to support your position.
   6. Give as many examples and illustrations as you can to clarify your main points.
   7. Incorporate other philosophers' views where needed, being sure to give credit where it's due.

Additional Exercises and Activities for Study and Discussion

1. Find an example from any source of each of the logical fallacies presented in this chapter, describing it in detail and telling why the author should not have used it.
2. Describe any situations or times when you have committed any of the logical fallacies in discussions or arguments with your family, your teachers, or your friends. Also describe any fallacies they may have committed.
3. In examining your own experiences, describe any situations when you have used inductive, deductive, or analogical reasoning, reductionism, or expansionism, and also describe any errors you may have made then that you can now see. About how often do you think you use any of these types of reasoning? Examine and describe a typical day in your life to answer this question.
4. Using the seven-step process of how to analyze philosophically, deal with a problem or issue of your choice or one that your professor has assigned to you. Some possible suggestions: dealing with a broken love affair or friendship, dealing with some ecological or environmental problem, dealing with some problem in a human relationship with a member of your family or a friend, deciding whether or not to drop a course you are not doing well in, deciding who or what to vote for in an important election, and dealing with a difficult situation at work.

5. Set up an analogical argument on any two things that will help to explain or clarify what something is like, and describe any problems or difficulties you had in doing this. Here again follow suggestions from your professor or use your own ideas. Some possible suggestions: God is like a poet, engineer, dynamo, father, mother, king (select one); human beings are like animals, computers, machines, gods (again select one); love is like a spring day; being in business is like being in a war; "All's fair in love and war" (this implies an analogy).

Footnotes

1. René Descartes, *Discourse on Method,* in *The Philosophical Works of Descartes,* trans. Elizabeth S. Haldane and G. R. T. Ross (Cambridge: Cambridge University Press, 1911).
2. These steps, which include five originally established by John Dewey, in *How We Think* (New York: D. C. Heath, 1933), can be found in Harold H. Titus et al., *Living Issues in Philosophy,* 7th ed. (New York: D. Van Nostrand, 1979), pp. 226–227, from which I have freely adapted them.
3. Francis M. Cornford, trans., *The Republic of Plato* (New York: Oxford University Press, 1945), pp. 227–235.
4. Ibid., pp. 1–53.
5. I am indebted to Perry Weddle's *Argument: A Guide to Critical Thinking* (New York: McGraw-Hill, 1978), Chap. 2, for this categorizing of fallacies, which I found very helpful.

Bibliography

Carter, K. Codell. *A Contemporary Introduction to Logic with Applications.* Encino, Calif.: Glencoe, 1977.

Copi, Irving M. *Introduction to Logic.* 5th ed. New York: Macmillan, 1978.

Cornman, James W., and Keith Lehrer. *Philosophical Problems and Arguments.* 2nd ed. New York: Macmillan, 1974.

Emmet, E. R. *Learning to Philosophize.* London: Penguin, 1968.

Flesch, Rudolf. *The Art of Clear Thinking.* New York: Collier, 1962.

Gorovitz, Samuel, *et. al. Philosophical Analysis: An Introduction to its Language and Techniques.* New York: Random House, 1965.

Hospers, John. *An Introduction to Philosophical Analysis.* 2nd ed. Englewood Cliffs, N.H.: Prentice-Hall, 1967.

Little, Winston W., *et. al. Applied Logic.* Boston: Houghton Mifflin, 1955.

Moore, W. Edgar. *Creative and Critical Thinking.* Boston: Houghton Mifflin, 1967.

Reid, Charles L. *Basic Philosophical Analysis.* Belmont, Calif.: Dickenson, 1971.

Scriven, Michael. *Reasoning.* New York: MrGraw-Hill, 1976.

Toulmin, Stephen, *et. al. An Introduction to Reasoning.* New York: Macmillan, 1979.

PART 2

The Nature of
a Human Being

CHAPTER *3*

Aspects of Being Human and Mind and Brain

The first issue or problem we will take up now is what is the nature of a human being, or what is a human being and how does "it" differ from other beings (plants, animals, inanimate objects) that are found in existence. This is obviously a metaphysical problem, and perhaps the most important of all metaphysical problems since it concerns all of us so intimately. There have been many attempts to describe and define human nature, and they range all the way from considering it to be a mere biological organism and physical-chemical machine to being a divine entity who is closely related to a god or gods. The one thing we will discover for certain, I believe, is that we are dealing with a very complex and mysterious type of being that does indeed resemble other beings that we know of and can observe, and yet, at the same time, that seems quite distinct and different from them. As mentioned in the last chapter, I now intend to indulge in a temporary expansionism. What I will be doing is to try to put together all the major views of human nature that have been described down through the ages—all of the main and persistent theories that have been stated about humanity—and treat them as if they were all aspects of what a human being is. I don't intend for this examination necessarily to provide the definitive description of human nature, but I feel it will be helpful to look at all human aspects as fully as possible, after which we may be able to arrive at some conclusions about what human beings actually are. At the least, you will have a wide variety of possibilities from which to choose a workable theory about human nature.

Aspects of a Human Being

THE PHYSICAL ASPECT

This aspect defines a human being as an animal with a body and a brain and in its extreme form stresses this to the exclusion of all other aspects. This view is called "materialism" which means that the whole of reality, including human beings, can be explained solely in terms of matter and energy (which is usually considered as merely another form of matter). From this viewpoint, any talk of humnan beings as having a mind, soul, self, personality, as if any of these things existed separate from their bodies and brains, is merely an expansionist "error" and really has no basis in fact. The strong form of this view would say that there is no god or supernatural, no mind, inner self, spirit, or person, but only a physical-chemical and biological organism, basically like other physical beings only somewhat more complex.

This aspect has traditionally been put forth by physical, natural, and some social scientists. I don't mean to imply that all scientists believe that there is only matter, but merely that the sciences have provided the origin and supporting arguments for this view since they are the subject areas that study the physical and biological aspects of the world and human beings. Let us now look at the strong materialist theories from the physical and natural sciences and from behaviorist psychology and the social sciences.

PHYSICAL SCIENCE.   As far back as Democritus and Leucippus (approximately 450 B.C.), as you remember from Chapter 1, the atomic theory of reality was presented, describing the elements of everything as small, indivisible particles of matter that are in constant motion in space or void. These atoms were considered eternal, so there was no reason to posit a supernatural world or being to have created them; according to science, they simply have always existed in their basic states and have evolved over billions of years by their constant changing and collision into the world we see today, including human beings and their brains, which are the most complex forms these atoms can take. In this view and others like it, then, everything in reality is the result of minute particles of matter, imbued with some sort of energy, that operate according to natural and physical laws.

Human beings, as a definite part of the physical world, are then physical bodies with physical brains, all of which operate and function through physical-chemical actions and reactions. Since most of these activities can be observed or at least traced in some way, there is no reason to presume any other "mysterious" force that causes human beings to act as they do—they are merely "machines" that operate according to the laws of physics and chemistry. For example, a close examination or analysis of any human being will reveal that "it" is composed of many physical and chemical elements (atoms, molecules, cells, enzymes, proteins, mineral salts, and so on). Such an analysis will also show that the body and its parts run by electricity—electrical charges released within the brain and throughout the nervous system. The physical sciences, then, state that whatever a human being is or does can be explained in terms of its physical makeup and the chemical or physical interaction of its parts. Even if some things cannot be fully understood at the present time, there is no reason to try to establish some mysterious force to explain them either from within human beings or outside of them in some supernatural world that no one can conclusively prove exists.

The proponents of this view say that we should remember that many things about human beings were not known or provable in earlier times but have since been explained quite clearly, causing many religious "superstitions" to be discarded. If we keep working in the sciences, they say, we will eventually find the answers to those remaining mysteries that we cannot yet answer. Since the only things that are observable and measurable are the body and its activities, then why try to complicate matters further by suggesting other things (God, soul, spirit, mind, self) that cannot be observed or measured? Therefore, this view says that human beings are strictly physical bodies and brains.

NATURAL SCIENCE.   Supporting the physical view but in a different way are the natural sciences—botany, zoology, and especially biology. The natural sciences define plants, animals, and human beings as animate, biological living organisms that are made up of cells that interact within the organisms. These organisms, in turn, interact with each other and with their environments. They are influenced by their environments, and their environments are influenced or affected by them. These organisms come into existence, live, and die all because of biological processes that are governed by the laws of nature. Human beings, after all, have a lot in common with all living organisms but, of course, have more in common with animals; therefore, according to this view, human beings are really another form of animal with a more complex brain and nervous system. When these arguments are added to the ones put forth by the physical sciences, the biologists then claim that you can account for almost everything that human beings are and do, and what you can't account for now, you probably will be able to in the future as all the sciences advance in technique and knowledge. Here again there is no need to talk about any mysterious substance or substances; rather, we should stay with what is observable and with what is experimentable—anything else is pure speculation.

SOCIAL SCIENCES.   The social sciences, accepting pretty much the natural and physical scientific view of human beings, examine the social and cultural existence and behavior of human beings, in order to explain how they interact with each other and within their social-cultural environments.

1. Behaviorist psychology is based totally on the materialist theory, saying that in addition to the physical, chemical, and biological activities of human beings, their behavior can also be observed and the results of these observations will round out the explanation of what human beings are and do. Behaviorism really started with the experiments of Ivan Pavlov (1849–1936) during which he established that animals can be conditioned to react to certain stimuli and that one can change behavior and even predict future behavior through the recognition of the animal conditioned reflex. In Pavlov's experiments with dogs, everytime he fed them, he would ring a bell. Finally he discovered that if he rang the bell without feeding them, they would nevertheless salivate as if food were present.

His theories were carried on further by John B. Watson (1878–1958), an American psychologist, who argued that human beings, like animals and even plants, behaved in certain ways because of certain stimuli received from their environments. In fact, the behavior of human beings was totally determined by external stimuli, so that what caused them to act and react in certain ways was not due to any self, mind, or soul but simply to their natural, social, and cultural environments. The most famous proponent of psychological behaviorism, whose work followed Pavlov's and Watson's, is B. F. Skinner (1904–   ), who developed the Skinner box and really invented the theory called "operant conditioning," in which he said that human beings are merely materialistic (body and brain) sets of responses to external stimuli and that the way they behave can be explained totally by looking at their environments and seeing how they react to them. There is no inner mind, soul, self, or inner being that is the causer of human behavior; rather, behavior is determined totally and solely by the stimuli coming from people's external environments.[1] Therefore, behaviorist psychologists accept completely the materialistic view of human nature and merely add what they believe to be the final scientific explanations for why these physical beings act and live the way they do.

2. Anthropology and sociology are other social sciences that sometimes take the physical view of human nature by stating that human nature arises and is developed only in a social-cultural context. They believe that human beings are solely a product of their acculturation

or socialization, and of course, they study these areas to find out all they can about human nature. This view of human nature does not have to be based only on the physical view of humanity, but it usually relies pretty heavily on it. Therefore, in addition to the physical and the behaviorist-psychological views of human beings, there is the effect of their culture and their social relationships on them to add to the description and definition of human beings as physical-social animals.

THE MENTAL ASPECT

Some views of human nature see it as totally or basically mental or rational; that is, they consider human beings as creatures of reason. From this viewpoint, human beings are considered as reasoning beings who are quite different from any other beings in existence because they have minds, which are more than, or different from, their brains and bodies.

THE CLASSICAL OR RATIONAL VIEW.   Beginning with ancient Greece and continuing through Roman culture, and later through the Renaissance and then the Enlightenment periods, human beings have been thought of as essentially reasoning or rational beings. Socrates and Plato thought of human beings as minds that were imprisoned in physical bodies, and Plato went so far as to deny the importance of empirical knowledge (knowledge gained through the five senses) in favor of a higher reason that could only be attained when one turned the mind on higher ideas and thoughts and did not concern himself or herself with the material world. Aristotle also emphasized the mind over the body and brain, but did not exclude empirical knowledge as Plato and Socrates had; however, he also agreed with them that the most important part of human beings was their reason and reasoning abilities.

What this view says, then, is that human beings have something special called "mind" that is quite distinct from brain and body and is therefore not physical but mental in nature. It also stresses that the basic source of all reality is not matter but mind. Somehow, underlying or lying behind everything that exists, there is intelligence that causes everything to exist and be what it is. In other words, if we were to look again at the atomic theory, for example, the mentalist view would say that the atoms, energy, and void are all caused by some intelligence or intelligent being. This view is generally called "idealism" and can be found in three forms, which will be described more fully later in the chapter in the discussion of mind and body. Briefly, however, they are (1) subjective idealism, which says that there is no matter, but only minds and their experiences (the most radical position of idealism, held by very few if any philosophers today); (2) objective idealism, which says that behind or within all reality is a mind or intelligence that originally caused and now sustains the world order; and (3) dualism, a more moderate form of idealism, which says that body and brain exist but there is also mind, which is more than the physical but related to it in some way. The academic areas that study and emphasize this particular aspect of human nature are philosophy and psychology (other than strict behaviorism).

THE EMOTIONAL ASPECT

Another popular and persistent view of human nature is that it is essentially emotional; that is, human beings are basically "feeling" beings. Used in this sense, the word "feeling" does not mean only that human beings feel pain, heat, or cold, but also includes a whole emotional or aesthetic way of living that animals and plants don't share. The point here is that human beings do not live in the world only physically or even only physically and mentally, but rather that their basic and most important aspect is their emotions or their aesthetic view of the world. For example, it is from this aspect that a recognition of beauty, happiness, love, and friendship arises. This emotional or aesthetic emphasis can be found in several areas of our cultural history.

ROUSSEAUIAN ROMANTICISM.   Jean-Jacques Rousseau (1712–1778) put forth the theory of the "noble savage," which stated that human beings were essentially good and beautiful in their natural state and only corrupted by their societies and civilizations. He felt that human beings should live as close to the state of nature and their feelings as they can. This view, which has been prevalent at various times throughout Western culture, is called "romanticism." It emphasizes the "higher" feelings of human beings and glorifies the aesthetic aspect of humanity. For example, according to the romantic, it's not the physical, biological, or mathematical description of the world that matters, but the beauty of the sunset, the stars, and rest of nature, as well as the love human beings have for one another.

EXISTENTIALISM.   Another view that emphasizes the emotional aspect of human nature is the twentieth-century philosophy called "existentialism," which sees the physical world as essentially the enemy of humanity and rationalization as abstracting or taking away from what is real. Existentialists state that human beings are forced to live in a physical world by circumstances outside their control and may use reason to understand their predicament to some extent, but the important life decisions are made from "gut feelings" and involve commitments that can't rely on any physical experimentation or rationalization when the chips are down, but only on what "feels" right. For example, Søren Kierkegaard (1813–1855), the first religious existentialist, said that all physical knowledge and reason must be suspended where a human commitment to God is concerned; one must simply make a "leap of faith" because God is unreachable by sense experience or reason.

ART AND AESTHETICS.   In addition to the subject areas of philosophy in general and some branches of psychology, the special area of philosophy that deals with the emotional aspect of human beings is called aesthetics. This field is essentially the study of art and art works and what they mean and what they express about humanity. There are many theories as to what art means, but essentially there is some agreement that through art, human beings, as artists, express what it feels like to live in the world. This type of expression is not a rational analysis of different events or aspects of the world, such as the sciences and other parts of philosophy present, but a symbolic presentation of the whole range of human feeling from the more basic sensual feelings all the way up to the more complex emotions, such as love and other profound human feelings.

THE SPIRITUAL ASPECT

From this view, human beings are considered as essentially spiritual beings imbued either with a divine spark from a supernatural creator (God in the Western religions) or sharing, like the rest of nature but in a special way, some sort of spiritual essence of an Ultimate Reality, which is nonmaterial in character (the general view of Eastern religions). The important aspect of human beings, from this point of view, is their souls or spirits, which are usually considered invisible and connected in some way to some higher order of reality. The field of study that usually deals with this aspect is religion, which includes theology (the systematic formulation of religious beliefs). There are several versions of this view, but I will limit myself to three: Platonism, Western religion, and Eastern religion.

PLATONISM.   Plato felt that the soul was a spiritual substance that was imprisoned in the body and that therefore had no relationship with the physical being or the external world. Through reason, the soul could rise above the shackles of its physical binding and attain a sort of rational-spiritual world beyond the natural world. In his view, then, human beings were essentially rational and spiritual beings whose souls entered their bodies at birth and left them at death, returning to the spiritual world from whence they originally came.

WESTERN RELIGION.   It is very hard to generalize about all the Western religions (Judaism, Christianity, and Islam), but they essentially agree that there has always existed a supernatural, spiritual being of great intelligence, power, and goodness who created the world and everything in it including human beings. This being has endowed human beings with something special, a divine spark or essence that animates them with intelligence and a basic striving for goodness and perfection. Much like Plato, the Western religious view believes that human beings must strive to go beyond their physical and even rational aspects to attain some sort of salvation in an afterlife, which is spiritual rather than physical. The Western religions believe that this supernatural being is "theistic"—that is it is either a person or stands in some sort of personal relationship to human beings. They believe that the ultimate goal of all humans is the release of their spiritual beings into a supernatural world to enter into some kind of intimate or close relationship with that spiritual being that created them.

EASTERN RELIGION.   It is even more difficult to generalize about Eastern religions, but one major difference between them and their Western counterparts is that the supernatural Ultimate Reality in their conception is essentially nontheistic, that is, more like a power source or ultimate destiny than like a personal being. They believe that this world is not the final existence for human beings but that there is some world or existence "beyond" the natural world which all human beings will eventually attain. Since their view of the Ultimate Reality is nontheistic, they believe in a kind of merging of all human beings with or into this Ultimate Reality rather than a relationship between human beings and a divine personal being. All these religious differences and theories will be discussed later in the chapters dealing with philosophy of religion (Part IV), but for the present, it is enough to know that the religious view of humanity sees its nature as spiritual rather than physical or mental.

THE SELF AND WILL ASPECTS

Two other aspects that at least should be mentioned are the aspect of a human being as self, person, or personality distinct from body, mind, emotions, and soul, and also the aspect of a human being who has a will and who therefore is self-directing.

THE SELF.   We will discuss this aspect in greater detail in the next chapter, but the claim being made here is that human beings are essentially persons or personalities and that there is some kind of persistent, yet private essence that differentiates each human being from another. In this view, self is not mind, body, emotions, or soul, but something other than these that develops and uses all of them in some way.

THE WILL.   The will is not usually considered as separated from the self or mind, and very few theorists think of human beings' essence as will. Nonetheless, I felt that it should be mentioned in this discussion of aspects of human nature. In many views of human nature, human beings are either considered as having "free wills" to direct their lives and their behavior or as not having any such thing but rather as being "determined" by external or internal forces. However, in much of human history, the concept of will has been important as a kind of directing and decision-making aspect of human beings and has been cited as one of the major differences between human beings and all other beings in the world. In other words, rather than being totally subjected to the forces of nature as animals and plants are, human beings can "will" to do otherwise, at least to some extent.

Before evaluating these aspects, let us look at what have been cited as some of the general differences between human beings and all other beings that can be found in reality.

DIFFERENCES BETWEEN HUMAN BEINGS AND OTHERS

ANIMATE AND ORGANIC.   Animals, plants, and human beings are animate and organic beings. Interestingly enough the word "animate" comes from the Latin word *anima,* which means soul, and *animate* essentially means alive or living (animated). Being organic also means being alive or living, but "organism" also implies a unified organization of parts that interact to make up the whole. The qualities of being animate and organic involve some sort of constant activity, an exchange of cells, chemicals, or fluids, that must continue to take place for the organism to persist. If for any reason this activity ceases, then the organism or animate being becomes inorganic or inanimate. For example, the heart must continue to beat, the lungs to respirate, and the brain to send its electrical messages to different parts of the body for an animal organism to continue to be organic and animate. If any of these fails, the rest of them fail, and the organism stops functioning. Therefore, there is a great difference between animate organisms and inanimate objects in that rocks, earth, and metals, for instance, are not animated or alive in any way. They can be considered "organic" only in the broadest sense of the word in that they are made up of parts that contribute to their unified wholeness, but there is no activity such as that which can be found in living plants, animals, or human beings. However, the distinction between organic and animate as opposed to inorganic and inanimate beings does not bring out the differences beween humans and plants and animals. Some of these differences are described next.

PHYSICAL DIFFERENCES.   Human beings differ physically from most of the rest of nature in that humans stand upright, have more flexible and greater use of their hands and arms, and have a larger brain and more sophisticated nervous systems. Some animals, particularly those of the family Pongidae (gorillas, chimpanzees, orangutans, and gibbons), have these attributes, but even they have them in significantly lesser degree.

SOCIAL, CULTURAL, AND INTELLECTUAL DIFFERENCES.   The wider gap between humans and animals and plants are those differences that involve the highly sophisticated, complex, and intricate cultures, societies, and human relationships that humans have developed. These seem to be largely due to (1) a more highly developed consciousness including a self-consciousness; (2) a very intricate and complex language ability, involving imagination, symbolizing, analysis, and intellectualization; and (3) an ability to step back or rise above nature and the world observing them as separate. These abilities have enabled human beings to establish history, cultures, traditions, ethical values, art, religion, philosophy, science, government, and ways of passing all this on to succeeding generations. It is important to realize that there are many other sophisticated cultures, abilities, and even communications systems among animals of all species, but there can be no doubt that the most complex of these pale beside those created and developed by human beings. With these differences in mind, then, let us now begin a brief and general evaluation of the aspects which were presented.

EVALUATION OF THE ASPECTS

THE PHYSICAL ASPECT.   It seems hard to refute, even if one wanted to, the fact that human beings have a physical existence and that almost everything they do depends largely upon their bodies and brains. As far as we know *for certain,* we have no existence outside of or apart from our bodies and brains. A recognition of our strong dependence on the physical aspect of our existence, however, does not mean that there is not more to human beings than just their bodies and brains, even if that "more" is caused by or dependent on the physical. Therefore, the problem often faced by the natural, physical, and social sciences, and behaviorist psychology is that their investigations and observations, although at times quite valid, do not explain everything. Human beings are composed of physical, chemical, and biological elements, and they also react to external stimuli causing them to behave in certain ways. The problem, however, is not that the physical view of human beings is invalid; it is just that there seem to be some areas of human life that are not totally explainable using only the physical aspect and the sciences that study it. Some of these differences will be discussed in dealing with the mind and brain controversy later in this chapter.

THE MENTAL ASPECT.   In its extreme form (subjective idealism), the mental aspect would seem to challenge common sense by stating that there is no physical world, objects, or body, only minds and their experiences; however, in its more moderate forms (objective idealism and dualism), it accounts well for the nature of human beings' experiences, such things as dreams and imaginings, and for consciousness that mentalists argue is much more than electrical discharges in the brain. As we shall see later in the chapter, the mentalist argues that physical occurrences just do not account for some parts of reality that humans experience. This aspect, however, is difficult to prove—much more difficult than the physical. For example, where is the mind? We can obviously locate and dissect a brain and body, but where is this thing called mind? Also, if we continue to talk about some sort of mind or intelligence that created and sustains the universe, how do we prove that, and where does *it* exist? Further, even though we accept humans as reasoning beings, is that all they are? What about their emotional and spiritual aspects?

THE EMOTIONAL ASPECT.   The critical analysis of this aspect asks that even though we have experiences of feelings and emotions, should we give them such importance? Isn't it more important to concentrate on our physical existence either with or without our mental existence without getting into such difficult things as emotions? Even if we have them, why should we place much importance on them? Aren't we always trying to control and suppress emotions by using reason? On the advantage side, emotions stop us from becoming merely cold, calculating reasoning machines and can also bring out more clearly some of the more beautiful, aesthetic parts of living. One of the real problems with the emotional aspect is that emotions are extremely difficult to define and describe. We can analyze the body, brain, or mind through the sciences and philosophy, but when we are dealing with emotions how can we be anything but inexact and imprecise?

THE RELIGIOUS ASPECT.   This aspect attempts to answer many questions about the cause of the universe and human beings. It further provides a loving, intelligent being as a creator, but also ties humanity in with this being. The problem with religion is that it is difficult to prove its claims conclusively. If we thought we had trouble locating mind, then how much more of a problem is it to locate and define "soul"! Can we experience soul in any sense at all as we can experience body or mind? Many will argue that religion at one time served a purpose in that it provided "storybook" answers to human questions, but now that we have science, which has answered many of these same questions, why should we bother ourselves about religion anymore? Even if it satisfies some psychological or emotional need that human beings have, shouldn't they realize, if this is all it does, that religion is really nothing more than a crutch of sorts? These are some of the problems with and criticisms of the religious aspect.

THE SELF AND THE WILL.   As for the self, many theorists, as we shall see in the next chapter, suggest that self is really a superstition and a delusion. After all, what is this self, and can it really be found or even experienced? Aren't we just multiplying our problems by suggesting that there is more than body, brain, and/or mind? Maybe this so-called "self" is really nothing more than a combination of the three, or even if it's only one of them (for example, mind), then why call one thing by two names? On the plus side, self stresses individualism, uniqueness, and personhood or personality, and shouldn't these be considered as very important when we are trying to define human beings?

As for will, it suffers from the same problems as self in that it is difficult to prove or to locate. Second, will is denied by determinist behaviorists as either nonexistent or merely as reaction to external stimuli. They say that when we act in certain ways, we do it because we are conditioned to do so, not because we will ourselves to do so. Its advantage is that it emphasizes human self-direction which has always been admired.

A TENTATIVE SYNTHESIS.   One of the purposes of expanding human-beingness to six aspects is to give us the widest view of humanity that we can have. Notice that all these aspects have been presented down through the centuries in one form or another: there has been the emphasis on the religious aspect since the earliest reaches of time and especially during the Middle Ages; the emphasis on the mind and rationality during the Grecian period, the Renaissance, the Enlightenment; the emphasis on emotions during parts of every century, but especially the nineteenth century; the emphasis on the physical during the twentieth century; and the discussion of self and will throughout all of these periods. All the views or aspects would seem to have some validity as long as—and this is the main difficulty with them all—one aspect is not considered the *only* correct view of humanity to the exclusion of all others. There are justifications for all of them to some extent or another, and my feeling is that all of these areas should be investigated thoroughly without rejecting any of them until one has found them wanting in some important way. We can learn a lot about the nature of human beings by looking into all of them before deciding whether or not they all fit together as parts of the whole or whether any of them should be eliminated from serious consideration. Another possibility is that they can all be absorbed into one, two, or maybe three of the aspects. For example, it's possible that all the aspects may be absorbed into or reduced to body and brain, mind and body, or mind, body, and self; we will look into such possibilities after we deal with the mind and brain problem and also with the self-no self issue in the next chapter. At that time, I will present to you a possible theory of synthesis which you can study and speculate about as well as analyze. First, however, we will examine the mind and brain controversy.

Mind and Brain

THERE ARE ONLY BODY AND BRAIN—MATERIALISM

In discussing the physical aspect, I presented a brief discussion of materialism; it is important now to elaborate upon it. The terms "materialistic" or "materialism" usually mean in their popular usage that someone is "money hungry" or always interested in material goods rather than in the intellectual or spiritual things of life. However, in philosophy or science "materialism" means that all of reality is composed of matter or matter and energy and that everything in reality can be explained in terms of natural and physical laws concerning matter and motion. Since the body and the brain are physical things, they are subject to the same laws as any other physical objects in existence. Being living pieces of matter, they are also subject to the biological laws applicable to living organisms. According to this theory, then, everything attributable to human beings in any way can be reduced to the physical-chemical-biological activities of brain and body—there simply is nothing else, and any attempt to bring forth other things, such as mind, self, soul, will, ghosts, or what have you, is just superstition or delusion.

REDUCTIONISM—THE MAIN PROBLEM WITH MATERIALISM

The major difficulty with materialism is that it runs into trouble because it tries to reduce everything to matter, which causes many problems to arise, especially when considering the nature of human beings. One of the main difficulties arising from materialism and its reductionism is that of identity. The materialist insists that human beings are merely brains and bodies, which means that human beings must be completely identical with their bodies and brains and that there is nothing else involved in their existence. Now the great advantage to this identity theory is that it is simple and uncomplicated. It says that there is only one thing that is "I" and that is my body (brain is of course considered a physical part of the body); therefore, humans *are* their bodies and nothing more, and when their bodies die, there is no more "they" or persons. This simplifies things a great deal since we do not have to contend with "ghosts in the machine" such as souls, minds, selves, inner men or women, and other such cumbersome ideas. It also does away with religion and many other human activities, but then so what? If there is only body, then why waste our time on non-existent things?

This would be fine, except that there is a real problem with this identity theory. If two things—I and my body in this case—are truly identical, then what can be said about one should be able to be said about the other with nothing left over. For example, there are indeed many things I can say about my body that I can also say about me— my height, weight, spatial location, date and place of birth all apply identically to both me and my body. However, is there anything true of me that is not true of my body; that is, can I say anything about me that I can't say about my body? It makes sense to say that I am moral or immoral, but does it make sense to say the same thing of my body or any part of it? For example, if I shoot and kill someone, is my body or the hand that held the gun immoral? It seems to be a very strange application of language to say that my hand was immoral. To be considered moral or immoral, it would seem at least human consciousness is involved, not merely being a physical organism.

Further, if I have profound wishes or desires or deep human or religious commitments, can I also say that my body has these same wishes or commitments? If I desire to write a book, create a painting, or become famous, for example, does it make sense to say that my body also wishes to do these same things (my body wishes to write a book, and so do I?). If I say I love God and worship Him, does it make sense to say that my body loves God and worships Him also? You can see that in order to say that I am only my body and nothing else and that my body is I and nothing else, I will have to say some rather strange things about my body. There are other problems resulting from this attempt at reductionism, but I will discuss them later under dualism.

THERE IS ONLY MIND—SUBJECTIVE OR RADICAL IDEALISM

This view was mentioned briefly earlier in Chapter 2 and under the discussion of the mental aspect in this chapter. This theory was put forth by Bishop George Berkeley, as noted earlier, and arose from his speculations about the privacy and limitations of human experiencing. The theory says essentially that the only things that exist in reality are minds and their experiences; therefore, there is no physical world, physical body, or matter that exists separate from some sentient being's experiencing of them ("sentient" means the ability to have sense experiences). Berkeley argued, in the tradition of the empiricists John Locke (1632–1714) and David Hume (1711–1776), that there is no knowledge or idea of anything without sense experiences. He went on to say that the only thing we can ever know or perceive are our own sense experiences. However, whereas most of us and other philosophers and scientists feel that many of the sense experiences we have are of an existent physical world with physical objects in it, Berkeley speculated that we have no justification for presuming such a thing. He thought we could never know anything except our own experiencing and theorized that therefore nothing existed but human minds and their experiences.

REDUCTIONISM—ALSO THE MAIN PROBLEM WITH SUBJECTIVE IDEALISM

Here again the problem with subjective idealism is that it attempts to reduce everything in reality to one thing, mind, and what it experiences, saying that since we can't know if anything exists if it is not experienced, then only that which we experience really exists. Berkeley was quite right in demonstrating how difficult understanding human perception really is. For example, how much of reality is really "out there" and how much of it is within our minds and their experiences? What is the world really like outside of our perceptions of it? Unfortunately, the answer to this has to be that we can't really know for sure. The real problem with Berkeley's reasoning, however, is that merely because we cannot perceive the world *un*perceived how can we say that it doesn't exist outside of our perceptions? Needless to say, a whole group of problems begins to surface for us if we accept subjective idealism. For example, if there is no physical world out there that is stable and persistent, then how is it that our perceptions have order and stability? When I go back into a room I have been in before, I see pretty much the same things, and how can that be if there are only my mind and its experiences? Berkeley, being a good Bishop, tried to say that God, the greatest of all sentient beings, perceived the world when human beings didn't and therefore provided the necessary order in our perceptions. However, then the question arises that if nothing exists unless some human being perceives it, who has perceived God? We will discuss idealism and Berkeley's contentions more fully in the chapter on perception later, but, at least at this point, the subjective idealism view of reality and human beings would seem to suffer the same or worse problems than materialism from its own form of reductionism.

THERE IS BOTH MIND AND BODY—DUALISM

The alternative to both materialism and subjective idealism is a theory called dualism, which says that there is body (including brain), and there is also something called mind, and they both exist in reality and are somehow related. After all, if they both exist (body and mind) and humans have them both, then they must be related in some way. The problem which now arises with dualism is how can two entirely different things (physical and mental) be related? If there can be no mind without the physical brain and the physical body in which it resides, then there has to be some relationship between the two, and the real question is what could such a relationship be?

Plato, whose view of mind is that it was a nonmaterial substance which really had no relationship to body except that it was imprisoned within it, was one of the first to put forth the dualistic viewpoint. In this view, mind is a nonmaterial substance related to an animal body as a possessor to a thing possessed, as a tenant to an abode, or as a user to a thing used. In other words, the theories set up to account for the relationship of two such disparate things as mind and body are possession, occupancy, or use. However, each of these theories has its problems when examined more closely.

POSSESSION. The problem with the possession theory is that possession is essentially a social or legal concept, and one's ownership (if one can call it that) over his or her body certainly arises from no human social customs or laws and is not alterable by them. If people buy houses or cars, they either pay money or enter into legal contracts to purchase them and thereby acquire ownership or possession. No such contract is entered into and nothing is paid for our bodies, however. A further problem with possession is that the loss of the body is in no way equivalent to the loss of any other human possession, but is regarded by humans, and rightly so, as a terrible loss or disaster equal to no other. If people lose their cars or houses as long as they have their lives and their bodies, they can survive: without their bodies, however, known existence, at least, is over.

OCCUPANCY.   The problem with occupancy to describe the possible relationship between mind and body is that it is a physical concept. One thing occupies another by being *in* or *upon* it. For example, if I occupy my car, it is because I am sitting on top of or inside it. However, in the dualist view, the mind is not a physical, but a mental thing, so how can it occupy space at all? One can say that the brain occupies the skull, but how can we clearly say that the mind is *in* or "occupies" the brain? Where indeed is it located? Since the mind is considered by the dualist as nonphysical, then it cannot be resting in or upon any physical body.

USE.   The problem with the use theory is that people simply do not use their bodies the way they use implements or tools. They sometimes use their limbs and other parts over which they have voluntary control, somewhat like they use tools, but many bodily parts are not within their control at all.

We must conclude, then, that human beings do not *have* a body in the way that they have anything else at all, and any comparisons of the body to material possessions or instruments or abodes are misleading. Whatever the connection between people and their bodies, it is far more intimate and metaphysically complicated than is anything else we can think of. People's bodies are at least parts of themselves, and we all believe that, but they are not part of us in the same way that an engine is part of a car or that even one of our legs is a part of our bodies. Notice that this whole problem of relationship between mind and body has arisen because we have abandoned (even if only temporarily) the materialist and subjective idealist reductionism. Perhaps you can see now why those theories have been put forth—if we can show that there is really only one thing (mind *or* body), then we do not have to show relationships between two things. If, however, two things cannot be reduced to one thing, then we are stuck with trying to show how they relate to one another or how they are connected. It behooves us, then to look further into the claim that there are really two different things that exist—the mind and the body. We will discuss these two things as mind and brain hereafter since the brain is a part of and included in the body and yet the physical part of the body that is most closely related to the mind.

Mental and Physical Events (Mind and Brain)

In his book, *An Introduction to Philosophical Analysis,* John Hospers presents a brilliant and precise analysis of what happens when human beings hear a sound. The description is as follows:

> What happens when you hear a noise? Unless you are just "Hearing things," in which case the auditory sensation is generated from within the brain itself, something first happens outside your body: soundwaves, alternate condensations and rarefactions of the air, cause air-particles to strike repeatedly on your eardrum, so that it vibrates. The eardrum is connected by three small bones to a membrane that covers one end of a spiral tube in the inner ear. The vibration of your eardrum is transmitted through this chain of three bones to the membrane at the end of the tube. The tube is filled with a liquid, perilymph, so that the vibration in the membrane attached to these bones causes a corresponding vibration to pass through this liquid. Inside the first tube is another one filled with a liquid called endolymph; vibrations in the perilymph cause vibrations in the membranous wall of the inner tube and waves in the endolymph. Small hairs stick out from the membranous walls into the endolymph, which are made to vibrate by the vibrations in the endolymph. The auditory nerve is joined to the roots of these hairs. The vibration of the hairs causes impulses to pass up the auditory nerve to a part of the brain called the auditory center. Not until the auditory center is stimulated do you hear a sound.[2]

Hospers goes on to say that all these events, no matter how minute or technically unobservable, are physically minute changes going on inside the human head, but what happens when the auditory center is stimulated, he adds, is something different altogether. The actual hearing of the sound, let us say a bell ringing, is no longer a physical event locatable inside the head, but something entirely different. It is an auditory sensation, a sound *experience,* and this is not a physical, but a *mental* event. Hospers goes on to say that "It is an *awareness,* a state of *consciousness*" and the same holds true for all other sensory experiences such as seeing, smelling, touching, and tasting.[3]

In view of the foregoing, it would seem that if you examine any process involving the senses and try to describe it, you will find that you have two descriptions—the scientific one, which describes the physical part of the process, and the experiential one, which describes the actual sensory experience that is mental, not physical. Why is this?

Are there really differences between physical events and mental events? If so, what are they?

DIFFERENCES BETWEEN MENTAL AND PHYSICAL EVENTS

In addition to the problem of identity, described as a criticism of materialism, there are two other differences which are claimed by the dualist: locatability in space and private versus public observability.

LOCATABILITY IN SPACE.   We can always locate physical things, events, and processes in space. They take place somewhere. In fact, one of the defining characteristics of any physical object is that it occupies and is locatable in space; that is, it is spatial. But where is the sensory experience located? Going back to Hospers' description, if you hear a bell ringing, then where is your auditory sensation—where is your hearing of the bell ringing located? It can't be in the physical soundwaves or the bell or between the bell and your ear, because all of these occurrences take place outside of you and are located in space. Would it be inside your head, then? The neural processes and electric discharges can certainly be located inside your head and may even be measured, but where is the auditory sensation? Is the bell ringing sound occurring inside or on your ear, or is there a tiny "bell ringing" going on in some part of your brain that someone else could observe or hear? It makes sense to talk about the physical-neural processes as occurring 2 inches behind or inside your ear, but does it make any sense to say that the ringing sensation is occurring 2 inches behind your ear?

The same problems arise if the sense experience you are having is not caused by objects outside of your body. Supposing you see spots or other configurations before your eyes or see things in your dreams— exactly where are they located? Since they do not exist in space at all, where do they exist? Certainly they do exist because you *do* in fact see them; they are as real as spots on a leopard or stain spots on a rug— yet they seem to have no physical existence, but only a mental existence. Therefore, as strange as it may seem, there are some "things" in reality that are not located in space—mental things. This idea is very hard for us to accept because we have been brought up with a strong empirical outlook, where we merely assume that everything that exists has to be physical and exist in space. If you examine your experiences, however, you cannot pinpoint any spatial existence for mental events at all.

PRIVATE VERSUS PUBLIC OBSERVABILITY.   Another difference between mental and physical events is that physical events are publicly observable but mental events are not. If, for example, a volcano is erupting somewhere, it is publicly observable to anyone who can get to where it is happening either in person or by our vast and sophisticated communications technology. It is possible, through modern photographic techniques, to observe the fertilization of a human ovum at conception and even to follow its embryonic and fetal development. Also, through microscopic photography, it is possible to observe the smallest capillaries of the human circulatory system and see blood cells moving through them, none of which can be seen by the naked eye.

However, these are all physical events; is there any way at all that I can have or observe any of your sense experiences? Can I, for example, by using the powerful microscope see in your brain the tree experience you are having? I can and certainly do have my own experiences; in fact, I usually presume, as you do, that when the two of us are observing a flower, for example, that we are having at least similar experiences of sight, smell, and touch. We cannot be having exactly the same experiences, however, because mine are mine and yours are yours. I can never *truly* share your experiences and you can never truly share mine. In other words, we cannot even be sure that we are indeed experiencing the same thing; we can only presume it, but in at least some sense, we can never have or exactly share the same experiences. Even if somehow I could be hooked up to your sensory system so that when your skin was cut somewhere I could also feel pain, wouldn't my sensation of pain still be mine and yours still be yours? Therefore, there is a real difference in the ability to observe physical events and mental events.

THE REDUCTIVE FALLACY

Given these two differences plus the problems with identity, described in the discussion of materialism, it would seem that both the materialists and subjective idealists are guilty of what is called the "reductive fallacy." That is, they have both tried to reduce either mind to brain or brain to mind, and because of their distinct differences, such reduction in either direction is fallacious. It would seem that states of consciousness or awareness, however closely correlated they may be with physical brain-states or processes, are not the same thing. When any two things, processes, or events X and Y always occur together (activity in the physical brain and some sort of sense experience in the mind), there is a great temptation to try to reduce the one to the other and say that one of them is "nothing but" the other (mental experiences are nothing more than physical brain states). To do this, however, is to commit the reductive fallacy.

When thoughts, imaginings, or sense experiences occur, neural (physical) processes are going on in the brain—no one can deny this. In fact, it seems to be true that thoughts never occur in the absence of neural processes and, moreover, that neural brain states or processes are absolutely necessary for the occurrence of thoughts and other mental events. However, to say that X is a necessary condition for Y is not to say that X and Y are the same thing. If one is going to say that X causes Y, then there are two things, the cause and the effect or result. X could hardly be the necessary condition for or cause of itself. Therefore, it would seem to be an empirical fact that mental life and mental events are utterly dependent on physical brain activity; however, to say that this is true is not at all the same as saying that mental life *is* in fact brain activity. The pain you feel in your cut finger is causally related to the stimulation of physical nerve endings, but your pain is *not* the stimulation itself. You feel pain whether or not you know anything about nerve endings.

Dualism—Mind and Brain: Mental and Physical Events

Then if we cannot reduce brain to mind or mind to brain, physical events to mental events or vice versa, what are the alternatives if we accept the existence of *both* mind and brain? Our difficulties now shift to how to account for the fact that these two very different things are related, and most important *how* they are related. A number of theories have been put forth ever since the concept of dualism was first accepted that may be placed under two headings: radical and moderate or synthetic dualism. Refer to Figure 3–1 for a pictorial diagram of monistic and dualistic theories about mind and brain.

RADICAL DUALISM

Radical dualists argued for the complete distinction between and separation of mind and brain. They felt that mind and brain were so different that they could not be connected in any way. How, they asked, could something entirely mental be connected with something entirely physical? Yet they recognized that there obviously was some relationship. They then surmised that the connection must be one of some sort of parallelism, that is, that mind and brain must exist somehow side by side in some sort of synchronization so that when a physical event occurs in the brain, a corresponding mental event occurs in the mind. They envisioned brain and mind as two perfectly synchronized watches or as two perfectly matched trains traveling side by side on

Figure 3-1. Mind-brain dualism.

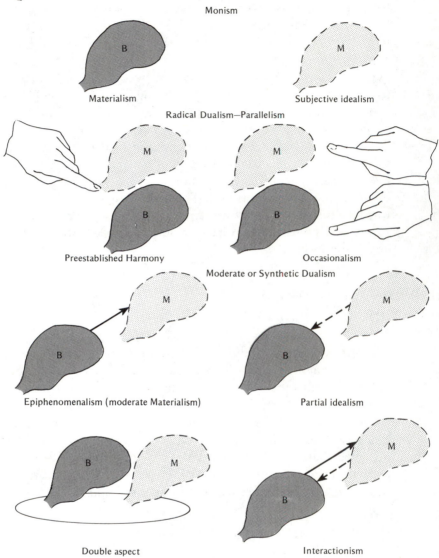

separate tracks at exactly the same speeds. Their idea was that there was a perfect coordination between mind and brain, but they were in no way connected or causally related (that is, one did not cause events to occur in the other). One of the problems they faced, of course, was how had this parallelism occurred and how it worked. There emerged two theories, both of which were dependent on the existence of God, an intelligent and powerful creator, who could establish such a complicated system.

PREESTABLISHED HARMONY.   One view stated that when God created human beings, He created the mind and the brain in perfect harmony so that whenever one event occurred in one, a corresponding event would occur in the other; that is, for example, when you cut your finger and your nerve endings were stimulated causing the pain center of the brain to become active, then because of the preestablished harmony set up by God, you also had the experience of pain in your mind.

OCCASIONALISM.   Instead of preestablished harmony from the beginning, occasionalism theorists stated that whenever you cut your finger, God would at the same time cause you to feel pain; that is, he constantly operated on every "occasion" to cause body and mind to work in perfect coordination because he was from moment to moment coordinating them.

EVALUATION OF PARALLELISM.   It is not totally impossible that parallelism or radical dualism is the case, but it seems farfetched for several reasons.

1. The theory is dependent on the existence of God, which is the cause of no little controversy in some scientific and philosophical circles, but even if we accept the existence of such a being, how can we know or be sure that He has established the mind and brain relationship in such a way? Further, as far as occasionalism is concerned, it seems even theologically questionable that God is constantly interfering in the world and causing moment-to-moment coordination between the human brain and mind.
2. The connection between brain and mind seems more intimate and more closely related than any sort of parallelism would suggest.
3. This is essentially only a theory and a theory that is in effect unprovable—how are we ever going to find out whether this is how brain and mind work or not? Perhaps in some afterlife we may, but this does us no good now, and what good reason do we have for continuing to believe such a theory, no matter how it's stated?

MODERATE OR SYNTHETIC DUALISM

This type of dualism sees brain and mind as both existing as distinct from one another but as interrelated in some intimate way. There are several theories presented here.

EPIPHENOMENALISM (MODERATE MATERIALISM).   The epiphenomenalist states that mind, as well as brain, does exist but that it exists because brain causes mind or mental events to occur in a one-way relationship. That is, mind comes about only through brain states or activities, and mind in no way can affect or cause anything to happen in the brain—the whole relationship is strictly a one-way street. Sometimes this form of dualism is described analogously as the mind is related to the brain in the same way as smoke is related to fire. In the larger metaphysical sense, this theory of moderate materialism states that matter or the physical comes first in reality and that mind and the mental come afterward as more highly developed forms of matter; that is, mind and mental events have evolved from matter and physical events.

PARTIAL IDEALISM.   This theory is the complete opposite from epiphenomenalism in that the belief is that mind controls the body and physical events in a one way relationship. For example, this view would say that our minds control our bodies, sometimes popularly described as "mind over matter." If I think that I am going to cross the street, then my mind and its thoughts "tell" my brain and body to take the necessary actions to do this. Metaphysically speaking, in the larger sense, this view would accept matter and physical events as existing but only as the result of a prior intelligence that created them and caused them to occur. This intelligence could be theistic (God), nontheistic, beyond nature, or within nature in some way. This view, then, does not deny the existence of matter or the physical, it merely says that it was created, operates, and is controlled by mind in some way and that mind comes before matter.

DOUBLE-ASPECT THEORY.   This view accepts that both mind and brain, the mental and physical, exist and that they are closely related because they are parts of the same underlying "substance." In this view, mind and brain are like two branches of the same tree trunk or two children of the same parents. The underlying substance could be described as anything, such as, soul, spirit, or self, or perhaps one could even say that mind and brain are two parts or aspects of the body that are the underlying substance.

INTERACTIONISM.   The last theory under moderate dualism is called interactionism because it states that both mind and brain exist in a very close interrelationship in which they both affect each other with equal power. For example, if one receives a blow to the head, then one becomes unconscious (physical event causing a mental event); on the other hand, if a person has a lot of mental anxiety, his or her hands begin to perspire (mental event causing a physical event). There can be variations in how brain and body came about, but once existing, they are both in constant interaction, one causing the other and vice versa at different times.

EVALUATION OF MODERATE DUALISTIC THEORIES

EPIPHENOMENALISM.   This theory has some validity in that there are many times when physical events obviously cause some sort of mental event to occur. For example, when a horse kicks us, we have pain, or when we get hit on the head, we become unconscious. Further, when the brain is destroyed in some way, as far as we know, there are no more mental events for the person whose brain that was. However, there are also some problems with this theory in that there seem to be some situations when the mind also affects the brain and the body. For example, some mental illnesses seem to have absolutely no physical basis, and yet the mentally ill people's bodies and brains seem to be affected—so-called "psychomatic" illness. Further, this theory does not account for such things as hypnotism, biofeedback, and yogic meditation, all of which seem to be cases of "mind over matter" or mind affecting brain and body. As for its larger metaphysical view that brain and body came first and then mind developed from them, there is no conclusive evidence to prove it, and even if it is so, it does not prove epiphenomenalism. A last point is that whatever reason can be found for saying the physical causes the mental will also hold good for saying that the mental causes the physical.

PARTIAL IDEALISM.   Many of the same arguments that apply to epiphenomenalism also apply to partial idealism only in reverse. It is true that there seem to be times when mental events or mind causes physical events or affects the brain and body, but, as shown, there are just as many times, if not more, where physical events or brain causes mental events or affects the mind. As for its larger metaphysical theory that mind or mental events come first in reality, the problem, as with epiphenomenalism, is how can this be proved? Where is this intelligence in nature or in the supernatural? Certainly many people *believe* that there is a god or some other intelligent power either beyond or within nature, but belief in itself is not proof. Also, as with epiphenomenalism, whatever reasons for saying the mental causes the physical will also hold true for saying the physical causes the mental.

DOUBLE-ASPECT THEORY.   This theory, of course, is also a possibility, but double-aspect theorists have really expanded the difficulties by proposing a *third* thing to contend with when there is no obvious evidence for such a thing's existence. We are having enough trouble with two things, mind and brain, and now with this theory we are forced to deal with a third thing, some sort of mysterious underlying substance! Even if we accept the premise that there is such a thing, then what is it, what is its origin, and how did it come to spawn both mind and brain? Certainly we are on very shaky ground when we propose that this substance is soul, spirit, or self; they seem even more indefinable than brain and mind, although we will attempt to define "self" in the next chapter. Even if we propose that body is the underlying substance, what have we accomplished? We do not fully understand the connection of brain to body, much less body to mind. This theory, then, really seems to complicate further the whole problem rather than to solve anything, and besides it is almost completely without proof.

INTERACTIONISM.   This theory would seem to be more feasible than the other three moderate dualistic theories in that it allows for mind and brain to affect each other, thereby doing away with the weaknesses of both epiphenomenalism and partial idealism that provide only for a one-way relationship. It also avoids the pitfalls of the double-aspect theory in that it deals with both brain and mind without dragging in a third unexplainable, indefinable substance. Its major problem, however, is that it does not show how this interactionism takes place. Since physical things and physical events are so different from mental "things" and mental events, how can such different things actually cause or affect one another? There are many theories in which it is believed that nonmaterial, spiritual, or mental forces can cause physical events, but there is absolutely no conclusive proof that any of these theories is valid. There is no clear explanation about how any interaction, if it indeed exists, works or where or how any interaction, if it indeed exists, works or where or how it takes place. Therefore, even though this theory does away with many problems that the other theories under both radical and moderate dualism, as well as the theories of materialism and subjective idealism, have, it still does not give a clear explanation of the relationship between brain and mind.

It is easy to see now why materialists and subjective idealists believe in their theories, for even though these theories have their problems, at least they do not have to try to account for a physical–mental relationship. What are we to do now? Must we retreat to materialism or subjective idealism with all their problems, or shall we select the best of the dualism theories? This is one of those points in philosophy where without further evidence we need, we will have to select the theory we feel is most highly supportable by reason and evidence, recognizing its drawbacks and yet striving to overcome them wherever we can. We also need to be open to any further developments in science, the social sciences, and philosophy that will shed further light on the problem. I will attempt to make some suggestions at the end of this chapter, but before doing that, let us look at various theories as to what the mind is.

Views of the Mind

PASSIVE VIEWS

Several views of the mind presented throughout history are of a passive nature; that is, they see the mind as a sort of receiver of sense impressions from external stimuli, which impressions are then stored up in the memory portion of the mind, and brought out later when needed. I would like to present three of these views now: those of John Locke, David Hume, and B. F. Skinner.

JOHN LOCKE AND THE MIND AS A BLANK SLATE.   John Locke, the father of empiricism (all ideas come from sense experience) in arguing that there are no innate or inherent ideas that human beings are born with, but only ideas based on sense experiences, described the human mind as a *tabula rasa* (blank state or chalkboard) at birth. He said that we are all born with a blank slate and that things get recorded on it only when we have sense experiences. According to Locke, for example, how could we have an idea of a tree, flower, or particular animal if we had never seen one? Further, how would we know what a ringing bell sounded like if we had never heard one? Could we know what the colors red, blue, and green were like if we had never seen them? Of course not, Locke said, so the mind at birth must be a blank slate that then becomes filled with ideas only when we receive experiences through our five senses.

DAVID HUME AND THE MIND AS A THEATER.   David Hume, who was also of the empiricist tradition, said that there could be no ideas without impressions, that is, no thoughts, ideas, or anything mental without some sort of sense experience to cause it. He thought of the mind as a theater on which and through which many perceptions came and went like players on a stage. He saw mind, in other words, as a large container or building for allowing various perceptions, ideas, thoughts, and so on, to make their appearances and disappearances.

B. F. SKINNER AND THE MIND AS COMPUTER.   Unlike Locke and Hume, Skinner really does not accept the theory that there is a mind or mental events in the sense that we have been discussing it under dualism. Remember he is a thoroughgoing materialist and believes only in body, brain, and behavior caused by external stimuli from the environment in which body and brain reside. When he talks about what we have been referring to as mind, he characterizes the brain as a kind of computer that, when programmed and fed proper information, yields a certain kind of output or information. He describes both mind and self (as we shall see in the next chapter) as a set of unified responses to stimuli. In other words, the brain receives stimuli from the outside world and then responds as a machine or computer does. The only thing mind would seem to do, in this view, is to sort, classify, and organize data fed into it and then to put this data out when stimulated to do so.

EVALUATION OF THESE VIEWS.   It is important for us to examine phenomenologically our own experiences of our minds to see if any of these theories squares with what we actually do experience. One difficulty that can be found with all these views is the fact that the mind is defined basically as a passive receiver or receptacle for sense experiences from outside of it. This is also a good time for us to apply a critical examination to the analogies presented to us in all three cases. First, what does a blank slate do? It can only do one thing—receive marks (sense experiences) put on it and hold them until erased. Does an examination of your own mind reveal that it does that and only that? Surely it is true that part of what your mind does is receive information and data from outside of it through the five senses; as a matter of fact, there is hardly a waking moment when this process is not going on to some degree or another. But the question is, Is that all that the mind does? What about connecting and relating these experiences? What about abstracting from them and generalizing about similar experiences? For example, if I see a number of red things—a shirt, a dress, a car, a strawberry—I can also think that they have that color in common (that they are several *red* things) and further that there is a general classification of redness to which all red things relate. Could a blank slate ever perform such analyses? How? In looking at David Hume's analogy of the mind as a theater, here again we are left with a passive receptacle that can do nothing but allow various perceptions to flow on and off of its stage. Is this what our minds do? Certainly there are many perceptions flowing through our minds constantly, but they do not merely hold them and let them go; they also relate, categorize, and synthesize them.

Skinner's concept of mind as a computer shows the mind to be somewhat more active than a blank slate or empty theater but really still has the mind only receiving and putting out data. Here again the mind certainly does these things, and what's in the mind is certainly many times a result of how it is stimulated from the outside and what it is sent and what it receives through the senses, but is that all that it does? How do these theories account for Mozart's creation of forty-one symphonies, all of them different? How do they account for Einstein's ability to abstract from any sense experiences his theory of relativity? How do they account for even the youngest child's ability to understand and grasp the concept that $2+2=4$ does not really apply merely to specific things such as apples and oranges, but is rather an abstract concept applicable to all of reality—any two things plus any two things will always equal four—and moreover that you do not need "things" at all to work this problem or others like it, just your mind! Therefore, even though these views have some validity, they do not fully square with the experience of our minds that we have by merely examining them for even a short period of time. All three of these views suffer from the emphasis on the mind as a passive receiver of information and only one of them adds that the mind also puts this received information out, which still seems to be too limited a view of the mind.

THE MIND AS ACTIVE AND INTENTIONAL

DESCARTES AND CONSCIOUSNESS.   When René Descartes was performing his creative skepticism, he put aside all beliefs, theories, and claims he had ever had and asked himself if he could arrive at any certain truths at all. He discovered that the one truth he could not doubt was that he was indeed doubting; that is, he was a conscious being who thought. He certainly wouldn't be able to doubt if he weren't conscious and couldn't think. He then came up with his first truth, which he stated as *cogito ergo sum,* or "I think; therefore, I am."[4] In other words, Descartes established consciousness as a basic and primary fact or truth of human existence. Edmund Husserl agreed with Descartes about consciousness being the basic and most important human attribute, but he felt that Descartes did not go far enough because he didn't describe the nature of consciousness, which Husserl felt was all important in understanding the human mind.

WHAT IS CONSCIOUSNESS?   Just exactly what is this thing we call "consciousness"? A definition of it, even though we are most intimately aware of it, is hard to come by and has even been described as indefinable. Sir William Hamilton has expressed this quite well when he stated

> Consciousness cannot be defined: we may be ourselves fully aware what consciousness is, but we cannot without confusion convey to others a definition of what we ourselves clearly apprehend. The reason is plain: consciousness lies at the root of all knowledge.[5]

Even though difficult to define, we think of it in several ways, one of which is the conscious mind as opposed to the unconscious or subconscious mind. Another rather simplified view is: "Whatever we are when we are awake, as contrasted with what we are when we sink into a profound and dreamless sleep, that is [what it is] to be conscious."[6] Consciousness would certainly include thinking, imagining, wondering, speculating, and analyzing, but it would also seem to come before all of them in the sense that to do any or all of these, one would first have to be conscious. Also, there are many things that our minds do of which we are not immediately conscious, such as controlling our autonomic nervous system (breathing, heartbeat, blood circulation, and so on), although through such activities as yogic meditation and biofeedback, we have discovered that we can also exert some conscious control over these. However, for the most part, the brain and mind seem to operate whether or not we are conscious of their operation. Nevertheless, our consciousness certainly has to be considered as basic to whatever we call mind. Sometimes, there is a distinction made between consciousness as an activity and consciousness as content; it is at this point we should return to Husserl for his description of the nature of consciousness.

HUSSERL AND INTENTIONALITY.   In opposition to the passivist theories of mind, Husserl proposed the concept of "intentionality." What he stated was that the nature of consciousness or the mind is that it is "intentional"; that is, it is always active, not passive, and reaching out to or pointing toward some thing or object (physical or mental). What he said was that consciousness is never without a content but always has an object; therefore, it is not merely a receiver for outside stimuli, but it actively searches out both internal objects (thoughts, imaginings, feelings) and external objects (trees, chairs, buildings). It certainly receives stimuli from within and outside of itself, but it receives these actively, constantly connecting, relating, and "weaving" all of them together into a constructed view of reality that is independently, uniquely, privately, and individually ours.

For example, if we are sitting on a beach watching the sun set over the ocean, what is our conscious mind doing. Of course, it is receiving all sorts of sense impressions through our five senses: the smell of the salt air and seaweed, the feeling of the cool seabreezes on our skin, the different colors of the ocean, sky, and the sun itself, the feeling of the warm or cool sand on our feet, and so on. At the same time we are receiving these impressions, our conscious minds are selecting, classifying, separating, and relating these impressions to experiences and internal feelings that we have felt in the past and are feeling at the moment. The conscious mind also directs itself selectively toward different impressions and outwardly toward different parts or aspects of the scene before us and around us. Now how could a blank slate, empty theater, or even a computer do this? It would seem that rather than having been born with a blank slate, empty theater, or mere collection of circuits and tubes, we have been born with some sort of potentially active mental capability that is never merely just conscious but is always conscious *of* something, whether that thing be physical or mental in nature. Because of this self-direction of consciousnesses and also the difference in our past experiences, each of our consciousnesses will have a different content and be uniquely ours rather than someone else's. For example, suppose that we are ill, tired, or upset for some reason; then our experiencing of the sunset will be different from that of another person who is sitting there with someone he or she loves, or someone who has no problems. We don't even have to talk about differences that are this radical; there will be a distinct difference for us if we have lived most of our lives near the ocean, or in the desert, the city, the country, or the mountains. It is true that these are environmental differences, but the conscious mind interweaves them with all other experiences, feelings, and occurrences, past and present, to construct a view of reality that is uniquely different from anyone else's.

Conclusions

What are we to conclude from all these observations and analyses? Certainly we must conclude that whatever else is true, human nature and especially the human mind and consciousness are extremely complex to the point of being quite mysterious. As to which of the theories of human nature you should accept as correct, you must try to discover which of these many theories fits best with what your sense experiences and reasoning reveal to you. You must, of course, examine your own minds to see which theory of mind squares with what you "see" there.

We have seen that all the theories have some validity and that they all also have certain drawbacks, which we must weigh carefully before deciding on which theory best fits what we experience as the nature of humanity and the nature of the human mind. The theories of materialism and subjective idealism give us the simplest, least complicated views of human nature and the human mind, but we must question whether that simplicity is warranted and justified by what indeed exists in reality. On the other hand, the dualistic views help us by including both mind and brain in our view of reality, but complicate matters further by presenting us with the extremely difficult problem of how to account for the intimate relationship between two seemingly quite disparate things—the mental and the physical.

Perhaps, however, before completing your analysis and selection of which aspect of human nature you feel most closely characterizes what a human being is and which view of the mind and brain controversy you should select, you should hold any final decisions in abeyance until we have examined and discussed another complex problem arising out of the question, "What is a human being?" and that is whether or not there is such a thing as self, and what theories there are about self, both pro and con.

Applying Philosophy—
Situations for Thought and Discussion

SITUATION 1

General Directions Concerning the Basic Question. In answering the following basic question, be as honest and sincere as you can. Also remember that beliefs not supported with evidence or reasoning are not philosophically sound, so do your best to present your philosophy rationally, giving evidence, illustrations, and examples from sense experience or supporting your beliefs through reasoning wherever possible.

The basic question: What is the nature of a human being and what aspects go into making up this nature?

1. Consider seriously the following questions as guidelines for answering the basic question well. You need not follow them point by point, but should instead write a clear, coherent essay:
   a. To what extent are any or all of the following "aspects" or parts of what a human being is? How do you know?
      (1) Body and brain—the physical or material
      (2) Mind—the mental or rational
      (3) Feelings—the emotional
      (4) Soul—the spiritual
      (5) Will—the decision-making process
   b. Explain the mind-body controversy and describe what you feel is the most acceptable version of mind and body and why.
      (1) Are there only body and brain and physical events?
      (2) Are there also mind and mental events?
      (3) If there are both, then what is their relationship?

SITUATION 2

Examine a 5- to 10-minute segment of your experiencing or experiences and describe in detail everything that is going on that you notice during this time, including what is happening to you as perceiver or experiencer. After you have done this, discuss what the implications are as far as what your human nature is, answering in detail the following questions:

1. To what extent did this examination indicate to you that you have any of the following: body, brain, mind, emotions, soul, or will? Justify your answer with evidence and argument.

2. To what extent did you discover that your mind, if you believe you have one, is passive or active? Explain.
3. To what extent could or can you locate your experiences in space? Exactly where did they seem to occur?
4. To what extent could or can these experiences be shared with others?
5. Which philosophical theory (materialism, idealism, dualism) best describes or supports what you discovered during your examination? If you accept dualism, then which of the forms of dualism best describes what went on and why?

SITUATION 3

Get together with a friend who is willing to do the following (your instructor may want to set this up in the classroom) and experience the "same" event or happening. The event should be fairly brief (5 or 10 minutes, no more), and neither experiencer should have to do anything but experience it as fully as possible. After experiencing the event, you and the other experiencer should do the following:

1. Write down in as much detail as possible *everything* you experienced during the period of time the event took place. That means everything—thoughts, feelings, sensations, and so on.
2. After having done this, compare what you have both written.
   a. How do the two written descriptions differ? How are they similar?
   b. What do these differences and similarities tell you about your brains, minds, bodies, emotions, and wills? Answer in detail.
   c. Are the experiences you both had locatable in space? If so, where? If not, how do you account for their existence?
   d. To what extent are the two sets of experiences private?
   e. To what extent do the differences or similarities depend on what you have both experienced in your lives prior to this experience?

Chapter Summary

I. Aspects of a human being.
   A. The physical aspect—body and brain. This view is supported in general by physical, natural, and to some extent social scientists.

1. Physical science—everything in reality is made up of matter and energy.
2. Natural science—plants, animals, and human beings are animate, biological living organisms made up of cells that interact within the organisms. Organisms then interact with each other and with their environments.
3. Social sciences—the social sciences basically accept the theories of the physical and natural sciences and then examine the social and cultural existence and behavior of human beings to explain their interactions with each other and their environments.
   a. In psychology, the behaviorist school is based totally on a materialist theory and believes that the behavior of human beings is additional scientific data.
   b. Anthropology and sociology also sometimes take the physical view of human nature.

B. The mental aspect—mind. Some views of human nature see human beings as totally or basically mental beings.
   1. The classical or rational view—starts with Greek and Roman civilizations and arises again in the Renaissance and Enlightenment periods. It essentially sees human beings as rational beings with minds that are quite distinct from their brains and bodies.
   2. This later develops into idealism, which may take three forms:
      a. Subjective idealism, which says that there is no matter but only minds and their experiences (the most radical form).
      b. Objective idealism, which says that behind or within all reality is a mind or intelligence.
      c. Dualism, which is a more moderate form of idealism, which says that body and brain exist but that there is also mind, which is more than the physical but related to it in some way.

C. The emotional aspect—feelings. This view holds that human beings are essentially feeling beings.
   1. Rousseauian romanticism—Rousseau felt that human beings were born perfectly in their natural state but were forever corrupted by their societies and reason. He believed in the "noble savage."
   2. Existentialism—reason is not the essential aspect of a human being but is a commitment of the whole of one's being. One must rely on one's feelings and faith to live in the world, which is the individual's enemy.

D. The spiritual aspect—soul or spirit. In this view, human beings are considered essentially spiritual in nature; that is, their essence is nonmaterial and somewhat supernatural. Three views putting forth this theory:
   1. Platonism. Plato feels that the soul was a spiritual substance imprisoned in the body.
   2. Western religion. There is a supernatural being who is a person or personal and that being has imbued each human being with a divine spark—the soul.
   3. Eastern religion. There is some sort of ultimate reality that is more than human beings, but human beings contain a portion of its essence in some way, and this forms their basic essence.
E. The self and will aspects.
   1. The self. Human beings are essentially persons or personalities, and self is something other than body, mind, or soul.
   2. The will. This is the decision-making aspect of human beings.
F. Differences between humans and other beings.
   1. They are basically animate and organic, but so are animals and plants.
   2. There are also very definite physical differences.
   3. Social, intellectual, and cultural differences are significant too.
G. Evaluation of the aspects of a human being:
   1. The physical aspect is hard to deny or refute, but is it really all there is to a human being?
   2. The mental aspect in its most extreme form, subjective idealism, would seem to challenge common sense and scientific research. There is also a problem with where mind is and how it works. Further, is reason really the only essential part of human nature?
   3. The emotional aspect is questionable because we wonder, even though we have feelings, whether we should not control them with reason. The advantage of this aspect is that emotions help us to avoid being machines.
   4. The religious aspect is hard to prove even though it does provide human beings with a sense that there is more to them than just the physical and even the rational and emotional. What is the evidence for the soul's existence, however? Where is it, and can anyone experience it?
   5. Self and will. Many theorists have denied the self's existence, saying that it really is a delusion. Again, where is it located, and what is it like? Its advantage is that it gives human beings more than other beings in existence—a person-

ality or personhood. Will suffers from the same problem as self as to location and makeup. It is also denied by determinists but is considered the seat of human freedom by free will proponents.

H. A tentative synthesis. All these aspects are considered significant by most humans, but we have to make sure that none of them is thought to be the only aspect of a human being. They may reduce to one or two aspects, but for purposes of investigation, perhaps none of them ought to be rejected.

II. Mind and brain.

A. Materialism states that there are only body and brain, nothing else and further that all that exists in reality is matter and energy. Everything else is superstition or unproved theories.

1. The main difficulty with materialism is that it reduces everything to one thing, matter, and not everything fits into that category.

2. Second, there is a problem with identity in that if I say that I am my body and nothing else, then I find that many things I say about myself are not applicable to my body, and they should be if we are identical.

B. Subjective idealism states that everything reduces to minds and their experiences, which denies the existence of matter or the physical and flies in the face of the sciences. Its problem, like that of materialism, is also reductionism.

C. Dualism. This theory states that both mind and body exist in some sort of relationship, but the problem with this is exactly what is the relationship?

1. Possession—the mind possessing the body—is one theory, but the problem with this is that it is essentially a social or legal concept, and no society or laws have established mind-body relationships. Also, humans do not possess their bodies in the way they possess anything else.

2. Occupancy is another theory, but this is a physical concept, and how can anything mental occupy anything since it is not a physical object in any way.

3. Use is another theory of the mind-body relationship, but the problem with it is that people simply do not use their bodies as they use any other objects or tools.

4. We must conclude, then, that whatever the relationship, human beings do not have a body as they have anything else.

III. Mental and physical events (mind and brain).

A. If you examine any process involving the senses and try to describe it, you will discover two descriptions:

     1. The scientific or physical one.

     2. The experiential one, which describes the actual experience and which is mental, not physical.

  B. Major differences between mental and physical events are the following:

     1. Physical objects and events are locatable in space, whereas mental events are not.

     2. Mental events are strictly private, whereas physical events are publicly observable.

  C. Since these differences are real and ineradicable, then both materialism and subjective idealism are guilty of the reductive fallacy—of trying to reduce two different and distinct things to one.

IV. Dualism—mind and brain: mental and physical events.

  A. If we cannot reduce mental events to physical events or vice versa, then we will have to deal with two things, and then the problem is, what is the relationship between them?

  B. Radical dualism or parallelism argues for the complete separation of mind and brain. Brain is one thing—physical matter—and mind is entirely different so that they must somehow operate on parallel paths.

     1. Preestablished harmony—this theory states that God set up mind and brain as two clocks in perfect synchronization so that when something happens in the brain, something corresponding to it happens in mind.

     2. Occasionalism—this theory states that God constantly intervenes in reality to ensure that brain actions cause mind events and vice versa.

  C. Evaluation of radical dualism or parallelism.

     1. It is dependent on the existence of a god, which is hard to prove conclusively. Even if we accept his existence, however, how can we know he has set mind and brain up this way?

     2. The connection between brain and mind seems more intimate and closely related than parallelism would allow.

     3. This is only a theory and one that is essentially unprovable.

  D. Moderate or synthetic dualism. This view sees both brain and mind as existing and distinct from one another, but as interrelated in some intimate way. Several theories attempt to show what this relationship is:

     1. Epiphenomenalism (moderate materialism) states that both brain and mind exist but that brain causes mind and that physical events cause mental events in a one-way direction. Mind has no effect on brain or body.

2. Partial idealism is completely opposite from epiphenomenalism in that it holds that there are both the physical and the mental but that the mental basically is the cause of the physical in a one-way direction.
3. Double-aspect theory states that brain and mind are both aspects of some underlying substance, like two branches are a part of the same tree trunk.
4. Interactionism. This theory states that both mind and brain exist in a very close interrelationship in which they both affect each other with equal power, in a two-way direction.

E. Evaluation of moderate dualism.
1. Epiphenomenalism has some validity in that many times physical events cause mental events, but often mental events do not seem to be caused in this way, and sometimes they seem to cause or affect physical events.
2. Partial idealism has the same objections as does epiphenomenalism except in reverse; also, it seems to argue that the mental comes first in reality, and there is no evidence to conclusively prove this.
3. Double-aspect theory raises a third problem in that we cannot account for the underlying substance mind and brain are both supposed to be a part of—it is guilty of unnecessary expansionism.

F. We can now see why materialists and subjective idealists argue so strongly for their monistic theories, for it is difficult to account for the relationship of mind and brain when they are considered two distinct things.

V. Views of the mind.
A. Passive views see the mind essentially as a receiver of data from outside it. There are three such views:
1. John Locke and his theory of mind as blank slate.
2. David Hume and his theory of mind as theater.
3. B. F. Skinner and his theory of mind as computer.

B. Evaluation of these views.
1. If we examine our minds and describe what they do or how they function, do we discover that they only receive data? What does a blank slate do except this? It cannot even make relationships among the data it receives.
2. If mind is a theater, then is the only thing it does is just let perceptions flow through it, on and off its stage?
3. Skinner says that mind is a unified set of responses to stimuli. This makes it more active than Locke's or Hume's theories, but again is the only thing that mind does is receive

stimuli and react to it? How does this view account for Einstein's theories or Mozart's compositions?

C. Mind as active and intentional.

1. René Descartes presumed this idea when he established his theory, "I think; therefore, I am."

2. Edmund Husserl stated that Descartes did not go far enough because Descartes did not describe the nature of consciousness, which is active, creative, and intentional.

D. What is consciousness? It is almost indefinable, yet it is essential to mind and lies at the root of all knowledge.

E. Husserl and intentionality. He said that the mind is not just there, as Descartes stated, but that it is active, intends or goes out toward objects (mental or physical), and is constantly creative. It is never without an object or a content and is directive in nature, not just a passive recipient.

F. One needs to examine one's own mind and consciousness to discover which of the many theories fits best with one's experience.

Additional Questions and Activities for Study and Discussion

1. Do a critical evaluation of B. F. Skinner's novel, *Walden Two*. To what extent do you feel such a society as he describes is possible or not possible, worthy or not worthy, interesting or uninteresting, and why? Would you like to live in such a society? Why or why not? Answer in detail.

2. Try as fully as you can to define and describe "consciousness" basically from your own experience of it.

3. Argue for and against materialism, idealism, and dualism, giving both sides of each theory and arriving at some conclusion about all three theories.

4. Read J. J. C. Smart's essay, "Sensations and Brain Processes," and critically evaluate it in view of what we've discussed in this chapter. Do you agree or disagree with his theory? Why? Be specific.

5. What is your opinion of what a human being would be like if he or she could have a brain transplant that would work? You might wish to read Robert Heinlein's *I Will Fear No Evil* or Barbara S. Harris' *Who Is Julia?* for some ideas. Do you think the recipients of such transplants would be totally new persons and have totally new natures, or would they retain some or all of their own natures? Why? How does your answer relate to the arguments for and against materialism, idealism, and dualism in the chapter? Be

specific. Presuming that one's human nature would be changed by such transplants, to what extent do you feel they should be allowed or encouraged (if they would work)? Why?

6. Read Plato's theories of knowledge and human nature in his *Republic,* and critically evaluate them in view of what's been discussed in this chapter. To what extent do you agree or disagree with his theories? Why?

7. Read Hermann Hesse's *Magister Ludi (The Glass Bead Game)* and describe how the ideal society depicted in the novel involves any or all of the aspects of human nature described in this chapter. Which ones are missing and how does their not being present affect the strived-for perfection of the utopian society in the novel? What do you think of this society and its goals? Answer in detail.

8. Read Henry David Thoreau's *Walden* and B. F. Skinner's *Walden Two* and compare and contrast them as to the different views of human nature depicted in each work. Which and how many of the aspects discussed in the chapter do you find the authors including in their appraisals of human nature? Give examples from the works to substantiate your views. Which view of human nature do you find most significant and why?

9. Read Jean-Jacques Rousseau's *Discourse on the Origin of Inequality Among Mankind* and Thomas Hobbes' (1588–1679) *Leviathan,* and compare and contrast their two views of human nature. Which view do you most agree with and why? If you agree with neither, then describe what your view is and why you think it's more accurate than theirs.

10. Read John Steinbeck's *Grapes of Wrath* and describe and critically evaluate his view of human nature. To what extent do you agree or disagree with him and why? Support your arguments with specific examples from the novel.

Footnotes

1. B. F. Skinner, *Science and Human Behavior* (New York: Free Press, 1965), pp. 30–31.

2. John Hospers, *An Introduction to Philosophical Analysis,* 2nd ed. (Englewood Cliffs, N.J.: Prentice-Hall, 1967), pp. 378–379.

3. Ibid., p. 379.

4. Frederick Copleston, S. J., *A History of Philosophy* (Garden City, N.Y.: Image Books, 1962), Vol. 4, pp. 100–101.

5. Dagobert D. Runes, ed., *Dictionary of Philosophy* (Totowa, N.J.: Littlefield, Adams, 1962), p. 64.

6. Ibid.

Bibliography

HUMAN NATURE

Arendt, Hannah. *The Human Condition*. Chicago: University of Chicago Press, 1958.
Fromm, Erich, and Ramon Xirau, eds. *The Nature of Man*. New York: Macmillan, 1968.
Harris, Barbara S. *Who Is Julia?* New York: Popular Library, 1977.
Heinlein, Robert. *I Will Fear No Evil*. New York: Berkley Pub. Corp., 1971.
Krutch, Joseph Wood. *The Measure of Man*. New York: Grosset and Dunlap, 1953.
Rogers, Carl, and Barry Stevens. *Person to Person: The Problem of Being Human*. New York: Real People Press, 1967.
Scheler, Max. *Man's Place in Nature,* trans. Hans Meyerhoff. New York: Noonday, 1962.
Sherrington, Charles. *Man on His Nature*. New York: Mentor, 1951.
Shostrom, Everett. *Man, the Manipulator*. New York: Bantam, 1968.
Skinner, B. F. *Walden Two*. New York: Macmillan, 1976.
Stevenson, Leslie. *Seven Theories of Human Nature*. London: Clarendon, 1974.

MIND AND BODY

Anderson, A. R., ed. *Minds and Machines*. Englewood Cliffs, N.J.: Prentice-Hall, 1964.
Borst, C. V., ed. *The Mind-Brain Identity Theory*. New York: St. Martin's, 1970.
Brain, W. Russell. *Mind, Perception, and Science*. Oxford: B. H. Blackwell, 1951.
Broad, C. D. *The Mind and Its Place in Nature*. London: Routledge and Kegan Paul, 1925.
Campbell, Keith. *Body and Mind*. Garden City, N.Y.: Anchor, 1970.
Ducasse, Curt J. *Nature, Mind, and Death*. LaSalle, Ill.: Open Court, 1951.
Flew, Antony, ed. *Body, Mind, and Death*. New York: Macmillan, 1962.
Gunderson, Keith. *Mentality and Machines*. Garden City, N.Y.: Anchor, 1971.
Hook, Sidney, ed. *Dimensions of Mind: A Symposium*. New York: Collier, 1961.
Laslett, Peter, ed. *The Physical Basis of Mind*. Oxford: B. H. Blackwell, 1951.
Lewis, H. D. *The Elusive Mind*. London: Allen and Unwin, 1969.
Lovejoy, A. *The Revolt Against Dualism*. LaSalle, Ill.: Open Court, 1955.
Rosenthal, David, ed. *Materialism and the Mind-Body Problem*. Englewood Cliffs, N.J.: Prentice-Hall, 1971.
Ryle, Gilbert. *The Concept of Mind*. London: Hutchinson, 1949.
Shaffer, Jerome. *The Philosophy of Mind*. Englewood Cliffs, N.J.: Prentice-Hall, 1968.
Shoemaker, Sidney. *Self-knowledge and Self-identity*. Ithaca, N.Y.: Cornell University Press, 1963.
Smythies, J. R., ed. *Brain and Mind: Modern Concepts of the Nature of Mind*. New York: Humanities Press, 1965.
Vesey, G. N. A., ed. *Body and Mind*. London: Allen and Unwin, 1964.
Wisdom, John. *Other Minds*. Oxford: B. H. Blackwell, 1949.

CHAPTER 4

Self, Being, and Courage

One of the most recurring ideas about the nature of a human being, and one that is thought to be the greatest difference between them and other beings in the world, is the concept of self or personhood. More than any other observable species in our world, we seem not only to be able to react to external stimuli and our environments, but also to have an awareness of ourselves or our own bodies and consciousnesses, which other species seem not to have. We constantly refer to ourselves, using the pronouns "I," "me," "mine," "my," "myself" as if there is something more that we are referring to than just our bodies that exist in space and are observable to others. Down through history, this concept has been very important, at least in Western culture. We have blamed it for making us egotistical, and religionists, both Eastern and Western, have blamed the concept for keeping us separated from God or from attaining oneness with some Ultimate Reality; yet, on the other hand, we have praised the concept of self for stressing our uniqueness, individuality, and autonomy and for the marvelous scientific discoveries, great philosophical systems, and magnificent art works we have created throughout history.

In the West, the concept of self has been pretty well at the center of any discussion of human nature until David Hume in the eighteenth century and more recently with B. F. Skinner in the twentieth century. There has always been a greater problem in defining what the nature of self is than in denying its existence, but one way of dealing with difficulties of the first kind, as we have seen in other types of reductionism, is to eliminate the object in question. The following pages will deal with questions about whether there is a self or not and presents theories about what self is thought to be. All the aspects of human nature—mental, physical, spiritual, emotional, self, and will—will be coordinated into a suggested synthesis, but first let us look at the attempts to deny the existence of self.

There Is No Self

There are three major theories that are anti-self in nature, and we have already noted two of them: B. F. Skinner's and David Hume's. The other comes from Buddhism.

B. F. SKINNER

There really is not much more that Skinner has to say about self than what was described in the last chapter concerning mind. He feels that self, like mind, is an illusory superstition that has been accepted by human beings down through the centuries to account for the unity that we feel and for the different things we do that could not be explained other than by positing a kind of "ghost in the machine." However, Skinner goes on to say that this belief may have been considered necessary prior to the time we had developed a proper science of behavior. To his way of thinking, however, all of Pavlov's, Watson's, and his own experiments with the conditioned reflex of animals and operant conditioning of humans revealed that in actuality there was no mysterious inner self or person. Basically what occurs, according to Skinner, is that human beings, like animals, are conditioned to be what they are by their environments and the stimuli they receive from them. Skinner proved that he could get birds, rats, and other laboratory animals to behave in certain predictable ways by rewarding appropriate behavior and either ignoring or not rewarding unwanted behavior.

Skinner's experiments with animals were so successful that he expanded his theories to human beings as well. He felt that humans behaved in certain ways not because they had an inner self that made them do so, but because they had been conditioned to behave these ways by the external forces and influences exerted on them from their social and cultural environments. Most people act in certain acceptable ways (acceptable to their societies) because this behavior has been constantly reinforced over a long period of time. If they did not behave acceptably, then they did not receive any rewards, were ignored or ostracized, or were punished in some way.

For example, if children do good work in school, they get good grades (reward), encouragement from their teachers (reward), and some sort of praise, a pat on the back, or even money from their parents (reward). On the other hand, if children do not succeed in school, then they can be ignored (no reward), be made to stay after school by their teachers (punishment), and also be spanked or denied privileges by their parents (punishment). The reward system is called "positive reinforcement" by Skinner, and the ignoring or punishment system is called "negative reinforcement." In this way, children (and adults later) are taught what is acceptable and nonacceptable behavior and most will respond in the appropriate way. From all of his experimentation, Skinner feels that the concept of self—the idea that all behavior is caused by a kind of inner person—is not only false but is also interfering with the great advances we could be making in attaining acceptable behavior and getting rid of unacceptable behavior. He feels that the problem up to now is that we have been conditioned only haphazardly, not scientifically, and if we can recognize how behavior is affected and can be molded and changed, then we can attain heights of civilization never before reached.

Skinner theorizes, then, that what we call "self" is really like mind, a "unified set of responses to stimuli." All we really do, as he stated in his theory of mind, is respond to stimuli from our external social and cultural environments. The fact that these responses are coming from one human being rather than another or are different is not due to our having inner selves, but rather because we are one set or "machine" which responds and reacts, whereas someone else is another. The unity of these responses is not due to unique selves but rather to the fact that we are separate human "animals" or biological—physical machines. We use personal pronouns such as "I" and "me," but they merely refer to what is understood in the science of behavior as this sophisticated set of responses. The word "self" is also just another way of using language that is now archaic but that has been with us for so long that we cannot shake it. Skinner feels that the sooner we rid ourselves of this notion of self, the sooner we can get to the center of the problem of how to create a good society and good human beings and solve it.

INITIAL EVALUATION OF THIS THEORY.   Most of the same objections concerning Skinner's theory of no mind apply to his theory of no self. He is quite right in saying that we respond to external stimuli and also that we are conditioned by our environments, but is that all we do, and are we only what we are because we have been conditioned to be so? I have already pointed out that mind and consciousness are more complex than Skinner is willing to acknowledge. As far as his theory that we are totally conditioned by our environments is concerned, like his theory of mind, it would seem to be too all encompassing and try to include too much.

For example, we might ask the question, "Who is it that responds to stimuli?" Skinner would answer that it is a sophisticated animal or machine, but can this really describe the complex activity that goes on when human beings receive and respond to stimuli? For instance, many people do not respond "appropriately" at certain times no matter how much they are rewarded, ignored, or punished. Is it possible, because they are conscious selves or persons, that they may choose to override the stimuli they are receiving? For example, people have been tortured and killed without behaving "appropriately" as they were commanded. Also, despite the ability to predict human behavior to a significant extent, it doesn't seem possible to predict it totally, because people will behave in certain ways despite their conditioning. However, this gets us into the problem of freedom versus determinism, which will be taken up in Chapter 5. Further, other objections to Skinner's theory of no self will be found in a discussion of Hume's theories and also in a description of the nature of self later in this chapter. At this point, suffice it to say that Skinner's attempt to reduce self to body, brain, and behavior is no more successful than is his attempt to do the same with mind; in fact, it will be shown to be even less successful before the chapter ends.

BUDDHISM

In Buddhism, self is described as something that is constructed by human beings and their cultures, but it is not what they really are and in fact gets in the way of what is real. Buddha stated that there is really *an-atta* (no self) and that human beings are a coming together or collection of five transient "streams" *(skandhas),* which are bodily sensation, feeling, perception, mental conception, and consciousness. Human beings are really nothing else, and trying to establish an "I" or "me" merely interferes with the goal of human beings, which, in Buddhist philosophy, is to merge these streams into the great "oneness" that is the Ultimate Reality. Buddha further described human-beingness as a flame that has no substantial existence but is merely passed on from candle to candle (person to person). The goal of Buddhism, then, is the extinction of any idea of soul, self, or ego, because it is felt that these are false constructs that stand in the way of total realization of and merging with the Ultimate Reality.

EVALUATION OF THIS VIEW.   Here again, a great deal of criticism against this view will be found in an examination of Hume's theories, which follow, especially since Hume's theories are very much like the Buddhist theories except more philosophical in nature. However, let me mention two problems. One question that arises is, What holds the five streams together, or what makes them mine rather then anyone else's? If Buddhism tries to say that the streams belong to no one, then how is it that I am having mine and you are having yours, only I can't be sure whether mine are anything like yours? What makes my "streams" different from yours? Do these streams just float freely in reality or are they one person's or another's? The second problem is that Buddha tried to eliminate the permanence and stability of self by likening it to a flickering flame, but what is the nature of this flame? Is it not something? Then what is it? Is it really any less permanent than self? Calling it a flame does not seem necessarily to deny self; for example, many believe that the self dies or "goes out" at death just as the flame is extinguished. Others believe that it continues to exist in some other supernatural state. At any rate, let us look at David Hume's antiself theory since it is the most fully presented of any in the history of philosophy.

HUME'S ANTISELF THEORY

Hume's theory about there being no self is best expressed in the following quote from his *Treatise of Human Nature:*

> There are some philosophers who imagine we are every moment intimately conscious of what we call our *self;* that we feel its existence and its continuance in existence. . . . For my part, when I enter most intimately into what I call *myself* I always stumble on some particular perception or other, of heat or cold, light or shade, love or hatred, pain or pleasure. I never can catch *myself* at any time without a perception, and never can observe anything but the perception. (Book I, Part 4, Chapter 6)[1]

According to Hume, then, what we call "self" is merely a "bundle" or collection of experiences or perceptions. From birth to death, these experiences occur in a temporally successive order, that is, one after another in time, from the past to the present and into the future. This whole series, moreover, constitutes the bundle or collection—there is no self beyond this bundle, and the bundle *is* simply the whole series of experiences. As it has sometimes been stated, "We are our experiences, and nothing more."

How does Hume arrive at his theory? First, in true empirical fashion, Hume says that we can have no ideas, that is, no thoughts or images of anything, without sense impressions or experiences. For example, he would say that we cannot have an idea or image of a tree unless we have first had a sense experience of that tree. So that to say we know something exists, we must have some sort of experience of it. Therefore, as he stated it, "If no impressions, then no ideas." He then goes on to argue that any clear idea of self must be derived from an impression (an experiencing) of it; however, self is not any one impression; rather, it is that to which our several impressions and ideas are supposed to refer. He states further that if any impression gives rise to the idea of self, it must continue invariably throughout our lives, but no impression is constant and invariable; therefore, there can be no such idea. The reason Hume said this is that he believed that each impression human beings have is distinct and separate, that is, each time we blink even though we are looking at the same thing, we have another and different perception or impression. If we look away and look back at something, each perception is different—separate and distinct. Since all impressions are like this, we can then discover no self apart from or underlying these impressions.

Remember, in discussing mind, Hume described it as a theater through which successive perceptions can pass, repass, mingle, and glide away. This theater has no identity except as a framework or container for our many impressions. We state, erroneously according to Hume, that there is a self because we confuse the idea of identity with the idea of a succession of related perceptions. He goes on to say that memory produces a "relation of resemblance" among our perceptions (that is, we think they resemble one another when they are really separate and distinct) and our imagination is carried along the chain of succession so that the chain itself appears to be a continuing and persistent object that we then label "self" or "personal identity." He feels, therefore, that it is memory that is the chief source for the idea of self or personal identity, and it then causes us to pretend there is a real uniting principle, a permanent self distinct from our perceptions when there really is not.

EVALUATION OF HUME'S VIEWS.   First, Hume states that thoughts, feelings, and ideas are found in bundles or collections, but how can there be thoughts or feelings without owners, without any person or self to have them? Can there be a thought without a thinker or an experience without an experiencer? How can this be? After all, there are no free-floating thoughts and experiences, are there? What would such things be like? Can you imagine a thought or experience just floating around in space without a thinker or an experiencer to think or experience it? Such a situation would seem strange indeed. If they are not free floating, then mustn't there be a something, an *I,* to whom these events belong? Isn't it true that every mental event must in some way or another belong to some individual, some center of consciousness? And wouldn't this be more than the collection of mental events themselves?

Secondly, since experiences are not free floating, then what is the principle of individuation that makes my experiences mine and your experiences yours? If the self is merely a bundle of experiences, then how does one distinguish the contents of one bundle from that of another? In other words, what makes this experience that I am now having mine, and the one you are having yours, even if we are experiencing similar things, like a baseball game?

Another problem is that Hume's own analysis seems to be self-contradictory. He writes, "I never catch myself . . . ," but to what or whom do the words "I" and "myself" refer? An owner of experiences? But Hume has already ruled this out. He says that he is aware only of certain states of consciousness (he calls them "perceptions") but not of the self that has them. What then makes them his? Are they his because they occur in a certain temporal succession? But so do yours and mine; therefore, what's the difference between yours, mine, and his? When he looks within himself, whose states of consciousness does he find? Presumably no one's, but rather just loose states of consciousness, but how is this possible? Surely he finds *his own* experiences, and if that is the case, we are forced back to the view that the "I" is something more than just a series of states of consciousness.

Finally, is it actually true, as Hume states, that I am really not aware of myself as a continuing entity beyond the series or collections of experiences? Is it true that when I have an experience, I am only aware of the experience, or am I also aware of myself as the owner or "haver" of the experience? Contrary to what Hume believes, it would seem that I don't experience something merely as an experience, but as *my* experience. Isn't the ownership of the experience or the experiencer a definite part of the total experience? It must be obvious, then, that to deny the existence of self, we must think and say rather strange things about our nature. Notice also that many of the arguments that attack Hume's theory also successfully attack the theories of Skinner and Buddhism. However, the fact that we have argued strongly against the theories that there is no self doesn't mean we have shown in any way that there is. What are some of the arguments and reasons for accepting the existence of self?

There Is a Self

One of the best descriptions of self comes from the eighteenth-century philosopher, Thomas Reid (1710–1796), who said

> My personal identity implies the continued existence of that indivisible thing which I call *myself*. Whatever this self may be, it is something which thinks, and deliberates, and resolves, and acts, and suffers. I am not thought, I am not action, I am not feeling; I am something that thinks, and acts, and suffers. My thoughts and actions and feelings change every

moment; they have no continued, but a successive, existence; but that *self,* or *I,* to which they belong, is permanent, and has the same relation to all the succeeding thoughts, actions, and feelings which I call mine. Such are the notions that I have of my personal identity. (From *Essays on the Intellectual Powers of Man,* Essay III, Chapter 4)[2]

Reid makes several assumptions about the existence of self that we will now examine, along with other important characteristics of self that have been presented at different times throughout history.

CHARACTERISTICS OF SELF

CONTINUITY AND UNITY.   The self provides continuity, unity, and some permanence and stability throughout a human being's life. As Reid said, thoughts, actions, and feelings change every moment because they have no continued or permanent existence; rather they merely follow or succeed one another. Self, however, is permanent and persists; it has the same relationship to all my thoughts, feelings, actions, and experiences. For example, one moment I may feel sad, another happy; I may now be looking at a tree and having the experience and perceptions of doing so; yesterday I was watching television; now I am swimming, and so on. These experiences, thoughts, feelings, and actions are all different and changing from minute to minute, sometimes second to second, but the "I" who is having them has persisted and continued throughout all of them, from the earliest memories I have as a child to the present, and until I die. This unity would seem to be more than merely the fact that all these experiences are collected or "bundled" in one place, for there is an active perceiver and experiencer who is involved with all of them and to which they all relate.

MORE THAN ITS WORLD.   Self is more or other than the world that it observes or to which it relates. Animals, plants, and inanimate objects seem to be immersed or submerged in nature. They do not seem to have the ability to "step back from" nature to observe, analyze, or speculate about it. Self involves consciousness or awareness of itself as separate from nature. For example, migrating birds seem to have no choice in changing their location with the seasons, nor do salmon have a choice in their spawning. These things seem to be "programmed" by nature to occur, and neither the birds nor salmon seem to have any choice in the matter, nor do they seem to be able to separate themselves from what is happening to observe it, analyze it, or change it in any way. Humans, on the other hand, although influenced by natural inclinations and urges, nevertheless can observe these things and separate themselves from them if they choose to. Human beings are indeed a part of nature and their cultures, but they also are separate from them and are aware of this separateness.

DISTINCT FROM ITS EXPERIENCES.   We are not, despite what Hume says, merely our experiences or perceptions. That they affect and influence us there is no doubt, but we are primarily observers, experiencers, thinkers, and feelers, not observations, experiences, thoughts, and feelings. For example, if I am hungry, then I am not the feeling of hunger itself, but I am that being that has hunger or that is hungry. What would it mean to say, "I am hunger"? Further, if I am thinking that $2+2=4$, what sense would it make to say that I *am* that equation? Rather, it only makes sense to say that I am thinking of or about that equation.

PRIVACY.   Self, like mind and perhaps because of it, is private and unsharable. I can share some of my organs with others, if I agree to transplant surgery, and I can even try to share my innermost thoughts and feelings with others, but I cannot *truly* share my "self" with anyone. I can share a lot of things, but I cannot share my individual selfhood or personhood. We all share many of our thoughts, feelings, and experiences with each other, but a great deal more of them are never shared at all. Can I ever truly know what you are thinking or feeling? Even if we are witnessing the same event such as the sunset over the ocean I described earlier, how can we know we are perceiving exactly the same thing, having the same feelings, or even having the same experience; as a matter of fact, we have to admit that our experiencings may be similar, but they can never be the same, for mine are mine and yours are yours.

SELF-CONSCIOUSNESS.   One thing we can do that most animals cannot do significantly is direct or turn our consciousness or awareness on itself. It is quite true that animals have consciousness—we can draw this conclusion from observing their behavior—however, there is little evidence that they can direct that consciousness on itself, as human beings can. For example, I can ask you to turn your consciousness inward phenomenologically to examine what it is you experience when you hear sounds or see colors. I can also ask you to examine your minds in other ways; I cannot, however, ask or cause animals to do this, and it is questionable whether they could even if I were able to ask them. I am not stating categorically that animals can have no consciousness of self, but the extent of such consciousness would seem to be a great deal less than even the most minor human examination of self.

Given all these characteristics, then, it would seem that we would have to at least strongly consider the possibility of the existence of self as opposed to accepting a nonself theory. The question then arises that if there is a self then what exactly is it—what is its nature? There are quite a few theories about self and its nature, but I will present only five of them here: Josiah Royce's (1855–1916) objective and personalistic idealism view, George Herbert Mead's (1863–1931) view of self merely as a social organism, and the existential view of self, which includes three subviews: Jean-Paul Sartre (1905–1980) and self as totally self-created, Martin Buber (1878–1965) and self as arising out of personal relationship, Paul Tillich (1886–1965) and self as the courage to be.

Nature of Self Theories

SELF AS PART OF AN ABSOLUTE SELF

Josiah Royce's version of self is related to two theories of idealism, which I have not fully described in my earlier discussions of subjective idealism and dualism. One of these is objective idealism, which puts forth the idea that there is in and behind all reality a mind or intelligence of some kind that has created everything that exists and has ordered reality logically and rationally. This intelligence can either be considered a person or personal, like human beings, or an impersonal force of some kind. The first view is sometimes called personal idealism, which means that the ultimate mind or intelligent being is not merely a force but also a self, a person, with whom there is a possibility for relationship with other selves or persons, namely, human beings. Royce essentially takes this viewpoint when he defines "self" as a "meaning embodied in conscious life, present as a relative whole within the unity of the absolute conscious life."[3] He seems to be saying that there is an absolute conscious life that is meaningful and personal; that is, it exists absolutely and is whole and complete. Then he goes on to say that within this absolute being there exist a number of relative, unified, and meaningful conscious lives or selves who take their meaning and existence from this absolute being in which they reside. He states further, concerning this absolute, that the "universe in its wholeness is the expression of a meaning in a life."[4] Because of the nature of this absolute being, the individual selves that reside within it are essentially unique because of their individuality, but they also have unity with and because of the absolute. That is, they are not just completely separate, isolated individuals because this individuality is transcended by its connection with the absolute. It has its final expression in some form of absolute consciousness (God or ultimate consciousness), which is different from and more than that which human beings now possess.

EVALUATION OF THIS THEORY.   This theory can be considered advantageous because it can provide philosophical support for a religious viewpoint, either Western or Eastern. For example, the Western religious viewpoint is that an intelligent, personal being created the world and human beings and has some sort of personal and special relationship with it and them—even more so with them since they are considered as having been "created in His image." This means that they share in His absolute and meaningful consciousness. In the Eastern sense, which does not stress the personal part as much, the individual self or consciousness can be seen to exist because of the Ultimate Consciousness, and it gains its meaning and significance from that source. Furthermore, one need not be specifically religious to accept Royce's theory, but just use it as a way of accounting for the significant differences between human beings and the rest of the world—they are different because they are products of an Absolute Conscious Self with meaning.

Despite its attractiveness to idealists or religionists, however, one has to ask what proof or arguments can be offered for the existence of an absolute conscious life as Royce describes it? His description of the individual self may have some validity, but his description of an absolute conscious life has no conclusive proof or support in reality for its existence. Where does this absolute consciousness reside? Is it a disembodied mind floating around somewhere in space and time, or what? Why couldn't this conscious life that human beings are said to possess have evolved over a long period of time, and why must one conclude that there has to be some absolute consciousness existing somewhere? Even if we cannot completely account for why the human self exists as it does, why must we posit an absolute consciousness? The real problem with Royce's theories, then, is that they rest on unproved assumptions, and even though they are interesting, they are nothing more than his speculations which are to a great extent unfounded.

SELF AS MERELY SOCIAL ORGANISM

George Mead describes self as basically a social organism and states that it does not even arise or exist outside of the social setting.[5] He describes self as separate from both the physical organism (body) and also from human intelligence. He states that the self is different from the body in that self is something that has a development. He feels, further, that the intelligence of the lower forms of animal life and a great deal of human intelligence do not involve a self. In making this separation and distinction between self and intelligence, Mead states that we must distinguish between immediate experience and the organization of it into the experience of the self. He even says that human beings can have pain and pleasure without there being an experience of the self. He goes on to say that one must be conscious of self in order to have it, and he describes a human being running away from someone, for example, as not being conscious of self. He feels that one must be able to get out of or step back from "self" and see it as an object, rather than a subject, to achieve selfhood.

He feels, further, that the only way this can be done is in a social setting. He feels that human beings experience themselves as such, never directly, but only indirectly, from the particular standpoints of other individual members of the same social group or from the standpoint of the group as a whole to which they belong. He describes human relationships as so many objects to other subjects that are objects to others and eventually objects to themselves. In other words, he sees the social process as consisting of people seeing others as objects and even seeing themselves as objects. He says that there are all sorts of different selves answering to all sorts of different social reactions and that it is the social process itself that is responsible for the appearance of the self; in fact, the self does not exist apart from the social process. Further, the unity and structure of the complete self reflects the unity and structure of the social process as a whole, and the organization and unification of any social group is identical to the organization and unification of any one of the selves within that group.

EVALUATION OF THIS THEORY.   First, is it really true that the physical organism is different from the self because the self is capable of development? Isn't the physical body also capable of development, and isn't it in fact constantly developing in some way or another. For example, don't physical organisms adapt to changes in their environments and therefore develop in some way?

Even more questionable is Mead's separating of self from intelligence. Isn't the very nature of self dependent on the human consciousness and also its intelligence? Further, can we actually separate self from any connection with its experiences? Is it true that we can experience pleasure or pain without having or being conscious of self? Who or what is doing the experiencing? Does it make sense to say that my body or mind is feeling pain or pleasure but that I (self) am not? Is it also true if I am running away from someone or performing some other activity that I am not conscious of self? It is true that I may be concentrating on getting away from the person who is chasing me, but what for if not to save my "self"?

In discussing the fact that people must see themselves as objects before they can become selves, is Mead describing anything that can really take place? Can one ever get outside of himself or herself? How? Doesn't consciousness in human beings always imply consciousness of self as well as of other things? Further, is it really creative or meaningful to think of one's self as an object? Isn't it dehumanizing to reduce oneself and others to the level of objects and not persons or subjects?

Finally, isn't Mead's definition of "self" just too narrow? Isn't there a self that exists before entering into various experiences, social and otherwise? It is true that it may find some of its most creative development in and through the socialization process, but does it in no way exist apart from these? What about great thinkers who have separated themselves from the actual social process for many years and still produce great works of science, art, religion, and philosophy? As for his statement that individual selves are merely reflections of their social groups, does this mean that this is all they are? There is certainly a relationship between the individuals of a group and the character of that group, but does this mean that the structure of the individual is *totally* like the structure of the group or vice versa? That self is creative and grows and develops in relationship to other selves in a social process would seem to be true, but what is it that grows and develops? Mustn't there be a self, even if only a potential self, prior to the social self or selves? We will see other views of the importance of the development of self through social relationships when we get to Buber and Tillich later, minus many of the problems with Mead's theories.

SELF AS INDIVIDUALLY CREATED

The existential view of self is heavily dependent, as you might expect, on the existentialist view of mind and consciousness as active, creative, and intentional. The existentialists believe that a human being creates his or her self either from nothing except the fact of existence or from some prior essence (nature or meaning). Therefore, there are really two types of existentialists (described in the paragraphs that follow), but they both believe that to know what the nature of a human being or reality is, humans must start with themselves as conscious beings. They should not start with a preconception of some sort of prior human nature, God, or the external world, but with human subjective consciousness itself and then see what can be arrived at in the process of investigation and examination.

EXISTENCE PRECEDES ESSENCE—ATHEISTIC EXISTENTIALISM. This version of existentialism, whose most prominent advocate is the late Jean-Paul Sartre, the twentieth-century philosopher, believes that there is no prior essence, nature, or meaning from which human beings acquire self, personhood, or *their* essence. There is only existence, and out of this existence human beings create their own essence or selves. Before going any further, it is important to elucidate the distinction between "existence" and "essence."

Both these terms relate to being, especially human-beingness, but to philosophers they can mean two different aspects of being. "Existence" refers to the fact *that* things or persons are, the fact of their being, the fact *that* they exist. "Essence," on the other hand, refers to *what* they are or their nature or meaning, and—in the case of human beings—their selves. No philosopher is necessarily trying to say that these aspects are truly separated in reality, for if something exists it has to exist in a certain way. For example, tables, animals, trees, and people do not just exist; they have certain natures and certain qualities or attributes—trees don't just exist; they exist as trunks with branches, leaves, roots, blossoms, and sap. John doesn't just exist; he exists as a tall, thin man with red hair and blue eyes. Existence and essence, however, are distinct and distinguishable from one another. We can describe and talk about them separately as Sartre indeed does.

In Sartre's view, human beings have existence over which they have no control; they are born into whatever family, culture, time, and circumstances in which they find themselves. However, out of this existence, they and only they, according to Sartre, can create their essence, their own human natures, their selves. Sartre states that other beings in the world have limited essence that is intertwined with their existence and that is determined by natural forces. Only human beings are different because they have consciousness, which makes them free. The assumption that human beings are determined by outside natural and cultural forces is, according to Sartre, a fallacy. He sees no prior essence, God, or already created human nature as truly existing. Only human beings and their existence, which includes consciousness, are present, and out of this basic "stuff" humans create what they are.

They can choose to let nature or society mold and determine them, but if they do, according to Sartre, they are acting "in bad faith" toward their freedom and what they can be. If they do this, however, they are responsible for what they become in the process. Sartre gives an example of a waiter who accepts the role in which he functions like a kind of automaton performing his special "waiter tasks." There is little that is human about this strict functioning in that any self that could be created is submerged beneath the role that society has created for him and to which he assents. As a human being who is free, according to Sartre, he must become aware through his consciousness of the fact that he is responsible for creating his own self, his own life and its meaning. If he doesn't do this, he is never a self but only an existent entity that merely thinks. Self, to Sartre then, is something that a human being creates out of consciousness and out of the awareness that he alone can create meaning or self. He creates it out of nothing more than his existence—there is no God, for example, who gives him a soul which is his essence or meaning.

EVALUATION OF THIS THEORY. Sartre's theory has some advantages in that it advocates individualism, freedom, creativity, and responsibility, which are all considered good by many human beings in encouraging individual human growth. However, there are also some disadvantages. Why should we accept Sartre's assumption that there is no prior essence (God, Ultimate Intelligence, or Ultimate Reality). After all, that's all it is, just an assumption. What's the reason for not accepting a prior essence other than the fact that Sartre says we shouldn't? Many people would argue that the concept of a prior essence is the only theory that can effectively account for such sophisticated human attributes as consciousness and intelligence. Even if we do accept it, however, isn't Sartre's theory *too* individualistic and isolating? What is the connection between one human being and all others if they are all off creating their own selves without regard to any unifying factor, such as God or human nature? Further, are we really as completely free as Sartre says we are? Aren't we really more determined by our genetic makeup and our social and cultural environmental conditioning than he is willing to admit? And, last, can human beings really create this meaningful self, which Sartre proposes, from mere existence without any kind of essence which has at least the potential for self growth and realization?

ESSENCE PRECEDES EXISTENCE—THEISTIC EXISTENTIALISM. This version of existentialism agrees with the other that human beings must start with themselves and that they are responsible for what they become and what they are, but the power and ability to do so comes from some creative source, some Ultimate Reality, which is also present in some way within us. According to this type of existentialist, we must start with a human as a conscious being, and then we will discover eventually that this human being has been preceded by some sort of Ultimate Being, Ground Being, or Being-Itself from which he or she draws the power of being that enables the individual to construct his or her self and reality meaningfully. The emphasis is still on human beings as creators of their "selves," but only because of the power of being that comes from some Ultimate Source (for example, God).

Human beings, then, are not isolated within themselves as Sartre's view suggests; rather they create themselves in unity with the Ultimate Being and with other human beings. There are two important philosopher-theologians who exemplify this view, Martin Buber and Paul Tillich.

MARTIN BUBER AND THE I-THOU RELATIONSHIP.[6]   According to Buber, human beings approach reality in two ways: one is the I-It approach; the other is the I-Thou approach. The I-It approach is subject to object in nature and involves practicality, use, and exploitation. For example, if I am hoeing a garden, my connection to the hoe that I am using is strictly that of I-It. The hoe is an inanimate object for me, as subject, to use, but I have no relation with it other than its practicality to me as an implement, a thing, an object. I can carry this I-It approach into other areas too. For example, if I am an employer of a secretary, I can see this person as some "thing" for me to manipulate and exploit for whatever reason I see fit.

According to Buber, the practical I-It approach to reality is necessary and significant, but if that is the only way we relate to reality and others, then we are living at a low human level. There is another type of approach which is necessary if we are to exercise our highest potentiality as human beings, and this he calls the I-Thou relationship. This relationship is not subject to object in nature, but rather subject to subject, person to person, and relational and reciprocal. Buber states that this approach is the highest form of human living and that out of such relationships the self is created and grows in vitality and significance. For example, if we reconsider the employer-secretary situation, when I relate to my secretary, not merely as a machine or an extension of his typewriter, but as a person with feelings—another human being—then I am approaching or meeting him as one person to another in a subject to subject relationship. I relate to him and he, in turn, relates to me as one human being to another. In the process of such relationships there is a give and take, a true meeting of selves, a personal contact out of which such human attainments as friendship and love arise.

Buber says that we can relate to almost anything or anyone in an I-It sense, but it is only when we attain the I-Thou, that our potential selves are actualized and realized. For example, Buber describes how human beings can perceive a tree in many different ways: physically, as a collection of atoms; botanically, as a growing plant; mathematically, as something to be measured and seen geometrically; and in a practical sense as a source of lumber or shade. However, Buber goes on to say that when we see the tree as a living, vital part of nature and "go out toward" it as a living thing of beauty and let it also relate to us, then the tree becomes more than just a thing, for our use and exploitation. It becomes for us, rather, another living thing to which we are related as we are or can be to the rest of nature. The I–Thou relationship, then, according to Buber, is the highest form of human relationships and is dependent on its source (what he calls the Eternal Thou), which is where the I–Thou relationship begins. Buber states that human beings need not turn to this Eternal Thou directly, but as they enter into I–Thou relationships with other human beings and the world around them, they are also making connection with or relating to this source. Buber stresses that this relationship with others is not conformity or collectivism but, rather, a dialoguic type of relationship in which both subjects or persons are truly meeting each other with friendship and love, not trying to dominate or be subordinate to one another, but vitally exchanging ideas and feelings. In this process, each self is able to realize its fullest potential.

PAUL TILLICH AND COURAGE AND BEING.   Paul Tillich starts by talking about the human condition that he describes as threatened by three major anxieties. He states that our development of self, or self-actualization or self-realization, is threatened by these three anxieties, which he describes as (1) fate and death, (2) emptiness and meaninglessness, and (3) guilt and condemnation.[7] Tillich says that every human being by the nature of his or her humanity is beset throughout life with one or the other of these anxieties that prevent full realization of self. Tillich describes these anxieties as "existential," that is, as a real part of existence rather than as "pathological," or disease oriented or caused. In the process of living our lives, he says, we are all, at one time or another, "anxious" about the fact that our fate or destiny is unknown to us and that the ultimate unknown is death; we are also threatened by the loss of meaning or the possibility of our lives being empty; and last, we are threatened by the awareness of guilt from our peers, from God, and even from ourselves, and of being condemned by any or all of these.

Let me give one example that will involve all three anxieties while stressing that they do not always occur like this. Suppose that a husband and wife have their first baby and the baby seems healthy but dies three months after birth from an unknown cause. This occurrence, of course, is one of life's cruelest disasters. In trying to deal with this tragedy, the couple may face all three anxieties. They had made many plans for their baby and themselves as a family, but fate stepped in and changed all of that. They didn't know that could happen; it was an unknown factor for them despite the plans they had made and the care they had taken to insure their baby would live. The death of their child also brings forth the unknown quantity and anxiety surrounding death itself. What does it really mean? What really has happened to their child, and how could it have happened?

Since they had planned a full life for themselves *with* their child, now their lives seem empty and even meaningless, especially if this baby had become the center of their family life, as most children do. They may even begin to question whether their lives can hold any further meaning for them now that their hopes and plans have been destroyed. They may also feel guilty and condemned, from their own feelings that there must have been something they could have done to prevent this terrible thing from happening. They might also feel that God has punished them for some reason they cannot identify. They may also feel guilty because family and friends seem to suggest that they could have been less "careless" in some way. Of course, with all this guilt, they may certainly feel condemned in some way.

Again, all this may not happen this way in every case, but it can at least show you the reality of such anxieties. It is Tillich's theory that whether such disasters occur or not, we face these anxieties every day of our lives in one way or another, whether they come about from concern over failing grades, moral guilt for having lied or cheated, the unexpected loss of a job, or the emptiness and meaninglessness we feel from a divorce or breakup of a love affair. He says that these are a real and continuing part of our daily lives and existence. That is why he calls them "existential" anxieties, meaning they are a definite part of our existence.

He goes on to say that these anxieties cannot be eliminated since they are a part of the human condition, so that one can only have the courage to be, live, or exist *in spite of* these threats to our self-realization, self-actualization, or human-beingness. He states further that this courage to be comes about in two ways: (1) the courage to be as oneself, or the courage of individualism, and (2) the courage to participate with others and the world in which we live, or the courage of participation. In the courage of individualism, individual human beings tap their potential and develop themselves as fully as they can, which may sometimes require a separation or escape from their society, culture, and other people. This development is something that can only be done by the individual alone and requires the courage to be alone and to face who and what he or she is and try to develop one's self and to *be,* despite threats to this development.[8] An obvious example of this type of courage can be found in Henry David Thoreau's one year spent away from civilization at Walden Pond in Massachusetts. During this time, in almost complete solitude, Thoreau spent time meditating about his nature and the nature of human beings and the world in general, reading, getting closer to nature, and just thinking about life and what was important to him about it without any interference from the society, culture, and other people he had left behind. It took courage on his part to isolate himself from all the comforts of civilization and the human relationships around him so that he could in effect construct himself as an individual from what he found in himself during his separation and isolation.

The courage of participation, on the other hand, involves finding the courage to be by participating in a society or various groups or institutions within it to be able to face and deal with the three anxieties. For example, by joining a particular religious group, one may be able to face the three anxieties because one can gain courage and strength to do this from the group. Many religions provide for an alleviation of all three anxieties. The anxiety about fate and death can be overcome, for example, because the group promises the participants that they need not worry about fate because God will provide for them and not about death either since they will never fully die; only their physical existence will end. They will, however, continue to live an even better life in another world. If their lives are empty and meaningless, then the religion can give them meaning and fill their lives because of what God has promised and also through the support of and social interaction with their fellow religionists. They may also feel guilty and condemned, but God and the religion can alleviate these too because they can be forgiven, not only by their fellow religionists in the group but also by God.

There are risks in both types of courage in that if human beings employ only the courage of individualism, they risk loss of connection with and participation in their societies and cultures. In other words, human beings who demonstrate this type of courage may isolate themselves from everything and miss the significant interchange and socialization that is certainly important to self and societal development. The risk of participation, on the other hand, is the possible loss of one's individuality or individual self in a collectivism or conformity in which the individual becomes merely a part of the group, a part of the mass. Therefore, what Tillich seems to imply is that the best approach in dealing with the three major anxieties is the courage of individualism and the courage of participation in interdependence.

Human beings should develop themselves as individuals as fully as they can, and this may require a separation from the rest of the society and from other people. However, once they have done this to the fullest extent possible, they should then have the courage to return to their world and participate in their societies and with other human beings. Referring back to Thoreau at Walden Pond, we must remember that after a year, he returned to his society and culture (no matter how reluctantly) and actively participated in it by writing about nature, humanity, and life so that all could read about these things. He even committed acts of civil disobedience in which he protested what he considered immoral acts by the government and other parts of society.

It takes courage to be an individual, and it also takes courage to participate, but, according to Tillich, it takes the greatest courage to be both an individual and a participant. Up to this point in his discussion, one could apply this theory strictly to human beings without concern about anything further, but Tillich, somewhat like Buber, stated that the courage and power of being that human beings can exhibit comes from what he calls the Ground of All Being, or Being-Itself, which is God in His purest form, or what Tillich refers to as "the God above the theistic God," which human beings have created in *their* own image.[9]

EVALUATION OF THESE VIEWS. That these views are interesting there is no doubt, and I feel that they have some validity and basis in experience. However, you will have to examine your own experience to see if they are relevant to you. Like Sartre's theories, however, they are theoretical assumptions that cannot really be proved conclusively. They improve on Sartre's theories in that they overcome his isolated individualism, but they cannot prove conclusively their concepts of the Ultimate Reality, and calling it the Eternal Thou, Being-Itself, and Ground Being does not change that fact. As I have suggested, all these theories should be subjected to greater investigation and evaluation to discover the extent of their relevance and validity.

A Synthesis of the Aspects of Human Nature— Brain, Mind, Self

In concluding this chapter, I would like to suggest a possible synthesis of many of the views that we have examined in this chapter and the previous one and try to provide you with perhaps a more all-encompassing view of human nature than any one of the theories we have examined.

ASSUMPTIONS ABOUT MIND AND BRAIN

I am forced to accept the dualistic point of view, but I accept only its moderate or synthetic form. Neither materialism nor subjective idealism seem to be valid theories to me because of their reduction of mind to brain or brain to mind. I can find no way around the fact that both brain and mind and both physical and mental events exist. Further, of all of the dualistic theories, I feel that interactionism generally describes the relationship between brain and mind the best, even though the theory itself does not explain *how* the relationship occurs. I feel that there are times when mind causes brain and obviously times when brain also causes mind, and I feel this relationship is much closer and more intimate than that described by any of the other theories.

Also, I generally accept the existential-phenomenological version of consciousness and basis for mind because it describes them as active and creative rather than passive. My experiencing of how my mind and consciousness work is much closer to that theory, with all of its vagueness and problems, than to the concepts put forth by Skinner, Hume, and Locke.

ASSUMPTIONS ABOUT SELF

I also accept the existence of self, because in turning my mind inward, I do not merely find perceptions, streams of consciousness, or responses to stimuli, but a personal identity that is uniquely "I" and no one else. The question of the nature of self is a difficult one to deal with—is it really the same thing as mind, body, soul, and emotions? If so, we can use "self" as a catchall term for all these things, but then how does it come to be or develop? This is a problem that has not been solved by any of the theories we have examined, at least, not to my satisfiaction. I feel that when we talk about self, we must think of it in two ways: (1) potential or potentialized self and (2) actualizing or realizing self.

POTENTIAL SELF.   I would describe potential self as human consciousness that is dependent on brain activity, so that in the chronology of development, brain and body come first. Somewhere in this development process the potential self, consciousness, arises, and the nature of this consciousness is intentional, active, creative, and directive in nature. This directional quality of consciousness is what we refer to as will. Consciousness is by nature directive, but as this potential self develops, the directive quality can become more self-directive in nature.

POTENTIAL SELF AND OTHER ASPECTS OF HUMAN NATURE (See Figure 4–1).   This potential self appears to work through or interweave with the other aspects of human nature described in Chapter 3. It works through its physical aspect—body, brain, and the five senses—to receive and gather information and to power all its other activities. It interweaves with mind to analyze, rationalize, and evaluate all the information it receives and to organize consciousness when needed. It connects with emotions to experience the world and itself aesthetically

Figure 4-1. A continuing process of self-actualization and self-realization.

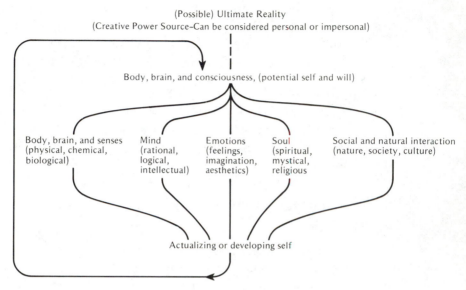

and to develop its human feeling. It uses its spiritual aspect to search out spiritual possibilities of other supernatural beings and to deal with the mystical and religious questions human beings have always had about their origins. Potential self enters into interaction with nature and culture because it lives in a natural world and also a world of other social beings.

All this "working through" can be done formally by the self through the natural and physical sciences for body and brain; through philosophy and psychology for the mind; through philosophy, psychology, and the arts for emotions; through religion and theology for the spiritual aspect; and through the sciences, the social sciences, and actual experiencing for the social and natural interaction. These formal approaches provide us with a systematic way of developing all human aspects as fully as we can. We can, of course, use these same aspects informally as well. For example, by interacting with another person, I can learn more about myself and others.

ACTUALIZING SELF.   All these activities are part of a continuing and developing process through which the potentialized self becomes actualized or realized more fully than it was before. Once it has become more actualized, it can continue back through the process to greater growth and creativity. Actualizing self can always return to potential self for its individuality and then work through the six aspects as needed and desired for yet greater actualization. I also believe that the courage of individualization and the courage of participation are involved in the whole process, in that self works through the first five aspects individually, although it can do this also by participating, and then participates by working through the sixth aspect (social and natural interaction). It is important to note that this process is not as clear cut or as strictly organized as my description might suggest. I see the whole process of interaction of self with the other aspects of human nature as very complex and not very clearly explainable overall.

THE QUESTION OF AN ULTIMATE REALITY. We will deal with this question much more specifically in the chapter on philosophy of religion, but one may upon speculation include some sort of Ultimate Reality in the total picture as a source for body, brain, and the potential self. This Ultimate Reality can be (and has been) characterized as God, Allah, Yaweh, Brahman, Nirvana, The Good, the Tao, or even just some sort of energy source. The important thing to remember here is to start, as the existentialists suggest, with human beings and especially human consciousness, and work from there always being sure to check assumptions and theories against your experiences, both internal and external.

You should note at this point that this suggested synthesis of all the theories and aspects of human nature is merely presented to show how one might go about trying to pull some of these things together. You should, as was suggested in the first two chapters, apply analysis and critical evaluation to my conclusions about the theories as well as my theory about the existence of self, in its two aspects, and its development through body, mind, emotions, spirit, and natural and social interactions. You are encouraged to come up with your own theories and to try to support them as fully as you can. If you select any of the theories that have been mentioned (for example, materialism, parallelism, self as social organism) as significant, do not forget to deal with the criticisms of them and any drawbacks or disadvantages that have been pointed out in this chapter.

One thing we can conclude for certain in having examined human nature is that whatever else is true about the nature of human beings, it is a mysterious and complex thing to deal with, and any attempt to oversimplify its complexity usually ends up in omitting certain important aspects of what it means to be human.

Applying Philosophy—
Situations for Thought and Discussion

SITUATION 1

To what extent do you agree with the antiself or proself theorists and why?

1. Is there a self? If not, then how do you account for personality?
2. If there is a self, then how does it come about and what is its nature?
3. If you believe that there are body, mind, and self, then how do they relate to and interact with one another?
4. To what extent do you agree or disagree with Paul Tillich's theories about the three major anxieties and the two types of courage? What part do these play in understanding the nature of a human being, and especially the existence of self?
5. How do Buber's theories of self square with your experience or nonexperience of self?
6. Which of the theories of self described in the chapter do you agree with and why? Why do you reject the others? Be specific.

SITUATION 2

Have the quotes of Hume (antiself) and Reid (proself) copied on sheets of paper and hand them out to your family, friends, co-workers, and fellow students. After they have read them, ask them which they accept as the most accurate and why (you may construct a questionnaire with specific questions on the subject for them to answer if you wish).

Which theory did they select and why? If they said they believe there's a self, then ask them

1. Where it is?
2. What is it made up of?
3. Where does it come from and how and when do they believe it first comes into existence in a human life?
4. How does it differ from and yet relate to body, brain, mind, emotions, and will?

If they believe there is no self, then ask them what they believe their essence to be—that is, what gives them personhood?

SITUATION 3

Read *The Sun Also Rises, A Farewell to Arms, For Whom the Bell Tolls,* and *The Old Man and the Sea,* all by Ernest Hemingway, and describe in detail how Hemingway's concept of self evolves from the first novel to the last (read them in the order I have set them down). What is his concept of self and how do you know? Give significant examples from the novels to substantiate your views. What is Hemingway's theory concerning the relationship of self to body, mind, emotions, and will? Here again give examples from his works. How important are relationships with other people and nature to the development of self, according to Hemingway? How do you know? How important are the courage to be as oneself and the courage of participation, as put forth by Paul Tillich, to Hemingway's concept of self? Explain in detail.

Chapter Summary

I. There is no self—three major theories.
   A. B. F. Skinner is a materialist and does not believe that anything other than matter, energy, and behavior exists.
      1. He believes that what we call "self" is nothing more than a "unified set of responses to stimuli."
      2. Human beings receive stimuli from their environments, and then they react to them, building up over a period of time certain familiar responses to recurring similar stimuli.
   B. Evaluation of this theory. He is right in that we do respond to external stimuli, but is this all we do? His theory would seem to claim too much and not encompass what actually happens.
   C. Buddhism says self is a construction of human beings.
      1. Buddha believed that there is really no self, just streams (bodily sensation, feeling, perception, mental conception, and consciousness).
      2. This is all that human beings are and any constructed self or ego must be eliminated for the individual to merge with ultimate reality.
   D. Evaluation of this theory.
      1. What holds the five streams together?
      2. Buddha tried to eliminate any self of substance by replacing it with the flame concept, but what is the flame?
   E. Hume's antiself theory.
      1. There is no self—merely a collection or bundle of perceptions.

2. How does he arrive at his theory?
    a. Hume says that we can have no ideas without sense impressions or experiences; one must have an impression before one can have an idea.
    b. There is no impression for self, merely various impressions of one or another perception.
    c. Mind is a theater through and onto which perceptions pass; there is nothing more.
F. Evaluation of Hume's views.
    1. How can there be perceptions without owners?
    2. What is the principle of individuation that makes your perceptions different from mine?
    3. Hume uses the words "I," "me," "myself"; if there is no self, then to what do they refer?
    4. Is it really true that we are not aware of ourselves as perceivers in addition to being aware of various perceptions?

II. There is a self (Thomas Reid).
  A. Characteristics of self.
    1. Continuity and unity.
    2. More than its world.
    3. Distinct from its experiences.
    4. Private in nature.
    5. Self-conscious; that is, it can be conscious of itself.

III. Nature of self theories.
  A. Josiah Royce: Self is a part of an absolute self.
    1. His view is one of objective idealism—he theorizes an absolute self that is meaningful.
    2. He then defines "self" as a "meaning embodied in a conscious life, present as a relative whole within the unity of the absolute conscious life."
    3. Both are meaningful and personal.
  B. Evaluation of this theory.
    1. Its advantage is that it can provide philosophical support for a Western religious point of view; however, one need not be religious to hold this view.
    2. Its disadvantage is that it is merely a theory that is not provable, and where the absolute self is and what its nature is are unresolvable problems.
  C. George Mead and self as merely a social organism.
    1. Mead defines self as only a social organism and separate from intelligence or body.
    2. He feels that animals and humans alike can exist without self.
    3. Self cannot arise unless human beings objectify it.

4. Self can only arise in a social setting; it does not exist otherwise; any social group is identical with any one of its selves.

D. Evaluation of this theory.
   1. Is it really true that the physical organism is different from the self?
   2. Can we really separate self from mind and intelligence?
   3. Can anyone ever see himself as an object? Is it ever possible for a subject to separate himself from his self and see it as an object?
   4. Isn't Mead's definition of "self" too narrow? Isn't there a self of some kind before social relationships are entered into? What is it, then, that enters such relationships?
   5. Groups reflect their members and individuals reflect their groups, but does this mean that they are wholly identical?

E. Self as individually created.
   1. Existentialism—two types:
      a. Existence precedes essence or atheistic existentialism. This view is held by Jean-Paul Sartre. There is only existence—no prior human nature or God—and humans create their own essence (or nature) out of this existence.
         (1) Existence refers to the fact that a thing or person is.
         (2) Essence refers to what a thing is, or its nature.
         (3) Human beings, according to Sartre, are completely free.
      b. Sartre's theory has some advantages in that it stresses individualism, freedom, creativity, and responsibility; however, why should we accept his assumption of no human nature or God? This is nothing more than an unprovable theory, an assumption. Further, many theories argue against unlimited freedom of human beings. Moreover, his theory is too individualistic and isolating. It is really possible for human beings to create their own essence?
   2. Essence precedes existence or theistic existentialism. This theory agrees with Sartre that human beings are responsible for creating who they are but disagrees in that it believes that there is a prior essence which gives humans power to do this.
   3. Martin Buber and the I-Thou relationship. Human beings approach reality in two ways:
      a. I-It relationship. This is subject to object in nature and involves practicality, use, and exploitation. This is nec-

essary, but if we live at this level alone we never rise to the heights of human ability and realization.

    b. I-Thou relationship. This is subject to subject in nature, person to person, and relational and reciprocal. This is the highest form of human living, and out of this relationship the self is created and grows significantly.

4. Paul Tillich and courage and being. The human condition involves three existential anxieties:

    a. Fate and death.

    b. Emptiness and meaninglessness.

    c. Guilt and condemnation.

    d. These anxieties cannot be eliminated, they are not pathological, but existential. They can, however, be faced and dealt with if one has the courage to be in spite of them.

5. There are two types of courage:

    a. The courage to be as oneself, or the courage of individualism.

    b. The courage to participate with others and the world, or the courage of participation.

    c. There are risks in both types of courage. One who uses only the courage of individualism risks the loss of one's world and others; one who uses only the courage of participation risks the loss of oneself.

    d. Tillich seems to suggest that the most significant approach to the problem is to use the courage of individualism and the courage of participation in interdependence.

6. Evaluation of these views. They are interesting and have some validity; however, each person must examine his or her own experiences and see if they are relevant. As with Sartre's theories, they are not conclusively provable, but they do avoid his overindividualism and also allow for the inclusion of a God.

IV. Synthesis of aspects of human nature.

    A. Assumptions about mind and brain.

        1. I accept dualism rather than materialism or idealism.

        2. I accept the theory of interactionism, which, although it does not explain how mind and brain interact, seems to present the view that best squares with my experiences.

        3. I also accept the existential-phenomenological version of consciousness and basis for mind because my experience leads me to accept mind as active and creative rather than passive.

B. Assumptions about self.
    1. I accept the existence of self because I do not find just streams of consciousness or bundles of perceptions, but a permanent perceiver who has these things. I see, however, two aspects of self:
        a. Potential self, which is human consciousness and is dependent on brain activity. It is active, intentional, and creative. This active and directional quality I call will. This potential self interweaves with the other aspects of human nature.
            (1) It works through its physical aspect—body, brain, and five senses—to receive and gather information and to power all other activities.
            (2) It interweaves with mind to analyze, rationalize, and evaluate all the information it receives and to organize itself when needed.
            (3) It connects with emotions to experience the world itself aesthetically and to develop human feeling.
            (4) It uses its spiritual aspect to search out spiritual possibilities of other, supernatural, beings and to deal with the mystical and religious aspects of reality.
            (5) It enters into interaction with nature and culture.
        b. All this "working through" can be done formally through all the appropriate fields of study for each aspect (e.g., physical and natural sciences for the physical).
        c. We can also use all of the aspects informally through, for example, various human relationships.
        d. Actualizing self is what is developed through this interweaving process; it is not static, but constantly growing, active, and creative. The process does not end but continues from potential self through the aspects to actualizing self and back to potential self for its vitality.
    2. An ultimate reality can be included in the process as the source of all power, or not; the process can stand on its own logically without the presumed existence of an ultimate reality.
C. The synthesis is merely suggested so that students can see how it is possible to put the aspects together. We can definitely conclude that whatever else is true about human nature, it is mysterious and complex.

Additional Questions and Activities for Study and Discussion

1. Read the book, *Dibbs in Search of Self,* and analyze and critically evaluate it in view of what we've studied in this chapter. How do you feel the author defines "self"? How can one go "in search of self"? Does Dibbs ever find "self" in the novel? How or how not? Show how the author depicts any relationships between self and any of the other aspects of human nature described in this chapter.

2. Read Erich Fromm's *Escape from Freedom,* and analyze and critically evaluate his theories in relationship to the development of the human self. To what extent do you believe that human beings have been and are still trying to "escape from" the freedoms they have acquired from the industrial and technological revolution, the rise of democracy, and the limitations of religious authority? To what extent does this "escape" affect self and its development?

3. Compare and contrast any child whom you know well with any adult, and delineate the differences in what self means and is to each of them. To what extent do you believe that self has developed or is developing in the child, and why? If you can, observe children at various ages—at least from babyhood through age seven—and state when you think self begins to develop and why? To what extent can you see more developed aspects of it in the adult and beginnings of it in the children? To what extent do you find that self is related to any or all of the other aspects of human nature described in this chapter? Which ones and why? Are there some present in adults that are not in children? If so, which ones and why?

4. Read Henry James' *Washington Square* or read or see the play or see the movie entitled *The Heiress* and show how the heroine's self develops throughout any of the works. Describe her self at the beginning and at the end. To what extent does her self change and why? Be specific. Do you feel that it has changed for the better or for the worse? Why?

5. Read Paul Tillich's *The Courage to Be,* and do a complete analysis and critical evaluation of his theories. To what extent do you feel that his theories about human existential anxieties and the establishment and growth of self through courage are accurate or not? Why? Be specific.

6. Read psychologist Rollo May's *Man's Search for Himself,* and analyze and critically evaluate it in relationship to this chapter. To what extent do you agree or disagree with the author's theories, and why?

7. Read Viktor E. Frankl's *Man's Search for Meaning,* and analyze and

critically evaluate his theories concerning self in that book. To what extent do you agree or disagree with those theories, and why?

8. Read two of Hermann Hesse's books, *Steppenwolf* and *Siddhartha,* and describe how they are in fact a search for self. Analyze and critically evaluate the concepts of self that Hesse presents in the two novels. Do you agree or disagree with his theories of self, and why?

Footnotes

1. Frederick Copleston, S.J., *A History of Philosophy* (Garden City, N.Y.: Image Books, 1962), Vol. 5, Part II, p. 106.

2. John Hospers, *An Introduction to Philosophical Analysis*. 2nd ed. (Englewood Cliffs, N.J.: Prentice-Hall), p. 407.

3. This description of Royce's theory of self can be found in Josiah Royce, *The World and the Individual* (New York: Macmillan, 1913), Vol. II, pp. 256–260 and 265–277.

4. Ibid., p. 270.

5. This description of self can be found in George H. Mead, *Mind, Self, and Society* (Chicago: University of Chicago Press, 1947), pp. 135–144.

6. These theories are presented in Martin Buber, *I and Thou* (New York: Scribners, 1958).

7. Paul Tillich, *The Courage to Be* (New Haven, Conn.: Yale University Press, 1952), pp. 40–54.

8. Ibid., p. 86, and Chapter 4, "Courage and Participation," and Chapter 5, "Courage and Individualization."

9. Ibid., pp. 182–185.

Bibliography

Buber, Martin. *I and Thou*. New York: Scribners, 1958.

Castell, Alburey. *The Self in Philosophy*. New York: Macmillan, 1965.

Hall, Calvin S., and Lindzey Gardner. *Theories of Personality*. New York: John Wiley, 1970.

Hesse, Herman. *Siddhartha,* trans. Hilda Rosner. New York: New Directions, 1951.

———. *Steppenwolf,* trans. Basil Creighton. New York: Holt, Rinehart and Winston, 1970.

Johnstone, Henry W., Jr. *The Problem of Self*. University Park, Pa.: Pennsylvania State University Press, 1970.

Myers, Gerald E. *Self: An Introduction to Philosophical Psychology*. New York: Pegasus, 1969.

Perry, J. *Personal Identity*. New York: Lieber–Atherton, 1975.

Rogers, Carl. *On Becoming a Person*. Boston: Houghton-Mifflin, 1961.

Sampson, Edward E. *Ego at the Threshold: In Search of Man's Freedom*. New York: Delta, 1975.

Shoemaker, Sydney. *Self-knowledge and Self-identity*. Ithaca, N.Y.: Cornell University Press, 1963.

CHAPTER 5

Determinism and Human Freedom

In dealing with the nature of a human being, as we have been in the last two chapters, it is important that we include a chapter on a problem that is both metaphysical and ethical in its implications—that of determinism versus human freedom—or putting the problem in the form of a question, "Are human beings really free, or are they totally determined by all the forces working on them from conception to death?" If there is a case to be made for freedom, then another important question will be, "To what extent are human beings free, and to what extent are they determined?"

If you think back to the last two chapters, you will discover that certain assumptions about freedom and determinism are definitely lurking behind the various theories about mind versus brain and self versus no self. For example, B. F. Skinner's theories concerning the nonexistence of mind and self are rooted in materialism and also determinism, whereas the existential or phenomenological (Husserl) theories are based on assumptions that human beings are free to some extent or another (Sartre, for example, states that human beings are completely free to create their own essence from their existence). In addition to the controversies concerning mind and brain, I have also mentioned the aspect of will, and any discussion of will must of necessity deal with freedom or "free will." It, therefore, behooves us to examine the rather complex problem of freedom and determinism.

As noted earlier, the problem of freedom and determinism is metaphysical and also has implications for ethics. The questions of whether there is universal causation (to be defined later) or not, and whether there is also freedom, especially human freedom, are obviously questions about reality and its nature: "Is everything in reality determined by prior causes or forces, or are there some 'things' or beings who are free either because universal causation is not true or despite its existence?" is truly a metaphysical question. However, whether or not human beings are free or are determined is also a definite problem or issue for ethics or morality, for how can human beings be held morally responsible for their decisions and actions if they are totally determined by forces or causes over which they have no control? For example, how can we hold a murderer responsible for killing his or her victim if it can be shown that the murderer was or is not free to act or even decide to act but, instead, is totally determined by his or her genetic structure and environmental conditioning to have committed the act of murder? Since we will be taking up the study of morality (ethics) in the next part and chapters, it is quite important to come to some conclusions about the issue of determinism and human freedom beforehand.

Definitions

Before presenting arguments for and against different aspects of this issue, it is important to state some key definitions.

Determinism actually means the same thing as "universal causation," which can be stated positively as follows: "For every effect, result, occurrence, event, or happening, there is a cause or causes." Stated negatively, "determinism" or "universal causation" means, "There is no such thing as an uncaused event."

Hard determinism is the form of determinism that states that universal causation is totally incompatible with freedom and that freedom is an illusion because everything and everyone are determined to be what they are by causes over which they have little or no control.

Soft determinism is that form of determinism that states that even though universal causation is indeed true, there can still be freedom, especially in the human realm. Soft determinists even go so far as to say that human freedom is possible only within the framework of universal causation. From this viewpoint, then, freedom is definitely not incompatible with universal causation.

Fatalism goes farther than determinism in both its forms in that it assumes that whatever occurs is outside of human control—everything is irrevocably fixed, no matter what human beings do.

Indeterminism is the theory that states that not everything has a cause or causes but that some things, especially human decisions and actions, are uncaused.

With these definitions in mind, then, we will first proceed with arguments for these theories, and then, after they have all been presented, each will be critically evaluated.

Fatalism

This theory has been held since early times, especially in the ancient periods of Greece and Rome, probably because much less was known about the physical, chemical, and biological nature of the universe than is known in our century. In the early Greek tradition, characterized in Homer's *Iliad* and *Odyssey,* human beings are seen as noble and magnificent creatures but under the control of the whims of nature as personified in the gods. For example, as strong and wiley as Achilles was in the attempt to hunt down and kill Hector, a god who favored Hector caused a fog to hide him, which enabled Hector to escape.

During these periods, fate and destiny were those unknown controllers of the lives and deaths of human beings. Human beings might think or feel that they had control or freedom over their own lives, but fate and destiny might have other things in store for them. This is beautifully presented in Sophocles' play, *Oedipus, the King.* In this play, Oedipus is able to solve the most difficult riddle of the sphinx, which indicates his great intelligence, and his strength and bravery as a ruler is later proved after he marries Jocasta, the queen of Thebes, and becomes its king. However, a prophet tells Oedipus that he will kill his father and marry his mother, two of the worst crimes in ancient Greek culture (patricide or matricide and incest). Unbeknown to Oedipus, he has already committed both deeds. Sophocles showed in this play that no matter how intelligent, strong, or decisive a human being was, his fate and destiny were already decided for him, and there was nothing he could do about it.

What this theory says, then, is that no matter how we plot or plan, no matter how we try to think out every decision or action, fate will somehow step in and run our lives for us; therefore, if, for example, we are due to die in a war, it doesn't matter whether or not we wear a helmet or stay in a bomb shelter or trench, for if we are meant to be hit by a bullet or a bomb, then it will "get us" no matter what we do. Many people state the theory this way, "No matter what I do or think, whatever happens will happen, and I have no control over it—anything that I do will make no difference—'Que sera, sera,' 'What will be, will be.'" People who talk this way are called "fatalists."

Indeterminism

Indeterminists will accept causality in all other parts of nature except the human realm, although they may argue that there is a certain amount of freedom even in the physical realm, especially at the subatomic levels of nature. They will also go so far as to accept some causality in the human realm, for example, in the area of our autonomic nervous systems and in reflex actions. However, they feel that to the extent we deliberate, choose, and act, our actions are not determined but free.

William James (1842–1910), a philosopher and psychologist, was a strong proponent of this theory. James felt that we should affirm our freedom as our first act of freedom, and he seemed to be saying that to be free, we *have* to affirm our freedom. To the extent that we do not do this, we allow ourselves to be determined, but we obviously (to his way of thinking) have freedom if we will merely affirm it. Another argument James gave for indeterminism was that the very fact that we human beings feel regret for some of our actions assures us that we are free. If we were not free, then why should we feel regret, since we could not be responsible for having done something for which we would have regret? A last argument he gave was the fact that many human actions cannot be predicted. Since our actions cannot be predicted with any accuracy as the actions of molecules and atoms can, for instance, then we must be free and unlike other parts of or beings in the universe.

Soft Determinism

The soft determinist accepts universal causation wholeheartedly but feels that freedom is possible within it. The soft determinist argues against indeterminism, saying that if some events are uncaused, they are not caused by anyone, and therefore the indeterminist's argument really does not give human beings freedom. What it does is replace causation-denying-freedom with freedom due to accident. The soft determinist argues that the very fact of universal causation allows for freedom because some of the causes can be attributed in large part to human beings. In other words, the soft determinist argues that within the web of cause and effect, human beings can cause some effects or that some results can come from human causes and, therefore, human beings can take some responsibility for having caused some events or occurrences.

The soft determinist feels that many beings in nature are determined but that human beings, because of their consciousness and reasoning abilities and the extent to which they have and use them, can choose to act in certain ways and be responsible for their choices and actions. Soft determinists do not believe that we have unlimited freedom, as the indeterminist seems to feel, but they do believe that we are sometimes free to deliberate, to make choices based on our deliberations, and then to act on our choices. This does not mean we have total control over our lives and actions, but we do have some, and to the extent that we do, we are free and responsible.

Hard Determinism

As has been noted in the definitions, hard determinism states that freedom in any sense is incompatible with universal causation because, since everything is caused, eventually causes for human actions will end up outside of humans and outside their control. True, say hard determinists, human decisions and actions may change or affect some events—which is why they disagree with fatalists—but those decisions and actions when traced back far enough are discovered to have been caused by something else and eventually by something over which they have no control. More arguments and evidence from all areas of human culture have been brought forth for hard determinism—especially in modern times—than any other of the foregoing theories, and we should look at them now.

RELIGIOUS DETERMINISM (PREDESTINATION)

This type of hard determinism states that everything that happens has been preordained or predestined by an all-powerful, all-knowing god. According to this view, because God created the universe and everything in it, including human beings. He has the power to do anything, and he knows everything that has happened, is happening, and will happen; therefore, everything in the world's past history, present, and future is foreknown and thereby predestined. If, for example, God has decided that I will lead a good life and "go to heaven," then I will; if, on the other hand, he has decided I will lead a bad life and "go to hell," then I will do that instead. I have absolutely no say over what I or anyone else does because everything has been predestined, programmed, predetermined by an almighty supernatural being. This theory of predestination was most strongly presented by the Protestant minister and theologian, John Calvin (1509–1564), who said that individuals cannot merely by their deeds ensure their own salvation—those who get to heaven have been chosen by God already. The only freedom any human being has if this theory is true is not knowing for sure whether or not he has been chosen by God to enter heaven; therefore, it would behoove him or her to do good works so that he may gain, at least partially, God's favor.

SCIENTIFIC DETERMINISM

Because the physical and natural sciences depend upon experiments, constancy, and prediction in their search for knowledge and truth, they must accept universal causation. This has led many scientists to presume further that such causation means that there is absolutely no freedom in the universe. Not all scientists accept this extreme point of view; nevertheless, some of the strongest arguments and evidence for determinism have been put forth in the twentieth century by the natural and physical sciences, especially as they have affected modern psychology.

PHYSICAL SCIENCE AND PHYSICAL DETERMINISM.   The greatest exponent of physical determinism was Sir Isaac Newton (1642–1727). He believed that nature and the universe are governed by natural laws (for example, the law of gravity) and that there is, therefore, no such thing as freedom. Since everything observable—even things unobservable to the naked eye, such as atoms and molecules—is physical in nature, then everything that occurs to these things and everything they do are caused by one or another physical law or event. Since, according to Newton, human beings are also physical in nature (Newton was a materialist, as it is defined in Chapter 3), they are subject to physical causes both within and outside of them. For them, freedom is merely an illusion.

BIOLOGICAL AND GENETIC DETERMINISM.   Biological determinism is best exemplified in Charles Darwin's theory of natural selection, which he presented in his most famous work, *The Origin of the Species*. Darwin (1809–1882) believed that various species in nature evolve at different stages in the history of the world and that only the fittest survive. For example, even though some prehistoric animals (dinosaurs, for instance) were extremely large and powerful, their brain capacity and mental ability were so limited that they did not survive, whereas smaller and more intelligent beings, such as humans, did. Darwin suggested that this process of natural selection essentially has nothing to do with freedom. He believed, rather, that it is nature that governs, through its various processes, the makeup, strength, and survival potential of the various species and that the species that emerge as dominant are determined by the stage along the evolutionary scale at which they appear.

A more modern and sophisticated version of this theory is concerned with genetic makeup, especially that of human beings. None of us has any say over the identity of our parents, from whom we will inherit our genes; and since our genes determine so much of our makeup—our sex, personality, and eye, hair, and skin color—how can we be said to be free in any real sense of the word?

HISTORICAL OR CULTURAL DETERMINISM.   Georg W. F. Hegel (1770–1831) developed a deterministic theory that was based on history. He believed that the various periods of the world's history are manifestations of an "absolute mind" that is trying to realize itself in a state of perfection. He also believed that the basic nature of reality and the world is rational and mental and that the physical world is merely a manifestation of the absolute mind's intellectual growth toward perfection. The implications of his theory are that we are neither responsible for nor able to control the period of history or the culture in which we are born. Rather, the character and actions of all individuals are determined by their own culture and all preceding cultures and historical events. Furthermore, since history is a manifestation of an absolute mind that exists in the universe and that is attempting to realize itself, then we, too, are a result or manifestation of that absolute mind. Even if we disregard Hegel's theory about an absolute mind, his arguments about our being determined by our own and preceding cultures are quite compelling.

ECONOMIC OR SOCIAL DETERMINISM.   Karl Marx (1818–1883), following Hegel's theories, believed that our characters and actions are not so much historically determined as they are economically and socially determined. Marx's theory, called dialectical materialism (see Chapter 2, dialectical reasoning, and again Chapter 3, materialism), states that human beings are determined by an evolutionary economic class struggle. According to Marx, this evolutionary process led from early agrarian economics, through monarchies and feudalism, through the rise of the middle class and industrialism, to capitalism and, eventually, to socialism. He believed that people cannot control the economic class into which they are born, and yet their natures are determined in every way by this event. He further believed, as Hegel, that there is an inevitable force in nature (economic, however, rather than historical) that human beings cannot control and that will eventually lead to the ultimate goal, which is a classless society.

PSYCHOLOGICAL DETERMINISM—FREUDIANISM AND BEHAVIORISM. Some of the most convincing of the arguments developed in the twentieth century in support of determinism, especially as it affects human beings, have come from psychology. In the nineteenth century, Sigmund Freud (1856–1939), the father of psychoanalysis, put forth the theory that human beings are determined, even prior to birth in the womb, by their unconscious minds and by various natural drives that their society's mores and customs required them to repress. For example, one of Freud's theories is that all sons are basically in love with their mothers (Freud called this the Oedipus complex) and that all daughters are basically in love with their fathers (the Electra complex). Because incest is forbidden in most societies, these unconscious yet natural drives must be repressed, affecting human beings in different ways and sometimes causing them to have severe mental and emotional problems. Therefore, if mothers or fathers give too much, too little, or the wrong kind of love to their sons or daughters, the entire mental and emotional lives of these children can be affected to the point where they become neurotic or psychotic.

This theory has been used many times in defending criminal killers, as when, for example, the defense claims that a certain man who has raped and killed a number of women has done so because they all resembled his mother and that his unconscious hatred of her compelled him to commit the crimes. Just as this man was "determined" by his unconscious drives of love and hate for his mother to perform terrible acts, so, a Freudian would argue, all human beings are determined by all their inner drives and unconscious motivations to behave the way they do.

In the twentieth century, psychological determinism has not been most significantly argued from the point of view of the inner psyche, as in Freudianism, but rather from the point of view of the influences of the external environment as in behaviorism. This approach is best exemplified in the work of B. F. Skinner (1904–   ), who described his theories in two books, *Science and Human Behavior* and *Beyond Freedom and Dignity* (an interesting title to say the least), and in his utopian novel, *Walden Two*. The theories of Skinner have been pretty thoroughly presented in Chapter 3, in the discussion of the mind versus brain controversy, and in Chapter 4, in the discussion of Skinner's antiself theory, so I see no need to reiterate what has been presented there. Suffice it to say that Skinner feels that human freedom is not fact but illusion and that everything we are and do has been predetermined and is continuing to be determined by the external stimuli we have received and are receiving from our environments.

These arguments for determinism from all areas of human culture and the whole theory of universal causation in itself have some rather powerful implications for any assumptions concerning human freedom or the lack of it. Hard determinists make the following assumptions based on their central theory of universal causation and all the arguments for determinism presented earlier:

1. Either human beings are free or they are not; there is no in between.
2. However, the evidence is overwhelmingly in favor of our not being free, as follows:
   a. We have no control over our genetic makeup, so any determinants that come through our genetic inheritance and make us what we are are not our responsibility—we are not free to choose our genetic structure.
   b. We have very little if any control over our early childhood environments out of which our original characters were formed.
   c. We have not much more control over our later environments during our school years because of the many strong influences or determinants imposed on us by our complex and powerful cultures at all levels.
3. All the preceding means that
   a. We may think that we are free, but freedom is an illusion; rather, we are totally determined by everything we have ever experienced.
   b. To be free, we would have to be able to have created our own original characters, but as anyone can see, that is impossible.
   c. We are compelled to act as we do, given all the factors that have determined and are determining us, and we simply could not have done otherwise than we did, nor can we do other than what we do.
   d. Everything is not outside of our control, as in fatalism, for we may choose to act, and the way in which we act can affect other people and events around us. But are we free to choose? Can we, for example, choose our desires?

Critical Evaluation of the Theories

It is appropriate at this time to evaluate critically all these theories and then try to come to some conclusion concerning the knotty problem of freedom and determinism.

FATALISM

There are certainly times in our lives when we feel that everything is outside our control and that, no matter how hard we have tried to avoid something bad happening, it happens anyway. It does seem to us that when this occurs, it is "fated" or somehow "predestined" by some power or powers outside of us, and that no matter what we did, the occurrence could not have been prevented.

However, there seem to be many more times when what we have done has made a great difference in what has occurred. For example, when we are in an accident, our lives might have indeed been saved because we took the precaution of fastening our seat belts. Further, although it is true that if we take a direct hit from a bullet or a bomb, wearing a helmet or getting into a foxhole or a bomb shelter probably will not make much of a difference; however, wouldn't we be foolish not to take those precautions since we know that our chances of getting injured or killed are somewhat decreased by taking them? People may talk like fatalists, but hardly anyone lives his or her life as if nothing he or she did would make any difference. If people really believed that fatalism was true, then they would never attend school, save money, try to woo a mate, plan to have children, or do anything but stay in bed all day. It simply is not true then that everything is really outside of our control and that nothing we ever do matters as far as it concerns directing our lives or making a difference in the world around us or in the lives of others.

INDETERMINISM

There are several criticisms of indeterminism that come mostly from soft and hard determinists. First, indeterminists suggest that some events—presumably those involving human beings and especially those in the area of mortality—are uncaused, but what would an uncaused event be like? It is true that we cannot trace each and every cause for every occurrence, but has anyone ever really witnessed an uncaused event? Can we even conceive of such a thing? Even though we cannot know the specific cause or causes of every event, does it not seem absurd to even suggest that some events are uncaused? If I decide to shoot someone in a fit of anger, is not the shooting caused by something? My anger, which was caused by something or someone else, which in turn was caused by something else, and so on? It does not seem to square with either logic or experience to say that some events or occurrences are not caused by something or someone. Further, even if some events were uncaused, this would not help to establish human freedom, would it? It would seem that the soft determinists were right in their criticism of indeterminism in that if some events are uncaused, then they are not caused by anyone or anything, including human beings themselves. Instead of being caused, these events would have to be considered as accidental, and how could any human being accept the responsibility for being morally good or bad if what he or she did merely occurred by accident?

The indeterminists are willing to state that actions occurring in nature and outside of human beings are caused, but aren't our deliberations, choices, and, therefore, our actions caused also, and many times by causes outside of our control? For example, if we are afraid of attending funerals because we had a very bad experience at a funeral when we were three years old, then isn't that fear caused by our previous experience? Also, isn't even our ability to control that fear dependent on causes that may lie outside of us? For example, maybe we can overcome the fear with the help of a therapist or with the support of a friend, and maybe we can't.

William James' affirmation of freedom is encouraging, but isn't it really just wishful thinking? If it is really true that human beings aren't free, then wishful thinking will not make them free. Wishing for something may help us to attain it, but we all know that much more is involved in attaining something than merely wishing for it—the old song, "Wishing Will Make It So," is a lovely thought, but it is certainly not true in and of itself. We may wish the earth were flat, but that cannot change the reality and truth that it is not. As far as the fact that we have regrets proving that we are free is concerned, our regrets may be due to our lack of awareness that we are truly determined and that the freedom we feel is really an illusion that can be easily destroyed by the evidence and logic of hard determinism.

James' contention that human actions cannot be totally predicted is not a conclusive argument against determinism either. Human actions are much more predictable than they ever have been in the whole history of the world. Many business firms, like banks and insurance companies, plan their entire business activities on actuarial statistics, which, if followed, cause them to succeed extremely well. Further, according to behavioral scientists, the more information we acquire about the science of human behavior, the more successful our predictions will be so that we may in the future be able to predict human behavior more completely than ever. It would seem then that the arguments for indeterminism are not successful in gaining us human freedom. Let us see if soft determinism can help us.

SOFT DETERMINISM

The indeterminist would argue that as soon as you accept the principle of universal causation, you have eliminated freedom, which is why he argues for some events being uncaused. The hard determinist agrees with this criticism, saying that the soft determinist is merely trying to create something that isn't there—he is really trying to squeeze freedom out of an intricate and complex web of interwoven and intertwined causes and effects. The hard determinist would argue that there is no such thing as limited freedom; either human beings are free or they are not, and once we accept universal causation, we rule out any possibility of freedom. The hard determinist says that if universal causation is true, then *everything* is determined—desires, thoughts, actions, feelings—because as you trace all causes back far enough, they end up outside of human beings and not within their control. Therefore, how can freedom be compatible with determinism?

Note that the hard determinist is *not* agreeing with the fatalist that everything is outside human control and what we do does not matter, but he is saying that if we keep tracing cause and effect back far enough, they end up outside of us. For example, I can change my environment and other people by my influences on them—I can build beautiful buildings that create nice environments in which people can live; I can also be kind or cruel to people and affect how they feel and act by my behavior. However, my abilities to do these things come from my genetic makeup over which I had no control—I didn't cause mine, my parents didn't cause theirs, my grandparents didn't cause theirs, and so on. My abilities also come from my environment influences in my early childhood, over which I had little or no control, and over which later I have some but not total control. Therefore, the hard determinist would argue, soft determinism is just as much wishful thinking as indeterminism—there simply is no such thing as freedom.

Does this mean that we must accept hard determinism since all alternative theories are refutable and since hard determinism seems to have so much evidence and logic on its side? Let us now take a critical look at hard determinism and then see if we can arrive at some conclusions about whether or not human beings are free or determined.

HARD DETERMINISM

First, we shall critically evaluate each of the various types of determinism; then, we shall examine hard determinism's assumptions and implications.

RELIGIOUS DETERMINISM (PREDESTINATION).   If we accept the existence of an all-powerful, all-knowing God, then predestination or religious determinism would seem to have some basis, but there are tremendous theological, as well as philosophical, problems with this theory. First, not all philosophers, scientists, or even religionists are willing to accept the existence of a god or one who is all powerful or all knowing. The proof for such an existent being is not conclusive, nor are its or his qualities or attributes. Second, even if we accept such a being, the idea that human beings are not free to choose good or evil would seem to negate the messages of many religions and plunge the whole God-human relationship into absurdity. It is ridiculous to think of an all-powerful, all-knowing, all-good being who would create beings who would think that they are choosing good or evil when in fact this being is causing them to choose. What is the point of blame, praise, punishment, or reward, if human beings cannot help what they do because they are forced by a supernatural being to do it?

Some religionists would argue that just because God has foreknowledge does not mean that he has caused human beings to act in certain ways. They describe God as if he were a person standing on a mountain top who can see two cars heading for a collision on a road below him. He can see and know what is going to happen, but he does not have the power to have caused them to be there, nor does he have the power to prevent the collision. Another possibility is that as God, he does not choose to prevent it. As you can see, all these possibilities throw doubt on two of God's supposed qualities—his power and his goodness. If he does not have the power, then he is not all powerful; if he chooses not to stop the accident, then there is a question about his goodness. Besides it is quite difficult to conceive of a being knowing what is going to happen and yet not having anything to do with causing it.

Most important, however, religions (especially the Western ones) would not make much sense if human beings are not considered free to choose good or evil. It is only with such freedom that any message of salvation makes sense. Human beings must be free to choose, or the concept of God becomes absurd—a master puppeteer manipulating puppets. Very few Christian sects accept the concept of predestination, and the evidence for it, generally speaking, is weak to say the least.

Scientific Determinism. Even though universal causation would seem to be a valid theory, there is no conclusive proof that every event that has ever occurred has a cause or causes. To know this conclusively, we would have to be able to trace all causes back to the beginning. True, we can posit a first cause like God or energy, or atoms, but we cannot know for sure that things have happened in the way those theories say they did. Therefore, we can look on the theory of universal causation as an assumption—one that seems to make the most sense, but an assumption nevertheless. We know that scientists definitely need to presume cause and effect, but we cannot know for certain that it is true in all cases or that it always works in the way scientists and hard determinist philosophers say it does.

Physical Science and Physical Determinism. This theory is not conclusively proved either, and even if it holds true for most of nature, human beings are quite different from other beings in nature, as we have noticed in Chapters 3 and 4. Critics of Newton argue that humans are not merely physical, but are also mental (and/or spiritual) beings, and that because they are more than physical, they are able to "transcend" physical laws. Furthermore, the discoveries of modern physics, exemplified most pertinently by Werner Heisenberg's quantum theory of physics, have raised serious doubts about Newtonian views of nature and the universe being strictly physical and mechanical. In such theories, the door has been left open for the possibility of freedom even for nonconscious entities such as atoms and molecules. Therefore, although science generally accepts universal causation, some of the more recent theories have indicated such possibilities as spontaneity and freedom even in the physical world.

Biological and Genetic Determinism.   There is no doubt that evolution in some form has had a lot to do with forming all human beings, and especially the genetic development and evolution of the human species. We know for sure that we acquire much of our cellular structure, hair and eye coloring, bone formations, sex, and so on from our genes, which are a combination of the genes of our parents. Here again, however, there are unanswered mysteries and questions.

We really don't know how evolution actually works as exemplified in the various "missing link" theories. Further, we really don't know how much of what we are can be attributed to our genetic makeup and how much to our environmental influences; this is especially true of such mysterious human attributes as intelligence. Just about the time evidence seems to be overwhelming that environment determines intelligence, something arises in the study of genetics that indicates that genes play a greater part than we thought before—and vice versa. It is probably true that they both have something to do with intelligence, but no one knows for sure which does what and how dependent humans are on either for the development of their intelligence.

Also, just as in the case of physical science, the biological-genetic theory tends to limit human beings to only the physical (in this case the biological and genetic), and, in comparison with other biological beings, humans are quite a bit more complicated and mysterious.

Historical or Cultural Determinism.   Obvious problems exist with Hegel's theory in that there is no conclusive proof that there is any such thing in existence as an absolute mind; as a matter of fact the phrase "absolute mind" is itself not very clear. Is there some sort of disembodied mind out there in the universe somewhere? As we have seen in Chapter 3, the problem of whether or not mind exists is difficult enough, but trying to separate it completely from brain or body does not square with any experience we have. Has anyone ever witnessed mind without any connection to some brain and body? What would be the nature of such a thing? Even if we accept Hegel's theory of an absolute mind, how do we know that it is connected to history in any way? Furthermore, there is no conclusive evidence that history really proceeds in the way Hegel described. There are many other theories of history that do not imply a total determinism such as Hegel presents.

It is certainly true that every culture is influenced by past cultures, particularly the culture nearest to it, and that all human beings in that culture are also influenced, but is it not also just as possible that the people in the present culture can change previous traditions and cultural actions? Doesn't that mean, then, that human beings and present cultures can rise above or transcend their past cultures? At best, historical or cultural determinism can only partly account for what present cultures and their members are and do.

Economic or Social Determinism. There are similar problems with this theory as with Hegel's. First, there is no conclusive proof for the existence of a process such as dialectical materialism. Also, as with Hegel's theory, there are many other economic theories just as plausible as Marx's that, however, do not espouse determinism. Second, even though there is no doubt that people are influenced by their individual economic status and that of their society, there are, as we have seen, many other influences that affect economics as well as human beings. For example, scientific and technological developments have a great deal of influence on the economic status of cultures and their members—probably more than economics itself has on science and technology. Also, economics is not the only influence that affects human beings; in fact, one could argue that human beings can affect or determine the changes in economics at least to the same extent that economics affects them.

Psychological Determinism—Freudianism and Behaviorism. In the twentieth century, these two forms of psychology have probably contributed more toward the argument for determinism, especially as it applies to human beings, than has any of the other theories mentioned earlier. First, we should recognize that there are many more psychological theories than just these two and that they do not support determinism but rather human freedom. Second, one must again be careful that any theory that tries to subsume all of human nature should be carefully questioned since very few one-sided theories can explain the complexities inherent in human motivations and actions. There are also specific objections and criticisms of both Freudianism and behaviorism.

The major criticism of Freud's theories is that they are too generalized to have any real basis in fact. That is, he has taken his experiences with a few abnormally disturbed patients and used them as a basis for establishing theories that are supposed to apply to all human beings. It may be true that some sons are in love with their mothers and that some daughters are in love with their fathers and, further, that these emotions have caused them a great deal of difficulty in their lives. There is, however, little conclusive evidence to show that these problems affect *all* human beings and that their lives are totally determined by such influences. As a matter of fact, most child-parent relationships seem to exist without any psychological incestuousness being involved. Here again, as with other theories of determinism, one theory about human motivations and behavior cannot seem to encompass them all.

One problem with Skinner's theories of behaviorism is that they are based on a total materialism, and, as we have seen in Chapter 3, this theory is refutable because it does not account for mental events, which are quite different from physical events. Moreover, as does Freud, Skinner carries sound premises too far in trying to apply them to all human motivation and behavior. It is quite true that people can be and are conditioned by various methods to behave in certain ways or to change certain aspects of their behavior. Weight, smoking, and alcohol control clinics, among others, are perfect examples that this can be done. The fact that conditioning works under some circumstances does not mean, however, that human beings merely react to external stimuli all the time, or that conditioning always works, or even that it should be applied in all instances. Another problem that exists with Skinner's theories is that they are based on a questionable view of the human mind—that it is a passive receptacle for outside stimuli only. As was stated in Chapter 3, this view of the human mind does not seem to square with our experiences of it as something more active and creative than he has described.

EVALUATION OF ASSUMPTIONS OF HARD DETERMINISM

Human Beings Are Either Free or They Are Not. This assumption is guilty of the false dilemma logical fallacy (see Chapter 2). As with many of the hard determinist's arguments, words are often pushed out of context.[1] To say that human beings are free, it is not necessary for them to have complete or unlimited freedom. To say that human beings are either completely free or they are not free at all creates a false dilemma and omits the possibility of other alternatives. Most advocates of human freedom recognize that human beings can in no way be completely free. For example, I cannot without help defy any of the so-called "laws of nature." Obviously, I am not free to change myself into a car or a dog or a rose. If I am constrained by chains, then of course I am not free to get up and walk away. However, none of this means that I cannot have limited freedom, and limited freedom is all that most freedom advocates are asking for.

We Have No Control over Our Genetic Makeup. It is quite true that we have no control over our genetic makeup and that very much of what we are and have become is due to our genetic "programming." However, given our genetic basis, is it not possible for us to develop ourselves beyond our genetic determinants at least to some extent? For example, if people are born mentally retarded because of genetic deficiencies, aren't they still able to go beyond their original deficiency to some extent through proper loving care, therapy, and education? If I am genetically determined to have a tendency to be overweight, can't I overrule this tendency by carefully watching what I eat and by exercising? Many things caused by my genetic makeup I cannot alter, but I am certainly not totally bound by genetic structure in everything I am and do unless I am severely damaged by genetic deficiency. Haven't we all seen people almost totally crippled and incapacitated by such deficiencies nevertheless function as artists, writers, and scientists? Our genes are important determinants of what and who we are, but they are not the only determinants, and we can often rise above them when they restrict us.

We Have No Control over Our Environment. It is true that we have little or no control over our early childhood environment and are certainly affected by our later environments, but does this mean we have no ability to compensate for early childhood experiences or to override later influences? How can one account for the fact that in a family where two children are subjected to abuse that one of them will forever be marked by this experience whereas the other, although marked by it, will nevertheless be able to rise above it? We are certainly influenced by our culture and society at every turn, but is it also not true that we can override such influence and even do some of the influencing ourselves?

For example, Martin Luther King, Jr. (1928–1968) was certainly influenced by the discrimination against black people in the South and other parts of the United States, but can anyone doubt the tremendous effect he and his followers had on the culture and society that influenced them? Does this mean that determinism works both ways? If so, then there seems to be a modicum of freedom for at least some human beings.

157

We Cannot Have Created Our Original Characters.   This is another example where the hard determinist pushes language out of context, and it assumes two things: (1) that we can know what "original character" means and (2) that once established, an original character is static and unchangeable. What exactly is our original character? Does the hard determinist mean our genetic makeup? If so, then he is refuted by the arguments just given. Further, isn't he asking the impossible? How could we ever create our own genes? We would already have to exist to do this, and wouldn't that mean we would already have a genetic makeup? The requirement that we create our own genes is too demanding and unreasonable.

By "original character" does the determinist mean a combination of our genetic makeup and our early childhood influences? If so, when would our original character be formed—at what year of our childhood, and how would we know when this has occurred? Further, how could we have created our own original character—whatever it is— since we would already have had to exist, and wouldn't that mean we would already have an original character? Here again the determinist is too demanding and unreasonable.

Finally, even if we accept the concept of an original character, is its nature as static as the determinist seems to suggest? Haven't we all experienced our characters developing and changing depending on our contacts with other people, education, and our own thoughts? If this original character, whenever it is supposed to have been formed, is not locked into place, then isn't it possible to talk about some freedom in its development and later formation?

We Are Compelled to Act as We Do.   Again the hard determinist pushes the meaning of words out of context. "Compulsion" means the act of forcing or compelling and may involve constraint or coercion. In psychology, it means an irresistible impulse to act, regardless of the rationality of one's motivation. To use this word, which has a specific meaning and applies to only certain types of instances in human behavior or events, to describe human behavior and events in general is to force it out of its proper context and dilute its rather specific meaning. For example, it makes sense to talk about a kleptomaniac's compulsion to steal, which he cannot control and which seems to come from within him, but not to describe a basically normal person's behavior as "compulsive." To say, as the hard determinist does, that we are *compelled* to act as we do, given all the factors that have determined and are determining us, and that we simply could not have done otherwise than we did, nor can we do other than what we do, is to confuse and blur the meaning of "compulsion."

The whole idea that we could not have done otherwise than we did is also an example of misuse of language by the hard determinist. Of course, if we had chosen to do something different, then we could have done otherwise. As we look back on events, can't we always remind ourselves that we could have done otherwise and either wish we had or be glad we hadn't? For example, if we are trying to choose between spending our vacation in the mountains or at the seashore, if we choose the seashore, can't we look back on our decision and say that we could've done otherwise if we had chosen to do so? What will the hard determinist tell us—that the fact that our parents abused us made us choose one over the other and that we "couldn't have done otherwise"? He would be hard pressed to prove any such statement.

Are We Free to Choose?   The hard determinist argues not that everything is outside of our control, as in fatalism, for he says that human beings may choose to act and the way they act can affect other people and events around them, but are they free to choose? Can they, for example, choose their desires?

John Hospers states this determinist argument well as follows:

> We can act in accordance with our choices or decisions [he will say] and we can choose in accordance with our desires. But we are not free to *desire*. We can choose as we please, but we can't please as we please. If my biological or psychological nature is such that at a certain moment I desire A, I shall choose A, and if it is such that I desire B, I shall choose B. I am free to choose either A or B, but I am not free to desire either A or B. Moreover, my desires are not themselves the outcomes of choices, for I cannot choose to have them or not to have them.[2]

Is it really true that we cannot choose or overrule any of our desires? We certainly cannot choose all of our desires, but can't we choose some or choose to (and successfully) override others? Even though Hospers agrees with the hard determinist that people are very often victims of inner urges and desires that they do not want and from which they cannot escape, he argues very effectively, in rebuttal, that

> Nevertheless, to a very *limited* extent (varying considerably from person to person) and *over a considerable span of time,* we *are* free to desire or not to desire. We can choose to do our best to get rid of certain desires and to encourage other ones; and to a limited extent we may be successful in this endeavor. People who greatly desire alcohol sometimes succeed, by joining Alcoholics Anonymous or by other means, in resisting the temptation to drink until finally they no longer desire it. So, it is not true that we are never free to desire or that we are always the victims of whatever desires we happen to have.[3]

The Human Mind, Consciousness, and Freedom

I totally agree with all the criticisms of hard determinism described by Hospers and also with all the others presented in the evaluation of hard determinism, but the strongest argument against hard determinism centers on the nature of human consciousness and the human mind.

When talking about universal causation, we must take into consideration the complexity of the human mind as it was described in Chapter 3. A rock is dependent on outside forces for its movement, change in shape, and change in color. Plant life is subject to forces outside and within it, and a plant grows, changes, and dies in reaction to these forces, which, as far as we can determine, operate at all times on some sort of biological (or botanical) instinct. Animals, too, although closer to human beings in their bodies and minds, are often governed by instinctual actions programmed down through the years by hereditary and genetic chances.

As we move along the evolutionary scale from inanimate to animate beings and from vegetative to animalistic beings, we see the element of freedom increase with each step. The rock, which has no freedom at all, is drastically different from the plant, which is affected by its own internal workings as well as by outside forces. Animals are much more mobile than are plants, have a greater observable consciousness, and can even be said to make some limited choices. For example, if a forest is on fire, the instinct to survive will cause an animal to attempt to escape by running away from the fire. Assuming that the fire is burning in a semicircle behind the animal, then it has approximately 180° of ground in front of it. This gives the animal a range of possibilities for the direction it may take, and what makes it take any one particular direction? There may be certain obstacles that limit its direction, but even with this, doesn't the animal, in a limited sense at least, "choose" a path of escape?

When we reach human beings on the evolutionary scale, we find they have a much more sophisticated consciousness and that their consciousness and minds are developed far beyond those of any other observable beings. This means that the possibility for freedom greatly increases, for it is consciousness, the human mind, and reasoning on which most soft determinists and indeterminists base their arguments for human freedom. As was presented in Chapter 3, under the heading of "The Mind as Active and Intentional" (in the theories of Jean-Paul Sartre, the existentialist, and Edmund Husserl, the phenomenologist), the mind is not merely a passive receptacle, reacting to and absorbing stimuli from the outside, but rather it is intentional, directive, creative, and active. I would refer you back to that chapter at this point and especially to the example of a human being experiencing a sunset at the beach.

Another example that might be helpful at this point is that of a person who drives along the same route from home to work and back every day. Each trip he takes in either direction is different in the sense that his mind notices different objects along the way and brings different previous experiences to the drive. Naturally, some of the external objects along the route *are* different, but even if they never changed, the human mind could direct itself in different ways, selecting among the objects outside it and its previous and present experiences and thus, in a sense, *creating* its own experience of the drive. If the possibilities are open-ended, even to some extent, then there are many to choose from. Since the human mind can select and direct itself differently, there are many more possibilities of choice available to the human than to the forest animal with the fire at its back. The level of sophistication of choices is, of course, also much higher.

Therefore, if the human mind can, even in part, create its own experience, then experience is not merely waiting in a deterministic sense to impinge itself on human consciousness. As Sartre pointed out, you may have been born crippled or blind, and you were not free to choose otherwise, but you are free in how you choose to live out your life with your infirmity. You are determined in your physical limitations, and you are even determined by the culture, economic level, and family in which you are born, but you are not completely determined—unless you *choose* to be—in how you live out your life, even though it has been influenced, in part, by all these things.

Building on the second Hospers quotation, cited earlier, this means that although I may have been born with a physical or psychological lack or urge that causes me to become addicted to alcohol when I drink it. I may become aware of this lack or urge and—with or without outside help—override this deterministic factor in my life. One might say that my consciousness is directing itself to a new life experience free from addiction to alcohol and all its attendant difficulties. I, then, to some extent *create* that life experience for myself even though I have, by my physical and psychological nature, been formerly determined very strongly toward the completely different life experience of a person who is addicted to alcohol. Almost all the groups that have been successful in the elimination of various drug addictions have stated that all they can really do is try to make people strong enough to make the choice for nonaddiction themselves and then to support and help them as much as possible. The choice, however, has to be the addicts', and until they actively choose the new life experience, their lives will probably not change very much.

Conclusion

This argument should convince us that there is such a thing as human freedom and that it is no illusion. Accepting that it exists, it is logical to assume that it applies to mortality as well as to choosing what clothes we will wear or where we will spend this year's vacation. With these conclusions in mind, it would seem that the only tenable position for one to hold in the controversy of freedom versus determinism is soft determinism, which says that universal causation, both by evidence and argument, is a strongly supported theory of reality that is compatible with limited human freedom.

Soft determinism is, therefore, the theory that I support. I feel that our freedom is limited and that there are many times when our actions are not within our control. We may be suffering from a psychological compulsion, such as kleptomania, and not be able to control our desire to steal. Under such a compulsion we cannot be held *morally* responsible for stealing something because our compulsion is outside of our control. Further, we may be forced at gunpoint to do something that we know to be morally wrong, or we may be constrained so that we cannot do something morally right. We may be powerfully affected by the way in which we were treated by our families, by our genetic deficiencies, by the century in which we were born, by the culture and economic level into which we were born—all these things may determine our characters to a great degree. But—paraphrasing Hospers—nevertheless, to some extent (varying considerably from person to person) and over a considerable span of time, we are free to desire or not to desire, to choose or not to choose, and to act or not to act.

With the acceptance of this viewpoint, it does make sense to assign moral responsibility to human beings when appropriate, and it also makes sense to praise, blame, reward, and punish them for their actions. We certainly should be careful to ascertain that people are not acting from uncontrollable compulsions or constraints before we assign praise or blame to them. Having discovered, however, that they have acted freely, it does make sense to talk of moral responsibility and its attendant rewards and punishments. We will do just that in the next three chapters concerning ethics, the study of morality.

Applying Philosophy— Situations for Thought and Discussion

SITUATION 1

Are you free or determined? To make the discussions in this chapter applicable to you and your everyday life, speculate on whether you are free or determined by examining your experiences to the fullest extent possible, and write a well-organized and coherent essay dealing with the following questions in any order you wish:

1. To what extent are you influenced or determined by the following?
   a. Your genetic makeup.
   b. Your early childhood and relationship with your parents and any siblings in your family.
   c. Your later childhood and adolescence—include here the influence of your teachers and student peers.
   d. Your economic and social status.
   e. Your religious or nonreligious background.
   f. Science and technology.
   g. The history (both the near past and long ago) and culture of your society.
2. Given the foregoing influences, to what extent are you free in any or all of the following areas of your life?
   a. Physical.
   b. Mental or psychological.
   c. Emotional.
   d. Spiritual or religious.

SITUATION 2

With your instructor's direction and guidance, read any of the following literary works and discuss the extent to which you think the main characters are free or determined: Albert Camus' *The Stranger;* Herman Melville's *Bartleby the Scrivener* or *Billy Budd;* Stephen Crane's *The Open Boat;* Joan Didion's *Play It as It Lays;* Fyodor Dostoyevsky's *Crime and Punishment;* Arthur Miller's *Death of a Salesman* and *After the Fall;* F. Scott Fitzgerald's *The Great Gatsby;* Ernest Hemingway's *The Sun Also Rises* or *For Whom the Bell Tolls;* or any others your instructor might want to suggest.

SITUATION 3

Research the background of some great men or women (for example, Albert Einstein, John F. Kennedy, Michelangelo, Picasso, Florence Nightingale, Mother Theresa of India, Eleanor Roosevelt) or some infamous men or women (for example, Josef Stalin, Adolf Hitler, Charles Manson, Lee Harvey Oswald, the Boston Strangler, Lucretia Borgia, Ma Barker of the Barker gang, Lizzie Borden) and discuss the extent to which their goodness or badness was determined by forces over which they had no control and to what extent you feel they were responsible for what they did and how they acted.

Chapter Summary

I. Introduction.
   A. Any discussion of the nature of a human being must include an examination of whether or not human beings are free or determined.
   B. This problem is metaphysical but also has implications for ethics in matters of moral responsibility, blame, reward, and punishment.
II. Definitions.
   A. "Determinism" means the same thing as universal causation, which in turn means that there is no such thing as an uncaused event.
      1. Hard determinism means that universal causation is totally incompatible with human freedom.
      2. Soft determinism means that universal causation allows for freedom.
   B. Fatalism states that whatever occurs is outside human control altogether.
   C. Indeterminism states that not everything has a cause.
III. Fatalism. This theory goes back to ancient times when it was felt either the gods or fate governed all human life. It states that no matter how we plot or plan, fate will somehow step in and run our lives for us—everything is outside of human control.
IV. Indeterminism. Indeterminists state that there may be causality in other parts of the natural realm but that humans are free. William James is the greatest exponent of this theory who felt that we had to affirm our freedom in order to be free, that we had to be free because we felt regret for some of our actions and also because many actions could not be predicted.

V. Soft Determinism. Proponents of soft determinism feel that universal causation actually makes it possible for us to be free and argue against indeterminism, saying that if some acts are uncaused, then they are uncaused by *anyone,* and therefore humans are not free in these actions either.

VI. Hard Determinism. This is not a form of fatalism because it accepts the fact that human decisions and actions can effect causes and results, but hard determinists do argue that the web of causation is so intricate that human freedom is ultimately impossible once universal causation is accepted.

A. Religious Determinism (Predestination). This type of hard determinism states that everything that happens has been preordained or predestined by an all-powerful, all-knowing God. Since He created the universe and has these attributes, then everything is foreknown and predestined.

B. Scientific Determinism. Because everything in the universe is governed by "laws of nature," everything is physically, chemically, and biologically determined.

1. Physical determinism states that the world and everything in it is governed by physical laws of nature.

2. Biological and genetic determinism states that everything is governed by a process of natural selection (Darwin) or is genetically determined—we are what our genes at conception say we are and have no control over our genetic makeup.

3. Historical or cultural determinism, through Hegel, states that everything in the human world is determined by prior historical events as well as by events in our own era.

4. Economic or social determinism, put forth by Marx, states that we are totally determined by our societies' economic struggles and those prior to us.

5. Psychological determinism says that we are determined by forces within us or by our environment.

a. Freudianism says that we are determined by our unconscious minds and various natural drives within us.

b. Behaviorism, through B. F. Skinner, states that we are totally determined by our environmental conditioning since we are merely "unified responses to stimuli."

C. Implications of all these arguments.

1. We are either free or we are not—there is no in between.

2. The evidence is overwhelming in favor of our being determined—genetically, socially, culturally, and religiously.

D. All these mean that

1. Freedom is an illusion.

2. We can not have created our original characters; therefore, we can not be free.

3. We are compelled to act as we do and could not have done otherwise.

4. We are not free to desire even though we may be free to choose or act on our desires.

VII. Critical evaluation of these theories.

A. Fatalism is weak as a theory because it quite often does make a difference what we do as far as what happens to us, and also it is not a practical theory to live by—no one is truly a fatalist.

B. Indeterminism is also impractical because we cannot even conceive what an uncaused event would be like. Further, even if some events are uncaused, how could that help us to be free? If they are uncaused, aren't they also uncaused by us? And isn't James' theory wishful thinking; furthermore, having regrets really does not prove anything.

C. Soft determinism is considered wishful thinking by the indeterminists and also hard determinists because they argue that as soon as you admit universal causation, you have eliminated the possibility of freedom.

D. Hard Determinism.

1. Religious determinism is rejected by most scientists, philosophers, and even religionists since most Western religions would not make much sense if humans did not have any freedom because praise, blame, reward, and punishment would have little point.

2. Scientific determinism is weak because there is no conclusive proof for determinism, and therefore it is an assumption, not conclusive fact.

a. Critics of physical determinism would argue that humans are more than the physical and therefore that they transcend physical laws. Further, some physical scientists have argued that the more we know about modern physics, the more we see that the possibility for freedom exists.

b. There are many critics, both religious and nonreligious, of evolution and the theory of natural selection because of missing link theories and other gaps in our knowledge. Further, critics would again argue against humans being strictly genetic or biological in nature.

c. Historical or cultural determinism has problems because there is no proof for Hegel's absolute mind concept, but further even though we are determined by history and culture, we affect them in many ways so that we can be said to determine them also.

d. Economic or social determinism fails for many of the same reasons that the historical and cultural theory does in that there is no conclusive proof for Marx's theories and many other economic theories which have validity do not exclude human freedom. Here again, human beings would seem to affect economics as much as they are affected by it.

e. Psychological determinism is limited basically to two theorists, Freud and Skinner, but there are many other psychologists who do not exclude freedom in their theories.

    (1) Freud tried to generalize theories he gleaned from working with abnormal people, and he goes too far with his applications to all humans.

    (2) Skinner's theories are based on a total materialism that can be refuted, and he too tries to make too large an application of his theory to all of human motivation, actions, and behavior.

f. Evaluation of hard determinism's assumptions.

    (1) "Either human beings are free or not" is guilty of the fallacy of false dilemma.

    (2) It is true that we have no control over our genetic makeup, but isn't the determinist demanding too much here, and further don't we often go beyond what our genes have determined?

    (3) It's also true that we don't have much control over our early and late childhood environments, but don't we quite often rise above these by our own efforts?

    (4) We cannot have created our original characters, but what actually is our original character, and is it never capable of changing once established? Again the determinist demands too much here.

    (5) "We are compelled to act as we do" tends to push the meaning of the word "compulsion" out of context. We are sometimes compelled or constrained, and sometimes we are not. To say that we are always compelled destroys the meaning of the word.

    (6) That we could have done otherwise is obvious too, when we look back over our experiences, at least in some cases, and if we had chosen to, things would have been different.

167

(7) Within limitations we are free to choose, but we are also free to desire. There are many examples where people have overridden desires, even compulsions, and desired something else.

V. The human mind and consciousness gives us freedom.

   A. We must take into consideration the complexity of the human mind when discussing universal causation.

   B. As we move up from inanimate to animate objects and from plants to human beings, we see a great deal of difference in the power to be free.

   C. By examination of our experiences, we discover that human consciousness is intentional, directive, and creative; and to the extent that it is, we have limited freedom. The human mind in many ways creates its own experience of the world around us.

   D. Therefore, there is such a thing as human freedom—it is no illusion—but it is limited by all the influences working on us from all areas. It would seem, then, that soft determinism is the most tenable position to hold in this controversy, but it also does make sense to hold human beings responsible for their decisions and actions, provided that they are not overly limited by other influences in their lives.

Additional Questions and Activities for Study and Discussion

1. Analyze any act you have committed for which you have strong feelings (for example, regret or pride) and argue to what extent you feel this act was freely done by you or determined by forces within or outside of you. Be specific.

2. Read any of the following books and discuss both how the authors view determinism and freedom and what you think of the societies created in these books: Aldous Huxley's *Brave New World, Brave New World Revisited,* and *The Island;* George Orwell's *1984;* Plato's *The Republic;* B. F. Skinner's *Walden Two;* Ray Bradbury's *Fahrenheit 451;* Robert Heinlein's *The Moon Is a Harsh Mistress;* Jean-Paul Sartre's *No Exit* and *Nausea.*

3. In examining the world around you, to what extent do you feel that human beings are subject to the same types of determinism as plants and animals? Be specific.

4. Research any of the following individuals and their works and explain in full the extent to which you think their theories are valid or invalid where freedom and determinism are concerned: Calvin

and predestination, Newton and scientific determinism, Darwin and biological determinism, Hegel and historical determinism, Marx and economic determinism, Freud and psychological determinism, Skinner and behaviorism, William James and indeterminism, and Sartre and freedom.

5. Compare and contrast B. F. Skinner's views found in *Science and Human Behavior, Walden Two,* and *Beyond Freedom and Dignity* with Joseph Wood Krutch's *The Measure of Man.* How do the two authors agree or disagree on the nature of human beings? To what extent do they agree on whether or not human beings are free or determined? Present both their views carefully and then evaluate them. What conclusions do you draw about the nature of human beings and whether or not they are free? Explain in detail.

Footnotes

1. John Hospers, *Human Conduct: An Introduction to the Problems of Ethics* (New York: Harcourt Brace Jovanovich, 1961), p. 513.
2. Ibid., p. 508.
3. Ibid., pp. 508–509.

Bibliography

Beardsley, Elizabeth L. "Determinism and Moral Perspectives." *Philosophy and Phenomenological Research* 21 (1960): 1–20.

Berofsky, Bernard, ed. *Free Will and Determinism.* New York: Harper & Row, 1966.

Bertocci, Peter A. *Free Will, Responsibility and Grace.* Nashville: Abingdon Press, 1957. This is a discussion of the problem from a Christian perspective.

Campbell, C. A. *In Defense of Free Will: With Other Philosophical Essays.* New York: Humanities Press, 1967.

Delgado, Jose M. R. *Physical Control of the Mind: Toward a Psychocivilized Society.* New York: Harper, 1969.

Dobzhansky, Theodosius G. *The Biological Basis of Human Freedom.* New York: Columbia University Press, 1960.

Edwards, Jonathan. *Freedom of the Will,* ed. Paul Ramsey. New Haven, Conn.: Yale University Press, 1957. This is a good presentation of Calvinistic predestination.

Farrer, Austin. *The Freedom of the Will.* New York: Scribners, 1958.

Hook, Sidney, ed. *Determinism and Freedom in the Age of Modern Science.* New York: Collier, 1958.

Hospers, John. *Human Conduct: An Introduction to the Problems of Ethics.* New York: Harcourt Brace Jovanovich, 1961.

————. *An Introduction to Philosophical Analysis,* 2nd ed. Englewood Cliffs, N.J.: Prentice-Hall, 1967.

James, William. *The Will to Believe and Other Popular Essays in Philosophy.* New York: Longmans, Green, 1912. The essay, "The Dilemma of Determinism," presents James' theory of indeterminism.

Munn, Allen M. *Free-Will and Determinism*. Toronto: University of Toronto Press, 1960. This book discusses freedom and determinism from the point of view of physics and physical science.

Sartre, Jean-Paul. *Being and Nothingness: An Essay on Phenomenological Ontology,* trans. Hazel E. Barnes. New York: Washington Square Press, 1964. This book presents Sartre's special point of view on existentialist freedom.

Skinner, B. F. *Science and Human Behavior*. New York: Macmillan, 1953.

————. *Walden Two*. New York: Free Press, 1962.

————. *Beyond Freedom and Dignity*. New York: Alfred A. Knopf, 1971.

Stillman, Peter G. "The Limits of Behaviorism." *The American Political Science Review* 69 (March 1975).

Thomsen, Dietrick, "Split Brain and Free Will." *Science News,* April 20, 1974.

Werkmeister, William H. *A Philosophy of Science*. Lincoln: University of Nebraska Press, 1965. Chapter 12 contains a discussion of freedom in relation to the laws of nature.

PART

3

Ethics: The Study of Morality

CHAPTER 6

Values and Where They Come From

Ethics, the study of morality in philosophy, is based on values, just as aesthetics, the study of art and beauty, is. It is therefore important to spend some time discussing values, what they are and where they come from, before getting into what morality or ethics is and does. One of the things that seems to distinguish human beings from other beings in the world is humans' desire and ability to value things in the world or to make value judgments, such as "the sunset is beautiful," "abortion is wrong," "children should not be abused or molested," and many others. It seems to be part of the nature of human beings to make such value judgments, and they do it all the time. One of the most difficult problems with all this, however, is, Can such judgments be valid, and if so, how? If not, then are such judgments meaningless? Many people argue that there is really no point in even discussing morality, because morality has no real basis in fact; others see in their moral rules, prohibitions, and commandments powerful absolutes that must be imposed upon all humans if they are to be human to the fullest extent. We will examine and discuss some of these questions and specific issues later in this and the next two chapters as well, but first it is important to examine the nature of values in general.

Facts and Values

The first important distinction to make is between facts and values. What is a fact? When we say, "It's a fact that . . . ," we are saying that something, some event really occurred, is occurring, or will occur. For example, if the sun is shining, then it is a fact that it is; if I have been measured as 6 feet tall, then that's a fact also; if I put on a blue sweater, then it is a fact that I am wearing a sweater of that color. Another way we can look at facts is that they are true statements or propositions we make about these events or occurrences; in other words, a fact is a statement or proposition that accurately describes an actual state of affairs or occurrence or event that really exists.

This use of the word "fact" is really closer to what we need in order to compare facts with value judgments. I will go into much more detail in Chapter 12, Knowledge, Belief, Truth, and Falsity, in explaining this distinction. Suffice it to say at this juncture that a fact is a statement that describes a state of affairs that was, is, or will be happening. Perhaps we should refer to these as factual statements as opposed to value statements or value judgments.

Examples of factual statements are "John beat up and killed Willis," "Inge had an abortion," "Fernando told the truth about what happened," "Maria saved me from drowning." Notice that even though all these statements could be interpreted as having something to do with morality (killing, abortion, lying, saving lives), they are merely statements about something that has actually occurred or happened—there is no judgment made about whether these actions were good or bad or whether or not the people should have done them. Any such claims would imply some sort of value judgment about them or their actions.

Now, if we went farther to make such judgments and said, "John *should not* have beaten and killed Willis and is a *bad* man or an *immoral* or *unethical* person," "It was *wrong* of Inge to have had an abortion because she took a human life," "It was *good* of Fernando to tell the truth, for lying is *wrong*," "Maria did the *right* thing in saving a human life and is a very *moral* person," then we would be making value judgments and, in these cases, moral value judgments.

Notice that the value statements have such words as "should," "good," "bad," "moral," "immoral," "unethical," "wrong," "right," whereas the factual statements do not. Therefore, value statements require judgments about whether something or someone is good, bad, right, wrong, moral, immoral, ethical, or unethical; or they *prescribe* behavior in some way, using such words as "should" or "should not," "ought" or "ought not," "shall" or "shall not."

PROBLEMS WITH FACTS AND VALUES

Several problems and misconceptions arise out of the differences between factual and value statements. Due largely to our heavy stress on scientifically supported knowledge in the twentieth century, we tend almost to worship "facts" and mistrust values or at least give them much less emphasis. It is certainly important for us to know when something is a fact. For example, to know that a certain road is slippery when it is wet may save our lives by causing us to slow down. It is also important for us to know that a certain bottle contains poison so that we will avoid ingesting its contents or we will keep it away from our children.

However, we should avoid slipping into the misconception that because value statements are usually not factual in content in the way that factual statements are, they therefore have no meaning or are not important. It is true that value statements may be harder to determine as true or false, but that does not mean that they are not as important as facts. There are times when values may contribute much more to human life and humanity in general than facts do. For example, is the fact that we and the Russians have enough atomic weapons to blow up the world several times over as important as whether or not we *should* keep stockpiling or ever use these weapons? Further, is the fact that we have less money as important as what uses we should put what money we have to—building government buildings or providing proper medical care for people and raising the quality of everyone's life?

This does not mean we should ignore true facts to establish values, but neither does it mean that we should rule values out as unimportant because they are harder to substantiate and support than many facts. We will discuss the significance of value statements further in the next two chapters and again in Chapter 12. For now, it is important to question where values come from.

Where Values Come From

Some people state that values come from outside of us, from some higher source (God, The Good, Allah, Brahman, Nature) and that values are strictly objective. This implies that even if no human beings were around, and indeed before they were in existence, values existed in the world totally independent of human beings. Others argue that values are strictly subjective and totally dependent on the human quality of valuing; that is, if there were no human beings, there would be no values. Let us examine both these arguments.

VALUES AS OBJECTIVE

Arguing that values are objective means one of three things: values exist in things whether or not human beings are around to value them, or they come from some supernatural source, or values exist in nature itself.

VALUES IN THINGS THEMSELVES.   Is it possible to be objective enough to stand outside ourselves temporarily and see if the world and all the things in it would have value even if we were not here to value them? If there were no human beings in the world, would water, trees, air, plants, flowers, mountains, rivers, and seas have any value, or would they be valueless without us to appreciate them? It is true that it is really impossible to separate ourselves completely from this question because even as we ask it we are placing values on the things of this world; however, if we look at the question from the points of view of animals, plants, and insects, we can see that there are values present. Water, trees, plants, and earth have a value for animals since they drink, eat, sleep, burrow, breathe, and climb to survive. True, we have no evidence that animals value these things in the same way that we do, but certainly they are valuable to them.

Further, when we reenter the world with our values, is it not appropriate to ask why we would value any of these things if they weren't at least to some extent valuable in themselves? There are, of course, many things in the world that only have value if there are human beings around to appreciate them. Of what purpose is gold to animals and plants, for example, and what good would automobiles and airplanes be to them except as possible shelters from the elements? Also, there are certain aspects of the world that seem to have value for human beings, such as the beauty of a mountain scene or a seascape, but don't the sea and the mountains have a great deal of value for animals, plants, and insects, even though they probably cannot appreciate their beauty as we do?

Does all this mean, then, that values are indeed objective and not really dependent on human beings? As we have seen, perhaps some things in the world, or aspects of them at least, can be said to have value whether we are here or not; however, others require human valuing to be valuable. This is especially true of anything that is man-made, such as culture, tools, art, governments, and so on. But maybe all these values, whether in things or within us, come from some supernatural being; let us look at arguments for this viewpoint.

VALUES COME FROM A SUPERNATURAL SOURCE.   Many people believe in a supernatural being, beings, or ultimate reality of some kind.

They usually also believe that this ultimate reality has in some way provided all the values there are, has created the world and all things in it, and has established both aesthetic and moral values for all beings, but especially human beings, to experience and follow. It is certainly possible that such beings exist and have done all this, but there is no *conclusive* proof for their existence; there is, of course, faith or strong belief, but this is not proof. Also, when we examine moral values, for example, as we will in the next two chapters, doesn't it seem just as feasible that a lot of them arise from human needs and desires out of a common aim to live together peacefully and creatively, as the theory that they have been imposed on us from some supernatural source?

Another problem arises when we start to consider the many and different types of such supernatural beings: Which set of moral commandments or prohibitions are we to follow? Plato's The Good? Allah's? Yahweh's? Jesus'? Buddha's? The Tao's? All these beings and the religions or philosophies surrounding them have moral systems connected with them, and in some cases they are similar, but often they differ and sometimes to a great extent. How do we know which supernatural basis is the correct one? We will discuss the problems with the existence of God arguments later, in Chapter 10, but right now let us say at least that there is no conclusive proof that morality *necessarily* has any supernatural basis.

VALUES COME FROM NATURE.   Sometimes separate and sometimes connected to the supernatural theory is the argument that says that moral laws are somehow a part of nature and the natural world. People will often argue that certain things are wrong because they "go against nature." We also often talk about "natural laws," meaning such laws as gravity, thermodynamics, and so on. The use of the word "laws" can be a bit confusing here because it is a quite different use when it is connected to nature than when it is related to human morality and culture.

First, so-called "natural laws" are descriptive rather than prescriptive; that is, they describe events in nature that happen to occur with extreme regularity. For example, we know that every time we drop something or throw it into the air, it will fall to the earth because of the earth's gravitational pull. When anything happens with such regularity and frequency in nature, science calls it a natural law, but this is not like a law that tells us what or what not to do; rather, it is a law that *describes* this regular and consistently occurring event. Further, natural laws seem to describe physical occurrences rather than moral ones.

If there are any natural moral laws, what would they be? Are there any laws set out by nature that tell human beings how they ought or ought not to behave? What are they and where are they to be found? Some people argue, for example, that homosexuality is morally wrong because it is unnatural. They seem to assume that nature only accepts heterosexuality, but a wide study of sexuality in nature shows that many animals are homosexual, some plants are asexual, and so on. In other words, we get into quite a bit of difficulty if and when we try to find morality in nature itself; therefore, it would seem that morality does not come from nature or the supernatural. Does this mean that values, then, are not objective but rather subjective?

VALUES AS TOTALLY SUBJECTIVE

The view of values as totally subjective means that if there are no human beings, then there are no values; everything is or would be valueless. As we have already seen, in the section dealing with values existing in things themselves, it would seem that values cannot be totally within human beings. However, the great value systems have obviously been created by human beings (Aristotle, Plato, Socrates, Immanuel Kant, St. Thomas Aquinas, St. Augustine), and we would also have to admit that probably most of what human beings value comes from within themselves; yet if something looks beautiful or tastes good, must not there be some quality in it that causes us to see its beauty or taste its sweetness? It would seem, therefore, that what we need in discussing values is some kind of synthesis.

VALUES AS BOTH SUBJECTIVE AND OBJECTIVE

If we examine the process of valuing, we usually find that we have not only a valuable thing or a valuing person in isolation, but rather both of them and a certain situation or milieu in which the valuing takes place. For example, for a human to appreciate or value gold, it has to be a beautiful and rare precious metal, but it also has to be appreciated by some being who can know that it is beautiful and also precious. Animals would not know such things.

The situation or milieu must also be such that the valuing can take place. If one is in a civilization or a setting in which other human beings can also value the gold, then it has some value, but on a desert island where there is little food or water and no one to trade the gold to, this metal would have considerably less value than would the necessities. So, in conclusion, it would seem that values are objective to some extent in that things have value in themselves. They are also subjective in that a valuer is needed for any valuing to take place. In addition to both the objective and the subjective viewpoints is the situation or milieu in which the valuing occurs.

How We Select or Decide on Values

We have seen where values come from, but how do we select the values we have, and why do we value some things over others? The whole process of valuing, to be sure, is a very complex one, but perhaps we can make a few generalizations about how human beings select their values, realizing, of course, that there are no hard and fast rules with no exceptions when it comes to a human activity such as this.

PERMANENCE

Some values are temporary, for example, a particularly good dinner, and some things are more permanent, for example, a good marriage and a family with children and grandchildren. We often tend to value more highly the permanent or lasting aspects of our lives. For example, some people might prefer a series of short, uncomplicated love affairs that are transitory and in which the individuals do not get overly involved, but most of us, it would seem, prefer the security and stability of a longer, deeper, more permanent relationship such as that found in marriage. Also, many people strive for jobs and professions that have a longer staying power and that give more long-range pleasure and security and stability than just any job that may give more money. Further, people often prefer intellectual and spiritual endeavors to those that are essentially materialistic and transitory. This is not necessarily true of all human beings, but generally, human beings have preferred those things that are more permanent in nature.

PLEASURE AND HAPPINESS VERSUS PAIN AND UNHAPPINESS

There is no doubt either that most human beings find those things valuable that bring pleasure and happiness, whereas they find those that bring pain and unhappiness not valuable. One has to be careful here also to make certain conditions and distinctions. Often we will undergo, even willingly, some pain and unhappiness to attain some long-range goal. For example, we will subject ourselves to the pain and discomfort of surgery to maintain our health and live a better life. We also may work temporarily at a job that is unpleasant and distasteful to achieve something the money from it will bring. Therefore, we do not always, regardless of situations, seek pleasure and happiness, but there is no doubt that we may try to seek them as much as possible.

A second distinction or condition that is important to make is that pleasure and happiness should always be defined in a very broad sense so that they are not limited to immediate and sensual gratification only. Many critics of pleasure and happiness seekers suggest that this activity is nothing more than "pig trough hedonism" ("hedonism" means the devotion to or search for pleasure) as characterized by the old saying, "Eat, drink, and be merry, for tomorrow we die." However, happiness and pleasure can also refer to less sensual activities as well, such as intellectual, spiritual, and humanitarian activities. Here again, I am not trying to state that sensual pleasures are valueless and should be avoided, but rather that the words "happiness" and "pleasure" have wide meanings that encompass any and all pleasure and happiness enjoyed by human beings. However, it is quite true that happiness and pleasure are important to human beings and that the values that bring them these feelings are certainly sought after.

SELF-CHOSEN VALUES

It would also seem to be true that those values that are chosen by individuals themselves have more importance than do those imposed on them from without. One might ask how any values can be self-chosen when we are born into such complex cultures and societies where values are already established for us. We start out by receiving values from our parents, then our schools, our peers, our governments, and so on. If this is so, how can any of our values be self-chosen?

Here again, a careful distinction needs to be made. Just because we are born into a family culture and a society that has an established pattern of values does not mean that we must, once we can reason for ourselves, accept them without testing or evaluating them. Neither does it mean that all of society's values are insignificant and should be discarded. What is really important here is that people should not blindly follow any system of values until and unless they have critically examined it and have made sure that they accept it as their own. A value system that has been tested in such a way will then have more meaning for the people who have examined it critically.

For example, if a woman has been raised in a certain religion all her life, but has never questioned or examined it to be sure she really believes everything that it stands for, she will only be superficially involved with its values, and the first time her belief is tested, she may be shocked to discover that she has no value system to fall back on because she has had to reject her traditional but unquestioned religious one. On the other hand, if she has researched and evaluated her religious beliefs and has established her own commitment, she can feel more comfortable that through her system she can deal with moral issues that confront her. Therefore, those values that people have carefully chosen to be their own will tend to have a greater significance for them.

EXCELLENCE

Another quality that affects those values we choose is excellence. Anything that is done well or approaches being the best of its kind is sought after by most human beings. For example, if one knows what an orange tastes and smells like and tastes a very fine orange from a certain crop or orchard, then added to one's preferred taste for oranges will be the excellence of this particular orange, making it more worth seeking out. Further, if one loves music, then when it is excellently performed, one will appreciate it more than when it is done amateurly or poorly. Therefore, excellence is another definite factor in choosing one's values.

CREATIVITY AND HARMONY

The last two factors that determine what values we tend to choose are those of creativity and harmony as opposed to lack of creativity and disharmony. Most human beings seem to prize harmony in their lives and surroundings and in relationships with other people. Further, some people definitely prefer situations in which they can be creative in their work and in their lives. For example, in the case where a person's job brings a good salary but where the person has to work in an environment that is very upsetting and that causes disharmony both at work and in his or her home life too, that person may decide that harmony is more important than money and quit this job, taking one for less money but with better working conditions on the grounds that his or her and the family's peace of mind is more important than the money to be earned doing that job under disharmonious conditions. Furthermore, if the job is very routine and does not provide an opportunity to be creative, the person may again take a job with less salary but with the opportunity for greater individual creativity.

A kind of corollary to creativity and harmony are those values that tend to be constructive rather than destructive. Most people will try to seek out those values that cause the former and avoid those that tend toward the latter. For example, a person may get a lot of enjoyment out of drinking alcohol and eating to excess, but may choose to eat and drink less when he discovers that basically his pleasures are destructive, not only to him, but also to those around him.

In conclusion, all these factors play a part in values we select and how we select them, so even though valuing is very complex, it is good to keep some of these criteria in mind when selecting our own values in the future or testing presently held values. The important thing is to ask yourself which of these criteria are most important and try to apply them systematically to your own value system.

Relativism

One of the most controversial areas of values discussions is the one having to do with the theory of relativism. Relativism actually states that there are no absolute values at all and that all values are relative to time, place, persons, and situations. In other words, if we in the United States believe that certain things are valuable, it is because we have been raised in this particular country with its own particular culture, society, and economic system. The values of Calcutta, India, or Nairobi, Kenya, or Peking, China, are also relative to those places and those people. There are no values that cut across all cultures and peoples that are not relative to the specific place in which they are held, according to the relativist.

FACTS ARE FACTS; VALUES VARY

Many people feel that, after all, facts are facts but that values vary greatly. For example, the fact that the earth is not flat is not subject to time, place, or person; it simply is an absolute, truthful fact. However, whether or not it is wrong to kill another human being is strictly relative to time, place, situation, or persons. Therefore, many people would argue that values really do not have much significance because they are like people's tastes—either you prefer oranges or you do not, and Howard may like them whereas Jeanne does not, and either you feel that it is wrong to kill or you do not; it is all really dependent on how you feel at any one particular time.

Of course, there is much to be said in support of at least some relativism, for the fact that values vary is certainly true. But must we then accept the assumption that there are really no lasting or permanent values at all? Some anthropologists do indeed make a strong case for the extreme relativism of values from culture to culture, saying that culture A believes in stealing and adultery whereas culture B does not, and therefore what is right in the first culture is wrong in the second, but they believe there are no general or absolute standards of morality that cut across all cultures. Other anthropologists, however, argue very effectively that perhaps the way in which values are carried out may differ from culture to culture, but the deeper human values are the same for all human beings. For example, they say that most human beings have similar needs such as those for survival, security, friendship, love, family pride, hunger, and sexual satisfaction. If this is so, and most human beings seem to value these things, then are values really relative?

ARE DIFFERING VALUES RIGHT?

A misconception concerning this issue is that because values vary, whatever a culture has deemed right is necessarily so. However, if a certain primitive tribe of humans believes in rape and child molestation, why must we accept what they do as morally right?

A common erroneous assumption is that if people are behaving in a certain way, then what they are doing is necessarily moral. People often use as an excuse for their questionable moral behavior the statement, "Everybody does it" or "If you did it so can I." There is, however, no direct or necessary connection between what people do and what they *ought to* do. It certainly is not impossible that "everybody" is acting immorally, so what people accept or do may or may not be moral. Therefore, it is possible that if most cultures are opposed to rape and child molestation, and a few differ, the few are acting immorally or vice versa. The important distinction here is not what people do, but what they should do, and some criteria must be established other than current or even acceptable cultural behavior to determine what is moral. It is, of course, possible that people are indeed behaving morally since many of our customs and practices are based on what has been worked out through careful moral reasoning and whatever evidence can be brought to bear that behaving in certain ways is moral; however, what is being done is no necessary guarantee that it is what should be done.

RELATIVISM'S IMPRACTICALITY

Another argument against relativism is that it is simply not practical to hold the theory especially in its extreme form. Certainly it is important to allow for cultural and individual freedom in deciding what values people should be allowed to follow, but is anyone really a relativist in practical living situations? Are any of us willing to say that people should be allowed to do whatever they want to do as long as they think it is right? If we ask ourselves that question, won't we discover that we definitely want to qualify it by saying something like "as long as they don't harm anyone else?"

In stating such a qualification, we may not be setting up absolutes, but neither are we totally accepting the theory that values are completely relative. Doesn't this need to qualify relativism suggest that there must be certain guidelines or limits within which all humans should behave? Most societies, for example, have laws or taboos against killing, rape, or child molestation and can usually give good reasons why such rules are in existence, one of which is to allow for enough security and stability so that people can live together peacefully, creatively, and cooperatively. If wholesale killing is allowed or performed, for example, then a society and the individuals in it will exist in constant chaos and danger and not be able to function effectively. Therefore, the practicality of living will not allow for a total relativistic point of view.

CONCLUSION

What, then, are we to conclude concerning this matter of relativism? It would seem that we would have to accept relativism up to a point, but we would also have to draw the line somewhere and further recognize that merely because values are to some extent relative, they are still significant, and what is more many of them tend to be lasting and permanent, if not absolute. We need some kind of prohibition or limits on actions that would harm or kill other human beings; otherwise, we would destroy ourselves and our world. How we decide on which values should be lasting or permanent is a matter for the next chapter, but let us at least recognize that values are important and not merely matters of personal taste.

The Significance of Values and Current Value Conflicts

It would seem to be an aspect of being humans to make value judgments. Values would seem to be thrust upon them so to speak. Do we ever merely perceive things or grasp facts for very long before we start to make some sort of value judgment? For example, when perceiving an old oak tree (notice that I have already inadvertently identified it as old and oak), it isn't long before we notice its beauty, majesty, and the pretty green of its leaves, the richness of its dark brown trunk, as well as the symmetrical shape of its branches. Therefore, values are with us in almost everything we see or do, so we really cannot completely escape valuing even if we wanted to.

This valuing becomes particularly crucial when we go beyond admiring trees and sunsets and deal with the many value conflicts that confront us in our daily living. Such values dealing with morality have been with us as long as we have been around, but many of them have

taken on even greater significance and importance in our highly technological and industrialized advanced societies of the twentieth century. We will examine briefly just a few of them now.

TECHNOLOGICAL DEVELOPMENT
VERSUS HUMAN SURVIVAL

It has often been the case that we have developed something new that
ended up revolutionizing our lives before we could determine that it
would do so, but never has this been such a problem as in the twentieth century when science and technology have developed more in one
hundred years than they have in the nineteen hundred years preceding
it. Inventions such as the telescope, gunpowder, and the steam engine
certainly had their effects on the societies of the world, but their effects were much more gradual than were those of the events and inventions of the twentieth century. Never before have we found ourselves with inventions, technology, or procedures that we were using
before we really had the chance to ask whether or not we should be
using them or even to what extent we should be using them.

The best example of this is the development of atomic energy. The
fact that atomic energy first entered our lives as the greatest destructive war weapon in the history of humanity immediately indicates the
moral issues we faced in first using the atomic bomb. And now a scant
four decades afterwards, there is enough atomic weaponry to destroy
the world a hundred times over. Especially in America, where we have
always prized "progress" and technological advancement, we are now
faced with protecting ourselves and our survival from tools we ourselves have created. We are not just faced with possible atomic extinction from war, but also from the pollution and destructiveness of atomic
waste even when this great energy source is used for peaceful means.
We are already too late in asking ourselves if we should be using atomic
energy merely because we have it. We have certainly come to realize
that we must not use it without safeguards, but so great an energy
source is extremely difficult to safeguard.

We are not merely dealing with knives, spears, maces, or even guns
and gunpowder; we are dealing with wholesale destructive power.
Every time we develop something new in technology, we seem to
threaten our own survival in some way. For example, the development of assembly-line technology and robotic devices may put more
people out of work, and unless we foresee the results of this and do
something about this problem, we may destroy the economic as well
as the humanistic meaning of many people's lives. So we can see that
every technological development, no matter how seemingly minor,
thrusts value problems upon us.

ECOLOGY

Along with and partly as a result of our technological development, we also have a problem with ecology. Both the Old Testament, which told us we had dominion over the earth and all its inhabitants, and Greek Platonic philosophy, which stressed the importance of the inner human intellectual world and minimized the significance of the external world, have caused us to think of nature as our unbounded well of resources and also something for us to manipulate and control to our heart's content. As a result, humans have done more to destroy nature, especially in the last two hundred years, than have all other species that have inhabited the world since the beginning of time. We seem to have proceeded, and still seem to be proceeding, on the assumption that nature's resources are eternal and unbounded. As we have greedily used up one resource after another and have destroyed and made extinct various animal species and plant life, we have come to discover that there is a limit to these resources, and we may never see some of them again unless we are more careful in using them.

Not all human societies have related to nature in this way, and most of them in the Eastern part of the world still do not. Recognizing that nature is made up of other living beings besides humans and that they deserve moral consideration, not just because they affect our own survival, but because they are valuable in their own right, many so-called "primitive societies," such as that of the American Indian, have treated nature with much more respect than have so-called "civilized" humans. The former group has taken from nature only what was needed to live and has not destroyed or fouled the environment around them. Value decisions affecting our relationship with nature, then, have been and are being thrust upon us almost daily, if for no other reason than that it has become quite clear a misuse of natural resources will definitely affect our own state of existence and survival.

MEDICINE

Probably no other area of our culture has brought value considerations to our attention more than medicine, perhaps because scientific advancement in this field seems to affect our lives and deaths more immediately than other areas. With the development of advanced sanitation techniques, wonder drugs, sophisticated surgical procedures, and so on, we have made it possible for more people to live longer than they ever used to. We have also created a tremendous population explosion to the point where we have had to develop birth control techniques ranging from the pill to abortion. The development of the pill itself has revolutionized the status of women in the twentieth century and has affected our cultures as no other invention has. We have respirators, heart machines, dialysis machines, and organ transplants that can extend the lives of many human beings sometimes for the good, but other times to the detriment of the individuals affected, their families, and society as a whole. No other area of human activity has had to ask itself, "But *should* we use these things just because we have them" more than medicine. We find ourselves, in addition to the good we are accomplishing, prolonging the deaths of people who are supposed to die and who would be better off if we allowed them to do so.

We have had to come to grips with the value problems of when human life begins, when it ends, and at what point it achieves or loses value. These are often the most difficult questions we have had to face in our modern-day living. Further, we have had to come to grips with the human conditions of dying and death themselves, which is not easy in a technological culture that seems to promise us an extension of life that approaches immortality itself. In medicine, therefore, we find ourselves making decisions about life, death, and treatment that we never before had to make.

BUSINESS AND ECONOMICS

Since in modern societies so much of our time and effort is taken up with our work and economic needs, we have also come to see that many value situations have arisen and arise each day. They have to do with relationships between employers and employees, employees and other employees, businesses and the public, and business and the environment. We have moved, down through the years, away from a totally agricultural environment and a split between masters and slaves toward a highly technological and industrial society in which owners, employees, and the populace in general all have a vital stake in business activities.

Just look at the effect that something like the shortage of oil, real or faked, has had on the auto industry, not to speak of the desires of the public to move from gas guzzlers to economy cars and especially foreign imported economy cars. According to one twentieth-century saying, "As General Motors goes, so goes the nation," and there certainly seems to be something to it. When the public changes its desires for certain types of cars to others, whole factories have to retool and many people are laid off. Further, and worse, when people decide to keep their old cars for a much longer time and stop buying new ones, car manufacturers have to cut down severely on their output and many workers become unemployed, thus affecting the entire economy and society in all its aspects.

Businesses have to weigh their profits against employee rights, public safety, environmental destruction, and the general well-being of the society in which they operate. Everything they do or even think about doing these days involves some value decision or another affecting a conflict of various interests from all segments of society. So even in business—in fact, especially here—values constantly come to the fore and have to be decided upon and balanced.

Conclusion

It is not hard to see, therefore, that we cannot escape valuing and making value judgments and decisions, many of which are the most important decisions in our lives. Our very lives and the complexity of living them require that such decisions be made and even depend on what decisions we do make. If we return to statements made in Chapters 1 and 2 concerning the difference between knowledge and wisdom and think over some of the issues that have been raised in this chapter and those that will be raised in the next two, we will see that values add a dimension to our lives beyond the facts we study and know and are indeed the most important aspect in attaining the wisdom we seek. To attain wisdom, we must recognize that values are an essential part of human awareness and human life.

Applying Philosophy—
Situations for Thought and Discussion

SITUATION 1

Using your own experience, as well as the information in this chapter, answer the question, "Where do values come from?" as fully as possible in a clear coherent essay, dealing with each of the following questions in any order you wish:

1. To what extent are values objective, subjective, or both, and why?
2. Speculate on how you think human beings began to have values and to value things. Support your answer.
3. How do you decide what has value and which values you accept or are going to accept? How much do the following affect how you choose the values you do?
   a. Permanence.
   b. Pleasure and happiness.
   c. The fact that they are self-chosen.
   d. Having excellence.
   e. Causing creativity.
   f. Causing harmony.
   g. Constructiveness versus destructiveness.
4. In the process of discussing these seven factors, describe, as fully as you can, how your own values have come about.

SITUATION 2

To what extent do you think that values are relative and to what extent do you think they are not? Answer as fully as you can, supporting your arguments with evidence and logic wherever possible. In answering this question, also answer the following questions in any order you wish:

1. It is a fact that values *do* indeed differ from culture to culture and even from person to person. To what extent does this prove that there are no permanent values?
2. If you can accept a strong relativist position, then can you also accept that there can be times when rape, murder, child abuse and molestation, and the like can be accepted as good or right? Give examples and be specific in supporting your answer.

3. If you take an absolutistic position, then what should be done with cultures and/or people who do not conform to these absolutes? Also, which absolutes should everyone follow, and where do they come from?

4. If you take a middle position between relativism and absolutism, then how do you decide what is permanent or absolute and when you can allow for relativism? Be specific and give examples.

5. Argue for or against the fact that because a particular culture has chosen certain values, such as cannibalism, infanticide, or human sacrifice as moral, we must accept them as moral. Support your answer with evidence and logic.

SITUATION 3

Show how values are deeply involved in any one or more of the following current problems facing human beings in the twentieth century: science and technology and human survival, ecology and environmental protection, medicine, and business and economics. Whichever ones you select, deal with the following in any order you wish:

1. Show carefully how these issues are not merely factual, technical, legal, or scientific issues but also involve values and value judgments. Be specific and give examples.

2. Isn't the imposition or involvement of values a detriment to progress and advancement in these fields, especially where values tend to be in conflict? Why or why not? To what extent should progress or advancement be slowed or halted where values are involved?

3. Why is it important to have values carefully established *before* we do something in any of these areas? Give examples of problems that have developed because we have not done this.

4. Since values, even in a homogeneous culture such as ours, differ, how can we establish a set of them to which we can relate all our activities? Make a list of such values to which you feel any of the foregoing activities could be related, dealing with acts such as cheating, lying, preserving life, and so on.

Chapter Summary

I. Facts and values.
    A. A fact is a statement that describes an actual state of affairs, event, or occurrence.
    B. Value statements are judgments about whether something is good, right, moral, or immoral; they prescribe behavior by using such words as "should" or "ought."
    C. Problems with facts and values in our time.
        1. Facts are almost worshipped, whereas values are mistrusted.
        2. We need to know facts certainly, but there are times when values may be even more important than facts, and just because they are more difficult to prove (if we can prove them at all), it does not mean they are not important.

II. Where values come from
    A. Values as objective—means one of three things:
        1. Values exist in things whether or not human beings are around to value them.
        2. Values exist in nature itself outside of human beings as valuers.
        3. Values come from some supernatural source.
    B. Values would seem to reside in things themselves at least to some extent, for if humans were not around the universe, the things in it would still be valuable.
    C. It is certainly possible that values come from a supernatural source, but there is no conclusive proof that such a source exists or that values come from it.
    D. It is very difficult to find morality, for example, in nature itself. There are things of value there and nature itself has values, but there do not seem to be any natural moral laws.
    E. Values as subjective means that they are completely dependent on the existence of human beings—no human beings, no values.
        1. As we have seen, there is a valid argument for values existing in things themselves at least to some extent.
        2. On the other hand, a great many things have value only because there are human beings around to value them.
    F. Values as both subjective and objective would seem to be a proper synthesis of the problem in that if we examine the process of valuing, we usually find three aspects:
        1. The objective or the thing of value.

2. The subjective or the valuer—one who does the valuing.
3. The milieu or situation in which the valuing takes place.

III. How we select or decide on values seems to involve several criteria or aspects:

A. Permanence—those values that are more permanent or long-lasting would seem to be of more value to us generally.

B. Pleasure and happiness versus pain and unhappiness—those things that bring us pleasure and happiness would be more valuable than those that do not; in fact, we tend to avoid the latter. There are several important distinctions to make, however.

1. We do not always merely seek pleasure; we will often undergo pain and unhappiness in the short run to attain pleasure and happiness in the long run.

2. Pleasure and happiness should also be defined broadly to include the spiritual and intellectual as well as the sensual.

C. Self-chosen values—those values are most significant that are self-chosen rather than merely imposed from the outside.

D. Excellence—things of value are often enhanced by the quality of excellence. If one loves music, for example, its value is always enhanced by the excellence of its performers.

E. Causing creativity and harmony—those things that tend to cause human beings to be creative or to bring about harmony are also to be valued. A corollary of these is that those things or activities that are constructive to human well-being rather than destructive would be valued.

IV. Relativism

A. Definition: there are no absolutes or permanent values at all, but all values are relative to time, place, persons, and situations.

B. Facts are facts, but values vary is an argument put forth by the relativists—the fact that the earth is not flat is absolutely true, but whether some human is good or not is a matter of taste or personal preference.

1. Some anthropologists support this view, pointing to the wide differences among most cultures.

2. Other anthropologists stress the commonality of such values and needs as survival, security, friendship, and love.

C. Are differing values necessarily right? This is a misconception centered on relativism, presuming that because a particular society approves of human sacrifice or cannibalism necessarily makes what they are doing moral or right.

D. Relativism's impracticality is quite obvious when we ask, "Can we really say that whatever anyone wants to do is right as long

192

as he or she thinks it is? Can we ever approve rape, murder, and child abuse or molestation?''

E. Relativism is not a proven fact, and although it is useful in allowing some freedom for individual and cultural differences, this allowance does not at all preclude significant limits and permanent values (if not absolute ones).

V. The significance of values and current value conflicts.

A. Values are thrust upon human beings; it is almost impossible to avoid valuing and value judgments even in the simplest acts of sense perception.

B. We are also confronted with many value conflicts in our daily lives, especially in the following areas:

1. Technological development versus human survival. The discovery of atomic energy is the foremost example of this.

2. Ecology. We have discovered that if we do not have a view of nature as valuable, we can destroy it and ourselves in the process.

3. Medicine. Since scientific advancement in this area seems to affect our lives and deaths more closely than any other, we have often been confronted with value conflicts in areas such as population control and prolonging death.

4. Business and economics. We have many value conflicts in relationships between employers and employees, employees with other employees, business and the public, and business and the environment.

Additional Questions and Activities for Study and Discussion

1. Examine closely any situation or event in which you have been involved and show how valuing was an integral part of it, trying to distinguish between the "facts" of the situation and its "values."

2. To what extent do you believe it is possible for you to have self-chosen values given the fact that you were born into a culture that already had established values and have been raised in a certain family, community, and school system? If you feel that you have indeed chosen your values, describe how this choosing took place and the bases for making your choices.

3. Define as clearly as you can "pleasure, happiness, pain, unhappiness," giving specific examples and illustrations of each. Do not use clichés or superficial aphorisms, such as "Happiness is a warm puppy." Try to give as clear a definition as you can of these words,

both for human beings in general, as far as you can determine it and also from your own individual point of view. After you have done this, describe in detail how great a part in your value system trying to attain pleasure and happiness and trying to avoid pain and unhappiness plays. Be specific.

4. Describe the values or lack of them of the following characters in the literary works listed and show how they affect their lives and what happens to them and others around them: Garp and his mother in *The World According to Garp* by John Irving; Meursault in Albert Camus' *The Stranger;* Willy and Biff Loman in Arthur Miller's *Death of a Salesman;* Quentin and Maggie in Arthur Miller's *After the Fall;* Raskolnikov in Fyodor Doestoyevsky's *Crime and Punishment;* Ivan Ilych in Leo Tolstoy's *The Death of Ivan Ilych;* Jack and Willy in Robert Penn Warren's *All the King's Men.*

5. Select what you think is a current value conflict that human beings face in their lives, other than those just listed, and describe it fully, showing why you think it is a value conflict. What do you think has to be done to resolve the conflict? How would you go about doing this if you were able? After doing this, describe carefully a value conflict or value conflicts in your own life and how you are or hope to be dealing with it, or them. Be specific.

Bibliography

Baylis, Charles A. "Grading, Values and Choice." *Mind* 67 (1958): 485–501.

Caws, Peter. *Science and the Theory of Value.* New York: Random House, 1967.

Cowan, J. L. *Pleasure and Pain.* London: Macmillan, 1968.

Fried, Charles. *An Anatomy of Values: Problems of Personal and Social Choice.* Cambridge, Mass.: Harvard University Press, 1970.

Hook, Sidney, ed. *Human Values and Economic Policy.* New York: New York University Press, 1967. A symposium of the New York University Institute of Philosophy.

Lewis, Clarence I. *An Analysis of Knowledge and Valuation.* LaSalle, Ill.: Open Court, 1946.

Margolis, Joseph. *Value and Conduct.* London: Oxford University Press, 1971.

Maslow, Abraham H., ed. *New Knowledge in Human Values.* New York: Harper, 1959.

Parker, Dewitt H. *The Philosophy of Value.* Ann Arbor: University of Michigan Press, 1957.

Pepper, Stephen C. *The Sources of Value.* Berkeley and Los Angeles: University of California Press, 1958.

Perry, Ralph B. *Realms of Value.* Cambridge, Mass.: Harvard University Press, 1954.

CHAPTER 7

Moral Theories and Decision Making

What Is Morality?

THE DIFFERENCE BETWEEN MORAL AND NONMORAL

Before dealing with various theories of morality and what is involved in moral decision making, it is quite important that certain distinctions be made and definitions be presented. As the title of this part states, ethics in philosophy is the study of morality. The word "morality" comes from the Latin *moralis,* which means "customs" or "mores," and "ethics" comes from the Greek *ethos,* which essentially means "character." Some use "morality" to apply to personal moral issues outside of professions, such as law, medicine, business, where the word "ethics" is used. Essentially, I feel that the two words and their counterparts "immoral" and "unethical" can be used pretty much interchangeably. For example, a rapist could be called either unethical or immoral (presuming we would agree that rape is an immoral or unethical act), and a business owner who cheats or is dishonest with the public can be referred to as either immoral or unethical. It seems to me that any finer distinctions between these two words is pretty much splitting hairs.

The first major distinction that needs to be made is between moral and nonmoral issues. Generally, when morality is involved, the value words cited in the last chapter, "good," "bad," "right," "wrong," "immoral," "unethical" and the prescriptive words, "should" or "ought" and "should not" or "ought not" will be used in moral value judgments. However, these words can also be used in a nonmoral sense, such as in the statements "This is a good steak," "Your answer to question 25 is wrong," "You should shave before going out." When used in sentences such as these, these words have very little or no moral import whatsoever; that is, they do state values and prescriptions, but they are not *moral* values or prescriptions. For example, when we describe a steak as "good," we mean that it is tender and that it tastes good. We do not mean that it is morally or ethically good as we would in the sentence, "Rick is a moral man because he never lies or cheats." In this example, we are talking about Rick's conduct or behavior, not how he tastes. Further, we are referring to his behavior in a moral sense; that is, we are talking to some extent about how Rick relates to other human beings morally. Therefore, inanimate things, such as tables, chairs, houses, mountains, and lakes and even certain animate things such as animals, plants, and insects are nonmoral. Human beings in certain aspects of their behavior and conduct are classified as moral; in some aspects, they are not.

THE DIFFERENCE BETWEEN MORALS AND MANNERS

Since morality centers on human behavior and conduct, we must make a second distinction between human behavior as it pertains to manners and morals. If someone is invited to a formal dinner party and comes dressed in jeans without shoes and a shirt, he is not being immoral or unethical, but he certainly is exhibiting bad manners. On the other hand, if this same person abuses a child by beating her, he can be said to be acting immorally.

In the first example, we are talking about a breach of etiquette or social custom in the way people behave if they are to be accepted in certain social situations. In the second example, we are talking about a breach of morality or ethics in that another human being's life is being threatened or harmed. The person in the first case is offensive in that he has violated a social custom or rule, but he is not immoral because he has not seriously harmed another person by lying, cheating, raping, stealing, or killing.

There can be a connection between morals and manners in that they both apply to human behavior and conduct, and we prefer that everyone acts in accordance with the rules for both, but it is important to distinguish between offenses against manners and moral offenses because they are different, both in quality and in seriousness. Most people that we consider moral also usually have good manners, but a person who is rude may nevertheless be moral, and one who has good manners may be immoral.

THE DIFFERENCE BETWEEN LAW AND MORALITY

Law is probably the clearest expression of social morality one could find in any culture, but despite this, law and morality are not necessarily the same thing. For example, there can be morally unjust laws that often provide the impetus, from moral concern, for their repeal or revocation. Laws such as those promoting slavery in the early history of our country may be considered immoral because they are unjust to some of the human beings of a particular society. Since the law denies these human beings freedom and other rights, such as the right to own property and the right to be treated humanely, it can be seen as being immoral. Further, some laws that brand certain behavior as immoral, such as laws prohibiting certain private sexual activities between consenting adults, may conflict with what is considered morally allowable by most members of a particular society.

It would seem obvious, however, that despite these differences, many of our laws have been established because of the social and legal need to make clear our moral concerns against acts such as killing, raping, stealing, lying, and cheating. When we feel a strong moral concern about something, such as the lack of strict control over drunk drivers and the many deaths resulting from them, then we lobby for stricter laws, and if the public outcry and concern is strong enough, the laws are often changed. The same thing happens when unjust laws are on the books. People who find such laws morally offensive challenge them to get them repealed or revoked. There is, therefore, a close relationship between morality and the law, but they are nevertheless not the same thing. One could establish a society based on a few moral principles and rules, and if the people were willing to keep such rules, a complicated legal system would not even be needed. On the other hand, when societies become as large and complex as ours is, it is often important that the moral feelings of the people get expressed and sanctioned (supported, upheld) in some clear public way, and that is the purpose and value of law and legal systems.

THE DIFFERENCE BETWEEN MORALITY AND RELIGION

There is no absolutely necessary connection between morality and religion. It is quite true that every religion, to my knowledge, has a moral system of do's and don'ts—commandments and prohibitions—but it is not true, in reverse, that every moral system is necessarily based on or connected to religion. One of the reasons people often confuse morality with religion is that they do not distinguish between social morality and religious morality. If a moral system has in it certain do's and don'ts that have to do with human beings in relation to some supernatural being or beings, such as in the Ten Commandments (Don't worship false gods, Keep holy the Sabbath, Don't take the name of the Lord in vain), these should be distinguished from commandments or prohibitions that govern socially moral activities, such as not killing, not stealing, not committing adultery, and so on. It is obvious that one can have a moral system that does not even mention the existence of a supernatural being or beings, but merely concerns itself with proper moral social behavior.

One such system is that of the American Humanist Association in San Francisco. Whether or not one agrees with its avowed morality, it is one example that there can be a moral system that has absolutely no connection with a supernatural and yet attempts to prescribe human behavior in the areas of protecting and preserving human life, stealing, lying, justness, and fairness, and nondiscrimination because of race, religion (or nonreligion), and sex.

Therefore, it seems obvious that, although religions may have moral systems connected with them, morality can certainly be established separately from it. One might even argue that the social morality of religions really does not necessarily come from a supernatural source (see previous chapter on values) but, rather, has arisen out of the human need to live together in a community, one aspect of which may be religious.

AMORALITY

One last distinction before trying to define "morality" or "ethics" is that of amorality. Amorality means essentially "indifference to morality" or the inability to distinguish between right and wrong. I would argue that morally uneducated babies should generally be considered as amoral until such time as they are taught some moral distinctions. Also, I feel that there are some human beings who fall into this category, even though they may have been exposed to morality both as children and as adults.

Certain criminals, for example, who constantly repeat their crimes and perform immoral acts and who cannot see that they have done or are doing anything wrong are to be branded as amoral. A person who can kill another innocent individual and feel absolutely no remorse or regret or not feel that he has done anything wrong at all I would call amoral. Amoral differs from nonmoral in that it applies to human beings who perform moral or immoral acts but do not see them as such.

WHAT MORALITY IS

So far we have stated how morality differs from manners, law, and religion, but we have yet to make a positive statement of what it is or give a definition of the word. "Morality" or "ethics" has to do with what is right or wrong or bad or good in a *moral* sense. Morality, according to the definition I gave of it in my book, *Ethics: Theory and Practice,* deals basically with humans and how they relate to other beings, both human and nonhuman—how they treat others to promote mutual welfare, growth, creativity, and meaning in a striving for what is good over bad and what is right over wrong.[1]

One of the problems that arises with this definition is how we define the term "right," "wrong," "good," "bad." For a definition of these terms and therefore a clearer definition of the terms "moral," "immoral," "ethical," "unethical," I will reiterate several of the criteria I cited for how we select our values in the previous chapter. That which is good, right, moral, or ethical brings human beings pleasure and happiness, arises out of excellence, creates harmony, causes creativity, and is constructive. On the other hand, that which is bad, wrong, immoral, or unethical gives human beings pain and unhappiness, is lacking in excellence, causes disharmony, fosters no creativity, and is destructive. These two definitions, at least, can provide a working definition for the meanings of these words as we deal with moral theories and issues in the remainder of this chapter and the next. You are encouraged to think deeply about how you define these terms and what they mean and to come up with any additional distinctions or definitions you find meaningful.

How Moral Decisions Can Be Made

Now that we have made careful distinctions and properly defined key terms used in ethics, it is time to discuss what is involved in making decisions; that is, How do human beings decide what is moral and what is immoral?

EMOTIONS AND REASON

Before discussing specific traditional ethical theories, it is probably important to see what part is played by emotion and what part is played by reason in moral decision making. Also, we will go one step farther and ask what parts they should play.

EMOTIONS.   It should be very clear to everyone that emotions play a big part in morality and moral decision making. All we have to do is listen to statements made by both sides of the abortion or capital punishment issues, for example, or listen to victims of murder or rape and their families, to see that moral issues bring out some of the strongest feelings expressed by human beings anywhere in their lives. The questions, however, are, "How much should our emotions influence the moral decisions we make? And to what extent should these strong emotions be tempered by reason?" The problem with using emotions to decide moral issues is that people's emotions vary, and if we go on feelings alone in arguing for or against a controversial moral issue, there is not much arbitration possible. For example, if Edward feels that capital punishment should be used for any crime where someone has been kidnapped or killed and Lois feels that taking another human life is not a solution to the problem of murder, how are their feelings to be dealt with?

Let us assume that they both feel very strongly about their positions to the point where they are shouting at one another. Is their rather violent expression of feelings really solving anything? Can they arrive at any useful conclusions if they never get beyond merely expressing their feelings? It would seem that something else is needed to come to grips with the issue of capital punishment than mere outpouring of emotions. This does not mean that one should not get emotional over moral issues; emotions definitely belong in and are a part of the human character (see Chapter 3), but they need to be tempered with reason.

REASON.   The ability to ask questions, seek evidence, and discuss and argue logically is due to another attribute called reason. When and if we start to use reason in dealing with moral issues (or any other issues for that matter), we can rise above the highly personal and individualistic quality of our emotions and approach some possible meeting ground where ideas can be discussed.

For example, to use the preceding example, instead of continuing to shout or in other ways pour out their emotions, Edward and Lois can begin questioning each other's positions, which will force them to give reasons for why they feel the way they do. This is the first step toward presenting a reasonable argument for their beliefs and makes them give a basis for their strong feelings. Once reasoning starts, there is a possibility to use careful and common methods (see Chapter 2), such as attacking fallacies, checking the logic of one's arguments, and demanding evidence for statements being made on either side. In this way, instead of a continual outpouring of feelings about the matter of deterrence in capital punishment, for example, both people can present, examine, and critically evaluate what evidence and arguments are available for whether or not capital punishment does or does not deter people from killing other people. Edward may find, for example, that his assumption that it has high deterrent value is not supported conclusively by either evidence or logical argument, even though he has always strongly felt that it does. Lois may be brought to realize, on the other hand, that it does indeed deter the killer and that there are few suitable alternatives to the release of murderers within a few years to possibly kill again.

Only by going beyond their emotions, which of course, they may still retain to some extent, can they arrive at any clear understanding of the issue and its ramifications. It is obvious, then, that reason should play a large part in moral decision making.

SYNTHESIS OF EMOTION AND REASON.   It would seem that the obvious solution to the split between emotions and reason in deciding morality would be to combine them in a constructive and creative balance. Using emotions alone would seem to get us nowhere and provide no middle ground between personal feelings for arbitration of opposing points of view. On the other hand, reason alone would reduce morality to cold calculation and eliminate part of the human element by excluding feelings from moral decision making. It would seem best to subject our feelings to rational examination, to seek all evidence we can about a certain moral issue, and to use all the tested methods at our disposal (again I refer you to Chapter 2) to arrive at the best solutions we can in dealing with important moral issues, such as capital punishment. Morality is a crucial part of human existence, and moral problems must be dealt with and resolved wherever possible. The best way to accomplish this is by approaching morality rationally and logically without eliminating or excluding human feeling and compassion.

Traditional Theories of Morality

There are two basic approaches to morality, one that is based on the consequences of one's decisions, actions, and moral rules and one that is based on something else, such as a supernatural source or a strictly rational structure. We will examine both approaches.

CONSEQUENTIALISM

Consequentialist theories of morality are based on the idea that what determines what is moral are the consequences or results of a choice, an action, or a rule. This essentially means that when we are trying to determine whether or not we are going to make a choice, act in a moral way, or establish a moral rule, we must try to calculate what the results or consequences of these will be. The assumption is that if what we choose or do will bring about the best good consequences, then it is the right or moral thing to do. On the other hand, if bad consequences will ensue, then it is the wrong or immoral thing to do. There is another question that arises that determines which form of consequentialism one accepts, and that is the question, "To whom should these good consequences accrue?"

One can look at the results of moral acts as affecting oneself or others, or to put it another way, we might ask to what extent does or should self-interest (egoism) or other-interestedness (altruism) play a part in determining what is moral? A self-interested approach to this would mean that what is moral is what is in one's self-interest, and self-interest is all that the agent (one who is acting) need consider. On the other hand, an other-interested approach would mean that what is moral is not what is in one's self-interest, but rather what is in the interest of others, and therefore the agent must essentially ignore what is in his self-interest and act totally in the interest of others.

For example, if a woman is pregnant and considering an abortion, she can consider only her own self-interests or those of others. She might, if she is considering only herself, decide to have or not have the abortion depending on whether or not she feels it suits her own self-interests. She need not consider the interests of the unborn embryo or fetus, the father of the child, her parents, or society in general. On the other hand, if she is altruistic in her approach to morality, she must put all these "others" first rather than her own self. It is important to note, however, that merely because she is taking a self-interested approach to morality does not automatically mean that she will choose abortion. She may, for example, feel that she would not be able to live with the guilt of abortion, or she may want to raise a baby whether or not it would be in anyone else's interest for her to do so. The important point to remember here is that her motivation for her decisions is self-interest rather than concern for others.

A good question to ask at this juncture is, "To what extent should these two concerns affect morality?" Some philosophers argue that morality does not even begin until other-interestedness is in the picture and that self-interest is a very low human motive for morality. They would argue that morality in its very essence must involve a concern for others, not self or at least not self alone. Egoists, as you will see shortly, disagree with this viewpoint, arguing that self-interest is the only reasonable basis for morality, considering our uniqueness and individual differences.

Let us look into two theories that stress the opposing views and critically evaluate them before making any decisions about what parts self and other interestedness should play in morality. There is really no ethical theory called altruism, but there is a theory that comes close, and it is called utilitarianism, which states that we should do what is best for everyone affected by what we do. After we discuss egoism, we will examine that theory.

ETHICAL EGOISM.   The major principle of ethical egoism is that people should always act in their own self-interests if they want to be moral. It does not preclude acting in the interests of others completely, but it does stipulate that people should not do this unless it is clearly in their own self-interest to do so. For example, the woman who decides not to have an abortion could be said to be acting in the interest of the fetus she is carrying, but the egoist would state that her decision must be in her self-interest, not that of the fetus. If the fetus happens to benefit by her decision, that's all right, but the choice or act *must* be primarily in the woman's self-interest or she shouldn't do it.

Ethical egoism comes in three forms:

1. Individual, which states "Everyone should or ought to act in *my* self-interest."
2. Personal, which states, "I ought to act in my own self-interest; I make no claims about what others ought to do."
3. Universal, which states, "Everyone ought to act in his or her own self-interest."

Let us examine and critically evaluate each of these.

Individual ethical egoism probably comes the closest to what we refer to in derogatory terms as "selfishness." It demands that everyone should act in one person's interest, which pretty obviously excludes the interest of everyone else. Aside from its total self-centeredness, though, there are some real problems with this version.

First, it is extremely individualistic and subjective and does not apply to more than one person, at least not in its essence. Second, wouldn't stating this theory work against the person espousing it and therefore (inconsistently) not be in his or her self-interest? If someone you knew stated openly that this was his theory, would you tend to satisfy his self-interest or would you avoid him like the plague? Of course, he could always lie and say that he was an altruist while secretly holding this ethical theory, but wouldn't lying, especially about one's ethical theory, be ethically questionable? Third, since the ethical egoist is also a consequentialist, what would the consequences be if everyone were an individual ethical egoist? Would anyone's self-interest be satisfied? And how would we resolve the millions of conflicts that would arise if everyone expected everyone else to operate in just his or her own self-interest? As we can see, there are some real problems with this version of egoism, not to speak of many ethicists' concern that any moral system ought to consider others as at least a part of its structure.

Personal ethical egoism is of course more moderate than is the individual form, in that the former allows others to follow what ethical system they want and does not demand that they act in only one person's interest. However, it is still a strictly one-person ethical system, and the same question arises as to whether the personal egoist's interest would be satisfied if he or she promulgated or laid out his or her theory. That is, wouldn't people, knowing that he was always going to be out for himself, be on their guard and tend not to serve his self-interests? This version, then, is not as seriously problem-ridden, but still has its defects.

Universal ethical egoism is the most commonly presented version because it applies to all human beings as most other ethical theories do. This form of egoism states that *everyone* of us ought to act in his or her own self-interest, which would seem on the face of it to give us all a high degree of freedom, individuality, and equality. The main problem with this version, however, is what is really meant by "everyone"? Does this type of egoist really want everyone's interest satisfied or just his own?

When conflicts about self-interest arise, how are they to be resolved? It would seem there is no clear method. All egoists would seem to have to keep seeking their own self-interest until something gives. This could lead to "might makes right," meaning that the person with the greatest power or force would win out, but many people would question this method of solving conflicts of interest. Further, what kind of moral advice is this type of egoist to give another egoist when their interests conflict? Is he to try to advise her to act in his, the first egoist's, interest or in her own (the second egoist's) interest? If he advises the first, isn't he really operating as an individual or personal ethical egoist? And if he advises the second, what happens to his own self-interest? If he is trying to satisfy everyone's interest, isn't he moving toward altruism or utilitarianism?

The advantage of universal ethical egoism is that it does stress individuality and freedom. Also, if everyone were self-sufficient, this theory might work, provided that various self-interests did not come into conflict too often. However, not all of us are self-sufficient; in fact, few of us really can be. We seem rather to be quite interdependent on each other for our livelihoods.

Farmers, ranchers, doctors, teachers, lawyers, police officers, fire fighters, telephone operators, and so on all depend on each other for the services or supplies they can furnish one another. Furthermore, what will happen to those less fortunate people in our society, such as the blind, crippled, mentally retarded, poor, and helpless? Can we merely rely on everyone's deeming it to be in his or her own self-interest to be charitable toward these needy people? If everyone is merely out to satisfy his or her own self-interest and this does not happen to include taking care of the needy, then a lot of people will not survive. True, we can dismiss this difficulty by merely saying, "That's their problem," but isn't that attitude ethically questionable? It certainly is in the view of many ethicists.

It would seem that ethical egoism in all its forms is not satisfactory; at least, it has serious enough problems so that we ought to look at other traditional theories before accepting it.

UTILITARIANISM. Utilitarianism, essentially fathered by Jeremy Bentham (1748–1832) and John Stuart Mill (1806–1873), states that if we want to be moral, we should always act in such a way that we bring about the greatest good consequences for everyone (self included, but not emphasized over others) concerned or affected by the action. For those who feel that others should be considered in morality, utilitarianism would seem to be a vast improvement over the self-centeredness of all three forms of ethical egoism. One of its disadvantages, which ethical egoism does not have, however, is the difficulty of trying to decide what would constitute good consequences for others. It is obviously much easier to decide what is in one's own self-interest than it is to decide what is in the interest of, let's say, twenty other people who have different likes and desires. The advantage it gains, however, is that it seems to be fairer to more people and it also provides a means of minimizing conflicts, since if everyone considers everyone else's interests, conflicts are less likely to arise. If and when interests do conflict, this theory states that one is to try to resolve them in such a way as to satisfy everyone's interest. Admittedly, this may not be easy to do, but at least the utilitarian starts with compromise in mind, whereas the egoist basically does not.

Utilitarianism has two forms: act and rule. Act utilitarianism's principle states that people should always do that act that will bring about the greatest good consequences for everyone concerned or affected by it. Rule utilitarianism, on the other hand, states that people should establish and follow *rules* that will bring about the best good consequences for all concerned. The act version allows for greater freedom and individuality in moral decision making, whereas the rule form provides more guidelines and stability.

The act utilitarian feels that every situation, person, place, and time is different and, therefore, that we should decide in each individual situation what is the best thing to do for all people in that situation. This type of utilitarian sees rules as restrictive and impractical in that there would have to be too many exceptions; therefore, "situation ethics" is felt to be the best way to approach morality, and as long as the act utilitarian is considering everyone's interest, then his or her actions would be moral.

The rule utilitarian, among other critics of act utilitarianism, believes, unlike his counterpart, that even though there are differences in people, places, and times, there are nevertheless many similarities that would justify the use of rules. Furthermore, the rule utilitarian feels that the act approach to ethics is too chaotic in that the act utilitarian would have no guidelines (except for doing what is in everyone's interest) either to go by or for teaching the young or morally uninitiated what is right or wrong. The rule utilitarian also feels that by virtue of the act utilitarian's theory, moral actions would have to be considered anew each time a situation arose, and this might result in loss of time and allow an immoral act to take place by not acting in time.

With these problems in mind, then, the rule utilitarian proposes that we should try to determine which rules would benefit everyone and then establish and enforce them, so that everyone's interest would be satisfied. For example, since most people value their lives and in fact can do very little else without them, there ought to be rules preserving and protecting them. To simply let each person decide whether to kill or not in each situation as it arises would not be in the best interests of everyone, according to the rule utilitarian.

The obvious problems with this rule approach, as stated earlier in describing the act approach, is the difficulty of establishing fair rules that will cover the many differences in human life. Along with this goes the problem of the restrictiveness of rules and laws. Being free in a situation to decide what is moral or not allows for flexibility and human creativity in solving problems. If, on the other hand, there are restrictive rules, then people's freedom to resolve moral problems is hampered. Another problem with rules is that they are often hard to establish and even harder to repeal or revoke when and if they are discovered to be ineffective, inappropriate, unjust, or immoral. As cited in the previous section dealing with morality and the law, laws condoning slavery or discrimination against minorities had to be challenged in courts and actually took many years to change.

Another problem that affects both forms of utilitarianism is what is often referred to as "the cost-benefit analysis" approach to morality. This arises out of the difficulty of always trying to satisfy everyone's interests. Since most of the time utilitarians would probably fall short of this goal, there is a temptation to settle for bringing about "the greatest good for the greatest number." Now on the face of it, this doesn't sound too bad, but what happens to those who are not among the "greatest number" or in the majority? Can we be sure, for example, that a few people will not lose their lives for the good of the many?

What is missing from utilitarianism is some sort of principle of justice that would guarantee just and fair treatment for *everyone,* not just most people. Another way of looking at it is that there may often have to be bad with the good, but it should be distributed fairly so that the same people do not always get the bad.

This approach can also be used to support an "end always justifies any means to attain it" attitude in morality. That is, as long as the cost is low and the benefit is high, any act is moral. For example, a recent experiment in the South came to light in which a number of black men who had syphilis were allowed to remain untreated in return for housing, food, and money to discover what the ravages of the disease could really do to the human body. These men, who were not informed of the nature of the experiment, obviously would suffer the effects of the disease and eventually death. The assumption on the part of the experimenters seemed to be that these black men were not very important to society or themselves so that letting them get sicker, when their disease could be cured, and letting them die was of no consequence. Someone had to receive the bad if such experiments were to be successful, so why not these "useless black men"? I stress that this is not really a principle of utilitarianism, only one of its dangers if it is carried too far in its attempts to bring about the best good consequences for everyone.

OTHER PROBLEMS WITH CONSEQUENTIALIST THEORIES. The main problem with consequentialist theories of morality is the difficulty of determining consequences. As we have seen, in particular this is more of a difficulty for utilitarianism than for ethical egoism because of the number of people to be considered in making moral decisions. However, it is often difficult to determine consequences whether for oneself or others, especially on a long-range basis. We may be able to determine immediate consequences of our actions, but can we know with any certainty what long-range effect or consequences our decisions and actions will have on us or anyone else? For example, in developing and using the atomic bomb during World War II, could the scientists or the politicians or the rest of us, for that matter, have foreseen all the consequences that have come about? President Harry S. Truman, at that time, could foresee that he could probably end the war in the Pacific and save many Allied lives, but could he have possibly foreseen the tensions of the long "cold war," the stockpiling of dangerous atomic weapons, the pollution of the atmosphere, and the dangers to human lives that have led to the anxious times in which we live?

One can never be sure what the consequences of any action will be, and sometimes the consequences are detrimental and destructive, or at least the bad effects are often as great as the good effects.

Maybe the basis for morality ought to be more stable and secure than simply satisfying someone's interest; maybe morality ought to be found or placed on a higher plane than its results. Perhaps we ought to be able to decide or discover what is moral and then adhere to this regardless of the consequences. There are moralists who put forth such theories, and they are called nonconsequentialists.

NONCONSEQUENTIALISM

Nonconsequentialists argue that morality is and should be placed on a much higher plane than merely satisfying people's interests. These theorists are mostly rule oriented in their approach to morality and tend to feel that what is right or wrong, good or bad, is absolute and not dependent on the whims, desires, or interests of anyone. They seem to feel that morality is based either on the religious and the supernatural or on some sort of higher reasoning and logic that is incontrovertible and unchanging in nature so that "what's right is right and what's wrong is wrong," and nothing in the lowly realm of human desires or actions should have any effect whatsoever.

DIVINE COMMAND THEORIES. Theories that argue that morality is based on something supernatural usually take the position that there is some ultimate good (a being or beings) from which divine commands have come down to humans, and whatever this ultimate being commands is right or wrong because "It" is the ultimate source and arbiter of all goodness and rightness. Many religions have such a system within their structure. In the West, our most obvious example is the Judeo-Christian ethics presented in the Old and New Testaments of the Bible in the Ten Commandments, the teachings of the prophets, the parables and Sermon on the Mount of Jesus, and such other writings and interpretations as the teaching traditions of Christianity and the Talmud of Judaism.

In this body of literature and teachings, an entire moral system of commands and prohibitions is established, and those who support the divine command approach to morality would say that, to be moral, we must follow this moral system without question and regardless of the consequences to anyone. After all, the ultimately good being has set this system up, and the task of humans is merely to follow it because it comes from the highest source of goodness and rightness that exists. Other religions have their own versions of this divine command theory, but the essence is the same: good and right are clearly established for human beings, and they must follow the rules set down for them to be moral.

Some of the same problems discovered in the previous chapter in discussion of the supernatural source of values apply here too. First, how do we know for sure that supernatural beings exist? We have only faith, no conclusive proof. Even if we accept their existence, how do we know for sure that they are moral and have really set down or put forth the commandments that are attributed to them? All these bits and pieces of morality have always come to us through human beings or, at least in Jesus' case, beings in human form. They claim to have been inspired by the supernatural, but there is no conclusive proof that these moral commandments were not really just presented by human beings for the good of other human beings and given strong sanction by being tied in closely with the religious views of their particular community.

Second, which moral system are we supposed to accept and follow? As I noted earlier, there are similarities, but there are also significant differences, and it all depends on which religion we were raised in or which one we have accepted on faith, which rules we think are moral. Third, what happens to those people who are not religious at all? Are they excluded from being moral or even morally acceptable because they do not believe in the existence of supernatural beings? It would seem ridiculous to ostracize human beings who appear to act morally because they do not have the same faith as we do.

Fourth, is it fair, or even moral, to follow an ethical system that completely ignores consequences and that cannot be questioned or adjusted? For example, what does "Thou shall not kill" really include or exclude? It is quite simply stated to the point where no exceptions or qualifications, such as "except in self-defense or in just wars or to protect the innocent," are even encouraged or allowed. Such exceptions point us again toward consequences, but the question, "Why should we follow rules with bad consequences?" should certainly be asked. We have absolutely no flexibility in moral matters, nor can we seek human advice or arbitration, since this moral system supposedly comes from a world we have no real knowledge of or control over.

KANTIAN DUTY ETHICS.   One significant nonconsequentialist theory that does not depend on the supernatural for its basis is the moral system established by Immanuel Kant (1724–1804), which is often referred to as "duty ethics" because of its heavy dependence on duty as the only real motivation for acting morally. Kant's system is probably the most highly rationalistic in the history of ethics. Kant felt that morality could be established on an absolute basis much like mathematics and logic through the higher aspects of human reasoning alone. He did not think that emotions or, as he called them, "inclinations" should have anything to do with establishing morality. In fact, he seemed to feel that morality was a kind of corrective to the irrationality and capriciousness of our wants, desires, and inclinations; hence, his emphasis on duty rather than on feeling as motivation for morality. Kant also thought that there were moral absolutes that we could discover just as we discovered the unchanging theorems, axioms, and postulates of geometry and all other forms of mathematics.

Kant established four major principles in his system calculated to form the background of morality. First, he felt that to be absolute, any moral rule would also have to be universal in nature; that is, it would have to apply to all human beings in all situations everywhere. If there were exceptions, or if a moral decision or action could not be universalized to apply to everyone at all times, then it would not be moral. He called this principle the "categorical imperative," which can be stated as follows: an act is immoral if the rule that would authorize it cannot be made into a rule for all human beings to follow.[2] For example, Kant argued we could not universalize killing because it would be contradictory to the meaning of life itself, and there would be no life and obviously no morality if we made a moral rule, such as "All human beings ought to kill each other." Therefore, Kant argued, killing is immoral because it cannot be universalized, whereas "All human beings should preserve and protect human life" can because it supports human life and all it stands for.

A second principle Kant presented was what he called the "practical imperative." This principle stated that no rational human life should be used merely as a means to an end but rather should be considered as a unique end in itself. This universalizes the uniqueness and significance of all rational human life and provides an antidote to the cost-benefit analysis problem that arose in utilitarianism. To use the example of the syphilitic black men again, Kant's principle would not have allowed the experiment. However, in another example, if a woman were dying of cancer and every method had been tried to cure her except one last experimental drug procedure, and if it could be shown that it might cure her, as well as provide valuable information for medical science, then Kant would probably have allowed it as moral. It is true that the woman would be used as a means to an end, but since the drug would be therapeutic for her, she would not *merely* be used as a means but would still be considered as a unique end in herself.

Another example that incorporates both of Kant's imperatives is his argument against suicide. Not only did Kant argue that "All human beings should kill themselves" obviously could not be universalized, but he also argued that suicide was an act that used a rational human being merely as a means to an end. If a human being wanted to kill himself to end his suffering or because he was in serious financial difficulty, Kant would say that he was using a human being (himself in this case) merely as a means to an end and was denying himself as a unique end in himself.[3]

Kant's third principle came about because of criticism leveled at his categorical imperative. Critics argued that universalizability would not necessarily make an action or rule moral. They said that it was possible to universalize something that may be questionably moral. Their example was, "Never help anyone in need." This could be universalized without too many problems since most human beings are basically self-sufficient, but, they argued, if we did not help needy people, would not our inaction be questionably moral? Kant agreed, but then he introduced what he called "the reversibility criterion," which said that another test of the morality of an action or rule would be to reverse its effect on someone else to oneself. He said that one should ask, "If I were in need, would I want to be helped or not? Yes, I would. Therefore, the rule: 'Never help anyone in need' could not be moral."

Kant's final principle is that to be fully moral, any action must be done out of a sense of duty regardless of our desires, wants, or inclinations. He went so far as to say that a person who was inclined to or felt like doing a moral act would not be as moral as he would be if he really were not inclined to do it but rather forced himself to do it out of a sense of duty, regardless of his inclinations. Kant said that in using the other three principles, we must develop moral rules that are absolute in nature, and then we must obey and follow them completely, without question and regardless of consequences or self or other interestedness—strictly out of a sense of duty. In doing all this, according to Kant, we would achieve a true moral life in the fullest sense of the word. By the way, Kant's moral rules when formulated look (interestingly enough) like the Ten Commandments of Judaism and Christianity: Never kill, never lie, never steal, never break promises, and so on.

There are some problems, as you might imagine, with a system that is so rigid and inflexible and that ignores consequences. First is the problem of universalizability. In addition to the criticism already presented—that rules can be universalized that may be questionably moral—there is the whole question of whether or not we can or should universalize morality to the extent that Kant demanded. Obviously the act utilitarian would disagree vehemently that we should try to establish a system of moral rules that would attempt to govern all humans and all situations.

Further, in introducing his reversibility criterion, as a kind of antidote to the problems of his categorical imperative, Kant actually brought consequences into a system that claimed to exclude consequences as too lowly a way by which to establish and apply morality. By saying that we should ask ourselves how we would feel if we were in need, isn't Kant asking "What would the consequences be to me if that rule were turned around?" In this case, then, he has violated his own basic assumption about what an ethical system should be and do.

Further, there are additional problems with this criterion or "the Golden Rule," as it is sometimes called. What does this criterion really tell us to do? It suggests that we "put ourselves in the other fellow's shoes," and this is not a bad method for recognizing the needs and welfare of others in making moral decisions. However, other than a method or a helpful attitude, what does it really mean? I am asking these questions because many people cite the Golden Rule as their only moral principle, and I am suggesting that it is not enough.

For example, suppose that I love physical contact that comes about from fighting and being fought; should I assume that since I want to be involved in such actions, others do too? I could, of course, apply the rule on a broader scale, and say that I should do for others what brings them pleasure since fighting and being fought is what brings me pleasure, but then I have the consequentialist problem of determining what constitutes pleasure for others. Even if I decide to use this approach, however, should what other people want and desire be the only principle governing my moral decisions and actions? For example, suppose that I know a sadistic person; should I allow myself to be beaten by him because it is what he wants? Furthermore, this rule is based on the assumption that people choose to live a certain life-style and that, if the situation were reversed, they would not want the results of that life-style to affect them, which may be erroneous.

For example, suppose that Brian is a clever and successful burglar and really loves stealing and all that goes with it. Why must we assume that he would not want to steal if someone burglarized him sometime? He might say, "Well, that's the breaks; but in no way do I intend to stop what I really like to do just because someone has done the same thing to me." The reversibility criterion, or Golden Rule, has much less content than most people think. I agree that it is a good technique to use in trying to be fair in making moral choices, but without other principles and as the sole moral principle, it is quite weak.

Another problem Kant had with universalizability is that he seemed not to realize that even though to universalize a moral action would allow for no exceptions, one could qualify the rule and still universalize it. For example, as I have said, Kant tended to establish inflexible rules, such as "never kill" and "never lie," but he did not seem to realize that rules such as "Never kill except in defense of the innocent or in self-defense" or "Never tell lies unless it would protect or preserve human life" could also be universalized. Notice that the difference is that with these latter rules the rule maker is not saying, "People should not lie or kill, but I can lie or kill whenever I want to," but rather, "People should not lie or kill except in certain specific instances." In other words, the rule is qualified to allow for a general exception for all people governed by it.

This problem indicates another, as when Kant stated that we should never lie, never steal, never kill but did not tell us what we should do when these "never" types of duties come into conflict. For example, what should we do if we have to choose between lying and breaking a promise or, more seriously, if not lying would cause a death? It would seem that according to Kant's system, we would have to not lie and allow the death to occur. Many ethicists, as well as ordinary people, would seriously question this approach to morality.

The last problem with Kant's ethics is his overemphasis on duty as opposed to inclinations as a motivation for morality. He makes a good point in that we do always admire people who disregard their own comfort and even their own lives to do what they feel is their moral duty. This is why we admire our heroes and heroines down through history, but Kant seems almost to say that if people are trained in such a way that they are inclined to be good and avoid being bad, somehow they are not as moral as those who constantly have to fight against their inclinations to act in accordance with their duties. This is not to denigrate the importance of duty in morality; rather, I think that we would all be just as happy or even happier if we knew that our neighbor was not inclined to lie or steal than if we knew that our neighbor was constantly in a violent struggle with himself not to do these things. I am sure we would all be rather upset to see him constantly holding himself back while eyeing, panting, and slavering over our wives and goods; we would much prefer that through his statements and actions he showed he was not inclined to do these things.

Finally, Kant does not tell us what we should do when our inclinations and duties are the same? If we feel like not stealing and it is also our duty, then are we only minimally moral, whereas if we really want to steal, but hold ourselves back, are we then fully moral?

ROSS' PRIMA FACIE DUTIES.   Before leaving the nonconsequentialists, we should examine Sir William David Ross' (1877–1940) theory called "prima facie duties." Recognizing some of the preceding problems with duty ethics, Ross found Kant's nonconsequentialism important but modified it somewhat to eliminate some of the difficulties, especially where ranking of duties is concerned. Ross agreed with Kant that there were certain duties we had that must generally be performed. He called these *prima facie* (this literally means "at first glance") duties, which means that people must, if they are to be moral, perform them unless some other important duty conflicts with them. Duties that Ross put forth include those that arise because of people's own acts, such as their duty to keep any promises they have made and their duty to correct or make reparation for any wrongful acts they have done to others, and those of the duty of gratitude, which is dependent, not on prior acts but on the prior acts of others. Other more future-looking duties are to[4]

1. Not do harm to anyone.
2. Promote the maximum possible good.
3. Distribute fairly and justly any good that is produced by my or any other's action.
4. Improve myself in both morality and intelligence.

Notice that Ross does not stress "always" or "never" when stating these duties. He says, rather, that these should be of primary importance in the decisions and actions of all human beings unless there are other duties that would somehow take precedence over them. However, this should occur only rarely. An important distinction between Ross and Kant on the matter of duties is that Ross tended to rank some of these duties as being more important than others. For example, both duties 1 and 2 are obviously at the top of the list of important duties, but Ross felt that 1 is always more important than 2 and that 1 should definitely take precedence. This means that it is much more important not to do harm to anyone than it is to do good, even though doing good is obviously very important. Presumably this means that if one is trying to decide on an action, such as the experimentation on the previously mentioned black men for the good of humanity, and if there is harm to someone in doing this, then obviously the harm that would be done takes precedence over any good that might be accomplished. Therefore, we would have to assume that Ross would not condone the experiment any more than Kant would.

Even though Ross' system improves over Kant's in several ways, there are still problems. Its advantage is that it is more flexible than Kant's, giving people a chance to override rules rather than adhere to them strictly and also ranking them so that, when there is a conflict, we can choose what should take precedence. However, the problems with his theories are that there is no clear way of establishing which duties are prima facie and which are not; furthermore, even though Ross gives us the flexibility to rank these duties, again he gives us no clear method by which this is to be done. He merely claims to know them to be true by reason of self-evidence; that is, we are to assume that everyone knows intuitively which ones are prima facie. This, of course, is not necessarily true. Not everyone will necessarily agree with

Ross on the truth of these, although he will probably find general agreement on most of them. He admits that if people cannot accept them as prima facie, then he cannot prove that they are. He can only ask them to reflect on them again until they know they are prima facie.[5] This is, of course, a rather weak foundation on which to base the major duties of one's ethical system no matter how appealing that system may appear to be.

Presumably, we are also to use some of the same type of intuitionism to decide which of them ranks higher in importance when our duties conflict, but here again, isn't this rather unclear and really too subjective a way of deciding issues that are this important? Therefore, even though Ross has improved over the deficiencies of Kant's system, his basis for morality and making moral decisions still does not seem to be as workable as that of the consequentialists.

CONCLUSION.   Despite the difficulties with nonconsequentialism, I would hate to see students dismiss these theories because of our emphasis in this century on situations and relativism in morality. There is certainly a problem in general with all nonconsequentialist theories arising in the important question about whether we should ever attempt to eliminate consequences from our moral deliberations, choices, and actions. As was shown in Kant's reversibility criterion, it is difficult to completely ignore consequences when doing morality. Despite all the grandeur of trying to set up a system of morality based solely on some higher basis, we have to ask ourselves what the real purpose of morality is if not to somehow bring about good consequences for human beings or to make our world a better place in which to live. This means that we cannot just do morality in a vacuum, but must be concerned about effects as well as causes and somehow apply morality to our daily lives.

On the other hand, the stability that is gained in a fairly clearcut moral system that is not going to change with every situation or human whim also seems to be advantageous. Further, there are some very fine ethical principles in both Kant and Ross that everyone of us should consider in the building of our own ethical systems. As has already been stated, the reversibility criterion, as long as it is not overused or is used alone, provides a workable attitude to consider. I think, also, that any moral system ought to include some element of universalizability since we do not live in isolation. Further, universalizing will give us stability and security in our morality; this should at least be a serious consideration when setting up a moral system. Even more worthy of consideration is Kant's practical imperative as a means of attaining justice and equality (equal worth of all human beings). Finally, despite the problems in the duties versus inclinations noted earlier, incorporating duty into any ethical system would seem to be important.

As for Ross' contributions, establishing important moral duties and ranking them is of great value despite the difficulty of trying to give them a basis on more than intuition. Maybe later we can find a better means by which to provide such a basis that will be more workable and satisfactory.

A Synthesis of Theories and Problems

After examining all these theories involving consequentialism, non-consequentialism, act and rule approaches to ethics, and self and other-interestedness, what are we to do about their advantages and disadvantages, their good points and their bad points? Will we merely have to select the theory with the least problems and try to ignore them, or can we possibly synthesize the theories in such a way that we can gain all the advantages and minimize or eliminate the disadvantages? I feel that synthesis is the best way to deal with all these differences, and I definitely believe that it is possible.

As presented in my previous book, *Ethics: Theory and Practice,* and as I would like to do now, much more briefly, here are my ideas for your consideration, discussion, and critical evaluation.[6] My purpose here is to help you think about and, I hope, set about organizing your own systematic approach to morality in general and moral problems in particular, not to indoctrinate you into any particular moral system.

SOME BASIC ASSUMPTIONS ABOUT ETHICAL SYSTEMS

If we look at the various criticisms and problems we have discussed in connection with all the traditional theories of morality, we will discover that certain patterns or ideas about what a workable ethical system should be begin to emerge. Before discussing how we might go about constructing any ethical system, however, we should make some of those assumptions clear.

RATIONAL BUT NOT WITHOUT EMOTION.   As discussed in the beginning of this chapter, reason and reasoning are extremely important to any moral system and to doing any kind of moral deliberation or decision making. All the ethical theories we have looked at have attempted to use reason to one degree or another. Kant's is without a doubt the most highly rationalistic of all the theories. As a result, his system seems probably more cold and calculating than any of the others; therefore, we can see that emotion or feeling, which is already involved in any moral issue, ought not to be entirely eliminated. Emotions should be tempered and tested, however, with the best evidence we can find and also the most careful logic and reasoning we can arrive at, so that we are not merely expressing emotions unreasonably but are also leaving room for compassion, love, friendship, and sympathy where they are called for. In other words, our morality must be governed by reason but not devoid of emotion.

LOGICAL CONSISTENCY WITHOUT INFLEXIBILITY.   Some of the problems with ethical egoism and act utilitarianism revealed that although there was individuality and freedom, there was also possible or actual inconsistency. In egoism, the inconsistency had to do with the difficulty of knowing how everyone's interest could be satisfied; in act utilitarianism, inconsistency was encouraged by always adjusting one's ethics to the situation and also by leaving situational ethical decisions in the hands of each individual without any more guidelines than doing what is in everyone's interest. On the other side of the coin, Kant's system was so consistent that it approached inflexibility using "never" and "always" and not allowing for exceptions or even qualification of rules. It would seem important, then, that we ought to be as consistent in doing morality as possible without being so inflexible that we cannot allow for the complexity of human living and exceptional situations that might occur.

UNIVERSALITY AND APPLICABILITY.   The idea that we should try to universalize our morality attempting to include all humanity and most situations we encounter, as I have already said, is a good idea; however, we also need to be able to apply morality to specific and actual situations in our lives. We cannot be so universal in our approach that we are merely abstract and theoretical. This is a very real danger in Kant's system; his ethics is so highly universalized that it is often difficult to apply it to specific situations. On the other hand, act utilitarianism and egoism are so highly individualized that there is little universality in either system. We need to strive for a balance, then, between universalizing our rules or principles and making it possible to apply our morality effectively to any situation that may arise.

TEACHABILITY AND PROMULGATION.   One problem that arose in our discussions of all forms of ethical egoism, but especially the first two, and also act utilitarianism, was that of teaching morality to children or to the uninitiated and also promulgating (laying out or setting forth) the theories for others to see. If you remember in discussing egoism, there could be problems for the egoist if he told people that everyone should act in his or her interest or that he was going to act in his interest and he did not care what others did. Even in universal ethical egoism, there was difficulty that it might not be in the egoist's interest to tell people to act in their self-interests when it might hamper his own. Also, merely to tell someone to act in his own self-interest doesn't teach him what really is in his own self-interest; in other words, specifics are missing. In the case of act utilitarianism, one can only teach people that they ought to do what is best for everyone in each situation they encounter, but what tells them what this "best" really and specifically is? There are no rules or other principles to go by, so teaching morality would be almost impossible. It is assumed, then, that we ought to be able to promulgate or state clearly our ethical theories and they ought to be constructed in such a way that they can be taught to anyone.

RESOLVING CONFLICTS.   One problem we found in universal ethical egoism was that it was extremely difficult to resolve conflicts of interest when they arose, and in Kant's system we discovered that he made no allowance for resolving conflicts in our various important moral duties. We also have to realize that human beings differ in many ways and that not everyone is going to embrace just one ethical system; therefore, any ethical system we propose must be able to at least attempt to resolve any conflict that may arise. In other words, there must be ways within any ethical system that is to be considered workable and livable to deal with and attempt to resolve conflicts among human beings, duties, and obligations.

With these assumptions in mind, then, how can we go about establishing an ethical system that incorporates them and also brings together consequentialist with nonconsequentialist views, self-interest and other-interest, and freedom and order?

THE SYNTHESIS—PRINCIPLES AND FREEDOM

Additional assumptions, some of which have already been made earlier, are, first, that we need to consider consequences of our moral choices, decisions, and actions. As has been suggested, consequences, or the way in which moral actions affect human beings, would seem to be one of the most important aspects of morality; otherwise, morality can become merely an abstract intellectual game. On the other hand, there seem to be times when consequences may have to be given a secondary priority, that is, when a certain action calls for a basically nonsequentialist point of view. For example, shouldn't rape and child abuse or molestation be considered immoral regardless of the circumstances? What would the circumstances allowing it be? It is true that a strong case can also be made against these acts on the basis of consequences, but should consequences be considered to make exceptions, such as whether the child who would be sexually molested desires it or does not mind and therefore the molester's pleasure should be considered as important? I am not suggesting here either that such a situation would necessarily arise, or that it is ever true that children would feel this way, only that there should not be consequentialist loopholes in such moral issues.

Second, both self and other interest ought to play a part in moral decision making. Because of this, it would seem that the utilitarian principle of the greatest good for everyone should be the guiding rule or principle since it manages to include the consideration of others without excluding self-interest.

Third, there must be a synthesis between the act and rule approaches to doing morality. We need the stability, security, and order of rules, and yet we also need the freedom, flexibility, and individuality of the act approach so that morality can be actually applied and lived with in a meaningful day-by-day way. How can all these be synthesized? The best way of doing this is to use broad rules—I call them principles rather than rules—and then incorporate freedom, or the act approach, into the system as one of these principles, while limiting it in deference to more crucial principles—those that are more prima facie. The important question arises, "What principles would we designate as prima facie and why? And we also need to rank these principles in order of importance and somehow decide where the principle of freedom fits into the overall scheme.

The first thing that we need to do is to try to decide what we consider important enough to be listed as duties all humans should adhere to if they want to be moral and create a moral life for themselves and others. Such decisions must be carefully thought through by each individual in the following manner: What do I consider most valuable in *my* life and in life in general and why? How can I form a principle that will include these values and exclude values that I consider detrimental to me and others? I would ask each one of you to perform this very important examination of your values and then attempt to formulate appropriate principles to embody them. I would like to suggest five basic ethical principles that I formulated after going through this process.[7]

FIVE BASIC ETHICAL PRINCIPLES

Value of Life Principle.   Since we cannot do anything without life and since each of us holds our own life in a very special and unique way, it would seem that the most important principle we should consider is one that would ensure that human life is preserved and protected. Without live human beings, morality would have little or no meaning. Just what does this principle involve, however? Does it mean that life must be prolonged at all costs, or does it mean that life can never be taken for any reason whatsoever, as Kant demanded in his duty, "Never kill"? There should be a strong emphasis on the word "value" in the title of this principle. There may be times when the value of life is of less importance than other principles and "value" will at times need to be interpreted. For example, a dying person could receive treatment that would prolong his life for a few weeks but that would cause him to be in pain and terrible discomfort. If he chooses not to accept such treatment, even though it would prolong his life, because he would rather live what time he has left without pain or discomfort, then he ought to have the right to refuse such treatment. I have interpreted this principle as "the value of life and the acceptance of death," which would allow for valuing life, but only with the realization of the inevitability of the death that will come to all human beings.

In many instances recorded in history, people have willingly overridden the value of their own lives for other principles, such as freedom, the good of others, the good of their country, and the importance of their religious commitments. Therefore, this principle can be overridden with good reason, but being the primary principle, it should generally be observed and upheld.

THE PRINCIPLE OF GOODNESS OR RIGHTNESS. Since the words "moral" and "ethical" mean good or right, any moral system must assume as an ultimate principle that of goodness or rightness, or as it is sometimes called, "beneficence." This principle demands that human beings attempt three things: (1) to promote goodness over badness, (2) to cause no harm or badness, and (3) to prevent badness or harm. Since "immoral" and "unethical" mean bad or wrong, you can see their prohibition expressed in all three demands. Since I have already defined "good," "bad," "right," "wrong," earlier in the chapter, I don't need to do it again here. Suffice it to say that this principle is secondary in priority only to the value of life principle.

THE PRINCIPLE OF JUSTICE OR FAIRNESS. Among the demands of the principle of goodness, nothing is said about the fair or just distribution of goodness, and when it is inevitable, badness among human beings, and yet this is an important principle to consider. Is it enough to do good and avoid or prevent harm? Isn't it also important to see that good and bad are distributed fairly and justly? Because there are many human beings to consider, and also if we accept Kant's practical imperative, then each person deserves a unique, individual, and personal consideration as an end in himself or herself. I stress that the type of justice I am discussing here is "distributive" rather than "retributive" (revenge or "an eye for an eye, a tooth for a tooth") justice. This would mean that if there are "goods" available, be they economic, medical, or educational in nature, but not enough to go around, some attempt should be made to distribute these goods as justly and fairly as possible to ensure that some human beings do not get all the goods while others get nothing.

There are three ways such distribution can take place: (1) according to need or ability, (2) according to merit or dessert (whether people merit or deserve goods or not), and (3) equally among people regardless of the other two ways. Just and fair distribution, especially in the third sense described, does not necessarily presume a socialistic or communistic system of distribution. It does mean, however, that human beings ought to have equal opportunity to attain these goods and also that goods that are essential for survival should be made as available as possible to everyone. It is quite interesting, in reference to socialism or communism, that Russia, for example, does not distribute the goods on the third basis, equally among all, as we might expect. In the hierarchical structure of the Soviet society, scientists, engineers, cosmonauts, and certain artists and athletes are given more goods than are ordinary workers, so the Russian system of distribution seems to be in accordance with ability, merit, or desert rather than equality.

THE PRINCIPLE OF TRUTH TELLING OR HONESTY.   Fourth in importance, at least as I have ranked it, is the principle of honesty and truthtelling, which is needed to establish trust in moral dealings, especially since most morality depends on rational discourse. It is important, for example, in making promises or other commitments, that people can believe what is told them. Promises or other statements made by liars are of no value and in essence destroy any real chance for morality. Anyone who has ever been lied to or cheated by someone he or she has trusted knows how difficult it is to ever trust that person again, especially if the lying or cheating has occurred more than once. One can only maintain the wariest of relationships with that person and will often discontinue it completely. Therefore, to establish principles and moral dealings at all, there must be honesty and truth telling.

THE PRINCIPLE OF INDIVIDUAL FREEDOM.   Last, but definitely not least, is the principle of individual freedom, which is how the act approach to morality becomes incorporated into my synthesized moral system. I have already given many reasons why freedom should be brought into and made a part of any ethical system, such as allowing for differences in people, places, and times and in general allowing for flexibility and the avoidance of rigidity in ethical decision making, but the main reason for establishing freedom is the very nature of human beings themselves. As we discussed in Chapters 3 and 4, our minds and selves are uniquely ours and are truly and in actuality unsharable; that is, I cannot experience your experiences or really "get inside of" your mind and self and you cannot get inside mine. In other words, the very nature of a human being is to be highly unique, individual, and subjective. No matter how much we try to share our inner lives or be objective about things, we are in a sense condemned to our own subjectivity. Because of this, we will experience and value things differently and some allowance must be made for these differences. Therefore, a principle establishing, allowing for, and even encouraging freedom in moral matters is essential.

How the System Works.   I have then attempted to bring consequences and nonconsequences, self and other interestedness, and now the act and rule approaches together by establishing principles to give order and stability to the system and by including individual freedom as one of its principles to allow for flexibility. However, it is still not clear how all this works or, put another way, how freedom can be limited and yet still allowed to avoid the inflexibility of the rule approach on the one hand and the possible chaos of the act approach, on the other.

The solution to the problem lies in the priority or ranking of these prima facie duties, and I have done this in the order in which the principles were set down. The first principles are ranked in order of importance as life, goodness, justice, and honesty and truth telling. The last principle, freedom, is generally overruled by the other four so that human freedom is allowed in moral matters to the extent that it does not violate the other four principles. Put in other words, people are free to do whatever they want except that they may not endanger or take a life, they may not do bad or wrong, they may not be unjust, and they may not tell lies or be dishonest. Any freedom that is exercised to such an extent that it violates the first four principles is to be considered immoral or unethical *unless* sufficient reasoning and evidence can be presented to justify such violation. In this way stability, order, security, and universalizability exist in the system because I have established and am using ethical principles that generally must be followed by everyone.

I have also allowed for flexibility, individuality, and creativity by incorporating freedom into the system and including it as the last principle. Finally, I have limited this freedom by giving the other four principles priority. The limiting of freedom further is workably specific, unlike the common practice of saying, "People are free to do whatever they wish to do provided they do not infringe on anyone else's freedom or harm others." This phrase, although commendable in spirit and attitude, does not clearly state what constitutes infringement or harm to others, and this makes it next to useless. My system, on the other hand, specifies in a somewhat broad sense what actually does constitute infringement or harm—violation of those duties or acts embodied in the other four principles. Let us look at how this whole approach to morality can be applied.

APPLICATION OF THE SYSTEM.   Let us take two examples and apply the system to them: (1) two adults living together in a husband-wife relationship without benefit of marriage and (2) the rape of a woman by a man.

1. Let us assume that these two people have agreed to live together without benefit of marriage and intend to practice birth control. There is no threat to human life, so they are not violating the first principle. The question of goodness is moot; they are not on the face of it causing any badness or harm, and they seem to feel that their relationship is promoting goodness for themselves. However, are they being just and fair to each other and to others? Let us assume that their parents, relatives, and some of their friends are unhappy about their relationship. Does this constitute injustice or unfairness on the part of the couple? One also needs to ask at what point are adults required to adjust their private styles to what others wish? The only element that could constitute injustice or unfairness would be offending others' tastes, and offense to taste does not necessarily constitute violation of this principle.

Are they being dishonest or lying? Obviously not, since everyone seems to know about their relationship, and, presumably, they have made certain agreements between themselves. Therefore, in this case, the principle of freedom may take precedence over justice since none of the other principles is violated.

2. In the case of rape, however, the principle of life is violated in that any person being threatened with rape is obviously subjected to bodily harm and often death. The only goodness that could be cited in such a situation would be the pleasure to be obtained by the rapist, but the badness arising out of such an act would far outweigh it. Obviously, the rapist's "goodness" would cause grave injustice to the woman and her family. Honesty and truth telling could be violated if the rapist lied to get his victim into a situation where he could rape her. The upshot of this analysis is that the freedom to rape must be limited because it violates all the other four principles and is therefore immoral.

In presenting these particular principles and the method of dealing

223

with freedom and its limitation, I in no way suggest that anyone is required to accept any of the principles. You may, for example, wish to use only one or two principles or add some that I have not presented. However, the purpose of this section, on the synthesis of all the theories and general moral problems, has been to show you how you might go about setting up your own moral system. It is my sincere hope that all readers will attempt to do so as soon as possible if they have not already, for moral or ethical issues are the most important ones we have to face in our lives.

The next chapter will present one major moral issue in several of its more important aspects—the taking of human life—which will allow you to apply whatever you have developed as a moral system in a meaningful way to some of the most serious problems involving the violation of the primary principle—the value of life.

Applying Philosophy—
Situations for Thought and Discussion

SITUATION 1

What is your basic ethical system and what reasons can you give to support it? To answer this question well and completely, deal with the following subquestions:

1. What is your basic ethical principle or principles and why?
2. Should everyone be free to pursue his or her own ethical system? To what extent, and how can individual differences be reconciled so that people can be ethical toward each other?
3. To what degree are the following specific actions moral or immoral, according to your system, and why? Show how your basic ethical principles relate to your views on these specific moral problems—do at least *six* of the following (Do not answer this question until you have read Chapter 8.)
   a. War.
   b. Defense of the innocent, including self-defense.
   c. Allowing to die, mercy death, and mercy killing.
   d. Abortion.
   e. Capital punishment.
   f. Suicide.
   g. Sexual intercourse before or outside of marriage.
   h. Rape.
   i. Adultery.
   j. Homosexuality and lesbianism.
   k. Pornography.
   l. Stealing.
   m. Breaking promises, contracts, or agreements.
   n. Cheating and lying.
   o. Use of stimulants and depressants (narcotics).
   p. Racial, religious, or sex discrimination and prejudice.

In supporting your basic principles of ethics and your views on these actions, do not rely *only* on religion, your parents' views, society's views, or your peers' views. The crucial question really is, Why do *you* believe these actions are right or wrong? *You* should have good reasons for holding your positions on morality; merely inheriting them from some tradition, religious or otherwise, is *not* a good enough reason for the purpose of this paper.

SITUATION 2

Examine, describe carefully, and evaluate critically any system of ethics or moral code with which you are familiar (for example, a religion's, your family's, any of your friends', any profession's, or business'), dealing with the following in any order you wish.

1. To what extent are the following assumptions embodied or carried out?
   a. Is the system rational and yet not devoid of emotion, or does it overemphasize one or the other?
   b. Is there logical consistency without inflexibility?
   c. Does it have universality and yet apply to particular situations?
   d. Is it teachable and promulgatable?
   e. Does it have the means to resolve moral conflicts?
   f. Does it consider and involve consequences?
   g. Does it satisfy both self and others' interests?
   h. Does it synthesize the act and rule approaches? If so, how?
2. To what extent does it embody any of the five basic ethical principles? What other principles, if any, does it use?
3. What do you feel are its advantages and disadvantages? Be specific.

SITUATION 3

In your own words and as carefully as you can, define "morality" and show how it differs from religion, manners, customs, the nonmoral, and the law, by giving specific examples and illustrations from your own experience and elaborating on them as completely as you can.

Chapter Summary

I. What is morality?
   A. The major difference between what is moral and nonmoral is that in morality such words as "good," "right," "bad," and "wrong" and such prescriptive words as "should" or "ought" are used, but in a value-laden, moral sense. In nonmoral situations these same words have no moral import but usually deal with taste differences or function (e.g., "A good car runs well").
   B. The difference between morals and manners is that manners concern what is or is not socially acceptable in certain situa-

tions where human behavior is involved, such as acting boor-
ishly at a formal dinner party, whereas morals affect people's
lives and well-being in a more serious manner, such as in rape.

C. The difference between law and morality is that even though
law is probably the greatest public expression of social morality, morality usually comes before the law and often changes
it. Also, there can be morally unjust laws, so morality and law
are not merely one and the same thing.

D. There is no absolutely necessary connection between religion
and morality. All religions have a moral system, but not all
moral systems are based on religion.

E. Amorality means essentially "indifference to morality" or the
inability to distinguish between right and wrong.

F. What morality is: morality has to do with what is right or
wrong, bad or good, in a moral sense, and it deals basically
with humans and how they relate to and treat other beings to
promote mutual welfare, growth, creativity, and meaning in
striving for what is good over bad and what is right over
wrong.

II. How moral decisions can be made.

A. People can and often do use emotions; most moral issues are
heavily laden with feeling, but the real question concerns the
extent to which emotions should decide moral issues.

1. Emotions vary to such an extent that arbitration is often not
possible.

2. Can reasonable conclusions to moral conflicts ever be arrived at if we never get past our strong feelings about them?

B. Reason involves the ability to ask questions, seek evidence, and
discuss and argue logically.

1. With this attribute, we can rise above the highly personal
and individualistic quality of our emotions and approach a
meeting ground for discussing ideas.

2. We must be careful, however, that by using reason to the
exclusion of emotion, we do not become too cold and calculating in dealing with moral issues.

C. A synthesis of emotion and reason would seem to be the solution to this controversy in that they could be combined in a
constructive and creative balance. To avoid the inability to ar-
bitrate emotions and the calculating aspect of using reason alone,
we should subject our feelings to rational examination and yet
let compassion and understanding also play a part in morality.

III. Traditional theories of morality.

A. Two basic approaches to morality:

1. Consequentialist, which states that what determines moral-

ity is whether there are good results or consequences en-
suing from a choice, act, or rule.

2. Nonconsequentialist, which is based on something other than
consequences, such as a supernatural good or higher reason.

B. Ethical egoism is one of the consequentialist theories and comes
in three forms:

1. Individual—everyone should always act in *my* self-interest.
2. Personal—I should always act in my self-interest; I make
no claim about what others should do.
3. Universal (the most commonly presented form)—everyone
should always act in his or her own self-interest.
4. Egoists, then, believe that consequences should accrue for
oneself in order to achieve morality.

C. Critical evaluation of all three forms:

1. Individual ethical egoism comes closest to what we call selfishness, and it is too individualistic and subjective as well
as being somewhat contradictory (Is it in your self-interest
to tell people that they should act in your self-interest?).
2. Personal ethical egoism is more moderate but is still too
highly individualistic and subjective and also there is still a
problem with getting one's interest satisfied once one reveals that one is an egoist.
3. Universal ethical egoism seems to be fairer, but the problem lies with the meaning of "everyone." How can we resolve conflicts of self-interest? Whose self-interest does this
egoist really want satisfied?
4. The advantage of ethical egoism is that it stresses individuality and freedom and might work in situations where most
people were self-sufficient and completely independent;
however, the disadvantage is that in a highly complex society most people are interdependent on each other for services and supplies. Therefore, ethical egoism is not satisfactory as an ethical theory.

D. Utilitarianism is another consequentialist theory that states that
if we want to be moral, we should always act in such a way
as to bring about the greatest good consequences, but this time
to everyone concerned.

1. The advantage of this theory over egoism is that it more
fairly considers others in performing any act.
2. Its disadvantage in relation to egoism is that it is more difficult to determine good consequences for others rather than
just for oneself.

3. It comes in two forms:
   a. Act utilitarianism, which states that people should always do that act that will bring the greatest good consequences for everyone.
   b. Rule utilitarianism, which states that people should establish and follow rules that will bring about the best consequences for all concerned.
   c. The act version allows for greater freedom and individuality in moral decision making, but the rule approach provides for more stability. The former can be too anarchistic, whereas the latter can be too inflexible or restrictive.
   d. The act utilitarian stresses differences in persons, places, and situations, whereas the rule type stresses similarities. Further, the rule utilitarian says that leaving it up to each individual to bring about good consequences in each situation would not in the long run bring about the greatest good for everyone.
   e. The act utilitarian, on the other hand, says that we cannot make rules to cover all situations; therefore, the best thing to do is just decide in each situation what is right.
4. The cost-benefit analysis approach is another problem affecting both forms of utilitarianism. It arises out of the difficulty of trying to do the best for everyone; when we cannot, the temptation exists to do the greatest good for the greatest number.
   a. This is in itself not a bad idea except that there is a tendency not to care too much what happens to those who are not counted in the greatest number—the minority.
   b. This approach is also often used to support "a good end always justifies any means used to attain it," and many ethicists often take issue with this approach, stating that any means used must also be morally good rather than morally bad.
5. Another problem with all consequentialist theories is the difficulty of determining consequences, especially future long-range consequences. This is worse for the utilitarian than for the egoist, but it is still a problem for both.

E. Nonconsequentialist theories argue that morality is and should be placed on a much higher plane than merely satisfying people's interests and should not be as subject to change or whim as consequentialism is. Most of these theories are rule oriented.

F. Divine command theories argue that morality is based on some sort of supernatural ultimate good being or beings from which divine commands have come down to human beings.

   1. The assumption is that these commands are right in and of themselves regardless of consequences, interests, or situations.

   2. Therefore, to be moral, one must follow these commands without question.

G. Critical evaluation of this theory:

   1. Again, as with the supernatural source of values argument, there is no conclusive proof but only faith that such a being or beings exist.

   2. Even if they do, how do we know that they are moral or that they really gave such commands? Maybe their human followers really created these commands.

   3. Which supernatural source are we to accept—there are many (Yahweh, Allah, Zeus, Jesus, Buddha, etc.)?

   4. Does this mean that if people do not have faith, they cannot be moral?

   5. Is it fair to follow a moral system that so completely ignores consequences?

H. Kantian duty ethics is an attempt by Immanuel Kant to establish morality on the basis of absolute reason alone and has four major ethical principles:

   1. Any rule that is moral would have to be universalizable, so Kant established his categorical imperative, which states that an act is immoral if the rule that would authorize it cannot be universalized so that it would apply to all human beings.

   2. Kant's practical imperative states that no human life should be used merely as a means to an end but, rather, should be considered as a unique end in itself. This universalizes the uniqueness and importance of all human life and nullifies any assumption of cost-benefit analysis.

   3. The reversibility criterion states that to test if an action is moral or immoral, people should reverse positions and see if they would want something done or not done to them.

   4. To be fully moral, any action must be done out of a sense of duty, regardless of desires, wants, or inclinations.

I. Problems with Kant's theory:

   1. Merely because a rule can be universalized does not mean that it is moral; in fact it is possible to universalize questionable moral rules. Further, should morality be universalized to such an extreme? The act utilitarian, among others, would certainly disagree.

2. Kant's reversibility criterion sneaks in consequences and as other than a moral attitude is questionably helpful—what does it really mean?

3. Kant did not differ between making an exception to a rule and qualifying it. "Never kill except in self-defense" can be universalized just as well as "Never kill," for example.

4. Kant's system never told us how to determine the importance of duties since they were all absolute—what are we to do if keeping a promise would result in someone's death, for example?

5. He also overemphasized duty over inclination. After all, isn't a person who is inclined to be moral actually as moral as someone who has to struggle to be so?

J. Ross' prima facie duties corrected one of Kant's problems by trying to rank duties by declaring them prima facie (at first glance, they are moral). Some of these duties are

1. Those that arise because of people's own prior acts, such as the duty to keep promises made and to make reparation for any wrongful acts they have done.

2. Those dependent on the acts of others, such as the duty of gratitude.

3. Other more future-looking duties, such as promoting the maximum possible good, not doing harm to anyone, distributing fairly and justly any good that is produced by my or anyone else's actions, and improving myself in both morality and intelligence.

4. Ross improves over Kant's system by not stressing "never" or "always" and by ranking duties, saying, for example, that it is more important not to do harm than it is to do good.

K. Problems with Ross' theory:

1. Even though his system improves over Kant's, Ross does not give us any clear way to establish which duties should be considered prima facie—he suggests that we should merely intuit what they are.

2. He also, except again for intuition, does not show us how we might rank such duties in order of importance.

L. General problems and advantages of nonsequentialist theories:

1. Should we ever completely ignore consequences? Isn't the whole point of morality, or at least one of the most major ones, to bring about good to as many people as possible?

2. One advantage of these systems is that there is a great deal of security and stability to them because they have clear rules to follow, but the disadvantage to this is that they are often too rigid and inflexible to apply practically to our daily lives.

3. Another advantage is that there are some very fine ethical principles within both Kant's and Ross' theories that can be applied, perhaps with some modifications, to many ethical systems.

IV. A synthesis of theories and problems.

    A. Basic assumptions about ethical systems:

        1. They should be rationally based but not without emotion.

        2. They should have logical consistency without inflexibility.

        3. They should be universal in scope and yet practically applicable to particular persons, places, and situations.

        4. They should be able to be taught and promulgated.

        5. They should have the ability to resolve conflicts among duties, obligations, systems, and individuals.

        6. They must consider consequences of moral choices, decisions, and actions.

        7. They ought to somehow combine self- and other-interestedness.

        8. They must also provide a synthesis between the act and rule approaches to morality because we need both security and stability on the one hand and freedom and flexibility on the other.

    B. The synthesis—principles and freedom. To achieve this synthesis we must use broad rules, or prima facie duties, which are well based and supported with reason and evidence but which somehow incorporate freedom as well. There are five basic ethical principles worthy of consideration:

        1. The value of life principle, which means a reverence for life but an acceptance of death.

        2. The principle of goodness or rightness, which demands three things of human beings:

            a. To promote goodness over badness.

            b. To cause no harm or badness.

            c. To prevent badness or harm.

        3. The principle of justice or fairness, which is concerned with distributive justice, states that any good or bad arising from actions must be distributed as fairly as possible so that the same people do not always get just the good or the bad. Distribution can be made in three ways:

            a. According to need or ability.

            b. According to merit or desert.

            c. Equally among people regardless of the other two ways.

        4. The principle of honesty and truth telling really is at the root of moral communication and discourse and is needed

if one is to be able to trust others to follow the other principles.

5. The principle of individual freedom is based on the uniqueness of each human being and states that human beings ought to be free in their valuing and in their moral decision making.

C. How the system works is that all the principles are set down or ranked in the order of their importance, as shown. Each principle is limited by the one above it, and the principle of individual freedom is limited by all the other four. Therefore, there is order in the system provided by the principles, and freedom is incorporated as one of the principles that is limited, however, by the other four.

1. People are free to do whatever they want *provided* that they do not violate principles 1–4; that is, they are not free to take life, do bad, be unjust, or tell lies and be dishonest.

2. Application of the system to two situations:

   a. Two adults living together in a husband-wife relationship without marriage can be considered moral in that their actions do not violate any of the first four principles enough to deny them freedom.

   b. The rape of a woman, on the other hand, is a violation of all five principles (the woman's freedom is also denied), and therefore the man's act is immoral and he should not have the freedom to do it.

Additional Questions and Activities for Study and Discussion

1. Do you think that human beings are essentially good, bad, or a combination of both? Why? In a well-organized essay, argue for and bring evidence to support the position you have taken. How does your position affect your approach to morality? For example, should a moral system be strict, clear, and absolutistic or permissive, flexible, and relativistic?

2. Do you believe that morality should or should not be based *solely* on religion? Why? Is it possible to establish a moral system without any reference to religion? If so, how? If not, why not? What could be the basis of such a system if not religion? Be specific and describe your position in detail.

3. On an episode of *M★A★S★H*, the popular television series, Hawkeye

Pierce performed an unnecessary appendix operation on a battalion commander merely to remove him from battle because, through his amoral overaggressiveness, he had the highest casualty rate of any other battalion commander. Every effort had been tried to get him to change his approach, but he was going on with his disastrous military actions anyway. Hawkeye figured that by performing the operation, he would probably save the lives of a hundred or more men. His fellow surgeon, B. J. Hunnicutt, argued that it was unethical for a surgeon knowingly to operate on a healthy body. He added "some things are always wrong." Hawkeye argued that many surgeons in the States did many unnecessary surgeries and their motives were to do them for money, whereas Hawkeye was trying to save lives. Hawkeye did the surgery, and the commander's appendix was completely healthy.

How do Hawkeye's arguments relate to the cost-benefit analysis approach to morality? To what extent do you feel that Hawkeye is justified in using the commander as a means to what he deems to be a good end? To what extent do you feel B.J. is justified in his nonconsequentialist rule that doctors should *never* perform unnecessary operations knowingly? Is there ever a time when a good end justifies *any* means used to attain it? If so, when? If not, why not? Which surgeon do you feel was right in his moral approach, and why? Answer in detail, and support your answers fully.

4. Read Joseph Fletcher's book, *Situation Ethics,* and critically evaluate his act utilitarian position. Keeping in mind that he offers no specific rules for moral behavior, what values and what difficulties do you see in his sole commandment, "Do what is the loving thing to do in any situation"? Are there problems with deciding what "the loving thing to do" is in some situations? If so, what are they? Is love really enough to be moral and always do the right thing? Why or why not? Describe a situation in which "the loving thing to do" can be clearly known.

5. Read Robert Heinlein's *Stranger in a Strange Land* and critically evaluate the ethical egoism advocated by the author through his main earth-born character. Perform a similar analysis on the protagonists of the author's other books, *The Moon Is a Harsh Mistress* and *I Will Fear No Evil.*

6. Analyze and critically evaluate U.S. national and foreign policies, attempting to determine whether they are based on egoism (national egoism) in any of its forms, act or rule utilitarianism, or rule nonconsequentialism. If you feel that a combination of these approaches is used, then show how, giving specific examples and illustrations. Support your arguments fully.

7. One of the advantages of rule nonconsequentialist theories is that they clearly state do's and don'ts, thereby lending a great deal of stability and order to morality. Adherents describe the benefits of this when they say, "We know just where we stand with this type of morality, and it gives us a great deal of security when compared with relativistic morality." To what extent do you feel that this advantage is an important one? Why? To what extent do you feel that this is a disadvantage rather than an advantage? Answer in detail.

8. Rule nonconsequentialist theories essentially state that there are certain moral absolutes that should never be violated (for example, rules against killing, mutilating, stealing, child molesting). To what extent to you agree or disagree with this idea? Are there certain do's and don'ts to which human beings should always adhere? If so, what are they, and why should they always be adhered to? If not, why not?

9. To what extent do you believe that Christians or Jews use the divine command theory approach rather than egoism or utilitarianism as a basis for their ethics? For example, do you believe that most Christians follow their religion's moral rules simply or only because they believe they were established by God, or do they follow them for other reasons? Answer in detail.

10. Do a complete and careful analysis of how you made a specific moral decision? To what extent did you use emotion, reason, or a combination of the two? To what extent did you use the act or rule approaches, and why? To what extent was your decision based on consequences or nonconsequential procedures?

Footnotes

1. Jacques P. Thiroux, *Ethics: Theory and Practice,* 2nd ed. (Encino, Calif.: Glencoe, 1980), p. 8.
2. Kant's actual formulation can be found in *Problems of Moral Philosophy*, 2nd ed., ed. Paul W. Taylor (Belmont, Calif.: Dickenson, 1972), p. 219. The version given here is my paraphrase.
3. Immanuel Kant, *Fundamental Principles of the Metaphysics of Morals* (New York: Longmans, Green, 1923), Sect. I, II, and III.
4. John Hospers, *Human Conduct: Problems of Ethics,* 2nd ed. (New York: Harcourt Brace Jovanovich, 1982), pp. 208–210.
5. Taylor, *Problems of Moral Philosophy,* p. 269.
6. Thiroux, *Ethics,* Chap. 6.
7. For a full presentation and support of these principles, see ibid., Chap. 6.

Bibliography

GENERAL READINGS ON ETHICS AND ETHICAL THEORIES

Baier, Kurt. *The Moral Point of View*. Ithaca, N.Y.: Cornell University Press, 1958.

Binkley, Luther J. *Contemporary Ethical Theories*. New York: Citadel Press, 1961.

Frankena, William K. *Ethics*, 2nd ed. Englewood Cliffs, N.J.: Prentice-Hall, 1973.

Hospers, John. *Human Conduct: Problems of Ethics,* 2nd ed. New York: Harcourt Brace Jovanovich, 1982.

Melden, A. I., ed. *Ethical Theories,* 2nd ed. Englewood Cliffs, N.J.: Prentice-Hall, 1967.

Outka, Gene, and John P. Reeder, Jr., eds. *Religion and Morality*. Garden City, N.Y.: Anchor/Doubleday, 1973.

Taylor, Paul W., ed. *Problems of Moral Philosophy,* 2nd ed. Belmont, Calif.: Dickenson, 1972.

Wall, George B. *Introduction to Ethics*. Columbus: Charles E. Merrill, 1974.

Wasserstrom, Richard A., ed. *Morality and the Law*. Belmont, Calif.: Wadsworth, 1971.

READINGS ON ETHICAL EGOISM

Alston, William P., and Richard B. Brandt. *The Problems of Philosophy,* 2nd ed. Boston: Allyn & Bacon, 1974.

Gautier, David P., ed. *Morality and Rational Self-interest*. Englewood Cliffs, N.J.: Prentice-Hall, 1970.

Medlin, Brian. "Ultimate Principles and Ethical Egoism," *Australasian Journal of Philosophy* 35 (1957): 111–118.

Olson, Robert G. *The Morality of Self-interest*. New York: Harcourt Brace Jovanovich, 1965.

Rand, Ayn. *The Virtue of Selfishness*. New York: New American Library, 1964.

READINGS ON UTILITARIANISM: ACT UTILITARIANISM

Fletcher, Joseph. *Situation Ethics: The New Morality*. Philadelphia: Westminster Press, 1966.

READINGS ON UTILITARIANISM: RULE UTILITARIANISM

Ayer, A. J. "The Principle of Utility," *Philosophical Essays by A. J. Ayer*. New York: St. Martin's, 1955.

Bentham, Jeremy. *The Principles of Morals and Legislation*. Several editions.

Mill, John Stuart. *Utilitarianism: With Critical Essays,* ed. Samuel Gorovitz. Indianapolis: Boss-Merrill, 1971.

Narveson, Jan. *Morality and Utility*. Baltimore: Johns Hopkins, 1967.

Smart, J. J. C. *Outlines of a Utilitarianism System of Ethics*. London: Cambridge University Press, 1961.

READINGS ON RULE NONSEQUENTIALISM

Kant, Immanuel. *Fundamental Principles of the Metaphysics of Morals,* 9th ed. New York: Longmans, Green, 1923.

————. "The Supreme Principle of Morality," *The Range of Ethics,* eds. Harold H. Titus and Morris Keeton. New York: D. Van Nostrand, 1966

Korner, Stephen. *Kant.* Baltimore: Pelican, 1955.

Paton, Herbert J. *The Categorical Imperative: A Study in Kant's Moral Philosophy.* Chicago: University of Chicago Press, 1948.

Ross, Sir William David. *The Right and the Good.* London: Oxford University Press, 1931.

————. *The Foundations of Ethics.* Oxford: Clarendon Press, 1939.

————. *Kant's Ethical Theory.* New York: Oxford University Press, 1954.

Shwayder, D. S. "The Sense of Duty." *Philosophy Quarterly* 7 (1957): 116–125.

Thiroux, Jacques P. *Ethics: Theory and Practice,* 2nd ed. Encino, Calif.: Glencoe Press, 1980.

CHAPTER 8

A Crucial Moral Issue: The Taking of Human Life

This chapter is designed to present one important moral issue in several of its aspects since all moral issues cannot be dealt with in only one section of an introductory text on philosophy. I would refer you to my earlier-mentioned text as well as to other texts listed in the bibliography at the end of this chapter, which deal only with ethics if you wish to delve deeper into other moral issues, such as human sexuality, lying, cheating, and breaking promises. The issue that will be dealt with here will be the taking of human life, which constitutes a violation of the first and primary principle that was presented in Chapter 7. The aspects of this issue I will deal with will include defense of the innocent and self-defense, abortion, and euthanasia and allowing people to die. The approach to all these will be similar in that the basic problem or issue will be presented, any key terms will be defined, and any important distinctions that have to be made first will be made, and the most common arguments for and against the issue will be presented, leaving the critical examination and evaluation of the issues to you, your classmates, and your instructor.

Definitions and Distinctions

As with any important issue, it is necessary to define key terms to be used in discussing it and also to make any necessary distinctions to eliminate as much confusion as possible.

KILLING AND MURDER

Killing means to put to death, slay, deprive of life, put an end to or extinguish, so that any ending of a person's life that is caused by another or oneself would be considered a killing. However, a person can also be killed by an object, such as a building collapsing, or an event, such as an earthquake or a hurricane, so that the cause would have to be determined carefully before the responsibility of any human being for a killing could be established.

Murder means the unlawful killing of one human being by another, especially with malice aforethought.[1]

Suicide is defined as an intentional taking of one's own life.[2]

Three other definitions or distinctions that should be made have to do with motives and circumstances surrounding any killing, and they often have a significant effect on what we determine to be the moral responsibility for any loss of human life.

Passion means that a killing or murder was done under extremely emotional circumstances. For example, if a wife has been abused and beaten by her husband over a long period of time and finally after one particularly severe beating loses control and, with great fear and anger, stabs him to death with a kitchen knife, this would be considered a crime of passion. Crimes of passion usually refer to those committed under intense emotional duress or strain.

Negligence in killing usually refers to some sort of carelessness on the part of someone that results in the death of someone else. A case where a driver who is in a hurry speeds through an intersection without making a stop hits another car and kills the driver would be an example of negligence. This is not a crime of passion, since the driver was not necessarily under emotional strain, nor is it premeditation since he did not plan to kill anyone.

Premeditation, then, is the thinking about and planning of the killing of another over a period of time before the act is finally committed. A situation in which a son who is in line for a big inheritance from his father's estate plots and plans to kill his father over a long period of time to get his inheritance and then does so would be an example of premeditation.

Usually, when assigning moral responsibility for an act of killing under these three conditions, one that has been premeditated is considered more immoral than is one due to negligence, and negligence is more immoral then is a killing due to passion. However, the responsibility may vary depending on the circumstances surrounding the act. For example, a person who is very emotionally or mentally disturbed, and who may not know right from wrong, may nevertheless carefully premeditate a murder. Also, the culpability for the death of someone due to negligence will depend on the extent of the negligence of the person responsible. Finally, even though a man kills another while extremely angry and emotional, it may be determined that the person was capable of controlling and should have controlled his anger at least to the point where he didn't do such severe harm to or kill the victim.

With these definitions and distinctions in mind, then, let us proceed with the aspects of killing, the first of which is that done in defense of the innocent, which includes self-defense.

Killing in Defense of the Innocent

Most people talk about killing in self-defense, but I prefer to expand upon this idea to include any killing that is done in the defense of any innocent person or persons, including oneself. It is, of course, important to define what "innocence" really means and to ensure that the person who is killing in defense of it is really innocent. A person who is innocent would generally be considered as "not responsible for or guilty of something wrong or unethical . . . not dangerous or harmful."[3] For example, if the husband who beats his wife kills her during a beating, he cannot be considered as having acted in defense of the innocent or self-defense since he was not innocent. On the other hand, when his wife during a beating killed him in trying to protect herself, what she did could be considered in defense of herself as an innocent person. Furthermore, any act taken against most children or handicapped people is considered an attack on innocent beings since these human beings are almost always considered helpless or innocent. Now the question is, "Is it ever morally justifiable to take someone's life in defense of the innocent?"

ARGUMENT FOR KILLING IN DEFENSE OF THE INNOCENT

This argument rests on two assumptions: (1) Even though the value of life principle advocates a reverence for human life, people have a right—some would say an obligation—to protect any innocent life, their own included, when it becomes clear that another human being, the killer, does not recognize the value of others' lives; and (2) the good of defending the innocent far outweighs the bad of killing a person who is threatening to kill or who actually does kill innocent people.

The essence of these two assumptions and the argument itself is that by threatening to kill or by actually killing others, perpetrators of such acts forfeit their rights to have their own lives considered as valuable, especially when their acts of killing cannot be prevented except by killing them. In other words, this argument would qualify the value of life principle, or rephrase it, so that it would state, "Human beings should not kill other human beings *except* in defense of the innocent, which includes themselves."

Proponents of this argument also come out against the pacifist position, which says violence and killing are always wrong, stating that it does not take into consideration all the complexities of human existence. They say that killing never is an admirable ideal, and most people adhere to this principle all their lives; but some humans—fortunately, a relatively small number—do not respect the lives of others, and innocent people, therefore, have the right to defend themselves and other innocent people against these killers.

ARGUMENT AGAINST KILLING IN DEFENSE OF THE INNOCENT

The argument against killing in defense of the innocent is based on the assumption that resorting to violence or taking human life is always wrong. This view is held by pacifists, Jainists (Jainism is an Eastern religion), and Kantian duty ethicists. Its advantage is that it is the most consistent ethical position possible in terms of following the value of life principle because it respects human life in all cases. According to this argument, all human life is to be revered and no one may ever be killed for any reason, even if one's life is threatened by another. If such a threat arises, people being threatened may do everything short of violence or killing to prevent their being killed, but they may not kill another even in self-defense or in defense of other innocent people.

Proponents of this argument would criticize the arguments for killing in defense of the innocent, stating that violence tends only to breed more violence and that once the killing of humans is allowed, even in defense of the innocent, no one knows where the violence will end (this is often referred to as the "domino argument": when dominoes are set up one behind the other, if you push the first one down, the next one will fall and then the next one, and so on).

Those who base their ethics on religion also argue that only God can create or take away life; therefore, killing is not the right of human beings under any circumstances. Their feeling is that the punishment of killers is God's province, not ours, and that punishing a killer by killing him only causes another immoral act and, as the old saying goes, "Two wrongs don't make a right."

Since both the domino and religious arguments will arise again in other aspects of taking of human life, it is important to evaluate them now.

THE DOMINO ARGUMENT.   Basically this argument has a good point because it causes us to be concerned about the effects of our moral decisions or acts in a more long-range sense. For example, if we are considering making laws against abortion or suicide less restrictive, will we cause other dominoes to fall that we really do not want down, such as mercy killing? In other words, by allowing one aspect of killing to become unrestricted, are we opening the door to letting all killing become so? It is always important to try to gauge the effects of our moral choices, decisions, actions, and rules or laws, but where there is no definite or conclusive proof that one thing *necessarily* leads to another, we should not use this argument as the *only* reason for not allowing something, such as killing in defense of the innocent. For example, there is no conclusive proof that when killing in defense of the innocent or in self-defense is allowed, any other type of killing is condoned or allowed. Most of our laws against killing will make allowances for these two types of killing, and yet there are still laws against mercy killing, for example, even if the "victim" requests it.

Furthermore, when rules or laws allowing some sort of taking of human life are written, specific exclusions of what we do not want to allow can be made, or if a domino effect occurs later, a new law can be written to forbid what is unacceptable. For example, when California's Natural Death Act was written, allowing people to refuse artificial life support and die if they wished to (once they were determined to be terminal), a clause was included to state that in no way was this act to be considered as condoning or permitting any sort of direct act to end a person's life.[4] In another example, even though our legal system found it difficult to have strict laws against pornography when a domino effect occurred because not only adults but children were used for pornographic purposes, a new law prohibiting the use of children in pornographic activities *was* passed. Therefore, although the domino argument works well as a cautionary measure in our moral decision making, it should not be the sole reason that something cannot be allowed.

THE RELIGIOUS ARGUMENT.   This argument, as described earlier, basically states that only God has the authority to give and take away life and that human beings are only loaned their lives to live as well, morally, and religiously as they can; they do not, under any circumstances, have the right to choose death for themselves or others. The first problem with this argument is that it would not be fair to apply this restriction to those who are not religious or who do not accept a particular religion that forbids ever taking human life. Second, it is scientifically, philosophically, and even theologically questionable that a supernatural being, if it exists, is constantly intervening and interfering in the affairs of the world. Is it really true that only God gives and takes away life? When a child is conceived, is not the cause of its conception the psychological desires and the biological actions of its parents?

When someone is allowed to die or is killed, are these acts done by God? Suppose, for example, someone, unable to make decisions, is dying of cancer and the doctors and relatives are trying to decide whether to give the patient extraordinary treatment or allow him to die? Is God making whatever choice is finally decided upon? If the people involved decide not to treat, are they really leaving the patient in God's hands? It would seem, rather, that they have decided to allow the patient to die and, therefore, must accept the responsibility for that decision. If you carry these assumptions far enough, you will have to blame God for the deaths of victims at others' hands as well as for the birth of a baby.

Daniel Callahan summarizes the extreme weakness of the argument that only God creates and ends life as follows:

> [This view] presupposes that God intervenes directly in natural and human affairs as the primary causative agent of life and death. Not only is this theologically dubious, it also has the effect of obscuring the necessity that human beings define terms, make decisions and take responsibility for the direct care of human life. Moreover, to say that God is the ultimate source of the "right to life," which is less objectionable theologically, still does not solve the problem of *how* human beings ought to respect that right or how they are to balance a conflict of rights.[5]

Therefore, even if people are religious, this argument is a very questionable one and in itself is not really sufficient to not allow people to die or even to not allow killing under certain circumstances.

CONCLUSION—IS IT MORAL TO KILL IN DEFENSE OF THE INNOCENT OR NOT?

After reading these arguments for and against killing in defense of the innocent, what is *your* decision? At this point, you should decide whether or not you deem this act as moral or not and under what conditions you would or would not allow it, given your particular ethical system. You should present your arguments and evidence to support your decision as fully as you can. In addition to stating your arguments as completely as you can, decide the morality of killing in the following situations:

SITUATION 1

Over the past two years, Barbara's husband, who drinks a lot, has been beating and abusing her. He has also beaten their children and has often threatened to kill all of them if they didn't act the way he wanted them to. On a Saturday night late he comes home extremely drunk, wakes them all up, and begins to beat Barbara and slap the children; he again threatens them all with death and starts to head toward the youngest child's room. Barbara, fearing for her life and the lives of her children, picks up a heavy doorstop and hits her husband on the back of his head and kills him. Was her act moral? Why or why not?

SITUATION 2

Tom, who owns a liquor store that has been robbed several times notices a teenager, sixteen or seventeen years old, head toward the door with a bulge under his coat that Tom knows to be merchandise. Tom yells at the boy to stop, but the boy starts out the door and begins to run down the street. Tom takes out a gun he keeps under the counter, runs out into the street, and fires three times into the retreating back of the teenager and kills him. Was what Tom did right? Why or why not? Notice that this is a killing in defense of property rather than innocent lives—does this fact make any difference in your considerations? Would there be a difference if the teenager were armed and had held Tom up? How important are property rights when they conflict with human life? Develop your answers in detail.

SITUATION 3

Elena is accosted by two men in an alley and is held by each while the other rapes her. Afterward, the two men escape, but Elena knows that they hang around a local bar. She gets her brother's gun from home, goes to the bar, and wounds one of the men but kills the other before patrons in the bar can stop her. She feels that she has acted in defense of herself as an innocent person, but the law charges her with murder, saying that since she shot the man about an hour after she had been raped, her act must be considered as premeditated and therefore murder rather than self-defense. Do you feel her act was morally justified or not? What difference would it have made if she had somehow been able to kill the man during or right after he had raped her? Can she logically claim self-defense or defense of the innocent an hour after the commission of the crime? Why or why not?

SITUATION 4

A wealthy farmer, who has been heard saying that he hates young "hippy" types with beards and long hair who camp out where his farm is located, is driving at night when he spots a car stopped in the road ahead that he knows belongs to two young men he has seen in the area. Since he cannot get by, he stops his truck, takes down the rifle he always keeps in his cab, and gets out of the truck. The two doors of the car open and the two men get out and come toward him. He can see that they have been drinking, and they start swearing about their situation and at him. They are both taller than he is, and he tells them to get back into the car and move it. They tell him they cannot, and if he doesn't like it, why doesn't he give them a push. He tells them again angrily to move the car, but they still keep coming toward him. As they approach, he shoots and kills them both. When the police arrive, he tells them he shot the two in self-defense and that he thought they were going to do him harm. When asked whether or not the men were armed, he replies that he didn't see any weapons in their hands or on their persons. Is what he did a moral act; why or why not? What do you feel the criteria for killing in self-defense or defense of the innocent should be? why? Suggest some examples when defense of the innocent is justifiable and when it is not.

Capital Punishment

Capital punishment is defined as the infliction of the death penalty for certain crimes.[6] These crimes, usually called "capital crimes," have varied, depending on the culture and times, from stealing to murder. Generally in the United States and Western Europe, capital crimes are murder, especially premeditated murder, kidnapping with intent to do bodily harm or kill someone, and sometimes treason, especially when it is determined to endanger the lives of the people of a nation. A capital crime, then, is usually considered so serious that the penalty for committing it should be death (capital punishment). This type of punishment in earlier days and cultures was used much more frequently and commonly than it is today. In the last twenty-five to fifty years in the United States and in other countries around the world, capital punishment has been thought, on the one hand, to be a barbaric, uncivilized way of dealing with serious crime, but on the other hand, many people have demanded its more frequent use, saying that it is the only fair and effective punishment for serious crimes. Obviously, then, it has been and is a very controversial moral issue as we shall see when we examine the arguments for and against it.

ARGUMENTS FOR CAPITAL PUNISHMENT

EFFECTIVE DETERRENT ARGUMENT.   People who argue for capital punishment claim that it is the only effective deterrent to serious crime. They argue with irrefutable logic that if a killer is put to death, he at least will never kill again. They also argue that, in a general sense, capital punishment acts as a deterrent for any criminal who may be contemplating a serious crime; in other words, they say that if a society has capital punishment, capital crimes will decrease. They point out that the reason that serious crime is on the increase is that we presently do not have effective and enforced capital punishment but instead have weak and ineffective jail and so-called "life sentences" from which many killers can be paroled after seven years, letting them out to perpetrate more serious crimes on innocent people.

ECONOMIC ARGUMENT.   They argue further that the cost of keeping killers in prison, even if they stay in for life, is prohibitive and that innocent taxpayers should not have to support anyone who has committed such a crime. If these killers are sentenced for a long while, they are usually not rehabilitated even though innocent people, who could become their future victims, have paid millions of dollars to keep them in prison. Basically, killers are not considered worthy of continued living and certainly not at taxpayers' expense.

RETRIBUTION.   Many people argue that the Old Testament saying, "An eye for an eye, a tooth for a tooth," should be followed in that it is only just that someone who has killed another should be paid back by being killed himself. In this way and only in this way can justice be done—if you kill me, then someone else (presumably the state) should kill you. Notice that this is not the same definition of justice that I discussed in the previous chapter. This is "retributive" justice, or justice based on avenging one crime with another similar one. The principle of justice, on the other hand, dealt with "distributive" justice or the proper distribution of goodness or badness rather than getting even.

FORFEITURE OF RIGHTS.   Another argument following upon the retribution argument is that killers, having violated both morality and the law, have forfeited their rights to be treated ethically and therefore their lives should not be valued, nor should killing them be considered immoral. Further, proponents of capital punishment would argue that it is just another form of defense of the innocent, except that it applies to the whole society. Just as individuals have the right to protect themselves against killers who threaten their lives and the lives of other innocent people, so has society the right to protect itself against anyone who has killed once by ensuring that he or she does not kill again. Therefore, by killing, one forfeits all rights to have his or her life valued.

ARGUMENTS AGAINST CAPITAL PUNISHMENT

VIOLATION OF THE VALUE OF LIFE PRINCIPLE.   Many argue against capital punishment on the grounds that it is a direct violation of the value of life principle. They maintain that capital punishment amounts to murder—social murder—directed by society against one of its members and that if taking human life is wrong in other instances, then it is also wrong in this instance. All capital punishment does is provide for retribution and revenge, which are considered by many people as primitive and barbaric in a civilized society. In a religious sense, they continue, the Old Testament retribution has been replaced by the New Testament teachings of Jesus, which say to "love your enemy" and "turn the other cheek." This implies that there should be no automatic forfeiture of rights even of criminals and that compassion must be applied in cases even where people commit heinous crimes.

Also, since killing criminals will not bring back their victims or in any way recompense the survivors of the victims, there is really no purpose in taking the criminal's life except to satisfy society's need for revenge. Opponents of capital punishment feel that this is not a civilized emotion and that all this type of punishment does is to encourage violence and murder in society at large.

INEFFECTIVENESS AS A DETERRENT.   Opponents of capital punishment attack the deterrent argument, stating that there is no conclusive evidence to support its claim. They point to history in support of their argument, stating that when capital punishment was used against thieves in England, pickpockets were operating throughout crowds of watchers who had gathered to see a thief hanged. They also question why, if this punishment works so well as a deterrent, executions by hangings, firing squads, and gas chambers are not shown on television or performed in the streets instead of being done in the relative privacy of prisons, and why is the entire populace not required to watch all executions? They point further to the fact that killings occur even in prison, right outside the execution chamber; therefore, they state, capital punishment does not, as its proponents proclaim, act as an effective deterrent to serious crime.

INEQUALITY OF CAPITAL PUNISHMENT.   Sometimes people accused of capital crimes are convicted mainly on circumstantial evidence, and it is therefore quite possible to execute an innocent person. If even one innocent person is executed, this argument continues, then capital punishment is a moral wrong. Furthermore, since rich people who are charged with capital crimes can afford better attorneys, the people most often convicted of capital crimes are poor people, many times members of minorities, such as blacks, Chicanos, and native Americans. This means that punishment by killing may be applied unequally to people who commit similar crimes. It is true that such inequality exists at all levels of justice, but at least the punishment for these lesser crimes is not death, and an exconvict, after release, has a chance to go on with this life.

DENIAL OF REHABILITATION.   This argument states that nothing is accomplished by capital punishment except the compounding of the badness already caused by the original crime: instead of one human life being lost, through capital punishment, there are now two. Wouldn't it be better for society to try to eliminate killing by reforming killers through education and other methods of rehabilitation? The opponents of capital punishment argue further that most killers have been shaped by a corrupt society or a poor early environment (child abusing parents, for example) and that if we could only reeducate them, they could become useful members of society.

CONCLUSION—IS CAPITAL PUNISHMENT MORAL OR IMMORAL?

Capital punishment has become extremely controversial in recent years because of the rise in serious crime, due to many factors such as overpopulation and overcrowding in our cities. This has caused greater poverty and frustration and anxiety, which has often led to violence. Further, with all the crowding of the courts and confusion within our legal system, many criminals have pleaded guilty to lesser charges (plea bargaining) and been released within a few years even after they have killed someone. In addition, life sentences have not meant life at all but often only five to ten years after which a killer is released, some of whom return to crime and kill again. Taxpayers have begun to balk at the costs of maintaining criminals in prison and the inefficiency (they feel) of rehabilitation and the inability of our legal system to prevent recurrence of serious crime.

The main problem seems to be that in the minds of many citizens, there just isn't a suitable alternative to eliminating at least more serious crime through the use of capital punishment. How, then, do you feel about this issue? You should now examine arguments on both sides of the issue very carefully and present your own arguments for or against it. Whichever side you choose, be sure to answer the criticisms of the other side and also to attack their arguments as well. If you choose to oppose capital punishment, then be sure to present alternatives so that the safety of innocent people is insured while the lives of capital criminals may still be protected. In addition, examine and critically evaluate the following situations.

SITUATION 1

In the famous Leopold and Loeb case, two intellectual college students kidnapped and killed a young boy for ransom money and as part of an intellectual game. They were caught, tried, and convicted and were to be sentenced to death, but the famous Clarence Darrow argued intensely and effectively for life imprisonment rather than the death penalty. While in prison, one of the killers was himself killed in a fight, but the other became a model prisoner, completing his college education, teaching other convicts, and even volunteering for possible life-threatening experiments by allowing himself to be injected with malaria germs to test out new drugs and treatment. After about twenty or thirty years, he was paroled, moved to another country, and continued to teach until his death.

Do you believe that this man should have been given capital punishment as had been originally intended, or do you feel that the greater good was served by allowing him to live? Why? If even one killer can be rehabilitated, do you think capital punishment should be abolished? Why or why not? Is there any way you would suggest how to weed out the people who can be rehabilitated from those who cannot?

SITUATION 2

Glenn, who had been abandoned by his parents when he was five, was constantly in and out of trouble, was moved from one foster home to another, then to various reformatories, and then to prison at eighteen where he was involved in several acts of violence with other prisoners, even killing one of them. After serving twenty-five years, he was finally paroled, got a job, and married a woman who had been visiting him in prison for several years. After being out of prison for six months, he assaulted and raped a woman, who identified him, after which he was tried, convicted, and sent back to prison.

Statements by Glenn and several psychologists and sociologists asserted that Glenn was the way he was because of his previous life and because his societal situation had made him that way. Since he seems to be unrehabilitatable, what should be done with him? Capital punishment? life imprisonment without parole? a long but determinate sentence like he had before? What can be done about society's responsibility for allowing him to become unrehabilitatable? Should he ever be allowed out into society again? If so, under what conditions? If not, why not?

SITUATION 3

Caryl Chessman was tried and convicted of crimes of kidnapping and rape. At the time in California, kidnapping was punishable by death, and Chessman was given the death penalty. He consistently claimed that he was innocent of any of the activities ascribed to the "red light bandit" (so named because the bandit used to shine a red light into the cars pretending he was a policeman; then he would beat and tie up the men and take the women away to another area— thus the charge of kidnapping—and rape them). No one was ever killed during any of these crimes, but one of the women raped was so damaged psychologically that she had to be placed in a mental institution. Even though Chessman had lived a life of crime, he claimed complete innocence as far as being the red light bandit and claimed not to have done any of those crimes. He spent twelve years on Death Row in San Quentin, staving off his execution, writing and having published two books about prison life, and generally studying his own criminality. He never showed any remorse or regret for the life he had lived, but he claimed that he had been convicted on circumstantial evidence. Finally, his appeals ran out, and the governor of California refused to commute his sentence. He was executed in the gas chamber.

Many people argued that he never should have been executed because (1) he never killed anyone, (2) he was convicted on mostly circumstantial evidence, (3) he proved himself to be an intelligent person who was rehabilitatable since he had learned a great deal about the law and was capable of writing books good enough to publish, and (4) he would have been a good person to study in order to learn about what caused him to be a criminal.

Do you think he should have been given capital punishment? Why or why not? Do you think kidnapping should be punishable by death? Would it have made any difference to your decision if someone had been killed in the commission of these crimes? Why or why not? If he had shown remorse or regret for the life he had led, would that have made any difference to you? Do you feel that the fact that he was intelligent, had studied law, and had written and published books should have made any difference in deciding whether to put him to death or not? Why?

Abortion

GENERAL STATEMENT OF THE PROBLEM

Abortion means the premature termination of a pregnancy prior to birth. A *spontaneous abortion* is the same thing as a miscarriage, whereas an *induced abortion* is caused either by the woman herself or by another, usually nowadays a medical doctor. In the latter case, it is often referred to as a *therapeutic abortion,* meaning that it is to be done for the woman's health or at least it is a medical procedure to be performed at the woman's request.

At the center of this issue are two major principles that we have previously discussed: (1) the value of life principle, obviously involving the unborn "conceptus," but also involving the quality of life of the woman; and (2) the principle of individual freedom, applying to the woman's rights over her own body and procreativity.[7] There are also two extreme sides to this issue: (1) the strong pro-life position, which holds that from conception onward, the conceptus is fully a human being, child, or person with all rights accorded any already born human being and whose life has equal value with any already born person; and (2) the strong pro-choice position, which states that an actual human being does not exist with full value and rights until birth and that until that time, the pregnant woman has rights that supersede the conceptus' rights until it is born.

One of the greatest difficulties faced in trying to discuss and resolve moral issues surrounding abortion is that both extremes consider the rights of their position to be absolute. When certain rights are considered absolute, there are *no* other rights whatsoever that can take precedence. The strong pro-life position states that the conceptus (they would probably say "child" or "person") has an absolute right to life, and this means that the woman has no rights at all that can be allowed to interfere with this absolute right. At the other extreme, the strong pro-choice position states that women have absolute rights over their bodies and lives and that the conceptus, until it is born, has no rights at all that can be allowed to interfere with women's rights.

As long as these rights are set forth as absolute, there is no compromise possible or any possibility of the two extremes meeting somewhere in the middle, and this means that there are only two choices: either abortion is completely wrong and should never be done or it is totally right and it can be done anytime. There are, of course, more moderate positions, such as allowing abortion under certain circumstances, but not under others, and limiting the period of pregnancy during which abortions may be performed. These will be discussed later. The main point to consider, however, is that when absolutes are held and enforced, there can be no compromises.

THE LEGAL STATUS OF ABORTION IN THE UNITED STATES

At the present time, and since 1973 when the U.S. Supreme Court ruled most state laws prohibiting abortion unconstitutional, abortion is essentially legal in the United States. The Court's ruling was that no state could prohibit a woman from getting an abortion up to the point of the viability of the conceptus. "Viability" is defined as that point in gestation when the conceptus could conceivably live outside of the mother's womb, generally to be considered when the period of gestation reaches the twenty-eighth week or later. States may pass laws restricting abortion after that time for the protection of the pregnant woman. Notice that hardly any consideration is given to the conceptus' rights and that the Court purposely did not rule on its status as a human being, saying that science, philosophy, or religion could not seem to come to any conclusions on this issue, so therefore the law could not decide such a matter on the basis of legality alone.

The abortion issue presents an excellent example where morality and the law are not necessarily the same, as described in the previous chapter. It would seem that, generally speaking, most Americans do not believe that abortions should be restricted by law; otherwise, such a decision by the Supreme Court would probably not have been made. However, there should be no doubt in anyone's mind who reads newspapers, watches television, or listens to the radio that many people are totally against abortion and believe that it is a form of murder of innocent human beings and therefore extremely immoral. This group, the strong pro-life people mentioned earlier, has succeeded in restricting federal funding for abortions, has campaigned against and defeated political candidates who have been pro-choice and pro-abortion, and is now striving to change the U.S. Constitution so that a human being and citizen is declared so from the moment of conception onward. Therefore, even though abortion is essentially legal, it is considered highly immoral by a large group in our society, and therefore it is not a dead moral issue at all.

WHEN DOES HUMAN LIFE BEGIN?

The strong pro-life position, as mentioned, believes in what is called the "genetic view" of when human life begins; that is, as soon as the female ovum is fertilized by the male sperm and the cells begin to divide, this view states, there is a human being present with all rights and values given any already born human being. On the other hand, the strong pro-choice position states that no human being, worthy of being valued and given rights on its own, is present until birth or very close to it. The interesting part of this controversy is that the biological facts are the same no matter which view one holds or even if one holds a different view somewhere in between the two extremes.

WHAT HAPPENS FROM CONCEPTION ONWARD?   After the ovum is fertilized, it becomes a single-cell zygote and after a day or so begins the process of cellular cleavage into first two cells, then four, then eight, and so on. During this process, the twenty-three chromosomes of the father are combined with the twenty-three of the mother to make the normal set of forty-six or twenty-three pairs that constitute the complete genetic makeup of every human being. Various cellular activity takes place during the first two zygotic weeks of gestation. From the second to the seventh weeks, when the conceptus is called an embryo, the fundamental body plan is established, the cardiovascular system begins to function, the foundation of all organ systems is established, and by the fifth week a face begins to appear along with primitive limb buds and brain vesicles. By the sixth week, a full complement of primitive organs is present; by the seventh week, the embryo will react to stimulation; and by the eighth week, when the conceptus is called a fetus (from now until its birth), there is discernible electrical activity in the brain. By the tenth week reflex activities are noticeable and the conceptus moves spontaneously without external stimulation; during the eleventh and twelfth weeks, its skeleton can be X-rayed, its heart can be picked up on an electrocardiograph, and its brain structure is essentially complete. Between the thirteenth and sixteenth weeks, the woman can usually feel the conceptus move. Birth usually occurs between the thirty-ninth and fortieth weeks.[8]

THE INTERPRETATION OF THESE DATA.   As has been said, these data remain the same, regardless of how we feel about the process or its result, but how are we to interpret them to decide when human life begins? We will have to consider the term *potentiality* as important, because we cannot deny that once conception and cellular division have begun, the conceptus has to be considered a human being *in potential-*

ity, at least. If allowed to progress without interruption, this active cell will not mature into a dog, cat, or oak tree; it will become a human baby with the full potential to grow into adulthood. The important question is when should it be considered an *actual,* rather than a potential, human being, and more important, when is it to be valued to the same extent as a baby that is already born?

The strong pro-life position believes it is to be valued from conception; the strong pro-choice position says from birth. If one feels that abortion in any way might be considered as murder, then the genetic view is the safest position to hold because the conceptus' life is protected completely even to the exclusion of the rights of the woman who is carrying it. On the other hand, in the strong pro-choice position, the woman's rights are protected and the conceptus is not to be considered her equal in value unless she chooses to give it such value.

THE DEVELOPMENTAL VIEW.   If we do not choose to accept either extreme of when human life begins because they *are* extreme, then at what point shall we decide to value the conceptus? as soon as its heart is formed and starts beating? when brain activity can be recorded? when its body is fully formed? when it begins to react to stimulation, show reflex activity, or move on its own? An argument could be presented for each of these points in the conceptus' development, but how can we decide?

Daniel Callahan and Sissela Bok have both described what is called the developmental view of human beingness.[9] This view essentially states that the conceptus is to be valued from conception onward but that its value increases as it develops, so that abortions done early in pregnancy may be permitted but they should be limited more and more as the conceptus develops and becomes more valuable because it is approaching full human beingness. Bok's position on abortion, based on this view of when human life begins, is that abortions may be allowed for any reason up to twelve weeks, or the first trimester of pregnancy, although they should be avoided where at all possible since human life is present in potential. From the thirteenth to the twenty-eighth weeks, abortion should only be allowed for very important reasons, such as severe malformation of the conceptus or to save the mother's life. After the twenty-eighth week, they should not be allowed unless the mother's life is definitely and actually in danger so that she would lose it if she were to go through with the pregnancy.

This view, although unacceptable to both extremes, provides a possible compromise for the rights of both conceptus and woman but limits those rights so that neither is automatically excluded from moral consideration. With all these possibilities in mind, let us look now at the most common reasons given for abortion and the arguments for and against them.

MEDICAL REASONS

One of the strongest reasons given for permitting abortion is endangerment to the health and, more important, the possible death of the woman if she goes through with her pregnancy. With our tremendous advances in medical procedures and technology, of course, such dangers have lessened a great deal, especially where sophisticated medical care is available, such as in large cities where modern medical centers exist. The conclusions of medical research into the major diseases or medical problems that can be seriously aggravated by pregnancy to the point of dangerously threatening the mother's health or life, cited by Callahan, are only a few: ulcerative colitis, chronic nephritis, and cancer of the bowel. This does not mean that there is no danger in a diabetic, epileptic, cardiovascular, or pulmonary disease–affected woman, but except for these cases, women can usually be brought safely through their pregnancies.

It is important to note, however, that the opinions on medical problems will vary from doctor to doctor and from hospital to hospital, so that a woman's doctor, trying to protect her health and life may advise her not to take any risks that he may consider too serious. Further, the woman and her family may also not wish to go through a pregnancy in which there is, for example, a 50 percent risk to her health and life. It would seem that when "push comes to shove," the mother's life is generally valued more by most people over the life of the conceptus. Therefore, medical reasons still can provide a valid reason for not continuing with a pregnancy, although they are not as powerful as they once were.

DANGERS OF ABORTION VERSUS DANGERS OF PREGNANCY.   The strong pro-life advocates state, as one might expect, that abortion is dangerous to the woman—much more dangerous than is going through with a pregnancy. The strong pro-choice people, on the other hand—again as one might expect—declare that abortion is basically a safe procedure and is much less dangerous to a woman than is going through a pregnancy. As we have seen, most women these days can be brought safely through a pregnancy even when they are suffering from a disease or some other physical problem. It is true, however, that during pregnancy, a woman goes through many hormonal changes that are bound to affect her entire physical being, and repeated pregnancies are bound to take their toll on a woman physically. Therefore, pregnancy is not a "piece of cake" nor, however, is it for most women a threat to health or life. Many women, for example, claim that, after the first three months, they were their healthiest during pregnancy; many others have discomfort and difficult times.

Abortion, too, seems neither to be as simple as the removal of a hangnail nor a grave danger to a woman when done in a sanitary medical setting under the care of a competent physician. To examine the risks of abortion, it is important to see what is involved in the procedure. Basically, there are two types of abortion performed these days, and they are as follows:[10]

1. *Uterine aspiration.* This method has generally replaced the old D & C (dilatation and currettage) method because it is safer, relying on plastic suctioning rather than on scalpel-like scraping of the woman's womb. In this method, a suction machine (aspirator), which consists of a plastic instrument at the end of a hose, is used to "aspirate" or suction off the conceptus and related material. There are possibilities of infection, but this method has less chance than does the D & C of perforating the walls of the uterus.

2. *Saline abortion.* This procedure is usually preferred and performed during later pregnancies (after the twelfth week). In this procedure, a needle is inserted through the abdominal wall of the woman into the amniotic sac where the conceptus is floating. Some of the amniotic fluid is drawn off and is replaced by a saline, glucose, or prostiglandin solution. Usually in about 20 hours, the uterus begins to contract and the woman goes into labor and then generally delivers a dead fetus. There is, of course, always some danger inherent in the injection of such substances into the amniotic sac. Also, even though the doctor performs the abortion procedure, he or she is not usually present during delivery, which causes problems when and if complications arise.

The conclusions of the researchers that Callahan cites in his book are that hospital-performed abortions are relatively safe but should not be undertaken lightly.[11] The possible effects of abortion on future pregnancies are the greater chance of miscarriages, inflammatory complications, possible sterility, and disturbance of the menstrual cycle. Also, risks are greater when the abortion is done later in pregnancy; when it is a first pregnancy, especially of a young girl; and when repeated abortions are performed. Generally speaking, however, abortion is a relatively safe medical procedure when done under proper conditions.

Therefore, medical reasons, including the risks in both carrying a conceptus to term or aborting it, should definitely be considered and not taken lightly in either situation, but they should not be considered as automatic reasons for either abortion or continuing pregnancy.

PSYCHOLOGICAL REASONS

Another set of reasons given for the need for abortion is psychological in nature, and therefore arguments for or against are much harder to substantiate. However, there are several areas involving both pregnancy and abortion that are worth investigating.

THREATS OF SUICIDE. Of course, threats of suicide or suicide attempts are to be taken seriously under any conditions. Women who claim to be so overwrought by pregnancy that they threaten or attempt to commit suicide certainly ought to be taken seriously and helped in every way possible including the consideration of abortion if their threats and attempts seem to be unresolvable any other way. However, from all research done on this issue, Callahan reports that "While a number of psychiatrists stress the *possibility* of suicide, on the basis of some threats and some genuine attempts, the evidence of the actual incidence of suicide suggests that it is in fact very rare."[12]

UNWANTED PREGNANCY OR UNWANTED CHILD. The basic reason probably for most desires for abortion is that both the pregnancy itself and the child are just not wanted. These may seem redundant, but they are really not, since a woman could go through a pregnancy without having to raise a child. Obviously the way a woman feels about pregnancy has to do with her general psychological attitude. No one, except a woman who has gone through pregnancy, knows what a joy, at times, and what a burden, at others, pregnancy can be. Many people, especially men, consider that pregnancy is merely a woman's lot and that she should be willing to go through it because it is the most natural of occurrences in her life. However, pregnancy, as I stated earlier, involves many hormonal and other physical changes to a woman's body. It also causes psychological changes and the ability to deal with these depends on many factors, such as the support of her husband and family, her own self-image, and her general situation at the time. The main point I want to stress here is that pregnancy should not be taken lightly, nor is the difficulty of the woman in going through it to be minimized, especially by people well past childbearing age, celibates, or other disinterested persons who have no intention of supporting the woman and her child either emotionally or economically.

By the same token, many women, when first discovering they are pregnant and in the first three months of pregnancy when morning sickness and other difficulties seem to be more prevalent, may be very upset that they are pregnant, but after this period is over manage to adjust well to both their pregnancy and the future of raising a child. What is important, where a woman is considering abortion or is undecided whether or not to go through with the pregnancy, is to provide careful and supportive counseling to help her through this period.

Another argument states that no unwanted child should be brought into a world that is already suffering from overpopulation and in which many other factors make it extremely difficult to raise a child. One question that pro-life people ask and rightly so is, "Unwanted by whom?" They declare that the child may indeed be unwanted by the mother who is to give it birth but that there are many potential adoptive parents by whom her child would definitely be wanted; in fact, since the Supreme Court issued its ruling, the availability of infants for adoption has definitely and dramatically lessened, especially in the largest desirable group—white male babies.

The pregnant woman would answer that she would still have to go through nine months of pregnancy, which is not easy, and then have to give up a baby instead of a fetus, which would be harder and more psychologically damaging for her. Another argument against this is that adoptive children do not always do as well as wanted natural children because of psychological insecurity due to their feelings of rejection by their natural mothers. It is certainly true that many adopted children do just fine, but many others, as evidenced by their restless search for their natural mothers and often difficult psychological adjustments, do not. Perhaps this is not as important as the alternative of aborting them, but none of these factors should be overlooked.

RAPE OR INCEST.   One of the strongest arguments put forth for abortion is that it should be allowed whenever a conception occurs because of rape or incest. Except for the strongest pro-life advocates, most people will allow for abortion when pregnancy occurs as a result of either of these. The argument is that there has been such psychological damage to the woman as a result of either of these two actions that she should not have to be forced to go through a pregnancy at all or bear a child conceived under such circumstances. The counterargument by the strong pro-life advocates is that these actions account for a very few pregnancies, and if the woman reports the occurrence soon enough, pregnancy can be prevented.

However, even if she gets pregnant in these ways, it is unfair for her to penalize the "fetus-child" for an act over which he or she had no control and murder him or her. The pro-choice advocates say that at least the woman should be able to make her own choice and decision here, since she has been through a terrible experience and only she knows how it is affecting and probably will affect her if she goes through with her pregnancy. There is one more psychological problem, which I will discuss later under fetal reasons for abortion, and that is the psychological effect of continuing a pregnancy when defects are known to be present in the conceptus or in giving birth to such a child.

PSYCHOLOGICAL EFFECTS OF ABORTION.   Pro-life advocates in discussing abortion cite the adverse psychological effects to the woman of going through an abortion, stating that they are and can be much worse than any psychological discomfort of going through a pregnancy. They describe the guilt feelings that women who choose abortion must feel knowing they have in essence murdered an innocent child. The regrets and remorse they must feel, the argument goes on, would far outweigh going through a pregnancy and either giving their child up for adoption to a good, loving family or keeping and raising the child themselves. At least women will be able to say, no matter how difficult it is to do either of these, that they have done nothing to take the life of an innocent human being, nor would they have to live with the guilt of such an act for the rest of their lives. Living with such guilt is bound to do psychological damage to any woman, and it is important that she be counseled about this possibility before she goes through with the abortion she may regret for the rest of her life.

Pro-choice advocates argue that it is not true that most women feel guilt that is long-lasting and powerful enough to cause them psychological damage of any consequence. In fact, they say, many women do not feel any guilt whatsoever and would have felt more guilt if they had brought a child into the world in less than optimum circumstances. Further, any guilt feelings that might or do arise can be alleviated by emotional support from family, friends, or, where needed, professional counseling.

In conclusion, as with medical reasons, psychological reasons concerning pregnancy and abortion are important and should not be ignored. More and more, health and well-being are considered to include psychological as well as physical aspects, and there is no doubt that anything in a woman's life as significant as pregnancy or abortion is bound to have an important effect on her body, mind, and life. But here again such reasons should not, without careful examination, be considered as automatically ruling out either going through with pregnancy or having an abortion.

FETAL REASONS

Another important set of reasons often given for abortion are those that concern the possible birth of a defective or deformed child. In the past, such conditions have only been suspected because of a pregnant woman's being exposed to German measles, having taken some drug known to give rise to birth defects, such as thalidomide, or having been exposed to radiation. At the present, however, due to advancements in medical technology, a procedure exists whereby a pregnant woman and her husband can be sure whether or not their child will be born with certain deformities, and this can be done prior to birth, when abortion can be performed.

AMNIOCENTESIS.   The procedure just mentioned is called "amniocentesis" and can be performed after the sixteenth week of pregnancy. The first part of the procedure is exactly the same as that used for saline abortions. A needle is inserted into the amniotic sac, and some of the amniotic fluid is withdrawn. It has been discovered that conceptuses shed dead cells into this fluid, which, when tested through a method called "karyotyping," reveals a great deal of information about the conceptus' genetic and chromosomal structure, and whether the conceptus has such defects as Down's syndrome (causing severe mental retardation) or Tay-Sachs disease (a progressively degenerative and terrible disease that sometimes occurs in the fetuses of Eastern European Jews), among others. Other information, such as the sex of the conceptus, can also be revealed. At the present, about 200 pieces of information about the conceptus can be garnered, and hopes are that the amount and type of information will increase dramatically in the future. The one problem with this procedure is that it has to be done late in pregnancy, and then it takes another four to six weeks to acquire the necessary information because that is how long it takes for the cells to be cultured. Therefore, any abortion to be performed as the result of such testing will have to take place late in a woman's pregnancy when the risks are higher, usually about the twentieth week or afterward.

THE ARGUMENT FOR ABORTION FOR FETAL REASONS.   The argument for fetal reasons states that, again given the difficulty of the world we live in, it is difficult enough for a normal person to survive much less one who is born deformed and will remain so for a lifetime, sometimes getting worse. Further, it is claimed that it is unfair to expect a family that has the option of aborting such a conceptus to go through with a pregnancy only to give birth to a seriously deformed child, requiring all kinds of medical support and maybe even institutionalization for most of its life. The birth of such a child may affect a family adversely from emotional, sociological, and economic points of view. The financial and emotional cost of raising such a child is hard to calculate, and the effect on other siblings in the family and the parents can be quite disastrous. Some families can and willingly do adapt to such a situation. In fact, many have had to do so in the past, prior to

261

amniocentesis. However, now that such a procedure is available, it is argued that families should be able to exercise their free choice and prevent such a child from being born. It is also argued that abortion for these reasons would also be done in the interest of such a child as well as its family and society. After all, the argument states, wouldn't it be better to prevent such a child from being born than to have it live a life of hardship and low quality?

THE ARGUMENT AGAINST ABORTION FOR FETAL REASONS. The argument against abortion for fetal reasons is that it constitutes a serious discrimination against the potentially handicapped and that even unborn people should not be murdered because they have serious deformities or defects. Proponents of this argument state often that dealing with a handicapped child is a very special destiny and should be undertaken with compassion and willingness—some who are religious even cite that God has chosen a particular family for this very special task. They go on to say that even if families feel that they can not raise such a child, they can give it up for adoption or place it in some sort of institution for its care. At least, any of these alternatives is better than murdering the child. They also argue that we can never know when we might eliminate some possible genius, such as Beethoven who had myriad defects and deformities when he was born, and we can never really predict how people will deal with their defects and what contribution they might make to society and the world.

The rebuttal to these arguments would be that the view of the specialness of such a child and the compassion of the family in caring for it is applicable only after such a child is born but not if its birth can be prevented; other than this, it is more sentimental than factual, realistic, or scientific. Opponents would also argue that since a conceptus is not a human being in the fullest sense, discrimination is really not an issue until after it is born. Further, very few people are willing to adopt such children and the quality of institutionalization in our society leaves much to be desired. Besides, why condemn any human being to a lifetime of institutionalization? As for the argument concerning the possible elimination of a genius like Beethoven, opponents argue that the chances of giving birth to a Dillinger or a Hitler are just as great as having a genius, and therefore this argument is weak.

One can only strive to avoid what is a reasonably predictable difficult situation, not presuppose the elimination of geniuses or villains, especially since both these are extremely rare anyway. What we would most likely be doing by not allowing abortion where it is desired, the argument states, is to force a troublesome life on a child and its family.

In conclusion, then, fetal reasons are definitely important in considering continuing pregnancy or having an abortion, and they cannot be overlooked in trying to come to some clear moral policy about abortion.

SOCIAL AND ECONOMIC REASONS

Many of these have already been suggested under the other three reasons, but to make them a little clearer, pregnancy and the raising of any child affects society at all levels—financially, politically, and socially. If a child is unwanted, unable to be cared for, or defective or deformed, the burden is greater. Advocates of abortion to prevent unwanted and defective births do not advocate the mistreatment of already born handicapped or unwanted babies or adults, but they feel that the prevention of such births whenever possible is moral.

The financial cost of giving birth to and raising a child these days is very high, and in most cases we are talking about an eighteen- to twenty-one-year period, not just childhood rearing. Socially the cost can also be quite high. For example, if an unmarried teenager still in high school becomes pregnant, her whole life can be adversely affected by going through with the pregnancy. Also, not just a teenager but even a married woman and her family living on a limited budget can be adversely affected by the birth of an unwanted child. Furthermore, there is the financial burden on society as a whole because of the need for state and government care for welfare and support of handicapped children and adults.

The answer to all these arguments given by pro-life people is that where human life is concerned, economics must take a back seat, and even though there is certainly social distress for both the teenager and the married woman already overburdened, the death of an innocent conceptus cannot be justified even under these circumstances. A counterargument to this is that it is wonderfully ideal, but too often, even financial help, much less emotional help, is not forthcoming. Many critics of this pro-life position also say that they do not want their taxes to be used to support any more unwanted or handicapped children than necessary, and if abortion is allowed, then they can concentrate on helping those who are already born.

Whichever side of the socioeconomic argument we take, we have to admit that these reasons for abortion are also important. In addition, it would seem that those who are adamantly opposed to abortion ought to "put their money where their mouths are" or at least provide viable alternatives to abortion. In other words, if they want to prevent abortion, are they willing to take effective action to spend a great deal of *their* money to provide real alternatives to it? For example, if a destitute woman does not choose abortion, will society or segments of it support her and her child at least financially through the pregnancy and afterward for eighteen to twenty-one years? A commitment along these lines would do a great deal toward making abortion less attractive. However, most pro-choice people are skeptical that society as a whole is willing to make such a commitment, even on a partial basis.

WOMEN'S RIGHTS

The last reason given for abortion is that women ought to have the same procreative freedom and rights over their lives and bodies as men. Since men never get pregnant, for most of them abortion is strictly academic unless they willingly accept responsibility for their own sexual behavior. Men can walk away from any sexual act, whereas a woman, if she gets pregnant, cannot. It is true that both women and men should be responsible for using appropriate contraceptives if they are going to be sexually active, but no contraceptive is 100 percent foolproof. Suppose that a woman dutifully uses a contraceptive but gets pregnant anyhow; wasn't she being responsible, and what is she to do now? The pro-life argument is that she must, regardless of the circumstances, have the baby. The pro-choice position, however, is that the woman ought to have absolute rights over her own body and life, just as men do, and since by a natural accident she is the one to bear the child, then she must have the right to abort the conceptus if she feels that she cannot or does not want to go through with her pregnancy.

ABSOLUTE RIGHTS OVER ONE'S BODY.   The pro-choice people argue that women have absolute rights over their own bodies, just as men do, as mentioned, and this means that the conceptus until it is born is a part of the woman's body and therefore dependent upon her choice or decision for its life. The way this argument goes, the woman has absolute say-so over whether the conceptus lives or dies.

There are problems with this position, however. It is true that most of the time, at least in free societies, rights over one's own body should be upheld wherever possible, but should they be considered *absolute?* For example, competent adults may either accept or refuse treatment, sometimes deciding for themselves whether they should live or die. But if adults are not held to be competent, for example, because of mental or emotional illness, then they do not have such rights. Further, if someone has the bubonic plague that could infect and kill many people and does not want to remain in isolation in a hospital, his rights over his own body must be limited for the good of society as a whole.

The difficult problem with women's rights over their own bodies when they are pregnant is that they now have residing within them another at least potential human life, and shouldn't they have to give some consideration to the rights of such a being? Rights over their bodies would certainly seem to be different from those when they are not pregnant. Here again, it is necessary to come to grips with the question of when unborn human life is to take on value to the point where its rights must be considered along with those of the woman, and as we have seen, there is no easy answer to this question; however, there should be a careful consideration of these rights. Two other issues arise with this argument, and they are the conceptus' being merely a part of the woman's body and the absolute rights of decision over whether another (even potential) human being may be born or not or may live or die.

It is true that the conceptus is a part of the mother's body and also dependent on her body for its sustenance, support, and life. However, it is not a part of or dependent on her body in the same way that any other growth or organ is; it soon develops its own cardiovascular, circulatory, and nervous systems that are separate and unique from the mother's so that it is really not the same as or merely a part of her body. A question should also be raised about the life or death of the conceptus being totally dependent on the woman's decision. There are few occasions in life when another's life or death is so completely dependent on one person, and the question about the mother's rights in this issue certainly has to be raised.

I am not trying to suggest that decisions for abortion do not have to or should not ever be made, but only that such decisions are extremely important and therefore should not be made casually. This is in no way like a decision to have a cyst or other growth removed. One wonders if the woman's rights over her children once born are also absolute so that she should be able to decide their lives or deaths as well. Therefore, the statement that women should have absolute rights over their own bodies and lives is certainly questionable. By the same token, women should have such rights, but they should not be considered absolute and therefore overriding any other rights that come into the picture, especially those of the conceptus to have continued life in the womb and eventual birth.

CONCLUSIONS ABOUT THE MORALITY OF ABORTION. It is obvious that abortion is still a very important moral issue in spite of its legality. There are very good reasons brought up on both sides of the issue, and they should all be taken seriously because abortion definitely involves the medical or physical, psychological, fetal, social, economic, and women's rights aspects of our lives. However, they should not be presumed to be automatic in deciding for or against such a serious act, nor should they be accepted or rejected superficially. In every abortion decision, at least two lives, if not more, are to some degree always involved, and they all deserve careful consideration.

As in the other moral issues having to do with the taking of human life, you should now consider the various problems, reasons, and arguments raised in this chapter and try carefully to work out your own conclusions based on your own ethical system and principles. In addition, again, consider the following situations dealing with this issue.

SITUATION 1

Teenage Pregnancy. Jane, age sixteen, and David, age seventeen, have had sexual intercourse, and now Jane is pregnant. Jane's mother, a Roman Catholic, wants Jane to go through with her pregnancy but give her baby up for adoption. Jane's father, an agnostic, wants her to have an abortion so that Jane can get on with her school and career. David and his family want Jane to have the abortion also and are willing to pay all expenses. Jane goes to the priest of her mother's church, to which she is only casually committed, and he tells her that to have the abortion would be a serious sin. She has also gone to an abortion clinic to discuss the abortion procedure, which to her seems scary, and its cost. She is indecisive about what she should do.

What do you think she should do and why—what do you think are her moral alternatives? How would you advise her or help her make the "right" decision? Answer in detail, and support your opinions. What would you do if this happened to you or someone close to you?

SITUATION 2

Fetal Reasons. Lupe and Rudy, both in their early twenties, are having their first child. Since Lupe had some problems early in her pregnancy, her doctor recommends that she have an amniocentesis. At four months of pregnancy she has the procedure, and the results six weeks later show that she will give birth to a Down's syndrome child. The results do not indicate how severe the mental retardation will be or if there will be any other deformities. She and Rudy both want children badly, but they would rather not have to raise a mentally retarded child with other possible defects, especially since they are young enough to try again for a normal child.

Remembering that this abortion would take place during the fifth or sixth month of pregnancy, what do you think they should do and why? What would you do if you were in their position? Answer in detail.

SITUATION 3

> *Unwanted Child*. Bill, age forty-two, and Marge, age forty, are married and have four daughters. Marge is using what she believes to be an effective birth control device because neither she nor Bill want any more children. The device, however, fails and she discovers she is pregnant. After adjusting to the idea, she and Bill decide it would not be so bad if they could have a son. Since she is forty, her doctor advises amniocentesis, which she has. The genetic counselor informs her and Bill that the child will be normal and also tells them that its sex is female. Bill and Marge decide they do not want another daughter, and Marge has an abortion, after which she has herself sterilized so that she can have no more children. Do you feel that she and Bill did the right thing? Why or why not?
>
> The genetic counselor felt terrible about their decision and wondered if she should not have told them the sex of the child? Do you think she should have withheld such information? Why or why not? Shouldn't Marge and Bill have the right to any and all information from such a test? What do you think of this reason for abortion compared with the reason cited in situation 2?

Euthanasia and Allowing to Die

The word *euthanasia* comes from the Greek *eu* meaning "happiness" or "well-being" and *thanatos* meaning "death." So when literally translated, euthanasia means a happy death, and in our modern sense, it often means a good death or death with dignity. To some people, it also means a mercy death or killing and is, therefore, a form of murder. Added to this are the distinctions of allowing people to die their own natural deaths, at their request or with their permission and also without it (because they are comatose, for example), and directly ending dying people's lives, again either with their permission or without it. When the same word ranges over all these differences and can mean anything from allowing people to die in peace to directly killing them, it is best to use other terms or phrases and avoid the confusion of such a word.

The three phrases I have chosen are as follows:

1. *Allowing people to die*—not starting, or stopping once started, any extraordinary means to keep dying patients alive which are deemed inappropriate in that they will only prolong death, not life.
2. *Mercy death*—taking a direct act to kill someone, such as shooting

them or giving them a massive dose of poison or drugs but at their request or with their permission.

3. *Mercy killing*—the same as mercy death, except without patients' permission or request, usually because they cannot give it due to coma, for example. In this situation, someone other than the patient decides to end the patient's life.

Just as recently as the last fifty years, this issue in its three aspects has become important and troublesome, due to the tremendous advances made in medical science, such as the development of miracle drugs, for example, penicillin and sulfa; the invention of the artificial respirator, pacemakers, and heart machines; and the greater sophistication of surgical techniques, such as open heart surgery and organ transplants. These advancements have extended the lives of many patients who would otherwise have died, and this has been a great blessing for many. Others, however, have been kept alive long after they should have been, leading to longer lives of very low quality and heavy emotional and financial burdens for them and their families.

Let us look at two examples. First, Ellie, age eighty-three, is suffering from metastasized cancer (spread throughout her body) and goes into cardiac arrest or renal (kidney) failure. With our modern equipment and methods, we can resuscitate her heart and get her on a machine to keep her heart going, or we can surgically put in a shunt and put her on dialysis (using a machine that functions as kidneys do when these organs fail), which would probably prolong her life another three weeks. Questions have to be asked, however: "What purpose will such actions serve?" "Will they cure her in any meaningful way?" It would seem that since she is dying anyway, the use of these procedures is not appropriate, and that the appropriate treatment is to keep her comfortable and pain-free until she dies her own natural death.

The second example concerns Richard, age twenty-five, who is brought into the emergency room with a severe head injury due to a motorcycle accident. The emergency room staff get him stabilized and he is put on a respirator to breathe for him and a heart machine to keep his heart pumping. After this is done, tests reveal that his brain has been almost totally destroyed with only minimal activity remaining. The only things keeping him alive are the two machines. The question then arises, "Should the machines be turned off to allow him to die his own natural death?" Note that as recently as twenty years ago, he probably would have died in the emergency room. Now, with these two machines, he could be maintained in his present state, especially since he is so young and since his heart and lungs are strong, for an indefinite period of time. Another question that arises and one that we will discuss later is, "Would turning off the machines be murder, or would they just be allowing him to die his own natural death?'' Before presenting the arguments for and against the three issues just defined, it is important to define and distinguish them from what has been called ''brain death.''

BRAIN DEATH OR IRREVERSIBLE COMA

Because of all our advancements in medical science, we have discovered that the former and traditional definition of death as that point at which the heart or lungs fail is no longer completely satisfactory since both these organs can be kept going even when a person's brain has failed. Human beings are made up of three major organ systems that are central to their continued living: the circulatory system, or heart and blood; the respiratory system, or lungs; and the nervous system, or the brain and nerves. In the past when any of the three failed, the others fell like dominoes. For example, if there was a severe head injury and the brain failed, then the heart and lungs would also fail because the brain could no longer send them messages. If the lungs failed, then no oxygen got to the brain; the brain would die, and the heart would stop. If the heart failed, then no oxygen would get to the brain; the brain would die, and the lungs would stop. As described in the second example, however, it is possible to bypass the brain and keep the other two systems going or transplant a new heart and even lungs to keep the brain alive. When the brain is bypassed, it is often discovered that even though a patient's heart is pumping and his lungs are breathing that his brain is dead or that he is in what is called ''irreversible coma.''

Because of the possibility of keeping a brain dead person alive and also because such patients or their families are often willing to donate organs for transplantation, the definition of death had to be expanded to include the death of the brain as well as that of the heart and lungs.

In 1968, an ad hoc committee was formed at Harvard University Medical School to develop criteria for determining brain death or irreversible coma. The committee's final report recommended four major criteria, which the medical community has pretty much used ever since to determine brain death: (1) unreceptivity and unresponsiveness, (2) no spontaneous movements or breathing, (3) no reflexes, and (4) a flat electroencephalogram (EEG).[13] The committee further recommended that these tests be carefully conducted twice in a 48-hour period, 24 hours apart, after which if they were all negative, the patient could be declared dead by reasons of brain death, and all treatment, including continuation of respirators and heart machines, could be discontinued.

The main reason this has been brought up is that many people tend to confuse brain death with allowing to die, mercy death, and mercy killing. They tend to make such statements as "once a person has been pronounced brain dead, then we can 'unplug' him from the artificial life support machines and 'allow him to die'." Others will claim that in disconnecting these devices, we are committing acts of mercy death or mercy killing. However, if you reread what I have just written about brain death and its criteria, you will see that these statements are contradictory and absurd.

If a person is pronounced medically and legally dead for any reason, you cannot allow him to die or kill him—he is obviously dead; therefore, any disconnecting of artificial life support systems will not kill him. I believe our confusion in this matter occurs because the person's body still *looks* alive since his heart is beating and his lungs are respirating; however, if he has been declared brain dead by the criteria given, transplanting organs or disconnecting equipment will not kill him anymore than will taking out intravenous lines on a person who succumbs to a heart attack. It is very important to remember this distinction, since once a person is properly declared brain dead, then allowing to die, mercy death, and mercy killing do *not* enter the picture in any way whatsoever. With this in mind, let us now proceed to the arguments for and against these three actions.

GENERAL ARGUMENTS FOR ALL THREE

INDIVIDUAL RIGHTS OVER ONE'S BODY AND LIFE.   Permeating all three actions, but especially those of allowing to die and mercy death, is the individual's rights and freedom over his own body, life, and death. This means that any individual ought to have the right to decide whether or not he should live, or if he wants to die, then he ought to have the right to do that too. I have already discussed the pro's and con's of these rights over bodies and lives in the abortion issue, dealing with the women's rights argument. As I pointed out, these rights are not absolute, but for the most part, competent adults are allowed to refuse medical treatment if they wish, and of course this may mean that they also choose to die instead of prolonging their lives with treatments. Therefore, where allowing to die is the issue, patients are usually given this option if they wish, even though some doctors do not approve for various reasons as you shall see shortly.

More questions arise, however, when mercy death is requested because, first, it is a direct act to kill someone, whereas allowing to die is generally not, and, second, someone else has to assist in the killing, that is, the person who is helping the patient to die. If the patient chooses to commit suicide, that is one thing of which people may or may not approve, but mercy death involves another person to help achieve the mercy death.

In mercy killing, the issue of freedom and individual rights is often blurred because the person usually cannot be asked since he is in a coma, for example. Further, the people who want to or do perform the mercy killing say that they know what the person would want if he or she could ask, but this always has to be somewhat of an assumption on their part. Therefore, there are some problems with the individual rights and freedom argument except when it has to do with allowing people to die their own natural deaths.

RIGHT TO DIE WITH DIGNITY.   Most human beings do not fear death as much as they fear dying and all the suffering that goes with it; therefore, many people feel that to die a long, drawn-out death would be to lose their dignity, and some kind of shortening of their lives would mean a more dignified end. First, it is difficult to define what "death with dignity" really means, since it may vary greatly from individual to individual. Second, some of the so-called "deaths with dignity," when examined carefully, may be questionably dignified. For example, in the book *Death of a Man* by Lael Wertenbaker, she describes the suicide of her husband Charles at the end of his bout with cancer of the colon. When he could not kill himself with an overdose of morphine, he then slit his wrists and bled into casseroles on his bed while his wife tried to help him.[14] What he went through and what he put his wife through, even though she agreed to it, was hardly dignified.

In another famous case, George Zygmaniak, in his twenties, whose spine had been severely injured in a motorcycle accident and who had begged everyone, including doctors to kill him, was shot by his brother Lester in a six-bed ward in a hospital, after which Lester had to stand trial for murder (mercy death). First, George was shot after only three days and before any additional physical or psychological therapy had been tried. Second, one wonders about the well-being of other patients in the ward. Third, his brother had to go through a murder trial. One could certainly question where the dignity in all of this lies except that George did not have to go on living.

GENERAL ARGUMENTS AGAINST ALL THREE ACTIONS

VALUE OF LIFE ARGUMENT.   Of course, the paramount objection to all three actions is the value of life principle. Aren't allowing people to die without doing everything possible to keep them alive and also directly killing people with or without their permission flagrant violations of this principle? After all, if one sees this principle in its clearest light, shouldn't we use all the science and know-how at our disposal to see that life is preserved and protected to the very end and never give up on any patient? If the principle is seen in this way, then of course none of the three actions would be moral. Remember, however, that this principle has been interpreted to mean "a reverence for life and an acceptance of death." This interpretation would at least condone allowing people to die their own natural deaths, if not the other two actions.

Another question that must arise in consideration of this principle is who should decide when life has value? We should all value life in general, but when it comes to an individual's own life, should he or she be the one to decide at what point life has or does not have value or should others decide this for patients? This brings up the "quantity versus quality" argument. Many people argue that life in and of itself, or life in quantity, is not as important as the quality of that life, and most would agree that individuals are essentially the best qualified ones to decide about the quality of their own lives. If this is an important consideration, then allowing to die can certainly be condoned where a competent dying patient wishes, for example, to live a shorter life of more quality without cancer treatment than a longer one of much lower quality because of such treatment.

This is also an important consideration in support of mercy death and mercy killing in that, in the first case, a person may choose to be "put out of his or her misery" rather than go downhill gradually with suffering and loss of dignity. However, there is still the question of killing someone rather than letting the person die. In the case of mercy killing, there is someone other than the patient deciding the quality of the patient's life, and this can certainly raise serious moral questions. So it would seem that the value of life principle does not necessarily rule out allowing to die, but neither does it condone mercy death and mercy killing because they pretty much constitute a direct violation of the principle, especially in the case of mercy killing where the act is done without the agreement of the person being killed.

THE RELIGIOUS ARGUMENT.   The religious argument, that only God can give or take away life, described and discussed in the beginning of this chapter is often used against all three actions, but it has the same philosophical and theological problems as with any other act involving the taking of human life. It is especially weak in the case of allowing to die, and many religions that would use this argument in other aspects of the taking of human life would nevertheless agree that allowing people to die their own natural deaths is within God's divine plan and not an immoral act.

The most famous religious statement of this was made in 1957 by Pope Pius XII while speaking to a group of anesthesiologists. He stated that it was not immoral to not start or continue extraordinary or heroic treatment on people who were near death and added that appropriate doses of medication, such as morphine, could be given to alleviate pain even if they might hasten the deaths of patients. Most religions, however, would definitely argue against mercy death and mercy killing because they are direct acts to take human life.

A last reminder here is that allowing to die cannot be truly said to "leave in God's hands" the death of a person. Remember, if we decide to do no treatment, or stop what we are doing, or decide to start or continue treatment, these acts are our responsibility, not God's, and we cannot use this argument to sidestep it.

THE DOMINO ARGUMENT.   We have already discussed this, but since this argument is used with these actions especially when talking about legalizing them in any way, we must examine it again. In fact, all these acts have been considered by many to be three very proximate "dominoes"; that is, if we allow people to die, won't that push down the next domino, which is mercy death, and if we allow that, then won't the third, mercy killing, fall also? The same criticisms, of course, apply here as to other aspects of taking human life. For example, allowing to die, unless it is due to criminal negligence, is generally accepted as people's individual rights, and appropriate medical decisions can be often made to effect this action. Therefore, it is not illegal in most countries. However, mercy death and mercy killing are illegal within the United States and most countries throughout the world. Further, consider how the California Natural Death Act, described earlier, was able to legalize allowing to die without in any way condoning mercy death or mercy killing.

Proponents of these last two actions have also argued that successful legal safeguards can be established to ensure that even they can be done in people's best interests without abuses, such as killing people for their estates, or because you merely want to be rid of them. For example, O. Ruth Russell in an article and also in a book published later, states that appropriate legal safeguards can be established that allow for "death with dignity" while protecting people against abuses or immoral and illegal acts. She lists no fewer than fifteen carefully stated provisions or safeguards, some of which are: such a law would be permissive rather than mandatory or compulsory; there could be no secrecy involved; there would have to be a written, notarized request; an advisory panel would be used; several doctors must be involved; a waiting period would be required; and it would be a criminal offense to falsify any documents, coerce patients or next of kin, or perform any mal-practice involving any act of euthanasia.[15]

Critics of this argument state that there is danger in even establish-ing such a precedent and that enforcing such safeguards would be dif-ficult. Further, they argue that these safeguards may protect people who request to die, but they might still lead to mercy killing without peo-ple's permission. Again, it is worthwhile to be aware of a possible domino effect, but that possibility in and of itself is no conclusive ar-gument against any of the three actions.

MEDICINE CAN NEVER CHOOSE DEATH.   Some doctors argue that by virtue of the nature of medicine, they can never opt for death but must always choose life. After all, the reason medicine exists is to save lives, not end them, and the minute doctors start making choices for death rather than for life, the very basis of medicine will be nullified. This will result not only in doctors becoming discouraged but also in an elimination of patients' trust in them.

However, this approach to medicine is deemed by other doctors and many patients and their families as extremely unrealistic and the cause of much pain and suffering. It is also seen as condoning the view of "doctor as God," which is totally unrealistic. Every reasonable doctor surely must realize that there is only so much medicine can do under certain circumstances and that death, after all, is inevitable for all of us. Critics also feel that there is a great difference between "choosing" death and "accepting" it when it is inevitable. Further, decisions over treatment of patients are not strictly medical in that they have to do with the quality of individual people's lives, and therefore many pa-tients and their families disagree that "everything must be done right to the end" to save them. They often object strongly to doctors' overriding their decisions about their own bodies and lives. They feel that they ought to have the final decisions about whether or not they want everything done right to the very end; they feel that if they de-cide they want this, then everything that can should be done; on the other hand, if they decide they would rather die their inevitable deaths without constant medical intrusion and suffering, then they should be allowed to make that choice too.

Doctors certainly have the right not to participate in such decisions, and they may take themselves off the cases of those patients who do not wish heroic treatment. Further, doctors certainly have strong ar-guments against condoning or participating in any acts of mercy death or mercy killing. Their arguments about the purpose of medicine are certainly much more cogent here, especially since such acts are illegal, but these arguments have much less force in the case of allowing to die.

POSSIBILITY OF FINDING CURES.   Another argument frequently offered against all three actions is that if we are too quick to let people die, or if we "end their misery" directly, we may be denying them the opportunity to be cured of their illnesses. New cures for diseases are constantly being discovered, and there are also so-called "miracle cures," those that occur in seeming defiance of all medical knowledge. Therefore, it is argued, if we continue every effort to keep dying patients alive, a miracle cure might occur or a scientific cure (a new drug or surgical procedure) might be discovered that would lengthen patients' lives or even cure them completely.

Not all doctors are willing to accept the existence of miracle cures, however, and many of them also argue that the time to be concerned with cures is when the disease is first diagnosed, not when the patient is almost completely destroyed by it. They would argue, for example, that the time to perform radical surgery, radiation therapy, and chemotherapy on cancer patients is not when the cancer has completely metastasized, but when such treatment can do some good, either in slowing cancer growth or in stopping it completely. Using "aggressive" medicine to treat completely metastasized cancer patients, they would argue, is closer to torturing patients than to healing them.

THE IRRATIONALITY OF WANTING TO DIE.   One argument that affects all three actions, but especially the first two, is that wanting to die has to be an irrational desire made under the tremendous duress of pain and suffering. It is inconceivable, the proponents of this argument state, that anyone should ever want to die—it is against the human instinct for survival and totally illogical. They go on to argue that because people who are terminal are suffering and often miserable, they cannot reason logically and are therefore deciding from emotions rather than from reason. They offer as support for this argument the fact that when patients are suffering they often say they want to die, but when the suffering is relieved, maybe even a few hours later, they change their minds completely and even make plans for the future. Therefore, the argument goes on, if people asking for death will just patiently wait to see what therapy and medical science can do for them, maybe they will adjust to the situation and change their minds about dying. At any rate if we allow them to die or kill them out of mercy, we might be doing them a wrong that we can never correct.

One of the criticisms of this argument is that it is perfectly rational to accept death since it is inevitable in all people's lives and that everyone must face and accept it. In fact, critics would argue, the fact that most of us do not accept death, when it is inevitable, is much more irrational than is rejecting it. Further, when people are really terminal and know that they are dying, they ought to have the right either to be allowed to die or to be helped to die in some way rather than having to suffer and waste away. Since they are going to die anyway, and the process of dying may be pretty terrible, anything done to shorten that process is very rational and any attempt to prolong it, on the other hand, is irrational. They would argue further that many requests for allowing to die and mercy death have come from people who have tried for some time to live with their tragic situations and who have carefully decided that death is preferable to suffering or a limited life of low quality. Moreover, is it really true that because people are suffering, they cannot make rational decisions about their lives or deaths?

Therefore, this argument would not in itself block allowing people to die their own natural deaths; as a matter of fact, it would probably be very difficult to prove that people who have been informed of their medical situation and considered all the alternatives are being irrational when they choose not to prolong their agony if they cannot be cured. It is not inconceivable, either, that people might want someone to help them to die to shorten their suffering. However, there is still the problem of a direct killing and of involving someone else in such an act. As the discussion condoning wanting to die as rational approaches mercy killing, it loses much of its force because it is more difficult to determine whether or not people being considered for mercy killing have made any choice at all. Since at least the final choice seems to be left up to someone other than the person to be killed, we could only discuss the rationality of killing people who cannot make decisions to live or die.

SPECIFIC ARGUMENTS AGAINST THE THREE ACTIONS

THE JUSTICE ARGUMENT.   This argument says that in two senses the principle of justice is being violated. First, the person who is allowing patients to die or is killing them is being unjust or unfair to them. This is hard to support, of course, when people request, permit, or agree to any of these actions, and therefore it would apply mostly to the act of mercy killing. In the second sense, injustice can be committed by people who want to die against others who do not want them to or who are being asked to help terminate their lives. For example, was it fair for George Zygmaniak to ask his brother Lester to kill him (perform mercy death)? First, Lester had to go to jail and undergo a court trial for murder. Second, what about the guilt Lester might feel for what he has done? Mightn't he wonder whether or not George could have lived with his injury if given more time? Presumably Lester knew his brother quite well and therefore may have had no misgivings, but since he was not a cold-blooded killer, he is bound to have had or perhaps may still have some concern over what he has done. One can then ask in such a situation whether it was just for George to ask Lester to kill him.

Even in allowing to die, if patients happen not to agree with their family members, should they have to consider whether or not they are being unjust to these other people in their lives? The criticism goes back again to whether any such injustice overrides an individual's freedom to decide his or her own life or death. After all, the individual is the one who has to suffer the pain and discomfort, not the family members, and the individual is the one who has to evaluate the quality of his or her life with or without treatment and live with his or her choice. It would seem then that the justice argument should be considered, especially in matters of mercy death and mercy killing, but it is not necessarily true that allowing to die is an unjust act especially since many family members will agree with the patient's choice.

ABANDONMENT OF PATIENTS WHO ARE ALLOWED TO DIE. Some people argue that not using or discontinuing any means that might keep dying people alive even a little longer is tantamount to refusing them proper medical care. They feel that if health care professionals (doctors, nurses, etc.) refuse to apply curative treatments, then they will abandon patients and their families to suffering and misery. This means that these professionals will say, in effect, "There is nothing more I can do, so I will treat you no further and allow you to die."

It is certainly possible that health care professionals could abandon patients for whom "nothing more can be done," and I'm sure it has been done in the past and is being done today. However, there is no reason why this should occur. Abandonment arises from an overemphasis on the aspect of medicine involving curing and healing patients and a deemphasis of the aspect involving comforting and caring for them. This distinction can be shown in the hospice approach to caring for the dying, which not only clarifies and puts into perspective allowing to die but also can eliminate the need for either mercy killing or mercy death.

THE HOSPICE APPROACH TO CARING FOR THE DYING

The concept of "hospice" is quite old in the Western world, dating back at least to the Middle Ages. In its modern form, it has been established and used extensively in the British Isles. The word "hospice" actually meant a refuge for wayfaring strangers, including those who are sick and dying. In the medical sense, this refuge is given to dying people who are completing their stay in this life and are traveling through the process of dying to "another life" or to death itself. In the religious sense, of course, this means an afterlife; for the agnostic or atheist, it may mean nothingness. In actuality, the modern hospice does not deal with acute cases or with emergency medical care; it seeks, rather, to help terminally ill patients and their families live as comfortably and meaningfully as they can until they die. This approach is now being used quite extensively in the United States and other parts of the world and consists of seven different aspects of patient care. Before describing these, however, it is important to know that hospice accepts allowing to die, but in no way condones either mercy death or mercy killing. The whole point of hospice is to eliminate pain, suffering, and misery so that patients can die their own natural deaths in comfort, peace, and dignity.

COMFORTING AND CARING FOR PATIENTS.   The hospice approach emphasizes "comforting and caring for" patients rather than "curing and healing" them. There comes a time in every terminal illness when the possibility of curing patients of their diseases no longer exists. At this point, medical care should not be discontinued, nor should patients and their families be abandoned; rather, the medical care should shift from "curing and healing" to "comforting and caring for." In this situation, the health care professionals should not stop giving treatment; rather, they should start giving *appropriate* treatment, which means controlling pain and discomfort and giving assistance at all levels to patients and their families until the patients die. It usually also means providing continuing assistance, when needed, to patients' families after patients' deaths.

TREATING ALL ASPECTS OF A HUMAN BEING.   Recognizing that humans have aspects or dimensions beyond the physical, which is the basic focus of medicine, the hospice approach utilizes a team concept in its care of the dying. The team includes patients, their families and friends, other patients, doctors, nurses, clergy, social workers, physical and occupational therapists, psychologists or psychiatrists, and various lay volunteers. Since sickness, dying, and death involve all aspects of a human being, his or her mental, emotional, social, and religious needs must be met along with the physical needs. Hospice assumes that dying patients and their families must have total care to get through what can be and often is a very difficult time.

PAIN AND SYMPTOM CONTROL.   Central to treating dying patients and their families is the need to eliminate the "misery" they ask to be put out of by controlling the pain and discomfort caused by the disease. The first thing to recognize is that pain is a very complex phenomenon involving the mental, emotional, social, and spiritual as well as the physical. This is why the hospice uses a team approach so that social workers can be used to help treat social pain and so on. The second thing to realize is that the pain of dying patients, when they have it, is not going to get better as the pain from surgery will, but will probably get worse as the disease progresses; therefore, a different approach must be used—preventive rather than reactive. Instead of reacting to pain when patients have it and giving them pain medication as needed, a regimen of pain control is set up to prevent the pain from occurring and to keep it under control at all times. The exact form of pain medication may differ from hospice to hospice; however, it is usually given orally, around the clock, and in an adequate enough dose so that the patients are kept free from pain without being sedated. Once such pain is controlled, it is obviously easier to minister to the social, psychological, and religious needs of the patients. A more detailed description of the hospice approach to pain control can be found in Sandol Stoddard's *The Hospice Movement*.[16]

OUTPATIENT AND HOME CARE.   Many of the mental, emotional, social, and religious problems of dying patients arise because they are taken out of their home environments where they feel most comfortable. Since they do not as a rule need extraordinary medical care, they can often be treated at home, and the hospice approach encourages this wherever possible, while at the same time providing for their medical needs through outpatient care and 24-hour support at home.

HUMANIZED INPATIENT CARE.   Where this type of care is not possible, many hospices provide an inpatient facility, which is not a hospital at all but a humanized, homelike, comfortable, and warm environment where patients are allowed many of their own belongings and where visitation by families is encouraged and very flexible. In such facilities, patients are given pain and symptom control and lots of "tender loving care" rather than extraordinary medical treatment, such as surgery, respirators, radiation, and chemotherapy.

FREEDOM FROM FINANCIAL WORRY.   All hospice care whether outpatient or inpatient, is performed on a nonprofit basis. Existing medical insurance, private or government sponsored, and grants or donations should pay for everything. Those patients who can afford to pay often contribute an amount that is within their means, but health plans or donations should be used to alleviate any and all financial worries. No patients should be denied hospice services merely because they cannot afford them.

BEREAVEMENT COUNSELING AND ASSISTANCE.   Helping dying patients and their families adjust to the fact of death before, during, and after its occurrence is an important part of the hospice approach. This is yet another reason that the team approach is used—so that social workers, clergy, trained volunteers, and other nonmedical members of the team can aid medical personnel in caring for the entire family unit. Too often in our society, the patient is cared for and the family is forgotten. When the patient dies, however, the grieving family remains, and its members often experience difficulty in dealing with the death of their loved one. If the patient *and* the family can be treated as a unit during the dying period, then much of the difficulty that might occur after the patient dies can be averted in that family members can go through at least some of their mourning while the patient is still alive.

SOME CONCLUDING COMMENTS.   Since the hospice approach allows patients to die their own natural deaths in peace and dignity with support from their families, friends, the medical community, and society in general, most reasons for "putting people out of their misery" through mercy death and mercy killings are eliminated. Allowing people to die their own natural deaths is an integral part of the hospice approach and constitutes an acceptance of death as well as life, and by accepting this plus eliminating most reasons for the other two actions, the hospice approach seems to be the most humane way of caring for the dying. All reasons for mercy death and mercy killing have not been eliminated in that some people may still rather die sooner than later whether they are to be treated by hospice methods or not, but most of the reasons have been eliminated and viable alternatives do exist.

CONCLUSION TO THE MORAL ISSUE OF EUTHANASIA AND ALLOWING PEOPLE TO DIE

It is now again your turn to try to deal with this issue in its three aspects. Try to decide which of these is moral or immoral and why, and be sure to keep the three major distinctions clear in your mind and in your discussions of this most controversial issue. Further, apply your ethical system to the following situations.

SITUATION 1

Allowing to Die. Rochelle, age forty-two, gave birth to a baby girl who had Down's syndrome (a disease that involves severe mental retardation), a hole in her heart, and an intestinal blockage (duodenal atresia). The heart defect made it difficult for the baby to breathe, and she would eventually need heart surgery. However, to keep her alive and from starving, she would first have to have the intestinal blockage removed, and this type of surgery is not too difficult. Rochelle and her husband, Charles, reasoned that if they gave permission for the surgery, their baby would still have to try to survive the severe heart defect and eventually have serious surgery, which she might not survive either. Further, even if she survived these two surgeries, she would still be severely mentally retarded; therefore, they decided not to sign the release for surgery and let her starve to death. Part of their reasoning involved that they wished to let nature take its course since before all our advanced surgical techniques, such multideformed babies would have died of starvation anyway—nature's way of ridding itself of its defective beings (so they reasoned).

First, do you agree with their decision or not, and why? Second, what would you do in their shoes and why? Consider the future of raising the child also in answering this question. The medical community has responded in two ways to such situations:

1. It has accepted the parents' decision and has allowed the child to starve to death over a period of eleven days, trying to keep it as comfortable as possible, but doing nothing to relieve the blockage.
2. It has succeeded in getting a court injunction over the parents' objection and then doing the intestinal surgery without the parents' permission, leaving them to deal with the remaining defects and mental retardation of the child.

Which action do you believe is moral and why? If you choose alternative 1, do you feel that mercy killing should be employed to hasten the child's death? Why or why not? If you choose alternative 2, do you think that society has any obligation, since it overruled the parents' decision, to provide free medical assistance and other financial help to these parents to help raise the little girl, or are the parents obligated to do all of this on their own? How do you resolve the conflicts among the following rights involved in this case:

1. The right of the baby, regardless of her problem, to medical care that could save her life.
2. The right of parents to decide whether or not their defective or deformed babies should be allowed to live, when, in the past, they would not have lived because of the lack of medical technology.
3. The doctors' and hospitals' rights to save lives when they know they can.
4. The conflicting rights of society to (a) protect its members (in

this case, the child) and allow them to live and (b) not be bur-
dened with defective and deformed children when the omission
of extraordinary care would allow the child to die of natural
causes.

SITUATION 2

Mercy Death. George, age twenty-four, who has a wife and child,
is paralyzed from the neck down in a motorcycle accident. He has
always been very active and hates the idea of being paralyzed. He
is also in a great deal of pain and has asked his doctors and other
members of his family to "put him out of his misery." After three
days of such pleading, his brother, Lester, comes into George's
hospital ward and asks him if he is sure he still wants to die. George
says yes and again pleads with his brother to kill him. Lester kisses
and blesses him, then takes out a gun and shoots him, killing him
instantly. Lester is later tried for murder and is acquitted by reason
of temporary insanity (legally this means that at the time of the
crime, he did not know right from wrong).

Was what Lester did moral, and why or why not? If someone
you loved asked you to "put me out of my misery," what would
you do and why? Do you think George should have asked Lester
to do such an act? Why or why not? Do you think that Lester should
have been charged with murder or brought to trial at all? Why or
why not? Do you think he should have been acquitted as he was?
Why or why not? Do you think that the law should be restruc-
tured to allow for mercy death? Why or why not? What safeguards, if any, should be included in such a law? Answer in detail.

SITUATION 3

Mercy Killing. Karen Ann Quinlan, age nineteen, went into a coma
because of a combination of alcohol and valium. She was given
emergency treatment at a hospital and was placed on a respirator,
which stabilized her breathing. She remained in a deep coma, and
when she was tested by neurologists, they discovered that about
70 to 80 percent of her brain was irretrievably damaged. She was
not at any time considered to be brain dead, however: she reacted
to pain, her eyes would sometimes open and her pupils would
contract; she would at times thrash about, and her EEG showed
some brain activity. Her family wanted her taken off the respirator
so that she could either live or die in a natural state. The hospital
refused, but finally, after a difficult legal battle, she was weaned
off the respirator and has continued to live without it for the past

seven years. Doctors have described her as being in a "persistent vegetative state," which means the cognitive part of her brain is not functioning and is irreversibly damaged, while the rest of her brain, the autonomic function, is normal. Her heart is strong, she breathes on her own, and she is getting normal bed care and nutrient feedings, but no other medical care, such as antibiotics. The doctors' prognosis is that she could last many more years because of her age and the strength of her heart and lungs. Most people would agree that she is living a life of very low quality, but any action taken to shorten her life would seem to involve an act of mercy killing (she obviously cannot request or permit any actions, being in a coma). Do you think that any act to end her life should be performed? Why or why not? If this happened to you or to someone you loved, what would you want people to do and why? Would you take some sort of action to end her life if Karen were your daughter? Why or why not?

It has been suggested to Mr. Quinlan, Karen's legal guardian, that he lower the nutrient level of her feedings and in effect let her starve to death. He says that he cannot do this because he feels it would be inhumane. Would you condone such an action if she were your daughter? Would you consider this as allowing her to die rather than mercy killing? Why or why not? What do you think ought to be done if her heart arrests, her lungs stop respirating, or her kidneys fail? There are medical procedures to be applied in all these cases—do you think they ought to be used on Karen? Why or why not?

Chapter Summary

I. Definitions and distinctions.
   A. *Killing* means to put to death, slay, deprive of life, put an end to, or extinguish.
   B. *Murder* means the unlawful killing of one human being by another, especially with malice aforethought.
   C. *Suicide* is defined as an intentional taking of one's own life.
   D. *Passion* means that a killing or murder was done under extremely emotional circumstances.
   E. *Negligence* usually refers to some sort of carelessness on the part of someone that results in the death of someone else.
   F. *Premeditation* is the thinking about and planning of the killing of another over a period of time before the act is finally committed.
   G. Usually when assigning moral responsibility for an act of kill-

ing under these three, one that has been premeditated is considered more immoral than is one due to negligence, and negligence is more immoral than is a killing due to passion.

II. Killing in defense of the innocent (including self-defense).

    A. Argument for killing in defense of the innocent rests on two assumptions:

        1. Even though the value of life principle advocates a reverence for human life, people have a right to protect any innocent life, their own included, when it becomes clear that another intends to violate this principle.

        2. The good of defending the innocent far outweighs the bad of killing one who intends to kill others.

        3. Proponents would argue against the strictly pacifist position that says killing is never morally justified and also say that killers have forfeited their right to life.

    B. Argument against killing in defense of the innocent:

        1. The argument is based on the pacifist assumption that resorting to violence or taking human life is always wrong.

        2. Proponents also argue that violence and killing only breed more of the same (the domino argument).

        3. Another argument from religion is that only God can create or take away life and that "two wrongs don't make a right."

    C. The domino argument states essentially that if we allow killing in defense of the innocent, we will start a chain reaction that will allow for other types of killing eventually ending up with all human life being threatened by death (if you set one domino in motion, it will knock down the next, and so on).

        1. It is always important to gauge the effects of our actions, but unless there is proof that this will happen, it cannot be used as the *only* reason for not allowing something.

        2. Laws can be written to allow one type of killing while forbidding all the rest.

        3. Furthermore, when other "dominoes are knocked over," laws or rules can be established forbidding them (after the fact).

    D. The religious argument basically states that only God has the authority to give and take away life.

        1. This would not apply to those who are not religious.

        2. It is also scientifically, philosophically, and even theologically questionable that God, if he exists, is constantly intervening and interfering in the affairs of the world.

        3. Furthermore, it is a way that human beings have of shirking their responsibilities in matters of life and death; the ac-

tual fact is that human beings make most of the decisions either to do something or not to do something that may or may not result in a death. Therefore, we cannot blame God or hold God responsible for what occurs.

III. Capital punishment.
  A. Definition—the infliction of the death penalty for certain crimes, usually murder, kidnapping with intent to kill, and sometimes treason.
  B. Arguments for capital punishment:
    1. It is an effective deterrent for those who have killed (obviously), but it also acts as a valid deterrent to those who might otherwise kill.
    2. Economic argument—innocent taxpayers should not have to keep killers in prison for life or even for shorter times; it is cheaper to kill them.
    3. Retribution or revenge is a good reason for capital punishment—"an eye for an eye, a tooth for a tooth."
    4. Forfeiture of rights. When a person kills, especially in cold blood, he has automatically forfeited his rights to have his life valued, preserved, and protected.
  C. Arguments against capital punishment:
    1. Capital punishment is a direct violation of the value of life principle.
       a. It still amounts to murder—social murder.
       b. The "eye for an eye . . . ." of the Old Testament has been replaced by "love your enemy" and "turn the other cheek" of the New Testament.
       c. Revenge is an uncivilized emotion and does not bring back the victim or in any real sense recompense the survivors.
    2. Ineffectiveness as a deterrent. There is no conclusive proof that capital punishment in any way really deters anyone from committing crimes.
    3. Inequality. Capital punishment is unequal in its application in that rich people get off, and poor people, usually minority races, get the brunt of being put to death. Further, there is no possibility of return to life for any innocent person convicted of a capital offense and killed.
    4. Denial of rehabilitation. If you kill criminals, then there is no opportunity to rehabilitate them; isn't it more civilized to do the latter?
  D. A problem with capital punishment is that there are not very many really satisfactory alternatives to the elimination of serious crimes and people who might kill again.

IV. Abortion.
   A. General statement of the problem.
      1. *Abortion* means the premature termination of a pregnancy prior to birth.
         a. *Spontaneous abortion* means the same as a miscarriage.
         b. *Induced abortion* is caused either by the woman herself or another, usually a medical doctor. When a doctor does it, it is usually called a *therapeutic abortion.*
   B. Two major principles are at the center of this issue:
      1. The value of life principle affecting not only the conceptus but also the quality of life of the woman.
      2. The principle of individual freedom, which applies to the woman's rights over her own body, procreativity, and life.
   C. Two extreme sides to the issue:
      1. Strong pro-life, which holds that from conception onward we are talking about a full human being with all the same rights of one who is already born.
      2. Strong pro-choice, which states that a human being is not actual and fully human until birth and that a woman's rights supersede those of any conceptus.
      3. The real problem with both of these positions is that they rest on absolute rights, which does not allow for compromise.
   D. Legal status of abortion in the United States. Abortion is essentially legal up to point of viability (twenty-eighth week of gestation—when the conceptus could conceivably live outside the mother's womb). States may or may not pass laws restricting abortion after this point because of the high risk to the mother's life.
   E. When does human life begin? This is at the core of the abortion issue and very hard to decide upon. The facts are the same regardless of what position a person takes on the issue, but it is very difficult to decide or know when a human being exists in a full sense and also when it is to be given value equivalent to the already born.
      1. The genetic view is held by the strong pro-life position, which believes in humanhood from conception onward.
      2. The life-begins-at-birth view is held by the strong pro-choice group, believing that until there is a born baby, there is no full humanhood.
      3. The developmental view is a moderate position between the two extremes and states that humanhood in at least potentiality exists from conception, but as the conceptus devel-

ops, it gains more actual humanity and also gains in value. One application of this, presented by Sissela Bok, is as follows:

   a. Abortions are permitted for any reason up to the end of the first trimester (twelve weeks).

   b. From the thirteenth to the twenty-eighth weeks, they should only be allowed for very important reasons, such as severe malformation of the conceptus or to save the mother's life.

   c. After the twenty-eighth week, they should not be allowed unless the mother's life is definitely and actually in danger.

F. Medical reasons for abortion.

   1. With our advancements in medical technology, there are few diseases or medical problems that would prevent a woman from going through with pregnancy; however, there are some, and medical factors should always be taken into consideration.

   2. The dangers of abortion versus the danger of pregnancy. Neither of these risks should be minimized, but for the most part they are not in themselves sufficient reason for not going through with either.

   3. Types of abortion:

      a. Uterine aspiration.

      b. Saline abortion.

   4. The conclusions by researchers is that abortions are not completely no-risk or minor procedures, but when performed in a proper medical setting, they are generally safe.

G. Psychological reasons.

   1. Threats of suicide must always be taken seriously, but most research into this area reveals that suicides from having to go through with pregnancies are very rare.

   2. Unwanted pregnancy, unwanted child. This is probably the reason given most often for abortion.

      a. This should not be minimized, especially by men or others who cannot get pregnant. Pregnancy, even under optimal circumstances, is not easy.

      b. Women, however, often feel worse when they discover that they are pregnant with an unwanted conceptus and in the first three months when morning sickness is often prevalent. Later, they often change their minds and adjust quite well to their pregnancies.

      c. There is also a problem with the unwanted child argument in that, even though the natural mother may not want it, there are many adoptive parents that do. There are two counterarguments to this:

(1) The woman still may not want to go through nine months of pregnancy and then give her child up for adoption.

(2) Adopted children are not always happy because they may have difficulty dealing with what they feel was initial rejection by their natural mothers.

3. Rape and incest. Except for the strongest pro-life position, abortion is mostly accepted for these two reasons because of the psychological damage to the woman of the incidents themselves that caused the pregnancy and then the further damage of having to go through pregnancy after such mentally and emotionally disturbing occurrences.

4. Psychological effects of abortion. Pro-life advocates state that the psychological effects of going through with abortion, because of guilt feelings mostly, are much worse for a woman than is going through with pregnancy. Pro-choice advocates, however, do not feel that most women have guilt to the extent that it is psychologically damaging or even long-lasting, and even if they do, they can get support from family, friends, or even professional counselors.

5. Psychological reasons in this issue are very important and should be carefully considered, but again they do not provide automatic reasons for abortion or pregnancy.

H. Fetal reasons are those involving the possibility of giving birth to a defective or deformed child.

1. Amniocentesis can be done now after the sixteenth week of pregnancy, and after another four to six weeks, information can be acquired about whether the fetus is or is not going to be born with serious defects or deformities. One problem with abortion in this situation is that it has to be performed late in pregnancy when the risks to the life of the mother are higher.

2. The argument for abortion for fetal reasons is that it is difficult enough to raise a normal child in such a complex world, much less one that will be deformed for its entire life.

3. The argument against abortion for these reasons is that it constitutes discrimination against a handicapped person and that the life of the fetus should be preserved and protected, regardless of any deformities or defects.

I. Social and economic reasons are very important considerations because of the high cost of living and the extremely high monetary and social costs of raising a child through eighteen to twenty-one years.

   1. The rebuttal to these arguments by pro-life people is that, where human life is involved, economic reasons should not be given emphasis.

   2. One problem with this is that there is very little effort to provide real financial alternatives to support a woman in giving birth to and raising a child.

J. Women's rights. The last argument for choice in abortion issues concerns the rights of women to decide their own lives, procreative and other wise, without hindrance, just as men can.

   1. Rights over one's body are not absolute; there are situations when such rights should be limited.

   2. Further, when a woman is pregnant, she has to consider that the situation has changed. She may have rights over her own body in most cases, but doesn't pregnancy involve a quite different situation?

   3. The conceptus is a part of the mother's body, but it also has a separateness that does not put it in the same class with a tumor or an organ, for example.

   4. By the same token, men and people past childbearing age must have sympathy for the woman's predicament, which is not fair when compared with theirs.

K. In conclusion, abortion is a serious moral issue and all the reasons and the arguments for and against it must be given careful consideration when trying to decide what is the moral thing to do.

V. Euthanasia and allowing to die.

A. Definitions.

   1. *Euthanasia* comes from the Greek meaning "happy death" or, in a modern sense, "death with dignity"; however, to many people, it also means mercy murder, and when one word tries to cover such a range of meaning, it is better to use different words or phrases, which I have done.

   2. *Allowing to die* means not starting, or stopping once started, any extraordinary means to keep dying patients alive.

   3. *Mercy death* means taking a direct act to kill someone with his or her permission or at his or her request.

   4. *Mercy killing* means the same as mercy death except without the patient's permission or request.

   5. Concern with this issue has intensified over the last fifty years because of tremendous medical and technological advances.

B. Brain death or irreversible coma is a relatively new (1968) definition of death in addition to the more traditional ones of heart and lung failure. This is again brought on by our technological advances where we can bypass failed heart and lungs by certain machines and then discover a patient has a completely nonfunctioning brain. There are four criteria used to establish this:

1. Unreceptivity and unresponsiveness.
2. No spontaneous movements or breathing.
3. No reflexes.
4. A flat electroencephalogram (EEG).
5. These tests are to be carefully conducted twice in a 48-hour period, 24 hours apart, and if they are all negative, then a patient can be declared "brain dead."
6. Brain death, however, should not be confused with any of the three actions, listed above, because if someone is dead by valid definitions, then you cannot allow the person to die, give him mercy death, or mercy kill him.

C. General arguments for all three actions.

1. Individual rights over one's body and life. This argument states that individuals ought to have rights and freedom over their own bodies, life, and death. The pro's and con's of it have already been discussed in the abortion issue under women's rights over their own bodies.
   a. These rights are not absolute, but for the most part, competent adults do have strong rights and freedom where it concerns allowing them to die.
   b. These rights are weaker in mercy death, first because it is a direct act to kill someone, even though the person has requested it, and second, because someone has to be the killer since it is not suicide, but rather assisted suicide.
   c. In mercy killing, individual rights and freedom do not come into the picture because the person usually cannot choose for himself if he is in a coma, for example.
2. Right to die with dignity. Most human beings fear dying and loss of dignity worse than death, so according to this argument, they ought to have the right to die with dignity.
   a. It is often difficult to determine exactly what "death with dignity" really means since it varies from individual to individual.
   b. Some of the so-called "deaths with dignity" are very questionably dignified for the people dying and also for the survivors.

D. General arguments against all three actions:
 1. Value of life argument. Aren't all three actions flagrant violations of this argument? This principle has been defined as "reverence for life and acceptance of death," and this could at least condone allowing to die, if not the other two.
    a. Who should decide when life has value? We should all value life in general, but to what extent may a person decide when his own life has value or not?
    b. Many people argue that it is the quality of life rather than its quantity that is important, and individuals should be able to decide this about their own lives.
    c. In the cases of mercy death and killing, a killing of someone is still involved whereas in allowing to die it is not; therefore, the value of life principle does not necessarily rule out allowing to die, but it does not necessarily condone the other two actions.
 2. Religious argument. This has the same problem as it did in other areas of taking of human life, and it is especially weak in the action of allowing to die. Many would say that allowing to die is really part of God's plan, and most religions would seem to accept this without condoning the other two actions. There is also still the problem that we must take responsibility for our actions and not try to lay them off on God.
 3. Domino argument. This argument is used quite frequently here because these three "dominoes" are very close together so that if one permits allowing to die, then next will come mercy death, and once mercy death is allowed, then mercy killing will inevitably follow.
    a. The same criticisms apply here as in other areas of taking human life.
    b. We can legally allow one of the actions without allowing the other two by excluding them from our laws.
    c. Once we discover that any breach has occurred, we can pass laws forbidding any abuse and also establish enough safeguards to protect people from the misuse of these actions.
 4. Medicine can never choose death. This argument states that because of the nature of medicine—saving lives and curing—there can be no acceptance of death or allowing to die.
    a. Many doctors and patients themselves, however, deemed this view as the doctor "playing god" and, therefore, unrealistic.
    b. It is also based on false views of medicine that it can

    prolong life indefinitely and also that its only job is to cure and heal and when it cannot do this, it no longer has meaning.

    c. The other part of medicine, however, is comforting and caring for, and when curing and healing are no longer possible, then medicine should keep the patient comfortable and care for him or her until death.

    d. This applies to allowing to die, but not necessarily to the other two actions, and most doctors will not participate in these last ones.

5. Possibility of finding cures. This argument says that if we practice any of the three actions, we might deprive the patient of a chance of late-discovered or miracle cures.

    a. Most doctors are not willing to accept the argument for miracle cures to the extent that they will keep unnecessarily treating patients to the very end.

    b. Also, they argue that the time for cures is when the illness is first diagnosed and in the earlier rather than the later stages. Using aggressive medicine to treat patients who are obviously and inevitably dying is tantamount to torturing them rather than curing them.

6. The irrationality of wanting to die. This argument says that wanting to die is always irrational and usually due to the extreme pain and suffering of seriously ill patients.

    a. Patients often change their minds depending on whether they are suffering or not.

    b. One criticism of this is that it is more rational to accept death than it is not to since it is inevitable for all of us.

    c. Further, isn't it more rational, the critics of this argument would continue, to accept and even choose death when one is suffering terminally and when that suffering could be shortened.

    d. Many people who want to be allowed to die and ask for mercy death have suffered with their situations for long periods of time and, therefore, are often in the best rational positions to decide these things.

    e. Therefore, this argument would not necessarily block allowing to die, although there is still the matter of the direct killing involved in the other two actions.

E. Specific arguments against the three actions.

1. The justice argument says that the principle of justice is being violated in two senses.

    a. People who are allowing patients to die or who are killing them are being unjust or unfair to them.

     b. Patients who want to die can be unjust to others around them who do not agree, and especially those whom they have asked to help them to die.

     c. The question is, "Should any injustice being done to others be considered powerful enough to override patients' individual freedom and rights?"

  2. Abandonment of patients who are allowed to die. Many argue that by allowing patients to die, we are in effect refusing them proper medical care and are abandoning them.

     a. This could be, but there is no reason for it to happen if medicine is seen in both of its two aspects. not just one—comforting and caring for as well as curing and healing.

     b. The hospice approach to care for the dying allows people to die and yet never abandons them.

F. The hospice approach to caring for the dying. This approach seeks to help terminally ill patients and their families to live as comfortably and meaningfully as possible until they die. This approach consists of seven aspects of patient care:

  1. Comforting and caring for patients rather than curing and healing.

  2. Treating the whole human being in all his or her aspects (mental, emotional, spiritual, sociological, as well as physical).

  3. Appropriate pain and symptom control to keep patients completely free from pain and discomfort but still mentally alert enough to enjoy what life they have left.

  4. Outpatient and home care wherever possible.

  5. Humanized inpatient care whenever home care is not possible.

  6. Freedom from financial worry for medical care.

  7. Bereavement counseling and assistance before, during, and after the patient's death for the patient and his or her family.

  8. If this approach is practiced, then dying one's own natural death can be allowed, and the necessity for mercy death and mercy killing should be eliminated since there would no longer be any misery to put patients out of.

G. In conclusion, all reasons for these last two actions have not been entirely eliminated because some patients may not wish to live even with hospice care, but certainly most of the reasons have been taken away.

Additional Questions and Activities for Study and Discussion

1. What are your general views on taking human life in defense of the innocent (self included)? Be as specific as you can and give clear examples and illustrations of situations where you feel such acts of killing are justified and where they are not.

2. Do you think that capital punishment is morally justified? Why or why not? If you believe it is sometimes justified, then when and when not? What possible alternatives to capital punishment would you put forth for dealing with convicted killers to the point where you might consider the elimination of capital punishment? Be specific and answer in detail. Suppose a member of your family for whom you cared very deeply killed someone in a moment of anger, but not selfdefense. Would you want him or her to receive capital punishment or not? Why?

3. Under what conditions do you feel that it is moral to have an abortion? Under what conditions do you feel that it is immoral? Be specific. What workable alternatives to abortion would you recommend and why? If someone you really cared for or you yourself were faced with having an abortion or going through pregnancy, what would you do to help her or yourself? Presume that going through with the pregnancy would cause many problems emotionally, financially, and socially.

4. Do you agree that if people are going to take a strong stand against abortion, they must do much more in the way of counseling and giving other kinds of assistance to the prospective mother? Why or why not? What kinds of assistance and counseling do you feel are necessary? Be specific. How do you propose such assistance be made available since many people do not wish to support such programs with their taxes or donations? Do you think that if such support is not forthcoming, that abortions must continue to be permitted? Why or why not?

5. Draw up a kind of "living will" for yourself describing all situations in which you might want treatment stopped or mercy death or mercy killing administered to you. Be specific. If you strongly object to making up such a document, describe why fully.

6. Disregarding the legal aspects, if someone you really cared for asked to be allowed to die or asked for mercy death or was in a position to be mercy killed (deal with each of these situations), to what extent would you be able to involve yourself in these actions? To what extent do you think any of them is moral or immoral? Answer in

detail, giving specific illustrations and samples and also evidence and reasons for your answers.

7. Read the play, *Whose Life Is It Anyway?* by Brian Clark, and answer the following questions:

   a. Is this a case of allowing to die, mercy death, or mercy killing? Tell why.

   b. Do you think that the main character in the play is mentally capable of making such a decision, or do you think that his request should be disregarded because of his tragic situation? Why?

   c. Do you think that the main character has a right to decide for death even though he can be kept alive and alert for an indefinite period? Why?

   d. If you were in his place, how do you think you would feel? Would you want to live or die, and why?

   e. If someone you loved were in his position and wanted to die, would you let him or help him? Why or why not?

   f. Critically evaluate how the hospital, doctors, nurses, and social workers treated him? Do you agree with the way they dealt with him? Why or why not?

Footnotes

1. William Morris, ed., *The American Heritage Dictionary of the English Language* (Boston: Houghton Mifflin, 1975), pp. 720 and 863.

2. Ibid., p. 1287.

3. Ibid., p. 677.

4. *California Natural Death Act,* Paragraph 7195 (Sacramento: State of California Printer, 1977).

5. Daniel Callahan, *Abortion: Law, Choice, and Morality* (New York: Macmillan, 1970), pp. 417–418. See also Chap. 9.

6. Morris, *The American Heritage Dictionary,* p. 200.

7. Callahan, *Abortion,* p. 44. I prefer to use this term, "conceptus," that really means "that which has been conceived," because of its neutrality.

8. Ibid., pp. 371–373.

9. Ibid., pp. 384–390, and Sissela Bok, "Ethical Problems of Abortion," *The Hastings Center Studies* II, no. 1 (January 1974): 42–52.

10. For a description of other methods of abortion, see Jacques P. Thiroux, *Ethics: Theory and Practice,* 2nd ed., (Encino, Calif.: Glencoe, 1980), pp. 215–216.

11. Callahan, *Abortion,* pp. 31–43.

12. Ibid., p. 62.

13. Henry K. Beecher et al., "A Definition of Irreversible Coma," *Journal of the American Medical Association* 205 (August 1968): 85–88.

14. Lael Wertenbaker, *Death of a Man* (Boston: Beacon Press, 1957), pp. 178–180.

15. O. Ruth Russell, "Moral and Legal Aspects of Euthanasia," *The Humanist* 34 (July–August 1974): 22–27. See also her book, *Freedom to Die: Moral and Legal Aspects of Euthanasia* (New York: Human Sciences Press, 1975).

16. Sandol Stoddard, *The Hospice Movement: A Better Way of Caring for the Dying* (Briarcliff Manor, N.Y.: Stein and Day, 1978), pp. 221–229.

Bibliography

CAPITAL PUNISHMENT

Beck, Robert N., and John B. Orr. *Ethical Choice: A Case Study Approach*. New York: The Free Press, 1970. See Part II, Section 7.

Bedau, Hugo. *The Death Penalty in America*. Garden City, N.Y.: Anchor Books, 1964.

Ewing, Alfred C. *The Morality of Punishment*. London: Routledge and Kegan Paul, 1929.

Hart, H. L. A. *Punishment and Responsibility*. New York: Oxford Press, 1964.

MacLagan, W. G. "Punishment and Retribution." *Philosophy* 14 (1939): 281–298.

Williams, Glanville. *The Sanctity of Life and the Criminal* Law. New York: Alfred A. Knopf, 1957.

ABORTION

Bok, Sissela. "Ethical Problems of Abortion." *The Hastings Center Studies* II, no. 1 (January 1974): 33–52.

Callahan, Daniel. *Abortion: Law, Choice, and Morality*. New York: Macmillan, 1970.

Chandrasekhar, S. *Abortion in a Crowded World*. Seattle: University of Washington Press, 1974.

Cohen, Marshall, et al., eds. *The Rights and Wrongs of Abortion*. Princeton, N.J.: Princeton University Press, 1974.

Feinberg, Joel. *The Problem of Abortion*. Belmont, Calif.: Wadsworth, 1973.

Gardner, R. F. R. *Abortion: The Personal Dilemma*. New York: Pyramid Books, 1974.

Rodman, Hyman, and Betty Sarvis. *The Abortion Controversy,* 2nd ed. New York: Columbia University Press, 1974.

EUTHANASIA AND ALLOWING TO DIE

Beecher, Henry K., et al. "A Definition of Irreversible Coma." *Journal of American Medical Association* 205 (August 1968): 85–88.

Behnke, John A., and Sissela Bok. *The Dilemmas of Euthanasia*. Garden City, N.Y.: Anchor Books, 1975.

Feifel, Herman, ed. *The Meaning of Death*. New York: McGraw-Hill, 1959.

Glaser, Barney G., and Anselm L. Strauss. *Awareness of Dying*. Chicago: Aldine, 1965.

Kohl, Marvin. "Beneficent Euthanasia." *The Humanist* 34 (July–August 1974): 9–11.

Pearson, Leonard, ed. *Death and Dying: Current Issues in the Treatment of the Dying Person*. Cleveland: The Press of Case Western Reserve University, 1969.

Robitscher, Jonas B. "The Right to Die." *The Hastings Center Report* 2 (September 1972): 11–14.

Ross, Elisabeth K. *On Death and Dying*. New York: Macmillan, 1969.

————. *Questions and Answers on Death and Dying*. New York: Collier Books, 1974.

Rossman, Parker. *Hospice*. New York: Association Press, 1975.

Russell, O. Ruth. "Moral and Legal Aspects of Euthanasia." *The Humanist* 34 (July–August 1974): 22–27.

————. *Freedom to Die: Moral and Legal Aspects of Euthanasia*. New York: Human Sciences Press, 1975.

Stoddard, Sandol. *The Hospice Movement: A Better Way of Caring for the Dying*. Briarcliff Manor, N.Y.: Stein and Day, 1978.

Wertenbaker, Lael Tucker. *Death of a Man*. New York: Random House, 1957.

Williamson, William P. "Prolongation of Life or Prolonging the Act of Dying." *The Journal of the American Medical Association* 202 (October 1967): 162–163.

PART 4

Philosophy of Religion

CHAPTER 9

What Is Religion?

It is important to understand that philosophy of religion is not the study of religion from a specific religious or nonreligious point of view, such as Judaism or atheism, but rather is a careful analysis and critical evaluation of the philosophical implications of religion. "Theology" differs from philosophy of religion in that theology is a rational inquiry into the nature of God and religious truth and an organized, formalized body of opinions concerning God and his relationship to human beings, but usually from within a particular religion or religious structure. For example, in Christianity, a formulation of dogma, such as the Trinity or the Incarnation (where God is believed to have become human) and the discussion of such dogma would be considered theology, not philosophy. On the other hand, the critical analysis and evaluation of such dogma, the meaning of religious language, and arguments for and against God's existence, would be examples of philosophy of religion.

Philosophy of religion, then, is an attempt from an objective point of view to analyze and evaluate critically anything having to do with religion in all its aspects, subjecting it to the same tests of evidence, logic, and reason as any other area of philosophy (ethics or metaphysics, for example) with no special axe to grind except to enlighten, clarify, and help readers and students to become more aware.

I wish to state at the outset that the purpose of this part of the book is not to destroy people's faiths or make them into believers or nonbelievers; rather, it is to help them to understand as deeply as possible all the implications of accepting or rejecting religion, thereby increasing their awareness. I hope that such enlightenment will also increase tolerance on both sides of the religious issue—that religious adherents

299

will become more tolerant of religious beliefs different from theirs and also of those people who are agnostic or atheistic (basically nonreligious) and that nonreligious people on their side will not reject out of hand the significance of other people's religious commitments.

Too often, for example, religionists hold their beliefs without ever having questioned or tested them against scientific and philosophical theories that conflict with them. In this way they are only superficially religious. It would seem, however, that if one continued to be faithful after having tested one's beliefs, they would have been strengthened rather than weakened. Also, if one's beliefs cannot stand up to rational scrutiny, then perhaps they are not held deeply enough in the first place.

On the other hand, many nonreligious, sometimes antireligious, people reject religion completely but on a superficial basis without having really examined its purposes, significance, and implications for human life in general. Rejecting theories without having fully examined them is as philosophically unsound as accepting them in this way.

Therefore, philosophy of religion strongly encourages people to think carefully about the subject of religion so that any choices they make for or against it, or somewhere in between, can be based on intelligent examination with full knowledge and from as unbiased a point of view as possible. The purpose of this part of the book and its chapters, then, is to provide for such an examination by first discussing what religion is and does, next presenting arguments for and against the existence of an ultimate reality, and then surveying briefly various religious and nonreligious viewpoints.

General Definitions

As with previous chapters and subject areas, it is always helpful to define any key terms we will be using in our discussion.

Religion means essentially to "bind back," coming from the Latin *re,* which means "back" or "again," and *ligare,* which means "to bind." It also comes from *religio,* which in Latin refers to the bond between humans and the gods.[1] Another possible implication of the reference to binding might be that religion, in many cultures, has attempted to "bind" people together in some kind of community by providing the spiritual "cement" needed to form the foundation for other aspects of culture. The fact that it has not always been successful does not take away from its goal to do so.

Ultimate reality is a phrase that I plan to use, especially in general religious discussions, to refer to the central core of any religion or religious viewpoint because the other terms—Jahweh, Jesus Christ, Allah, Brahman, Tao, Zeus, The Good, Nirvana—are so different in character and yet ultimate to those who believe in them that a more neutral term is needed.

Ultimate concern is a phrase, created by the Protestant theologian and philosopher Paul Tillich, which means both an Ultimate Reality of some sort and the ultimate concern of human beings basically *for* some ultimate reality. This will be explained more fully later.

Other definitions will be made as needed when specialized terms and phrases are used.

Views of What Religion Is

The word "religion" means many things to many people; some define it very broadly to mean anything anyone believes in strongly, as characterized by the phrase, "He paid his insurance premiums *religiously.*" Others define it much more narrowly to mean that which involves only a supernatural being or beings; and still others narrow it further by saying that there is only one real religion, and it is Islam (for example). All others are accused of making false claims to being a religion. Let us now look at these two types of definitions.

THE BROAD VIEW

This view states that whatever any human being believes in strongly is considered a religion. People could devote themselves, for example, to rock music, art, communism, science, or whatever, and as long as they believed in it strongly or devoted their lives to its pursuit, then it would be their religion. Under this category, atheism is also a religion and, as has been mentioned, so is communism. Communism may not have any supernatural godlike ultimate reality, but it does have the ideal state concept that all communists can revere and strive for. This view, of course, has the advantage of allowing anyone with a strong belief to be considered religious, but it has the disadvantage of watering down or blurring the definition so that the word "religion" includes too much. How do we distinguish between the devoted Jew, Christian, Muslim, Hindu, or Buddhist and anyone who chooses to believe in just anything? Generally speaking, it would seem that what we refer to as religion or religious involves something more than just strong belief in anything. Let us look now at the other view.

THE NARROW VIEW

This view describes religion as having to do only with relations between human beings and a supernatural being or beings, and the nar-

rowest view would say that it applies only to one religion as characterized in the statement, for example, that "Christianity is the one true
religion," implying that all other beliefs are false or not really religions at all. This is more definitive, but it also causes problems in that
there are many more religions than just one (than just Christianity, for
example) and further that there are some very famous world religions
that do not stress the existence of supernatural beings, such as Confucianism, Buddhism, and Taoism.

PAUL TILLICH'S CONCEPT OF ULTIMATE CONCERN

In his book *Dynamics of Faith,* Tillich defines religious faith as "being
ultimately concerned" or as "ultimate concern."[2] With this view, he
encompasses both the narrow and broad views, although he actually
settles on a narrow view at the end of his discussions. When asked
whether he meant by "ultimate concern," the fact that a human being
was "ultimately concerned" about someone or something or whether
he was referring to the object of that human concern (for example,
God or Allah), Tillich said, in effect, both. He said that ultimate concern involved a certain attitude on the part of human beings in that
they were ultimately concerned *about* something or someone, but he
stated that the phrase also referred to the *object* of that human concern,
so that ultimate concern is both the human activity of being ultimately
concerned and also that *about* which one is ultimately concerned (God,
for example). Perhaps what he meant will become clearer as we examine the characteristics of ultimate concern as Tillich saw them.

CHARACTERISTICS OF ULTIMATE CONCERN

IT HAS THE HIGHEST PRIORITY OF VALUES OR CONCERNS.   By "ultimate" Tillich meant "unconditional, absolute, unqualified," and he said
that the ultimate concern has top priority in the system of concerns or
values that constitutes a personality. This means that it gives meaning,
purpose, and direction to a human life, and in a crisis a human being
will sacrifice all other values or concerns, including life itself, for it. It
also tends to unify both individual lives and the life of a community,
society, or culture. Further, Tillich states that all ultimate concerns or
values take on *religious significance,* whether or not they can actually be
called religious. It is with this latter statement that Tillich includes the
possibility, at least initially, of anything that a person believes in strongly
being an ultimate concern and taking on, if not actually having, religious importance.

Good examples of a religious type of ultimate concern are any of the famous martyrs from Christianity or other religions. Their over-riding concern was for God and doing what they believed He commanded to the point where they would even sacrifice their lives rather than be unfaithful to their ultimate reality and its wishes. A nonreligious example would be that of a strong patriot who would sacrifice his life and even the lives of his family "for the good of his country," his ultimate concern. Even though the patriot is not religious, yet as Tillich has pointed out, his ultimate concern has religious significance for him just as the religious martyr's does for him.

PERVASIVENESS. Ultimate concerns are by nature total and all embracing, according to Tillich. The Christian statement that is sometimes heard, "Everything I do is for the greater glory of God," is a good example of how pervasive they can be. Persons involved with ultimate concerns sometimes are said to "eat, drink, and sleep" their work, their art, or their religion. Such concerns, then, permeate a person's whole life at all levels.

HOLINESS OR SACREDNESS. There is always an emotive or affective attribute or accompaniment to ultimate concerns and commitments. For its adherents, an ultimate concern always contains an element of the experience of fear, wonder, awe, or mystery, and their reverence is a powerful expression of the holy. In fact, this characteristic may be one of the most definitive aspects of what religion is. One might even ask whether some concern can really be called ultimate or religious if it lacks this particular quality of the holy or if it is not a "system of holy forms," that is, patterns or structures of human attitudes, beliefs, or practices that are organized ways of thinking, feeling, and acting. Some examples of such forms or structures are myth (legends, stories); ritual, which is overt behavior and enactment before religious objects or symbols; morality or various codes on how or how not to behave (do's and don'ts for leading a good life); and the religious community, which provides for public and communal as well as private or personal expression of religious feeling. This is most often exemplified in various religions in their major services, such as the Catholic Mass and the Jewish, Protestant, Islamic, Hindu, and other religious worship services.

There is an aura of awe, reverence, wonder, and sometimes fear embodied in all these activities because the ultimate concern is conceived of as powerful, holy, great, and good. This can be seen even in nonreligious ceremonies such as patriotic activities in celebration of nations' independence or establishment and on other significant occasions.

SYMBOLIC EXPRESSION.   As already described briefly, religious experience takes place in a context of powerful symbolic objects and words that elicit a participant's religious responses. The participant often feels that the holy or sacred actually dwells in these symbolic objects and words. For example, Roman Catholics believe that when the priest pronounces the words of Jesus at the Last Supper, "This is my body . . . this is my blood . . ." over bread and wine during the Mass, that these are *really* and *actually* turned somehow into the body and blood of Jesus in a mysterious process called "transubstantiation." Symbols when used in these contexts are poetic or imaginative words or other kinds of significant objects (statues, scrolls, crosses, and incense, for example) that have the power to evoke and sustain deeply moving forms of experience for participants. If you have ever seen or have been in a famous cathedral, temple, or church with beautiful stained glass windows, statues, and carved altars, such as the Chartres Cathedral in France, or have ever read passages from a religious work, such as the Bible, the Koran, the Talmud, then you know how impressive all these symbols can be.

RELIGIOUS PRACTICE AND RITUAL.   Religious experience is both celebrated and lived. Individually it is said to give meaning and unity to a human being's life, and culturally it signifies the convictions that create the life of a culture and also make it a shared life or "community." For example, in Christianity and Judaism, there are rituals, such as baptism, marriage, confirmation, or bar or bas mitzvah to celebrate the acceptance of new members into the religious community, the important conjoining of husband and wife to continue the community, and the coming of age of the young. And every religion, even in the most primitive cultures, has similar rituals that not only have meaning for the individuals involved but for the community, commemorating such important events in their lives as the ones mentioned, plus the planting and harvesting of crops, the acceptance of people into the ministry or priesthood, and the mourning of the death of members of the community.

In describing all these characteristics, I do not mean to suggest that one would have to accept Tillich's views, but I believe that they are helpful in trying to understand what religion is and does. His approach helps, at least to some extent, to synthesize the broad and narrow views of what "religion" means. For Tillich, however, the ultimate concern has to be what he calls Being-Itself or Ground Being, but what we could probably best characterize as the Christian or Jewish concept of God in the fullest sense of the word.

PERSONAL RELIGIOUS FEELING
AND ORGANIZED RELIGION

There is one more important distinction that must be made and that is between personal religious feeling, or that feeling or sense of commitment that resides within a religious person, and organized religion, or the organization of various people's religious feelings into a community-oriented structure of laws and rituals.

PERSONAL RELIGIOUS FEELING.   To my way of thinking, this is where religion begins for human beings, even if one accepts the existence of an ultimate reality. It is, after all, the effect on human beings that we are concerned with when we discuss religion. Many anthropologists and historians feel that humans are the creators of religion, so their feelings about the powerful mysteries of the universe are what lead to the ultimate concern Tillich talks about when he refers to the human attitude. As far as we can tell, religion is one of the oldest of human activities or practices, preceding philosophy, science, and perhaps even formalized language. The only other human activity that seems to be as old as religion is art, which appears to have been closely intertwined with religion from its beginning as a kind of magical expression of religious feeling.

I will discuss the origin and development of religion a little later, but it is important to understand that religion, even at its most public, is basically a very personal thing with most human beings. Religious feeling would also seem to precede any type of organized religion. That is, religion as a structural system or as an organization would seem to occur after the personal feelings of its adherents and functions as a way of expressing them in community.

ORGANIZED RELIGION.   An organized religion, such as the Greek or Roman religions, Hinduism, Islam, Judaism, and Christianity, comes about when individuals' personal feelings have a common basis, such as the fact that the people come from the same area or culture or have many of the same needs or desires. All these similarities become organized by the leaders and/or priests of a tribe or culture into a set of patterns, forms, or structures, which include rituals, symbols, ethical practices, methods of worship, prayers, myths, and legends, which, because of their similarities, have significant meaning for the members of that particular tribe or culture. As long as the organized religion successfully expresses the personal religious feelings of its members, it is useful and important, but when feelings change and the organized structures do not, there is often a gap that causes rifts within the organization and new religious splinter groups arise if the original organization does not adapt or change with the feelings of its followers.

A good example of this has occurred many times in the history of Christianity and Judaism. There is no doubt that Christianity has its roots in Judaism, but with the coming of Jesus, there was a new religious feeling to which Judaism would not and could not adapt. Even after Christianity was formed, the Roman Catholic tradition was its strongest expression after the split with the Eastern Orthodox churches (Greek, Russian, Armenian, etc.); however, beginning with Martin Luther's attack on the Roman Catholic church and what he felt were corruptions of basic Christian ideals, Protestantism arose and over the years has experienced many, many more schisms (splits) of which we are all aware.

Therefore, it is very important to distinguish between personal religious feeling and organized religion. Many times critics of religion confuse the two, rejecting "religion" in its entirety because of some corruption or problem within a particular religious organization. Also, there are many religious people who do not belong to any specific organized religion but who nevertheless have strong personal religious feelings. It would behoove organized religions to be aware of this difference, for many times they become outmoded and fail to express adequately the religious feelings of their followers. This very often results in people dropping out of the organization and sometimes starting up new ones. It is a vital and living religious organization that recognizes these changes in feelings and, at least within reason, allows for or adapts to these changes, especially when they are valid and important. Too often, then, these two are confused, but it is important to recognize that, for both religious and nonreligious people alike, these two aspects of religion are indeed different.

Origin and Development of Religion

It is, of course, very difficult to really know how religion first began. There are many myths in many different religions about how the world came about or was created and where human beings came from. They all involve the acceptance of some sort of source or power behind nature and everything in the universe, but of course nobody knows for sure what the very first religious expression of a human being was or whether religion actually came from some supernatural source, from humans themselves, or from some combination of the two. We can, however, to some extent trace some of the early religious expressions through studies that have been made of ancient cultures and their primitive counterparts in our own time. Without presuming to accept or deny the existence of an ultimate reality of any kind, let us attempt to understand how religion might have evolved, strictly from the human point of view.

MANA, ANIMISM, AND SPIRITISM

Since we, even in our time of sophisticated scientific knowledge, still have reverence for the power of nature and the mysteries of the universe, it is not unreasonable to picture primitive humans holding out their hands and feeling the warmth of the sun, or witnessing the great forces in nature, such as floods, earthquakes, tornadoes, and storms, as well as its beauty. Obviously, these forces and even the beauty was and is outside of human control; that is, human beings did not cause any of them—they just occurred. Since these primitive humans did not have any real scientific knowledge about atoms, molecules, cells, or bacteria, they presumed that there were powerful spirits in the universe that caused rain, sunlight, tree and plant growth, and so on. These unseen but felt powers that primitive humans recognized have been called "mana" by anthropologists who have studied this development of human beings and cultures. This mana created and caused awe and reverence in human beings. We still have many of these same feelings, for who of us today on witnessing a storm at sea, a tornado, a hurricane, or an earthquake or on looking out on some majestic scene in the mountains, at the seashore, or on the desert does not feel this power and majesty and have a sense of awe or reverence? Therefore, it seems valid to assume that these feelings were even stronger and more frightening for primitive humans.

It also seems quite natural that these primitives would want to exert some control over these powers so that they could acquire more of their good effects and prevent bad effects from occurring. What better way to do this than to try to see these powers as persons in some way, albeit unseen persons, so that humans could relate to and communicate with them just as they could each other. They felt that if they could placate the powers' fury and encourage their friendship or even love, then perhaps they could protect themselves from the storms and yet acquire the warmth, coolness, or food, for example, that they needed to survive.

It seems that primitive humans first saw that there were spirits in every tree, animal, plant, the sea, the sun, and within the earth itself. They felt, in other words, that everything in reality was inhabited with unseen spirits, and this phenomenon is called "animism," which comes from the Latin *anima* meaning "soul" or "spirit." When these spirits were thought of as free or mobile and able to appear anywhere and not just be imprisoned within a tree, for example, then the phenomenon is called "spiritism."

POLYTHEISM, PANTHEISM, AND HENOTHEISM

When the urge to relate to these spirits as persons arose, then spiritism became *polytheism* (many personal gods); that is, these spirits were seen as personal and could be related to by human beings as real persons of whom they could make requests for good things to occur and also for bad things to be prevented. For example, if there was a drought that caused plants, animals, crops, and even humans to die, humans would talk or "pray" to the rain spirit or god to send rain. If they were on the sea and a terrible life-threatening storm came up, they would pray to the sea spirits or sea god to calm the seas and thus save them from drowning.

Whether good things or bad things happened, people seemed to feel that they had to give these spirits or gods sacrifices or to somehow allay or prevent their fury from harming them or ruining their environments; therefore, they prayed, worshipped, danced in honor of, atoned for their sins, real and imagined, and otherwise revered these gods to get and keep them on their side.

To understand better and get them to do what they wanted, these early humans often fashioned statues or idols that looked somewhat like them and in front of which they could perform their obeisances. They sometimes also adopted certain animals, such as snakes, bears, or antelope as specially imbued with certain powers or luck, and they then protected and worshipped them. The American Indian, for example, reveres most animals, but especially the eagle, and certain other cultures also selected one animal as their magical power "connection" with unseen powers or as a particular manifestation of the gods.

Pantheism suggests that there is spirituality in all of nature and that these spirits may appear in human, although godlike, form to mere mortals; for example, in the Greek and Roman cultures, Poseidon or Neptune was god of the sea, Ares or Mars was the god of war, Eros or Amor was the god of love, and so on. There was a god or goddess for every aspect of nature, and many lesser spirits such as dryads and hamadryads inhabited many different parts of the forest, such as trees and streams. This approach to religion, as I stated earlier, is called "pantheism" from *pan* meaning "through all" or "in all" and *theism* meaning person or personal. Some gods were considered more important than others, for example, the father god or king of gods Zeus, in Greek religion, and his queen Hera (in Roman religion they were called Jupiter and Juno). When a religion has many personal gods, it is called "polytheism," since *poly* means many. When one god is more important than the rest in a religion but other gods are not denied, it is called *henotheism*.

When religious spirits or persons are located within the common world of nature and culture, then the religion is called a nature-culture religion, and it almost always involves a plurality of religious spirits or gods and polytheism, pantheism, or henotheism. As you no doubt realize, most of our modern-day Western world religions do not have this quality, but have instead a one-god concept, which is called *monotheism*. We will discuss that type of religion in a moment, but we can see that religion, certainly at its inception and from all the evidence available from the study of ancient cultures, seems to have been very closely connected with nature and that the relationship between humans and their ultimate reality seemed to be intimately intertwined with nature and the world around them.

MONOTHEISM

Differing from nature-culture religions, a more abstract view of the power behind everything is that of monotheism, which refers to the believing in and the worshipping of one god who is a person or who stands in some sort of personal relationship to human beings and the world "it" has created. This is generally considered, especially by monotheists obviously, as a more sophisticated type of religion than one that is mixed up or "confused" with various objects and processes or events in nature. This concept is more logically simple and pure, in that there is one power that is unseen and abstract, an intelligent being (this accounts for the order of the universe) who is also a person or personal. This view would also conflict less with science and philosophy in that it would be separated from instead of all mixed up with nature. I am not trying to say that science and philosophy have no objections to monotheism—in fact their objections are quite serious in certain areas as we shall see—but rather that the whole concept, generally speaking, has at least been more appealing to most modern-day humans than have the other views previously mentioned.

It is hard to know when monotheism first began. There seems to be some slight evidence of it in Egyptian times with at least one pharaoh, but it seems to be more of a Greco-Judaic view beginning with Socrates and Plato and their views of some sort of ultimate reality, which Plato referred to as "The Good" (only one "o" removed from God?). This being was more in the form of a source of abstract thought and also goodness that Plato posited as the Ultimate Idea or Truth in his transcendent world of ideas. This being is not clearly delineated either by Socrates or Plato, and Plato discusses it in the section of his

Republic called "The Myth of Er." By calling it a "myth," Plato seems to place it in literature rather than in philosophy, where the rest of the discussion in *The Republic* is embodied.[3]

Aristotle, as will be discussed later, also had a concept of something called the Prime or Unmoved Mover, but this seems to have been a necessity of logic for Aristotle to account for the motions of the planets rather than some theistic or personalized God-type being. The most clearly presented monotheistic view is that of Judaism, which seems to have arisen independently of the Greek culture. This ultimate reality, referred to as Jehovah or Yahweh—according to Jewish teachings as found in the Old Testament of the Bible, the Talmud, and other sources, including interpretations of the many Jewish scholars down through the ages—is the creator of the universe and everything in it. He is the Holy Other, a transcendent god, who will not permit worship of any other gods. According to Jewish teachings, this being has spoken to the Jewish people through various prophets and has made a covenant or agreement with the Jews, whom he has chosen as his own people. Therefore, this being, although not of this world, nevertheless has a personal relationship with the people in it. This same being is also the God of the Christians later, although his oneness is somewhat complicated by the addition of Jesus and the Holy Spirit, all of which we will discuss later.

In the Islamic religion, which comes after Judaism and Christianity in time, the god, Allah, is similar in concept to the Jewish monotheistic God. Hinduism also has a one-god concept, but it is more henotheistic in that it accepts other gods as well; it accepts them, however, as manifestations of Brahman, which is the name of its ultimate reality. All these particular versions of monotheism will be discussed more fully later. Let us now take a look at the nature of such a monotheistic ultimate reality.

THE NATURE OF THE MONOTHEISTIC ULTIMATE REALITY

Most versions of such a being characterize it as the creative power source from which the universe and everything in it have come. It is intelligent and logical in its creative power, although it has also been characterized as forceful and even artistic. It is generally considered as the Holy Other or transcendent; that is, it stands apart from its creation and is more than or other than what it has done. This particular assumption may, of course, put this being far beyond human attainment. However, this being can also be seen as "immanent" or as residing to some degree within the world and intervening in its processes.

The degree of immanence may vary from being a part of everything, but especially humans, to operating merely as a force in nature.

Its last general quality is that it can be seen as impersonal, the way in which it is accepted in most Eastern religions, or personal, as it is in Western religions. There are advantages to both views. The Eastern view avoids the problems of anthropomorphism (making the ultimate reality humanlike or even into a glorified human), but, of course, it also provides a lesser possibility for a close personal relationship between God and humans, which the Western view encourages. Some arguments also present this being as both transcendent and immanent, which means that although it is a separate being from its creation, it inhabits this world or at least human beings in some mysterious way. This is exemplified in such statements as "The kingdom of God is within you" and by such concepts as Atman-Brahman in Hinduism and the existence of individual souls in Christianity. We will go into much more detail concerning these views of the ultimate reality in the next two chapters. At this point, let us examine the possibilities for the nature of the religious relationships between human beings and the ultimate reality.

THE NATURE OF RELIGIOUS RELATIONSHIPS

MYSTICISM. The mystical approach to the ultimate reality definitely sees it as transcendent, Holy Other, and unreachable by most human methods. In this respect, the ultimate reality is thought of as some being that cannot be conceptualized by human reason; it can be experienced only through some sort of mystical awareness. This approach would eschew all references to rationalizing this being, such as arguing for or against its existence, but would claim rather that its presence is felt in some mysterious way, usually by some nonrational process through meditation, contemplation, or private vision. The advantage of this approach is that it bypasses any criticism from a rational point of view since it admits at the outset that communing with this being is not accomplished through reason or at least not through analytic reason. On occasion, the claim is made that humans use a higher form of reason, sometimes called intuition.

The mystical claim is that one can only experience this being himself or herself and, therefore, that there is no objective analysis possible by others. The disadvantage of such an approach is that it puts the ultimate reality totally beyond human conception in general. Incidentally, this way of conceiving of the ultimate reality has not been as popular in Western religions as in the Eastern ones. There are to be sure some strands of mysticism in Western religions, such as Hassidism in Judaism and St. John of the Cross and St. Theresa of Avila in Christianity, but generally the Western approach has favored a more theistic, anthropomorphic, and rationalistic approach. Eastern religion, on the other hand, has tended toward the derationalization of the ultimate reality, placing this being in whatever form they see it, far beyond human beings and reachable only through some sort of meditative exercises, such as Zen in Buddhism.

THEISM AND ANTHROPOMORPHISM.   As has been described earlier, "theism" conceives of the ultimate reality as a person or as personal. "He" relates to human beings much as they relate to each other and is capable of many humanlike emotions, such as anger, love, mercy, and so on. This being is definitely felt to be reachable through human activity such as prayer, ritual, and other overt actions. He can be talked to and he will answer. He can be asked for help or protection, and he will provide it. This approach seems to be much more satisfactory to Western religionists, for they are more comfortable with thinking of this being as their "father" or "brother," only in a deeper sense than in human life, and in feeling that they can relate to him in a close personal way as they can with any human loved one or friend.

One problem with this approach is that Western religion often tends to anthropomorphize the ultimate reality so that it is sometimes more human than godly, with all the attendant difficulties that might accrue to such a vision. For example, does this being have a body, like human beings only perhaps more glorified? If not, then how can we say that it is male or any other gender? Another problem is knowing where this being resides and what it looks like. Some forms of Christianity complicate matters in their conception of the ultimate reality as three persons with one divine nature—the Trinity of the Father, Son (Jesus Christ), and the Holy Spirit. This is deemed a mystery and rightly so, but it does make the personification of this being even more difficult. At any rate, one can see that there are problems with anthropomorphizing the ultimate reality.

RELIGIOUS ATHEISM.   Another way of looking at the ultimate reality is in a nontheistic, impersonal way. I call this "religious atheism," which must sound like a contradiction in terms, but actually "atheism" merely means "against theism." This can mean the rejection of any ultimate reality, which I call "nonreligious atheism," but it can also mean the acceptance of an ultimate reality, which is *not* a person or personal in any way. A good example of this is the "Tao" of Taoism, a Chinese religion. This Tao (pronounced "dow" as in "how"), sometimes translated as "The Way," is a kind of life force that flows through and

exists within all reality. It is a power that is believed to be everywhere, but it is not a person or personal as the Western God is.

Taoism states that what one must do is sort of "go with the flow"
and not assert oneself in any way. One should just try to fit in with
the natural flow of things and not try to analyze or symbolize or personalize the Tao in any way. Of course, this view of the ultimate reality has the advantage of avoiding all the pitfalls of theism and anthropomorphism, but it also has the disadvantage of the loss of personal
relationship and identity with an ultimate reality. The Tao is much
more like an impersonal energy or force that operates in all aspects of
nature and reality.

DEISM.   Somewhere in between theism and religious atheism is deism,
which sees the ultimate reality as an intelligent, powerful source that
once created the universe and everything in it but now has no personal
relationship with what it has created. It is a kind of God-as-scientist-
or-engineer viewpoint. The deistic god has no personal interest in his
creation, but his existence does account for the logical order of the
universe in all its aspects. This view, which is close to Aristotle's Prime
Mover concept, was very popular in the eighteenth century (called the
Age of Enlightenment), for it satisfied the need of that century to account for order and reason in the universe without involving what many
people thought of as the superstitious and anthropomorphic aspects of
theism.

As noted before in discussing other matters in this chapter, more
will be said later about the various views of the nature of the ultimate
reality in the next two chapters, but now it is important to discuss
some of the general problems that occur when dealing with religious
language and concepts.

Problems with Religious Language, Concepts, and Meaning

One of the main difficulties that occurs in discussing religion is that
language and concepts used in connection with it are often times different from those used in science and philosophy and other areas of
culture. It is best then that we realize these problems before continuing.

THE NATURE OF RELIGIOUS LANGUAGE

One of the problems in dealing with religious language, especially as
it is found in various "books" that form the backbone of a particular

313

religion's tradition, is that it is often not scientific or philosophic but, rather, is symbolic, poetic, or literary in form. A great deal of religious feeling is expressed in myth (defined here as "story" or "legend"), fable, or parable, mainly because most religions have their roots in oral traditions long before written language was available, and stories and poems are easier to remember than are nonpoetic or nonliterary prose as the former can be pictured in the mind or memorized with the help of rhythm or rhyme.[4] When we deal with this type of literary language, we do get significant meaning from it, but it is also quite difficult to analyze it or to distinguish fact from fiction.

Another problem with religious language is how it relates to non-religious or ordinary language. Does it mean exactly the same thing to use the word "love" in connection with God as it does to use it in connection with human beings, or is the meaning of the word entirely different when used in the two contexts?

RELIGIOUS LANGUAGE AS UNIVOCAL.   When religious language is said to be exactly the same as ordinary language, the relationship is univocal (literally one voiced). If we try to take this viewpoint, we have difficulty almost from the outset. Referring back to the discussion about God's gender, for example, how can it mean exactly the same thing to say that God is male and that President Reagan is also male? God would not seem to have a body, as President Reagan does. Also, to say that President Reagan is Maureen Reagan's father cannot be exactly the same as saying that God is the father of the human race. There does not seem to be any biological or genetic relationship in the second situation as there is in the first.

RELIGIOUS LANGUAGE AS EQUIVOCAL.   Does this mean, then, that the words "male" and "father" are not *at all* the same in meaning or are equivocal (literally separate voiced)?[5] If so, then it is almost impossible for us to use human language sensibly when talking about the ultimate reality or God. If the words have completely different meanings, then what *is* the relationship? It is almost as if we are speaking nonsense. If we call God our father or describe him as male, then exactly what do we mean? The meanings of these words are perfectly clear when used with President Reagan or any other human male, and if they completely lose their meanings when used with God, then what purpose do they serve and why do we use them in talking about God?

RELIGIOUS LANGUAGE AS ANALOGICAL.   A third and generally more acceptable version is that religious language does not mean exactly the same as ordinary language, nor is it completely different; rather it is analogical.[6] This means that the words when used in both contexts have similar and related but not identical meanings; rather, they are analogous to one another. For example, when we describe a dog as a male and a father to his pups, we use the terms somewhat analogically to that of what we mean when we use these in a human context. However, when we use these same words in connection with humans, we obviously mean something more since maleness and fatherhood are not the same in the canine and human realms. This may be why dog breeders use the term "sire" rather than "father" when speaking of the relationship betwen a male dog and his pup.

One can see how the analogy works further when we begin to speak more abstractly, for example, in using the word "intelligent." We speak of animals as being "intelligent," but we certainly do not mean exactly the same thing by the word when we speak of our fellow human beings, nor do we mean something entirely different. We are speaking analogically, that is, in a *comparative* manner. We are saying, in effect, to speak of Bowser as intelligent means something like speaking of Plato as intelligent, but it does not really mean the same thing.

This seems to be a more workable theory than the univocal or equivocal, but it has one serious problem. In speaking analogically of dogs and humans, we can accept or reject the analogy because we can see both of its parts; that is, we can compare the dog we are calling intelligent with human beings we call intelligent and see how well the analogy fits. In using the analogy with human beings and an ultimate reality, however, we have before us only one part of the analogy—the human one. Any analogy between humans and God, for example, has to be one-sided so that we can never really fully test the analogy to see if it is accurate. What we end up with, then, is a literary device that, however, still seems to work better than the other two theories. We say that the sentence, "God is our father," means that God has the same attributes, *symbolically speaking,* as our human fathers. He created us originally, albeit mysteriously; he protects and guides us; and we respect and love him as he loves us, his sons and daughters. However, we have no conclusive proof that God is really our father or that this relationship is not just in our minds rather than truly a part of external reality.

THE PROBLEMS WITH RELIGIOUS CONCEPTS

Related to the problems with the nature of religious language is the problem with religious concepts due again a great deal to the nature of the basis of religion. First, much religious practice is symbolic and ritualistic rather than scientific or philosophical. For example, a good deal of what is expressed by religious people toward their ultimate reality is done in nonrational ceremonies such as masses, services, sacraments, and rites and also in more concrete symbols such as statues, church buildings, stained glass windows, paintings, and ritualistic movements and gestures. When I call these nonrational, I do not mean *ir*rational or mad; I mean that all these things are very difficult to analyze and even define in some scientifically or philosophically rational sense. For example, how can you scientifically or philosophicaly rationalize that pouring water on people or immersing them in it actually makes them spiritual members of a particular religion? I do not mean to say that this activity is meaningless or insignificant; rather, its meaning or significance is not solely found in the realm of reason. It is something quite different and therefore difficult to rationalize.

Further, much so-called religious "knowledge" or information is "revealed" and not experienced or reasoned as scientific and philosophical knowledge is. Almost all religions are based on some sort of revelation or revelations from some source, usually outside of nature. There are many such revelations claimed, and they differ in many ways even though they are sometimes similar. It is very difficult, without using faith, to know which of these revelations should be accepted as knowledge or whether any of them should. Many religious people find such revelations and the evidence surrounding them sufficient with their faith to convince them that a particular ultimate reality exists and that they should live their lives as it tells them to, but there is no clearly rational way to examine these as we can a particular scientific or philosophical theory that can be observed and tested by rational means. Further, as we shall see in Chapter 13, "The Sources of Knowledge," there is some question whether or not revelation and faith can really be considered as valid sources of knowledge at all.

All these special aspects and attributes of religion—its language, concepts, and meaning—then present some problems for philosophy of religion in that in any analysis, examination, and evaluation that we attempt in this area of human life, we must be aware of the pitfalls and confusions that may occur whenever religion is discussed. This may be why many people will often be heard to say, "Never discuss politics or religion," meaning that they are too controversial and that there really are no clear answers for us in these areas. However, from the philosophical point of view, to refuse to examine and discuss any question is tantamount to remaining ignorant of its implications, and therefore we should not avoid critically analyzing religion. We should, however, be wary of the problems we may encounter in doing so.

Cultural Purposes of Religion

In trying to see where religion fits into the various aspects of human culture and what purposes it fulfills, we find that there are several needs that it has met and also several uses to which it has been put—some constructive and some detrimental to human beings.

CONSTRUCTIVE PURPOSES

One of its most important contributions to cultures at all levels and sizes (for example, family, tribe, city, nation) has been to attempt to unite all members into one community, thus giving them order, security, and a peaceful existence. It attempts to do this physically, mentally, emotionally, and spiritually, thereby organizing the life of the community at all levels of its existence. The spiritual and emotional aspects are, of course, taken care of in the rituals, ceremonies, dedications, and other religious activities that are embodied in its practice. For example, religion anoints and sanctifies the community's leaders, thus tying them into the spiritual world and also giving them the significant authority they need to rule the community in this world.

It also incorporates the physical in that it provides ceremonies to celebrate the seasons, crops, and the need for rain, sunshine, and children, for example. It provides for political and social control by tying the community and its government in with whatever supernatural existence or existences are believed to exist. It provides education in the traditions and lore of the community in its religious practices and in many of its teachings. Mentally it tries to give meaning to the existence of the whole culture and everyone in it by defining its values, and it attempts to provide psychological satisfaction for all its members in that it gives them and their culture meaning and purpose and also staves off the three anxieties described by Tillich (see Chapter 4): fate and death, guilt and condemnation, and emptiness and meaninglessness.

Moreover, it provides a code of morality and a sanction for what is morally acceptable or unacceptable in that particular community. It sets up laws or rules in the form of commandments and prohibitions, do's and don'ts, so that members know how to act and so that everyone's life, freedom, and happiness can be enhanced, preserved, and protected. The sanction is greater than that set down by human laws alone, for if the spirit(s) that govern the world can provide the sanctions, then laws have more force. Obviously, ten years in prison in this life is not as powerful a punishment as is an eternity of suffering after one dies, anymore than a reward of money in this life is equivalent to eternal bliss in some sort of heaven. If morality and religion are both tied together, then there is obviously more unity and order in the community than if they were not.

As you can see, then, religion can organize and unify an entire culture's life and the individual lives of all its members, not only providing security in this life but also promising a continued existence afterward of total happiness and goodness. The natural is incorporated with the supernatural, and the attempt is made to consolidate all aspects of human beings and their culture. When religion functions well, it has tended to do this and has often been a beacon light of hope and realization in oppressive societies that were corrupt and decadent. However, religion, as with any other human institution—and it is always a human institution, regardless of its supposed supernatural connections—has also been seen as destructive by many of its critics because of its own corruptions, which have often led to persecution, human degradation, and death.

CULTURAL PROBLEMS WITH RELIGION

PERSECUTION OF OTHER BELIEVERS OR NONBELIEVERS.   In the history of every religion, there has been some persecution of others, who either belonged to other religions or who believed in no religion. No religion is exempt from this. Persecution probably arises, when it does, because of some of the very things that contribute to religion's efficacy. For example, the unity and order inherent in most religions also generally means that there is a goodly amount of control exerted by the religion and its leaders over the rest of the members of the culture. This control does of course provide unity, but it also makes it difficult for any dissension to be accepted by the status quo. Most religions, being somewhat dogmatic and absolutistic in their structure, tend not to encourage or often allow for questioning or dissension. It is as if the religion would crumble if legitimate questions were allowed, especially when some of its tenets have been successfully challenged by scientific discoveries or philosophical reasoning. What is often difficult for religions is to let go of those beliefs and tenets that are definitely outmoded or proved wrong without fearing that the whole religion will collapse.

For example, when Galileo Galilei (1564–1642), the Italian scientist and philosopher, theorized from his observations in astronomy that the sun and not the earth was the center of our universe, he was unfairly persecuted for his discoveries because his findings did not square with the notion that earth and, therefore, human beings were the center of the universe as held by the major religion of Western Europe at the time, Roman Catholicism. The problem with that religion's taking this hard line is that its essential dogma is that God created the world and humans, not where he placed the center of the universe; however, religions often feel that if they change one thing, they will have to change everything. This viewpoint has caused more difficulty for religion, especially in the nineteenth and twentieth centuries with the tremendous rise of science and its discoveries, than has any other which it holds.

POLITICAL AND SOCIAL CONTROL.   Another criticism that has been leveled at religion by Karl Marx and Friedrich Nietzsche (1844–1900) among other critics is that it has exerted political and social control to such an extent at different times throughout history that it has become corrupt and decadent and has also encouraged poor and downtrodden people to remain that way, thereby giving ruling and financial power to the few. Many religious-political leaders have ruled well and fairly, but many others when given absolute authority sanctioned by an ultimate reality of some kind, have been cruel tyrants.

Marx called religion "the opiate of the masses," meaning that it was used by religious-political leaders to keep most of the people down either as slaves or as cheap labor to maintain a rich and powerful hierarchy both in the state and within the religious organization. This is usually not contained within the ideals of the religion, but it nevertheless has occurred throughout history. For example, when Jesus was teaching Christianity, he encouraged his followers to give up worldly things and follow him in living a spiritual life; however, when you look at the carrying out of the various religions organized in his name, you often find extremely powerful institutions that are concerned with worldwide finances and political strength and that rival even the biggest secular business conglomerates. These organizations often gain their stature at the expense of people in general but especially the poor of all nations.

Both Marx and Nietzsche argued that religion requiring blind belief, which it calls faith, urges human beings to deny their rationality and intelligence and become robots who will merely do what they are told without question. Further, by tying the secular authority in with its supernatural counterpart, it manages to subjugate people to the wishes of the rich and powerful, often denying the people freedom and rights. Marx argued that each human being ought to have equal access to the wealth and goods of the world and felt that an economic, political, and social system that concentrated on equalizing the opportunities of everyone, and excluding what he called superstition and fairy tales that promoted wealth and power for the few, was what human beings needed, not religion.

Nietzsche felt that religion, especially organized Christianity, denigrated human beings and human intelligence, making them puppets of superstition and those in power who really had no true moral values. He encouraged the elimination of religion and all its teachings, declaiming that "God is dead," and saying that human beings must use their own intelligence to establish their own moral values, which would not be tied to corrupt organizations, religious or secular.

CONCLUSION

It is easy to see that religion has served and is serving many purposes in cultures and for individuals, some of them constructive and creative, others destructive and oppressive. It would seem that as an organized religion attempts to maintain the central core of its dogma without denying the real religious and social needs of its members, it can promote the first types of purposes and avoid the latter. It would seem important for an organized religion to recognize that it is a means for the expression of the personal religious feeling of its members, and to ensure that it continues to do this and still maintain its integrity, it must allow for questioning and also often adapt to the needs of its members.

As we have seen in this chapter, no matter how we attempt to define "religion," the most significant definition seems to involve some sort of ultimate reality. The next chapter will be devoted to the arguments for and against the existence of such a being and some of the problems arising out of the belief in its existence.

Applying Philosophy—
Situations for Thought and Discussion

SITUATION 1

Set aside for the moment any beliefs you have or do not have concerning some sort of ultimate reality, and picture yourself as an intelligent but primitive human being in a natural setting without any knowledge of science or technology. What in yourself and in your environment would lead you to believe in the existence of some ultimate reality or realities? Be specific and describe to what extent and why you might believe in any of the following: mana, animism, spiritism, pantheism, polytheism, henotheism, or monotheism. How would such a belief or beliefs affect how you would act from day to day? Are there any reasons, other than the need to explain what happens around you and why, that you would need such a belief or beliefs? Explain in detail.

SITUATION 2

Assume that you are the leader of a primitive culture living close to nature. Would you attempt to establish some sort of religion as a part of your culture? Why or why not? What kind of religion would you establish and why? To what extent would it contain any of the following and why? What exactly would each of these that you would include be like and why? Describe in detail.

1. What would the nature of the ultimate reality or "ultimate concern" of your religion be and why? How would you describe "it" to your people? As impersonal, personal, one or many, and why?
2. What laws would you have governing general social behavior?
3. What would your moral laws or code be and why?
4. What rituals would you establish celebrating special occasions such as birth, coming of age, marriage, death, the death of an old chief and the establishment of a new one, planting and harvesting of crops, preparing for a hunt to gain food, and so on? Include as many as you feel are necessary explaining why you chose each one.
5. What regular worship services including what rituals would you feel would be necessary and what sacrifices would be required and why? How often would you have such rituals performed?

6. How would you deal with new knowledge that might make any of your beliefs or rituals obsolete? How would you allow for incorporation of new knowledge into your culture's belief system?
7. How would you encourage the members of your culture to accept this belief system, and how would you allow for any dissension or different beliefs to persist?
8. If you believe that religion should be avoided in establishing your culture, what would you have in its place and why? Explain in detail.

SITUATION 3

Describe to what extent you believe that every human being has an "ultimate concern." Do you believe that we actually have only one concern that is ultimate, for which we will even lay down our lives, or do we have many concerns some more important to us than others but really no one concern that is ultimate? What are some of your more important concerns and to what extent are they ultimate in nature? Describe them in detail and also explain why they are important to you. To what extent would you describe them as being religious in nature? For what concerns would you sacrifice everything including your life, if you had to, and why? Be sure you look over the section of this chapter dealing with the characteristics of ultimate concern before you answer these questions.

Chapter Summary

I. General definitions.
   A. Philosophy of religion is not the study of religion from a specific religious or nonreligious viewpoint but rather a careful analysis and critical evaluation of the philosophical implications of religion.
   B. Theology is a rational inquiry into the nature of God and religious truth and an organized, formalized body of opinions concerning God and his relationship to human beings, usually from within a particular religion.
   C. Religion means to "bind back," or sometimes it means a "bond between humans and the gods."
   D. "Ultimate reality" is a neutral phrase used to refer to the central core of any religion.
   E. "Ultimate concern" is a phrase created by Paul Tillich that

means an ultimate reality of some sort and the concern of humans for such a reality.

II. Views of what religion is.

   A. The broad view states that whatever a human believes in strongly is considered his religion. This can include everything from supernaturally based beliefs to rock music.

      1. Its advantage is that anyone with a strong belief can be considered religious.

      2. Its disadvantage is that it blurs the definition so that the word "religion" includes too much.

   B. The narrow view states that religion has to do only with relations between humans and a supernatural being, and in its most narrow form, it is limited to one particular religion.

      1. Its disadvantages are that it excludes many people from being religious, especially in its narrowest form.

      2. Its advantage is that it appropriately limits the meaning of religion to something related to some sort of ultimate reality.

   C. Tillich's ultimate concern.

      1. It stands for both the ultimate object of human concern and also the act of being concerned.

      2. Characteristics of ultimate concern.

         a. It has the highest priority of all values or concerns for an individual.

            (1) It gives meaning and purpose to human life.

            (2) It takes on religious significance whether it is religious in nature or not.

      3. Pervasiveness. It is total and all embracing.

      4. Holiness or sacredness. There is always an element of the experience of fear, wonder, awe, or mystery, and the reverence of its believers is a powerful expression of the holy.

      5. Symbolic expression. Religious expression takes place in a context of powerful symbolic objects and words (holy books, sculptures, stained glass windows, music, etc.).

      6. Religious practice and ritual. Religious experience is both celebrated and lived through the various services, sacraments, and rites performed within each religion.

   D. Personal religious feeling and organized religion. There is a difference between what a human feels in a religious sense and an organized religion.

      1. Personal religious feeling is where religion begins for human beings.

      2. Organized religion comes about when individuals' personal feelings have a common basis and all their similarities of

belief and living become organized by leaders or priests into a set of patterns, forms, or structures.

    a. When organized religion no longer provides appropriate expression for its people, then rifts and schisms occur and often new sects or religions are formed.

    b. It is important to distinguish between personal feeling and organizations so that people do not criticize religious people instead of the possible corruptness of a religious institution.

III. Origin and development of religion.

  A. Mana, animism, and spiritism.

    1. Mana refers to the unseen but felt powers in nature and the world recognized by primitive human beings.

    2. Animism is the phenomenon of human beings assuming that there were spirits in everything in reality, such as plants, animals, the ocean, etc.

    3. Spiritism occurs when these spirits are thought of as free or mobile and are able to appear anywhere.

  B. Polytheism, pantheism, and henotheism.

    1. Polytheism arose with the urge to relate to these spirits as persons or as personal (polytheism means "many personal gods").

    2. Pantheism suggests that there is spirituality in all of nature and that spirits may appear in human, although godlike, form to mortals. Greek and Roman religions are characteristic of both this and polytheism.

    3. Henotheism occurs when one god is more important than the rest in a religion but other gods are not denied.

  C. When religious spirits or persons are located within the common world of nature and culture, then the religion is called a nature-culture religion and almost always involves a plurality of spirits or gods.

  D. Monotheism refers to the believing in and worshipping of one god who is a person or who stands in some sort of personal relationship to human beings and the world "it" has created.

    1. This is considered, especially by its followers, as a more sophisticated type of religion than the other types.

    2. Given the rise in science to account for most happenings in nature, many also feel that this view more intelligently replaces the nature-culture types of religion.

    3. How monotheism began:

      a. There was one example in Egypt with one of the pharaohs.

      b. Socrates and Plato believed in an ultimate reality that they called "The Good."

      c. Aristotle believed in the Prime or Unmoved Mover, which he posited to account for the motions of the spheres.

      d. The Jews and Christians believed in Jahweh.

      e. Islam believed in Allah.

      f. Hinduism also has a one-god concept called Brahman, but Hinduism tends to be more henotheistic in its approach.

E. The nature of the monotheistic ultimate reality.

    1. It is generally considered as the creative power source from which the universe and everything in it has come.

    2. It has been characterized as intelligent and logical, forceful, and even artistic in its creativeness.

    3. It is usually thought of as the Holy Other or Transcendent, standing apart from its creation.

    4. It is also sometimes seen as "immanent" or as residing to some degree within the world and intervening in its processes.

    5. It is seen as personal by its Western believers or as somewhat more impersonal by its Eastern believers.

      a. The advantage of the Eastern view is that it avoids anthropomorphism and its problems, but its disadvantage is that it does not provide as personal a relationship as the Western.

      b. The Western views are just the opposite as far as advantages and disadvantages are concerned.

F. The nature of religious relationships.

    1. Mysticism approaches the ultimate reality as Transcendent, Holy Other, and unreachable by most human methods.

      a. It states that the ultimate reality cannot be conceptualized and is unapproachable through usual rational means.

      b. It approaches this reality rather by some nonrational process through meditation, contemplation, or private vision.

      c. The advantage of this approach is that it bypasses any criticism from a rational point of view, but its disadvantage is that it puts it beyond the realm of reason where most other human activities can be dealt with.

      d. Mysticism believes, rather, that the ultimate reality can be experienced only by individuals who contemplate it.

2. Theism and anthropomorphism.
   a. This view provides for a more personal relationship and also makes the ultimate reality more conceivable and reachable by the human mind.
   b. One of its problems is that it anthropomorphizes the ultimate reality so that it is sometimes more human than godly with all of the attendant difficulties.
3. Religious atheism conceives of the ultimate reality as nontheistic and impersonal like a creative power force. This has all the reverse advantages and disadvantages of theism.
4. Deism is the theory that the ultimate reality is an intelligent, powerful source that has created the universe and everything in it, but has no personal relationship with what has been created—a sort of a god-as-engineer-or-scientist view. This is somewhere between the personal and the impersonal views.

IV. Problems with religious language, concepts, and meaning.
   A. The nature of religious language is that it is often not scientific or philosophical but, rather, is symbolic, poetic, or literary in form, which makes it difficult to analyze or to distinguish fact from fiction.
   B. Another problem with religious language is how it relates to nonreligious or ordinary language.
      1. The theory that religious language is univocal means that it is exactly the same as ordinary language. However, we have problems immediately because how is God the Father the same as a human being's father, for example?
      2. When religious language is considered equivocal, it is thought of as completely different from ordinary language so that the words "father" and "male" when used to describe god mean absolutely nothing like what they mean when used to describe humans. This would mean that when we are talking about god, we are talking nonsense.
      3. When religious language is considered analogical, it does not mean the same thing as ordinary language, nor is it completely different; rather, it is *analogous* to ordinary language. One serious problem with this view is that we do not have both sides of the analogy to compare and contrast God and man. We can surely see the human side, but how can we know how that compares or contrasts with God when we can never see "Him"?
   C. Problems with religious concepts.
      1. As mentioned earlier, much of religion takes place in unanalyzable situations using rites, symbols, and rituals.

2. Also, much religious "knowledge" is revealed and is not experienced or reasoned as most of our other knowledge is.

V. Cultural purposes of religion.
   A. Constructive purposes.
      1. It provides unity for all its members, thus giving them order, security, and a peaceful existence.
      2. It provides a meaning of life for its members and a way of dealing with the three major existential anxieties described by Tillich.
      3. It also provides a code of morality and a sanction for what is morally acceptable or unacceptable in a community.
      4. It unites the supernatural with the natural and all aspects of human beings, god, and nature when it functions at its best.
   B. Cultural problems with religion.
      1. All religions have had some history of persecuting other religious or nonreligious nonbelievers in their point of view, and this has been destructive.
      2. Political and social control. When used for the good of all human beings, religion has had a beneficial effect on politics and society, but it has too often been used to oppress and subjugate the many for the benefit of the few who are rich and powerful.
         a. Marx called religion "the opiate of the masses" and advocated a social system for the good of all humans without the superstition of religious institutions that he felt oppressed most humans.
         b. Nietzsche said that religion denied the beauty of human reason and made most people into mindless sheep following corrupt leaders. He felt that what was needed was to declare god was dead and urge all human beings to develop their own intelligences to the fullest.
   C. It is seen, in conclusion, that religion has been constructive for civilization and it has also been destructive and stultifying to the growth and creativity of human beings.

Additional Questions and Activities for Study and Discussion

1. Study the history of any one particular religion and show carefully and clearly how it has helped and hurt humanity. Be as honest as you can in doing this. What is your overall evaluation of whether this religion has been beneficial to humans or not? Dis-

cuss how it is a creative and constructive force in today's world or not and try to describe why.

2. Read or see the play or film of John Osborne's *Luther,* and analyze and critically evaluate the difference between personal religious feeling and organized religion and discuss how they affect each other.

3. Carefully examine scientology, the Reverend Sun Myung Moon's Unification Church of God (Moonies), and/or transcendental meditation, and describe how each fits the definition of religion. You will first have to define "religion" in the light of what has been discussed in this chapter. Tell why you believe they do or do not fit the definition of what religion is.

4. Describe in detail how you believe religion began and has developed after having read as many viewpoints of this phenomenon as you can from sociological and anthropological as well as religious history sources.

5. Read, analyze, and critically evaluate William James' *The Varieties of Religious Experience* as fully as you can.

6. Read as many religious versions of how the world began as you can find. Almost all religions have a theory or story of creation, but you might look up the stories in the following religions: Judaism (Genesis of the Old Testament), Hinduism, Taoism (Lao Tzu's *The Tao De Ching—The Way and Its Power*), Islam (the Koran), ancient Greek religion, and various religions of the American Indian, people of the South Seas, and so on. After you have examined them, compare and contrast them as to similarities and differences, any validity they might have, based on human experience, and their relationship to the particular culture out of which they have arisen. Which ones do you like best and why? In the light of present scientific discoveries and advancement, how effective do you feel any of these "stories" of creation are and why? Be as objective about all of this as you can be.

7. Read Nathaniel Hawthorne's *The Scarlet Letter* and describe how the religious viewpoints described in that book affect the individual characters and the culture in which they live. To what extent do you feel their religion is constructive or destructive and why?

8. Read *The Chosen* and *The Promise* by Chaim Potok and discuss how personal religious feelings can differ radically even though people are committed to the same religion. Also examine the difference between a basically mystical and nonmystical approach to religion as exemplified in the two boys and their fathers in these books.

9. Read *Siddhartha* by Hermann Hesse and discuss to what extent you feel Siddhartha's quest and its realization is a religious one. Also

describe the difference between personal religious feeling and organized religion that you find in the story.

10. Read *I and Thou* by Martin Buber and analyze and critically evaluate his description and theories about the ultimate reality. To what extent do his theories relate to what we have discussed in this chapter and to your own beliefs about the nature of the ultimate reality and its relationship to human beings? Answer in detail.

Footnotes

1. William Morris, ed., *The American Heritage Dictionary of the English Language* (Boston: Houghton Mifflin, 1975), p. 1099.
2. Paul Tillich, *Dynamics of Faith* (New York: Harper, 1957), pp. 1–4.
3. Francis M. Cornford, trans., *The Republic of Plato* (New York: Oxford University Press, 1945), pp. 348–351.
4. See Eric Havelock, *Preface to Plato* (New York: Grosset and Dunlap, 1967), for an interesting discussion of the Greek oral tradition.
5. John Hick, *Philosophy of Religion,* 2nd ed. (Englewood Cliffs, N.J.: Prentice-Hall, 1973), p. 69.
6. Ibid., pp. 70–71.

Bibliography

Adams, James L. *On Being Human Religiously: Selected Essays in Religion and Society.* New York: Beacon Press, 1976.

Altizer, Thomas J. J., et al., eds. *Truth, Myth, and Symbol.* Englewood Cliffs, N.J.: Prentice-Hall, 1962.

Buber, Martin. *I and Thou.* New York: Scribners, 1958.

Cheney, Sheldon. *Men Who Have Walked with God.* New York: Delta, 1974.

DeVries, Jan. *The Study of Religion.* New York: Harcourt Brace Jovanovich, 1967.

Eliade, Mircea. *Patterns in Comparative Religion.* New York: Sheed and Ward, 1958.

———. *Myth and Reality.* New York: Harper, 1968.

Hick, John. *God and the Universe of Faiths.* New York: St. Martin's, 1973.

———. *Philosophy of Religion,* 2nd ed. Englewood Cliffs, N.J.: Prentice-Hall, 1973.

James, William. *Varieties of Religious Experience.* New York: Mentor, 1958.

Kitagawa, Joseph M. *Religions of the East.* Philadelphia: Westminster, 1968.

Miller, Edward L. *God and Reason: A Historical Approach to Philosophical Theology.* New York: Macmillan, 1972.

Murray, Henry A., ed. *Myth and Mythmaking.* Boston: Beacon, 1968.

Needleman, Jacob. *The New Religions.* New York: Doubleday, 1970.

Smith, Wilfrid C. *The Meaning and End of Religion.* New York: Mentor, 1964.

Streng, Frederick J., et al. *Ways of Being Religious.* Englewood Cliffs, N.J.: Prentice-Hall, 1973.

Tillich, Paul. *Dynamics of Faith.* New York: Harper, 1957.

Tremmel, William C. *Religion: What Is It?* New York: Holt, Rinehart and Winston, 1976.

Weinberg, Julius R., and Keith E. Yandell. *Philosophy of Religion.* New York: Holt, Rinehart and Winston, 1971.

CHAPTER 10

Arguments for and Against the Existence of an Ultimate Reality

Almost everyone believes in some sort of ultimate reality even if it is only basic components of matter and energy. Materialists (see Chapter 3) usually reject the existence of any sort of supernatural being, but they do believe in the existence of matter and energy, and most of them believe that some component of them has existed for a long time if not forever. In other words, their concept of the ultimate reality is that it is matter and energy in some form.

It is certainly hard to refute their existence because they can be experienced in many forms, and almost everything in the universe seems to be either directly or indirectly related to these two components of reality. For example, even though arguments were presented in Chapter 3 to support the view that matter and energy were not the only existent things in reality and that there were also mind and mental events, it is difficult to support any view that mental events and mind exist apart from the physical and material brain and body. Even when one accepts the existence of a spiritual entity such as soul, it is mostly thought to inhabit the physical body in some way even though it is believed to exist outside of the physical as well (prior to and after physical life). Therefore, it is pretty difficult to deny the importance and significance of matter and energy as lying somewhere and some-how at the base of whatever is considered ultimate reality.

Many people, however, are not willing to settle for just these two components, no matter how basic they are. They either want to posit an intelligence (idealism—again see Chapter 3) or some sort of per-sonal (theism) or impersonal (religious atheism) creative power source. That is, something *more* is thought to exist that has caused matter and energy and somehow has interwoven them into the magnificent, log-ical, and intelligible order that we call the universe, topping the whole thing off with the most complicated and greatest of all of creations—human beings. It is very difficult for many people to accept a straight materialism; most seem to feel the need for and, of course, really do believe in some sort of intelligent being, personal or impersonal, that somehow has had a hand in what exists.

I described some of the nontheistic and theistic views of the ulti-mate reality in the last chapter, but allow me to explain them in more detail now before presenting the classic arguments for and against the existence of such a being.

Nontheistic Views of an Ultimate Reality

PLATO'S "THE GOOD"

Plato believed that the physical world and everything it it was merely a shadow copy of another world that existed beyond it and that was attainable through the higher reason of human beings. He believed that there was a world of ideas or "forms" that were the ultimate patterns for everything in the physical world. For example, he felt there was an abstract reality called "honor," "itself by itself" from which all acts of honor came and to which they related. In other words, he believed that for each collection of similar things in this world there was some sort of ultimate source or pattern that existed in the "world of ideas." He further believed that truth existed not here in the shadow copy world of things but in the world of ideas.[1]

The ultimate form or the highest object of reason and knowledge, according to Plato, was something he called "The Good," which he refused to define, probably because he felt it was basically indefinable. He does indicate that he feels that this ultimate reality is the basic "form" for or cause of everything and that it is reachable through the highest levels of human reason, which he called the "dialectic" (see Chapter 2). He discusses all this in "The Allegory of the Cave" and "The Four States of Cognition: The Line" in his *Republic*.[2] Basically, however, what Plato presented as the ultimate reality was some sort of intelligence or at least ultimate object of human intelligence that was not personal but that also was not in any way considered material or physical.

ARISTOTLE'S "PRIME OR UNMOVED MOVER"

Further, as mentioned in the last chapter, Aristotle also posited an ultimate reality that was based on his need for a logical universe and also his need to account for what he observed to be the regular and consistent motion of the planets and stars around earth (he felt the earth was the center of the universe rather than the sun) (see Figure 10-1).

Aristotle argued that for something to move, it had to be moved by something else and, therefore, that each of the heavenly or planetary spheres was moved by the next one outside of it. He then wondered what would cause the outermost sphere to move because he felt that the spheres could not merely go on forever in infinite regression; that is, there could not be an infinite number of spheres—they had to end or stop somewhere. This meant that there had to be a cause of the outermost sphere's movement, which itself did not need a cause, and he called this "being" the "First (or Prime) Mover," which was itself unmoved by anything else. Aristotle, as Plato, did not define this being very clearly except to say that it must be a kind of intelligence that

Figure 10-1. Aristotle's concept of the universe.

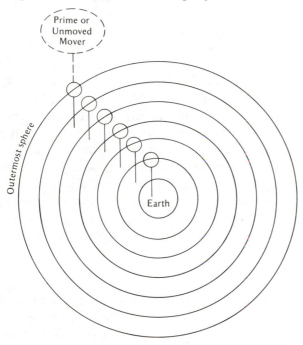

moves the outermost sphere in not a physical but a mental way and that it consists of "life and mind."[3] So as in the theories of Plato, Aristotle's concept of an ultimate reality was essentially a mysterious intelligence which caused the motions of the spheres.

This is, essentially, the deistic view of the ultimate reality, as described in the previous chapter as the view of God held in the eighteenth-century Age of Enlightenment. The scholars of this period saw the ultimate reality as a kind of master scientist or engineer who was not personal in any sense and did not relate to his creatures except as their initial creator.

HEGEL'S "ABSOLUTE MIND" CONCEPT

Georg W. F. Hegel (1770–1831) was an objective idealist, as opposed to the subjective idealism of Berkeley (see Chapter 3), in that he thought that there was an absolute mind or spirit that was the whole of reality and nature and that contemplated itself in an intellectual way. As it did this through the dialectical process (see Chapter 2), it manifested itself through the history of the world, which proceeded in a logical way (dialectically, Hegel believed). Therefore, Hegel accounted for the logic and order in the world by positing an absolute intelligent being or spirit, which was not personal, but a kind of an intellectual force or energy throughout all aspects of nature. It was the cause of the order in the universe, but it had no apparent personal relationship with human beings in it.[4]

LAO TZU AND THE "TAO"

Lao Tzu (604 B.C.) was the mysterious "Grand Old Master" who was presumed to have written the *Tao Te Ching* (translated usually as *The Way and Its Power*), which presented the ultimate reality as the Tao, which is the ground of all existence, the womb from which everything springs and to which everything returns. It is beyond all reason and can only be known through mystical insight. It is the "way of the universe; the norm, the rhythm, the driving power in all nature, the ordering principle behind and in the midst of all life."[5] The Tao is then a powerful life force that runs through and is in everything in nature. It is not a person or personal in any way, but a kind of living power that causes and sustains everything in the universe.

BUDDHISM AND "NIRVANA"

Siddhartha Gautama, the Buddha (560–480 B.C.), established his religion, Buddhism, which was unlike any other religion, as you will see in the next chapter where it is discussed. There was no God or even soul as the West has presented these in its religious traditions. What Buddha posited as the ultimate reality was something he called Nirvana. Actually the word means "to bow out" or "to extinguish," and it refers to the necessity of eliminating the human ego to attain the ultimate reality. Buddha said that Nirvana is really indefinable, incomprehensible, indescribable, inconceivable, and unutterable, which certainly does not give us much to go on.[6] Obviously his approach was one of mysticism (see Chapter 9) and difficult to reason through, but we can assume that it is a kind of state of oneness achieved by humans with the ultimate reality and that state and unity *is* in fact the ultimate reality. Whatever else Nirvana is, it is not a person or personal in any way. It is probably the most highly mystical view of the ultimate reality there is, but here again it is a kind of ineffable state that exists when one extinguishes ego or self and is absorbed into that reality that is ultimate and beyond all else.

HINDUISM AND "BRAHMAN"

There are elements of Brahman that include the personal and even a manifestation of itself as personal gods, but the major thrust of the Hindu concept of the ultimate reality is a great power source that contains everything (creativity, preservation, and destruction) and that is more like a "godhead" rather than a god. It is beyond all definition, like Nirvana, but it can and does manifest itself in and through persons. Somewhat like the Tao, Brahman is that from which the world arises, into which it returns, and by which it is supported.[7]

Theistic Views of an Ultimate Reality

JUDAISM'S AND CHRISTIANITY'S YAHWEH OR JEHOVAH

The name "Yahweh" is derived from a form of the verb "to be" in Hebrew, and the Jews understand Yahweh to be truly existent as characterized by two phrases found in the Old Testament, "Before all else I am" and "I am Who am." His name is often further interpreted to mean "the cause of everything that exists."[8] In Judaism, God (Yahweh) is definitely a person and also relates to human beings on a personal level, as exemplified by all his believed contacts with Moses and the prophets. As a person—the greatest of all persons—God has the following characteristics.

ONE AND UNIQUE.   Judaism is definitely a monotheistic religion and makes one of the earliest and clearest statements of this concept. "I am

God, and there is none else; I am God, and there is none like me!" (Isaiah 46: 8–9). "Before Me no God was formed, nor shall there be any after Me" (Isaiah 43: 10–11), and "I am the first and I am the last; beside Me there is no God" (Isaiah 44: 6–7).

CREATOR OF ALL.   It is the belief of the Jews that only God existed from the beginning and that he caused or made the whole universe and everything in it as described in Genesis of the Old Testament and again in Isaiah 44:24: "I am the Lord, Who made all things, Who stretched out the heavens alone, and Who spread out the earth."

ALL KNOWING, ALL POWERFUL, AND ETERNAL.   The Jews believe that God knows everything there is to know and is therefore the supreme intelligence in reality. No matter how intelligent human beings are or can be, God is the perfect intelligence (omniscient). As creator of the world and everything in it, he is also the greatest source of power in reality (omnipotent); he is always described in this way and is often referred to as the "Almighty" one. He is eternal in that He has always existed and will always exist, and therefore he is the first cause of everything.

THE RULER OF HISTORY.   In this respect, God has given the world and human beings a destiny or purpose and has set history in motion; he gives the world and humans purpose for existing.

SACRED AND HOLY.   He is often referred to as "the Holy of Holies": he is sanctified and he sanctifies, and he is therefore the only being worthy of worship.

RIGHTEOUS AND JUST.   In this respect he is the great lawgiver (the Ten Commandments), and he provides for justice in the world that goes beyond the human concept of justice.

MERCIFUL AND CARING TOWARD HUMAN BEINGS.   This is where the personal aspect of God is most exemplified. God is not merely deistic or impersonal toward his creation and his creatures, but he relates to them—cares what happens to them—and extends his great mercy toward them.

THE ULTIMATE GOOD.   God created morality and provides the ultimate good for humans to strive for. God is all good (omnibenevolent) and beneficent and therefore provides the source and the goal for all morality. We will discover later in this chapter that there are some serious problems in trying to reconcile God's ultimate power with his ultimate goodness; nevertheless this is how he is portrayed by the Jews.[9]

Christianity pretty much accepts all these views and characteristics and agrees with them. It actually personalizes God even further by accepting the belief that God somehow manifested himself as a human being (considered a great mystery in Christianity) and reinforced his personhood further and also his mercy, justice, and goodness by being the savior of all human beings. Christians also believe that, in his human form as Jesus, he taught all human beings more about himself and more about what we should be and do to be moral and religious people. These teachings can be found basically in the Sermon on the Mount and in various other parables and examples given throughout the New Testament.

ISLAM'S ALLAH

Islam is probably more fiercely monotheistic than even Judaism. The very word for Islam's ultimate reality exemplifies this—Allah, which literally means "The God." For the Islamic worshipper, God did not create the world and human beings; *The* God did. This may seem a minor distinction between Yahweh and Allah, but it does point up the unquestionable monotheism of Islam.[10] This is also characterized in the famous Muslim (the followers of Islam are called Muslims) creedal formula, especially in its first line, *la ilāha illa Allāh,* which means "There is no god but Allah."[11] The characteristics are much like Yahweh, but some additional aspects are mentioned.

Allah is considered immaterial or nonmaterial and therefore invisible; in addition, Allah is "a unified Personal Will who overshadows the entire universe with his power and grace. Allah is almighty, omnipotent, Lord of the worlds, the Author of heaven and earth, the Creator of life and death in whose hand is dominion and irresistible power." He is also merciful, forgiving, and compassionate.[12] He, like Yahweh, "stands alone and supreme, He existed before any other being or thing, is self-subsistent, omniscient, omnipotent [all seeing, all hearing, all willing]."[13]

It is easy to see, then, that the theistic version of the ultimate reality is similar in at least three of the world's religions. This being is intelligent, powerful, good, just, and merciful and is either a person or stands in some sort of personal relationship to what "it" has created and, of course, is considered worthy of worship and sacrifice. Let us now examine the arguments that attempt to prove the existence of such a being; afterward there is a critical evaluation of those arguments.

Arguments for the Existence of a Theistic Ultimate Reality

THE ONTOLOGICAL ARGUMENT

St. Anselm (1033–1109), one of the great scholars of the Middle Ages, was the first to form the ontological argument. *Ontology* in Greek essentially means "the logic of being" or "the study of being *as* being."[14] Anselm's argument was probably called that because it attempts to prove the existence of the ultimate reality by the fact that its existence must be because it cannot be conceived in any other way by human beings. The argument goes something like this:

The Ultimate Reality is a being than which no greater can be conceived; that is, if we try to conceive of a perfect being, in order to be perfect and ultimate, it must be one of a kind and such that no greater being can be conceived. We have an idea or conception of such a being, the argument continues, and such a being *must* exist; otherwise, there could be yet a greater being that *did* have existence. Even the lowliest of things in the world has existence, so to be perfect, this being must exist.

To reiterate (1) we humans can conceive of a perfect being, greater than all others; (2) to be perfect and greater than all others, it must have existence; (3) therefore, an ultimate reality does exist.[15]

THE CAUSAL-COSMOLOGICAL ARGUMENTS

This argument for the existence of an ultimate reality really consists of two arguments or parts: (1) the causal argument, which argues for the existence of a first cause of all other causes; and (2) the contingency argument, which argues for the necessary existence of one ultimate being. Both arguments were presented best by St. Thomas Aquinas (c. 1224–1274), who was perhaps the greatest scholar of the Middle Ages. There is no doubt that Aquinas relied very heavily on Aristotle's philosophical speculations in metaphysics and then added his own Christian theological reasonings.

THE CAUSAL OR FIRST CAUSE ARGUMENT.   Two arguments comprise Aquinas' first cause argument. First is the argument from motion, in which he stated that nothing moves without first being moved, so that everything that moves or is in motion must have a mover to move it or start its motion. If all things in motion have to have a mover, then motion must go back in infinite regression without any sort of starting place, but this seemed illogical to Aquinas. Therefore, he speculated that there must be at least one mover that is not itself moved or an ultimate mover to have caused the first movement or motion in the universe but who is prior to all motion. I trust that this argument sounds familiar because it is practically the same argument as Aristotle's concerning the motions of the spheres in which he arrived at the assumption of his Prime or Unmoved Mover.

The first cause argument is, of course, a widening of the argument from motion to include the presence of cause and effect in the universe. The argument states that there is no such thing as an uncaused event or happening or anything—everything has a cause (remember the theory of determinism in Chapter 5?). The universe is some *thing* and must also have a cause, but the same problem of infinite regression exists unless we accept the existence of a first or uncaused cause; therefore, there must be an ultimate reality that is the first and uncaused cause of everything that exists.

THE CONTINGENCY ARGUMENT. This argument centers on the necessity of there being a first being that existed before all other beings or things in existence and prior to which no other beings could have existed. Aquinas argued here that in human experience all beings are "contingent," that is, either temporary in nature or dependent on other beings for their existence. In other words, no being *has* to be, but is contingent or temporary in nature. Further, all beings, as we have observed, come into being and die or go out of being. If all this is true, then the original being had to come from nothing, and this is a very difficult concept to accept, for how can something come from nothing? Therefore, there had to be one being that is not contingent, but necessary or that always had to be and from which all other beings could come. This being is the ultimate reality or the ultimate being.

THE ARGUMENT FROM DESIGN

Aristotle had argued quite separately from his Prime Mover discussions that everything on earth had a purpose or that reality was teleological in nature; that is, everything seemed to have some sort of purpose or end that it worked or strove to attain. For example, if an acorn was planted, it "strove" to become an oak tree, and barring any accidents or interruptions, it usually did. Once a human was conceived, it also strove to become a baby and then an adult, and again, barring any accidents or interruptions, it attained its end or goal. Aristotle did not seem to connect his theory about the teleological nature of the world with the Unmoved Mover of the outermost heavenly sphere, but Aquinas did, stating in effect that since everything had a purpose, goal or design, there must have been a designer for something as complex as the universe in all its aspects. He argued this way:

Everything in the universe that is observable to humans is ordered, intricate, and complex to the point where it just simply could not have happened by chance. Since there is such order and complexity, there must have been an intelligent designer; therefore, there must be an ultimate being who has the intelligence and power to have designed the universe in all its aspects.

This is without a doubt the most popular argument for the existence of an ultimate reality, and it has appeared in many forms even up to the present. If you remember, one of the more popular versions of this argument appeared in Chapter 2, when discussing the argument from analogy, and that is the watch and watchmaker argument. It states that if one were to walk along a road and discover a watch, open it up, and see its complex workings, one would have to presume that such a thing could not have happened by accident and that it must have had a designer. Since the universe is perhaps 100 or 1,000 times more complex and intricate than a watch, then how much more obvious that the world in all of its ordered beauty must have had a designer.

THE ARGUMENT FROM PERFECTION

Aquinas' last argument is somewhat similar to Anselm's ontological argument, but Aquinas stated that it appears only after God's existence has been proved through the other four arguments and, therefore, does not start with one of God's attributes (goodness or perfection) but comes only after his existence is first proved. This argument proceeds on the basis that there are gradations or degrees of bad and good from bad to good to better and to best. Aquinas argues that these gradations would not make any sense if there were not an ultimate good or perfection for the degrees to proceed to; therefore, there must be a perfect being to provide the ultimate degree of goodness—perfection.[16]

THE UTILITY OR MORAL ARGUMENT

This argument is sort of a corollary to the argument from perfection in that it claims that a belief in God, the ultimate all-good, perfect being, is a great and indispensable influence without which human beings would not live good lives. To have morality, according to this argument, there must be an ultimate all-good being to provide the source and the impetus for human morality. All morality, it goes on to state, really comes from a supernatural source (see Chapter 6, in reference to values as objective from a supernatural source). For example, the Jews and Christians would point to the Ten Commandments as the basis for all significant human morality, and other religions would do the same. As noted in Chapter 6, all religions seem to have a moral system, and most also accept some sort of supernatural force as a source for their morality.

THE ARGUMENT FROM RELIGIOUS EXPERIENCE

As John Hospers characterizes this argument, "I and other persons have experiences of a peculiar nature, which are so profound, so meaningful, and so valuable, that they cannot be explained on any natural hypothesis; they must then be due to the presence of a supernatural being, God, who inspires such experiences."[17] These experiences are of two types: (1) public experiences, during which many people have experienced similar things, such as at Lourdes, Fatima, or Cana; and (2) private experiences, which one person usually has and which convince him or her that there is some sort of supernatural ultimate reality. These experiences, which seem to be unexplainable in any other way, must, by virtue of their occurrence, prove the existence of an ultimate reality, who had to have caused them.

THE ARGUMENT FROM MIRACLES

Again, Hospers describes this argument very well: "Miracles have occured at various times in human history, and how could such events be accounted for in any other way than by saying that God intervened in the natural course of events?"[18] A miracle would generally be considered a very unusual event or occurrence that defies all possible scientific explanations. Many miracles are described in the Old and New Testaments, for example. There are the appearances of God to Moses and the prophets and the parting of the Red Sea in the Old Testament, and the changing of water into wine at Cana, the multiplication of loaves and fish, the curing and healing of incurables, and even raising people from death in the New Testament. Since these events often occur through a holy man of some kind (Jesus and the prophets, for example), such miracles must prove the existence of some sort of ultimate reality that can set aside the laws and patterns of nature to cause them.

Critical Evaluation of These Arguments

THE ONTOLOGICAL ARGUMENT

The first problem with Anselm's argument is that he attempts to define God into existence, and this cannot be done. Merely because I can conceive of a perfect anything does not mean that it exists. For example, I can define what a unicorn is, but we all know that unicorns do not exist except in our imaginations. The thoughts, images, pictures, and descriptions of unicorns really do exist, but there is no such existent being itself. Critics of Anselm's argument suggested that they could conceive of all sorts of perfect things, such as a perfect island, but only the conception existed, not the island. Anselm retorted that there is really only one perfect being, and that is God. However, in truth, Anselm is still trying to define God into existence; even Aquinas said that Anselm was doing this.

The second major criticism of the ontological argument was best presented by Kant in which he argued that Anselm tried to make existence into a property of a thing, such as color, size, hardness, or shape. Kant argued that existence is not a property of anything. Something exists, and it also has certain properties. Existence is not a property of something but rather a relationship between the concept of that thing and the world.[19]

THE CAUSAL-COSMOLOGICAL ARGUMENTS

THE CAUSAL OR FIRST CAUSE ARGUMENT.   The first question one wants to ask upon hearing this argument is, "What's the cause of God?" and we are led to that question by Aquinas' beginning assertion that "Everything has a cause." If *everything* has a cause, then God must have a cause also, but this of course is not the intent of Aquinas or his argument. If he changes his first premise to "Everything *but God* has a cause" and then goes on to state that God is the first (uncaused) cause of everything, then he is guilty of circular reasoning or begging the question (see Chapter 2 for a description of this logical fallacy). What he does is to already assume that God exists in his first premise, and if he already assumes it, then the argument has no force; that is, it does not prove that God exists, that he is the first cause, or that he caused anything.

Critics have also argued against Aristotle's and Aquinas' rejection of infinite regression. Why can't there be infinite regression, they ask? No one knows how far back the causes go and whether they go back infinitely or not. The universe might be a continuous circle that has always existed—a circle is certainly logically conceivable. However, even if one accepts a first cause for everything in reality, why must that first cause be God? Couldn't it be, as Democritus described it, matter, energy, and space?

And that brings up two more points. First, why just one cause? Democritus stated that the basic components of reality were atoms (matter), which was always in motion (energy), and space. Second, why do we have to assume a cause for the universe, which is really not a thing but many things? Can't we just argue that each thing in the universe has its cause and that its cause had a cause and so on, without presuming a first cause for the entire universe?[20]

THE CONTINGENCY ARGUMENT

What is the meaning of "necessary being"? Does necessary here mean that the positing of such a being is necessary because again we cannot accept an infinite regression of contingent beings? The argument still has some force when we think of the first being as having to come from nothing if there were not at least one being that was permanent, that had to be and from which all other beings had to come. Again, though, if there has to be one being that always existed, why can't it be the universe itself or matter or energy or a combination of both of them? Whatever the argument proves, it does not prove the existence of a supernatural ultimate reality.

THE ARGUMENT FROM DESIGN

First, it is not really clear what the words "order" or "orderly" mean. Some things, for example, paintings or musical compositions, appear orderly to some people but not to others. Further, doesn't any group of objects spread out in space have order? If you pick up a handful of pebbles and throw them into the air, won't they fall down to the ground and appear to have some sort of order? Couldn't some giant explosion way back in time have scattered everything in the universe in some sort of order? Then it's not necessarily true that order has to come from design. Even if we assume a designer, what is "its" personality? Benevolent? Malevolent? Indifferent? Is there any proof that it has a personality at all—couldn't it merely be a power source? Also, we have already seen, in Chapter 2, that the argument from design depends heavily on analogy, but as was pointed out there, we only have one side of the analogy; we have evidence that watches, buildings, or cars are designed, but we have never seen anyone design a universe such as the one that we are in. This is David Hume's major objection to the argument, that order can be known to come from design *only* if it has been observed to have come from design.

THE ARGUMENT FROM PERFECTION

There is no obvious or necessary connection between the fact that humans recognize or establish gradations of good, bad, right, or wrong and the fact that there has to be an ultimate perfection or an ultimate imperfection. Further, as has been presented in Chapters 6 and 7, there is no conclusive proof that there is any connection between human morality and any kind of supernatural being. If human beings are largely responsible for valuing, even though things do have value in themselves, then they are also responsible for the degrees of bad, good, better, and best, not any supernatural being of any kind. That is, it is not necessary for there to be an ultimate perfection for there to be values or gradations of goodness.

UTILITY OR MORAL ARGUMENT

Again as described in Chapters 6 and 7, there is no conclusive proof for the existence of an all-good supernatural being, and there are certainly alternate views of how morality came about without any sort of dependency on religion. We can give many good reasons why people should be moral, such as a better environment and society, a fairer and better treatment of everyone, and a fuller achievement of human ideals, as humans, without once having to turn to a supernatural being for support. This of course does not in any way prove the nonexistence of such a being, nor is it intended to, but it does indicate that there is no *necessary* connection between a supernatural being and human morality.

ARGUMENT FROM RELIGIOUS EXPERIENCE

PRIVATE RELIGIOUS EXPERIENCES. As far as private religious experiences are concerned, these are of course not actually sharable with others, so at best they would convince only the person who is having or who has had such an experience. Another problem with such experiences is not that people actually have them or not, but rather with the conclusive proof that the experience has actually come from some supernatural being. People may have visions of Jesus, the Virgin Mary, Buddha, or Allah, and the fact that they really did have the experience may not be in doubt at all. However, except for personal interpretation, how do they know that these visions really came from God or any other supernatural being?

PUBLIC RELIGIOUS EXPERIENCES.   Public religious experiences affect more people than just one, but there is always the problem of mass hysteria or mass hallucination. Further, there is always also the possibility of legend building from a particular occasion during which an intense religious experience occurred involving a charismatic leader and many of his more-than-willing-to-believe followers. Here, again, even if many people witness an unusual happening or occurrence, how does this prove the existence of a supernatural being? Granted the experience is real and may be unexplainable, but there is no necessary connection between such an experience and any sort of god. Another factor that is often present in such mass experiences is a very strong desire on the part of the people having it to believe it.

OTHER PROBLEMS WITH THE RELIGIOUS EXPERIENCES ARGUMENT.   Is not the basis or evidence for any religious experience the same, namely, that someone has a private experience or that several people have a public experience of such intensity and significance to them that they interpret it as coming from an ultimate reality? If so, then must we not accept every religious experience on equal terms? If not, why not? If we accept all of them, and some of them yield conflicting information or teachings, then how are we to determine which ones are true and which ones are not? There just do not seem to be any valid criteria that would help us to decide the validity of any of these experiences as there is for deciding most empirical experiences, such as whether it is raining or not.

Further, is a certain kind of experience by itself a guarantee that any objective thing or person corresponding to that experience exists? For example, suppose that we have a dream or vision in which we are surrounded by unicorns and minotaurs (mythical beasts that are half man and half bull). Is there any necessary connection between the dream or vision and real existent unicorns or minotaurs? Is a vision in which religious figures are experienced anymore necessarily truthful than that containing mythical beasts? As Hospers states, "When a statement that seems to be simply about an experience asserts, however covertly, the existence of something beyond the experience itself, then the occurrence of the experience alone can never guarantee that the thing beyond it exists."[21]

ARGUMENT FROM MIRACLES

Miracles are of course often related to religious experiences, but one of the real problems with them is defining exactly what constitutes being a miracle. Is a miracle merely any unusual event? There have been in past history many unusual events that were attributed to some sort of supernatural being or beings and that have later been explained by science or in other ways. However, even if an unusual event occurs that is unexplainable by science or any presently known information we have, does that mean that it must have been caused by a supernatural being? Actually, is it not merely an unexplained event? What evidence can lead us conclusively to the existence of an ultimate reality?

Here again as in the case of religious experiences, how much does already believing or disbelieving in God affect whether or not we believe miracles prove his existence? If I believe in God, and I am the only one who survives an airplane crash, then won't I almost immediately assume that God has performed a miracle? On the other hand, if I am atheistic or agnostic, mightn't I believe that I was lucky or that my survival was a happy coincidence? Suppose that absolutely nothing could be found to have caused the crash but that 350 people died while I survived; why isn't the loss of the 350 a miracle whereas my survival not? Further, most of the miracles centered in religion have happened hundreds of years ago and require us to believe in the hearsay of others and also have faith in the existence of a god who inspired the biblical history recounting these events. The miracles of course may have occurred, but they still do not provide conclusive proof that any such being exists unless we already believe it. Therefore, miracles themselves may not be questionable, but they do not provide decisive proof for the existence of any supernatural being.

Characteristics of a Theistic Ultimate Reality and Their Problems

CHARACTERISTICS

In attempting to establish the existence of a theistic ultimate reality, all the arguments also imply certain characteristics that are generally attributable to such a being, and it is important to understand what these characteristics are and to analyze and evaluate them critically.

OMNIPRESENCE.   The ontological, contingency, miracles, and religious experience arguments tend to imply that God is the ultimate existent being—Paul Tillich refers to this quality and to the ultimate reality as Ground Being or Being-Itself—that God has always existed (is eternal) and has never come into existence and will never go out of existence. He is immortal as well as eternal. This omnipresence is often interpreted in two ways: (1) God is transcendent or the Holy Other, a being separate from his creation and his creatures; and (2) God is immanent or everywhere and in all things, or is intimately involved with human beings (His creatures) and the world (His creation). Some views emphasize his transcendence, such as Judaism, Islam, Eastern Orthodox Christianity, and Hinduism (so far as one can interpret Brahman as theistic), whereas others emphasize his immanence (many forms of Christianity other than the Eastern Orthodox). Still others synthesize the two qualities and state that God is both immanent and transcendent (Roman Catholicism and some Protestant Christian sects).

OMNISCIENCE.   The causal and design arguments imply that God is omniscient or all knowing, the ultimate and supreme intelligence who knows everything and uses his knowledge to create and design the universe in all its complexity. His intelligence is also the source for human intelligence. He is also the reason, of course, why the universe in all its aspects is ordered and intelligible.

OMNIPOTENCE.   The causal and design arguments also imply that God is omnipotent or all powerful in that he can cause and design the universe in all its aspects without help from anything or anyone. He is the source of all power, and he has created matter and energy that are the building blocks of everything. To have created this universe and human beings in all their complexity, he would have to have ultimate power, so he is the most powerful of all beings.

OMNIPERFECTION AND OMNIBENEVOLENCE.   The ontological, perfection, and utility or moral arguments imply that God is perfect and complete in every way, that he needs nothing or depends on anything or anyone, and also that he is the ultimate good from which all morality comes. Without him in all of his goodness, there would be no morality at all.

PROBLEMS WITH THESE CHARACTERISTICS

ANTHROPOMORPHISM.   All these views tend to anthropomorphize God, that is, make him like human beings in every way. As a matter of fact, many critics of theistic religion state that all these qualities or attributes are really anthropomorphic extensions of human characteristics based on human wishful thinking. For example, humans exist in a very special way; therefore, God is the ultimate form of this existence. Humans are intelligent; therefore, God is the ultimate intelligent and all-knowing being. Human beings have power through their minds and bodies to intervene in and control other aspects of nature, but God has ultimate and total power. Human beings can be excellent and strive toward perfection in many ways. For example, certain athletes are the best there are in their particular sports, Bach and Beethoven among others approach perfection in their music, and Einstein is almost the perfect theoretical physicist. Therefore, God constitutes that perfect being and perfection toward which all human beings strive. Human beings seem to be the only beings capable of moral choices and actions, but God is the ultimate moral being, the Ultimate Good.

One might ask, "What's wrong with all of this?" After all, according to many religions, God has created humans in his own image, so it is not strange that they would have all his attributes only to a less perfect degree. Many critics of religion have stated, however, that matters are really reversed in the case of these attributes; that is, human beings have always desired to personify the powers they believe to be lying behind nature and themselves, and, therefore, they have created God in *their* image. This, of course, does not mean there is no God or even that God does not have many of these attributes, but it may mean that, if there is an ultimate reality, it may not be theistic except in the way that humans conceive of him.

Several other problems arise when we anthropomorphize God. For example, isn't it really difficult if we think about it carefully to conceive of *total* and *absolute* existence, knowledge, power, goodness, and perfection? What would these really be like? We have only experienced those things in imperfect states, and there is nothing in these imperfect states to lead us necessarily to assume that there are perfect states of any of them. We have experienced various degrees of intelligence, power, goodness, perfection, and existence, but has any of us ever experienced perfection in any of these? Then, how can we presume that any such perfect states exist or that any one being could have them?

Further, if the ultimate reality is complete and perfect, then why does it "need" human beings' love and adoration? I once heard a rather beautiful description of how the Holy Trinity (God the Father, the Son, and the Holy Spirit) came about. It was described as the effect of the overflow of the perfect love of God the Father into the other two beings, and then this love was extended to the creation of angels and then human beings. However, if a being is total, perfect, and complete in itself, then why would it need to overflow at all, and certainly the question has to arise, why would such a being need love and adoration and obedience from anyone or anything? If God doesn't need it but chooses to need it, what does that mean? Wouldn't it seem illogical or at best a kind of game that he is playing? Of course, if God were not complete or perfect, then he would have needs like us humans, but that is not how he is described.

Most descriptions of the ultimate reality present it as nonmaterial in form, that is, without any physical body or brain or structure at all. This viewpoint presents several problems. One problem that was raised in Chapter 3 is, Do we have any experience at all of disembodied minds? Isn't all our experience based on minds that function through brains and bodies? Then how can we even conceive of a mind somehow wandering loose in space and time without any connection to a physical brain and body? Even if we say that intelligence runs throughout nature, we have a difficult time—does God's mind somehow exist in trees, rocks, and earth as well as in humans and animals? How? Such a situation is extremely difficult to conceive of.

Moreover, if there is no body, then how can we call God he or she? Doesn't gender depend on the existence of physical characteristics? We could of course be using "he" and "she" metaphorically as we do with inanimate things, such as ships, cars, or buildings, but none of these is very godlike, and furthermore, many religious people really do mean that God is their father or that Jesus is their brother. How can this be, if God has no physical body?

These are only some of the problems arising out of trying to make God humanlike, but one of the most difficult of all problems to resolve in the theistic concept of the ultimate reality is the problem of evil, which we will take up next.

The Problem of Evil

One of the knottiest and most difficult problems to deal with in a theistic view of the ultimate reality is the problem of evil in the world. As you will see, evil is only a problem if one accepts two of God's traditional theistic attributes: omnipotence and omnibenevolence. This problem is usually stated in the form of a dilemma and was best presented in Part XI of David Hume's *Dialogues Concerning Natural Religion*.

THE DILEMMA AND ANALYSES OF IT

Hume stated the dilemma as follows:

> If evil is from the intention of God, then he is not benevolent.
> If evil in the world is contrary to his intention, then he is not omnipotent.
> Either it is in accordance with his intention or contrary to it.
> Therefore, either God is not benevolent or he is not omnipotent.[22]

THEORIES ATTACKING HUME'S PREMISES

THERE IS NO EVIL IN THE WORLD.   One argument presented against Hume is that there really is no evil in the world and what we think is evil is really an illusion because we really cannot see God's plan or the "big picture" in its entirety. In other words, God's goodness is different from ours so that perhaps what we consider evil is really good when seen from the vantage point of God's omniscience. This argument takes us back to the previous chapter when we discussed the possibility that language when used in a religious sense is really equivocal, that is, completely different from when we use it in an ordinary sense. This raises definite problems in that if what human beings truly think goodness and morality and badness and immorality are is entirely different from God's view of them, then what indeed is the connection between us and God?

Further, what kind of morality does God have if murder, violence, rape, mayhem, and so on are really considered in the long run good? Can human beings be that far off in their understanding of what morality is? Another problem that arises here is why has God taught us such a moral system if it is so completely different from his? It would certainly seem to destroy totally the moral or utility argument as it stands. Another criticism that John Hospers brings up in connection with this position is that if God is infinitely good, then shouldn't infinite goodness still be goodness, even as infinite space must still be space? [23]

If one even tries to suggest a stronger position that there is really no evil in the world, one would seem to be putting forth a totally implausible theory. How can there not be any evil in the world when children and other innocent people are tortured, raped, and murdered and where something like the holocaust could have taken place in World War II? It is absurd even to suggest that evil does not exist.

EVIL IS NECESSARY TO THE GREATEST GOOD.   Another theory attacking Hume's premises is that evil is necessary to the greatest good; that is, we could not have good in its fullness if there were no evil. A corollary to this is that this world in which we live is the best of all possible worlds; that is, God could not have made it any better. Presented with this view, we again have to ask why nature or the world would have to be set up in such a way when God is omnipotent and omnibenevolent? Human beings are imperfect and not like God is supposed to be, but wouldn't most of them attempt to alleviate pain and suffering if they could? They only have limited power and benevolence, but God has it infinitely. Doesn't this fact have to raise questions about God's good intentions or power? And if God couldn't set the world up in any other fashion so that the only way we could have good would be to have terrible occurrences of evil, then isn't he less than omnipotent?

Further, the good that comes out of evil is often hardly sufficient to justify it, and isn't it possible for the good to have come about without all of the evil out of which it grew? For example, if parents who are sensitive to other people's needs after losing a child become more sensitive to the needs of other parents who have also lost children, is the good that comes out of the evil of their losing their child sufficient to justify their loss? Perhaps one should ask such parents; I doubt, however, that they would agree with this theory. In addition, to argue that good sometimes comes out of evil is no more true than it is to argue that evil sometimes comes out of good. For example, a certain mother may give her son a great deal of love and affection but make him dependent on her to the point where he resents her and becomes psychotic and then goes around killing other women who remind him of his mother.

Also, if the purpose of evil is to make us good or virtuous, then the world is not really organized to do this. For example, often some of the best people seem to get all the pain and suffering, whereas those people who seem to need to be made virtuous by evil do not have anything bad happen to them at all. Further, even when evil people have bad things happen to them, they sometimes become worse than they were before. For example, a thief may go to prison and be punished for several years, and then when he comes out of prison he may become a murderer. Therefore, the world, as it is set up, is inconsistent with a being that is supposed to be both all powerful and all good. Further, if God could not have allowed humans to become good without there having to be extreme evil, then he is questionably omnipotent.

EVIL IS THE ABSENCE OF GOOD. Another argument put forth is that evil is really the absence or privation of good. St. Augustine advanced this theory that evil is negative and good is positive. He argued that there is no evil, but rather the comparative absence of good. What does this really mean? Would it be any different to say that good is the comparative absence of evil? This claim really does not seem to clarify anything much. Aren't good and evil both real? Does it change any facts to say that one is the absence or privation of the other? That suffering and pain exist there is no doubt, and neither is alleviated by saying that it is merely negative or an absence of happiness and pleasure.

EVIL IS DUE TO HUMANS HAVING FREEDOM. One of the most serious attacks on Hume's premises is that human beings could not really be free or have free will if they did not have the freedom to choose evil as well as good. The argument from theism in this instance says that God did not create puppets or robots who merely do what he tells them to because they cannot help themselves, but rather he created free human beings who have real choices of doing good or evil.

And even though God wants them to choose good, he allows them freely to choose evil. He wants them to choose to do what he wants them to freely, not because he has forced them to. As a matter of fact, the whole idea of salvation would not make much sense if humans were not free to choose evil as well as good (refer back to the arguments against predestination in Chapter 5).

First, it is important to distinguish between two types of evil:

1. *Natural evil*—that kind of event that occurs in nature without human intervention or cause, such as earthquakes, floods, hurricanes, forest fires and electrocutions caused by lightning, and so on. If, of course, these are merely considered random or even ordered happenings in nature, and there is no God or God merely lets nature take its course, then one would not have to consider them evil. However, if God is both all good and all powerful, then he should be able to prevent such occurrences, at least where they result in the wounding and deaths of innocent human beings.
2. *Moral evil*—that kind of evil inflicted on humans by other humans. The argument may certainly apply here—and we will examine this type of evil—but this still would not explain the existence of natural evil.

In reference to Chapter 5, again, it was argued that human beings are free, but in a limited sense only; that is, humans are not free to do just anything they want, but within certain limitations and all the influences working on them, they are free to at least some extent. Since we are limited in certain areas, then why could we not have been limited, for example, in our ability to create the worst degrees of evil, such as the gassing of six million Jews in World War II? In other words, is freedom worth such a price as all the evil humans are allowed to inflict on each other? Which of us would not curtail the freedom to rape, abuse and molest children, murder in cold blood, and commit other terrible evils if we but had the opportunity? I cannot believe that any sensitive, compassionate human being would not agree to the elimination of all such evils by limiting the freedom to commit them. Further, if God could not devise a system in which humans are free yet not evil, then he is not truly omnipotent.

Certainly we expect God to do what is logical, and it might be logically impossible to have freedom if there is *no* evil at all, but, as described, could he not have given us limited freedom to choose and do evil and still allow us to be free? For example, if he is both all good and all powerful, couldn't and shouldn't he have intervened in the World War II holocaust to stop the evil from getting so out of hand? Again, wouldn't most of us imperfect humans have done so if we had the power? If the proponents of the argument that evil is necessary for freedom state that God chose not to intervene, then isn't this rather a cruel game he is playing with humans as the unfortunate pawns, and isn't his goodness then questionable?

ELIMINATION OF THE DILEMMA BY ALTERNATE VIEWS

THERE IS NO GOD.   As mentioned earlier in connection with natural evil, if there is no God, but just nature, and nature is neither moral nor immoral, then of course what happens in the universe at the natural or human level is either due to natural occurrences or to lack of human morality. In this atheistic view, humans are responsible for creating and living out their human morality, and they must take full responsibility for what they do or do not do. Evil then is due strictly to human lacks and is correctible only through human means. At least, we would know the cause of evil and strive to correct it. Evil would be due either to natural events or imperfections in human nature, and we must at least strive to eliminate the latter wherever we can. However, we cannot blame a nonexistent supernatural being or nature that is in itself neither moral nor immoral.

DITHEISM.   Ditheism as a theory puts forth the idea that there are two gods of equal power, one good or benevolent and the other bad or malevolent. Evil and good in the world are due to the struggle between these two fairly evenly matched powers, and the outcome is unknown. Neither one of these gods is omnipotent, but one is good and the other is evil. This was referred to as the Manichean heresy in the Middle Ages, and St. Augustine at one time was quite enamored of this view. He later accepted the mainstream view of Christianity and chose to explain evil as I have just described. Ditheism would, of course, solve the problem because omnipotence and omnibenevolence in one theistic god has been eliminated. Christianity does describe two powers, God and Satan, but Satan has limited powers, and the traditional teaching is that God could overpower him at anytime and eventually will. Satan, therefore, has limited power, whereas God does not.

THE OMNIPOTENT BEING IS MALEVOLENT.   One could also account for evil by positing an all-powerful being who was malevolent or evil, but then we would have the same problems of accounting for good as we now have in accounting for evil with an all-powerful benevolent being.

OMNIPOTENCE WITHOUT PERFECT GOODNESS.   If God is seen as basically good but not all good or perfectly good, then even though he were omnipotent, he would still have to strive for perfection. How-

353

ever, he would not already be perfectly good, and, therefore, evil would be accounted for by his "grand struggle" to achieve perfect goodness. In this way, he is striving to be moral, albeit on a higher plane, in the same way that we are. This view, of course, although resolving Hume's dilemma, would not really be satisfactory to most theists who believe that God constitutes the moral perfection toward which all humans are constantly striving.

BENEVOLENCE WITHOUT OMNIPOTENCE.   There is also no problem if God is seen as all good but not all powerful. God may indeed be fully benevolent and perfectly good but may not have the total power to prevent or stop evil. Therefore, there is evil in the world because although God is good and desiring that there be no evil, he is not powerful enough to prevent it. One would have to ask, if he believes that God had power enough to create the world, how God would not have power enough to prevent evil.

DEISM.   If God is deistic in nature, that is, if he designed and caused the world and everything in it, but left it to run on its own without his interference or intervention, then he no longer takes any personal (theistic) interest in it or its inhabitants. Since nature would "take its course" and human beings would be free to choose good or evil, it would be possible for evil to exist in the world because God would not choose to interfere in any way. This of course would not be satisfactory to those who would want to have a personal relationship with the ultimate reality—God in this view would not be approachable or have any meaningful relationship with human beings.

POLYTHEISM.   If there were many gods, then there would not have to be one that is all good or all powerful. Expanding upon ditheism, there could be many gods who might feud with each other, and there would be times when humans would be caught in the middle and therefore subject to evil occurrences. For example, as in Greek mythology, there were many gods and they often chose sides in human events and would help the side they favored and hinder the side they opposed. This would account for evil in the world, because there would be many powerful forces vying for control of portions of the world and of human beings. None of them would have absolute power, nor would they be perfectly good. In the Greek view, the gods were immortal and powerful, but they were not perfect and not always good.

The problem with this view, however, is that the main thrust of the Western religious view is that there is only one God and that he has all the attributes noted earlier. The view of many gods is considered by modern religionists to be primitive and unsophisticated and flies in the face of their religious teachings in the Bible and the Koran.

CONCLUSION.   The problem of evil, therefore, seems to be unresolvable if we insist that God has both the attributes of benevolence and power totally. We can, of course—as many theologians indeed do—simply classify this dilemma as a mystery to which only God has the answer; maybe when we die, we will know the truth about this dilemma, although we must face the fact that we may never know. This problem, however, remains one of the most difficult ones that theists have to cope with. One can, of course, have faith in God's existence and in the ultimacy of his power and goodness, but it is difficult to say that there is any clear explanation for the dilemma other than some of the alternative theories presented here.

Reason and Faith

As we can see from all these arguments for the existence of a theistic or even nontheistic ultimate reality, they cannot conclusively prove any such existence, at least, not by any standards using sense experience and reasoning in the way we would attempt to prove anything else we are aware of. In other words, there are definite difficulties if one attempts to apply reason and rational arguments to the whole religious question, including God's existence or nonexistence. Of course, we have not conclusively proved either that there is no ultimate reality, theistic or nontheistic, but isn't this really the argument from ignorance described in Chaper 2? Isn't the burden of proof on those who would have people believe that there is a theistic god rather than claiming he exists because we cannot prove he doesn't?

Another possibility, of course, is that God really cannot be attained by sense experience or reason but, rather, by what religious people call "faith." The first thing we would have to discover is exactly what faith is and how it may be defined.

FAITH

Søren Kierkegaard (1813–1855), the religious existentialist, came to the conclusion that humans could not reach God by reason, that rationality simply would not take them far enough. The only way to reach God, according to Kierkegaard, was to make an "inductive leap of faith." He described this decision-making process as that of a human being looking into the chasm of darkness, nothingness, and meaninglessness and either accepting these as the end of everything or making the leap of faith across the chasm to God.

One of his favorite examples of this kind of faith was when God was supposed to have tested Abraham's faith by asking him to kill his son, Isaac. Kierkegaard asked, "How could such a request from a just and merciful God make any sense at all?" It is, in fact, totally absurd, and yet Abraham, with blind faith, accepted the command and was about to commit this terrible act when one of God's angels stopped him. Kierkegaard stated that Abraham had a decision to make and that reason could not have helped him to do it; he had to make an inductive leap of faith toward God, and he did. This, of course, in many ways solves all the problems with the fact that none of the rational arguments for the existence of God conclusively proves his existence. One does not need arguments; arguments merely support the faith that one already has that God exists. But what is faith?

FAITH AS BLIND BELIEF.   In the Bible, faith is defined as "belief in things unseen, yet hoped for."[24] "Faith" is generally defined by many scientists and philosophers as "a firm belief in something for which there is no evidence. We do not speak of faith that 2 plus 2 equals 4 or that the earth is round. We speak of faith only when we wish to substitute emotion for evidence."[25]

When faith is defined in this way, there is no obligation that one believe anything for which he has no conclusive evidence. Thomas Huxley (1825–1895), the renowned English scientist, who coined the word "agnosticism," stated the agnostic principle this way: "it is wrong for man to say that he is certain of the objective truth of any proposition (claim or assertion) unless he can produce evidence which logically justifies that certainty."[26] In other words, if faith is merely blind belief, then why should anyone cling to it unless it is psychologically or emotionally satisfying? However, the fact that any assertion or claim is satisfying in these ways has nothing at all to do with what is true or false.

FAITH AS AN ACT OF THE WILL.   Another possible definition of "faith" is that it is an act of the will (voluntarism) that bridges the gap between reason and the unknown truth or falsity concerning God's existence. Two philosophers have presented this view in somewhat different ways.

Blaise Pascal (1623–1662), a French philosopher, mathematician, and scientist, stated this voluntaristic view in the form of a wager. He said, in effect, that if we wager our lives that God exists, we stand to gain eternal salvation if we are right and to lose little if we are wrong. If, on the other hand, we wager our lives that there is no God, we stand to gain little if we are right but to lose eternal salvation and happiness if we are wrong. He then states, "Let us weigh the gain and the loss in wagering that God is. Let us estimate these two chances. If you gain, you gain all; if you lose, you lose nothing. Wager then without hesitation that he is."[27]

Many religious people would object to this approach to faith in God because they feel it is extremely crass and crude and that God, knowing all, would see through it right away and definitely object to it. They also feel that faith ought to be deeper than mere selfish survival and more substantial than a mere act of gambling. Nonreligious people would object to its lack of rationality. Why should people force themselves to believe anything at the level of a wager? Either God exists or he does not, and wagering will not affect the truth or falsity of the matter. These people would want to wait for more evidence or better arguments before accepting God's existence.

Others, however, might argue that as a means of developing one's faith into something deeper, Pascal's wager might not be such a bad place to start, and—they might add—Pascal does have a point that people have a lot to lose if they are wrong and a lot to gain if they are right, depending on how they wager. Other critics might add that people could have a lot to lose if they lived strict religious lives and avoided doing many things they would like to do that would not be acceptable in certain religions.

William James (1842–1910), the psychologist, philosopher, and founder of pragmatism as a philosophy, stated the voluntarist case somewhat more philosophically than did Pascal. James agreed that there can be no conclusive evidence either way as to the existence of God, but he felt that this matter is of such extreme importance that anyone who so desires has the right to believe strongly that God exists and to will himself to believe where he has doubts. He states that

> We cannot escape the issue by remaining skeptical and waiting for more light, because, although we do avoid error in that way *if religion be untrue,* we lose the good, *if it be true,* just as certainly as if we positively chose to disbelieve. . . . To preach skepticism to us as a duty until "sufficient evidence" for religion be found, is tantamount therefore to telling us, when in the presence of the religious hypothesis, that to yield to our fear of its being an error is wiser and better than to yield to our hope that it may be true. . . . Dupery for dupery, what proof is there that dupery through hope is so much worse than dupery through fear? I, for one, see no proof; and I simply refuse obedience to the scientist's command to imitate his kind of option, in a case where my own stake is important enough to give me the right to choose my own form of risk.[28]

Again the criticism leveled at Pascal might also be leveled at James, although perhaps with less intensity; that is, doesn't James' version of faith lack the kind of living religious faith and commitment, which is expressed in the Bible?

George Santayana (1863–1952), the Spanish-born American philosopher, said about James' voluntarism, "There is no sense of security, no joy, in James' apology for personal religion. He did not really believe; he merely believed in the right of believing that you might be right if you believed."[29]

Another criticism of James' position is that it constitutes an unrestricted license for wishful thinking. An idea might be true although it did not appeal to James; that is, for him it would not be "a matter of such extreme importance." However, if the idea were true, how would James ever come to know it by his method, or would his method only result in everyone's becoming more firmly entrenched in his or her own current prejudices? Doesn't this amount to an encouragement to us all to believe, at our own risk, whatever we wish? Will James' universal permissiveness help us, however, if we would really prefer to strive to believe what is *true* and not merely what we *like?*

FAITH AS ULTIMATE CONCERN.   We already discussed Tillich's concept of ultimate concern in the previous chapter, but the action part of his theory is what he calls faith; that is, for Tillich, "faith" is being ultimately concerned.[30] It is not blind belief, nor is it even an act of the will; it is, rather, an act of commitment or witnessing. In this respect, Tillich fits into the mainstream of Protestant theology, which states that faith is an act of witnessing or testifying toward God. Faith, in this view, is an activity—the most important of all activities—that of being ultimately concerned about the ultimate reality.

For Tillich, as a religious existentialist such as Kierkegaard, faith is not merely an act of reason or emotion, but a centered act involving one's entire being—a total commitment to what concerns a human being ultimately—the ultimate reality or God. As was pointed out in Chapter 9, the ultimate concern (God) demands total and absolute commitment, and humans respond by having faith or being ultimately concerned; therefore, faith is not merely belief, but commitment.

The difficulty with Tillich's theory is that saying that faith is an act of commitment or an act of being ultimately concerned shows us that perhaps there should be more of an active quality to faith, but is it really any stronger proof of or reason to believe in God's existence? Maybe it is less passive than blind belief and more satisfying than the voluntarist view, but it still would not necessarily cause one to reach God anymore easily unless he already believed that God existed, and even if we accept the activeness of Tillich's view, aren't we really back to faith as blind belief?

FAITH NOT USED ONLY IN RELIGION.   Some religionists state that faith is not merely limited to religious matters but that human beings use it in all endeavors, and even in science and philosophy. They claim that the scientist has faith in the law of gravity, for example, which is why he can conduct experiments that involve it. They would also say that the mathematician has faith that 2 plus 2 equals 4 and that the philosopher has faith in the principles of logic.

But aren't such people guilty of the fallacy of "changing meanings" (see Chapter 2)? Does "faith" really mean the same thing when used in religion and these other areas? The scientist knows that inductive reasoning yields only probable certainty, which is dependent on the continued validity of the law of gravity; however, how often has gravity not been in effect? Never, as far as we know, so that there is a very high degree of probability that any experiment based on its validity will be predictable. How is this the same as religious faith? No one has ever really seen God, and only few have claimed to have done so, so how do we know with any degree of probability that God exists?

The mathematician does not need any proof that 2 plus 2 equals 4; he does not need to test this anymore than the geometrist needs to test that all circles are round or that all triangles are three-sided. Everytime the mathematician uses the preceding equation or any like it or following from it, it yields the same results, and further it applies to everything, not just apples and oranges—that is, it is universal in scope.

As far as philosophers having "faith" in the principles of logic goes, the principle of identity, for example (A is A or a thing is what it is, such as "A table is a table"), there is no way that people can observe anything or use language about it at all if they do not accept this principle. It is simple, yet very necessary to all human beings. Even in religion, one could not use the word God or the sentence "God is God" if the principle of identity were not true.

There are two other principles of logic to be discussed in the next part dealing with knowledge, but suffice it to say that they are absolutely necessary and ultimate to any kind of language usage or reasoning. It would be contradictory to say "A is *not* A," and any situation derived from that contradictory assertion would be logically impossible. What would it mean to say "A table is not a table"? It would also be contradictory to say "God is not God," but it would not be contradictory to say "God does not exist." It might be false, but it would not be contradictory, and we would have to have much more sufficient evidence than we do to make that statement or its counterpart, "God exists." The reasons why this is so will also be discussed in the next part.

It has sometimes been claimed by theists that we live our whole lives having faith in quite ordinary things. For example, we have faith that the sun is going to rise every morning and set every evening, but is that faith? How many times have we experienced these occurrences and reasoned inductively that they will happen again tomorrow? This is hardly faith "in things unseen but hoped for" because there is high inductive probability that they will occur because of past occurrences. As John Hick puts it, in discussing the bracketing together of religious and scientific "faith," "A scientist's 'faith' is significant only as a preliminary to experimental verification. But religious faith . . . can hope for no such objective verification."[31]

Conclusions

What exactly are we to conclude concerning these arguments for and against the existence of a theistic ultimate reality? It would seem that we would have to accept the fact that there are definite difficulties if we attempt to apply reason and rational arguments to the whole religious question including God's existence or nonexistence. What then are the alternatives if one still sees religion as important, significant, or necessary?

EMOTIONAL OR PSYCHOLOGICAL SATISFACTION. One reason for believing in an ultimate reality of some kind is that it can be emotionally satisfying, and therefore reasonable or not, one should believe. In this respect, maybe James had a point in saying that we should have faith and suspend reason in at least this one crucial instance—incidentally we do not have to do this in any area of our lives other than religion. However, we sometimes do suspend reason in other instances, for example, in committing ourselves to another person in a love relationship. Such a commitment is never a strictly rational act on our part, but often involves an emotional and perhaps even a "faith"-type commitment to the one we love. Could this be the true religious meaning of faith, that we love God a great deal and that this is a crucial existential situation like human love? It is true that we risk the danger of being wrong or in error if we suspend reason, but maybe our commitment is more important than the possibility of error in believing God exists when he may not.

BEING BORN AND RAISED IN A RELIGIOUS TRADITION. Many people are religious because they have been born and raised in a particular religious tradition; that is, their parents and maybe grandparents, and perhaps even great-grandparents, have always belonged to the Baptist Church, for example. This is in itself not a weak or poor reason for being a Baptist oneself, provided that—in true philosophical fashion—one has fully examined this religion and has really made it his or her own: in other words, as long as the *only* reason for believing in it is not mere inheritance of a tradition by the accident of having been born into it.

BELIEF IN A SACRED BOOK.   Many people believe in a particular religion and ultimate reality because a certain book (Bible, Koran, Vedas) that claims to be inspired says that they should. Again, this in itself is not a problem as long as these believers are aware of the circular reasoning fallacy (see Chapter 2) in which they say that they believe the Bible is true because God inspired it. In other words, one does not conclusively prove the other because this would be a circular argument. However, when the sacred book and its related ultimate reality are accepted on faith, one could have a good personal reason for accepting both. Here again, one should not merely accept anything without careful questioning; however, when the point of the "leap of faith" is reached, people may, of course, make it.

HUMANS NEED SOMETHING MORE THAN THEMSELVES.   One reason that is given for being religious is that human beings have always needed to reach beyond themselves to an ultimate being of some kind because they need something "more" than just themselves, this world, and this life. It certainly seems to be true that probably most human beings have felt they needed this, but not everyone has always believed this way. Some people have argued that striving to better their own lives and the lives of others in their society and in this world during their time on earth is enough for them, and the only reaching beyond themselves that they do is toward higher and higher goals to better this world. Therefore, they do not feel the need for some other being or afterlife beyond them. This again would seem to be a matter of personal choice and would depend on what human beings feel comfortable with—some people need religious belief, and some do not.

FAITH HAS AN EFFECT ON ONE'S LIFE.   Another reason given for being religious is that religion, including belief in God and an afterlife, has a significant effect on people's lives. They argue that their lives had no real meaning until they became religious and even go so far as to say that no human being's life can possibly have meaning if there is no belief in some religious ultimate reality.

This has always seemed presumptuous to me—that a human life could not possibly have meaning without religion in some form. Many people who definitely seem to me to have real meaning in their lives have been atheists or agnostics. Certainly Bertrand Russell (1872–1970), the great English mathematician and philosopher, was an avowed atheist all his very long life, as was the earlier-mentioned Jean-Paul Sartre, and yet both men devoted their lives to trying to better humanity and society, published many significant writings, and contributed a great deal to humankind in general. How can anyone sit in judgment of them and say that their lives were meaningless?

On the other hand, many religious people, such as Albert Schweitzer (1875–1965), the great Swiss musicologist, philosopher, and humanitarian, St. Thomas Aquinas (already described), and many others have also lived meaningful lives. Further, it is quite clear that many people feel that *their* lives would not be meaningful without their faith in an ultimate reality.

Some philosophers, John Wisdom, for example, have questioned whether or not belief in a religious ultimate reality really makes any difference in human beings' experience of the world. He argues in his famous parable of the gardener that if two people both return to their neglected garden and find some plants flourishing, and one believes that their flourishing is caused by a mysterious gardener who is never seen, but the other can find no conclusive evidence for this theory, what exact difference in their experiences can be discovered? Don't they both observe exactly the same things, the plants flourishing among the weeds? Whether the mysterious gardener caused this state of affairs or whether there are other scientific explanations or even no explanations, what difference does that make to their experience?[32]

In one sense, the religionist would agree that they experience similar things, but in another sense—he would probably say a more important sense—he would insist that the truly religious person's life is enriched and different because of his faith. He would argue that such a person, believing in a theistic ultimate reality, for example, would live his life and also live in the world differently from the atheist or agnostic and that his life and world would be enhanced by his belief.

CONCLUSIONS TO BE DRAWN

What conclusions can be drawn from all these reasons and all the issues we have examined in this chapter?

THE PERSONAL QUALITY OF RELIGIOUS BELIEF.   It seems quite obvious in examining the many reasons just given for believing in an ultimate reality that religious faith and belief are very powerful personal decisions involving deep feeling and thought and also strong commitment. If this is so, then shouldn't all people be free to decide for themselves which religious or nonreligious commitment they should choose without fear of condemnation or being ostracized.

Is it possible, in this respect, for the religionist to admit that all people do not necessarily need religion or to believe in God for them to lead moral and meaningful lives? Is it also possible for the nonreligious person to admit that some people need to believe in an ultimate reality and that to do so they need not be considered ignorant or unintelligent? In fact shouldn't it be possible for both these groups to coexist without either group needing to feel morally or intellectually superior or inferior to the other?

A BROAD BASIS FOR UNDERSTANDING AND TOLERANCE.   In reference to Chapter 7, what we seem to need is a broader basis than any particular religious commitment for relationships among all human beings who are searching for the truth about religion and an ultimate reality. We also need a tolerance for those who have or have not arrived at a clear commitment. Isn't it more important that we act morally toward each other while we are in search of meaning and truth rather than feel the necessity to convert people to our particular way of thinking?

This broad view is a difficult one to maintain when a particular religious person or atheist is militant and evangelical in his or her approach, but if we are to maintain the significant pluralism of a democratic society, it would seem that we must not impose particular religious or nonreligious values on others against their will. How to do this without watering down all religion is not an easy task, for no religionist wants to consider all religions the same in value and significance; otherwise, why would he or she be strongly committed to his or her own? It would be insulting to tell someone who is committed to a particular religion that his religion is no different from anyone else's. On the other hand, who can stand in judgment of someone's religion as long as that person is moral and not harming others?

Therefore, there must be "courage to be" on both sides of this issue to allow everyone continually to search and question in the area of religion so that there can be a free flow of ideas and a creative growth of all people toward self and societal realization. We must strive for that delicate balance between our strong, deep commitments and our allowing others their own commitments, religious or nonreligious.

In the next chapter, we will briefly survey some of the world's great religions so as to understand what some of these commitments consist of.

Applying Philosophy—
Situations for Thought and Discussion

SITUATION 1

Nontheistic Views of the Ultimate Reality. Compare and contrast all the nontheistic views of the ultimate reality described in this chapter and, *regardless of your own beliefs,* describe which view or combination of views you feel is most significant to you and to humanity in general. Be sure to deal effectively with all views and give reasons and evidence for your choice or choices. In other words, you may put together your own synthesized view of a nontheistic ultimate reality.

SITUATION 2

Theistic Views of the Ultimate Reality. Compare and contrast *all* the theistic views of the ultimate reality described in this chapter as fully as you can. For the purpose of this exercise, *disregard your own theistic belief* (if you have one) or your atheism or agnosticism, and describe which view or combination of views you feel would be most significant to you and to humanity in general. Give reasons and evidence for your choice or choices.

SITUATION 3

The Problem of Evil. Describe and critically evaluate as fully as you can the problem of evil as it is presented in this chapter. Deal with the dilemma itself, all the arguments attacking the dilemma and their criticisms, and then all the alternatives presented to resolve the dilemma. After you have dealt with all of these, present as completely as possible your own viewpoint on the problem of evil being careful to deal with all the criticisms that might possibly attack your resolution of the problem.

Chapter Summary

    I. Nontheistic views of an ultimate reality.
       A. Plato's "The Good" is the ultimate form or highest object of reason and knowledge in his "world of ideas or forms." His concept of the ultimate reality was a kind of supreme intelli-

gence or at least the highest object of human intelligence that was not personal nor material or physical.

  B. Aristotle's "Prime or Unmoved Mover" was a result of a need to explain the logical functioning of the universe, especially the motions of the planets or "spheres." His view, like Plato's, was also of an intelligence of some kind.

  C. Hegel's "absolute mind" was again an intelligence that was the whole of reality and that expressed itself through the dialectic that was manifested in the history of the world.

  D. Lao Tzu's "Tao" was the ground of all existence, "the womb from which everything springs and to which everything returns." He felt that it was the power running through all of nature and reality, causing and sustaining them.

  E. Buddhism's "Nirvana" was not personal or a person in any way but a kind of ultimate state of oneness with the ultimate reality that human beings can achieve; it is basically indefinable and indescribable.

  F. Hinduism's "Brahman" is a kind of godhead rather than a god, but it does come closest of any of these theories to a theistic ultimate reality. It is a great power source that contains everything (creativity, preservation, and destruction), and it is beyond all definition, like the Tao and Nirvana.

II. Theistic views of the ultimate reality.
  A. Judaism's and Christianity's Yahweh or Jehovah is the ultimate existent being ("I am Who am"), which has the following characteristics:
     1. He is the creator of everything.
     2. He is all knowing, all powerful, and eternal.
     3. He is the ruler of history.
     4. He is sacred and holy.
     5. His is righteous and just.
     6. He is merciful and caring toward human beings.
     7. He is the ultimate good.
     8. Christianity generally accepts all these characteristics but personalizes God even further by accepting the belief that he manifested himself in human form as Jesus.
  B. Islam's Allah is even more monotheistic than is the god of the Jews and Christians. Allah has characteristics much like Yahweh, with some additions:
     1. He is nonmaterial and, therefore, invisible.
     2. He is a unified personal will who overshadows the entire universe with his power and grace.
     3. He is lord of the worlds, the author of heaven and earth,

and the creator of life and death and is all powerful as well
as compassionate.

III. Arguments for the existence of a theistic ultimate reality.

A. The ontological argument states that God exists because we can
conceive of a perfect being than which none greater can be
conceived, and such a being must have existence or it would
be an imperfect being.

B. The causal-cosmological argument comes in two parts:

1. The causal or first cause argument states that everything has
a cause; the universe is something so it must have a cause,
but if we keep going back for causes we end up with infinite regression; therefore, there must be a first cause that is
itself uncaused but that is basically the cause of everything
else.

2. The contingency argument centers on the issue that all beings
are temporary and contingent, but argues that, if this is so,
then originally something had to have come from nothing.
This would seem to be absurd; therefore, there must be at
least one being that has always existed, that is not contingent or temporary, but is permanent.

C. The argument from design states that the universe is so logical, ordered, and intricate that it could not have just happened,
but must have been the result of a designer.

D. The argument from perfection states that since there are degrees of goodness from good to better to best, there must be
a perfect being to which these gradations can lead.

E. The utility or moral argument states that morality has to come
from an ultimate, good being who is supernatural; it could not
have its basis in the mere imperfection of humanity.

F. The argument from religious experience states that people have
had experiences of a peculiar nature that cannot be explained
naturally; therefore, they must have come from a supernatural
being who inspires them.

G. The argument from miracles states that unaccountable events
have occurred in human history and that they are so unusual
that they cannot be accounted for by any possible scientific explanation; therefore, they must be caused by a supernatural
being.

IV. Critical evaluation of these arguments.

A. The ontological argument.

1. It is an attempt to define God into existence, and you cannot define anything into existence; merely because you can

define something (e.g., a unicorn) does not mean that such a being exists.

2. The argument tries to make existence a property of things when it is not; something exists and it also has certain properties.

B. The causal–cosmological arguments.
    1. The causal or first cause argument has four problems:
       a. It begs the question or is a circular argument—either God also has a cause or you are assuming that God exists before you even start the argument; either way His existence cannot be proved by this argument.
       b. Critics have also argued against the rejection by Aquinas and Aristotle of infinite regression. Why couldn't things go back infinitely or exist in a closed circle, for example?
       c. Even if one accepts a first cause, why need it be just one cause or a personal god? Why couldn't it be matter and energy?
       d. Why can't the universe itself be the first cause—why couldn't it have existed eternally?

C. The argument from design:
    1. "Order" is not very clear. Doesn't order occur whether it's designed or not (like throwing up a handful of rocks)? Therefore, order does not have to come from design.
    2. Even if we assume a designer, what is its personality and how do we know?
    3. Couldn't it be an impersonal power source rather than a personality?
    4. This whole argument is based on analogy, but we only have one part of the analogy—to say that the universe is a result of design, we would have to observe a universe being designed.

D. The argument from perfection. There is no necessary connection between the fact that we recognize gradations of goodness and that there has to be an ultimate perfection or imperfection. Also, there is no conclusive proof that there is any connection between human morality and any supernatural morality.

E. The utility or moral argument. There is no conclusive proof for the existence of an all-good supernatural being, and there are several viable alternative views of how morality came about without any dependence on religion. We can give many valid reasons why people should be moral whether or not we accept a god.

   F. Argument from religious experience.

      1. Private religious experiences are not actually sharable with others, so they prove nothing.

      2. Public religious experiences do affect more people, but there is always the problem of mass hysteria or hallucination.

         a. Legend building can result from an intense mass experience.

         b. Even if such an experience is not explainable, there is no necessary connection between it and the existence of any supernatural being.

         c. There is often a very strong desire or expectation to have and believe such an experience.

         d. Since there are many religious experiences from different religions, then don't we have to accept them all on equal terms? How do we determine which are true? There are no clear criteria for doing this.

         e. It is usually true that the experience itself exists or existed for the people having it, but how does this prove that anything beyond the experience exists? Merely having such an experience cannot prove this.

   G. The argument from miracles. Miracles are often related to religious experiences, but how do we define what a miracle is? Even if an unusual event occurs that is not presently explainable by science, why should we call this a miracle? Further, how can we prove that this unusual event was caused by any supernatural being or that such a being exists?

      1. How much does already believing in God lead us to believe that some unusual experience is a miracle caused by Him?

      2. Can't bad things or occurrences be called a miracle as well as good? For example, if 350 people die in a plane crash for which there is no explanation and one survives, then is the loss of 350 lives a miracle where the one survival is not?

V. Characteristics of a theistic ultimate reality implied by these arguments and their problems.

   A. Omnipresence. The ontological, contingency, miracles, and religious arguments imply that God is the ultimate existent being, immortal as well as eternal. This omnipresence can be interpreted in two ways:

      1. God is transcendent or the Holy Other, separate from his creation and creatures.

      2. He is immanent or everywhere and in all things and intimately involved with human beings and the world.

B. Omniscience. The causal and design arguments imply that God is omniscient or all knowing, the ultimate, supreme intelligence. He is the reason why the world is intelligible and also why humans have intelligence.

C. Omnipotence. The causal and design arguments also imply that God is all powerful in that God caused and designed the universe without help from anything or anyone else, and He is also the source of all power.

D. Omniperfection and omnibenevolence. The ontological, perfection, and utility or moral arguments imply that God is perfect and complete in every way, needing nothing or anyone and that God is the ultimate moral good from which all morality comes.

E. Problems with these characteristics.

1. Anthropomorphism. All these characteristics tend to make God like human beings in every way, that is, a sort of superhuman. Many critics state that humans have made God in their image rather than the other way around.

   a. Can we really conceive of all these human characteristics as absolute or total? We have no real experience of such realities.

   b. If this being is complete and perfect, then why does God "need" humans to love and worship him? If God doesn't need these but chooses to need them, what does this mean? Is it a game God plays?

   c. God is generally presumed to be nonmaterial in form. How then can there be a mind without brain and body? If there is no material body, how can we presume that God has gender?

VI. The problem of evil is one of the most difficult that religion has to deal with.

A. Hume's dilemma. If God intends evil, then he is not all good; if evil exists contrary to his intention, then he is not all powerful. It is either one or the other; therefore, either God is not all good or he is not all powerful.

B. Theories attacking Hume's premises.

1. There is no evil in the world—evil is an illusion. That is, God's goodness is different from ours.

   a. If his goodness is so different that terrible evil really appears good to him, then what is the connection between us and him?

   b. What kind of morality is it if murder, violence, rape, and mayhem are really considered good in the long run? This would essentially destroy the utility or moral argument.

369

      c. Isn't infinite goodness still goodness even as infinite space is still space?

      d. Who can seriously accept the stronger implication that there really is *no* evil in the world? Isn't this almost totally implausible?

2. Evil is necessary to the greatest good, and this is the best of all possible worlds. If God is all powerful and all good, why does the world have to be set up this way?

      a. Humans are imperfect, but don't they try to eradicate evil, and wouldn't they eliminate most of it if they had the power?

      b. The good that comes out of evil is hardly sufficient to justify it—couldn't good have come about in any other way? If not, then God is not all powerful.

      c. Is this position any more true than that evil sometimes comes out of good—what is the difference?

      d. If the purpose of evil is to make us good, then the world is not really organized to do this.

3. Evil is the absence of good. This really has little significant meaning. What is the difference between saying this and saying that good is the absence of evil? Aren't they both real rather than the absence of one or the other? How does this change the fact of their actual existence?

4. Evil is due to humans having freedom, and humans could not be free unless there were evil for them to choose.

      a. There are two types of evil:

         (1) Natural evil, for example, earthquakes and floods, occurs in nature without human intervention. How can these be due to human freedom?

         (2) Moral evil is that kind of evil inflicted on humans by other humans.

      b. Humans are limited in their freedom in many other areas, why not also in morality as well?

      c. Couldn't the worst evils, like murder, be eliminated and humans still be free?

      d. Is all this so-called "freedom" really worth the terrible extent of evil? Wouldn't most of us give up a little more freedom to prevent the more heinous crimes?

      e. If God could not devise a system in which humans are free yet not evil, then God is not truly all powerful.

C. Elimination of the dilemma by alternate views.

1. There is no God, or atheism. If there is only nature and human beings, then natural evils are just coincidences or due to natural causes, unexplainable in any other way. Also,

human lack or imperfection causes moral evils, but there is no supernatural involvement.

2. Ditheism presents a theory that there are two gods of equal power, one good and one evil, and they are struggling to win.

3. The omnipotent being as malevolent presents the view that there is an all-powerful being, but he is basically evil rather than good. However, with this view we would have the same problem accounting for good as we now have for accounting for evil.

4. Omnipotence without perfect goodness. If God is basically good but not all or perfectly good, then even though God were omnipotent, he would still have to strive for perfection.

5. Benevolence without omnipotence. If God is all good but not all powerful, then the dilemma is also resolved. God is powerful, but not all powerful, so he has to struggle for goodness and he cannot prevent evil from existing. However, if God is not all powerful, then is there a being more powerful, and how could this being have created the world?

6. Deism states that God caused the world but no longer relates to it, and this also would resolve the dilemma; however, this view would not be satisfactory to those who desire a more personal or theistic god.

7. Polytheism states that if there were many gods, then there would not have to be one that is all good or powerful. This is an expansion on ditheism. The gods would be very powerful, but not necessarily totally perfect, and they would be immortal. This view would be too primitive and unsophisticated for most Western religionists.

VII. Reason and faith.

   A. All the arguments are inconclusive as far as proving that there is a God, so maybe humans have to use faith.

   B. Kierkegaard held the view that reason could not get humans to God; one would have to make a "leap of faith."

   C. Faith as blind belief is a "belief in things unseen, yet hoped for," in a religious sense, and a "firm belief in something for which there is no evidence," in a scientific or philosophical sense. The principle of agnosticism—that people should not say they are certain of any proposition for which they have no conclusive evidence—would object to either sense.

   D. Faith as an act of the will. In this view the will is used to bridge the gap between reason and the unknown truth or falsity about God's existence.

1. Pascal wagered that one would lose all and gain nothing if one did not believe in God and God really did exist, and lose nothing and gain all if one believed, and God did exist; therefore Pascal said one should bet on the odds.

2. William James stated that God's existence or nonexistence was a matter of such importance that one had the right to suspend the need for evidence and reasoning in this one instance only.

3. Criticisms of these views:

   a. Pascal's approach is too crass for most religionists; namely, faith ought to be deeper and more substantial than mere selfish survival. Also, why should atheists or agnostics accept anything as true on the basis of a wager?

   b. Isn't James' concept of faith also lacking in vitality and commitment? Further, his view constitutes an unretricted license for wishful thinking—wouldn't truth then become something that is satisfying rather than something that is true?

E. Faith as ultimate concern—Paul Tillich. Faith is not merely blind belief or even an act of the will, but a centered act of the whole being, a total and ultimate concern for the ultimate reality. This may be less passive than the other two versions but is it any stronger proof of or reason for believing in God?

F. Faith is not only used in religion, according to some religionists, but we all have faith in something—even scientists and philosophers.

   1. Should the word "faith" even be used in science and philosophy? We do believe that the sun will rise each morning in the future, but is this merely faith? Don't we have a lot of evidence, and highly probably evidence, that it will? Each area, such as science, mathematics, and philosophy has its basic principles, but these are usually ultimate, like the principles of logic. Also, aren't there a number of possible explanations for the world and human existence without necessarily depending on the existence of god?

VIII. What are we to conclude concerning the arguments for and against the existence of a theistic ultimate reality?

A. There are real difficulties in applying reason and rational arguments to the whole religious question.

B. Reasons for believing in God, despite these difficulties:

   1. Emotional or psychological satisfaction. We can believe in an ultimate reality because it can be emotionally satisfying.

      a. Maybe James was right and anything that is so momentous in our lives can be believed in despite rational objections.

    b. When we make commitments in love relationships, for example, we sometimes suspend reason or at least use some other criterion than reason—maybe love of God is an extension of this.

2. Being born into and raised in a religious tradition. This in itself is not a poor reason, but one should have investigated the tradition for oneself and made it one's own.

3. Belief in a sacred book. People often believe in a particular religion because they accept a sacred book like the Bible or Koran. One should be aware of the circular reasoning that is often used to prove that such a book is truly inspired by an ultimate reality, but if one has faith, in the ultimate reality *and* believes in "his" book, then this, of course, can be an acceptable reason. However, one again should not accept either without careful and sincere questioning.

4. Humans need something more than themselves. Religionists often give as a reason for believing that all humans need something more than just themselves and this world. If some people feel this way, then this is the same as the psychologically satisfying reasons just given, but it is quite presumptuous to assume hat all humans need something more. Therefore, this would be a matter of personal choice.

5. Faith has an effect on one's life. Another reason given is that religion in all its aspects has a significant effect on people's lives and even is said to give them meaning where before it did not exist. This, again, is a matter of personal choice, and it would be presumptuous to assume that a human life would have absolutely no meaning without a religious faith.

IX. Conclusions to be drawn.

    A. The personal quality of religious belief. If religion depends so heavily on personal decisions involving deep feeling and thought, then shouldn't we allow wide freedom for such choices?

      1. Shouldn't the religionist admit that all people do not necessarily need religion to lead moral and meaningful lives, and shouldn't the nonreligionist admit that some people do need religion without considering them to be ignorant or unintelligent?

      2. Shouldn't it be possible for both these groups to coexist without either group needing to feel morally or intellectually superior or inferior to the other?

373

B. A broad basis for understanding and tolerance. What we need is a broader basis than any one particular religious commitment for relationships among all human beings who are searching for their own truths about religion and an ultimate reality. We also need a tolerance for all as long as they are essentially moral toward each other.

1. It is not easy to be tolerant and yet still maintain a strong commitment to one's own religious belief without feeling the need to convert others against their wills.

2. It is insulting to tell someone that his or her religion is no better than anyone else's, and yet who can stand in judgment of another's religion as long as that person is moral and is not harming others.

3. We must therefore have the "courage to be" on both sides of this issue to allow for a free flow of ideas and creative human growth—we must achieve that balance between our strong and meaningful commitments and tolerance of others' commitments, religious or nonreligious.

Additional Questions and Activities for Study and Discussion

1. Which arguments for a theistic ultimate reality go the farthest toward convincing you that there is such a being, and which are the least convincing? Be sure to give reasons why you find them convincing or unconvincing. Also, how would you deal with the problems and weaknesses of those that are convincing? Answer in detail.

2. Do some research on the nature of cause and effect and infinite regression, and discuss your own position on this issue. Among others, I would suggest that you read David Hume on this matter and John Hospers' section on cause in *An Introduction to Philosophical Analysis*. Present the arguments for and against the existence of cause and effect, and then give your own position on the issue. After you have done this, apply what you have learned to the causal-cosmological arguments for the existence of an ultimate reality. Do you find the arguments more or less convincing now that you have done the research? Why?

3. Define the following characteristics of a theistic ultimate reality as fully as you can, and describe what they imply concerning such a being's qualities and abilities: omnipresence, omniscience, omnipotence, omniperfection, and omnibenevolence. Describe as best as you can how any being could be said to have such attributes and

what such a being would be like. To what extent do you feel such a being would need any of the aspects of a human being described in Chapters 3 and 4 (i.e., body, brain, mind, emotions, soul, self, will) and why?

4. Define "faith" as fully as you can. To what extent do you think that every human being has it? To what extent do you feel that it is blind belief or emotional in nature? To what extent do you feel that it is as significant as evidence and rational argument and why?

5. Read what Martin Buber has to say about the Eternal Thou in his book *I and Thou* and what Paul Tillich has to say about "The God above the theistic god" (Ground Being or Being-Itself) in *The Courage to Be* and *Dynamics of Faith* and describe in detail what you think of their views of the ultimate reality. Can you relate well at all to their versions or not? To what degree do you find their views more acceptable and less anthropomorphic than the more traditional views described in this chapter?

6. Read any one or more of the following works of literature and describe in detail how the authors present and deal with evil in the world. Also describe how their presentations and views on evil relate to the problem of evil as presented in this chapter. Select from among Herman Melville's *Billy Budd* and *Moby Dick;* John Irving's *The World According to Garp* and *The Hotel New Hampshire;* Arthur Miller's *After the Fall;* John Steinbeck's *East of Eden;* the chapter entitled "The Grand Inquisitor" from Fyodor Doestoevsky's *The Brothers Karamazov* and also his *Crime and Punishment;* Joseph Conrad's short story, "The Heart of Darkness"; and Nathaniel Hawthorne's *The Scarlet Letter.*

7. Do as much research as you can on the "holocaust" of World War II (the killing of six million Jews by Hitler and his Third Reich of Germany) and discuss in detail the problem of evil in connection with it (how God could be both omnipotent and omnibenevolent and still allow this to happen). Read works by Elie Wiesel and Rudolf Hoess' *The Commandment of Auschwitz* as well as these works of fiction: William Styron's *Sophie's Choice;* Leon Uris' *Exodus, Mila 18,* and *QB VII;* Friederich Duerrenmatt's *The Quarry;* plus Adolf Hitler's *Mein Kampf* and any other works you can find on the holocaust. After doing the necessary research, describe how you think that there could or could not be a theistic god with the two attributes required while such evil was still allowed to exist and continue.

8. Research, as fully as you can, the so-called "miracles" at Lourdes and Fatima or any other "miracles" that you know about or have experienced and discuss in detail how they do or do not prove the existence of a supernatural ultimate reality.

Footnotes

1. Francis M. Cornford, trans., *The Republic of Plato* (New York: Oxford University Press, 1945), pp. 180–181.
2. Ibid., pp. 227–235 and 221–226.
3. Frederick Copleston, S.J., *A History of Philosophy* (Garden City, N.Y.: Image Books, 1962), Vol. I, Part II, p. 59.
4. Ibid., vol. VII, Part I, pp. 206–207.
5. Huston Smith, *The Religions of Man* (New York: Harper, 1958), p. 199.
6. Ibid., p. 125.
7. Ibid., pp. 72–74.
8. Rabbi Sylvan D. Schwartzman and Rabbi Jack D. Spiro, *The Living Bible* (New York: University of American Hebrew Congregations, 1962), p. 21.
9. Ibid.; all these can be found on pp. 37–38.
10. Smith, *The Religions of Man,* p. 218.
11. John G. Noss, *Man's Religions,* 4th ed. (New York: Macmillan, 1969), p. 527.
12. Smith, *The Religions of Man,* pp. 230–232.
13. Noss, *Man's Religions,* p. 527.
14. Dagobert D. Runes, ed., *Dictionary of Philosophy* (Totowa, N.J.: Littlefield and Adams, 1968), p. 219.
15. Saint Anselm, *Saint Anselm: Basic Writings,* trans. Sidney N. Deane (LaSalle, Ill.: Open Court, 1962), Chaps. 2–4 of Anselm's *Proslogion.*
16. These arguments can be found in St. Thomas Aquinas, *Summa Theologica,* in *Basic Writings of St. Thomas Aquinas,* trans. Anton C. Pegis (New York: Random House, 1945).
17. John Hospers, *An Introduction to Philosophical Analysis,* 2nd ed. (Englewood Cliffs, N.J.: Prentice-Hall, 1967), p. 444.
18. Ibid., p. 450.
19. Immanuel Kant, *Critique of Pure Reason,* trans. Norman Kemp Smith (London: Macmillan, 1933), pp. 505–506.
20. This argument is presented in David Hume, *Dialogues Concerning Natural Religion,* ed. Norman Kemp Smith (Edinburgh: Nelson, 1947), p. 18.
21. Hospers, *An Introduction to Philosophical Analysis,* p. 448.
22. Ibid., p. 461.
23. Ibid., p. 471.
24. Hebrews 11:1.
25. Hospers, *An Introduction to Philosophical Analysis,* p. 141.
26. Thomas Huxley, *Science and Christian Tradition* (New York: Appleton, 1896), pp. 309–318.
27. Blaise Pascal, *Pensées,* trans F. W. Trotter (New York: Dutton, 1932), p. 67.
28. William James, *The Will to Believe and Other Essays* (New York: Longmans, Green, 1897), pp. 26–27.
29. George Santayana, *Character and Opinion in the United States* (Garden City, N.Y.: Anchor Books, 1958), p. 47.
30. A full discussion of this theory can be found in Chapter 1 of Tillich's *Dynamics of Faith* (New York: Harper, 1957).
31. John Hick, *Philosophy of Religion,* 2nd ed. (Englewood Cliffs, N.J.: Prentice-Hall, 1973), p. 57.
32. Ibid., p. 86. The parable in its entirety is quoted here.

Bibliography

Ballou, Robert O., ed. *The Portable World Bible*. New York: Viking, 1944.

Campbell, C. A. *On Selfhood and Godhood*. New York: Macmillan, 1957.

Christian, William A. *Meaning and Truth in Religion*. Princeton, N.J.: Princeton University Press, 1964.

Doestoevsky, Fyodor. *The Brothers Karamazov*. New York: Signet, 1971.

Gilson, Etienne. *God and Philosophy*. New Haven, Conn.: Yale University Press, 1941.

Hartshorne, Charles, and William L. Reese. *Philosophers Speak of God*. Chicago: University of Chicago Press, 1953.

Hick, John. *Faith and Knowledge,* 2nd ed. Ithaca, N.Y.: Cornell University Press, 1966.

———. *Arguments for the Existence of God*. London: Macmillan, 1970.

———. *Evil and the God of Love*. New York: Harper, 1966.

———, ed. *Faith and the Philosophers*. New York: St. Martin's, 1964.

Hospers, John. *An Introduction to Philosophical Analysis*. 2nd ed. Englewood Cliffs, N.J.: Prentice-Hall, 1967.

Knox, John. *Myth and Truth: An Essay on the Language of Faith*. Charlottesville: University of Virginia Press, 1964.

Martin, James A., Jr. *The New Dialogues Between Philosophy and Theology*. New York: Seabury, 1966.

McKeon, Richard, ed. *The Basic Works of Aristotle*. New York: Random House, 1941.

Murray, John C. *The Problem of God, Yesterday and Today*. New Haven, Conn.: Yale University Press, 1964.

Novak, Michael. *Belief and Unbelief: A Philosophy of Self-knowledge*. New York: Macmillan, 1965.

Ogden, Schubert M. *The Reality of God and Other Essays*. New York: Harper, 1966.

Pike, Nelson, ed. *God and Evil*. Englewood Cliffs, N.J.: Prentice-Hall, 1964.

Ross, Sir David. *Aristotle*. New York: Barnes and Noble, 1966.

Smith, John E. *Experience and God*. New York: Oxford University Press, 1968.

———. *The Analogy of Experience: An Approach to Understanding Religious Truth*. New York: Harper, 1973.

Temple, William. *Nature, Man, and God*. New York: St. Martin's, 1953.

11

Western Religions

It is important to realize that two chapters in an introduction to philosophy textbook certainly cannot hope to present in any depth even one of the world's great religions much less several from the East and the West. What I hope to do in these chapters, however, is to present you with a very cursory, but essential survey, of the religious commitments of human beings both from the Western and Eastern cultures so that you will have at least some grasp of what religion is and does in our world. I hope also that you will want to pursue your studies in this area further, perhaps by reading more complete works on the various religions or by taking a course or several courses on the world's great religions.

With these disclaimers in mind, I will now proceed to present introductions to and insights into the three great Western religions—Judaism, Christianity, and Islam—in this chapter and the Eastern religions—Hinduism, Buddhism, Taoism, and Confucianism—in the next. (Note that I will not cover even all the Eastern religions.) In the next chapter, I will also discuss atheism—both religious and nonreligious—agnosticism, and secular humanism.

The purpose in presenting you with these views is twofold: (1) to help you expand your knowledge of religious and nonreligious viewpoints other than your own, so that you can become more tolerant and understanding of others' viewpoints and (2) to show you that there are many possibilities in the area of religion from which to choose. In other words, there are viable alternatives to a straight acceptance of the Western religious viewpoint.

It is even possible for you to synthesize several views to arrive at a position concerning religion with which you feel comfortable. Too often, because of the ethnicity of our traditions, we see ourselves as having only two choices: to believe in a Judeo-Christian viewpoint of some kind or not to believe at all. I hope by now that you have seen that there are many more options than these two; at any rate, these chapters are designed to present some alternative viewpoints as well as to enlarge your understanding of religion in general. These chapters are in no way an attempt to denigrate or reject any of the religious or nonreligious beliefs presented; rather they are designed to enlighten you on this interesting and significant aspect of human nature.

Judaism—Meaning in Monotheism

Judaism as the oldest monotheistic religion in the Western world forms the early basis for Christianity; Judaism is even linked to Islam by Muhammad, Islam's great prophet, in that Muhammad accepted the Hebrew prophets as well as Christianity's Jesus as part of the prophecies and bases leading up to the Islamic religion. In other words, Judaism is one of the most significant and influential religions in the world's history and in the world today. What, then, forms the basis for such a significant religion?

THE QUEST FOR MEANING AND PURPOSE

The great Jewish teachings seem to begin with the presumption that no human beings really believe that humanity brought itself into being and cannot help realizing that they have limited powers. Therefore, they cannot help wondering about the characteristics of an ultimate source, power, or reality. In this respect, one of the strongest driving forces behind Judaism is the refusal of the great Jewish teachers, leaders, and prophets to deny meaning and purpose in the universe and the world. The great Jewish thinkers simply could not accept a prosaic, chaotic, amoral, or hostile universe of senseless matter determined by blind, impersonal laws. They felt, on the contrary, that the forces of nature, life in all its aspects, fertility, birth, death, mind, and human ideals cannot be explained as mere bits of matter regulated by mechanical laws. They felt that these were all parts of a world that is heavy with feeling, meaning, and purpose in all of its aspects.

THE UNIVERSE IS CONNECTED WITH PERSONHOOD. From the beginning, as described in Genesis, the ultimate reality is conceived as a person "walking" in the Garden of Eden. Was this such a naïve or absurd idea? The Jews felt that reality was really more like a person than a machine. The world is intelligible and ordered, and although parts of it are threatening and can be destructive, overall the Jews conceived of the universe as benign, nurturing, and caring. Jewish thought seemed to find the greatest depth and meaning in persons and personhood; therefore, they tended to focus their personalism in a single, supreme, nature-transcending will—God. They felt, then, that life was consistent and unified and that there was a meaning and purpose to it that is exemplified and can be found in God, who personifies the unifying, transcendent principle.

THE UNIVERSE IS MORAL.   The Jews felt that human social life is sustained by moral behavior, but if ultimate reality were not moral, then human beings would have no ultimate meaning and purpose for a moral way of life. As stated in Genesis, "In the beginning God created the heaven and the earth . . . and created man in His own image . . . male and female created He them. . . . And God saw everything that He had made; and behold, it was very good."[1] This describes the divine unification that necessarily combines for the Jews, power, value, and goodness. All existence created by God has enduring worth and reflects his eternal power, meaning, and goodness; therefore, no matter how desperate life becomes for the Jews, life itself is never despaired of, for meaning is always there, and there was always opportunity for a creative response to it.

This ultimate goodness or morality is passed down to humans by an ultimately moral being through the Ten Commandments, which were also adopted by Christianity and were accepted by Islam as well. These commandments provide a minimum standard by which human collective life can endure, for they cover main points of conflict within any group—murder, adultery, stealing, and lying. The great Jewish prophets had a twofold conviction about imbuing their civilization with morality: (1) the future of humanity is dependent on a just and moral social order, and (2) individuals are responsible for the conditions of their society as well as for their personal lives.

NATURE IS IMBUED WITH GOD'S MEANING.   "And God saw everything that he had made; and behold, it was very good."[2] This statement, again from Genesis, implies that nature has meaning and purpose and is not merely blind, mechanistic, particles of matter operating at the whim of energy and natural laws. The physical components of existence are not illusory, defective, or unimportant in Jewish teachings. Nature is good, and in Genesis, there is expressed an appreciation of nature blended with confidence in the power of human beings to transform nature for good. This view has many implications. This view of nature and human beings provided the motivation for science as first realized in the Western world. It seems quite clear that the Jewish approach, coupled with the Greek and Roman views, have led to a greater interest and advancement in science than in the Eastern world where this view was not held. Another implication is a strong motivation for concepts of self-determinism as real and vital in transforming nature and human beings toward purposeful goals.

Further, Judaism, Christianity, and Islam are not basically mystically oriented, but tend to accept the body and physical nature along with the soul and spiritual aspect of reality. All three religions emphasize the material aspects of reality in areas of social service and humanitarianism. These are also symbolized in such teachings as the resurrection of the body, the kingdom of God on earth, and the Incarnation (in Christianity only). Therefore, Judaism finds meaning in the human situation and also accepts the limited but divine human vitality. This limitation is in the spirit, in that human beings sin or miss the mark, falling short of their basic nobility, goodness, meaning, and purpose; however, the potential for attaining all these does really and truly exist.

Judaism, in its belief in self-determinism, also accepts that human beings are free, and this is a basic assumption held by all Jews. Inanimate objects are seen as determined and not free, but human beings make or break themselves; they create their own destiny through their choices.

HISTORY IS A GOD AND HUMAN-CENTERED SET OF OCCURRENCES

Judaism sees history as a God-manipulated teaching experience for humanity and especially the Jews, His chosen people. The biblical view of history is that God is found within the limitations of the world of change and struggle. History, however, is not a world of illusion, nor is it merely a circular process of nature, but rather the arena of God's and humans' purposeful activity. Eden, the flood, the years of wandering in the wilderness, and even the sufferings of the Jews in modern times are all shaped by God into teaching experiences for those who have the wit to learn. God has directly intervened at critical points in history, according to Jewish theology, to guide his chosen people through challenges that teach them. Meaning in history, therefore, was and is important to the Jews. The Jews were convinced that the total way in which life is lived affects that life in its fulfillment. History, for the Jew, is not merely evolution is nature or the rise and fall of social cultures, but the contact between God and his creatures in many meaningful events.

REVELATION.   For the Jews, God revealed himself mostly in what he did rather than in what he said. The Jews were aware of God's saving power, mercy, and love for humanity in the Exodus, during which the Jews were saved from total and mass genocide by the Egyptians. The Jews had not perceived God; rather, God had disclosed or revealed himself to them as a God of power, goodness, mercy, justice, and love as well as a God of vengeance. He revealed himself, therefore, through the historical events in which the Jews were involved. Their history, then, was not merely a series of chronological events, but a real-life drama between them and God.

THE COVENANT.   For the Jews, God made his contact with them explicit through the various covenants he made with them throughout history. As we shall see later, Christianity also accepts all the Jewish covenants and even calls Jesus the "New Covenant." As early as Noah and the Great Flood, the Jews felt that God established a covenant (an agreement or contract) with Noah that was to apply for all times to the whole human race (Genesis 9:8–17). For his part of the covenant, God promised never to cause another flood. In return for this promise, God commanded Noah not to murder or eat meat cut from a living animal, to establish courts of justice, and to avoid idolatry, blasphemy, adultery, and robbery.[3]

Further, the Jews also believe that God entered into a succession of covenants with the patriarchs, first with Abraham, to whom he was said to have stated, "I am God Almighty . . . walk before Me and be blameless. And I will establish My covenant between you and Me, and will multiply you exceedingly," at which point Abraham "fell on his face, and God said to him, 'Behold My covenant is with you'" (Genesis 17:1–4). This covenant was renewed with Isaac (Genesis 26:2–5) and Jacob (Genesis 28:13–22).[4] The most famous and complete of all the covenants, however, was the one God made with Moses in Exodus (19:1–8, 23:25–31), when He gave him the Ten Commandments and further commanded that the Jews worship only Him and carry out His commandments. He agreed in turn to defeat the enemies of the Jews, keep them from sickness, and secure the land of Palestine for them and their descendants.[5]

OTHER SIGNIFICANT ASPECTS OF JUDAISM

There are significant aspects and symbols of Judaism other than the just-mentioned ones, and they include the great literary works, the Torah and the Talmud, plus the concept of "The Land."

TORAH. The word "Torah" means "instruction," and in the narrowest sense, it applies to the scroll of the five books of Moses (Pentateuch) found in every synagogue (Jewish temple or church). In its broadest sense it is the compendium of instruction, the guide for life, the evolving body of teachings that is Jewish "heritage."[6] To the Jews, the Torah represents both the divine and the human aspects of their religion through God and Moses: "out of human experience, in man's confrontation with God, Torah evolved. Out of Jewish history, God is made manifest."[7] The Torah consists of the five books of Moses—Genesis, Exodus, Leviticus, Numbers, and Deuteronomy—the first five books of the Old Testament of the Bible.

TALMUD.   Since the Torah was such a central part of Jewish belief, there was a constant and deep search for meaning and the understanding of it through debate, decision, and commentary by the great rabbis (teachers) down through the ages. This was basically maintained through an oral tradition until it was written down in about 200 B.C.E. and known as the Mishnah (Review). This then became the source for additional commentary, the Gemara (Addition), which was completed in Babylonia. Both the Mishnah and the Gemara make up what is called the Talmud (Compendium of Learning) and is sometimes called "the encyclopedia of the Jew."[8] The Torah and the Talmud, then, form the great sacred teaching books of the Jews.

THE LAND.   Another very powerful central concept of Judaism is that of "The Land." This refers to the Land of Israel, to which the Jews always felt their destiny was linked. As early in Jewish history as Abraham, whom God told to migrate to the Promised Land—the only place where he could fulfill himself as servant and herald of God—the concept of The Land has been a central part of Judaism. The Jews feel that only there, in the Promised Land, could the Torah be translated freely into the life of an independent nation.[9] The strong desire to return to the "promised land" of Israel and set up a nation is called Zionism, and Jews are pretty well agreed now that there must be an Israel that is a land as well as a common community of people. Some Jews today feel that all Jews everywhere should try to return to Israel; that is, they see The Land as a physical concept. However, besides probably being an impossibility, many Jews, for example American Jews, are proud of being members of another nation and do not wish to settle physically in Israel; they do, however, support the nation of Israel and its people and derive from the Land of Israel "spiritual uplift and inspiration."[10]

MITZVAH.   *Mitzvah* essentially means "commandment," and it is through mitzvah that the Jew responds to God. There are two kinds of mitzvot (plural of mitzvah): (1) those between human beings and God and (2) those among human beings themselves. Thus, as in

Christianity (as we shall see later), the two greatest mitzvot are to love God and to love one's neighbor as oneself (Leviticus 19:18). Mitzvah, therefore, *is* social justice, reverence for God, and a means for Jewish self-identification and realization and forms the cornerstone of Judaism. The goal and hope of Judaism through mitzvah is that one day both Israel and all humanity will no longer be blocked from freely fulfilling the mitzvot in freedom, love, and justice toward each other and also will be redeemed from war and persecution.[11]

THE MESSIAH AND THE MESSIANIC AGE.   As far back as Isaiah (Isaiah 11), the concept of a Messiah (the word means "anointed") has been a part of Jewish thought and belief. In the prophecy of Malachi, God's anointed would come to create order and perfection on earth. Orthodox Jews believe that this Messiah will be a person, a man, but Reform Jews see in the Messianic age the symbol for a future in which all humanity will be united in brother and sisterhood. The modern philosopher Hermann Cohen describes the concept of the Messiah as

> the future of world history. It is the goal, it is the meaning of history. . . . It is humanity itself which has to bring about this age of the Messiah. Men and cultures must learn to think and hope for the ideal of human life, the ideal of individuals and nations, the future of the Messiah as something in the *future* of the human race. The realization of morality on earth, its tasks and its eternal goal, this, and nothing else is the meaning of the Messiah for us.[12]

This differs from the Christian view of the Messiah, as you will see later, in that it is future looking rather than centered in the past. Also, it is considered more of a spiritual and moral infusion of God's will rather than a person. Even the Orthodox view does not stress the personal aspect of the Messiah as Christianity does. Again, as you will see, this concept of the Messiah is a real sticking point between Judaism and Christianity in that the latter is based on the assumption that the Messiah has already come in the person of Jesus, whereas the Jews do not accept Jesus in this light, but look for the Messiah or Messianic age to come later.

TYPES OF JUDAISM

There have developed over the years three types of Judaism—Orthodox, Reform, and Conservative—based on the conflict between adherence to original principles of the religion and the changing world down through the centuries in which the Jews found themselves.

ORTHODOX.   This form of Judaism, as you might imagine, adhered to all the original principles pretty rigorously, tended not to blend in too closely with the non-Jewish world around it, and maintained strict worship, ethical, and dietary laws that hearkened back to Moses, the early prophets, and the other great rabbis. Orthodox Jews believe strongly that their religion is revealed and that its core is mitzvot. Moses Mendelssohn (1729–1786) accepted this view and worked at ways to relate meaningfully to non-Jewish cultures and environments in which Jews found themselves during the eighteenth century but only in the sense of discovering how to express Orthodox Judaism to the gentiles (non-Jews).[13]

REFORM JUDAISM.   Abraham Geiger (1810–1874) is generally thought to be the founder of Reform Judaism, and to him the scientific human simply could not accept revelation because there is no proof within the scientific method for such a thing. This rejection of revelation and also any revealed doctrines (Torah and mitzvot), and The Land concept, shows the major differences between Reform and Orthodox Judaism. Geiger emphasized the deep-seated sense of kinship of the Jewish people so that to him the Torah became the source of ethics but no more, and the performance of mitzvot became a matter for individual decision, not binding as it is under Orthodox Judaism. Thus one might say that under Geiger, Judaism became much more secular in its approach. What was a deep-seated religion with worship and powerful laws and commandments became a basic system of education, worship, and sermons to promote the teaching of ethics to the world. This type of Judaism was of course popular in modern democracies and especially had its impact on American Judaism.[14]

CONSERVATIVE JUDAISM.   Zacharias Frankel (1801–1875) felt that Reform Judaism was essentially not a positive but rather a negative Judaism, destroying too much of what was central to the vitality and meaning of the Jewish religion. He too accepted the validity of science but felt that Jewish history was an evolving process rather than a static concept. He felt that the Torah belonged to the people and that between its instructions and the changing conditions of modern living there was a constant creative tension. He felt that the Jewish people could creatively adjust the Torah to life as it was lived, not life in the abstract, and he felt that the Talmud was one powerful example of just this type of adjustment. In this view, the Torah was not anchored in the unchanging word of God, but in the people who develop it; therefore, Torah, mitzvot, Talmud, and The Land doctrines are retained, but not with the rigidity of the Orthodox version of Judaism.[15]

CONCLUSION

It is easy to see that Judaism is probably the most important and influential of the Western religions, particularly since the other two Western religions have their roots within the Jewish tradition. It is a very vital and significant religion, and it has affected Western religious societies and cultures in a secular and ethical sense as well as religiously. It is important to keep the basic doctrines, history, theology, and ethics of Judaism in mind when studying influences on the Western world in general and on Christianity and Islam in particular. We will next examine the former, which grew directly out of Judaism.

Christianity

No other religion has ever had such a dynamic influence on the world or the cultures in it as Christianity did, and today it has the largest number of adherents of any single religion, Eastern or Western. Christianity, as I stated earlier, owes its foundation to Judaism. Its leader was in fact Jewish, and very little else is known for sure about him except that he was born somewhere around 4 B.C. during the reign of Herod the Great. He grew up in or near Nazareth, was baptized by John, a dedicated prophet of great intensity; in his early thirties Jesus was believed to have a career of teaching and healing that lasted from one to three years basically in Galilee, after which he incurred the hostility of both the Jewish and Roman establishments of the time and was put to death by crucifixion.[16]

There is really very little clear and accurate historical information available about Jesus. It may be shocking to most Christians and in fact everyone else who has been used to seeing pictures of Jesus down through the ages, but there is really no accurate description of what he looked like, how tall he was, or anything else about his physical appearance. His biographical data are not much more revealing; in fact, they are terribly scant, and most of what has been written about him was done long after he died (there is some disagreement on this issue, but it is basically accepted as true). Like its precursor, Judaism, Christianity is basically a historical religion. In the finest Jewish historical tradition, Christianity sees God as continuing to speak and relate to his creatures, human beings, through historical events just as he did in Old Testament times.

The birth, life, and death of Jesus are inextricably interwoven with the Jewish history and prophecies from its beginning, and Jesus is seen by the Christians as the Messiah that was mentioned in the Old Testament. As has been stated earlier, the Jews are not in agreement about the Messiah; some Jewish scholars thought of the Messiah and the Messianic promise as a realization of the Jewish goals of peace, love, and goodness. Other scholars thought of the Messiah as personal or as a person. The Christians obviously chose this latter meaning and saw Jesus of Nazareth as the Christ (Messiah), who had fulfilled all the prophecies mentioned in the Old Testament writings. If you remember the discussion, previously, concerning the covenants between God and his people, Christians have called Jesus the "New Covenant" and have described him as the last covenant and the fulfillment of all of God's promises to the Jews and to humanity in general. They actually saw God as speaking not just to the Jews but to all humanity through Jesus.

WHAT JESUS WAS LIKE

Despite the lack of clear physical and biographical information about him, Jesus, as revealed through the descriptions of his teachings and the three years or so when he was active in and around Galilee, comes across mostly as a humble, gentle, and charismatic man who constantly attacked hypocrisy, material goods, and public fame and instead espoused the causes of goodness, social justice, humility, and love of God and one's fellow human beings. He was a very interesting teacher in that he avoided philosophical or theological language in his teachings and instead used parables or stories and generally taught in the ordinary language of the Jewish people of the time. His stories were always connected to the kinds of work most of the common Jewish people were doing, and they understood his references very clearly. He walked among the common people and taught and preached in the fields, by the sea, in the hills and in the marketplaces, very seldom using churches or any other important buildings or locations for his presentations.

His Claimed Divinity.   Jesus never denied that he was a man and even called himself "The Son of Man," but he also claimed to be divine and called himself "The Son of God." Most Christians believe in Jesus' divinity, in that he was not just another prophet, like Moses, Abraham, and so on, who never claimed to be anything but men inspired by God, but God's divine son, and actually God himself. As a matter of fact, it was this claim that finally was the ultimate blasphemy to the Jewish priests of the time and cited as the main reason why Jesus was crucified. The Jews felt that it was an unbelievable claim by any man that he could be God or even partially divine and also a serious dilution of the strong monotheism in which they believed.

HIS SOCIAL MESSAGE.   One of the major thrusts of Christianity is its social message. As you have seen, the Jews had a strong social message also, but Jesus' social teachings were and still are quite revolutionary when taken seriously. He stressed following "the spirit of the law" rather than "the letter of the law." He emphasized that there really are only two commandments; to love God and to love your neighbor as yourself. As we have seen, this is not really different from the major thrust of Judaism, but in the way Jesus exemplified and taught this message, he was extremely controversial to the Jewish priests and leaders of his time. This message is exemplified in parables, like the one about the Good Samaritan and in Jesus' teachings in the Sermon on the Mount.

In the parable of the Good Samaritan, Jesus says essentially that people must have compassion for the outcasts of society and even for their enemies.[17] Perhaps Jesus' two most startling teachings—and the most difficult to follow for even the most devoted Christians—are the two from the Sermon on the Mount, which state that people should forget the Old Testament teaching, "an eye for an eye, a tooth for a tooth," and instead turn the other cheek when slapped, and also that they should forget the other old teaching of "loving one's friends and hating one's enemies" and instead "love one's enemies" as well as one's friends.[18]

These teachings seem to have been clearly stated and yet many Christians in the past and also today accept or even advocate violence, revenge, and the other Old Testament teachings. What Jesus seemed to be teaching was a very difficult moral system that urged human beings to strive for an almost supernatural perfection. Even more startling for the people of the time is that Jesus himself, from all accounts, was a living example of what he taught; that is, he was humble, compassionate, caring, and basically nonviolent toward others to the point that he even let the authorities (his enemies) crucify him rather than resist or fight back in any way. Is it any wonder, then, that Christianity became such a dynamic force in the Western world during and after the time when Jesus was alive and teaching?

CHRISTIAN DOGMA

It is not difficult to see how a man like Jesus could be a great moral teacher; after all, Buddha, Gandhi, Muhammad, Confucius, and many others were charismatic teachers of ethics, but none of them ever claimed to be divine and certainly not God. Most of the teachings about Jesus stress his divinity, and this raises a whole raft of questions, such as how and why would God choose to manifest himself as a human being? Why would he allow himself to be crucified when he is all powerful? How can there be three divine persons with only one divine nature?

Within Jesus' teachings and long after he died, even up to the present, these and many other questions have been raised, discussed, and debated by Christians as well as non-Christians.

The basic answers from within Christianity have been stated in the form of "dogmas," which are beliefs and principles presented and believed in by a particular religion—in this case Christianity. These dogmas or "truths" are accepted and believed by most Christians with varying degrees of emphasis and explanation.[19] Since they are very unusual and difficult to prove or accept, they are often called "mysteries"—mysteries of the Trinity, the Incarnation, Crucifixion and Atonement, and the Resurrection. Before dealing with the various types of Christianity, it is important to understand these dogmas.

THE TRINITY.   To explain how God could become human and still remain God and how the Holy Spirit could be left in the world to do God's and Jesus' work and there still be a monotheistic God (a one-god concept) and also to resolve all the controversy of Jesus' place in the heavenly kingdom, the doctrine or dogma of the Trinity was formed. Jesus referred to the Trinity in his sermons in that he spoke of God his Father, of himself as the Son of Man, the Son of God, and as God Himself, and of the Holy Spirit, the Paraclete, which he promised his disciples that he would send down to them to inspire them in carrying out his and his Father's teachings and ways.

The actual doctrine of the Trinity was not, however, formed or at least fully theologically stated until the Nicean Council, convened by the Emperor Constantine in 325 A.D., to finally put aside the Arian Heresy, which attacked Jesus' divinity. Out of this council came the Nicene Creed, which stated the belief in all three members of the Trinity and described them as one God. The dogma is that the Christian God is a "triune" God, consisting of the Father, the Son (Jesus Christ), and the Holy Spirit. These are three divine persons with one divine nature—a difficult concept to comprehend. This evidently means that the Ultimate Reality of Christianity is an essence that manifests itself in three ways: as the godhead, as divine-human or God-man, and as spirit.

There is no way that any mortal can understand this mystery. Even St. Thomas Aquinas, who was willing to base most of the proof for God's existence on empirical evidence and logical proof, stated that knowledge about the Trinity could only have been revealed by God himself. No human being could discover the Trinity by empirical or logical means. As one can see, this has to be a matter of faith, not reason, and one can also see how Judaism, which is based on a strong monotheism, rejects strenuously the concept of the Trinity, saying that it waters down the sacred oneness of Yahweh. Christians, of course, argue, that God is still monotheistic by virtue of his one divine nature, even though there are three divine persons. Anyone proceeding on the basis of logic or empirical reasoning would have to ask how this can be, and the answer would have to be that no one but God knows—it is a mystery.

THE INCARNATION—GOD BECOMES MAN.   Another mystery of Christianity is the very fact of Jesus Christ himself. Jesus is not merely a manifestation of God, as in other religions, such as Hinduism, but is God himself. For some mysterious reason known only to God himself, God chose to become man so that he could be the ultimate sacrifice in atonement for human sins. Looking at this objectively, Jesus has more power and significance than does any other religious leader in the history of the world.

Jesus was certainly man—he even said he was—but he is also divine, according to this dogma, and somehow he appeared to human beings, not merely as a great prophet, such as Moses, Muhammad, or Lao Tzu, but as God himself! The why and how of this occurrence is difficult to imagine much less to reason out, but this is one of the major cornerstones of the Christian faith. One might even ask if any religion can call itself Christian if it does not accept Jesus as the divine God.

CRUCIFIXION AND ATONEMENT.   Even if one accepts the strange fact that God has allowed himself to become human, that he would then allow himself to be tortured and killed by other humans boggles the mind. The dogma states, however, that this is the only way that the ultimate sinfulness of human beings can be eliminated. In the Old Testament, human beings were created by God in his image and therefore in a perfect state; however, they fell from his grace by disobeying his commandment not to reach beyond themselves to try to be like him (the sin of pride). Once they had fallen from grace, something was needed for them to be able to be redeemed; that is, since they had separated themselves from God, they needed a means to become one with him as they had been before the fall. They needed to achieve atonement with God, and the term really means at-one-ment, to be one with him. The teachings of Christianity state that no mere human being could atone for having fallen from grace, only God could; therefore, human beings could only be saved by some sort of divine sacrifice—the ultimate sacrifice. Therefore, God became man; taught love, obedience, and atonement; and then sacrificed himself for the sins of all human beings by allowing himself to be crucified by human beings. This fulfilled one of Jesus' most powerful teachings: "Greater love hath no man than this, that a man lay down his life for his friends."[20]

The ultimate love, therefore, must be for God to become human and lay down his life for his creatures. God has asked for sacrifices throughout the Old Testament from human beings—usually sacrifices of animals, especially lambs in the Jewish tradition. In Christianity, Jesus is often referred to as the "Lamb of God, Who takes away the sins of the world." At one point, if you remember as I described earlier, he even asked a terrible sacrifice from Abraham to test his faith—his son Isaac—but God's own sacrifice of himself has to be the highest sacrifice possible.

RESURRECTION.   The real testing point for God's divine plan through Jesus Christ, however, is the Resurrection. God not only sacrificed himself (as the Son of God) for human sins, but also pointed the way for human beings to rise above their own sinfulness through the symbolism of Jesus' resurrection from the dead and ascension into heaven. Several points are contained in this belief: (1) Human sins were and can continue to be atoned for through God's ultimate sacrifice, (2) death is inevitable because of human sinfulness, and (3) human beings can conquer death by believing in Jesus who conquered death for himself and all humanity through his resurrection. Never before in the history of any religion had there been such a conquering of sin and death through the resurrection of a man (especially God-man) from the dead. It is important, of course, for Christians to believe in the other dogmas, but the Resurrection is the most important in the long run because it, according to Christians, is the ultimate proof for Jesus' being God.

Thus with the Incarnation, Crucifixion and Atonement, and the Resurrection of Jesus, the Christ (this also means "the anointed one"), human beings are truly raised above the merely physical world and existence of nature, plants, and animals and are reimbued with the divine spark with which God had originally endowed them. After his resurrection, Jesus, as he promised, sent the Holy Spirit (the third person of the Holy Trinity) to dwell in each human being and in the world, thus making human beings and the world sacred. The basic message of Christianity, then, is that human beings are once again divine, restored to God's image, and capable of entering into heaven with God. How these dogmas and teachings and ideals are manifested has been different down through the ages after Jesus died, and we shall now look at those differences as they appear in the three major forms of Christianity: Roman Catholicism, Eastern Orthodox Christianity, and Protestantism.

ROMAN CATHOLICISM

In 380 A.D., after an uphill battle and many persecutions for its beliefs, Christianity became the official religion of the Roman Empire in the form of Roman Catholicism—"Roman" because of its centrality to the empire and Rome itself and "Catholicism," coming from the word "catholic," meaning universal. Roman Catholicism (hereafter I will refer to this religion as Catholicism) accepted all the aforementioned dogmas, that is, the Incarnation, Crucifixion and Atonement, Resurrection, and of course the Holy Trinity and, in addition, stressed the virgin birth of Jesus through the Virgin Mary, his earthly but sanctified mother (she was believed to be conceived without sin), and also her assumption into heaven. The Catholic church also believed in its own holiness and its infallibility in the interpretation of all Christian matters, events, and dogmas.

TRADITION AND THE PAPACY.   In Catholic theology, "tradition" means the teaching ability and power of the church. Unlike Protestantism, Catholicism does not allow its followers to interpret the Bible freely for themselves; only the church has the power and the God-given authority to decide how the Bible should be interpreted. So it is not just the Bible that forms the backbone of Catholicism, as in Protestantism, but the Bible *with* tradition.

This teaching authority is believed by Catholics to have been established by God through St. Peter, the first great apostle and Jesus' favorite disciple, and passed down from generation to generation through the various popes who are the titular heads of the Catholic church on earth. This teaching authority has further been established as infallible, that is, without error, when dealing *in matters of faith and morals*. This latter distinction is important because the pope may make many suggestions or recommendations or even interpretations to Catholics, but unless the pope is speaking *ex cathedra* (literally "from his chair"), church members are not bound to follow what he says, although the church teaches that it is dangerous for Catholics not to do what he says. However, when the pope does speak *ex cathedra,* Catholics *must* obey. If there is a serious obstacle between Catholicism and Eastern Orthodoxy and Protestantism, it is this infallibility doctrine that Catholicism claims to have through its popes. In fact, it was one of the main reasons for the first great schism in the Catholic church between it and Eastern Catholicism, and it was also a very important difference between Martin Luther, the founder of Protestantism, and the Catholic church.

One of the difficulties encountered by most people with this doctrine is that they believe that no human being is perfect and that all human beings are capable of making errors—even serious errors. Since popes are only men, and since they are elected by the next higher circle of hierarchy in the church, the cardinals, who are also merely men, then how can one accept them as infallible or even their teachings as such? It may be for this reason that recent popes have not, even in their encyclicals (letters to the faithful), spoken *ex cathedra*. However, those same popes have continued to uphold past teachings on faith and morals stated by previous popes in matters of divorce, abortion, birth control, celibacy of the clergy, and so on.

SACRAMENTS.   One of the keystones of the Catholic church in its teachings and also in its rituals is the seven sacraments: baptism, confession, Holy Communion, confirmation, holy matrimony, Holy Orders, and anointing of the sick (sometimes called last rites). It is through these sacraments that Catholicism "hallows the everyday" or makes the important stages and events in life sacred.

Baptism is of course also central to most other forms of Christianity, as we shall see. In Catholicism, however, it is considered absolutely necessary that a child be baptized as soon after birth as possible, and if there is any chance that its life is in danger, immediately. Catholicism believes very strongly in the theory of Original Sin; that is because of the act of disobedience of Adam and Eve toward God, all human beings are born "with the stain of Original Sin." The only thing that can remove this, according to Catholicism, is the sacrament of baptism. At the same time, when a child is baptized, he or she is also formally accepted into the Catholic faith. The water that is used in performing the sacrament in essence washes away Original Sin. This can be a very simple act in that anyone can perform it by merely having the intention and saying the words, "I baptize you in the name of the Father, the Son, and the Holy Spirit." However, this is usually and preferably done by a Catholic priest in a more complex ceremony.

Confession is a sacrament in Catholicism that often has found strong disfavor among Protestants because it essentially requires one human being to confess his or her sins, no matter how serious they are, to another human being, the priest. The teaching of Catholicism is that baptism removes Original Sin, but something else is needed to remove sins committed or wrongs done after baptism. Through confession, the church tells its followers that God, through his ordained priests, recognizes the request on the part of his fallen children for forgiveness and their experssion of remorse for having sinned and then absolves them (absolution) from those sins.

Confession can be a two-edged sword in that it can increase strong guilt feelings on the part of Catholics who have committed what the church and they feel to be serious sins; on the other hand, however, confession can be almost therapeutic for sinners, in that they can admit their sins in confidence to someone who can listen and even advise them on their moral lives and then they can receive forgiveness for these sins and feel that their guilt has been lifted by the priest and, through him, by God himself.

One of the strongest criticisms from outside of Catholicism is that confession merely provides a hypocritical way of sinning and then receiving forgiveness; that is, people can do terrible things all week, but as long as they confess on Saturday night and go to church on Sunday, everything is all right, and they can then start the next week by continuing the same wrongful ways.

This, of course, is not the intention of the sacrament, but a misuse of it. Wrongdoers are supposedly sorry for what they have done and also promise to try to do better in the future; it is on this basis that wrongdoers are absolved of their sins. At any rate, confession is required of all Catholics at least once a year and must be done before entering into the church's central sacrament, Holy Communion.

Holy Communion is the central and most important part of the Catholic ritual or service, which is called the Mass. It is actually a reenactment of the Last Supper between Jesus and his disciples before Jesus was crucified, and it is based on his statements as he broke the bread and passed around the chalice of wine, "This is my body that was broken for you. . . . This is my blood that was shed for you."[21] As I described earlier, this is not merely a symbolic gesture of commemoration for Catholicism, but, through transubstantiation, the bread and wine were and are miraculously changed into the body and blood of Jesus Christ and therefore provide the Catholic who partakes of this sacrament in good faith with God's spiritual power. In other words, at each partaking of Holy Communion, Catholics believe that Christ somehow mysteriously enters into them and resides within them, thereby sanctifying them and giving them the power to live a Christ-like existence.

Confirmation is the sacrament that ritualizes and commemorates the coming of age of the young and is similar to bar and bat mitzvah in Judaism and the coming-of-age rites in other societies and religions. In this sacrament, the young people (usually around the age of twelve or thirteen) take certain vows and make a commitment to their faith that was only started at their baptisms as babies. At this point, young people have usually learned more about their faith and are now ready to accept some of the responsibility for their own commitment to it.

In matrimony and Holy Orders, the main vocations of the Catholic church are ritualized. Matrimony, of course, sanctifies the union of a man and a woman in marriage and also sanctifies the continued propagation of the species, especially the Catholic part of the species. Holy Orders is the ordination of young men (only men can enter the priest-hood in Catholicism) into the priesthood to perform the various sacraments and carry on the teachings of the Church. These men must dedicate their entire lives to the priesthood and, therefore, must take a vow of celibacy; that is, they may not ever marry while priests, and they are expected to remain priests for their entire lives. The priest-hood is considered a very special calling within the Catholic Church.

Just as baptism commemorates birth and confirmation sanctifies coming of age, the sacrament of anointing of the sick sanctifies one's final moments on this earth and the preparation for what Catholics believe to be the continued journey into the afterlife, hopefully heaven. Confession and absolution are usually a part of this ritual, and other rites are performed to sanctify people when they are seriously ill in case they die. This sacrament used to be called extreme unction (last anointing) or last rites, but the church has since attempted to use it more as a blessing of the sick and as a preparation for possible death than as a last rite.

MARIOLOGY.   Another aspect of Catholicism that has a much greater emphasis than in Protestantism is the preoccupation with and worship of the Virgin Mary, so called because in Catholic teachings Jesus was conceived within her by God through the Holy Spirit, and she never had any sexual contact with a man. She herself was supposedly conceived without sin (Immaculate Conception) unlike any other human being save Jesus himself. She carried Jesus and gave birth to him without any human sexual contact, as I have stated, and when she died, her entire body along with her soul was said to have been "assumed" into heaven (the assumption) again unlike any other human being except Jesus through his resurrection. This mariology, or what Protestant critics of Catholicism often have called "mariolatry," or overemphasis on the mother of Jesus, provides another strong difference between Catholicism and other forms of Christianity.

EASTERN ORTHODOXY

Between 380 and 1054 A.D., when the Eastern church broke with Roman Catholicism in the first great schism in the latter's history, the Catholic church consisted of both the Western part, centered in Rome, and the Eastern part, centered in Constantinople, named after the Emperor Constantine who really was the Eastern church's founder. Eastern Orthodoxy includes the churches of Albania, Bulgaria, Greece, Romania, Serbia, Armenia, and Russia. Eastern Orthodoxy is very similar to Roman Catholicism in that its members accept the same seven sacraments, believe in the teaching authority of the church, and of course accept Jesus as the Christ, the Trinity, the Incarnation, Crucifixion and Atonement, and the Resurrection.

They differ, however, in that they believe that the church's teaching authority is limited to interpreting of issues only mentioned in scripture. They disagree with Catholicism that any church can initiate any new dogma, such as the Immaculate Conception and assumption of the Virgin Mary. Further, the Eastern church leaves many more points open to individual interpretation than does the Catholic church. The Eastern church also objects strenuously to the power of the pope in Roman Catholicism and feels that the spirit of God preserves the teaching authority throughout the whole church, not merely in its hierarchy or leaders; however, the Eastern Church does believe that the church is the appropriate interpreter of most of Christianity, with the foregoing freedoms included. In other words, they believe that God's truth is disclosed through "the conscience of the Church," through the consensus of Christians in general.[22] This consensus would, of course, have to be focused by the church, but does not rely on the infallibility of human beings.

Another difference, cited by Huston Smith, is that the Eastern church places a much greater emphasis on what he calls "the corporate nature of the Church."[23] It is a common view in most forms of Christianity that the church is the mystical body of Christ; that is, just as arms and legs and other parts of our bodies are joined together in one united whole, so is each Christian a part of the mystical body of Christ. Catholicism believes this too, but stresses its hierarchy of pope, cardinals, bishops, priests, and laypersons more than the Eastern. The Eastern church emphasizes the interrelationship of all Christians, believing that each Christian can only be saved with others, even though an individual can be "damned alone."[24]

The Eastern church believes that "the conscience of the people is the conscience of the Church" and that the Holy Spirit's truth comes into the world diffused through the minds of Christians as a whole. In this respect, priests and laity are all individual cells of the mystical body of Christ, and whereas the Roman church is avowedly hierarchical, the Eastern church is much less so.

As Huston Smith states, "Even the titular head of the Eastern Church, the Patriarch of Constantinople, is no more than 'first among equals,' and the laity is known as the 'royal priesthood.' "[25] In this respect, the laity of each congregation elects its own clergymen, priests need not remain celibate, and laypersons may read the Bible in formal worship and even preach.

One other difference is that the Eastern church emphasizes mysticism more than Catholicism. Catholicism seems to feel and teach that mysticism or immediate and intuitive contact with God or any other member of the Trinity is reserved for a very few people, for example, saints such as Augustine, Aquinas, Theresa, John of the Cross, and others. Catholicism neither urges nor discourages this mysticism in its followers; however, along with the other equality in the Eastern church's view of its members, both priests and laypeople, mysticism is encouraged for everyone. The church feels that the aim of every life, priest or lay, ought to be the desire to share in the divine life of God, and everyone is urged to try to satisfy his or her aims in this respect.

PROTESTANTISM

After the great schism with the Eastern church in 1054, the next serious split came in 1517, when Martin Luther (1483–1546) posted his famous Ninety-five Theses attacking the excesses of the Roman Catholic church, such as the selling of indulgences, the pomp and wealth of the clerical hierarchy, and the rights of the individual Christian to interpret the Bible for himself. In this act, Protestantism was born.

Most people think the word "Protestant" strictly means "one who protests" against something; however, Huston Smith states that this is a negative way of putting what he calls the "Protestant principle." He says that Protestantism, in a positive way, "protests against idolatry because it testifies for (pro-testant = one who testified for) God's sovereign place in human life."[26] Therefore, the word "Protestant," in its positive sense, really means one who witnesses or gives testimony to God.

Protestantism, however, probably shares as much with Roman Catholicism and Eastern Orthodoxy as Christianity in the beginning did with Judaism—actually probably more. Its two most distinguishing features, according to Huston Smith, however, are (1) justification by faith and (2) the Protestant principle. The faith found in Protestantism is actually very close in essence to Tillich's concept of the action aspect of ultimate concern. It is not merely assent by the mind or an act of the will or feelings, but actually all three—that is, it is a centered act of the total being of a person, involving mind, will, and affections. The other aspect of this type of faith is that it is very much an individual thing. As Luther said, "Everyone must do his own believing as he will have to do his own dying."[27] As such, Luther felt that the Catholic Church actually did not encourage or nurture this individual commitment but stood in its way by stringing up in front of it obstacles of authority, trappings of ritual, and religious symbols that become important as ends in themselves rather than as means to fostering this individual faith and love of God.

Along these lines, the Protestant principle, as Smith calls it, warns against absolutizing the relative or falling into idolatry. Protestants felt that the secular (nonreligious) aspect of the world absolutized the human intellect and self, making it into a kind of "god," and that the religious aspect, as represented by the Catholic church, had absolutized dogmas, sacraments, the Church, the Bible, and personal religious experience. Protestants did not and do not reject these as means of attaining closeness to God, but they tried to stress the truth that the means weren't God himself. It was their feeling that the Catholic church became bogged down in both secular and religious absolutizing and that Protestants wanted to be able to hold up any symbols or institutions of human beings—secular or religious—to scrutiny and critical evaluation.

DIFFERENCES BETWEEN PROTESTANTISM AND THE OTHER TWO FORMS OF CHRISTIANITY.   As you have already seen, there are several differences between Protestantism and Roman Catholicism and Eastern Orthodoxy. To state them more clearly, there are, first, no real intermediaries between God and human beings. Protestants tend to deemphasize any kind of priesthood or hierarchy that is found in Christianity's two other forms and instead emphasize that each human being is his or her own priest in a sense. Ministers may lead congregations in prayer and advise them in matters of faith and morals, but all humans' consciences are their own, and their relationships with God are private matters between themselves and God himself. For example, when Protestants on rare occasions have an atonement for sins, their confession is very generalized and is recited by the whole congregation, not privately conducted by a priest as in Catholicism, and sins of individuals are not revealed.

Second, the Protestants emphasize much more strongly than do Catholics and the Eastern church the importance and significance of the Bible as the backbone and basis of their faith. As a matter of fact, according to Smith, one of the areas that Protestants have to be wary of is absolutizing the Bible or being guilty of "bibliolatry," that is, worshipping the Bible as if it were God himself when it is really only one of the means to reach him.[28] This emphasis on the Bible varies from a very strong fundamentalist interpretation of its words, to a more liberal attempt to understand its essential meaning. For example, Fundamentalists tend to interpret Genesis literally concerning the creation of humans and the world so that science and evolutionary theories are totally rejected. On the other hand, more liberal Christians find the *essence* of Genesis to state that God created the world and human beings, but they accept that he may have used a creative evolution to do it. You must realize that it is very hard to generalize in these matters, and you should, if you are interested, investigate many of these Protestant forms of Christianity to understand these variations of belief in the Bible and interpretations of it.

Third, the Protestants often have a much stronger social action emphasis than do the other two forms of Christianity in that Protestants often tend to believe less in ritual, statues, and other symbols and more in the relations among human beings. They feel that Jesus did not operate with fancy religious symbols or in gigantic church buildings, and therefore, many Protestant churches deemphasize these things and concentrate rather on the social relationships among human beings in their church activities and even in their services. Some powerful examples of this in our century are the involvement in the civil rights and antiwar movements of the 1960s and 1970s. I do not mean to suggest that other religions were not involved but that a large element of these movements was the Protestantism of such people as the Reverend Martin Luther King, Jr. (1929–1968).

TYPES OF PROTESTANTISM. There is a much greater diversity in Protestantism than in the other two forms of Christianity, due no doubt to the stress on individual commitment and the deemphasis of the priesthood and hierarchy. It is also very difficult to generalize about the many different sects of Protestantism because it is possible to classify all of them in different ways. If you are interested in a specific sect or in learning about all of them, then you obviously need to do much more reading and research than can be available in a small part of one chapter in a text. I hope, therefore, to perhaps pique your interest and give you a kind of overview so that you can distinguish Protestantism at least in a general way from other religions. You should be aware that these designations are mine and therefore may not agree with those of others. I will divide Protestantism by sect into general categories and then will describe briefly some of the main movements or trends in Protestant Christianity.

The Protestant sects, such as the Church of England, Lutheranism, and Episcopalianism, I would call "orthodox Protestantism." What I mean by the use of this term in this particular situation is that they most resemble the Catholic and Eastern Orthodox churches in much of their ritual, prayer, and hymns. They, of course, differ too in that they deny many teachings of the Catholic church; however, they tended to retain much more of Catholic practices, modifying them to suit their new and revised theological positions concerning God and human relationships with him.

Calvinism, Presbyterianism, Methodism, Baptists in England, and Anabaptists, such as the Mennonite Church, seemed to follow a harsher, more puritanical line than did the orthodox sects. They relied heavily on the Bible in a somewhat literal fashion and tended toward a serious nonfrivolous approach to life, emphasizing work, prayer, and service. This group probably provided the mainstream of Protestantism, which was less closely tied to the Catholic and Eastern churches. They tended to deemphasize ritual and pomp in church ceremonies and instead emphasized a more severe and spartan approach to prayer and services and to life itself.

Fundamental Protestantism arose largely in America and involves many segments of the Baptist Church here as well as Assembly of God and many others. These churches tend to rely on a very literal interpretation of the Bible and are therefore against anything that smacks of the orthodoxy of Catholicism, such as the hierarchy, church "tradition" as equal with the Bible, fancy ritual and ceremonies, objecting to them even in Protestant churches, such as the orthodox ones I have mentioned. Fundamentalists are generally against any attempts to reinterpret the Bible from its original writings, for example, in trying to fit evolution into God's plan when the Bible states clearly that he picked up dust and blew the breath of life into it to create man. In addition to being a collection of sects or churches, Fundamentalism is also one of the major movements in Protestant Christianity emphasizing the infallibility of the Bible, Jesus as divine, his resurrection, and the Second Coming, when Jesus will come to judge the world, and the world as we know it will be ended.

Another main movement in Protestantism is Liberalism, in which more emphasis is placed on the essence of the Bible rather than interpreting it literally, word for word. This group believes that Christianity is not static as the fundamentalists would have it, but a growing, changing, developing, and creative religion that is subject to change and wide interpretation. They also see God's revelation as progressive and continuing, not as just a one-time thing during the time of Jesus. They feel that God works through the history of the world. They also emphasize God as personal rather than the totally Holy Other of Fundamentalism, and they emphasize human dignity and a strong social action program in their approach to Christianity.

The fifth main movement, which is somewhere between Fundamentalism and Liberalism, is called Neoorthodoxy. Unlike the Liberals and more like the Fundamentalists, this group feels that the original revelation is the main and most important source of the truths of Christianity. They are also somewhere between the two extremes as far as the Bible is concerned, feeling that it is the word of God but that it also may be interpreted to some extent. This group also tends to emphasize that God is transcendent and Holy Other, more like the Fundamentalists than the Liberals who seem to stress His immanence.

It is really difficult to state which specific Protestant religion fits into what category or follows which trend or stream. If you can keep the essential aspects of each of the movements in mind, and then examine whichever religion you are interested in, you can then see how it fits into any or all of these categories. It is not even safe to cite one particular Protestant religion because it may have three different factions, each of which stresses one or the other of the main trends. For example, some Episcopalians may be highly conservative and orthodox, whereas another faction or group of the same church may lean very strongly toward Liberalism. At any rate, it is clear that Protestantism—probably the largest religion in America today—is quite diverse and multifarious in its structure while still holding to the mainstream of Christianity followed by Roman Catholicism and Eastern Orthodoxy.

Islam

The word *Islam* essentially means "to accept," "to submit," "to commit oneself," and "to surrender," and when a person declares that he is a Muslim (the proper name for one who embraces the Islamic faith), he means by this that he has committed, submitted, and surrendered himself to Allah, the one God, which I described in detail in the last chapter.[29] Islam is the newest of the world's great religions, having arisen in the sixth and seventh centuries A.D. Its charismatic leader is the great Islamic prophet, "The Seal of All of the Prophets," Muhammad (c. 571–632 A.D.), "the Last of All of the prophets," according to Muslims, for whom the only real miracle was that Allah chose him, an uneducated man, to receive the beauty and truth of the Islamic holy book, the Koran (sometimes spelled Qu'ran). Islam accepts the fact that Allah created the world and the first man, Adam. Islam accepts all the great Hebrew prophets and also Jesus as a prophet, but feels that Muhammad is the last of the prophets, who presented clearly to the Islamic people all the truths and teachings they would ever need. Muslims believe that through Abraham, God revealed the truth of his oneness or monotheism; through Moses, God revealed the Ten Commandments; through Jesus, God revealed the love of one's fellowmen; through Muhammad, God revealed definite laws for the realization of all the above.[30]

FIVE PRINCIPLES OF ISLAM

THE STRAIGHT PATH.   The Islamic Creed is very clear and definitive: "There is no God but Allah, and Muhammad is His prophet," and every Muslim is required to say this meaningfully and with full belief at least once in his lifetime. As one might expect, however, Muslims repeat this many times every day.[31] Muslims believe that Allah reveals his will and guidance of human beings in three distinct ways: (1) through Muhammad, his messenger; (2) through the Koran, his revelation; and (3) through the angels. From these clear and definite teachings, the Muslim's path or way is clear.

PRAYER (SALAT).   The practicing Muslim prays at least five times a day, using a special prayer rug and facing Mecca, Islam's Holy City. In addition, on Friday, all males are required to pray publicly, and under the leadership of an Imam (prayer leader), they prostrate themselves before Allah.[32]

CHARITY OR ALMSGIVING.   Every Muslim is of his free will to give an offering to the poor, the needy, debtors, slaves, wayfarers, beggars, and other charities of various kinds. It was first considered as a "loan to Allah," but is now voluntary, although everyone is expected to give.

RAMADAN.   Ramadan is Islam's holy month to commemorate Muhammad's commission from Allah and the beginning of his mission. The month rotates around the year in the Arabian lunar calendar. During this month, the religious Muslim tries not to partake of any food or drink from sunup until sundown. After sundown, he may eat moderately. The idea of fasting makes one think and meditate on spiritual things, aids in self-discipline, and sensitizes one toward the poor and hungry.

THE PILGRIMAGE (HAJJ).   Once in a lifetime every Muslim is expected to make a pilgrimage to Mecca, unless it is impossible, which of course constitutes another sacrifice for Muslims, especially those who are living far away from Mecca. Further, it is a chance for the most powerful of devotions at the greatest of all Islamic shrines.[33]

ISLAM'S SOCIAL TEACHINGS

ECONOMIC TEACHINGS.   Muhammad and the Koran taught that the wealth of Muslim societies should be widely shared. It does not deny a human being the right to work hard and accrue wealth, but it does insist that competition and the desire to acquire wealth be balanced by fair play and compassion. Also, as noted, one must give to the poor, sick, needy, and other charities.

WOMEN'S RIGHTS.   It is often felt that Islam tends to treat women as lesser beings, and in some ways compared with other Western cultures, perhaps they do, although women have been notoriously treated as less than men even in the supposedly democratic United States. Women, prior to Muhammad, were treated as chattel to be used or abused by their fathers and husbands in any way they pleased. After Muhammad, however, these conditions were changed. He forbade infanticide of daughters and required that they be included in their fathers' inheritance, not equally, but to receive half of what the sons got. This is, of course, not truly fair and just, but before Muhammad, women were eliminated from any inheritance whatsoever. The Koran opens the way for such things as their education, right to vote, and the right to careers; however, as it happens in any system where ideals are stated, actions often fall far short of these ideals. A lot depends on the advancement of the particular Arab country as to how many rights are given to women. For example, in Egypt, mostly due to Mrs. Anwar Sadat, the wife of the late Egyptian leader, women have a great many more rights than they do in other Arab countries where the leaders are not as liberal or enlightened.

RACIAL EQUALITY.   Islam stresses absolute racial equality, and Muhammad was said to have been married to a black woman. Intermarriage is not forbidden, and the popularity of Islam in such areas as Africa and Asia, as well in essentially white countries, is a testament to this racial equality.

THE USE OF FORCE.   The Koran does not teach pacificism, as the New Testament does, but it does teach forgiveness and the return of good for evil when feasible. It allows full punishment of wanton wrongdoing to maintain moral standards without becoming sentimental or too tolerant of people who commit serious moral wrongs.

In war, Muhammad was quite clear about several points: (1) agreements are to be kept, (2) treachery is to be avoided, (3) wounded and dead enemies are not to be mutilated or disfigured, (4) women, children, and the old are not be slain, (5) crops and sacred objects are to be spared, and (6) a morally just war must either be defensive or to right a serious wrong. As Muhammad stated, "Defend yourself against your enemies, but attack them not first; God hateth the aggressor."[34]

RELIGIOUS TOLERANCE.   The Koran stated, "Let there be no compulsion in religion. . . . Unto you your religion, and unto me my religion."[35] In enforcing these teachings, Muhammad said that all peoples may freely practice their religion and should be protected from insults and vexation: "Wilt thou then force men to believe when belief can come only from God?"[36] Here again we can always notice the falling short of ideals, as seen in the recent upheavals in Iran and in the war between Iran and Iraq. Many Muslims admit that their record is far from pure in religious toleration; however, they see the Christian record of persecution during the Crusades, the Inquisition, burning people at the stake, and devastating religious wars all done in the name of Christ and God as being much more serious and evil.

It is ironic that Jews, Christians, and Muslims share so much in common in their monotheism and yet still have an extremely difficult time getting along in matters of religion, politics, and culture in many parts of the world today. It would seem that differences in religious doctrine and social structure could be allowed to exist while still discovering a common meeting ground to achieve peace and resolve problems. All three major Western religions and all their sects need to work toward these goals.

Applying Philosophy—
Situations for Thought and Discussion

SITUATION 1

Select one of the three major Western religions with which you are not affiliated and research it as fully as you can, both historically and theologically, and analyze and critically evaluate it as a culturally effective force for the people involved with it and those affected by it. Describe what you feel are its strong and weak points, supporting your contentions with as much evidence and argument as you can muster. Objectively speaking, to what extent could you accept such a religious point of view and why? Do you feel that it deserves its designation as one of the world's major and great religions? Why or why not? What are its basic rituals and ceremonies and to what extent do you find them significant and why? Desribe its ethical and social teachings and state to what extent you find them significant or effective and why?

SITUATION 2

Compare and contrast Christianity with either Judaism or Islam, describing how they are different and how they are alike. Do you believe that these religions have similar roots—what are they? Do you believe it is possible to have a strong commitment to one of these religions and still live in peace with the other? How can this be achieved if they conflict in so many ways? Present a plan in detail of how you feel these two religions could allow each other to exist and still also allow for strong commitments to their own beliefs without changing the other's.

SITUATION 3

Examine the Middle East conflicts and crises from the point of view of the clash of the religions involved—Judaism, Islam, and Christianity. To what extent do you feel that these different religious beliefs are basic causes for all the conflicts that have occurred and are occurring? Answer in detail. Here, again, do you feel that there will ever be a possibility of resolving these religious differences and conflicts? Why or why not? How do you feel that this could be accomplished and why? Draw up a detailed plan for resolving re-

ligious differences without destroying any of the three religions'
commitments to their beliefs.

Chapter Summary

I. Introduction. Purpose of the survey of major religions in these two
chapters is to present students with various religious and nonreligious views.
   A. To expand knowledge of religious and nonreligious viewpoints different from their own, hoping to increase tolerance.
   B. To show them that there are many possibilities in the area of
   religion to choose from, not just theism or atheism.
II. Judaism—meaning in monotheism.
   A. The quest for meaning and purpose—great Jewish leaders and
   teachers refused to deny meaning and purpose in the universe.
      1. They believed that the universe is connected with person-
      hood in some way.
      2. They believed that the universe is moral.
      3. They believed that nature is imbued with God's meaning.
      4. Judaism, along with Christianity and Islam, is not basically
      mystically oriented so that it accepts this world and nature
      as significant and not as something to be shunned.
      5. Judaism also believes in self-determination and therefore
      human freedom.
   B. It sees history as a God and human-centered set of cocur-
   rences.
   C. God revealed himself to the Jews not so much in what he said
   but rather in what he did.
   D. The Jews also believed that God had made several covenants
   (agreements) with them through their prophets, from Abraham to Moses.
   E. Other significant aspects of Judaism.
      1. The Torah is the Jews' holy book, consisting of the first
      five books of Moses.
      2. The Talmud is a compendium of learning that is an inter-
      pretation of the Torah.
      3. The Land is a central concept of Judaism linking their his-
      tory to the land of Israel.
      4. Mitzvah is the ethical and social justice document of the Jews.
      5. The Messiah and Messianic age is another concept of Ju-
      daism; to some Jews the Messiah will be a person; others
      believe it will be an infusion of God's spirit in the world
      achieving peace and morality for all human beings.

    F. Types of Judaism.
1. Orthodox—a strict adherence to original principles.
2. Reform—a denial of revelation, seeing the Torah not as a divinely revealed book but as a source of ethics. A more secular approach.
3. Conservative—accepting the validity of science, but not denying the divinity of the Torah, stating that revelation is a dynamic process rather than static. It retained all the aspects of Orthodox Judaism without its rigidity.

III. Christianity
    A. No religion has had such a dynamic influence on Western culture.
    B. There is very little known about Jesus, its leader.
1. He seemed to be humble, gentle, and charismatic.
2. He taught in parables and stories rather than with philosophy or theology so that the common people understood him.
3. He claimed to be divine.
4. He had a revolutionary social message to love one's neighbor and even one's enemies.

    C. Christian dogma.
1. The Trinity—there are three divine persons with one divine nature: God the Father, God the Son (Jesus Christ), and God the Holy Spirit.
2. The Incarnation—God became man.
3. Crucifixion and atonement—God allowed himself to be crucified by men to atone for their sins and especially for the original sin of Adam and Eve in the Garden of Eden.
4. The Resurrection—Jesus arose from the dead and ascended into heaven, thus overcoming death for all humankind.

    D. Roman Catholicism.
1. Tradition and the papacy in this form of Christianity is one of the major differences between it and other forms—it believes in the Bible *plus* tradition (the church as teacher and interpreter of Christianity through its popes).
2. Sacraments—there are seven:
    a. Baptism, which erases the stain of Original Sin and welcomes the newborn into the religion.
    b. Confession, which involves repenteance, remorse, and absolution from all sins after Original Sin.
    c. Holy Communion, which is based on the Last Supper and is a mysterious means whereby Catholics receive the spirit of Jesus Christ into their very being.
    d. Confirmation, which is a coming-of-age sacrament for

the young adolescent who makes his or her own commitment to Catholicism.

    e. Matrimony and Holy Orders, which sanctify two vo-
cations within the religious community—the joining of
husbands and wives and entering the priesthood.

    f. Anointing of the sick, which blesses the sick and helps
them while they're dying.

3. Mariology is a very deep concern that Catholicism has for
Mary, the mother of Jesus.

    a. They believe that she was conceived without sin (Im-
maculate Conception).

    b. She conceived Jesus without sexual intercourse but
through the Holy Spirit directly from God.

    c. She was assumed bodily into heaven.

    d. Protestants often accuse Catholics of an overconcern with
Mary—mariolatry.

E. Eastern Orthodoxy.

1. Accepts Jesus as divine, the Trinity, the Incarnation, Crucifixion and Atonement, and the Resurrection.

2. It differs from Roman Catholicism in that it rejects the pope's
authority and claimed infallibility and also rejects such pa-
pal proclaimed doctrines as the Immaculate Conception and
the assumption of the Virgin Mary.

3. It also accepts the teaching tradition as "the conscience of
the church" rather than as the infallibility of men.

4. It differs further in that it stresses the "corporate nature of
the church," that lay people in the church have a greater
equality with priests than they can have in Catholicism.

5. The last difference is that the Eastern church emphasizes
mysticism for all levels of worshippers more than Catholicism.

F. Protestantism.

1. "Protestant" does not merely mean "one who protests" but
rather one who gives testimony that God is the supreme
being and the central part of human life.

2. It is certainly closely related to the other two major forms
of Christianity discussed earlier, but its two most distinguishing features are as follows:

    a. Justification by faith, which is much like Tillich's action
part of his theory of Ultimate Concern.

    b. The Protestant principle, which warns against absolutiz-
ing the relative either in the secular or religious world,
that is, taking the symbols that lead to God to be God
himself.

    3. Differences between Protestantism and the other two forms of Christianity.
       a. No intermediaries between God and human beings.
       b. The Bible is really the backbone and basis of Christian faith, not tradition or other religious aspects.
       c. Protestants generally have a stronger social action emphasis than do the other two.
    4. Types of Protestantism.
       a. Orthodox Protestantism includes such churches as the Church of England, Episcopalianism, and Lutheranism because they most resemble the Catholic and Eastern Orthodox churches in their rituals and some of their theology.
       b. The harsher, more spartan, and more puritanical line is followed by Calvinism, Presbyterianism, Methodism, Baptists in England, and Anabaptists, such as the Mennonite Church.
       c. Fundamentalism arose largely in America and involves many segments of the Baptist Church, the Assembly of God, and many others. These churches tend to rely on a more literal interpretation of the Bible and reject anything that smacks of the orthodoxy of Catholicism.
       d. Liberalism emphasizes the essence of the Bible rather than its literal words and accepts creative evolution. It also tends to emphasize God as more personal and also has a strong social action program.
       e. Neoorthodoxy is halfway between fundamentalists and liberals both in its views of the Bible and revelation.
       f. You can only view the foregoing as trends and tendencies and you are likely to find mixtures of these in different sects of even the same Protestant religion.

IV. Islam—the word means "to accept," "submit," or "commit oneself."
  A. Its Ultimate Reality is Allah; the Islamic conception of this being is strongly monotheistic.
  B. It accepts all the great prophets of Judaism and Christianity including Jesus, but it feels that its own prophet, Muhammad, "the Seal of All the Prophets," is the greatest and last of all.
  C. Five principles of Islam.
    1. The straight path—Muslims believe that there is no God but Allah who reveals his will in three ways: (1) through Muhammad, his messenger; (2) through the Koran, his revelation; and (3) through angels.

2. Prayer must be said at least five times a day with a special prayer rug and facing Mecca.

3. Charity or almsgiving is required to express the compassion of Allah for the poor and needy.

4. Ramadan is Islam's holy month to commemorate Muhammad's commission from Allah and the beginning of his mission.

5. The pilgrimage (hajj) to Mecca is required of every Muslim at least once in his life unless it is impossible.

6. Economic teachings are that Muslim wealth should be widely shared and that competition and the desire for wealth should be balanced by fair play and compassion.

7. Women's rights. Even though women's rights may not be considered by the West to be much under Islam, they are much greater than before Muhammad.

8. Islam definitely believes in absolute racial equality.

9. The use of force is not emphasized even though Islam is not a proponent of pacifism. Muhammad stated that force should only be used in defense or to right a serious wrong.

10. Religious tolerance is supported in the Koran, and persecution is forbidden.

D. It is recognized that the ideals of Islam are often not attained and are even thwarted; however, the same could be said of any religion, including Christianity or Judaism.

Additional Questions and Activities for Study and Discussion

1. Examine the history of the Civil War in Ireland and describe and evaluate what part the clash between Roman Catholicism and Protestantism plays in the long-standing conflict. Answer all the same questions posed in situation 3 concerning the Middle East conflicts.

2. Read Flannery O'Connor's short story, "Displaced Person," and discuss the part religion plays in the story. Both Protestantism and Roman Catholicism can be found in the story; to what extent do you feel that O'Connor thinks either form of Christianity is effective in solving human problems and alleviating human suffering? All the people who watch the tragedy that occurs near the end of the story are Christian, at least by affiliation; why do you think they do nothing to avert the tragedy? Shouldn't they as Christians have tried? Why or why not?

3. Read Ernest Gaines' short story, "The Sky Is Gray," and analyze

and critically evaluate the part that Christianity, and religion in general, plays in the story. Especially concentrate on the discussion between the old and young black men in the dentist's office about religion and nonreligious atheism. Is the old man's treatment of the younger man truly Christian? Why or why not, and why do you think he acts as he does? What is the point Gaines makes about Christianity and racial prejudice? Is racial or religious prejudice wrong in the Christian tradition? Why or why not? Be specific in backing up your positions.

4. Examine all the events and forces leading up to the deposing of the Shah of Iran and the takeover by the Ayatollah Khomeini, including the taking of hostages from the American Embassy, and show how all these actions fit or do not fit with the teachings of Islam. To what extent were and are the causes of these occurrences religious in nature? Answer in detail. Does the Koran condone and do you think Muhammad would condone what occurred under the Ayatollah? Why or why not? If there is a clash between the present religious policies and those of Muhammad, how do you account for them? Again, answer in detail.

5. Examine carefully the Mormon Church (The Church of Latter Day Saints), its history, and its teachings, and determine to what extent you would call it a form of Christianity or list it as a separate church in its own right. Be sure to substantiate your position with evidence and argument as fully as you can, listing the differences and similarities between Mormonism and other forms of Christianity.

6. Do research on the events leading up to and surrounding Martin Luther's posting of his Ninety-five Theses and describe and support to what extent you feel that his protests against the Roman Catholic church were or were not justified. Do you feel that the great schism between the Roman Catholic church and Martin Luther and his followers could have been avoided? If so, how; if not, why not? Do you feel that Protestants, Catholics, and Eastern Orthodox followers could ever be united into one Christian church? Why or why not? How or how not? After you have discussed this possibility, do you feel that Christians and Jews could ever get together—again why or why not and how or how not?

7. Examine the history of the persecution of the Jews by various groups including other religions, and describe why you think that they as a people have been persecuted so much. To what extent do you feel persecution has been caused by their religious beliefs? Why? To what extent were Christians and Christianity involved in these persecutions, especially during the holocaust of World War II? Can such persecution be justified either in Christianity, in all its forms, or in Islam? Why or why not?

Footnotes

1. Robert O. Ballou, ed., *The Portable World Bible* (New York: Viking, 1944), pp. 235–237.

2. Ibid., p. 237.

3. Rabbi Sylvan D. Schwartzman and Rabbi Jack D. Spiro, *The Living Bible* (New York: Union of American Hebrew Congregations, 1962), p. 45.

4. Ibid., pp. 45–46.

5. Ibid., pp. 44–45.

6. Leo Trepp, *Judaism: Development and Life* (Belmont, Calif.: Dickenson, 1966), p. 2.

7. Ibid.

8. Ibid., p. 16.

9. Ibid., pp. 4–5.

10. Ibid., pp. 5–6.

11. Ibid., pp. 6–7.

12. Ibid., p. 134.

13. Ibid., pp. 48–49.

14. Ibid., pp. 50–51.

15. Ibid., p. 51.

16. Huston Smith, *The Religions of Man* (New York: Harper, 1958), pp. 302–303.

17. Ballou, *The Portable World Bible,* pp. 410–411.

18. Ibid.; The Sermon on the Mount can be found on pp. 385–393, and the Good Samaritan parable on pp. 410–411.

19. One modern-day example of rejection of one of these dogmas can be found in John Hick, ed., *The Myth of God Incarnate* (Philadelphia: Westminster, 1977), in which a group of respected Protestant theologians deny the Incarnation.

20. Ballou, *The Portable World Bible,* p. 406.

21. Smith, *The Religions of Man,* p. 336.

22. Ibid., p. 339.

23. Ibid., pp. 339–341.

24. Ibid., p. 339.

25. Ibid., p. 340.

26. Ibid., p. 346.

27. Ibid., p. 343.

28. Ibid., p. 346.

29. John B. Noss, *Man's Religions,* 4th ed. (New York: Macmillan, 1969), p. 514.

30. Smith, *The Religion of Man,* pp. 235–236.

31. Ibid., p. 236.

32. Noss, *Man's Religion,* pp. 532–533.

33. Ibid., and Smith, *The Religion of Man,* pp. 236–241.

34. Smith, p. 248.

35. Ibid., p. 249.

36. Ibid., p. 250.

Bibliography

JUDAISM

Baron, S. W. *A Social and Religious History of the Jews,* 3 vols. New York: Columbia University Press, 1952.

————, and Joseph L. Blau, eds. *Judaism: Postbiblical and Talmudic Period.* New York: Liberal Arts Press, 1954.

Blau, Joseph L. *Modern Varieties of Judaism.* New York: Columbia University Press, 1966.

Finkelstein, L., ed. *The Jews: Their History, Culture and Religion.* New York: Harper, 1960.

Graetz, H. *History of the Jews.* Philadelphia: Jewish Publications Society of America, 1891.

CHRISTIANITY

Bainton, R. *Here I Stand, A Life of Martin Luther.* New York: Mentor, 1950.

Beach, W., and H. Reinhold Niebuhr, eds. *Christian Ethics: Sources of the Living Tradition.* New York: Ronald, 1955.

Brantl, George, ed. *Catholicism.* New York: Braziller, 1967.

Brauer, J. C. *Protestantism in America: A Narrative History.* Philadelphia: Westminister, 1954.

Denzinger, H. J. D. *The Sources of Catholic Dogma.* New York: Herder, 1957.

French, R. M. *The Eastern Orthodox Church.* New York: Hutchinson, 1951.

Hopkins, C. H. *The Rise of the Social Gospel in American Protestantism, 1865–1915.* New Haven, Conn.: Yale University Press, 1940.

Lossky, V. *The Mystical Theology of the Eastern Church.* New York: James Clarke, 1957.

Rouse, R., and S. C. Neill, eds. *A History of the Ecumenical Movement.* Philadelphia: Westminster, 1954.

Walker, Williston. *A History of the Christian Church.* New York: Scribners, 1959.

Watts, Alan. *Myth and Ritual in Christianity.* New York: Grove, 1960.

ISLAM

Gibb, H. A. R. *Modern Trends in Islam.* Chicago: University of Chicago Press, 1947.

————. *Mohammedanism, An Historical Survey.* New York: Mentor, 1955.

Goldziher, I. *Mohammed and Islam,* trans. K. C. Seelye. New Haven, Conn.: Yale University Press, 1917.

Guillaume, Alfred. *Islam.* New York: Penguin, 1954.

Schacht, Joseph, and C. E. Bosworth, eds. *The Legacy of Islam,* 2nd ed. Oxford: Clarendon Press, 1974.

Smith, W. C. *Islam in Modern History.* New York: Mentor, 1959.

CHAPTER 12

Eastern Religions and Nonreligious Views

Hinduism

The word *Hindu* really means "Indian" and also refers to a geographical area around the upper branches of the Indus River. Hinduism, like Christianity, is a religion of multiplicity, and it is very difficult to pin down all expressions of this complex and ancient faith. India is an ancient culture that dates back to around 2500 B.C. Hinduism is usually traced through four major periods: (1) The early period of the Vedas (the word *Veda* literally means "sacred knowledge" or "wisdom") and polytheism; (2) the Brahmanic period, which marked the end of the Vedic period and began to stress a form of monism if not monotheism (see the previous chapter); (3) the Bhakti period (*Bhakti* means "the way of worship and devotion"), which began about 200 B.C.; and (4) the modern period, which involved the East's relationship with the West.[1]

Hinduism is one of the few religions that very practically starts with the wants and needs of human beings as it moves into its religious teachings, and the expression of these wants and needs are put forth in two paths: (1) the Path of Desire and (2) the Path of Renunciation.

THE PATH OF DESIRE

The Path of Desire involves two main values that are worldly and secular: they are those of Kama (pleasure) and Artha (wealth, fame, and power).

PLEASURE.   All human beings want to experience pleasure and happiness or the hedonistic aspects of life involving gratification of the senses. Surprising as it may be to most Westerners, who think of the Indian culture and religion as extremely ascetic, pleasure is accepted as a significant value; however, it is also recognized as transitory in nature, and if overemphasized, it can be destructive. After all, the world and life can be enjoyable, and there is no reason why human beings should not desire or pursue pleasure as long as they do it with moderation. As long as the rules of morality are observed, people are free to seek all the pleasure they wish. The Hindu belief is that after human beings have sought this goal, they will realize that it is not the be-all and the end-all of life. Since it involves essentially gratification of the self, it is too narrow a view of life to sustain human beings for very long.

WEALTH, FAME, AND POWER.   Here again Hinduism sees these as worthy goals that often contribute to social success and a civilized culture. In fact, these goals involve other human beings more than does the desire for pleasure, so that they are often considered as somewhat more worthy than pleasure per se. Hinduism recognizes again that the drives for possession, status, and power are very strong in all of us, and it does not suggest that human beings never seek them. However, it again warns against pursuing them to too great a degree because (1) wealth, fame, and power are competitive and therefore also transitory in nature; (2) as a lifelong goal, they can never be satisfied and therefore tend to leave one wanting; (3) they are less self-centered than pleasure, but they still emphasize the self more than others; and (4) their achievements are ephemeral—that is, they "can't be taken with you" when you die. The Hindu feels that the human vision is not only centered in this life but also reaches toward eternity, that is, beyond this life and even himself as a worldly being to what the future holds for him beyond this world.

Again, Hinduism does not view the foregoing values as immoral or worthless, nor does it believe that the desire for them should be repressed or denied; however, it considers them as toys when compared with the deeper human values that can be attained through the Path of Renunciation.

THE PATH OF RENUNCIATION

The second path of Hinduism is based on what this religion assumes human beings really want—*mukti* (liberation). This liberation involves three corollary wants: (1) being, existence, and life; (2) knowledge and awareness; and (3) peace and self-realization. Humans do not merely want these, but they want them to an infinite degree, which is why they are all counted under the concept of liberation—a complete release from the countless limitations that press so closely upon the present existence of human beings.[2] Since human beings are considered finite, then is not their hope for infinite being, knowledge and awareness, and peace and self-realization really an idealization rather than something that is attainable?

Hinduism states that not only is this infiniteness attainable, but what is even more surprising, it says that it is already in the possession of human beings if they would just realize it! To understand this statement, it is important to understand Hinduism's conception of the ultimate reality that exists both beyond and within human beings—Atman-Brahman.

ATMAN AND BRAHMAN

ATMAN.   In Hinduism, the individual self stands self-proved and is always immediately felt and known. Whatever else one is uncertain of, he or she is absolutely certain of the existence of self. This self, in Hinduism, is not the mind, body, feelings, or will, but resides in pure consciousness (refer back to Chapter 4)—it is more than any of these most important human aspects. *Atman* originally meant "life-breath," which is interesting in that the Greek *psyche,* meaning "soul" or "self," also originally meant the same thing. Atman is that which pervades everything, that which is subject and which knows, experiences, and illuminates objects, and that which is immortal and unchanging. Atman is the ground or basis for all waking, sleeping, and dream states, but it transcends them all. It is universal, immanent as well as transcendent, and the ultimate subject that can never become an object. Where does Atman acquire these qualities?

BRAHMAN.   From the objective side, ultimate reality is called *Brahman,* that from which the world arises and is sustained and that into which it returns—that from which all beings come, by which they live, and into which they are eventually reabsorbed. Brahman is the supreme reality that transcends all, yet that underlies everything as its background. It is the universal self, and it makes all other selves possible (refer to Royce's theories of self in Chapter 4).

ATMAN-BRAHMAN.   The same reality exists from the subjective side (Atman) and from the objective side (Brahman). The absolute and ultimate reality manifests itself as the subject and the object and transcends them both—it is certain as the Atman and as infinite as the Brahman. "That thou art (tat tvam asi)" is the great saying of the

Upanishads (the great holy book of the Brahmanic period, written about 800–600 B.C.)—"I am Brahman; Atman is Brahman; I am that; I am the nondual bliss." In other words, the fullest realization possible is Atman and Brahman together, that is—to speak in Western terms— the Atman is similar to the divine soul that exists in each individual human being, whereas Brahman is the equivalent of God the Father, or the godhead. Infiniteness already exists in human beings in the form of Atman, which resides within them and which is the same thing as Brahman, which exists beyond them, and the complete realization of infinite bliss would be the perfect merging of Atman with its source, Brahman, and this is only possible through the Path of Renunciation. This is why Hinduism feels that although the Path of Desire is not in itself evil or in need of repression, yet human beings must go beyond this path to satisfy their real wants and needs. To achieve this, Hinduism prescribes four yogas or ways to the ultimate goal.

FOUR WAYS TO THE GOAL

Yoga is a method or means of attaining union of Atman with Brahman, and there is a yoga for every type of human personality—the reflective, emotional, active, and experiential. Hinduism again here exemplifies its wide approach to individual realization and integration with the ultimate reality.

JNANA YOGA—THE INTELLECTUAL WAY.   This yoga aims to achieve oneness with Brahman through knowledge. Human beings like Socrates, Plato, or Buddha are the types of human beings who would be most inclined to use this particular yoga. With this yoga, Hinduism provides a series of meditations and logical demonstrations designed to bring the thinker to the realization that there is more to him than his own finite self. This method involves three steps: (1) hearing and listening to the great wise men, scriptures, and the great philosophic treatises of the ages; (2) thinking—a prolonged, intensive reflection to make the abstract concepts of Atman and Brahman into reality; and (3) meditating as profoundly as possible on one's identity with the eternal spirit, which is Atman and Brahman.

BHAKTI YOGA—THE EMOTIONAL WAY.   This is often referred to as the way to Brahman through love and is more suitable than Jnana yoga to the person who is more affective or compassionate in nature. It differs from the intellectual approach in that it sees Brahman more definitely as Holy Other, an object of love and, therefore, as more of a person or personality, unlike the abstract ultimate reality that would interest the philosopher. The person's relationship with Brahman will be one of an outpouring of love rather than intellectual realization.

There are three features of this approach that enable the Bhakti to attain his goal: (1) "Japam," which is the practice of constantly repeating the name of Brahman, during all of one's life activities; (2) "ringing the changes on love," which is essentially utilizing all the modes of love—love of children, parents, brother and sister, friend, and beloved—and directing them toward Brahman; and (3) the worship of Brahman as one's chosen ideal that is beyond all the human modes of love in a very special way.

Karma Yoga—The Way to God Through Work. This yoga stresses the fact that people do not have to retire from the world to attain oneness with Brahman; they can also realize the ultimate reality through their everyday actions, sort of like Martin Buber's urging to "hallow the every day." Hinduism states that people should throw themselves into their work with everything they have, but that they should do so wisely to bring the highest rewards, not just trivial accomplishments. Hinduism feels that every action performed in the external world has its correlative internal reaction, and as each task becomes a sacred ritual in relation to Brahman, it approaches just that relationship. The people who follow Karma yoga will try to do each task as it comes and as if it were the only thing they have to do. They will seek to concentrate fully and calmly on each task as it presents itself and do it thoroughly and as perfectly as possible before moving on to the next.

Raja Yoga—The Experiential Way. This is really a psychological approach to self-realization and realization of Brahman. When Westerners think of "yoga," this is the way they are most aware of and have heard of the most. Because of its powerful inner experiencing, it has often been called "the royal road to reintegration."[3] Behind this yoga lies the Hindu assumption that human beings are "layered beings." First is the layer of the body; next is the layer that is that part of the mind that is a person's conscious personality; third is one's subconscious mind; and last and underlying the other three is Being-Itself, or the core of an individual.

To get to this core, one has to retire from worldly things and, through profound meditation and spiritual practices, try to attain that direct personal experience of "the beyond that is within," or Atman-Brahman. The method this yogi (a person who practices a yoga) uses is a willed introversion, which is the attempt to "drive his psychic energy into the deepest part of his being and activate the lost continent of his true self."[4] There are eight steps that the Raja yogi must follow: (1) abstention from injury of others, lying, stealing, sensuality, and greed; (2) the observance of cleanliness, contentment, self–control, studiousness, and contemplation of the divine; (3) a working through the body to the mind through various physical postures and positions (the most famous of which is probably the lotus position), which are intended to transcend bodily awareness and arrive at pure consciousness; (4) controlled breathing; (5) the turning of one's concentration totally inward; (6) control of the mind and its internal wanderings; (7) merging of subject and object in which the dualistic knower and known are united; and (8) attaining the final state, Samadhi (total absorption in Brahman), in which the mind is completely absorbed in Brahman because the yogi has penetrated through everything to full realization and oneness—Atman-Brahman.[5]

THE FOUR STAGES OF LIFE

Hinduism stresses differences in individuals, as can be noted from the discussion of the four different yogas to fit one's character and chosen life-style. It also sees every life as passing through different stages; how people live their lives also depends on which stage they are in.

THE FIRST STAGE—STUDENT.   In India, this stage usually begins after the rite of initiation, somewhere between the ages of eight and twelve, during which time the student lives in the home of his teacher, serving him in payment for his being taught. This is a stage of preparation when the student is supposed to listen and learn everything he can. Students learn not factual information but also good habits and character formation.

THE SECOND STAGE—HOUSEHOLDER OR PRACTICAL PERSON. Usually beginning with marriage, this stage involves family, vocation, and functioning in one's community. This is a time of practicality in which one strives for pleasure, success, and to do one's duty.

THE THIRD STAGE—RETIREMENT.   Anytime after the birth of his first grandchild, a person may withdraw from previous social obligation. This is a time of contemplation of life's total meaning and a time to work more fully on oneself toward greater realization.

THE FOURTH STAGE—SANNYASIN.   The word *sannyasin* is defined as "one who neither hates nor loves anything." Having achieved eternal reality through his retirement, one now returns but as a totally free person in a world he has transcended. Such wisemen often become homeless but respected beggars, independent of obligations, belongings, society, and so on. They live in the state of Atman–Brahman and behold nothing else.

THE CASTE SYSTEM AND ITS PERVERSIONS

It seems strange that in a religion and country where differences are so readily recognized and accepted that this would eventually resolve itself into such a thing as the caste system. It is hard to know where the caste system came from. Some argue that it is connected to the Hindu concepts of *karma* and the transmigration of souls or reincarnation. These two beliefs state that rather than there being one soul in one body that leaves it at death and goes to another world (heaven or hell) upon dying, as the Western religious view sees it, a soul transmigrates through various reincarnations toward fulfillment until it finally is released to be one with Brahman.

No one knows how many reincarnations exist for any particular soul, but the theory has it that this all depends on the deeds one performs in one's life, or his karma. The responsibility for one's future life is decided by his own actions and is based on his deeds. If he is immoral, then he will continue to be reborn until he finally achieves a moral state. In this respect, many Hindus feel that it is possible for someone to be reborn in a worse state than his previous life because he did not live that life in a moral or significant way.

It is possible, therefore, that the great unwashed, poor, and diseased people of India in the lower classes are the result of their own previous bad karma. It is also more probably due to differences in politics, social standing, economics, education, and intelligence. It is certainly not unusual in any culture to draw significant lines between classes—even our own supposed democratic culture has its upper classes, middle classes, and lower classes—its glorious residential areas and its ghettos and barrios; therefore, it is not so unusual that India would have a caste system.

Traditionally, there were four classes: (1) the Brahmins or seers, India's intellectual and spiritual leaders; (2) the administrators with an ability for organizing and promoting human affairs; (3) the producers, who are craftsmen, artisans, farmers; and (4) the followers, who are unskilled laborers, hard workers, but not skilled or usually very well educated or intelligent.

Besides the undemocratic aspects of having a caste system at all, there were several other problems that arose with such a system. First, there emerged a fifth and lower class called "untouchables," who were considered outcasts from the other castes in the system. Second, there was a proliferation of subcastes (about three thousand), which of course placed human beings into untold numbers of gradations and degrees of status. Third, there were strict prohibitions against intermarriage, and even interdining made social intercourse between the castes nearly impossible. When this happens, the upper classes begin to pull far away from the middle and lower ones to the point where political and social unrest often arises, as it did indeed in India. Fourth, as so often happens in strict class systems, the upper and middle classes profited from the system at the expense of the lower classes. Last, caste distinctions became hereditary, and families were almost forced to remain in the caste into which they had been born.

The caste system was and is an unfortunate outgrowth of Hinduism as it became applied to the social and cultural scenes; however, Buddha, as we shall see, Gandhi, and Nehru all were opposed to the caste system and felt that it was a perversion of the great Hindu ideals. Its rigidity has been lessened, and India in the modern world is working toward a greater awareness of the uniqueness of each individual human being, which has always been one of the theological and philosophical cornerstones of the Hindu religion.

In concluding our cursory description, it is important to stress that Hinduism, perhaps more than any other major world religion, has had and does have a strong tolerance for other religions. For centuries, Hinduism has shared its land of India with Parsees, Buddhists, Muslims, Sikhs, and Christians. In its basic religious structure, it accepts the concept of "many paths to the same goal" much more than do many other religions, such as Judaism and Christianity. Hinduism accepts almost all the world's great religious leaders as manifestations of Brahman; that is, Hindus believe that Brahman has appeared as Yahweh, Jesus, and Muhammad and in the form of the various religious prophets as well as in the forms of Vishnu (the Preserver), Shiva (the Completer), and Krishna (the leading Hindu incarnation of Brahman). Hinduism feels that Brahman is ultimate unity that chooses to manifest itself in diversity. As Sri Ramakrishna stated,

> God has made different religions to suit different aspirants, times, and countries. All doctrines are only so many paths; but a path is by no means God Himself. Indeed, one can reach God if one follows any of the paths with wholehearted devotion. One may eat a cake with icing either straight or sidewise. It will taste sweet either way.[6]

How much more effectively can religious tolerance be expressed? Many of the world's religions could learn a lot about religious freedom from Hinduism.

Buddhism

Buddhism is named after its founder, just as Christianity was named after Jesus, who was called Christ, and evidently Buddha was, like Jesus and Muhammad, a charismatic leader of great intensity who had a tremendous effect, not only on India but on the entire Far Eastern cultures as well as on Europe and America, especially in the twentieth century. Siddhartha Gautama of the Sakyas was born around 560 B.C. and died in 480 B.C. He acquired the name "Buddha," which means "the enlightened or awakened one" from his own description of himself when he was asked whether he was a god, an angel, or a saint. His reply was, "I am awake," and since the Sanskrit root "budh" denotes both to wake up and to know, he afterward became known as the Buddha.[7]

Buddhism is probably the strangest and most difficult for Westerners to grasp of all the Eastern religions. We have already discussed briefly the Buddhist concept of no-self in Chapter 4, but this "religion" also believes in no god and no soul or no spirit—Buddhism is a religion devoid of the general religious characteristics that we have seen in religions we have already discussed. In the Hinduism faced by Buddha, authority and the caste system had become a source of great wealth and privilege for the Brahmin and also the administrator classes; ritual, tradition, and speculation had become techniques of domination of the lower classes. Buddha abhorred the caste system, the hierarchy, and the power exerted by the few over the many in the name of religion. I trust that all this sounds familiar to you, for many religions have begun in reaction to a prevailing religious system that has been felt by a new, exciting, and charismatic leader to have become decadent and destructive of human beings in general. Christianity began in reaction to what is considered to be Jewish and Roman decadence, and Protestantism arose in reaction to what it believed to be the excesses of Roman Catholicism.

BUDDHA'S APPROACH TO RELIGION

Buddha believed in direct personal experience that involved intuition, a higher form of reason. He was not concerned with the institutions, cultures, or other structures, or opinions or beliefs arising from them, but rather with the feelings of equal individuals and the resolution of those feelings from suffering to its ending. He felt that religious activity had to be individualized, and told his followers, "Be ye lamps unto yourselves," by which he meant that each individual must do his own seeking, be his own tradition, and his own authority.

REJECTION OF COMMON RELIGIOUS ASPECTS.   Huston Smith lists six aspects of which Buddhism is devoid and that most religions have as their cornerstone and seven aspects that characterized its approach to religion.[8] The six aspects of which Buddhism is devoid are

1. There is no authority in Buddhism as there is in Catholicism, Judaism, or Islam; instead, Buddha challenged each individual to do his or her own seeking.
2. There is very little ritual in Buddhism except for individualized meditative techniques.
3. There is very little theological or philosophical speculation involved in Buddhism. Buddha was not concerned with the nature of reality either in the physical or spiritual world, but rather with the release from suffering and a spiritual realization for each individual human being.
4. There is very little emphasis on tradition in Buddhism. Buddha, as mentioned before, rejected most of the traditions of Hinduism and really attempted a fresh start with his religion aimed at individual self-realization. With this approach, tradition could only get in the way.
5. He preached a religion of intense self-effort, in that he believed that no gods, books, or rituals would give individuals any sort of realization; they had to rely on themselves, only, for any such attainment.
6. And, finally, Buddhism is totally devoid of any supernaturalism. As has already been stated, Buddha rejected any sort of divine being or beings and any sort of supernaturalism connected with human beings, such as soul or spirit. He rejected prayer, soothsaying, miracles, and any sort of supernaturally connected duties or rituals.

POSITIVE ASPECTS OF BUDDHISM.   The positive aspects of Buddhism, on the other hand, are as follows:

1. Buddhism is much more empirically based than is any other religion; that is, it emphasizes direct, personal experience as the final test for truth, rather than reasoning, inference, or argument.
2. Therefore, it is scientific in approach, a search for cause-and-effect relationships and a knowledge of reality as it is experienced by each individual human being.
3. It is pragmatic in that it is concerned with problem solving rather than with obtuse theological or philosophical speculation; for example, Buddha was concerned with how to eliminate suffering, not with the problem of evil in the universe.
4. It is therapeutic in that its major concern is for relieving suffering and making individuals "well" in the fullest sense of the word.

5. It is psychological in approach, in that it begins with human beings rather than with the universe and works at dealing with their problems, their nature, and the dynamics of their development.
6. It is democratic in that it rejects governments, caste systems, and any other ranking of human beings; each individual is important and unique in his own right, regardless of class or any other cultural status.
7. As has been stated or implied, Buddhism is directed toward individuals, stressing that each individual should attain his or her own enlightenment.

THE FOUR NOBLE TRUTHS

In keeping with Buddhism's pragmatism, empirical approach, and experiential emphases, Buddha very practically set up his religion on the basis of "Here is the problem, and here is the solution." He started by stating what he called the Four Noble Truths, and then described the Eightfold Path to deal with them.

DUKKHA.   This word is usually translated as "suffering" and means that life itself is suffering, dislocation, and an incompleteness that seeks fulfillment. From the trauma of birth to the terror and disintegration of death, all of human life is steeped in suffering. Buddha stated that in some way human life has become estranged from reality, and this alienation prevents the attainment of real happiness until it can be overcome. The first prerequisite for overcoming this estrangement is to be aware and have knowledge of its cause.

TANHA.   The word is usually translated as "desire." Buddha means by "desire" selfish and self-interested separation from the rest of reality. This activity is exemplified by the human desire and activity of separating itself from the rest of nature and the world in a subject versus object approach to life. For example, most humans see themselves (especially in Western culture) as subjects separate from and in conflict with nature, which is considered as something to be manipulated and controlled. Since Buddha believed that all reality is one, then anything that tends to separate human beings out as isolated from the rest of reality causes suffering.

OVERCOMING DESIRE.   The third Noble Truth follows on the second one, in that it states that if the cause of life's dislocation is selfish desire, then its cure is the overcoming of Tanha, or such desire.

THE EIGHTFOLD PATH.   The last Noble Truth is that suffering due to desire can be overcome through the Eightfold Path, as follows:

425

1. *Right Knowledge.* To deal with life's problems and especially the general problem of human suffering, one must know that suffering exists and is extensive, that it is caused by the desire for a separate existence and fulfillment, that it can be cured, and that the means of cure is the Eightfold Path.
2. *Right Aspiration.* If we must be aware in our minds and need to have right knowledge, we must also be sure "in our hearts" that what we want is freedom from desire and fulfillment—we must aspire to overcome desire and to attain fulfillment.
3. *Right Speech.* We must avoid lying or deception because language helps to form character and also reveals character. We must not use language wrongly to promote deception and block our real selves from coming through.
4. *Right Behavior.* Human beings must understand their behavior and its motives to improve it. Contained within this path is the Buddhist equivalent to the ethical implications of the Ten Commandments: do not kill, do not steal, do not lie, do not be unchaste, and do not drink intoxicants.
5. *Right Livelihood.* Human beings must not choose an occupation or career that would lead them to further alienate or separate themselves from reality. For example, working for an unethical business firm would thwart a Buddhist's drive for fulfillment.
6. *Right Effort.* One must have the will power to attain one's aspirations in striving for the Buddhist goals of attainment.
7. *Right Mindfulness.* A Buddhist must strive for awareness and therefore maintain a continuous alertness and self-examination. The mind must always be in control of the senses, and it must be directed to seeing things as they are and toward overcoming ignorance, for Buddha believed that if ignorance could be resolved, then fear and wrong desires could also be resolved. For example, if someone is afraid of death, then full concentration of the mind on death and all its aspects should alleviate that fear that is really due to ignorance of what death is.
8. *Right Absorption.* This final path comes about after the elimination of delusion, desire, and hostility has been achieved; and at that point, the Buddhist is absorbed in his meditation and moves toward freeing himself and attaining self-realization and fulfillment.

BASIC BUDDHIST CONCEPTS

NIRVANA.   Nirvana is the closest that Buddhism comes to having an ultimate reality. The word literally means "to extinguish" and involves the blotting out of the ego so that the true self comes through and merges with everything that is. This is a very difficult concept for Western religionists to understand, because it sounds to most of them as something negative rather than positive, as meeting with God or attaining heaven would be. Nirvana is not absolute nonexistence or life denying but, rather, the elimination and denial of ego. Nirvana is achieved when the boundary of the finite or limited self—the source of private desire—is extinguished and boundless life, incomprehensible and unutterable, is achieved. That's what Nirvana is and means.

Nirvana is not a god in the sense of a personal being but a state of being in which the self is merged and eternal harmony is achieved. Nirvana is indescribable and cannot be achieved in some group or mass form, but only individually through a kind of blissful experience after the ego self is extinguished and the true self is allowed to emerge and join with ultimate reality.

KARMA.   Buddha denied Atman or soul, but he still believed in karma or the causal sequence in which what happens to a person depends on his own actions. Buddha described karma as the passing on of a flame from candle to candle rather than a soul that is transmitted through different lower or higher forms. It seemed that he felt that the influence rather than the substance was transmitted along the causal chain. Buddha also believed in reincarnation, as Hinduism does, but the difference between the two religions lies in the conception of the nature of that which is affected by deeds and is transmitted from one form to another. In the case of Hinduism, it is the Atman; from Buddhism's point of view, it is a spiritual essence that seems to be centered in the ideas of the mind rather than in some other substance such as soul.

TWO TYPES OF BUDDHISM

As Buddhism developed, two major strands emerged determined by two different emphases: (1) the intellectual and (2) compassion. The first is called Theravada Buddhism; the second is referred to as Mahayana Buddhism. It is the latter, however, that has prevailed, possibly because it was Buddha's compassion for human suffering and the overcoming of it that seemed to be the most important thrust of his religion. It is said of Buddha that he had the opportunity to attain complete, perfect, and everlasting Nirvana at one point in his meditations, but he chose to wait and to return to this world to teach and assist all human beings in reaching Nirvana before he himself did. Because of this aspect of his life and teachings, he is often referred to as the "Compassionate Buddha."[9]

Theravada Buddhism tends to emphasize the intellectual and philosophical (*bodhi,* meaning "wisdom") aspects of Buddha's teachings, whereas Mahayana Buddhism emphasizes the compassionate *(karuna)* aspect. Therefore, the two types differed in many respects as follows:

1. Theravada emphasized that human beings determine their own realization completely alone; the Mahayana emphasized that their realization was contingent upon their relationships to others and their realizations also.
2. In the Theravadic view, human beings must be totally self-reliant, and there is no help or aid from an ultimate reality; in the Mahayanic view, the ultimate reality is in everyone as a potential aid for realization of all.
3. Theravada stresses wisdom and withdrawal, whereas Mahayana stresses compassion and association of individuals with each other.
4. Theravadic ideal is the disciple who proceeds independently to Nirvana, but the Mahayanic ideal is the disciple who approaches Nirvana but returns to the world to aid his fellow human beings in also attaining Nirvana.
5. Theravada sees Buddha as a saint whose personal influence ended when he entered Nirvana, whereas Mahayana sees him as a world savior who leads all human beings to Nirvana.
6. Theravada Buddhists opposed speculation and tended to emphasize and use meditation; Mahayana Buddhists elaborated upon and used speculation, ritual, and petitionary prayer more than the former.

With all these differences, the Theravadists tended to be more popular with the highly intellectual or mystical Buddhists, whereas the Mahayanists tended to be more popular with lay people because of their particular emphases. Probably the most popular form of Mahayana Buddhism is its intuitive school, which is called Zen Buddhism.

ZEN BUDDHISM

This form of Buddhism was based on Buddha's supposed Flower Sermon. At one time when Buddha had his disciples around him, instead of using any words whatsoever, he merely held aloft a golden lotus, and that was his sermon—no words, no preachings, no writings, just the ineffable beauty of the flower exposed for all to see. From this aspect of Buddha's teaching, Zen Buddhism was born on the assumption that words construct a substitute world that belies or dilutes the truth of intense, direct experience. Conforming to this false world constructed by words obscures, impedes, and destroys the transcending mind or the mode of experience that goes beyond the need for words. As Zen describes it, words and reason form a ladder "too short to reach reality."

Therefore, Zen is most concerned with the limitations of language and logical reasoning, which it sees as mere human constructs, and the transcendence of these constructs form the central intent of Zen's methods. In Zen, then, acts, not words, are the means to attain insight, awareness, and self-realization. Zen survives by the direct transmission of a specific state of awareness from mind to mind, like a flame passed from candle to candle, as in Buddha's concept of no soul. There are three major activities that characterize the Zen method: zazen, koan, and sanzen.

ZAZEN. This is seated meditation, usually in a lotus position and in a large meditation hall. Zen monks or students sit for hours on platforms in large halls, maintain silence, meditate on their koans, and also strive for a pure state of intuitive insight and awareness.

KOAN. This is a problem-solving device intended to break the hold of language and analytic reasoning over the human mind. Koans are sort of like riddles with no really clear answer available. The correctness of the answer depends on the interaction between Zen master and his pupil—only the master knows when his pupil has attained the correct answer or response to his assigned koan. Some examples of koans that have been used are "What was the appearance of your face before your ancestors were born?" or "We are all familiar with the sound of two hands clapping. What is the sound of one hand?" [10] If the pupil would protest that one hand can't clap, then he would fail the koan completely because he hadn't gotten the point of koan training.

This kind of thing, of course, seems very foolish to most Westerners who have been brought up on the need for "commonsense" or analytical and scientific reasoning, but the breaking of these false human constructs, which the Zen Buddhist sees as interfering with the attainment of full self-realization, is exactly the point of the whole thing. By being forced to wrestle with what his reason views as absurd, the student's exhausted rational mind will transcend itself and the limitations of thinking *about* something and will progress to thinking *within*, attaining insight within himself.

SANZEN. This aspect of the Zen method involves consultation with the Zen master by the pupil. The pupil states his koan answer, and the master motivates, validates, or invalidates the student's answer. The master, of course, does not teach with logical words, but often by actions, such as hitting or clapping, and tries to lead the student to an intuitive grasp of reality that is revealed by his answers to the koan. In other words, the master does not teach in the ordinary Western sense of the word; rather, the approach is pretty much nonverbal.

SATORI.   Satori is the goal to be attained by the three activities just described. Satori, like Nirvana, is indescribable and ineffable; it is an intuitive grasp of reality, a realization of the religious quest. Zen attempts to introduce the eternal into the now and to establish a relation between the utlimate reality and the individual self. There is no praying for salvation or eventual heaven; satori is a realization *now* of one's relationship with reality as a whole. There is no more dualism caused by language and reason, but only a direct experience of awareness and insight. Satori, however, is not an end in itself, but a progressive process in which life and the awareness that forms it are experienced to be a common good that is dependent on the welfare of all. Therefore, the purpose of satori is not to separate human beings from the world and reality but, rather, to allow them to live in this world and in their worldly selves more meaningfully. To achieve this, the Zen student or trainee must separate himself from the confusions of the outside world and the language and logical reasoning to which he is susceptible, but after attaining satori, the Zen training is not complete until the trainees make application of their experiences in their daily lives, both for themselves and for others.

Chinese Religion

It is very difficult to characterize Chinese religion because of the heavy influence of communism and its doctrines on a great part of China today; therefore, I will have to be content to present two important religions that influenced and still do influence what Chinese religion is still practiced. China, of course, has been influenced by Christianity and also some Zen Buddhism, but its mainstream of religious thought down through the ages has been Taoism and Confucianism.

TAOISM

For Westerners, Taoism is probably one of the strangest religions from the point of view of how it got started. It in itself is really not a practiced religion much anymore, but its influences are still felt in the overall Chinese religious viewpoint. The founder of Taoism was a legendary man named Lao Tzu, who was born about 604 B.C., and not much is really known about him except that he really did exist, since Confucius was known to have visited and been impressed by him. Lao Tzu, which literally means "the Grand Old Master" or the "Old Fellow," never preached or organized any church; he is known only through a book called the *Tao Te Ching,* Taoism's bible, and which is translated usually as *The Way and Its Power.* I described the Tao (remember it is pronounced "dow") in Chapter 10 when I was discussing atheistic views of ultimate reality, but it is important to realize that, even though it means path or way, there are three senses in which it can be understood.

TAO AS THE WAY OF ULTIMATE REALITY.   This is the way I described it in Chapter 10, but to reiterate somewhat, in this sense Tao is the ground of all existence, the womb from which everything springs and to which it returns. It exceeds the reach of the senses and reason and can be known only through insight. It is ineffable and transcendent, yet immanent or dwelling within.

TAO AS THE WAY OF THE UNIVERSE.   In this sense, it is the power behind or within all life and all things. It imparts its inexhaustible vital power to transitory material forms in the world, including human beings. It is also seen in this respect as a benign, eternal, and creative force of energy and life. In this respect it is often referred to as the "mother of the world," and can be seen to be similar to the Westerner's reference to Nature or Mother Nature.

TAO AS THE WAY HUMANS SHOULD ORDER THEIR LIVES.   This last meaning of the Tao is that human beings should fit in with and not try to conflict with or combat the Tao, Ultimate Reality, and the force of life. This way of fitting in with the Tao is called *wu wei*, translated as "creative quietude" or "supreme activity and supreme relaxation." Essentially, Taoism seems to be saying that nature and the Tao are good in and of themselves; they need no control or manipulation, as our Western science and even our religion would suggest ("Go forth and multiply . . . and have dominion over the earth"), but rather should be related to with as little interference from us as possible. The Beatle song title, "Let It Be," would seem to present a popularized description of the Taoist principle.

In further description of the Tao as ultimate reality, it may be seen to contain everything including opposite forces, which are described in Taoism as *Yang* and *Yin*. Yang is the active or male principle; Yin is the passive or female principle. In the Tao, there is a relativity of all values; that is, total reality includes opposites, such as good and evil, active and passive, positive and negative, light and dark, summer and winter, male and female, and so on. They are symbolized in Figure 12-1.

Even though these opposites are in tension, they are not completely in opposition, for they complement and counterbalance each other. If you look at the diagram carefully, you will find that each invades the other's hemisphere and establishes itself in the very center of its op-

Figure 12-1. The Yang and Yin principles and symbol.

posite's territory. However, in the end, they are both resolved in an all-embracing circle, which is the symbol of the final unity of the Tao. In other words, just as there are opposite poles, such as negative and positive and North and South, all of reality is itself polarized, as described, but the polarization is really unified by the totality of the Way (Tao).

This polarity and unity, and how human beings should live their lives in connection with it, is best expressed in Chapter 2 of *The Tao Te Ching* (pronounced "dow day ching"):

When the people of the world all know beauty as beauty,
There arises the recognition of ugliness.
When they all know the good as good,
There arises the recognition of evil.
Therefore:
Being and non-being produce each other;
Difficult and easy complete each other;
Long and short contrast each other;
High and low distinguish each other;
Sound and voice harmonize each other;
Front and behind accompany each other.
Therefore the sage manages affairs without action
And spreads doctrines without words.
All things arise, and he does not turn away from them.
He produces them but does not take possession of them.
He acts but does not rely on his own ability.
He accomplishes his task but does not claim credit for it.

It is precisely because he does not claim credit that his accomplishment remains with him.[11]

As you can see, the idea is not to interfere with but to blend in with the forces of reality, maintaining a balance between activity and relaxation. Human beings who are aware of and know the nature of the basic life force know that it will sustain them if they integrate themselves with it. In this respect, Taoists reject all forms of self-assertiveness and competition and feel that human beings should avoid being aggressive and oppressive not only toward other human beings but also toward nature in all of its aspects. We in the West view nature as an antagonist to be dominated, controlled, and conquered; Taoism, however, befriends nature and seeks to be in tune with it, much as the American Indians sought to do so. Taoism is obviously an ecological approach (mutual relationships between organisms and their environment), an organic philosophy of nature that, today, science has been finally forced to adopt after three centuries of mechanistic manipulating.

Therefore, Taoism provides an interesting contrast to the Western aggressive, competitive, and at times, oppressive approach to nature, the world, and human beings. Although not really being practiced as a religion today, Taoism has had a definite influence on many religions of the East and also of the West, not to speak of the new environmentalism, which has arisen in the West in the midst of the possible destruction of nature and human life through the misuse of chemicals, atomic energy, and other environmental resources.

CONFUCIANISM

Almost everyone in the West has heard a saying prefaced with "Confucius say . . . ." probably mostly from old Charlie Chan movies, but not everyone knows the significance of Confucianism as a religion and ethical system on China in particular and on the world in general. In fact, even though Confucianist teachings have been submerged in recent times while Chinese communism has had its greatest influences on China and its people, there is some indication that certain important teachings and tenets of Confucianism are returning as they are seen to fit in with Chinese communism in its postrevolutionary phase.

Confucius was born around 551 B.C., and when he grew up he was a teacher and then held several governmental positions. In these latter activities, he faced what he felt to be the overriding problem in China during his time and its preceding history, that of social anarchy caused by rampant individualism. He struggled with the problem of how to attain social cohesion or, put another way, how human beings can learn to live together in harmony. Confucius felt that although the "herd instinct" ensures reasonable peace and cooperation in the animal world, human beings, "the animals above instincts," require added glue to hold society together and to keep them in harmony with each other.

The "glue" that is needed, according to Confucius, is traditions, customs, and mores that inform human beings how to act in harmony with their fellow human beings. If proper ethical and social principles can be inculcated in all human beings, then socialization becomes spontaneous, requiring little force and few laws or controls. He felt that force is inadequate in sustaining total human life because human relationships require more than just force—they require things like love, friendship, and marriage. Confucius, however, was no sentimental romantic; he felt that love was vital to human beings, but he also felt that it required implementation in social structures to function well for us. He saw that reason and love could go beyond the social world, but he also saw that in doing so reason and love could prove to be dangerous instruments for rationalized self-interest. He felt that mind (reason) and heart (emotions) should concentrate on the social world of values, a world determined by the individual's relationship to his or her society.

To attain the ideal society of goodness and harmony, Confucius felt that a deliberate tradition that was disseminated by cultural institutions and inculcated in each individual of that culture would have to be established. The content of the deliberate tradition involves five basic ideals put forth by Confucius.

JEN. This word is usually translated as "human-heartedness" and was the "virtue of virtues" in Confucius' plan. Jen involves a feeling of humanity toward others and also respect for oneself—in other words, an indivisible sense of the dignity of human life wherever it appears. It involves compassion, charity, empathy, and magnanimity in one's dealing with others.

CHUN-TZU. This concept of a human being is the opposite of meanness, pettiness, or smallness in dealings with others. The chun-tzu is the ideal man, and only as persons who make up the society are transformed into chun-tzus can the society attain peace, goodness, and harmony.

LI. This word means both propriety, or what constitutes the right or appropriate behavior and attitude, and also it means a kind of ritual or stylization of life to achieve propriety constantly. Confucius felt that knowledge of how to behave correctly and appropriately was the very basis of any society, and he sought to order an entire way of life so that no one properly raised need ever be left to improvise his responses to situations because he did not know how to behave. Attaining li involved several assumptions.

First, one must know what the relations among words, thoughts, and objective reality are; therefore, speaking and writing carefully and precisely were terribly important to achieving li.

Second, Confucius felt that human beings must seek and achieve *chun yung* or the mean between life's extremes to avoid excess or paucity of anything. Li requires that human beings seek to avoid excesses before they occur, such as the "pride that goeth before the fall" of Western Christianity. One can avoid "the fall" by avoiding pride in the first place and by achieving instead the perfect balance and harmony between the extremes.

One example of the application of chun yung is in the five relationships within the Confucian social structure: (1) father and son, (2) elder brother or sister and younger brother or sister, (3) husband and wife, (4) elder and junior friends, and (5) ruler and subject. In this scheme, Confucius prescribed the following responses for humans involved in these relationships. A father should be loving and a son reverential; an elder brother or sister gentle, a younger brother or sister respectful; a husband good, a wife "listening"; an elder friend considerate, a younger friend deferential; a ruler benevolent, a subject loyal.[12]

Third, Confucius emphasized a respect for one's elders and also for age. The Chinese felt that age meant wisdom, maturity, value, and dignity. Contrast this to the American youth cult concepts that tend to relegate the aging to nursing homes, reject their experiences or maturity, and generally consider them to be a useless drag on society. In addition, as presented in the previous paragraph, Confucius emphasized the importance of the family—since three of the five relationships deal with family-oriented relations—and the older members of the family were to have the greatest respect and consideration to be accorded any of the family members.

Last, when all these were understood, the idea of li as ritual or lifestyle was to be realized. All these things—appropriate use of language, striving for the mean between extremes, the five relationships, the family, and respect for age—were to be achieved by providing stylized ways of ensuring that all human beings—from children to aging adults—in the society were given the means to achieve them by ordering all aspects of daily life.

TE.   The fourth concept of the deliberate tradition was te. This word literally meant "power," but Confucius did not mean by this force or oppression; on the contrary, he meant just the opposite. He felt that there were three essentials of government: (1) economic sufficiency, (2) military sufficiency, and (3) the confidence of the ruled in their rulers. He actually felt that the third essential was the most important. If leaders and their government did not have the trust, consent, and confidence of the people they ruled, then the government would not stand for very long. Consent of the governed is necessary for high morale, which, in turn, supports the rulers in their tasks. Rulers must also set the highest of moral examples for those whom they govern. Only in this atmosphere can a society be ordered, harmonious, and peaceful.

WEN. Wen is usually translated to mean "the arts of peace." To Confucius, the arts of peace were the fine arts, that is, music, the visual arts (painting, sculpture, architecture), and literature and poetry. He valued them highly but mostly as a means for moral education. He felt, perhaps a little too idealistically in a world like his and ours, that rather than military might, culture might provide a lasting civilization among civilizations. He felt that the nation that had the highest wen, the highest culture—the finest arts, the noblest philosophy, the grandest poetry, and the greatest moral excellence—would be the most victorious and the most enduring among nations. He believed this because he thought that these things really were the most highly valued by human beings everywhere. No one can doubt the grand idealism and optimism of such a view or deny the value in striving for such a culture. Whether it could be attained or could survive in this world is hard to tell.

CONFUCIANISM—MERE ETHICAL SYSTEM OR RELIGION?

So far, the description of Confucianism would seem to be nothing more or less than another ethical or social system for humans to live by. Why then is it or should it be called a religion? It is important to examine Confucius' metaphysics, that is, his view of reality.

In Ancient China, the emphasis had always been on ancestor worship, that is, those souls who had lived on earth that were now dead and had gone to heaven. These relatives of each family were asked to intercede for the living with Shang Ti, the great ancestor (ancestors were referred to simply as Ti). Confucius did not eliminate this religious tradition in China, but he did shift the emphasis from ancestor worship and ritual to the living and making them as moral and culturally harmonious as possible. For example, when he was asked which should come first, the claims of the living or those of the spirit world through lavish sacrifices, he answered that although the living should not neglect the spirit world, the living should always come first. He saw heaven and earth not as separate entities, as they are seen in Christianity, but as parts of a continuum. To him, the worship and respect for ancestors was just a part of the deliberate tradition that made human beings morally and socially excellent. There is no doubt, however, that the greatest emphasis in Confucianism is on this world and the improvement of it.

CONFUCIANISM'S IMPACT ON CHINA

From somewhere between 206 B.C. and 220 A.D., Confucianism became, in effect, China's state religion and remained so until the establishment of the Republic of China in 1912. Statesmen were trained under the teachings of Confucius, and schoolbooks were based on the great master's teachings. Throughout China's history until 1912, there has been great family solidarity, respect for elders, striving for the middle way between extremes, and a practicing of the arts of peace.

Since the rise of communism in China, it is difficult to know if the effects of Confucianism have been completely eroded under the new socialism and industrialism. There is no doubt that many of Confucianism's tenets would have to be rejected in favor of a more revolutionary stance, which modern China has obviously taken. However, it is hard to believe that any type of deeply ingrained civilization of twenty-one hundred years would merely disappear in all its aspects. The long-term results of Chinese communism as they have affected Confucianism are not readily discernible at this time in history, but maybe in the future, this dynamic and interesting phenomenon—the clash between revolution and tradition—will yield its outcome to world historians.

Nonreligious Viewpoints

Chapters on the philosophy of religion would not be complete without presenting nonreligious alternatives to the religious point of view and the various religions, East and West, that have already been presented. These viewpoints basically encompass atheism—religious and nonreligious—agnosticism, and secular humanism.

ATHEISM

RELIGIOUS ATHEISM.   As stated in an earlier chapter, "atheism" actually does not mean antireligious; rather, it denotes nonbelief in a personal god. As we have seen in an examination of some of the Eastern religions, in this sense Easterners are atheistic; however, some of them still believe in an afterlife and even an ultimate reality of some kind. They just do not see this ultimate reality as a person or even a personal force. Therefore, in this sense atheism is not antireligious.

NONRELIGIOUS ATHEISM.   Nonreligious atheism, which most people think of when they hear the word "atheism," usually rejects any belief in any kind of supernatural existence or reality whatsoever. What form it takes in its expression varies with the personal viewpoint of the religious nonbelievers.

For example, it may take the form of naturalism, a scientific view that there is only nature and nothing else. It can also take the form of materialism, as described in Chapter 3, or it can take the form of secular humanism, as we shall see later. This view, then, rejects any belief in a god, soul, afterlife, miracles, or anything else supernatural. It generally accepts only this life as we know and experience it, without any suppositions about a previous life or afterlife with any sort of supernatural implications.

AGNOSTICISM

Like atheism, agnosticism can be seen in two different senses: one I call epistemological agnosticism, and the other is agnosticism as a belief. As mentioned in Chapter 10, agnosticism refers actually to a suspension of judgment where the existence of a supernatural reality, an afterlife, a god, or a soul is concerned. What the agnostic essentially says is that the evidence for or against the existence of such things is not conclusive; therefore, the only position a rational human being can take, who is not convinced by what evidence there is, is one of suspending judgment until further evidence in either direction is forthcoming.

EPISTEMOLOGICAL AGNOSTICISM.   This form of agnosticism argues that no one really *knows* in the strong or weak senses of the word "know" whether or not there is or is not a god, afterlife or supernatural reality of any kind (see Chapter 14 for the definitions and discussions concerning the senses of the word "know"). Philosophical and scientific reasoning suggest that there is no conclusive evidence either way for the existence or nonexistence of a supernatural being to be known in any sense of the word "know"; therefore, every human being starts from this epistemological basis.

The argument that is put forth, then, is that no human being knows for certain whether god exists or not; therefore, he or she must start from this point of ignorance and then decide on which position to take—religious theism, religious atheism, nonreligious atheism, or agnosticism as a belief. In other words, sufficient proof or logic does not exist; so we must choose from our point of ignorance about the supernatural which belief we will hold concerning these matters. We must remember, however, that they are just that—beliefs—and no more.

AGNOSTICISM AS A BELIEF.   Agnosticism as a belief is a choice made by some people who are not convinced by any of the evidence or arguments that there is or is not an ultimate reality or any of its accompanying aspects; therefore, an agnostic believer chooses not to commit himself or herself to being a theist, atheist, or anything in between. Agnostics merely suspend judgment until more convincing evidence or arguments come along—they straddle the fence between theism and its alternatives but continue their lives in this world as they find it, not denying or accepting anything for which they do not have conclusive evidence. Many have called agnostics cowardly atheists, saying that they really reject religion, but are too cowardly to accept atheism, and therefore do not commit to anything. This may be true of some agnostics, and also I think it is true that the agnostic tends to lean more toward atheism than toward religion; however, it is also perfectly possible that one simply cannot be convinced of the position put forth by either side and therefore strongly feels that one's only rational choice under these circumstances is to not choose until more evidence is available.

SECULAR HUMANISM

The word "humanism" merely means related to human beings or concern for human beings. There are many types of humanism, such as naturalistic humanism, scientific humanism, religious humanism, and secular humanism, and the term, especially most recently, has come in for some rather undeserved "bad press," shall we say? As I have indicated, if being concerned with human beings at any level is wrong, then one must accept almost every human endeavor or aspect of human culture as wrong also.

This, of course, is absurd. Humanism generally takes a nonreligious stance, saying that there is no world or life beyond this one and that human beings everywhere are responsible for creating out of this life the most moral, significant, humanitarian, and creative existence possible both for their own present generation and also for generations to come. As a humanist, one cannot pass off the immorality or destructiveness of this world on God or disobedience of human beings toward God, but must take the responsibility of fighting it everywhere and eradicating it only through human efforts. One cannot rely on any other power or supernatural being for the creation of a better world; people living now and on this earth must make any changes that are to be made to improve the world.

Because of this point of view, humanistic alternatives must be found to Judeo-Christian ethics, which are based mostly on the existence of the supernatural. Humanists therefore ground their ethics in reason and empirical evidence only, and not on alleged supernatural commands or prohibitions. They emphasize the empiricism and logic of the sciences and philosophy to try to improve this world and allow for all the positive human values, such as freedom, security, happiness, progress, and peace, to come to fruition.

The most organized and outspoken of these groups is The American Humanist Association, incorporated in 1941 and located in San Francisco, California, which states its position as follows:

> Ethical humanism sees man as a product of this world—of evolution and human history—and acknowledges no supernatural purposes. Humanism accepts ethical responsibility for human life and conduct, emphasizing human interdependence.[13]

This association has published Humanist Manifestos I and II in its magazine *The Humanist,* published six times a year. What the association presents is a nonreligious alternative to ethics—humanist ethics. The association and the concept of secular humanism in general have recently come under heavy attack from certain of the more fundamentalist religious groups, sometimes referred to as the "Moral Majority." Whether or not these attacks are justified at all should be discovered by a careful study of the association's manifestos and other writings found in its magazine and the various books published by members.

"Humanism," of course, should not in itself be considered a pejorative term in that even religious leaders had a strong concern and compassion for human beings—much of Jesus's message, for example, can be said to be humanistic in nature in that he talks about how one's fellow human beings should be dealt with and treated, and he did definitely have strong concern for all human beings, even his enemies and including people of the world rejected by most societies and governments.

It is true that humanists tend to be atheists or agnostics in their religious beliefs, and naturalists, materialists, and empiricists in their approach to the world and human beings, but that should not mean that they and what they believe in should be rejected out of hand merely because they are not basically religious. We already discussed in the chapters on morality that it is definitely possible to have a moral system and be ethical whether one is religious or not; therefore, just as one should examine religious viewpoints to understand the whole idea of religion and what it means to human beings, so should atheism, agnosticism, and secular humanism be studied carefully before accepting or rejecting them.

Conclusion

In concluding this part on philosophy of religion, I hope that both religious and nonreligious students have been enlightened at least enough to continue their studies to discover the most that they can about this very important aspect of human nature and human culture. Philosophy of religion in no way attempts to indoctrinate any person in either religious or nonreligious points of view; rather, it sets out to analyze and evaluate critically everything about religion and its opposition to gain the deepest insights possible into this area of human activity. Just as Americans should know as much as they can about cultures other than their own, so should both religious and nonreligious people expand their knowledge about other religions and also nonreligious viewpoints. Only in this way can religion and its alternatives be understood and fitted into one's life and philosophy. I hope, at least, that some tolerance has been achieved toward those points of view that oppose your own and that you understand the bases for all points of view in this area of human life better than you did before.

Applying Philosophy—
Situations for Thought and Discussion

SITUATION 1

Given the last four chapters on philosophy of religion and in view of all the ideas and arguments you have been exposed to in the text, lectures, outlines, and discussions on the problems of religion, in your own words, explain and support in detail what your own belief and viewpoint are on the religious question. In answering this question well, deal with the following:

1. If you are religious, can the basic points of your religious belief be proved? If so, how and to what extent? If not, why do you believe them? Be honest and answer in detail. Also, if your belief accepts an all-good, all-powerful God, how do you deal with the problem of there being evil in the world? If you use any of the arguments in Chapter 10, be sure to deal with the criticisms of them.
2. If you are nonreligious, then how do you explain the nature of man and the universe, and what, essentially, *do* you believe in if not some religion? Be honest and answer in detail.
3. What do you think (depending on your religious or nonreligious position) about any or all of the following, and why? Be specific, supporting your beliefs with evidence and arguments.
   a. Theism in any or all of its forms.
   b. Atheism in any or all of its forms.
   c. Agnosticism.
   d. Voluntarism.
4. What is your view concerning people who do not believe as you do; that is, how do you reconcile your religious or nonreligious viewpoint with others who do not believe as you do?

SITUATION 2

Do careful research on the Republic of China today and relate in detail, in your opinion, to what extent the Chinese people are still affected by the teachings of Confucius, Taoism, and any other previous religion. To what extent has Chinese communism eradicated all the earlier religious ideas and ideals, and to what extent do these ideas and ideals still persist? Give specific examples of the

442

persistence or elimination of these religious tenets from the research you do.

SITUATION 3

To what extent do you feel that Eastern religions can fit in with Western religious traditions? Do some research on the effect of Eastern religion and philosophy on American religion and philosophy and evaluate critically to what extent Western thought has been changed because of Eastern religion's impact. Are there significant ideas that you feel can be incorporated into our Western culture? If so, which ones and why? If not, why not? To what extent do you feel that Eastern and Western religions can coexist without the need to convert Easterners to Western religions? Why?

Chapter Summary

I. Hinduism. Hinduism is one of the few religions that really starts with the wants and needs of human beings, and it presents these in two paths: the Path of Desire and the Path of Renunciation.
    A. The Path of Desire involves two main values that are worldly and secular: (1) kama (pleasure) and (2) artha (wealth, fame and power).
        1. Pleasure—all humans want pleasure and happiness.
            a. Hinduism accepts this as a significant value and does not forbid it.
            b. However, it also recognizes it as transitory in nature and, if overemphasized, destructive.
        2. Wealth, fame, and power—even though these are less self-centered than pleasure, they are also transitory as pleasure is. Hinduism does not forbid these desires, but again does not find them lasting or as significant as other aspects of human nature.
    B. The Path of Renunciation is based on what Hinduism assumes human beings really want—*mukti,* or liberation, which has three corollaries:
        1. Being, existence, and life.
        2. Knowledge and awareness.
        3. Peace and self-realization.
        4. They not only want these things, but they want them infinitely. Hinduism says not only is their attainment possible on an infinite basis, but it is already in the possession of humans if they would just realize it.

    C. Atman and Brahman.
1. Atman is the individual self that stands as self-proved; it is not ego, mind, feelings, or body, but pure consciousness—it is similar to the Western concept of soul.
2. Brahman is the Hindu version of the Ultimate Reality and gives Atman its divine power and existence—it is the ground of all being, the source of all creation, from which everything comes and to which it will return.
3. Atman-Brahman is the combination and interdependent merging of subject and object in a oneness that transcends them both. This is attainable only through the Path of Renunciation, and there are four ways (yogas) to this goal.

    D. The four yogas or ways:
1. Jnana yoga—the Intellectual Way—attempts to attain oneness with Brahman through knowledge and involves three steps:
   a. Hearing and listening to the great wisemen, scriptures, and great philosophic treatises of the ages.
   b. Prolonged, intensive reflection to make the abstract concepts of Atman and Brahman a reality.
   c. Meditating as profoundly as possible on one's identity with the eternal spirit of Atman and Brahman.
2. Bhakti yoga—the Emotional Way—is often referred to as the way to Brahman through love, which involves three features:
   a. Japam, which is the practice of constantly repeating the name of Brahman.
   b. Ringing the changes on love, which is the utilization of all the modes of love—of children, parents, brother or sister, friend, and beloved—and directing them all toward Brahman.
   c. The worship of Brahman as one's chosen ideal.
3. Karma yoga—the Way to God Through Work—stresses that humans do not have to retire from the world to attain oneness with Brahman; rather they can do so through their everyday actions.
4. Raja yoga—the Experiential Way—is the most common form of yoga Westerners think of. It is the approach to Brahman through meditation and willed introversion. This involves eight steps.
   a. Abstentions from injury of others, lying, stealing, sensuality, and greed.

      b. Observance of cleanliness, contentment, self-control, studiousness, and contemplation of the divine.

      c. Working through body to mind through various postures.

      d. Controlled breathing.

      e. Turning one's concentration totally inward.

      f. Control of the mind and its internal wanderings.

      g. Merging of subject and object.

      h. The final state, Samadhi, which is total absorption in Brahman.

E. The four stages of life.

  1. The first stage is student, which is a stage of preparation in which one learns knowledge and also good habits and character formation.

  2. The second stage is householder or practical person, which usually begins with marriage and involves family, vocation, and functioning in the community.

  3. The third stage is retirement, as when one becomes a grandparent, one may withdraw from previous social obligations.

  4. The fourth stage is sannyasin, in which one becomes a wiseman without home and totally free from all worldly obligations or commitments.

F. The caste system and its perversions. Somehow, maybe because of the Hindu concept of karma and reincarnation, the caste system evolved. There were basically four classes:

  1. The Brahmins or seers.

  2. The administrators

  3. The producers—workers, craftspersons, artisans, and so on.

  4. The followers—unskilled laborers.

  5. Problems with the caste system:

      a. A fifth class emerged called the untouchables.

      b. There was a proliferation of about three thousand subcastes.

      c. There were strict prohibitions against intermingling of any kind, which separated the classes even more widely.

      d. The upper and middle classes profited from the system at the expense of the lower classes.

      e. Caste distinctions became hereditary and condemned whole families to generations of servitude and poverty.

G. Hinduism is one of the most tolerant of all religions, seeing all other prophets and leaders of other religions as manifestations of Brahman.

II. Buddhism.
    A. It is a religion devoid of most of the more common religious characteristics; it has no god and no belief in soul, an afterlife, or a supernatural being or force.
    B. Buddha reacted against the caste system and all other structures of religion or government and concentrated instead on the personal experience of each individual.
    C. Positive aspects of Buddhism.
        1. It is much more empirically based than is any other religion, emphasizing direct personal experience.
        2. It is more scientific in approach than are most religions.
        3. It is pragmatic and concerned with problem solving.
        4. It is therapeutic, attempting to relieve human suffering.
        5. It is psychological in approach, beginning with human beings rather than the universe.
        6. It is democratic, rejecting all authority and class distinctions or stereotyping.
        7. It is directed toward individuals, not masses.
    D. The Four Noble Truths.
        1. Dukkha—life itself is suffering, dislocation, and incompleteness that seeks fulfillment from birth to death.
        2. Tanha (desire)—suffering is caused by desire, which causes self-interested separation and alienation from the rest of reality.
        3. Overcoming desire is the solution to suffering.
        4. The Eightfold Path is the way of overcoming it:
            a. Right knowledge—one must know the Four Noble Truths.
            b. Right aspiration—one must aspire to overcome suffering.
            c. Right speech—one must avoid lying or deception because language forms and reveals character.
            d. Right behavior—one must understand behavior and its motives and must not kill, steal, lie, be unchaste, or drink intoxicants.
            e. Right livelihood—one must choose an occupation or career that will help one to fulfill oneself.
            f. Right effort—one must have the will power and strive to overcome desire.
            g. Right mindfulness—the Buddhist must strive for awareness and self-examination.
            h. Right absorption—freeing oneself to attain self-realization and fulfillment in Nirvana.

E. Other Buddhist basic concepts.
   1. Nirvana—the closest Buddhism comes to an Ultimate Reality. It means to extinguish; however, it is not nihilism but rather the elimination and denial of ego. It is the attainment of oneness with reality.
   2. Karma—a causal sequence in which one's life past, present, and future is determined by one's deeds. Buddha does not see a substance, such as a soul, passed on through reincarnation, but rather the ideas of the mind like a flame from one candle to another.

F. Two types of Buddhism—Theravada (the intellectual) and Mahayana (the compassionate). The latter has been the most popular. They differ as follows:
   1. Theravada emphasizes the self-determination of individuals with no help to or from others; Mahayana emphasizes the significance of vital human relationships.
   2. Theravada emphasizes that individuals must be self-reliant and not dependent on an Ultimate Reality; Mahayana stresses the existence of the Ultimate Reality in everyone.
   3. Theravada stresses wisdom and withdrawal; Mahayana stresses compassion and association of individuals with one another.
   4. The Theravada ideal is the disciple who proceeds independently to Nirvana; the Mahayana ideal is the disciple who approaches Nirvana but then returns to bring others to it with him.
   5. Theravada sees Buddha as a saint whose personal influence ended when he attained Nirvana; Mahayana sees Buddha as a world savior who leads all humans to Nirvana.
   6. Theravada opposes speculation and emphasizes meditation; Mahayana elaborates upon and uses speculation, ritual, and prayer.

G. Zen Buddhism—the most popular form of Mahayana Buddhism—is sometimes called its intuitive school.
   1. It is based on Buddha's flower sermon in which Buddha unfolded the golden lotus and merely showed it to his disciples with no other comment. Zen, therefore, believes that words and reason are a "ladder too short to reach reality."
   2. Zen, therefore, sees language as a human construct that impedes direct experience, and it must be transcended if one is to attain reality.
   3. In Zen, acts, not words, are the means to attain insight, awareness, and self-realization. There are three parts to the Zen method:

447

      a. Zazen. This is seated meditation, maintaining silence, and meditating on koans.

      b. Koan. This is a kind of riddle that attempts to break down the student's dependence on words, logic, and reason. Example: "What is the sound of one hand clapping?" As the student strives to answer this, he goes beyond words to reality.

      c. Sanzen. This is consultation with the master concerning his koan.

    4. Satori. This is the goal to be attained by the foregoing three steps, and like Nirvana in Hinduism, it is indescribable and indefinable. Each person must attain it for and by himself or herself. All the master can do is lead the student there. This is not an end in itself; rather, it is a progressive process, which is then applied to life and to other humans.

III. Chinese religion is mostly comprised of two religions: Taoism and Confucianism.

    A. Taoism is based on the teachings of Lao Tzu as found in the book the *Tao Te Ching,* which means *The Way and Its Power.*

    B. Tao can be understood in three senses:

      1. As the Way of Ultimate Reality. In this sense it is the ground of all existence from which all things spring and to which they all return.

      2. As the Way of the Universe. In this sense it is the power behind all life and all things—a benign, eternal, and creative force of energy and life.

      3. As the Way Humans Should Order Their Lives. In this sense, it describes how human beings should mesh and merge with the Tao, not compete, conflict with, or try to control it. Humans should practice *wu wei,* which is "creative quietude."

    C. Yang and Yin. The Tao contains all opposites within it, such as dark and light, positive and negative, and so on. These opposites are in tension, but they are not completely in opposition. Instead, they complement and counterbalance each other; therefore, Taoism says that reality is really a unity of poles and that humans should see their oneness, not their separateness.

    D. Confucianism was a humanistic religion established by Confucius, who wanted to overcome the rampant individualism that led to anarchy in government and culture, so he looked for the "glue" that would hold society together and keep human beings in harmony with each other.

    E. He felt that this glue was a deliberate tradition that once established, could be disseminated by cultural institutions and inculcated in each member of the culture. This tradition consisted of five basic ideals put forth by Confucius:

1. Jen. This means "human-heartedness" and was the virtue of virtues in Confucius' plan. It involved a feeling of humanity toward others and respect for oneself.
2. Chun-Tzu. Is the ideal man, the result of the deliberate tradition.
3. Li. This means propriety and also the ritual or stylization of life that achieves it. In other words, li is proper human behavior, and it involves several assumptions:
   a. One must know the relationships between thoughts, words, and objective reality so that one can write and speak carefully and precisely.
   b. People must seek the *chun yung,* or the mean between two extremes especially in dealing with members of one's family. The family is important as the basic unit of society, and one must know the appropriate behavior in the various family relationships.
   c. There must be respect for one's elders.
   d. When all these were realized, then li would be attained and spread throughout the entire society.
4. Te. This meant power based on the trust of one human being for another, for example, of the ruled for their rulers. Rulers must set high moral examples and must have the confidence of those whom they rule.
5. Wen. This means "the arts of peace," by which Confucius meant all the peaceful arts, such as philosophy, the fine arts, and literature, as ways of teaching morality.

F. Confucius' metaphysics accepted the religion of his time, which consisted mainly of ancestor worship. These ancestors (Ti) were asked to intercede for the living with Shang Ti, the Great Ancestor.
   1. Confucius accepted heaven but saw it as a continuum with earth.
   2. He also accepted ancestor worship, but placed his greatest emphasis on the creation of a harmonious world for the living.

G. It is difficult to know the impact today of Confucianism on modern China, but it is hard to believe that a religion that lasted for twenty-one hundred years has been completely eliminated by Chinese communism.

IV. Nonreligious viewpoints.
   A. Atheism comes in two forms. It literally means "a nonpersonal god concept."

1. Religious atheism is not antireligious; it simply means that the Ultimate Reality is not a person or personal. As we have seen, many of the Eastern religions seem to take this particular point of view and are still considered religions.
2. Nonreligious atheism rejects any belief in any kind of supernatural existence, afterlife, soul, or anything else that is religious.

B. Agnosticism also comes in two forms.
   1. Epistemological agnosticism takes the position that all human beings start from a position of not knowing for certain that any supernatural, theistic or atheistic, exists because of the lack of conclusive proof; therefore, we all start from this point and then either believe or do not believe in the existence of an Ultimate Reality.
   2. Agnosticism as a belief states that once one has to choose, since there is not sufficient evidence to prove either the existence or nonexistence of an Ultimate Reality, then the only choice one has is to suspend judgment until further evidence either proves or disproves such as existence.

C. Secular humanism.
   1. "Humanism" merely means related to human beings or concern for human beings; can such a concern or relationship be considered bad in itself, as it has often been recently?
   2. There are many types of humanism—even religious.
   3. Basically, however, secular humanism does not accept most religious points of view, denying that anything supernatural exists. For secular humanists, there are only nature and human beings, nothing beyond them.
   4. Humanists basically see human beings as a product of this world, of evolution and human history, acknowledging no supernatural purposes. They also accept ethical responsibility for human life and conduct, emphasizing human interdependence.
   5. The American Humanist Association, located in San Francisco, California, is the major organization of humanists and has published Humanist Manifestos I and II, which present ethical stances on a variety of moral issues affecting modern human life, such as suicide, abortion, euthanasia, liberty, and so on.

Additional Questions and Activities for Study and Discussion

1. Read a history of Buddha's life and teachings; then read *Siddhartha,* by Hermann Hesse, and compare both works. To what extent do you believe that Hesse gets across the essential thought and meaning of Buddha and his teachings? To what extent can you utilize any of Buddha's teachings and theories in your own life? Which ones and why? Which ones can't you relate to and why? To what extent do you believe that Buddhism is really a religion, given the fact it has no god, soul, or afterlife concept?

2. Read the *Tao Te Ching* in its entirety, and describe to what extent you feel that America in the twentieth century could use any or all of Lao Tzu's ideas and teachings. Since he is basically opposed to competition, aggressiveness, and the manipulation of nature and reality in all its aspects, how could his ideas fit in with our culture? Do you feel that it is always important to be making progress, especially technological progress, or do you think that sometimes it might be better to not be so actively progressive as we are? Why or why not? As you look back on some of your experiences, do you feel that sometimes it would have been better for you not to conflict with nature or the forces around you and just sort of "go with the flow"? Describe in detail such experiences or situations and critically evaluate them in light of the *Tao Te Ching*.

3. After doing careful research, compare and contrast one Western religion with one Eastern religion and show how they are alike or different. List their respective strong and weak points in your estimation, and tell why you have selected these points as strong or weak. Do you think that it is at all possible for either religion to absorb or blend its strong points with the other's and vice versa? Why or why not?

4. To what extent do you feel that Confucianism is a religion or just a system of ethics and cultural teachings? Why? In the process of presenting your point of view, delineate carefully what you feel any religion should be and do to be called a religion. Be sure to give good reasons for your requirements. What do you think of Confucius' plan to establish a "deliberate tradition"? Do you think we in America should do more in this direction since we tend to allow traditions to evolve more haphazardly than Confucius would have liked? Do you think that one can try to establish a deliberate tradition and still allow for individual freedom? How could this be done? Answer in detail. Do you admire Confucius' concern with family relationships and respect for elders? Why or why not? How

does this compare with the values of our present culture? If you feel that Confucius' values are significant, is there any way that you can see them established or reestablished in our culture? How? Answer in detail.

5. Study the caste system in India through various credible sources and delineate to what extent you feel that Hinduism and its religious values have contributed to it? In your opinion, could the caste system be eliminated in its entirety and Hinduism still function as a religion? Why or why not? To what extent do you feel that the Hindu values of karma and reincarnation have contributed to the caste system? Answer in detail, giving reasons to support your positions.

6. It is often said that most Eastern religions are much more religiously tolerant of other religions than are the Western religions. Do some research on this topic and present your own views on whether or not you think the statement is true. If you believe they are indeed generally more tolerant, then why do you think this? If you think they are not more tolerant, then cite instances of both Western and Eastern religious intolerance to support your point. Do you feel that religious tolerance is important or not? Why? Answer in detail.

7. Describe in detail the *moral* teachings of Western and Eastern religions and compare and contrast them—to what extent are they similar and different? If there could be some kind of merging of these two different types of religions, to what extent do you believe that it could be accomplished at the moral level? Is it possible that this could also form the basis for religious tolerance among all the world's great religions? How and why, or how not and why not?

8. To what extent do you feel Buddha's evaluation of the nature of the human predicament (that all of life is suffering) and his solutions to it are valid or invalid? Answer in detail. If you believe that life involves a lot of suffering, to what extent do you feel we in the West attempt to overcome it and how? How does our approach to the problem differ from Buddha's and which do you think is more effective? Answer in detail.

9. What do you think of Hinduism's estimation of life as consisting of the two paths, desire and renunciation? To what extent do you feel that Hinduism has correctly characterized the human predicament and why? Hinduism seems very tolerant of human desires for pleasure and happiness and fame, wealth, and power. Do you think that this religion is more realistic about these desires than the Western religions are? Why or why not? Show how Western religions attempt to deal with what Hinduism considers very nor-

mal desires of human beings. To what extent are the approaches similar or different? Which do you think is more effective and why?

10. Read Henry David Thoreau's essay, "On Civil Disobedience," and his book, *On Walden Pond,* and describe in detail to what extent he incorporates many of the ideals found in Hinduism, Buddhism, and Taoism. Be specific and quote short passages to exemplify your position either for or against this contention. It is said that Thoreau's essay on civil disobedience formed the basis of Mahatma Ghandi's nonviolent but effective protest against British colonialism in India. Research this possibility to find out the similarities between the two great thinkers.

Footnotes

1. For a fuller discussion of these periods refer to I. C. Sharma, *Ethical Philosophies of India,* ed. Stanley M. Daughert (Lincoln, Nebr.: Johnson, 1965).
2. Huston Smith, *The Religions of Man* (New York: Harper, 1958), pp 25–27.
3. Ibid., p. 51.
4. Ibid., p. 53.
5. Ibid., pp. 36–61 for a fuller description of the different yogas.
6. Ibid., p. 86. I would strongly suggest that students read Smith's entire Chapter 2 on Hinduism.
7. Ibid., p. 90.
8. Ibid., pp. 104–109.
9. Ibid., p. 15.
10. Ibid., p. 146.
11. Wing-Tsit Chan, trans., *The Way of Lao Tzu* (New York: Bobbs-Merrill, 1963), p. 101.
12. Smith, *The Religions of Man,* p. 183.
13. *The Humanist* 33, no. 6 (November–December 1973): 3.

Bibliography

EASTERN RELIGIONS AND PHILOSOPHY IN GENERAL

Kitagawa, Joseph M. *Religions of the East.* Philadelphia: Westminster, 1968.

Koller, John M. *Oriental Philosophies.* New York: Scribners, 1970.

Radhakrishnan, S. *Eastern Religions and Western Thought.* New York: Galaxy Books, 1959.

Raju, P. T. *Introduction to Comparative Philosophy.* Carbondale: Southern Illinois University Press, 1970.

Yutang, Lin. *The Wisdom of China and India.* New York: Random House, 1942.

HINDUISM

Eliade, Mircea. *Yoga: Immortality and Freedom*. New York: Pantheon, 1958.
Gandhi, Mahatma. *An Autobiography; or The Story of My Experiments with Truth,* trans. Mahadev Desai. Boston: Beacon, 1959.
Ghurye, G. S. *Caste and Class in India,* 2nd ed. Bombay: Popular Book Depot, 1957.
Monier-Williams, M. *Brahmanism and Hinduism*. New York: Macmillan, 1891.
Morgan, K. W., ed. *Religion of the Hindus*. New York: Ronald, 1953.
O'Malley, L. S. S. *Popular Hinduism*. New York: Macmillan, 1935.
Renou, Louis. *Hinduism*. New York: Washington Square, 1963.
Zimmer, H. *Philosophies of India*. New York: Meridian, 1956.

BUDDHISM

Boas, Simone B., trans. *The Life of Buddha*. Middletown, Conn.: Wesleyan University Press, 1963.
Burtt, E. A., ed. *The Teachings of the Compassionate Buddha*. New York: Mentor, 1955.
Conze, Edward, trans. *Buddhist Scriptures*. New York: Penguin, 1959.
Hamilton, C. H., ed. *Buddhism, a Religion of Infinite Compassion*. New York: Liberal Arts Press, 1952.
Kalupahana, David J. *Buddhist Philosophy: A Historical Analysis*. Honolulu: University of Hawaii Press, 1976.
Suzuki, D. T. *Zen Buddhism,* ed. William Barrett. Garden City, N.Y.: Doubleday, 1956.
Thomas, E. J. *History of Buddhist Thought,* 2nd ed. New York: Alfred A. Knopf, 1951.
Watts, Alan. *The Way of Zen*. New York: Random House, 1957.

TAOISM

Blakney, R. B. *The Way of Life: Lao Tzu*. New York: Mentor, 1955.
Chan, Wing-Tsit. *Religious Trends in Modern China*. New York: Columbia University Press, 1953.
Fung, Y. L. A. *A History of Chinese Philosophy,* trans. Derk Bodde, 2 vols. Princeton, N.J.: Princeton University Press, 1952.
Lang, Olga. *The Chinese Family and Society*. New Haven, Conn.: Yale University Press, 1950.
Yang, C. K. *Religion in Chinese Society*. Berkeley, Calif.: University of California Press, 1961.

CONFUCIANISM

Creel, H. G. *Chinese Thought from Confucius to Mao Tse-tung*. Chicago: University of Chicago Press, 1953.
Waley, Arthur. *The Analects of Confucius*. London: Allen and Unwin, 1938.
——————. *The Ways of Thought in Ancient China*. Garden City, N.Y.: Anchor, 1956.
Yutang, Lin. *The Wisdom of Confucius*. New York: Modern Library, 1938.

PART **5**

Epistemology: The Study of Knowledge

CHAPTER *13*

Knowledge, Belief, Truth, and Falsity

If you remember as far back as Chapter 1, concerning what philosophy is and does, you will remember that there were three major areas of philosophy, two of which we have already dealt with: metaphysics, ethics, and epistemology. This part and its chapters will be concerned with the last of the three areas that was touched upon only briefly in Chapters 1 and 2. Epistemology, the study or problems of knowledge, is an extremely important part of philosophy because philosophy is essentially a search for knowledge and wisdom. Further, philosophy uses language, logic, and reasoning as its major tools in examining anything that is of interest to human beings. Therefore, it is very important for philosophers to be able to distinguish between belief and knowledge, to discover what can actually be known, if anything, and to know what constitutes truth or falsity. If philosophers (and scientists) are interested in knowledge and in knowing what is true or false in reality, then it is important to know what all these things are and what they relate or pertain to. In this chapter, therefore, we will examine these very important distinctions, words, and human activities and see if we cannot arrive at some clear understanding about human knowledge and truth and falsity.

What Does Knowledge Mean?

When we use the word "know," what exactly do we mean by it? Depending on how and in what context we use the word, it can mean at least three different things.

KNOWLEDGE AS ACQUAINTANCE

When we use "know" in a sentence such as, "I know John well," "I know what Paris is like," or "I know what you're talking about," we are using it in the sense of acquaintance. "I know John" essentially means "I am acquainted with John," and the same goes for "knowing what Paris is like" or "knowing what somebody's talking about." Using "know" in this sense means that I or you or anybody else is acquainted with something or someone, that is, that we have experienced someone or something in some way and can relate our language to it or him.

KNOWLEDGE AS ABILITY OR KNOWING HOW

When we use "know" in a sentence such as "I know how to change the oil in my car" or "I know how to fly a plane," we are using it in the sense of having some kind of knowledge or ability to perform some kind of action or task.

KNOWING THAT—PROPOSITIONAL SENSE

When we use "know" in the sense of knowing that . . . something is the case, such as "I know the sun will rise tomorrow" or "I know that 2 plus 2 equals 4," we are using "know" in its *propositional* sense, and this is the sense that philosophers and scientists are really most interested in because it forms the bases for both areas of endeavor. Scientists and philosophers are searching for knowledge about things— whether they exist, what their nature is, how they function, and how they relate to other things with which they come into contact. For example, if I want to know at what temperature water boils, I will experiment until I discover that it boils at 212° Fahrenheit at sea level. Then I can make the statement (or state the proposition), "I know *that* water boils at 212° Fahrenheit at sea level." "Knowing that," then, is the propositional sense of knowing and the most important sense of knowing for our purposes in philosophy, as well as for scientists. Before going any further with a discussion of knowledge and the word "know," it is important to understand what the terms "proposition" and "propositional," which I have been using, mean.

Propositions and States of Affairs

To understand what truth and falsity are and to what they apply, it is important to be able to distinguish among events, happenings, occurrences, and states of affairs and human judgments about them.

STATES OF AFFAIRS

Events happen in reality, such as the sun rising, water boiling, doors being closed or open, and rain falling or not. These events, occurrences, or happenings are neither true nor false; they either occur or they do not occur; that is, they are either actual or not actual, or they happen or they do not. These can be referred to under the major phrase "states of affairs," and the only thing we have to determine is whether or not they are actually happening, have happened, or will happen—we shouldn't ever use the words "true" or "false" with states of affairs because those words, as you will see, apply only to propositions, which will be defined in a moment.[1] Therefore, events or happenings occur or they do not both within us and outside of us in the external world, and we may or may not perceive them. Nevertheless, the only thing we have to determine about states of affairs for purposes of knowing something about them is that they either actually occur or they do not. This determination, as you shall see, affects our knowledge of them and the truth or falsity of any judgments or claims we may make about them.

PROPOSITIONS

A proposition is a meaningful sentence that makes a claim or asserts something about reality and has the quality of being either true or false. Actually it is propositions to which truth and falsity really apply, and only to propositions, not states of affairs, as I have already mentioned. Let us look at each part of the definition of "proposition" to see if we can understand it more fully.

SENTENCE MEANING.   There are many sentences that may or not be meaningful to us; most of them, of course, are because we use language, mostly in the form of sentences, to communicate ideas, thoughts, feelings, and knowledge to one another. The sentence, bad or good, is our main form of presenting words intelligibly for understanding and meaning. However, for a sentence to be called a proposition, it must be meaningful. A nonsense sentence, such as "Glops furgulate eleatically," could not be a proposition because no one knows what it might mean unless each of the words were defined to have meaning by the person who stated the sentence. It sounds like it could be a meaningful sentence (for example, note the similarity of "Turbines operate erratically"), but it isn't. Also, if someone said that John was standing between the post, he would also not be stating a meaningful sentence because before someone can "stand between . . .," there must be two things; one cannot stand "between" one thing. These are perhaps too far off the beaten track, but other sentences, such as "Listen to the warm," "Happiness is a warm puppy," and "Love means never having to say you're sorry," come very close to being meaningless sentences unless one does an awful lot of translating or restates the sentence in such a way so as to make it meaningful.

ASSERTION OR CLAIM REQUIREMENT.   Further, to be a proposition, the meaningful sentence must make some sort of claim or assertion about reality. Many meaningful sentences, such as commands or questions, could not be propositions because they do not satisfy this requirement. For example, the command, "Go to the store," and the question, "What's that girl's name?" cannot be considered as propositions because they make no claim about reality but merely command or state questions. Sentences like "The sun is shining," "His sweater is blue, not green," and "It is raining," all make some claim or assert something about reality, or describe a state of affairs. This is an important point; as propositions, they all describe a state of affairs. Remember, states of affairs are *not* true or false; propositions *about them* are.

THE QUALITY OF BEING EITHER TRUE OR FALSE.   Since it has already been stated that truth or falsity applies only to propositions, it remains to discover how we determine which quality applies to which proposition. We will discuss this shortly when we get to the various theories of truth. In the meantime, it is important to distinguish between types of propositions.

TYPES OF PROPOSITIONS

There are four types of propositions that I will define at this point.

ANALYTIC PROPOSITIONS.   The first type of proposition is called analytic because its meaning and truth or falsity can be determined merely by knowing the definitions and analyzing the meaning of the words in it. Many analytic propositions are mathematical in nature, such as 2 plus 2 equals 4, "All triangles are three-sided," and "A circle is not a square." Analytic propositions can be nonmathematical as well, however. Such sentences as "All bachelors are unmarried men," "All black cats are black," and "All women are female" are examples of analytic propositions. If you look at or analyze them carefully, they stand uncontested. Such propositions do not require sense experience, other than one's being able to hear or read words, to be understood.

INTERNAL SENSE PROPOSITIONS.   These propositions are assertions or claims we make about what we experience within us, and some examples are "I have a headache," "I feel pain," "I am happy," "I believe in God." Note that all these statements make some statement or claim about one's own thoughts, feelings, or beliefs rather than about mathematics or geometry or states of affairs that occur in the external world.

EXTERNAL SENSE OR EMPIRICAL PROPOSITIONS.   These are propositions about external reality, such as "Ronald Reagan is president of the United States," "The door is open," "It is five o'clock in the evening," "She is 5′ 7″ tall." Such propositions make assertions or claims about external reality rather than internal sense experience or abstract analytic thoughts.

MORAL PROPOSITIONS.   As was pointed out in Chapter 7, moral propositions either state a moral value judgment, such as "John is a morally upright person" or "Abortion is morally wrong," or they prescribe human moral behavior, as in a proposition such as "Human beings should not kill other human beings" or "Human beings ought to treat each other morally."

TRUTH AND FALSITY OF THE TYPES OF PROPOSITIONS.   How truth and falsity apply to the foregoing propositions, and how we can know whether they are true or false and under which conditions, will be a matter for discussion after we have examined the nature of these two qualities and also after we learn what constitutes knowing whether or not a proposition is true and whether or not we can know truth or falsity at all. This will be dealt with fully in the next chapter, and at that time, we will attempt to discover to what extent we can know that the four types of propositions are true or false.

Truth and Falsity—What Are They?

Like the word "know," there are several senses in which the word "truth" can be used. First, it can be used to mean about the same thing as "real," such as in the sentence, "This is *true* coffee." It also has special uses in certain fields like carpentry, such as in the phrase "true a line," which means to make something fit along a straight line. It can also be used figuratively or poetically as in "Jesus is the way, the *truth,* and the life." As we have already seen, this would not be a propositional use of the word "true," as Jesus could not be truth, although he could be the source of it, or he could speak it.

The word "false" can also be used in similar ways, as in the sentence, "He put up a false front," meaning that he hid his real self or feelings behind a false façade. One could also say that "The box has a false bottom in it," meaning that there is a fake bottom set on top of the real bottom of the box. So it can also refer to something being phony or fake.

However, truth and falsity in the propositional sense, which is the basic sense in which we are interested, applies only to propositions being true or false, as in the sentence, "The statement 'It is raining' is true because it really is raining."

THEORIES OF WHAT TRUTH IS

THE CORRESPONDENCE THEORY OF TRUTH.   This theory says that a proposition is true if it "corresponds" with a fact and false if it does not. The first problem we have here is with the word "fact." Does fact mean a true proposition, such as in the sentence, "It's a fact that it is raining"? If it does, then all we are saying is, "A proposition is true if it is true," which of course says nothing and gets us nowhere.

If by "fact" we mean state of affairs, then the problem arises of how a set of marks or sounds can be said to correspond to any state of affairs. For example, if someone takes a photograph or does a very good painting of you, then we can say that these items "correspond" to you, the real person. Or if someone sculpts an exact likeness of you, then we can say that the sculptured you corresponds to the real you as a physical being. If we match your red sweater with the same shade of red in a pair of socks, then we can say that the shades of red "correspond." How can we say, however, that the proposition, "A plane is flying overhead" corresponds to the actual state of affairs? Do the words make engine noises, have wings, or soar? It would not seem so, and therefore, the correspondence theory of truth seems inadequate.

THE COHERENCE THEORY OF TRUTH.   This theory is based on the interdependence of a set of propositions on one another and the fact that one set of propositions makes another set true. This theory states that it is not the relationship between the proposition and a state of affairs that determines its truth but, rather, the relationship of one proposition to another or to others. All these propositions "cohere," or hang or stick together. For example, to state that the proposition, "The sun will rise tomorrow" is true is dependent on other true propositions concerning the earth's rotation around the sun, the sun's heat and light, and many others. It is certainly true that many propositions are dependent on others for their truth at least to some extent. For example, in geometry, mathematics, or logic, one can derive theorems once certain axioms are assumed to be true, such as "the shortest distance between two points is a straight line." And in logic, everything we say is dependent on the principle of identity, that A is A, or a thing is what it is. However, does being dependent in this manner really make the proposition, "This table is made of oak" true?

Another problem with this theory centers on whether just because propositions are mutually coherent, that they prove anything. For example, is the proposition, "Charles Lindbergh made the first transatlantic flight" true because there were witnesses who saw him take off and witnesses who saw him land and witnesses in between who saw his plane fly overhead? It is true that the witnesses and their propositions all provide evidence that he made the flight, but what if they were all mistaken in some way? Isn't what really makes the proposition true is that it describes a state of affairs that actually occurred— the state of affairs of his actually having made the flight?

A final problem concerns the condition that a group of propositions could be mutually coherent and still not be true. For example, any one of us could make up a series of coherent propositions about an imaginary world with imaginary people in it, but none of them would be true. We can state a number of propositions about unicorns, but none of them could support the key proposition, "Unicorns really exist."

THE PRAGMATIC THEORY OF TRUTH.   This theory is sometimes called the "truth is what works" theory. First, one has to ask what is meant by the word "works" when used in this context. It is perfectly understandable to describe a piece of machinery as "working," or even a plan, meaning that it was actually workable. But what does it mean to say that truth works? If it is raining outside, and I say, "It is raining outside," what makes this proposition "work"? Isn't what makes it true that it describes an actual state of affairs? In other words, if it "works," isn't it for some other reason that is not in any way like the lawn mower I have fixed that now "works."

Another way of stating the pragmatic theory of truth is to say that if certain propositions yield good consequences for human beings, then they are workable and therefore true. This, of course, claims way too much for truth. For example, suppose that believing in pink elephants, unicorns, minotaurs, and gorgons works in that it gets me a lot of attention and also makes a lot of people keep their distance from me, which is what I want. Suppose further that I am relieved of all my responsibilities since people think that I am incapable of shouldering them now that I believe in all these things, and I wanted to be relieved of them. Now these beliefs and all of my statements about them have all "worked" for me and have brought me the consequences I desired. What has any of this to do with the truth of any of the propositions? As a matter of fact, all my propositions about these imaginary things are probably false.

Another example of this has to do with William James' voluntarist theory in the discussion of faith in Chapter 10. Remember that James, a pragmatist and founder of that particular philosophy, said that one can believe that a proposition is true if one feels that one can gain from it in some way. At the time, if you remember, the statement was made that believing in what we want to has nothing whatever to do with truth.

WHAT CAN WE CONCLUDE?   First, there is some merit to all the theories, and perhaps we can, if we are careful, utilize them all to some extent in arriving at true or false propositions. For example, it is true that there has to be a relationship between a true or false proposition and an actual or not actual state of affairs; the problem is that correspondence is weak and has to be replaced with another relationship.

Second, the coherence theory is certainly valid to the extent that propositions often do depend on other propositions for their mutual truths or falsities, so it is important to marshal a group of true propositions that are logically related. For example, to arrive at some conclusive truth about whether one should change jobs or not, it would be important to know a series of coherent propositions about the old job, the new job, family needs, chances for advancement or promotion, and so on. To arrive intelligently at the conclusion that "I ought or ought not to change jobs," it would be important that a series of coherent propositions were known to be true or false.

Third, it is not entirely the case that true propositions don't work for us in some way or don't yield good consequences. Sometimes, just knowing we have knowledge of what is true and what is false can bring us satisfaction and "work" well for us in our lives. If we know which answers on a test we are taking are true and which are false, for example, we can be satisfied that we know something about the material we have studied and at the same time get a good grade on the test and in the course we are taking. How much more pragmatic can truth get? In other words, as long as we are careful and aware of the pitfalls of each of the foregoing theories of truth and falsity, we can use them to some extent. However, there is one other theory that will not interfere with the other theories, when they are applicable, and that will yield perhaps a better foundation for determining whether or not a proposition is true or false.

THE DESCRIPTIVE THEORY OF TRUTH.   This theory, presented by John Hospers in his *Introduction to Philosophical Analysis,* is what I call the "descriptive theory of truth" and is a modification of the correspondence theory without its pitfalls. What Hospers says—as has been noted at various times—is that a true proposition *describes* (not corresponds to) a state of affairs that was, is, or will be actual or that has occurred, is occurring, or will occur. A false proposition, on the other hand, describes a state of affairs that was not, is not, or will not be actual or that has not occurred, is not occurring, or will not occur.[2] I have used "was," "is," and "will be" because we state propositions (or make claims) about reality in the past, present, and future, and therefore all three verb tenses must be available for use. This theory would seem to eliminate the difficulty of trying to make our propositions "correspond" to states of affairs and yet give us a clear method of determining whether propositions are true or not. For example, if the door in my room is open and I state the proposition, "The door to my room is open now," then my proposition is true because I am describing a state of affairs that *is* actual. If it rained last night, and I state, "It rained last night," then my proposition is true because it describes a state of affairs that *was* actual. If in either of these cases the opposite proposition were stated—"The door to my room is closed now" or "It did not rain last night"—then it would be false because it described a state of affairs that *is not* or *was not* actual.

IS TRUTH RELATIVE OR ABSOLUTE?

One of the more confusing aspects of truth and falsity is whether or not they are absolute or relative. In discussing morality, we had to deal with the problem of relativism, that is, the theory that morality is strictly relative to time, place, culture, and even individual. We saw that moral relativism was difficult to sustain with any force at all, but what about truth? Often you hear people saying such things as, "If you believe it, then it's true for you at least" or "To me it's true; to you it may not be." Others state with equal intensity that there are certain truths that are absolute. I recently heard a member of the Moral Majority ask a television interviewer, "Will the sun rise tomorrow?" When the interviewer answered, "Yes," then the interviewee said, "Then, isn't that an absolute—don't tell me there are no absolutes!"

Just what, then, is the status of truth and falsity? Do they vary from situation to situation, from time to time, from place to place, from culture to culture, and from person to person, depending on belief, thought, feeling, or knowledge, or are they absolute and unchanging (what's true is always true, and what's false is always false)? The first distinction we have to make is between stating propositions and stating beliefs.

There is a great difference between the propositions "God exists" and "I believe that God exists." Referring back to types of propositions, the first is an external sense or empirical proposition (some philosophers would disagree—this will be discussed later); the second is an internal sense proposition. A person may believe that a proposition is true when it isn't, and a proposition may be true whether or not anyone believes it to be. For example, many people believed that the earth was flat (some still do—there is, believe it or not, an organization functioning today called "The Flat Earth Society"), but that had nothing to do with the true proposition, "The earth is not flat." So one must distinguish between belief propositions and propositions that make an actual claim or assert something about reality.

To try to come to some conclusions in this matter, let us take a proposition and examine its status: "It will rain tomorrow, January 3, 1983, in San Francisco."

Let us presume that the date on which this proposition is stated is January 2, 1983. I have purposefully stated this proposition in the future tense for a specific reason that I will disclose later. The question now is what is this proposition's status on January 2, 1983? Several possibilities have been put forth by people in trying to determine the proposition's status, and they are as follows:

"As far as I'm concerned, it is true (or false)."

"To me it is true; to you it may not be."

"It is true until it is proved false or false until it is proved true."

"It is neither true nor false—it has no status."

"It is either true or false when it is stated."

The first two possibilities are dependent on what people believe is true. For someone to say, "As far as I'm concerned it is true," means actually that he believes it to be true, but, as we have seen, it is quite possible for one to believe that a proposition is true while it is actually false ("The earth is flat"). The second possibility seems to imply that if one believes that a proposition is true, then it is, and if someone else believes that it is false, then it is that too. If we take the proposition "The earth is flat," again, what does the truth of the proposition really have to do with whether people believed it was true or not? Is it really true that "wishing (or believing) will make it so"? It doesn't seem so, for the earth was not flat no matter who believed the proposition to be true or false.

The third possibility states that any proposition must be seen as true (or as false) until it is proved otherwise, but what in fact does this mean? Was it really the case that "The earth was flat" was really true at anytime before it was proved false? Isn't the case rather that the proposition was and has always been false? Try this test with any proposition and see if it in any way holds true; you'll find that it doesn't.

In looking at the proposition just stated, we find that we have trouble with the fact that it is set in the future, and therefore we are tempted to say that at the present time (on January 2) it has no status or that it is neither true nor false, but let us presume that it is now January 3 and it is raining in San Francisco. As we look back to January 2, when we stated the proposition, what really was its status? Wasn't it really true at the time we stated it? Remember we said, "It will rain tomorrow, January 3, 1983, in San Francisco," and it did rain, so we will have to say that the proposition was true at the time we stated it, even though we did not *know* whether it was or not at that time. But, you see, *knowledge* of whether the proposition is true or false does not have anything more to do with its actual truth or falsity than *believing* it is true or false.

What is the proposition's actual status on January 2, when it is stated? It is either true or false at that time; we just don't know which it is, and it doesn't really matter what we believe at the time we stated it. It is quite obvious, then, that propositions when stated carefully and precisely are absolutely true or absolutely false and that truth is not relative in any sense of the word, but absolute! Belief or disbelief has nothing to do with making propositions true or false; belief is indeed relative to the person holding it. Further, knowledge, or the lack of it, of whether a certain proposition is true or not also has nothing to do with its actual truth or falsity. Knowledge also is relative to time, place, and individuals. For example, if in 1800, some far-seeing individual stated, "Human beings will walk on the moon," the proposition was absolutely true when it was stated, regardless of whether anyone believed it or knew it was true or false.

What does this discussion mean to us, then? It means that truth and falsity really do exist and do not change, when carefully stated, which is why I used a specific date, year, and place in my example proposition. Anyone can readily see that a proposition such as "My car is parked in the driveway" will not *always* be true because sometimes it is parked there and sometimes it is not. If one specifies, however, a time or date, then the proposition is true. Even "It will rain tomorrow" cannot be always true because we do not have the date on which the proposition is stated.

What are the implications for knowledge if truth and falsity are absolute and unchanging? First, it makes the search for truth significant because it might mean (although not necessarily) that the truth can be known and that we can go beyond belief to knowledge, if true knowledge is possible (we shall investigate this in the next chapter). Second, if we can set up valid requirements for knowing whether propositions are true or false, we may find that we can really attain some truths because they really do exist and do not change whimsically.

At any rate, our problems actually center on our *knowing* which propositions are true and false and how we can know, and, as I have said, these are matters for the next chapter, which deals with the sources and nature of knowledge.

Applying Philosophy—
Situations for Thought and Discussion

SITUATION 1

Interview as many people as you can—family, friends, coworkers, employers, fellow students, and teachers—and ask them to define truth and falsity; also ask them to what extent they think that truth and falsity are relative or absolute. You may construct some sort of survey form or questionnaire if you wish.

After you have completed your interviews or survey, write a detailed summary of what you discovered about people's awareness or knowledge of truth and falsity. To what extent did you discover that most people are quite ignorant about what these two words mean? To what extent did you find they were able to distinguish between assertions or claims (propositions), beliefs, and knowing whether or not propositions are true or false? How many did you find using any or all of the theories of truth presented in this chapter? Did they seem to recognize the pitfalls involved with the theories or not? Critically evaluate their responses, your own theories, before and after reading this chapter, and the theories stated in the chapter.

SITUATION 2

Read the play *Death of a Salesman* or *After the Fall* by Arthur Miller and describe in detail how the ability or inability to distinguish between truth and falsity affects the lives of the main characters. To what extent do you see them using one or the other of the three major theories of truth and with what results? To what extent does the truth appear as absolute or relative in either of these two plays? Select some of the major propositions stated in the plays and show how they are false or true and what means you used to decide. To what extent are these major propositions analytic, internal sense, external sense, or moral in nature? To what extent can or can't the major characters distinguish among truth, belief, and knowledge? Give examples.

SITUATION 3

Analyze and critically evaluate the following quote from the Declaration of Independence: "We hold these truths to be self-evident, that all men are created equal, that they are endowed by their Creator with certain unalienable Rights, that among these are Life, Liberty, and the pursuit of Happiness." To what extent are these truths because "we hold them . . . to be self-evident"? Are the truths really self-evident? What does that mean? Answer in detail. What kind of a proposition is the quotation? Support your answer with evidence and agrument. To what extent would you call the proposition true or false (e.g., Are all men really created equal? In what way? Support your answer)? Are these really "truths," or are they only beliefs? Why?

Chapter Summary

I. Introduction.
   A. Epistemology, the third major area that philosophy emphasizes, has to do with the study or problems of knowledge.
   B. Since knowledge, truth, falsity, and belief are all so important to the philosopher and the scientist in their search for knowledge and truth, it is important to be able to distinguish among them all.

II. What does knowledge mean?
   A. Acquaintance. When I say, "I know who John is," I am talking about being acquainted with him.
   B. Knowing how. When I say I know how to do something, I am talking about ability or understanding the means of how to do it.
   C. Knowing that . . . something is the case is the propositional sense of "know," and this is the most important sense of "know" as far as philosophers and scientists are concerned.

III. Propositions and states of affairs.
   A. States of affairs are occurrences, happenings, and events that take place in reality; they are actual or not actual, but they can never be considered in themselves true or false—they either occur or they do not.
   B. Propositions are meaningful sentences that make a claim or assert something about reality and have the quality of being either true or false.
      1. To be propositions, sentences must be meaningful.
      2. Some sentences—commands and questions—are meaningful, but they make no claim or assertion about reality; therefore, they cannot be propositions.
      3. If the two foregoing criteria are satisfied, then usually the qualities of truth or falsity will apply.

470

C. Types of propositions.
   1. Analytic—those whose meanings and truth or falsity can be determined merely by analyzing the definitions and meanings of the words in the sentence.
   2. Internal sense—those that are stated about our internal thoughts, feelings, and beliefs.
   3. External sense or empirical—those that make some sort of claim or assertion about external reality.
   4. Moral—those that either make some sort of value judgment or prescribe moral behavior.
   5. How truth or falsity applies to these different types of propositions and to what extent we can know their truth or falsity will be discussed in the next chapter.

IV. Truth and falsity—what are they?
   A. Different senses of the word "truth."
      1. True can mean "real," such as "This is true coffee."
      2. It can be used in special crafts or fields, as in the phrase, *"true* a line."
      3. It can also be used figuratively as in "Jesus is the way, the *truth,* and the life."
      4. It is most importantly used in the propositional sense when it is applied to such propositions as the types just described.

V. Theories of truth.
   A. The correspondence theory. This states that a proposition is true when it "corresponds" to a fact.
      1. There are problems with both of the words "fact" and "corresponds."
         a. Fact can mean either the same thing as proposition or it can mean a state of affairs. Either way it does not help much with determining the truth of a proposition.
         b. "Corresponds" makes sense when talking about photographs of a person or matching shades of colors, but a proposition does not correspond to a state of affairs in any meaningful way.
   B. The coherence theory. This theory states that the truth of any proposition is determined by its relationship to other coherent propositions.
      1. There is some validity to the theory in that some propositions cohere, but is that really what makes them true or false?
      2. Even if propositions are coherent, does that prove that they are true? If many witnesses all say that something occurred, is that what makes the proposition describing it true? Isn't it the fact that the event really did occur that makes it so?
      3. Propositions may be coherent and not be true.

    C. The pragmatic or truth-is-what-works theory. The truth is what "works" or what brings about good consequences or satisfaction to human beings.

       1. What is the sense of "works" when used with "truth"?

       2. Believing that a proposition is true may bring about good results, but that does not make it true.

    D. What can we conclude?

       1. There is some validity to all the theories, and as long as we are aware of their pitfalls, we may use all three of them to some degree.

       2. There is a modified form of the correspondence theory that avoids its word confusion and fits in with all three theories.

    E. The Descriptive theory of truth.

       1. A proposition is true if it *describes* a state of affairs that was, is, or will be actual or that occurred, is occurring, or will occur.

       2. A false proposition describes a state of affairs that was not, is not, or will not be actual or that did not occur, is not occurring, or will not occur.

       3. All three tenses—past, present, future—are needed because we describe states of affairs in all three tenses.

VI. Is truth relative or absolute?

    A. There is a difference between the propositions "God exists" and "I believe God exists"—one is an external sense proposition, while the other is an internal sense proposition. Therefore, there is a difference between the truth or falsity of a proposition and believing that it is true or false.

    B. Different views about the status of the proposition "It will rain tomorrow, January 3, 1983, in San Francisco." Presuming that this is stated on January 2, what is its truth status on that date?

       1. "As far as I'm concerned, it is true (or false)."

       2. "To me it is true; to you it may not be."

       3. "It is true until it is proved false or false until it is proved true."

       4. "It is neither true nor false."

       5. "It is either true or false when it is stated."

    C. Problems with these views.

       1. The first two are based on differences in beliefs that have nothing whatever to do with a proposition's truth or falsity.

       2. The third possibility just isn't true; whether or not the proposition is true or false may not be known, but then we would have to suspend judgment and not take a position until proved otherwise.

3. The fourth possibility cannot be correct, for all we have to do is look back on what we said after January 3 arrives, and if it rains as the proposition said it would, then it was true when we stated it; if it does not, then it was false—it had a status, but we just did not know what it was.

4. The fifth possibility is the correct one. At the time the proposition was stated, it was either true or false, not both or neither—we just did not know which it was.

D. Therefore, truth when carefully and precisely stated in propositions is absolute, not relative, and believing or knowing propositions has nothing to do with their truth or falsity. Propositions are either true or false whether or not we believe or know them to be true or false.

E. What does this mean to us, then? It means that the search for truth is worthwhile because there is a chance, since it is absolute, that once discovered or known, it can be known for certain. However, we must discover whether or not such knowledge is possible, and that will be discussed in the next chapter.

Additional Questions and Activities for Study and Discussion

1. One of the possibilities in trying to discover the status of the proposition given was "It is false until it is proved true, or true until it is proved false." Even though there were some problems with that statement, to what extent is it as valid as our legal concept of justice in which a person charged with a crime is "innocent until proved guilty"? Wouldn't this support the former statement? Why or why not? What does the latter really mean and how is it related to what might be the truth in the legal situation? Answer in detail.

2. Analyze the following and state which ones are propositions or not; for those that you select as propositions, tell which type they are and why.
   a. I like Scotch.
   b. John likes Scotch.
   c. All three-sided figures are triangles.
   d. There is life on other planets.
   e. I believe there is an afterlife.
   f. I am depressed.
   g. All squares are four-sided.
   h. The door to my car is open.
   i. Stealing is wrong.
   j. All men are mortal.

    k. I think I'm going to be sick.

    l. The United States is composed of fifty states.

    m. A rectangle is not a triangle.

    n. All albino rabbits are white.

    o. All blackbirds are black.

    p. All black birds are black.

    q. My back hurts.

    r. I love my wife.

    s. My dog is suffering.

    t. Jesus Christ is God.

    u. Come home to me now.

    v. Ferngratz heints plotz.

    w. Where are you going in such a hurry?

    x. Saturday is red (consider Saturday as a day of the week here).

    y. All widows are female.

    z. P is p.

3. How would you answer a person who said, "At one time the proposition, 'Whales are fish' was true, but now that we know they are mammals, the proposition 'Whales are *not* fish' is true"? Explain in detail what you would say to such a statement.

4. Explain in detail what you think the definition of "truth" is when it is used in swearing in a witness: "Do you swear to tell the truth, the whole truth, and nothing but the truth, so help you God?" What does the court really expect of you with such a statement? What if one of the key propositions in your testimony about something you had witnessed turned out not be be true; would you be guilty of perjury? Why or why not?

5. If truth is absolute, how do you allow for the fact that innocent people have been convicted on the "true" testimony of several witnesses and then later found to be innocent because someone else who resembled them confessed to the crime?

Footnotes

1. I am indebted to John Hospers, An *Introduction to Philosophical Analysis*, 2nd ed. (Englewood Cliffs, N.J.: Prentice-Hall, 1967), p. 114, for the term "states of affairs."

2. Ibid., pp. 114–115.

Bibliography

Ayer, A. J. *Language, Truth, and Logic*, 2nd ed. New York: Dover, 1936.

Blanshard, Brand. *The Nature of Thought*, Vol. 2. London: Allen and Unwin, 1940. See Chap. 25 and 26.

Ewing, A. C. *The Fundamental Questions of Philosophy*. London: Routledge and Kegan Paul, 1951.

Nagel, Ernest, and Richard B. Brandt, eds. *Meaning in Knowledge*. New York: Harcourt Brace, Jovanovich, 1965. See Chap. 2.

Russell, Bertrand. *The Problems of Philosophy*. London: Oxford University Press, 1959.

Summer, L. W., and John Woods, eds. *Necessary Truths: A Book of Readings*. New York: Random House, 1969.

White, Alan P. *Truth*. Garden City, N.Y.: Anchor, 1970.

CHAPTER 14

Sources and Nature of Knowledge

After discussing truth, falsity, belief, and propositions, we can now look into the sources and nature of knowledge itself. Such questions as, "Where does our knowledge come from?" "What does knowledge consist of?" "To what extent can we know anything?" "Is there such a thing as certain knowledge—can we know anything for sure, or will there always be doubts?" will all be dealt with in this chapter, for since knowledge forms the basis for philosophy, science, and other areas of human activity, it is most important that all such questions be answered, or at least wrestled with in searching for answers.

In this chapter we will first look at alleged sources of human knowledge; we will then look at the requirements for knowing any proposition is true or false, and this will lead us to examine knowing in the weak sense and knowing in the strong sense. Finally, we will apply our conclusions to the various types of propositions that were described in the previous chapter.

Sources of Knowledge

When we say that we know that a proposition is true (or false), how do we *know* this? On what basis do we claim to know something? Another way of posing this question is to ask, "Where does knowledge come from?" Many sources of knowledge have been claimed by philosophers, scientists, artists, religionists, and other representatives from various cultures down through the ages. It is important that we examine these sources and then critically evaluate them for their reliability in making our knowledge claims.

SENSE EXPERIENCE

One of the most obvious ways we gain knowledge about the outside world and even the reality within us is through our sense experience, and there are two types on which we rely.

EXTERNAL SENSE EXPERIENCE.   As we *perceive* the world around us through our five senses (sight, touch, smell, taste, and hearing), we gain experiences of what things look like, feel like, smell like, taste like, and sound like. Our external senses have often been called "windows looking out on the world" by poets. How do we have any knowledge of what an orange tastes like or what the sound of the ocean is? We gain it through our senses, and therefore a good deal, and in fact perhaps most, of what we know, at least in a sort of raw sense, is gained through these external senses. Some philosophers and scientists, as you will see in the next chapter, state that the only way we can know anything is through our senses.

INTERNAL SENSE EXPERIENCE.   We live most intimately within our bodies to the extent that we are really the only ones who know how and what we think, feel, imagine, or wonder about (refer to Chapter 3, again, concerning the privacy of both types of sense experience, but especially the internal). How do we know when we have a headache? We experience a pain in our heads. How do we know when we are sad, happy, excited, or sick? We have these experiences within ourselves; therefore, almost all the knowledge we have about our own inner states—our own inner lives—is gained through our internal sense experience. No one can truly deny the importance and significance of both types of sense experience as fairly reliable sources of knowledge.

REASON

Even with sense experience, we need to make rational judgments, or use reasoning, to arrive at more than just raw sense experience. We can also gain knowledge largely from reasoning alone. As mentioned in Chapter 2, there are two basic types of reasoning, which I will briefly reiterate here.

INDUCTIVE REASONING.   This type of reasoning, if you remember, moves basically from the particular instance to a general conclusion. For example, because we observe that things, when dropped each time, fall to the ground, we then generalize that *everything* when dropped will fall to the ground.

DEDUCTIVE REASONING.   This type of reasoning moves in the opposite direction from that of inductive in that it goes from a general true premise or proposition to a particular instance. If you remember, in Chapter 2 I gave you the famous syllogism, "All men are mortal; Socrates is a man; therefore, Socrates is mortal," as one example of deductive reasoning.

Both types of reasoning will yield knowledge that goes beyond sense experience even though they both may be directly or indirectly based on it. For example, we can know that an orange has a pungent aroma and a tangy taste, but after we have smelled and tasted several of them, we can generalize that all oranges will taste and smell in a way similar to those few we have already tested. This is general knowledge that we cannot gain merely from experiencing one orange. Further, we are able to gain knowledge about what particular things fit into what classes by finding general qualities they have in common and *deducing* that the particular thing we are observing fits into the same class with other like things.

THE PRINCIPLES OF LOGIC.   Another aspect of reasoning that should be discussed now is the three major principles of logic without which we could have no logic. These principles are ultimate to any type of reasoning whether it comes from sense experience or from within the thinking process. These principles are (*A* stands for *any* thing or *any*-one):

1. The principle of identity: A is A.
2. The principle of noncontradiction: nothing can be both A and not-A.
3. The principle of excluded middle: everything is either A or not-A.

Why are these principles fundamental or ultimate to any type of reasoning? Actually, we cannot even speak or think rationally without them. Everything we think, say, or write presupposes the principle of identity. If you think or speak about the sun, you have to presume that the sun is the sun; otherwise, what are you thinking or talking about? If you think or say that the sun is not the sun, again what are you thinking or saying? Further, the sun cannot be both itself and not itself at the same time; this would be contradictory, and this is the principle of noncontradiction. To say, for example, that a triangle is a circle would violate the principle of noncontradiction because you are saying that the figure (triangle) is both three-sided and not three-sided. This principle, then, says that something cannot both be itself and not itself, but to avoid its falling between the cracks of logic and being *neither,* there is the principle of the excluded middle, which says the thing either is itself or is not itself; it cannot be neither.[1]

INTUITION

Another source of knowledge often claimed by some philosophers and religionists is intuition. Intuition can mean many things to many people, from hunches and wild guesses, to mystical insights, to a higher form of reason. Because of this variety of meanings, I have chosen to consider it separately from reason, sense experience, and other alleged sources of knowledge. In general, intuition means a kind of quick, direct, or immediate perception of knowledge and insight. There are several ways, as I have suggested, in which different thinkers see intuition and its reliability as a source of knowledge.

FEELINGS OR HUNCHES.   When the phrase "women's intuition" is used, or when statements such as "I had a hunch he would do that" or "I had a feeling that would happen" are made, the implication is that there is some sort of special kind of knowledge available (to the person himself or herself, at least) through the way one feels or through some other unexplainable means. The reliability would depend, of course, on how often "intuitions," hunches, or feelings paid off to the extent that people who had them were right about any claims they had made from this source.

QUICK PERCEPTION.   Some philosophers claim that intuition is really just another name for the quickness of the trained minds of intelligent people. For example, a person with a good mathematical imagination, and lots of training and experience in mathematics, may see a difficult mathematical problem and almost at a glance be able to arrive quickly at the correct answer. Or a brilliant composer might, after having composed many musical works, be able to compose music quickly and somewhat effortlessly. Wolfgang Amadeus Mozart (1756–1791) was said to have composed in this way. Few of his scores show that he made any corrections; he just seemed to have the music in his mind and was able to put it on paper quickly and without having to make any changes. Of course, if this is what intuition is, then we would be better off calling it mental quickness or advanced ability to reason.

A HIGHER AND DIFFERENT FORM OF KNOWLEDGE.   For Henri Bergson (1859–1941), intuition and intelligence, reasoning, and logic, are in different categories altogether. He felt that we can use our trained intelligence, reasoning ability, and logic to deal with basic problems of science and mathematics through our sense experience and inductive and deductive reasoning. He felt, however, that intuition was somehow a higher form of knowledge that was able to touch our inward lives in the areas of appreciating the arts, love and friendship, morality, and developing the inward self. He seemed to state that sense experience and reasoning, although functional in the activities of the everyday world, nevertheless were not suited to taking the human spirit to higher realms of knowing, which placed us way beyond plants and animals.

MYSTICISM.   We have discussed mysticism before in the chapters on religion, and if you remember aspects of Hinduism and Buddhism, you remember that a higher form of reasoning or a nonreason is often prized. Remember that in Zen Buddhism, in particular, every effort was made to break the hold that the senses and logical reasoning and analysis have on people so that they can rise to higher forms of insight and intuition to attain *satori*. In this respect, then, intuition is similar to Bergson's theories about it but more religious and mystical in intent.

IMMEDIATE KNOWLEDGE.   Some philosophers see intuition as an immediate awareness rather than as a rational process like reasoning and logic. They would list such things as our awareness of our own consciousness, awareness of self (see Chapter 4), abstract thought, and the ability to see relationships in mathematics, logic, between propositions, and between thoughts, ideas, and feelings as forms of intuition. All these things, they state, are above and beyond the regular type of reasoning and sense experiencing we do in our daily lives and, in fact, make them possible.

AUTHORITY

There is no way that we can experience everything in the world so that we can have extensive knowledge of any kind, but one of our sources, authority, can make it possible for us to gain knowledge without having to experience it for ourselves. For example, how could we ourselves possibly experience what happened during Greek or Roman times? The only way we can do this is through the expertise of authorities in the fields of history, anthropology, archaeology, the arts, and the sciences. If we want to know what the Greek civilization was like, we can read books, take courses, or listen to lectures by "expert" authorities in the field. In this way, we can gain a great deal of knowledge about Greece that would be impossible to acquire any other way.

If we need vital information about our health, moral issues, legal issues, science and technology, raising children, or the workings of our automobiles, we go to doctors, who are authorities in medicine (we can even seek out specialists!), ministers or ethicists, attorneys, scientists and technologists, psychologists or counselors, and engineers or auto mechanics to acquire the knowledge we need. It is impossible to be experts ourselves in all these fields; therefore, we get our knowledge from books, educational institutions in all their aspects, different media (newspapers, magazines, radio, television, and films), and various people who are experts in their fields.

REVELATION

As we have seen in discussing the various religions, revelation is considered by many to be an important source of knowledge and the only source that can bring certain kinds of knowledge to human beings. Revelation can be public, as that which is found in the Bible and Koran, for example. It can also be private and allegedly given to certain persons by some sort of supernatural source. If you remember, St. Thomas Aquinas, who felt that God's existence could be proved through sense experience and reasoning, stated that certain pieces of knowledge, such as the existence of the Trinity, could only be known through revelation. Mostly, then, what revelation means is that some supernatural being or beings has "revealed" certain knowledge to human beings that they could not have discovered through any other sources.

FAITH

Many religious people also feel that they gain knowledge about God, the soul, afterlife, and other supernatural things through their faith. Faith and revelation are certainly tied very close together. When a religious person is asked why he believes the Bible or revelation, he states that it is because he has faith they contain true knowledge that has come from God. Religious people see faith as a source of knowledge, partly because it makes supernatural knowledge possible and partly because they believe that if they have faith that certain propositions are true, they will be, and the faithful will then have special knowledge they wouldn't have otherwise.

TRADITION AND COMMON SENSE

The last source of knowledge we will discuss is somewhat related to authority. Much of the knowledge we have has been taught to us through our various cultural and societal traditions and institutions. Most of the information we get is based on the whole Western tradition, which has its sources in the Greek and Roman civilizations and in the Judeo-Christian traditions. Our laws, our morality, our science, and our social sciences can be traced to these sources, and they do provide us with knowledge. We also have our particular American traditions through our Declaration of Independence, the Constitution, and the many laws and descriptions and history of the various traditions and customs that have been passed down to us. Many times when we ask questions about where some knowledge came from, we may be told that it is "traditional" in some way.

Common sense is often also described as a source of knowledge. It is even distinguished from higher intellectual knowledge, for example, in the description of one who is highly educated but who "has no common sense." It is hard to define exactly what commonsense knowledge really is. It is supposed to be knowledge held "in common" by all human beings that usually helps them to function in their daily lives and in their society effectively. It is generally considered very practical, down to earth, and basic in nature. Often its importance is stressed by people when they say such things as, "Common sense will tell you that you should never loan money to a friend or member of your family."

EVALUATION OF THE SOURCES

SENSE EXPERIENCE.   Although sense experience is considered one of the most reliable of sources of knowledge by philosophers, scientists, and people in general (remember the old saying, "Seeing is believing"?), there are some problems in relying on it for knowledge. Let us discuss external sense experience first.

Our senses often deceive us through optical illusions, hallucinations, and defects in our sense organs. Second, we often make what John Hospers calls "perceptual errors", that is, we mistake one thing for another, such as a cat for a small dog, because we have not been attentive enough. The point is, how can sense experience be reliable when optical illusions cause us to see things not as they are, such as seeing water in the road ahead and finding that it is caused by heat waves; when the distant mountains appear purple to us, but when we get closer we find they are really green or brown; when if we are color blind, we mistake gray for green; and so on? We will discuss these problems in more detail in the next chapter dealing with perception and the external world.

Internal sense experiences are deadly accurate where our own internal feelings, ideas, and sensations are concerned, but they are limited *only* to those internal states and may have no relationship or effect on external reality. That is why, for example, believing that a proposition is true has nothing to do with its being true. Belief is an internal sense activity and proves nothing about the world outside of us. You can say, for example, that it is going to rain because you "feel it in your bones," but your statement has little reliability. Even if it does rain, it may have nothing to do with "the feeling in your bones," so such a statement really only has the reliability of belief. You would have been more accurate if you merely had said that you *believed* that it was going to rain, and of course, belief or nonbelief has nothing to do with whether it will rain or not.

REASON.   I discussed some of the problems with both inductive and deductive reasoning in Chapter 2, but let me reiterate briefly that inductive reasoning can yield only probable knowledge, never certain knowledge. This form of reasoning, however, is still reliable to the extent that it has higher probability—the higher the probability, the more reliable it is. Deductive reasoning, if its premises are true and the argument is valid, will yield certain knowledge. The biggest problem with this type of reasoning is trying to decide whether or not the premises are true, and it is often the case that the truth of the premises is based on induction and we are back again to the degree of probability. Often, too, deductive reasoning yields knowledge that seems trivial, such as that discovered in the syllogism concerning Socrates and mortality, quoted earlier.

The principles of logic would seem extremely important to any type of thinking we might attempt, and to discard them would destroy the validity of our thinking, speaking, and writing. They are analytic propositions, which I described earlier. Again, however, the knowledge they yield, once understood, is basic but not terribly profound or extensive. Despite these problems, we really could not function without reason in all its aspects, just as we cannot deny the importance of sense experience. The important point here is to be aware of the drawbacks and not be trapped by low probability or illogical reasoning.

INTUITION.   If intuition means feelings or hunches, then its reliability definitely has to be questioned. I am not trying to say that feelings are not important or that even hunches should not be considered, but I am saying that in themselves, they do not provide reliable knowledge. If I have the feeling or hunch that the person who is approaching me wants to mug me, then I should certainly be wary and cautious, but unless there is other evidence (sense experience), for example, that he or she is brandishing a knife or a club, I cannot presume that my feeling or hunch is reliable. Usually, when we deem it reliable, it is actually because of sense experience and reasoning, such as in seeing the knife or club. We have all had feelings or hunches about people, things, and events that have been reliable and many that have not. If this is all intuition is, then without sense experience and reasoning, it is nothing.

If intuition is merely quick perception, then it is basically an accomplished ability to use sense experience and all the aspects of reasoning quickly and accurately. It does not seem at all mysterious or "intuitive" that poets, musicians, mathematicians, lawyers, or doctors, who have practiced their professions steadily and over a fairly long period of time, are able to write music or poetry quickly, make even complicated legal distinctions easily and quickly, make accurate diagnoses in a short time, and work the most complicated mathematics problem very fast.

Bergson's theories about intuition being a higher form of knowledge can also be questioned because many other philosophers think that he makes too great a claim for intuition. They say that what he ascribes to it is really nothing more than sense experience and reasoning. For example, do we really appreciate the arts through some magical inner intuition, or does such appreciation really come about through lengthy observations (sense experience) of art and the development of reasoning and judgment based on those observations (reasoning)?

It is also true that love and friendship are based on more than logic and reason, but could this not really be a combination of feelings or emotions and sense experience and reasoning? For example, we become acquainted with someone through our sense experiences—seeing, hearing, and touching; then our emotions enter the picture, and we also use our reason to decide that we care for that person to some degree. Why do we have to ascribe this activity to something called "intuition"? Isn't this just unnecessarily expanding and overcomplicating the process (see expansionism in Chapter 2)? Further, we have already talked about how morality can be based on sense experience and reason as well as having emotional involvement. Why do we have to posit "intuition" to account for rational decisions that in order to survive and live together, we need moral standards? Is this so mysterious a process?

If intuition is merely mysticism, then it is limited to individual mystical experiences that certainly can be questioned as knowledge. The mystic has certain experiences, but how reliable are these experiences as knowledge? In the first place, only the mystic has the experience, and if various mystics have different experiences, as they surely do, then how are we to evaluate any of these as knowledge? Which mystic's experience is the evidence of the truth or falsity of any proposition (for example, "God exists," "Brahman is the ultimate reality," "Allah is the supreme power")?

Intuition as immediate knowledge can be questioned also. What indeed is immediate knowledge? Isn't sense experience of any kind immediate knowledge provided it isn't a remembering? Proponents of this view state that we know our own consciousness, our awareness of self, and abstract thought and relationships only through intuition. Certainly there is a difference between being aware of our own consciousness or self and being aware of the sky's being blue, but isn't this just the difference between external and internal sense perception? Further, if one reads Plato and books about his attempt to get the Greeks to think abstractly, one will come away with the notion that abstract thinking is not inborn but has to be taught, and it is not an easy task.[2] Moreover, there is no doubt that our minds have the ability to see relationships between our different sense experiences, but why does that have to be called intuition? Can't that just be considered a part of the mind's analytic and abstracting ability, especially when it is encouraged and expanded through learning?

AUTHORITY. Authority as a source of knowledge is very often reliable, but its reliability depends on several requirements. First, the authority must really *be* an authority. For example, if someone states what he or she calls a scientific truth and the individual has no training or experience in science, then his or her authority should certainly be questioned. We often have to be careful, too, that because we admire a famous person in his chosen field in which he is an expert (motion picture actor, musician, scientist), we do not let his abilities in that field convince us that he is also an authority in other fields, such as religion, politics, or morality. For example, movie stars often take strong positions on scientific or moral matters and just because they are famous, their positions or opinions may be given more credibility than they deserve. The common person may be more of an authority than these famous people because he or she may have done more research and thinking about these things than the stars.

Second, even when the authorities are really authorities, when they disagree, it is wise for us to withhold judgment. For example, Dr. Edward Teller (1908–) and Dr. J. Robert Oppenheimer (1904–1967), both renowned physicists, disagreed concerning the proper use of atomic energy; therefore, we must take this serious disagreement into consideration before committing ourselves to one side or the other in the controversy.

Finally, to be reliable, any authority's statements must be able to be checked, if necessary, by using sense experience and reasoning. For example, if a scientist states that a certain substance causes cancer in rats, then we ought to be able to be taken through the steps of the experimental process to see for ourselves that the substance does indeed cause cancer. If these three requirements are observed, whether the authority be a person, a book, a tradition, or an institution, then authority can be considered as a reliable source of knowledge.

REVELATION AND FAITH.   Since these two alleged sources of knowledge are so closely related, I will evaluate them together. First, many of the problems with these two sources have already been discussed in Chapters 9 and 10 on philosophy of religion, but the major difficulty with both is that there are many different revelations claimed for different religions, and which are we to believe? Second, many of these revelations are private and not observable to others for verification. Third, one has to depend largely on faith to accept any of the revelations as knowledge because they are not usually verifiable in the ways other claims are, through sense experience and reasoning. We have also already discussed the possible meanings of faith, and if it means "belief without evidence" or "blind belief," then it is merely that, and belief is not knowledge since we all believe many propositions that may not be true. If it means witnessing or commitment, then it is hardly a source of knowledge, but really more of a human activity based on strong belief.

TRADITION AND COMMON SENSE.   Traditions are generally significant and well worth preserving and adhering to; however, if they are untested by sense experience and reasoning, they may become outmoded or be based on beliefs that are untrue. For example, until Copernicus and Galileo, it was traditional to believe that the earth was the center of the universe; however, these two scientists proved that the sun, not the earth, was really the center. In this case, and in many others, tradition was not a reliable source of knowledge because it was based on false assumptions. One must constantly check, then, the reliability of tradition and not just accept it because it has been a tradition for a long time.

It is hard to define "common sense," but here again one must be wary when someone says "It's common sense; anybody knows that." To accept common sense as reliable knowledge, any claim being made under its aegis must be subjected to sense experience and reasoning. Many things that are considered common sense turn out to be "old wives' tales" and are often completely invalidated by scientific investigation and the resulting evidence it yields. For example, some people have claimed that it is common sense for a baby who is large to be prevented from walking too soon or its legs will be bowed. This is completely false, according to all scientific data available. Further, common sense is often used to discriminate against certain races or religions. For example, "everyone knows" or "it's common sense" that all Mexicans are lazy, all blacks are less intelligent than whites, and all Orientals are inscrutable. None of these of course is true even though some Mexicans may be lazy, some blacks may be unintelligent, and some Orientals may be inscrutable, just as some whites may also be any of the three.

CONCLUSION

It would seem that the most reliable sources of knowledge, even with their problems, are sense experience and reasoning. In most cases where other sources are claimed, these two sources have to be used to verify their reliability, and further in using sense experience and reasoning, some standards can be set up for reliability and verifiability. For example, if the light is not very good, if our sense organs are somewhat impaired, or if we are too great a distance from an object being observed, then we will have to adjust all these until the conditions for observing are optimum.

The important thing is that we can establish such conditions. For example, we can make sure that we are observing an object in bright sunlight; we can put on our glasses to eliminate our blurred vision, and we can check out what we see by using the sense of touch to ensure that the object we are observing is not a hallucination or an image projection, but a solid, three-dimensional object. Even authority, which is probably our next most reliable source of knowledge when the three requirements I mentioned are satisfied, still has to be verifiable through sense experience and reasoning. We may certainly use some of the other sources of knowledge as long as we are cautious and ever ready to check them by the two most reliable sources.

Now that we have examined and critically evaluated the sources of knowledge, let us look into what actually constitutes knowledge; that is, what does it really mean to say that we know that something is the case? What constitutes knowledge, and how does it really relate to and differ from belief, even strong belief?

The Nature of Knowledge

REQUIREMENTS FOR SAYING "I KNOW THAT . . ."

John Hospers sets up three requirements for knowing a proposition, any proposition, is true or false. They are the objective requirement, the subjective requirement, and the evidence requirements.[3]

THE OBJECTIVE REQUIREMENT.   For us to *know* that any proposition is true, the proposition must really *be* true. How else could we say we know it? If the proposition is really false and we say we *know* that it is true, then we of course could not really *know* the status of the proposition. For example, for me to say, "I know that the earth is not flat," that proposition would *have* to be true for me to be able to say I *know* it to be so. How could I know otherwise? This differs from believing any proposition is true, for to believe it, it need not be true as in the case of those who, prior to 1492, believed that the earth was flat.

THE SUBJECTIVE REQUIREMENT. Belief, however, is related to knowledge in that for me to say "I know the earth is not flat," I must also believe it. What would it mean for me to say "I know it is true, but I don't believe it"? We sometimes say things like this—for example, "I know he was shot, but I don't believe it"—but we can't really mean that we know it, if we don't actually believe it. In such statements, we are usually expressing our shock at the knowledge, but we really do know it. With these two requirements met, we have achieved a state called "true belief," but true belief still doesn't mean that we know any proposition to be true or false. For example, prior to 1492, Columbus believed that the earth was not flat, and the proposition "The earth is not flat" was true; however, at the time he uttered the proposition (prior to 1492), he could not really say he *knew* that it was true. Therefore, true belief is not enough for one to say he knows any proposition is true.

THE EVIDENCE REQUIREMENT. It is not enough that a proposition is true or that I believe it is true; I must have *evidence* that it is true. This is undoubtedly the hardest of the requirements to meet in knowing many propositions, for how much and what kind of evidence is required before we can say we *know* any proposition is true? "Some" evidence would not seem to be enough, because this would only give us part of what we need to know.

How about "all the evidence there is"? Is this even possible? Would it mean that we would have to have all the knowledge there is to have to acquire this kind of evidence? If this is the requirement, would we ever be able to say that we would ever have all the evidence there is? Some philosophers, as you will see later in the discussion of empirical propositions and whether or not we can know any of them for certain, take this nearly impossible position, while some do not. What about "enough" evidence? But what would constitute enough? This would seem to be too vague. I have used the phrase "conclusive evidence" throughout this book in discussing matters of religion, but what does "conclusive evidence" mean? Can we set criteria to establish what would constitute conclusive evidence? Before examining different types of propositions or going any further with this discussion, it is important to look at two senses of the word "know" when used in the propositional sense, and here again, I am indebted to John Hospers for his designations and the criteria for establishing them.[4]

THE STRONG AND WEAK SENSES OF "KNOW"

THE WEAK SENSE.   Hospers argues that we most often use this sense of "know"; in fact, this may be what most of our knowledge is. This sense of "know" really seems to be based on the "some evidence" criteria. For example, when we are at work, and we say things like, "My car is in the parking lot" or "I have a Steinway piano in my living room" or "My wife's at work," these statements would be classified by Hospers as the weak sense of "know."

The criteria he establishes for this sense are three: (1) I believe that the proposition is true, (2) I have good grounds on which to base my belief, and (3) my belief is indeed true. For example, using the first proposition, when I make the statement, "My car is in the parking lot," I believe it, because I put it there myself in the morning when I drove to work. Besides that bit of evidence, I locked it and gave no one else the key. And objects like cars are not in the habit of being moved from parking lots once they are parked and locked, so I have good grounds for my belief. The final criterion can be fulfilled if I take you out to the parking lot and we find my car parked where I left it.

In this way, Hospers says, I have fulfilled all the requirements for having known the proposition was true when I originally stated it. Again, as Hospers points out, much of our knowledge is like this. We may be inside of a room without windows, for example, but we "know," in the weak sense, that there is a tree outside the room because we saw it when we came in; because trees don't have a habit of moving, being moved, or disappearing; and because we can go outside to check or *verify* our claim. I'm sure you could think of many more examples that would fit this criteria.

I find one problem with it, however. Could we always say that we "know" such propositions even in the weak sense? Let me give you an example of what I mean. Let us say that I claim "I know my car is in the parking lot" (in the weak sense, of course) at 9:00 A.M. in the morning for all of the "good" reasons listed. Let us suppose, however, that at 8:45 A.M. someone broke into my car, "hot wired" it, and drove off so that the car was gone by 9:00 A.M. Let us say that someone saw this person and reported the theft and that the criminal was apprehended and my car brought back at 9:30 A.M. At 9:00 A.M., when I stated the proposition, did I really know, in any sense, that my car was in the parking lot, or did I only believe it, no matter how strongly? After all when I arrived in the parking lot at 9:30 A.M., my car was there. What are we to make of this situation? True, it probably would seldom happen, but it does pose the possibility of the weak sense of knowing being even weaker than we thought. I would probably be better off saying something like, "I am pretty sure that my car is in the parking lot because . . ." and give all the grounds for my belief.

If we take the propositions "God exists" or "God does not exist," which many people believe and some say they *know* either in the weak or strong sense, there are further problems. I may believe strongly that either of the propositions is true; and I may consider that I have good grounds for my belief; but how can the third criterion be fulfilled? It could be fulfilled after I die and go to heaven or hell or have some other meeting with God or not, or it may not because the assumption that consciousness persists after one has died is not itself provable. Further, presuming that consciousness does continue, how would my evidence be any stronger if I came face to face with a powerful figure or heard a strong voice or saw or heard nothing? At any rate, even if conclusive evidence were available for me one way or the other after I died, that would still not entitle me to say now that I know God exists or does not exist in the weak sense. Let us now look at the strong sense of "know."

THE STRONG SENSE.   In the search for certain knowledge, that is, trying to discover whether or not we can know that any proposition is true or false for sure, philosophers (and scientists) are most interested in this sense of "know." The criteria for this sense, as you might expect, are much more stringent than are those for the weak sense. To know whether any proposition is true in the strong sense of "know," three criteria must be fulfilled: (1) the proposition must be true, (2) I must believe it, and (3) I must have absolutely *conclusive* evidence that it is true.

Can we ever know any proposition to this extent? It seems very difficult to say yes to this, especially after seeing what trouble we can have even in determining whether we can really know a proposition to be true in the weak sense; however, we do have a chance with the weak sense. Is there even a chance for certain knowledge, however, especially considering the last criterion? We have already discussed the difficulty in trying to define "conclusive evidence," but let us examine the strong sense of "know" in connection with the different propositions that were presented in the last chapter: analytic propositions, internal sense propositions, external sense or empirical propositions, and moral propositions.

ANALYTIC PROPOSITIONS.   Remember that analytic propositions are those like "All triangles are three-sided," "No circle is a square," "All bachelors are unmarried men," and "All black crows are black." The propositions are true, aren't they, and you must believe them, mustn't you? But what about the "conclusive evidence" requirement? Is there any doubt in your mind when you analyze the words in such propositions and know their definitions that the propositions are true? Do you need to check all the triangles or circles in the world to see if propositions about them are correct? Do you need to check all bachelors or all black crows to see if they are unmarried or black, respectively? Of course you don't. It would seem that analytic propositions satisfy all the requirements for being able to be known to be true in the strong sense of "know."

Some philosophers even state that these types of propositons are either true or contradictory rather than false, and indeed if you deny them, you are being self-contradictory. Saying that "all bachelors are *not* unmarried men" is tantamount to saying that "all unmarried men are not unmarried men," and this would be contradictory. To say that "all circles are squares" would also be contradictory, because we know the definitions of a circle and a square and they are totally different. Therefore, analytic propositions can be known for certain.

One might ask, "So what? The information is really trivial—who cares about circles or squares or triangles?" However, they do present at least one type of proposition that can yield certain knowledge, and remember that the principles of logic that form the basis for all language, logic, and reasoning are analytic propositions, along with certain mathematical, algebraic, geometric, and logical formulas. Without analytic propositions, much of our higher reasoning would be impossible.

INTERNAL SENSE PROPOSITIONS.   Remember that these types of propositions are about our own internal states, describing things like pain, pleasure, imaginings, beliefs, wonderings, thoughts, ideas, and dreams. Such propositions as "I have a headache," "I believe that God exists," "I am sad," and so on are examples of these types of propositions.

To what extent can we know such propositions are true—in the weak sense? In the strong? How do they fit the criteria for the strong sense of "know"? It is impossible not to believe them because they are there and they are actual regardless of their cause or causes. For example, is the evidence for your headache conclusive or inconclusive? Do you feel pain, sadness, or pleasure, or not? Do you believe in God or not? Do you wonder whether your friend lied to you or not? The evidence for internal sense propositions seems to be immediate and self-evident. The only evidence you need for the proposition "I have a headache" to be true is to really have a headache; therefore, the proposition is true; you believe it; and you do indeed have absolutely conclusive evidence it is true. Even if your doctor says, "You can't have a headache, there is no cause for it," that doesn't alter the fact that you do indeed have a headache, nor does it make your proposition false. Generally, also, we will believe the internal sense propositions of others because we know that they generally *know* for certain how they feel or believe. They could, of course, be lying to us about their headaches to get out of work, for example, but generally we accept what they say about their own internal states. Whether we do or not, however, we do know what *our* internal states are, and therefore we know propositions we state about them are true in the strong sense of "know."

EXTERNAL SENSE OR EMPIRICAL PROPOSITIONS.   These propositions make claims about the external world and are dependent upon our external sense experiences and our rational judgments about them. When I say "I am holding a pencil in my hand," "I am standing in front of the Empire State Building," "My daughter is ten years old," or "There's life on other planets," I am stating propositions about external reality. Many of these, for example, the last one, can only be known in the weak sense; in fact, I would be more likely to state that proposition as a belief as would most other people probably, if they were even willing to commit themselves that far.

There is little doubt whether or not such propositions can be known in the weak sense, but can any of them be known in the strong sense? There is conclusive evidence for knowing the first two types of propositions for certain, but what about empirical propositions? Philosophers have disagreed whether such propositions can ever be known for certain or not. The skeptics in this area of knowledge (see Chapter 2 for a discussion of skepticism) state that there could *never* be conclusive evidence that any external sense or empirical propositions could be known for certain to be either true or false because the evidence concerning the external world is always open ended. In other words, new evidence could always be forthcoming or turn up that would invalidate what we thought we knew before.

Other philosophers state that we can know certain external sense or empirical propositions in the strong sense, whereas we can know others only in the weak sense. Still others we may believe but not know. Let us look at some of these propositions and apply our criteria.

Suppose that I am sitting out in the sunlight holding a book in my hand and reading it. I am not drunk or dreaming or under the influence of other drugs besides alcohol. If I state the proposition, when someone asks me what I'm doing, "I am reading a book," do I know this proposition in the strong or weak sense or do I just believe that it is true without knowing it? What kind of further evidence would I need to be able to say I know, in the strong sense, this proposition to be true? The light is good; my visual organs are working; I have feeling in my hands; I know I'm not dreaming because I woke up from a night's sleep in which I had several dreams only several hours ago, and there is a definite distinction between my dream states and my waking states; and, finally, I can examine the object in my hand extremely carefully to make sure that it is a book.

After all these bits of evidence have been examined and checked for accuracy, does it make any sense to say, "I doubt that I am reading a book; I only believe that I am, but I really don't know that I am"? Wouldn't that make much less sense than saying, "I know that I am reading a book"? In other words, once optimum conditions are achieved concerning knowing external sense or empirical propositions then we can indeed know them in the strong sense. If the optimum conditions are not achieved, then we can know them only in the weak sense, or if there is less evidence, then only believe them. For example, if I am making statements about external reality, such as "My car is in the parking lot," that I cannot state with absolute certainty because I cannot for the moment observe my car there, then, I can only believe that proposition to be true or know it in the weak sense depending on how good my grounds for believing the proposition is true are.

Returning to the proposition "God exists" and its counterpart "God does not exist," which we had trouble knowing in the weak sense, we would also have to say that we cannot know them in the strong sense either. As I have said throughout this book, we do not have absolutely conclusive evidence to say that we know either of them. Note, however, that if we state the different propositions, "I believe that God exists" or "I believe that God does not exist," we can know either proposition for sure because they are internal sense propositions. It is quite possible that "God exists" is true, and it can certainly be possible that I can believe it strongly, but the conclusive evidence requirement cannot be met. Therefore, we cannot *know* whether God exists or not, which is why I said in Chapter 12 that we all start from the position of epistemological agnosticism.

MORAL PROPOSITIONS.   These types of propositions, such as "Human beings should not kill other human beings," "Abortion is morally wrong," "Fred is a morally good person," or "Students should never cheat on tests," are also seen differently by different philosophers. Some philosophers say that we cannot know such propositions at all—we can only believe them; others say that we can only know these in the weak sense; still others, such as Kant (see nonconsequentialism in Chapter 7), say that we can know them in the strong sense.

Whether we can know these propositions to be true or not is much more difficult to determine than are the other three types of propositions, but this difficulty does not mean that they are meaningless, as some philosophers have suggested (see, in particular, A. J. Ayer and his books *Language, Truth, and Logic* and *Problems of Knowledge*).

What is different about moral propositions, of course, is that some sort of value judgment or moral prescription (should or ought) is involved (see Chapter 6), whereas in the cases of the other three types of propositions, factual, not value, claims are being made about some aspect of reality. However, let us examine some of these value propositions to see if we can discover whether or not they can be known to be true or false in either sense of the word "know." It is obvious that belief constitutes no problem whatsoever since people can believe anything they want, although it would seem to be futile and perhaps even dangerous to believe something that flies in the face of the truth. For example, if a person believes that if he jumps off of a ten-story building he will be able to fly to the ground without assistance and without being injured or killed, then he could lose his life. However, as we have seen, in general, belief statements are internal sense statements and can be known to be true—"I believe human beings should not kill other human beings" is true if the person saying it really does believe it. As we have also seen, belief statements are quite different from other claims about external reality, such as "Human beings should not kill other human beings." It is with the status of this latter type of proposition that we are concerned here.

Let us first apply the criteria for knowing in the weak sense to this proposition, which could also be stated as "Killing human beings is wrong." We certainly can satisfy the first criterion that we believe it. Perhaps we can also satisfy the second that we have good grounds for our belief. If human beings kill other human beings—and since most people consider human life as valuable because without it we can do nothing—then we can say we have good grounds for our belief. If every human being attempted to kill every other human being, then there would probably be no human beings around. The threat of being killed at every moment would also make life extremely hard to live at any sort of level except strict survival. From history and from experience, we know that life at the strictly survival level is not as satisfying, creative, or meaningful.

If we know this from experience, then can't we say that we have good grounds for our belief? How do we find out if our belief is true, however? Here again, sense experience and reasoning can be applied to all the significant differences between life lived during wartime and that lived during peace, for example. When life is constantly threatened, there can be little creativity, there is little harmony and very little if any pleasure, while there is a great deal of pain and unhappiness. Therefore, except for a few instances, such as those few people who enjoy killing and care little if they are killed, or issues such as killing in defense of the innocent, it would seem that a case could be made for saying that we can know in the weak sense, "Human beings should not kill other human beings" is true. If it seems too general a proposition to be known as true, then we can state it more precisely to include significant exceptions such as in "Human beings should not kill other human beings except in defense of the innocent" (including self-defense). So it would seem to me that at least some moral propositions can be known to be true (or false) in the weak sense, depending on what evidence is available and how convincing it is.

Can such propositions be known in the strong sense, however? Here again, it would depend on whether or not one can discover absolutely conclusive evidence. Some propositions could be known in this way, and some could not. For example, "Rape or the molestation of children is always wrong" would seem to be able to be known in the strong sense. What evidence could be brought to bear to prove that such a proposition is false? In what situation would these actions ever be morally right? Could you say that as long as a woman consented, it would be moral? The definition of the word "rape" means forced sexuality, not sexuality that is consented to. When would child molestation be acceptable? If the child consented? But we generally consider children as not able to consent to adult activities unless they are exceptionally mature, and despite this, we protect them by age limits from having the responsibility for such decisions as consenting to sexual activities with an adult. Therefore, couldn't we say that we know the foregoing proposition in the strong sense to be true?

This discussion would probably be challenged by many philosophers and perhaps even nonphilosophers, but I do believe that the issue of whether or not moral propositions can be known to be true or false is well worth considering, since they affect our lives sometimes even more significantly than do any of the other three types. My own personal conviction is that these propositions are really a type of external sense or empirical proposition with the value aspect added in. Therefore, I believe that when stated precisely and when convincing evidence is available—conclusive or nearly conclusive—moral propositions can be known to be true in the weak sense and sometimes in the strong sense. Regardless of how you feel about this issue, I think it can provide significant discussion because it is important to see to what extent moral propositions can be known to be true in either sense.

Conclusion

We have discovered that knowledge is quite different from belief although belief is related to knowledge in that you cannot have the latter without also having the former; that does not, however, work in reverse—believing does not mean that you know anything except that you do believe a proposition to be true or false. We have seen that we can know propositions in a weak sense and also in a strong sense and that we can know analytic and internal sense propositions in the strong sense as well as external sense or empirical propositions in either the weak or strong sense. I would say that we have also discovered that we can know moral propositions in the same ways, but I leave that for your continuing investigations and discussions.

External sense or empirical propositions are so important to almost every claim we make to knowledge that I feel that it is important to examine the basis for them, that is, perception; therefore, the next chapter will be given over to a discussion of what constitutes perception, what we actually perceive, and how reliable our claims are about knowing external reality when based on our sense perceptions.

Applying Philosophy—
Situations for Thought and Discussion

SITUATION 1

Interview your family members, friends, coworkers, fellow students, and teachers, and ask them what they know and if they know anything for certain. Ask them also what criteria they use for being able to say "I know that . . ." something is the case. After they have answered your questions, describe to them the weak and strong sense of "know," according to Hospers. Ask them now to restate what they know and what they know for certain (in the strong sense). Was there any difference between their two descriptions? If so, what? If not, why do you think not? How many of the propositions they said they knew in either sense fell under which of the four types of propositions? How many *beliefs* did they describe as knowledge in the weak and strong senses? Why, do you think? Describe the various sources of knowledge to them. Which sources did they find most reliable and which not? Try to find out why. After you have finished your interviews (again you may construct a questionnaire, if you wish), write your conclusions as to how most people you interviewed see knowledge, its sources, and its relation to belief and truth.

SITUATION 2

After having read this chapter and the one on truth, present in detail your views on truth, falsity, belief, the four types of propositions, knowledge in both senses, certain knowledge, and the sources of knowledge and their reliability. With which of the positions do you agree in all these matters and with which do you disagree—answer in detail and give evidence and substantiated reasons for your views on these matters. To what extent have your views on what you believe and what you can know changed since reading these chapters? In what ways and why? Describe in detail your reactions to the statements that "God exists" and "God does not exist" cannot be known in either the weak or strong sense, but only believed. Whether you agree or disagree, support your position fully.

SITUATION 3

Read Ryūnosuke Akutagawa's short story, "In a Grove," or see the motion picture *Rashomon* if possible, both of which show how elusive knowledge, especially certain knowledge, can be.[5] Analyze and critically evaluate each of the witnesses' knowledge and description of the truth. Which do you think is the correct one, if any, and why? What do you think happened and why? Answer in detail. What do you think the problems were with each version presented and why? Can evidence presented by a number of witnesses to any event bring us knowledge in either sense? Under what conditions can knowledge claims based on this kind of testimony be considered reliable, and why?

Chapter Summary

I. Sources of knowledge.
   A. Sense experience.
      1. External sense experience is that which we experience through our five external senses (sight, touch, smell, taste, and hearing).
      2. Internal sense experience deals with our internal states, such as feelings, thoughts, imaginings, wonderings, and beliefs.
   B. Reason involves rational judgements of our sense experiences as well as special thought processes, such as abstracting, logic, and making relationships.
      1. Inductive reasoning moves basically from the particular to general conclusions.
      2. Deductive reasoning moves in the opposite direction, from general assumptions to particular instances that follow from them.
      3. Another aspect of reasoning is the principles of logic:
         a. Principle of identity: A is A.
         b. Principle of noncontradiction: nothing can be both A and not-A.
         c. Principle of excluded middle: everything is either A or not-A.
         d. These principles are fundamental to any type of reasoning, speaking, thinking, or writing and, therefore, are considered ultimate to any type of reasoning.
   C. Intuition is considered a special type of knowledge and is defined in different ways by different philosophers:

1. Feelings or hunches.
2. Quick perception.
3. A higher and different form of knowledge involving things like appreciating the arts, love and friendship, morality, and developing the inward self—basically the theory of Henri Bergson.
4. Mysticism.
5. Immediate knowledge and awareness of self, ability to think abstractly, and the ability to see relationships.

D. Authority has to do with experts, books, histories, and institutions that are authorities on certain areas since we cannot possibly witness or learn about everything ourselves.

E. Revelation is that source of knowledge through which certain kinds of knowledge are revealed to human beings, usually through some sort of supernatural source.

F. Faith is often claimed as a source of knowledge through which religious people claim to know, for example, that God exists.

G. Tradition and common sense constitute the last source of knowledge, and they come to us through our cultural traditions or through common sense or common knowledge to which all people are supposed to have access.

II. Evaluation of the various sources.

A. Sense experience.
1. We are often deceived by our external sense through illusion, hallucination, dreams, and defects in our sense organs.
2. Internal sense perceptions are limited to just that, and no outside claims can be made. For example, I can believe God exists, but my internal sense—in this case, belief—has nothing to do with God's actual existence or nonexistence.

B. Reason.
1. Inductive reasoning can yield only probable knowledge, the reliability of which is in proposition to the degree of probability.
2. Deductive reasoning's problem is that its major premise is often based on inductive reasoning with all its attendant problems.
3. The principles of logic are basic and even ultimate; however, they are also somewhat trivial. That is, their certainty is often considered basic, but not profound.

C. Intuition.
1. If it is just feelings and hunches, then its reliability has to be questioned and cannot be verified without further checking through sense experience and reasoning.

    2. If it is merely quick perception, then again it is basically no more than an accomplished ability to use sense experience and reasoning quickly and accurately.

    3. Bergson's theories about its being a higher form of knowledge can also be questioned because again the kinds of knowledge he ascribes only to intuition other philosophers say we acquire through sense experience and reasoning.

    4. If it is merely mysticism, then it is limited to individual mystical experiences that have to be questioned as knowledge. Various mystics have had various experience that often do not agree, and which are we to accept as knowledge?

    5. As immediate knowledge, how is it different from sense experience? Isn't sense experience also immediate knowledge, and aren't the things we are supposed to know immediately really just sensed (except for memory)?

D. Authority is reliable, provided that

    1. The authority really is an authority.

    2. When authorities disagree, we should withhold judgment.

    3. The statements of any authority must be checkable through sense experience and reasoning if necessary.

E. Revelation and faith. The major problem with both of these is that, like mysticism, many different revelations are claimed, and which are we to believe? There is no standard by which any of them may be verified.

    1. Many of them are also private in nature and not observable to others for verification.

    2. If faith means "blind belief," then it is not knowledge; if it means witnessing or commitment, then it is still not a source of knowledge, but rather a human activity that really yields no knowledge.

F. Tradition and common sense.

    1. Traditions can become outmoded or be discovered to be based on untrue belief; therefore, we should not keep them up merely because they are traditions.

    2. What is common sense? Whatever its claims, its reliability would have to depend on being verified through sense experience and reasoning.

G. Conclusion. Even with their faults, the most reliable sources of knowledge would have to be sense experience and reasoning.

    1. We need to establish optimum conditions when knowledge through sense experience would be most reliable, such as good light for observation and further verification of visual experiences by touch experiences.

      2. If we are careful in our reasoning to avoid fallacies and other faulty logic, then reasoning can be a most reliable source of knowledge also.

III. The nature of knowledge.
- A. Three requirements for knowing any proposition is true or false.
  1. The objective requirement: the proposition must really be true.
  2. The subjective requirement: I must also believe it.
  3. The evidence requirement: requirements 1 and 2 are not enough—they are merely "true belief." We must have evidence that the proposition is true. But how much evidence?
     a. Some evidence would not be enough.
     b. All the evidence there is makes too great a demand on knowledge—would we ever know anything if this were our standard?
     c. Enough evidence? But what constitutes enough—this is too vague.
     d. Conclusive evidence? But can we establish what would constitute evidence that is conclusive?
- B. The strong and weak senses of "know."
  1. The weak sense has three criteria:
     a. I believe the proposition is true.
     b. I have good grounds on which to base my belief.
     c. The belief is indeed true.
     d. Much of our knowledge is in the weak sense.
     e. One problem is that we could be wrong in assuming that we know a proposition in this way since we often do not verify what we claim to know in the weak sense right away. Some event could occur that would nullify our claim to knowledge.
  2. The strong sense of "know" is the sense most philosophers and scientists are interested in—is there any certain knowledge? The criteria for this sense of "know" are:
     a. The proposition must be true.
     b. I must believe it.
     c. I must have absolutely conclusive evidence that it is true.
- C. Can we know any of the types of propositions in the strong sense?
  1. Analytic propositions can be known to be true or false in the strong sense because they are self-evident; that is, no further evidence is needed, and they fulfill all three requirements.
  2. We can also know internal sense propositions in the strong sense because the only evidence we need is having the pain,

belief, thought, or feeling. No further evidence is needed for us to know that any internal sense proposition we state about our own internal states is true.

   3. External sense or empirical propositions. Philosophers are not agreed on this type of proposition.

     a. Some state that we can never know any such proposition in the strong sense.

     b. Others argue that when optimum conditions are in effect for "knowing" such propositions to be true or false, it would be nonsensical to state that we still have doubts or only believe that these propositions are true or false.

     c. We cannot know the propositions "God exists" or "God does not exist" in either the weak or the strong sense, which is why we all begin as epistemological agnostics.

D. Moral propositions are more difficult to decide on because of the added problem of value judgments or moral prescriptions.

   1. In my opinion, some can be known in the weak sense to be true.

   2. A few can also be known to be true in the strong sense, such as those having to do with rape and child molestation.

   3. However, further examination, analysis, critical evaluation, and class discussion are urged concerning this type of proposition.

IV. Conclusion.

A. Knowledge is quite different from belief.

B. We can know analytic and internal sense propositions in the strong sense.

C. We can know external sense or empirical propositions in both the weak and the strong senses, depending on the proposition.

D. In my opinion we can also know moral propositions in the same way as external sense propositions.

Additional Questions and Activities for Study and Discussion

1. Read Shirley Jackson's short story, "The Lottery," and analyze and critically evaluate it in connection with tradition and common sense as a source of knowledge. What dangers does the story reveal in relying on tradition, common sense, and authority? What do you find good about tradition and common sense as sources and what do you find bad about them? When and how can reliability be determined for these two sources? What do you feel should have been done in the town about the lottery, and why? Have you noticed

any of our American traditions that are questionable? Which and why? Which of our traditions do you find to be meaningful and helpful and why? How can we constantly evaluate traditions and common sense so that as sources of knowledge they can be most reliable?

2. The words "know" and "knowledge" are used by Arthur Miller in two of his plays, *Death of a Salesman* and *After the Fall*. At the end of the first play, Biff, Willy's son, says that Willy didn't *know* who he was; he also said that he (Biff) knew who *he* was. What did he mean by these statements? What part does knowledge or the lack of it play in the events that occur in the play? Give detailed examples and illustrations to support your answer. At the end of the second play, Quentin says he *knows* several things: that we are very dangerous, that we know how to kill, that the people who built the concentration camps during World War II were his brothers and so were the victims who died there, and that love is not all or enough and neither is knowing. What does he mean by all these? Do you feel that he is right or wrong in his statements? Why? To what extent is the entire play really Quentin's search for knowledge and the truth about himself, others and the world? Why? Give examples from the play to support your position.

3. Do extensive research on intuition as a source of knowledge, reading Henri Bergson's theories on that subject as well as others, and analyze and critically evaluate it fully as a reliable or unreliable source of knowledge. To what extent to do you think there is such a source of knowledge, or to what extent do you think there is such a source of knowledge, or to what extent do you feel it is just part of sense experience and reasoning? Why? Give examples from your own experience in your thinking, imagining, wondering, and so on, that would support your views on intuition. Analyze and critically evaluate "women's intuition." Do you believe that women are generally more intuitive than men? Why or why not? What does "intuition" really mean when used in this latter sense?

4. Read Chapter 11 of John Hospers' *An Introduction to Philosophical Analysis,* and analyze and critically evaluate the significance and importance, or lack of them, of the principles of logic. State the principles clearly and give concrete examples of how they form the basis of all knowledge and reasoning. To what extent do you find them to be ultimate? Why? To what extent do you feel they require faith on the part of anyone who believes them to be true? To what extent is believing and knowing these principles similar or dissimilar to believing in and knowing God exists? Answer in detail and support your answer with evidence, reasoning, and ex-

amples as much as you can. Show how you use all three principles in your everyday thoughts and activities.

5. Show how all of us use authority as a source of knowledge and give several examples of authority that you depend on and also how one can guard against unreliable authority. Give several examples of unreliable authority that you can find in everyday life. Why are they unreliable, and to what extent do you feel people generally accept authority without question? In this connection, look up all the material you can find on the Milgrim experiment or read George Orwell's *1984* and show how authority can be used to give people false knowledge.

6. To what extent do you believe that faith and revelation are reliable sources of knowledge? If you believe that they are, then how do you answer the criticisms leveled at them? Be sure that you answer such criticisms in detail. If you do not believe that they are reliable, then tell why in detail, giving examples wherever you can. To what extent does it make a difference whether or not the revelation is private?

7. Fully discuss, analyze, and critically evaluate moral propositions and whether or not they can be known in either of the two senses. Give full evidence and arguments to support your point of view, and be sure to present which moral propositions you believe can be known in either sense, if any. You may do any research you wish examining other philosophers' points of view on this issue.

8. Argue as fully as you can, analyze, and evaluate the two propositions, "God exists" and "God does not exist," as to whether or not they can be known in either sense. Give the strongest evidence and reasoning to support whichever point of view you take. Can anyone say that he or she can *know* in any sense that either proposition is true? Why and how or why not and how not? Show in detail how these two propositions differ from "I believe that God exists" and "I believe that God does not exist." Do you agree that all human beings start from a position of epistemological agnosticism (define the phrase carefully) where the first two propositions are concerned? Why or why not?

9. Tell which of the following propositions can be known to be true or false in either the weak or strong sense and which ones can only be believed. Be sure to give reasons for your answers:

> There is life after death (an afterlife).
> There is life on other planets.
> I think I've been wrong about you.
> There is a heart in my body.
> A rectangle is not a circle.
> My dogs are in the backyard at home (said while I'm at work).

> I believe there's an afterlife.
> The earth is flat.
> I love my grandchild.
> All married women are wives.
> $25 + 25 = 50$.

10. Consider the skeptic's statement that we can never really know that any external sense or empirical proposition is true because we might always be dreaming. How would you attack the position that we could be always dreaming? Do you believe this or not? Why or why not? Is there any way that any of us can tell the difference between waking states and dream states? If so, how? If not, why not?

Footnotes

1. See John Hospers, *An Introduction to Philosophical Analysis,* 2nd ed. (Englewood Cliffs, N.J.: Prentice-Hall, 1967), Chap. 11 for a fuller explanation of these principles and arguments as to why they must be considered as ultimate principles to all thinking.

2. See Eric A. Havelock, *Preface to Plato* (New York: Grosset and Dunlap, 1967), for a description of the almost impossible task of getting the Greeks to think abstractly.

3. Hospers, *An Introduction to Philosophical Analysis,* pp. 144–149.

4. Ibid., pp. 149–157.

5. Ryūnosuke Akutagawa, *Rashomon and Other Stories,* trans. Takashi Kojina (New York: Liveright, 1952).

Bibliography

Ayer, A. J. *Language, Truth, and Logic,* 2nd ed. New York: Dover, 1936.

———. *The Problem of Knowledge.* New York: St. Martin's, 1956.

Chisholm, Roderick. *Theory of Knowledge.* Englewood Cliffs, N.J.: Prentice-Hall, 1956.

Dewey, John. *The Quest for Certainty.* New York: Putnam's, 1929.

Ewing, A. C. *The Fundamental Questions of Philosophy.* London: Routledge and Kegan Paul, 1951.

Hamlyn, D. W. *The Theory of Knowledge.* Garden City, N.Y.: Anchor, 1970.

Lewis, Clarence I. *An Analysis of Knowledge and Valuation.* LaSalle, Ill.: Open Court, 1947.

Malcolm, Norman. *Knowledge and Certainty.* Englewood Cliffs, N.J.: Prentice-Hall, 1963.

Nagel, Ernest, and Richard Brandt, eds. *Meaning and Knowledge.* New York: Harcourt Brace Jovanovich, 1965.

Roth, Michael D., and Leon Galis, eds. *Knowing: Essays in the Analysis of Knowledge.* New York: Random House, 1970.

Russell, Bertrand. *The Problems of Philosophy.* London: Oxford University Press, 1959.

Santayana, George. *Scepticism and Animal Faith.* New York: Dover, 1955.

Shaffer, Jerome A. *Reality, Knowledge, and Value.* New York: Random House, 1971.

Yolton, John W. *Theory of Knowledge.* New York: Macmillan, 1965.

CHAPTER 15

Perception and the External World

As I mentioned in the last chapter, sense experience is probably the most common way in which we receive knowledge and one of the two most reliable of all the claimed sources of knowledge. I also mentioned that there are some problems with the information that we receive through our senses not always being reliable because of perceptual errors, defective sense organs, less than optimum conditions for perceiving, and illusions and hallucinations. One of the most enigmatic questions philosophers have dealt with in epistemology, or the study of knowledge, is the nature of perception and its relation to the external world. That is, when we have a perception or perceive something, exactly what are we perceiving, and how close really are our perceptions of the external world to that world as it actually exists? For the most part, this probably already appears to you as a somewhat heady thing to be investigating. Why can't we just accept the fact that "What we see is what we get" or that we simply see the world as it is and not bother with any further confusion concerning the matter?

As you will see in a moment, this is part of the view called naïve realism, which is the view that most people accept concerning perception and the external world. We will, however, see that the whole problem of perception is not that simple at all and that there are some rather disturbing questions if we take this view at face value without questioning it seriously.

Before we start to deal with the problems surrounding perception and its relationship to external reality, it is important to define a few key terms that we will be using throughout the chapter.

Definitions

PERCEPTION.   When I use the words "perceive" or "perception" in this chapter I am referring to what is perceived through any of the five external senses described in the last chapter; however, human beings are basically visual beings, and so a good deal of what I will say will concern the sense of sight. The important point to remember, however, is that "perception" refers to all five senses.

Another distinction of importance is that there are different levels of perception. Hospers divides these into three levels:

1. Perception I—the passive "drinking in" of sensations—having sensations, for example, a particular visual experience. We are always, when we are awake, perceiving myriad sensations, many of which we do not even notice or bother to interpret. Examine any one minute of time while you are awake, and you will find as you think back on the seconds that are passing that you have had and are having a number of sensations that you may notice or not. It is the nature of our senses to be constantly perceiving in this manner, as long as we are conscious beings.
2. Perception II—at this level of perception, we notice some particular thing, a tree for example, and in this way we have singled out one particular perception or set of perceptions (if we look at a tree and several parts of it for a minute, don't we have more than one perception of the tree?) to notice or to concentrate on. We do this by directing our consciousnesses toward a particular perception or set of related perceptions, and sometimes our consciousnesses are directed by the fact that the perception "intrudes" on our perception I. For example, if a dog barks, our attention may be drawn to it, which means we notice it.
3. Perception III—at this level, we not only have passive sensations and we not only notice them, but we also somehow verify or see them correctly; that is, by combining perception I and perception II, we get perception III, which involves seeing something, noticing it, and then interpreting what we see and notice correctly.[1]

For example, we are standing in an open field "drinking in" many sensations (hundreds or thousands?)—the firmness of the ground on which we are standing, the trees, the grass, the bees buzzing, the birds chirping, the warmth and light of the sun, the sound of the wind in the trees, the smell of flowers—this is perception I, essentially. We hear a dog bark, and we notice it in the left part of our visual field—this is perception II. We then interpret what we have seen and ascribe the noise we heard to the dog. We may then further interpret and think,

"That dog over to the left just barked." We probably don't form a proposition so strictly as that just given, but something like that thought may cross our minds. We may then ask why the dog is barking, and we will move on to more perceptions. The process is much more complex than what has just been described, but at least you can get an idea of the distinctions that must be made among the three levels of perception.

PHYSICAL OBJECT.   This phrase is used to refer to any object that occupies space and is physical in nature, that is, something that is made up of matter and energy in some sort of combination. It is presumed to exist in the external world whether or not we perceive it and is considered not to be merely in our minds, but "out there." Such things as tables, chairs, clouds, houses, trees, plants, our bodies, animals, and mountains are physical objects.

SENSE DATA.   These are not physical objects, but rather our perceptions or experiences *of* them. In other words, I am distinguishing between the table in front of me in this room and my perception or experience of the table—its length, width, four-leggedness, hardness, color, shape, the fact that I can lay my pencil on it, and so on.

REALISM.   There exists a physical world that is real, and our perceptions of it are essentially accurate because of its essential stability. In this theory, what we perceive is the physical world and the physical objects in it.

IDEALISM.   I have already defined this in Chapter 3, but for the purposes of this chapter, idealism, especially as it is found in the theories of George Berkeley, is the theory that what we actually perceive is our experiences and nothing else but our experiences. Berkeley even denies that a physical world or physical objects exist separately from our perceptions (experiences).

PHENOMENALISM.   This theory of perception states that there is a physical world and physical objects, but we never experience either directly; what we perceive is our sense data, that is, our experiences of them. This is kind of a middle ground between realism and idealism.

EMPIRICISM.   This is the theory that *all* knowledge comes from sense experience and that there is no such thing as innate ideas or ideas that have not come from experience. Interestingly, John Locke, David Hume, and George Berkeley all started out as empiricists. Berkeley just went one step farther, which is why we call him an idealist. Locke and Hume remain two of the most important empiricists in the history of philosophy. Realism is the most closely related theory of perception to empiricism.

Naïve Realism

Now that we have appropriate distinctions and definitions under our belts, so to speak, it is important to get on with how we perceive external reality or the physical world, and also what exactly we do perceive. Most people will probably ask, "What's so difficult about that?" There is a physical world outside us and we perceive it as it is—that's how we know it, in fact. This view is called essentially "naïve realism" and involves five beliefs.

THE FIVE BELIEFS OF NAÏVE REALISM

1. There is an external world of physical objects.
2. We can know propositions about this world through our sense experience.
3. This world and its objects exist independently of our perceptions— the external world exists unperceived.
4. We perceive the external world pretty much as it really is.
5. Our perceptions or experiences of this external world are somehow caused by it and the physical objects in it.[2]

These beliefs should all sound or appear to be pretty familiar to most readers in that they all pretty much describe how people, in general, feel about the external world and our perceptions of it. However, each of these beliefs has been attacked and criticized by many philosophers who have thought systematically about them. Remember, as philosophy students we are interested in the truths about reality and our experiences of it, not in just accepting common or naïve beliefs about how things are; therefore, let us examine some of these criticisms of naïve realism to see what they reveal about perception.

CRITICISMS OF NAÏVE REALISM

DEPENDENCY ON SENSE ORGANS.   Isn't what we perceive dependent at least somewhat on the nature of our sense organs? What if all humans were color blind? What if we had eyes in the sides of our heads like horses? What if we could hear only high-pitched sounds? What if we were all blind? If anything were seriously different in our sense organs, wouldn't the world and external reality appear different to us? We know that we don't perceive everything that other beings, such as insects, animals, and birds can; are we then really able to perceive the external world with any accuracy at all? This certainly throws doubt on beliefs 2, 4, and 5.

ILLUSIONS.   Even with our sense organs being the way they are, there are many illusions where we think we perceive one thing, but it's really another. I already mentioned the mountains looking purple in the distance, but green or brown up close, and the illusion of water in the road ahead being caused by heat waves when there actually is no water there. If we immerse a rod or stick in water, it looks bent. We really do have these perceptions, and yet they are really not the way things are; the stick, for example is not really bent at all even though that is what we perceive.

HALLUCINATIONS.   Sometimes we perceive things that aren't even there. A person with *delirium tremens* (D.T.s) caused by excessive drinking may see bats or rats climbing up the walls when there is really nothing there. If you press the side of your eyeball while you are looking at an object, you will see two objects instead of one. You may hear the phone ring when it really did not ring, just because you are expecting a call. These are not just illusions having to do with things that are already there that we do not perceive as they are; these are perceptions (real perceptions) of things that are not there at all.

CONSTANT DECEPTION?   If we are deceived in some situations, how do we know that we are not being deceived in many more that we are not aware of; in fact, how do we know we are not being deceived most of the time or all of the time?

René Descartes when he was using his creative skepticism (see Chapter 2), and got to his doubts about his senses being deceived, wondered how he could know that he was not being constantly deceived by some evil genius or demon who was in charge of ordering his perceptions. Further, as I suggested in the additional questions in the last chapter, maybe we are really living in a dream world and will someday wake up to find that all our perceptions and experiences were part of a lengthy dream.

We all know how real our dreams appear to us while we are having them. When, for example, we perceive a mountain in our dream, the *perception* is real, isn't it? We really do have it, don't we? Needless to say, naïve realism may be comforting, but there are several problems with it that constitute a challenge to this rather simple view of something obviously more complex than when we first thought about it.

Representative Realism

JOHN LOCKE AND HIS THEORIES

John Locke, the father of modern-day empiricism, who has already been discussed in Chapter 3, was also disturbed by these difficulties, especially the ones dealing with the dependency of our experience of reality on our sense organs. To deal with these problems, he established a theory called "representative realism."

Being an empiricist, Locke, of course, accepted without question the existence of a physical world but felt that our experiences of it were really representations or resemblances of what really exists out there. For example, there is a chair in this room, and I am standing in front of it and perceiving it. What I perceive, my experience or perception of the chair, *resembles or represents* the chair as it actually is. This representation or resemblance is accurate because the chair in some way causes me to see what I see; that is, there are some qualities that reside in the chair and some that reside in my senses and in me that bring this representation about. These two different sets of qualities or attributes, Locke called primary and secondary.

PRIMARY QUALITIES.   Locke felt that certain qualities, properties, or attributes are really in any physical object that causes us to see the object as it really is. The object has these qualities whether we are perceiving it or not. Locke described these qualities as size, shape, height, and weight. These qualities can be dealt with in science because they can be measured—they are a part of or intrinsic to the object itself.

SECONDARY QUALITIES.   But there are other qualities, such as smell, taste, color, and a tactile quality (smoothness of surface, for example) that seem much more dependent on our senses for their existence. For example, if a human being is color blind, then he cannot see certain colors even though others can. Also, color varies whether there is bright sunlight, less light, or darkness. Other perceptions, such as smell and taste, also will depend on the condition of our organs of taste and smell and also what we have tasted or smelled just prior to our present perception. For example, a piece of candy will taste sweeter if we have just tasted something sour than it will if we have just eaten some ice cream.

Because of these differences and the heavy dependency on human sense organs, Locke felt that these were secondary qualities that resided within human beings, somehow in their sensory apparatus and brains. He felt that these secondary qualities were not in objects at all, but that there were "powers" in objects that could produce in perceivers sensations of color, sweetness, smoothness of touch, and so on. How then do we perceive primary qualities that do exist in objects themselves? Locke felt that physical objects somehow caused us to have sense experiences or perceptions that resembled their primary qualities. For example, the table that is 6 feet long, 3 feet wide, four-legged, and holds the book we just laid on it enables us to have a 6 feet long, 3 feet wide, four-legged book-holding perception of it. In some ways, it's as if our perception of it is like a photograph of a physical object when compared with the real thing.

CRITICISMS OF LOCKE'S THEORIES

As we have been going over these, you have probably had some questions concerning Locke's admirable attempt to relate perceptions to a physical world that he accepted without question. There are indeed many problems with his theories, which George Berkeley set forth in detail.

VARIABILITY.   Berkeley first agreed with Locke that the qualities he called secondary indeed varied from person to person, depending on their different sense organs and on the conditions (e.g., bright light or darkness) under which they were perceived. However, Berkeley also argued that primary qualities varied no less than did secondary qualities. For example, Berkeley stated that a book looks different in shape and size depending on whether you are holding it in your hand, looking down on it, looking at it from 3 feet away, and looking at it from 30 feet away from a corner of a room. Therefore, Berkeley argued that the difference that Locke tried to distinguish was not between primary and secondary qualities but rather between physical objects and our perceptions or sense experiences of them. In this way, Berkeley felt that *all* qualities of any physical object were dependent on our sense organs and sense experiences, not just secondary qualities.

QUALITIES ARE NOT SEPARABLE.   Berkeley argued further that Locke's so-called "primary" and "secondary qualities" could not really be separated as Locke attempted to do. How can you separate color from shape, for example? There is no such thing in reality that is not found in some shape. If you put a brush stroke of red paint on a wall, it is found in the shape of your brush stroke, isn't it? Do you ever perceive color that isn't also in some sort of shape. You don't merely see red, you see a red sweater, a red car, a red swatch of material (in a square shape), or a jagged red brush stroke. Berkeley argued that shape was really the boundary of color. With this argument, he stated that Locke's separation of primary and secondary qualities was an artificial one that really did not exist.

RESEMBLANCE.   Locke said that the reason our perceptions were accurate is that they resembled the primary qualities in the physical object. Berkeley already showed that Locke could not account for secondary qualities in this way because if these qualities did not exist in the objects themselves, but only powers to cause them, then how could resemblance take place. How could things like taste, smell, and colors resemble "powers"?

Berkeley went on to say, however, that even if they did, there is absolutely no way we could ever know that our perceptions resemble physical objects or their qualities in any way. To be able to prove Locke's theory of resemblance, we would have to be able to compare the physical object with our perceptions of it, but how could that be done? How can I compare my perceptions of the table in front of me with the table as it is, *unperceived?* Since the only way we can know anything about the table is through our perceptions (a basic tenet of empiricism), how can we compare our perceptions of it with the table itself unperceived? Obviously, this is impossible, and Berkeley argued, then, that the only resemblances we can ever validly discuss are those between and among perceptions and experiences. That is, I can compare my perceptions of the table in front of me today with the table in front of me yesterday (the same table), but I can in no way whatsoever compare my perceptions of it on either occasion with the table itself, unperceived. Therefore, Locke's theory of resemblances is an empty theory that cannot be verified in any way.

CAUSATION.   Locke also theorized that the reason we had perceptions is that physical objects and the external world *caused* us to have them in some way. He said there were powers in them that caused us to perceive secondary qualities, such as taste, smell, and color, and obviously he thought there were primary qualities in the object that caused us to perceive things like size and shape. However, if the only thing we can perceive are our perceptions or sense experiences, and if we cannot examine physical objects unperceived to see how they cause us to perceive them, then this theory is empty also. Causes are sometimes hard to determine or may even be hard to perceive (they may have occurred, for example, when there is no one around to perceive them), but usually we can see how my arm and hands can cause the pool cue to move and how the cue then causes the billiard ball to move. However, to say that A causes B, we must be able to experience both A and B to see the correlation between the two.

Even if we theorize that somehow physical objects cause us to perceive them, how could this causation work? Do they send out pictures? Do they emit electrical vibrations? Again as in Chapter 3, how can physical things cause mental images or mental things, such as sense perceptions? At any rate, there is absolutely no way to check, so Locke's theory for the causation of perceptions is also empty.

Berkeleian Idealism

Berkeley might have summed up his attack on Locke by saying,

> Locke . . . is committed to skepticism regarding a physical world: he cannot know that it exists, even if it does; and he is inconsistent, because he assumes that it exists and makes claims concerning it yet cuts himself off from the possibility of knowing it—which invalidates the arguments about physical objects and their qualities that he had given just before.[3]

Berkeley then concludes that because of his refutation of Locke's theory of representative realism that no good reason exists for us to say that a physical world or physical objects exist outside of our minds, since there is no real way to check this. He then moves to the startling conclusion that the so-called "physical" world and the "physical" objects in it do *not* exist at all! All that exists, according to Berkeley, are minds and their experiences.

At this point, we must feel that Berkeley has lost his mind—no external world, no trees, tables, or people that exist outside of us? How can this be? First, we should, as was suggested in Chapter 2, not reject any theory of reality—no matter how strange—out of hand without investigating it; we never know when we might learn something about the nature of reality or knowledge when we examine a theory that may seem to us strange at first glance. Second, we should understand what Berkeley is really claiming here. He is not saying that trees, tables, or people do not exist; he is saying that there are no physical objects apart from minds and that these "things" we call physical objects are really families or patterns of sense experiences, and we can never get away from our minds and their experiences, so why should we presume there is a physical world with physical objects in it? Let us realize that all we ever perceive are our experiences which occur most of the time in an orderly pattern, sequence, or relationship. Let us look now at Berkeley's arguments concerning his theories.

THE NATURE OF EXPERIENCES

If we again consider this now-famous (or infamous) table that I have had in front of me several times in this chapter, we will find that my experience of it has the following characteristics:

SYSTEMATIC VARIATION.   As I stand over it, move away from it to either side of it, back from it, or around it, its apparent size and shape vary systematically with my angle of vision and my distance far from or close to it. As I repeatedly move away or close to it or change my angle of vision, my experiences of it change in an orderly fashion, not haphazardly. After I have done this a number of times, I can predict how my experiences will vary and this predictability can be tested again and again.

RESEMBLANCE OF EXPERIENCES.   All of these experiences that differ as I move close to, away from, or around the table are different and varied, but they all resemble each other to the point where I will say that I am looking at the "same" table from many different angles. This kind of resemblance is verifiable and observable, unlike Locke's theory of resemblance between physical objects and my experiences of them, for this resemblance is among experiences, not between unobservable physical objects and human experiences of them.

CONTINUITY.   As long as I do not blink or turn away, there is no lack of continuity in this series of experiences; it is continuous and uninterrupted. The table experiences do not disappear and reappear, but continue to persist while I am having them.

CENTER OF EXPERIENCES.   Another quality that my experiences of the table have is that there is an apparent center from which all changes progress as I move about. My perceptions of the table do not fly around the room but seem to have a center from which they change in an orderly manner.

SEEING IS VERIFIABLE BY TOUCHING.   If I have any doubts that I might really be experiencing a mirror image or some kind of projection of the table, I can approach it and touch it, thus verifying my visual experiences.

All these observations led Berkeley to state without a doubt that a set of experiences, like my experiences with the table, forms an orderly series; he then concluded that "A physical object is nothing more or less than a *family of sense experiences.*"[4]

HALLUCINATIONS, ILLUSIONS, AND DREAMS

If all we can perceive are experiences and there are no physical objects, then how can we distinguish between these so-called "physical objects as families of experiences" and other mental events such as hallucinations, illusions, and dreams? If we assume that there is a physical world and objects, we can say that our experiences are of them and that hallucinations, illusions, and dreams are of something else. However, if all of our experiences are in our minds, then how can we distinguish the "physical object" ones from the dream, illusionary, and hallucinatory ones? Actually, Berkeley claimed that his theories really explained hallucinations, illusions, and dreams better than realism did. Let us examine how he distinguished between these two types of perceptual experiences.

HALLUCINATIONS.   According to Berkeley, the way we can tell a hallucination from a veridical ("true" perception) experience is to see if it does or does not fit in with a family of sense experiences.[5] If it is what Hospers calls "wild," that is, if it does not fit in with one of the families of sense experiences, then it is a hallucination. For example, if after taking a drug, I see my famous table expanding to twice its size and then contracting back to its original size, I know that it does not fit in with the family of sense experiences I associate with tables, and I presume I am having a hallucination. It is a "wild" experience; it simply does not fit in with the appropriate family or relate actually to most sense experiences that I have concerning any object like a table (any physical object). Berkeley also put the greatest emphasis on touch experiences as the confirmation of visual experiences that are veridical. If I think that I see two books on the table, but I can feel only one, then I am having some sort of hallucination because touch is the final test of whether there are really two books or one before me.

ILLUSIONS.   Sometimes our sense experiences belong to a family, unlike hallucinations. For example, when we put a stick in the water and it appears bent (the part under water), we cannot say that this is a hallucination because it means to be a part of regular perceptual stick experiences. However, when we run our hands down the stick, we feel that it is in fact straight. Further, we are able to account for its bent look because science has discovered information concerning refraction.

DREAMS.   How do we distinguish between families of sense experiences and dreams, which often involve families of sense experiences as well. Hospers discusses many possible criteria for distinguishing dream states from waking states but finally concludes that what is really distinctive of dream experiences is that they don't "fit in."[6] Our waking states form an ordered pattern. For example, most of our days are spent in a similar pattern. We have experiences at home; then we go to school or work and have those types of experiences; then we return home for more of the home types of experiences. We, of course, may have other experiences, such as "going out to dinner" experiences and so on. Each set of these experiences is a family of its own and all form a larger family that constitutes our daily lives.

Interrupting this orderly pattern and not fitting in with it are the dream states we have, most often at night when we are asleep. We may dream about a dead relative, or we may dream we are in some house that we have never seen; and we may do and say things that do not make sense to us after we wake up. We may move in slow motion, which we never can do when we are awake, and so on. If we tried to state that all life is a dream, that there are no waking states, but only dream states, then we would blur the distinction between dreaming and waking and also try to say that two dissimilar things (dream and waking states) are really similar, which would not square with our experiences.

BERKELEY'S ARGUMENTS
ON PERCEPTION AND EXISTENCE

All these arguments led Berkeley to state that "to be is to be perceived"; that is, if something is not perceived by some sentient being (some being who is able to sense and have perceptions), then there is no evidence that it exists. Berkeley is the philosopher who posed the famous "tree falling in the forest" question. He asked that if a tree falls in the forest, and there is no being there who can hear, then does the tree make a sound? Part of the problem is a verbal one having to do with the word "sound." If by this word one means "sound waves," then it is possible (if you are not Berkeley) for the tree to make sound waves when it falls. However, if you take the word to mean "sound experience," then of course it could not make a "sound" if there were no sentient being to hear or experience it; that is, there would be no sound *experience*. Even with this distinction cleared up, Berkeley would say that we have no proof that there are even sound waves because all we can ever know or experience are our experiences. We never hear sound waves; we only have sound experiences—we only hear the sound of the tree crashing to the ground.

What then can reality be like if it or any part of it can only *be there* if someone perceives it: Does this mean that when no one in your house is at home, your house and all the objects in it do not exist? But what accounts for the orderliness of our perceptions that Berkeley has already agreed that they have? How is it that whenever we arrive at a certain place—our street, and our lot—that there is a house standing on it fully furnished? How could this order exist if it were constantly disappearing whenever no sentient being was around? Certainly, there have to be times when there is no sentient being around—what happens and how?

Some critics of Berkeley's view have said, suppose that you set up a video and audio tape machine in a room at home or at work and turn it on and tape the room when no sentient beings are there. Then suppose that everyone who is sentient leaves the room with the TV camera and tape machine going. After an hour, we all come back, rewind the tape, and project it on a monitor. We can then perceive the room experiences as having existed while no one perceived them. Berkeley and other idealists would probably argue that all these things—setting up the TV camera and video tape machine, turning it on, leaving the room, returning to the room, running the tape, and observing what is on it—are merely more experiences and not proof of an external world.[7] How they would account for what we see after the tape is rewound and run forward—a room with things in it—I don't know. Would they consider it a hallucination or an illusion?

Other than these possibilities, what could account for our seeing the room with all its things? True, the seeing of the pictures is also an experience, but what happened in the gap between the time we were in the room and when we came back? Didn't the camera record a room and things that were, at least for a time, not perceived by any sentient being? Berkeley would not doubt this, but he would account for it in a different way, as we shall see shortly. Let us look now at his essential arguments for there being no physical world or objects.

WEAK AND STRONG IDEALISM.   Hospers characterizes the two implications of Berkeley's claims and arguments as weak and strong idealism. Weak idealism states that even if physical objects do exist unperceived, we have no reason for believing that they do—we could not know if they do, but they still could whether or not we knew it. Strong idealism states that physical objects do not exist at all, nor does a physical world.[8] Berkeley even goes so far as to state that it is contradictory to say that physical objects exist. Let us look at his basic logic, again as characterized by Hospers.

BERKLEY'S LOGIC.   Hospers states Berkeley's logic in the form of two syllogisms:

1. We do have acquaintance with physical objects.
2. All we can have acquaintance with is experiences.
3. Therefore, physical objects are experiences (that is, families of experiences).

Most of us would accept the truth of (1), and (2) is the basic tenet of empiricism, which, again, most of us accept, and certainly what Locke and Berkeley both accepted. Now (3) becomes the first premise of the second syllogism, as follows:

3. Physical objects are experiences.
4. Experiences cannot exist unexperienced.
5. Therefore, physical objects cannot exist unexperienced.[9]

CAUSATION. Before presenting criticisms to Berkeley's arguments, let us look at one more necessary aspect of his theory, and that is what causes sense experiences. Remember that Locke believed that sense experiences were caused by physical objects in some way because they had certain qualities in them and powers to cause other qualities. Most of us also believe that the reason we have experiences of an external world and its physical objects is because they really to exist for us to perceive. We see a table or a tree because they are there actually existent in reality whether or not we perceive them. We may not see them as they actually are, but we do see them in some way, and that is because they actually do exist and are present for us to see.

Since Berkeley has effectively refuted Locke's arguments for the causes of sense experiences and since he has eliminated the physical world and all physical objects from his theories, then how does he account for the fact that our sense experiences are ordered and patternlike (he, remember, fully accepts this view in his arguments for physical objects being families of sense experiences)? That is, when we return to a certain area at our workplace each day, there is a room full of physical objects pretty much as we have left them. How can this be if there is no sentient being to observe them when we are not there? As Hospers points out, Berkeley might have simply said,

> Physical objects are families of sense-experiences, as I have shown in my arguments. In any other sense, they do not exist; indeed, to say that they did would involve self-contradiction. Causality is a relation among sense-experiences; the concept of cause cannot be employed to connect sense-experiences with anything besides other sense-experiences. Therefore, it cannot be used to connect sense-experiences with non-observable causes-of-sense-experiences. Period.[10]

However, Berkeley did not say this; instead, he stated that there is a sentient being who is always observing all our experiences and that is God, who causes us to have our experiences and even is responsible for giving them the order they have. He has created this real world of sense experiences and he constantly perceives it, and in this way, it is there for us to perceive. The reason, for example, that we see the room and its things after we have used the TV camera and video tape machine and see the results on our TV monitor is that God continued to perceive the room and its contents when we were not perceiving it, thus allowing us to perceive it as an ordered family of experiences when we saw the tape. What we really have assumed is a physical world, then, is really a world of families of sense experience caused and perceived by God.

CRITICISMS OF BERKELEY'S ARGUMENTS

HIS THEORY OF CAUSATION. Berkeley's second premise was "All we can have acquaintance with is experiences," but what is our experience of God? Berkeley posited God as a cause of our experiences, and yet we have no direct experience of God. We can have experiences of people talking about Him or we can experience reading about Him, but what is our actual experience of Him? Berkeley has, in effect, refuted one of his main arguments by his own logic. If he insists that we can know God even though we cannot experience Him directly—that is, that God is the one being beyond our sense experiences—then why can't we presume the existence of physical objects beyond sense experiences, that is, unperceived. If you open the door for one thing that can exist unperceived, then you open it for all things.

Further, even if Berkeley had not posited God as cause, there would be a problem with the existence of other minds. If all I can know are my experiences, then how can I know that other minds exist? I have experiences of what I used to call physical objects because I can perceive them, but how can I perceive other minds? Yet Berkeley asserts that all that exists is minds and their experiences. Maybe all that exists is *my* mind and its experiences, which is called "solipsism." This is what Berkeley's logic brings us to if we follow it out.

This, of course, would be absurd. Why would I be writing this book for other humans with minds to read, if there were only my mind and its experiences? Berkeley said that "to be is to be perceived" applied only to physical objects not to other minds, but as with the God positing, if you let minds in unperceived, then why not physical objects? Besides, how can Berkeley or any of us say that we *know* that other minds exist when we have no sense experiences of them. It is true that we hear people talking (sense experience) and we read what they have written (sense experience), but those sense experiences are different from that of someone's mind.

THINKING OF PHYSICAL OBJECTS. Berkeley implied throughout his arguments and actually stated "Physical objects cannot be thought of as existing apart from a thinking mind," which is an ambiguous statement. If he means that we cannot have thoughts about such objects or our experiences of them without a thinking mind, he is quite right. As I pointed out in the "tree falling in the forest" example, there could be no sound *experience* without an experiencer. In the same way, there could be no thoughts about a physical world and objects without a mind. However, it is certainly possible to think about a physical world and objects existing without any mind being present to observe them—Locke did this and so do we constantly; that is where naïve realism came from, and most of us accept that view until we investigate further. Of course, just because we can think of them as existing apart from our perception of them does not mean that they exist in reality, but neither does it mean that they cannot exist *unless* we do think of them.[11]

BERKELEY'S SECOND AND THIRD PREMISES.   As we examine Berkeley's two syllogisms, we discover that there is a weakness in two of his premises—2 and 3. In premise 2, he states, *"All* we can have acquaintance with is experiences." But this is an assumption of radical empiricism; obviously we have acquaintance with our experiences—they are ours, aren't they? However, this does not mean that we cannot also have acquaintance with physical objects that we may also be experiencing. We may have acquaintance with physical objects as well as our own experience; in fact, that assumption provides exactly the difference between internal sense propositions and external sense or empirical propositions. We believe that the former describe things that are within us whereas the latter describe what exists outside of us.

In premise 3, Berkeley also goes too far in that he states, "Physical objects are experiences." Even if we were only acquainted with experiences, that does not mean that physical objects are only experiences. They, of course, could exist even if we did not experience them. It is true that we may not know in the *strong sense* that physical objects exist unperceived, but they still could exist whether we know for certain or not. As we said in Chapter 13, propositions can be true or false whether we know that they are or not.

STRONG AND WEAK IDEALISM.   These criticisms certainly bring into question Berkeley's commitment to strong idealism that states that there is no way that physical objects or a physical world could exist. Obviously, there could be a physical world. By saying that there could be a God and other minds, Berkeley has certainly left the door open to there being a physical world. But what about weak idealism, that even if physical objects exist, we have no reason for believing they do? Do we really have *no* reason? If we start a fire in the fireplace and leave the room for a period of time and then return and find the fire has burned down to embers and ashes, isn't this at least some evidence that the physical world exists unperceived (assuming that there was no sentient being in the room while the fire burned down)? Further, isn't

Berkeley's God theory of causation really much harder to accept than the assumption that a physical world exists unperceived, and when we are present, then we do indeed perceive it? It is certainly possible that God could have constructed a world of sense experiences, perceives it constantly, and orders it for us to perceive—after all, God is considered all powerful—but given scientific investigation and its results, isn't this view of the world and our perception of it, really much more farfetched than believing that it exists unperceived?

It seems to me, and I'm sure to you, a much better explanation for order in the world that there is a world that exists out there and that it is full of physical objects and events that are observable by us through our five senses, than that some supernatural being has perceptions that we can also perceive. Even if we buy the theory, how could we perceive someone else's (even God's) perceptions? We cannot even perceive each other's, so how could we perceive God's?

CONCLUSIONS

What are we to make of all this discussion? Should we assume that "philosophy makes you crazy" and that Berkeley is just another of its victims? First, we have learned a great deal about the complexity of perceiving an assumed external reality to the point where we can never really return to naïve realism. Second, Berkeley certainly refuted most of Locke's theories about how we perceive the external world, even if he did not successfully refute the external world or physical objects. We cannot return to Locke's theories, because they have serious lacks and problems with them; nor can we (and most of us do not want to) accept Berkeley's farfetched theories about our perceptions being caused by God's ordered perceptions. We still do not know what we perceive, how we perceive, and the causes of our perceptions. There is a third theory called phenomenalism, which tries to bridge the differences between realism and idealism; let us look at it now.

Phenomenalism

In idealism, at least in Berkeley's idealism, "to be is to be perceived" is the major tenet; that is, existence is tied to the presence of some sort of sentient being. Phenomenalism, however, changes Berkeley's statement to "to be is to be perceivable," which means that there are not just actual sense experiences, as Berkeley insisted, which are found in families or patterns, but *possible* sense experiences that any sentient being could have if he or she were to be in a certain place at a certain time. For example, Berkeley implied that if no sentient being were present in the room, it would not exist—this at least was the implication until he posited God as constantly perceiving the world. The phenomenalist, however, states that if a sentient being were to approach the area where the room is, he or she would perceive it and everything in it. The room provides a *possibility* of perceptions; it exists even when it is not perceived, but when its "possibilities are realized," then it can be perceived. Phenomenalists, then, do not deny that a physical world and objects exist; neither do they claim to know what it is *really* like. They claim that it must exist for us to be able to perceive it, but what they say we perceive is not physical objects directly; rather, it is something they have called "sense data."

LEVELS OF REALITY

Phenomenalists describe three levels of reality:

1. There is the perceiver, experiencer, or knower—a sentient being.
2. There is the act of perceiving or the process they call sensation (for example, the seeing of a color).
3. Then there is the "thing or object perceived," and this is where the complications begin.

Locke said that we perceive physical objects in a physical world although he would not deny that we also perceive mental things (hallucinations, illusions, dreams, our own ideas, thoughts, imaginings, and so on). Berkeley, on the other hand, said that we could only perceive our experiences and that physical objects and the world did not exist except as our experiences. Phenomenalists say that there are physical objects and the physical world, that there are perceivers, and that there are the sense data they perceive. As Locke did, they feel that the physical world and its objects can be perceived, but they feel that they can be perceived only *indirectly;* that is, we may be sensing a physical object, but all we ever really perceive are our sense data of it.

Sense data may be related to a physical object or they may be hallucinatory, illusory, dream perceptions, or some other mental perception not directly connected to a physical object (for example, a thought, feeling, or imagining). However, the point the phenomenalist makes is that whatever we say we perceive—physical object, dream, hallucination, thought, feeling—what we actually perceive are sense data. Let us examine the process of perception from the phenomenalist's point of view.

WHAT WE PERCEIVE

Let's assume we are back in the room with my famous table, and it is on a raised platform at the front of the room. I am perceiving it, and I ask everyone else in the room to direct their attention to it also (Isn't this exciting?). Now the first thing the phenomenalist will say is that there are as many sense data of that table as there are perceptions of it. If there are twenty of us in the room, then there are at least, numerically, twenty different perceptions of the table. Second, we all perceive the table from different angles and different distances. I am standing over it, Ruth is way back in the corner of the room, and Roger is sitting in front of and a little below it.

We would all agree that we are seeing the same table or the same physical object; however, the phenomenalist would say that we are not seeing the same sense data. From my position, I can only see its top; from Ruth's position, she can only see perhaps two legs and a diamond-shaped top and front; from Roger's position he can see two legs, parts of the other two legs, the front of the table, and maybe a little of the top's underside. The phenomenalist would argue that what we are all *actually* seeing is various sense data of the table but not the table itself directly.

Further, when we perceive something and there is no physical object, such as hallucinations, illusions, or dream perceptions, we are still sensing sense data, only there is no relationship of it to physical objects. For example, if we are having a hallucination of bats or rats climbing up the walls of our room because we have the D.T.s, there may be no physical objects (bats or rats), but we are certainly perceiving rats and bats; that is, we are perceiving sense data rats and bats. If we have a dream that we are flying through the air unassisted, then we truly perceive this event—we really do have the perception—but there are no actual physical objects related to the sense data we see.

Even when there is a physical object present and we perceive an illusion, such as the bent stick in water, we are actually perceiving the bentness of the stick; that is, we actually perceive that particular sense data even though the stick is not really bent. When we press our eyeballs and see two books before us, we really do see two books; that is, we perceive two sense data of the actual one book. Further, if we walk around our famous table and look at various angles and aspects of it, we perceive myriad sense data that may all be related to actual parts of the table. We see the legs, one at a time; we see the table top, the underside, the corners, the front, back, and side. (By the way, do you realize we never see any physical object completely? We can only see parts of it at any one time.) All these sense data, when put together, would allow us to describe the table, or at least all our sense data of the table.

EVALUATION OF THIS THEORY

This would seem to be a more reasonable theory of perception and the physical world than naïve realism, representative realism, or idealism, since it accepts the difficulty of knowing whether our perceptions of the physical world and objects are accurate or not and the fact that we would never know it. Also, it allows for a middle point between the observation of physical objects directly, as in realism, and sense experiences only, as in idealism. It also explains quite well the fact that some of our sense experiences have no relationships to physical objects (illusions, etc.). It does have its problems, however.

RELATIONSHIPS. What is the relationship among the three levels of reality in phenomenalism? We have the perceiver, the act of perceiving, and the "thing" perceived. Further, phenomenalists say there is the physical world, sense data of it, and the act of sensing itself. Does the perceiver perceive only sense data or does he or she in fact perceive physical objects? Does the perceiver perceive the physical objects *through* his or her sense data? If so, how does that work? If not, then how does the perceiver "get to" physical objects?

Moreover, what is the relationship between sense data and physical objects? Are sense data lying all over the surface of a physical object merely waiting to be discovered? Do they lie somewhere in between the physical object and the observer, or are they found in the human mind? There seem to be no clear answers to these questions.

CAUSATION OF SENSE DATA. Next, what causes sense data? If the physical object is out there, does light striking it cause its qualities to impinge themselves on our sensory apparatus (the apparatus of our five senses) and then through seeing, noticing, and interpreting experiences through our minds, do we then *perceive* the physical object?

Phenomenalists do not cite God as the cause of what we perceive as Berkeley does, but then what are the causes of perception? Are sense data not caused by physical objects at all, but rather by other sense data? How would this work, and what would cause the original sense data? Would this take us back to some form of representative realism? Maybe there is a combination of causes, but what would that combination be?

These questions and problems all show phenomenalism to be an unproved theory of perception. I should stress that there is much more to this theory than I have time to present in this chapter. There is a whole discussion, for example, over the certainty of sense data–type propositions as opposed to external sense or empirical propositions. If you are interested, you might want to look up and read some of the texts suggested in the bibliography at the end of this chapter.

Conclusions

1. We have certainly discovered that perception is a very complex process not readily understandable or provable.

2. Accepting the existence of a physical world and physical objects would seem to be the best way of explaining the order and stability of our perceptions; however, we cannot conclusively prove its existence.

3. We do not know that our perceptions are an accurate view of the physical world because we cannot (that is, it is logically impossible to) perceive it unperceived, so that we can compare it with our perceptions to see if they are accurate.

4. What we perceive is highly dependent on the way our sense organs are constructed, how well they work, and the conditions for observing the physical world.

5. We know that our sense experiences or perceptions of physical objects are not the same as the objects themselves—by nature they must be two different things.

6. We don't know what the connection between our perceptions and physical objects is, nor do we know for certain what causes us to have perceptions or to perceive things as we do.

7. We can only assume that our propositions about the physical world are accurate based on our perceptions, and we have to be careful when we are setting up criteria for perceiving the world. We need to establish optimum criteria for perceiving the world and strive to attain them to gain the greatest and clearest knowledge possible.

As you have seen, this is one of the most complicated areas of investigation in epistemology, and yet it is one of the most interesting for many philosophers and psychologists. Since so much of our lives and our knowledge is based on perception, continued investigation and research should be done to arrive at whatever truths we can about this area of philosophy.

Applying Philosophy—
Situations for Thought and Discussion

SITUATION 1

After you and your classmates have read this chapter and have done any other research on perception directed or suggested by your instructor, select some physical object or portion of the physical world to observe and perceive and describe in a detailed written report, as best you can, what process was involved in your perceiving it and how what you have described fits in with representative realism, idealism, or phenomenalism. After the reports are written, all class members should read theirs to the others and then the entire class should discuss the nature of the different processes described and see if a clear conclusion can be reached, with which everyone can agree, as to what happens when human beings "perceive the physical world."

SITUATION 2

Examine extremely carefully five areas or aspects of the physical world and evaluate them carefully and in detail as to whether or not there are primary and secondary qualities; to what extent do you think you perceive the physical world as it really is; to what extent is what you perceive dependent on *your* sense organs rather than on what is "out there"; if things look different from different angles, positions, and distances, then what constitutes the "veridical" (true) perception? To what extent are you fooled or deceived into thinking you are seeing one thing when that thing is really something else? How do you account for being fooled—what caused it? For at least one of the aspects you examine, look at some object with the naked eye and then under a microscope. Which do you feel would be the most veridical perception of the object? Why?

SITUATION 3

With the permission of your instructor, or on your own outside of class, stage a confusing and unexpected event, such as having someone come into the room and attempt to rob somebody or start a fight. Try also to tape what happens using a TV camera and a video tape machine. After the event is over, have everyone in the room write down what they saw happen and a detailed description of the person or persons who came into the room. How different were the reports? How close were they to what actually happened as recorded on the tape machine? Analyze carefully why the perceptions were different—why some were accurate and why some weren't—and what conditions affect the ability to perceive with accuracy.

Chapter Summary

    I. Definitions.
      A. Perception—that which is sensed through any of the five senses.
      B. Different levels of perception:
        1. Perception I—the passive drinking in of sensations.
        2. Perception II—noticing.
        3. Perception III—perception I plus perception II plus interpreting what is sensed and noticed correctly.
      C. Physical object—any object that occupies space and is physical in nature, that is, made up of matter and energy.
      D. Sense data—not physical objects but our perceptions or experiences *of* them, coined by phenomenalists.
      E. Realism—the theory that a real physical world exists and our perceptions of it are essentially accurate.
      F. Idealism—the theory that all that exists are minds and their experiences and that we never perceive anything else but our experiences.
      G. Phenomenalism—accepts a physical world but believes we never experience it directly and that all we ever really experience are sense data. It is a kind of middle ground between realism and idealism.
      H. Empiricism—the theory that *all* knowledge comes from sense experience.
   II. Naïve realism.
      A. This is what most people believe about the physical world and our perceptions of it.
      B. Five beliefs of naïve realism:
        1. There is an external world of physical objects.
        2. We can know propositions about this world through our sense experience.
        3. This world and its objects exist independently of our perceptions—the external world exists unperceived.
        4. We perceive the external world pretty much as it really is.

5. Our perceptions of the external world are somehow caused by it and its objects.

C. Criticisms.

1. Dependency on sense organs—what we perceive is dependent in part on our sense organs.

2. Illusions—we do have illusions.

3. Hallucinations—we sometimes perceive things that are not even there.

4. Constant deception—if we are deceived in some situations, perhaps we are deceived in all situations.

III. Representative realism.

A. This is a theory put forth by John Locke, the empiricist, who said, in effect, that what we perceive is a representation of the actual physical object that resembles it.

B. Primary qualities, according to Locke, are qualities, such as size and shape, that exist in physical objects themselves.

C. Secondary qualities are in us but are triggered by powers in the physical object. Examples of these qualities are color, taste, and tactile sensations.

D. Criticisms of Locke's theories, basically by Berkeley, are as follows:

1. Variability. Berkeley agreed that what Locke called secondary qualities varied from person to person, but Berkeley also argued that primary qualities vary in the same way.

2. Separability. Berkeley argued further that so-called "primary" and "secondary" qualities are not separable; that is, there is no color that is not found in some shape; in fact, shape is the boundary of color, according to Berkeley.

3. Resemblance. Berkeley said that Locke's theory of resemblance was not possible since we can never compare our perceptions with the world unperceived—this is logically impossible.

4. Causation. Berkeley stated that this theory was also empty because there is no way, again, we could find out how physical objects could cause us to have perceptions since we cannot perceive them unperceived.

IV. Berkeleian idealism.

A. The nature of experiences: if we consider any physical object, we discover that it has the following characteristics:

1. Systematic variation. As I move around or away from the object, its size and shape vary systematically with my angle of vision and distance.

2. Resemblance of experiences. All these experiences are different but they also resemble each other. The resemblance,

however, is among experiences not between the object and our experiences of it.

3. Continuity. As long as we do not blink or turn away, there is a continuity to our experiences.

4. Center of experiences. There is an apparent center from which all changes progress as I move about.

5. Verification by touch. Most doubts concerning visual experiences can be verified by touch experiences.

6. All these led Berkeley to state that physical objects were nothing more or less than families or patterns of sense experiences.

B. Hallucinations, illusions, and dreams.

1. Hallucinations. Berkeley says that we can tell a hallucination from a veridical perception in that hallucinations do not fit in with families of sense experiences—they are "wild."

2. Illusions. Illusions do belong to families of experiences; however, touch, here again, helps us to distinguish between these and veridical perceptions.

3. Dreams. Dreams do not fit in with our waking states even though they are often members of a family of sense experiences (in the dream itself). Our waking states form an ordered pattern within which dreams do not fit.

C. Berkeley's arguments on perception and existence.

1. Berkeley stated that "to be is to be perceived" and that there is no physical world or objects—only families of sense experiences that depend on the perceptions of sentient beings for their existence.

2. Weak and strong idealism.

   a. Weak idealism—even if physical objects exist unperceived, we have no reason to believe that they do.

   b. Strong idealism—physical objects and a physical world do not exist at all.

3. Berkeley's logic:

   a. We have acquaintance with physical objects.

   b. All we can be acquainted with is experiences.

   c. Therefore, physical objects are experiences.

   d. Experiences cannot exist unexperienced.

   e. Therefore, physical objects cannot exist unexperienced.

4. Causation. Berkeley said that God, the ultimate sentient being, has created the world of sense experiences, sustains them by constantly perceiving them, and orders our perceptions.

D. Criticisms of Berkeley's arguments.

1. His theory of causation is refuted by his claim that all we

can have acquaintance with is our experiences—what is the experience of God? If we can accept God's existence unperceived, then why not accept the existence of a physical world unperceived?

2. Even if he had not posited God, there would still be a problem with knowing other minds exist, since they cannot be experienced.

3. Thinking of physical objects. Berkeley said that physical objects could not be thought of as existing apart from thinking minds; however, this is ambiguous.
   a. If he means that we cannot think of it (or anything) without a mind, he is right.
   b. However, we can obviously think of physical objects existing whether minds exist or not—we do it all the time.

4. His second and third premises.
   a. The second is not proved—obviously we can have acquaintance with our experience, but this does not mean we cannot also be acquainted with physical objects.
   b. The third premise goes too far. Even if we were only acquainted with experiences, that does not mean that physical objects are only experiences.

5. Strong and weak idealism.
   a. These criticisms challenge Berkeley's strong idealism that a physical world or objects could not exist.
   b. In the case of weak idealism, do we really have *no* reason for believing they do not exist? When we start a fire, leave it for a while and return to find it burned down, isn't that some reason to believe that the physical world exists unperceived?

E. Conclusions.
   1. Is Berkeley crazy and all his arguments worthless?
   2. He showed us that we cannot return to naïve realism because perception is a very complex process.
   3. Berkeley also refuted or successfully challenged most of Locke's theories.

V. Phenomenalism.
   A. Its major tenet is "to be is to be perceivable."
   B. It accepts the existence of the physical world and its objects and states that this existence provides the "possibility of perception."
   C. It also believes that we do not perceive physical objects directly but only indirectly.
   D. Three levels of reality for the phenomenalist:

1. The perceiver, experiencer, or knower.
2. The act or process of perceiving—sensation.
3. The "thing or object perceived."

E. What we actually perceive, according to phenomenalism.
1. Not physical objects directly, or only our own experiences, but sense data.
2. We see these whether or not we are having illusions, hallucinations, or dreams or are perceiving physical objects—what we see in all these cases are sense data.
3. We all perceive the same physical object, for example, but we do not all perceive the same sense data.
   a. First, there are as many sense data being perceived as there are perceivers; that is, our sense data are numerically different.
   b. Second, we perceive the object from different angles, from different distances, and with different sense organs; therefore, our perceptions differ even though the object might be the same.
4. We really *do* see our sense data whether they are veridical or not, that is, whether or not they constitute true perceptions of the object. They are veridical in themselves in that we do really see the "bent stick," whether it is really bent or not.

F. Evaluation of this theory.
1. This seems in many ways more reasonable then naïve realism, representative realism, or idealism since it accepts the difficulty of knowing whether our perceptions of the physical world are accurate or not and the fact that we could never really know this.
2. It also allows for a middle point between the extremes of realism and idealism.
3. It does have its problems, however.
4. Relationships. What are the relationships among the three levels of reality in phenomenalism? Second, what is the relationship between sense data and physical objects?
5. Causation. What causes sense data?
   a. Is it caused by the physical object being struck by light and then impinging itself on our sense apparatus?
   b. Phenomenalists do not believe that God causes them in the Berkeleian sense.
   c. If sense data are caused by other sense data, then what causes the original or first sense data?
   d. If there is a combination of causes, what would that combination be?

V. Conclusions.
   A. Perception is very complex and not readily understandable or provable.
   B. Accepting the existence of a physical world and its objects seems to be the best story, but we cannot prove it.
   C. We cannot know that our perceptions are an accurate view of the external world because we cannot compare them with the world unperceived.
   D. What we perceive is highly dependent on how our sense organs are constructed, how well they work, and the conditions for observing the physical world.
   E. We know that our sense experiences or perceptions of physical objects are not the same as the objects themselves, and by nature they must be two different things.
   F. We do not know what the connection between perceptions and physical objects is, nor do we know what causes us to have perceptions or to perceive things as we do.
   G. Perception is a very complicated area of our existence, and continued research and investigation should be done.

Additional Questions and Activities for Study and Discussion

1. Referring again to Akutagawa's "In a Grove" or the film *Rashomon,* to what extent do you find the problems in the various conflicting witness reports in the story due to problems in perception? What kind of problems? Specify in detail. To what extent do your conclusions support any or all of the theories of perception we have discussed in this chapter? Which ones and how?

2. Referring to the character of Willy Loman in Arthur Miller's *Death of a Salesman,* how are his confusions between illusion and reality due to perceptual problems? Describe in detail the extent to which Willy is perceiving the physical world and its objects and the extent to which he is having illusions, hallucinations, and dreams. Be specific and support your claims with examples from the play.

3. Read Berkeley's *Three Dialogues Between Hylas and Philonous* and any commentaries on them you wish, and, regardless of how you feel about his theories, argue *in favor of them* from your modern-day perspective. Afterward, attack your own and Berkeley's arguments, again from your modern-day perspective.

4. Read and critically evaluate G. E. Moore's essay, "The Refutation of Idealism," in his *Philosophical Studies.* To what extent do you

agree or disagree with him? Do you feel that his views in that essay are still applicable to the present? Why or why not?

5. Do a complete and critical analysis and evaluation of the beliefs of naïve realism. Do you continue to believe any of them after doing this? Which ones and why? Which ones don't you believe and why? How would you restate these beliefs to coincide with what you feel perception really is and how it relates to the physical world and its objects? Support your beliefs with evidence and argument whenever you can.

6. Present as clear and concise an argument as you can supporting your theory of what causes us to perceive things as we do. What parts do our sense organs, brains, minds, emotions, physical objects themselves, and other external events, such as light, play in this process? To what extent can you supply evidence and reasoning to support your contentions? Support your views as fully as you can.

7. We all dream, daydream, and imagine things and events "in our minds," where there is no physical object to which they can be related. How would you describe this aspect of the process of perception? Do we really perceive them "in our mind's eye" or what (what is our "mind's eye?")? Some of them are, of course, due to memory, but what is that? Many of them have very little to do either with perceptions of the outside world or with memory—how can they be accounted for? Explain these processes as well as you can supporting your positions with evidence, arguments, and examples wherever you can. Do any research you wish or that is suggested by your instructor on these matters.

8. Select an art form to which you can relate and find meaningful (painting, sculpture, architecture, music, drama, fiction, poetry, film, dance, photography) and an especially meaningful example of it (to you) and analzye what exactly you *perceive* when you are experiencing it. Art is generally considered as more than just shape, colors, sounds, movements, and structure. Even though you perceive some or all of these things—and so describe what you do perceive in this sense—what else do you perceive, if anything? In other words, is there more to perception in connection with the arts than just perceiving physical objects in all of their aspects? Does this mean there is also more to perception in everyday life than just these things? Answer this question as fully as you can.

9. Examine a short segment (no more than 5 minutes) of your process of perceiving and describe what happens in this process at perception levels I, II, and III as accurately as you can. Do you find any other levels of perception in the process? If so, explain what they are. If not, explain how the process works among the

three levels—is there a moving back and forth, for example, or does your perception always go from I to II to III? Give plentiful examples of this process as clearly as you can. What exactly are you perceiving at the different levels, especially level 1?

10. Dr. Samuel Johnson (1709–1784) when told about Berkeley's theories about perception and the physical world, and especially that no physical world or objects existed unperceived, kicked a stone in front of him and said, "I refute him thus!" To what extent did he refute Berkeley's theories and to what extent did he prove them? How and in what way? Be specific in your answers. To what extent does the TV camera and video machine left running in a room where there are no sentient beings disprove Berkeley's theories? Be specific in your answer. If neither of these can disprove his theories, what does, if anything?

Footnotes

1. Once more I am deep in John Hospers' debt. He presented these levels of perception in a lecture in February 1969 at the University of Southern California. The designations are mine, however; Hospers used See[0], See[1], and See[2].

2. John Hospers, *An Introduction to Philosophical Analysis,* 2nd ed. (Englewood Cliffs, N.J.: Prentice-Hall, 1967), p. 494.

3. Ibid., pp. 506–507.

4. Ibid., pp. 508–509.

5. Ibid., Hospers uses the word "veridical" on p. 510.

6. Ibid., pp. 514–517.

7. Ibid., p. 518.

8. Ibid., p. 520.

9. Ibid.

10. Ibid., pp. 522–523.

11. Ibid., pp. 525–526.

Bibliography

Armstrong, D. M. *Perception and the Physical World.* London: Routledge and Kegan Paul, 1961.

Arner, Douglas C., ed. *Perception, Reason, and Knowledge: An Introduction to Epistemology.* New York: Scott, Foresman, 1972.

Austin, John L. *Sense and Sensibilia.* London: Oxford University Press, 1962.

Ayer, A. J. *Foundations of Empirical Knowledge.* New York: Macmillan, 1940, Chaps. 1, 2, and 5.

————. *The Problem of Knowledge.* New York: Macmillan, 1956.

Berkeley, George. "Three Dialogues Between Hylas and Philonus," in *The Works of George Berkeley,* ed. A. C. Fraser Oxford: Clarendon, 1901.

Chisolm, Roderick. *Perceiving: A Philosophical Study.* Ithaca, N.Y.: Cornell University Press, 1957.

Hirst, R. J. *The Problem of Perception*. London: Allen and Unwin, 1959.

Lean, Martin, E. *Sense-Perception and Matter*. London: Routledge and Kegan Paul, 1953.

Locke, John. *An Essay Concerning Human Understanding,* eds. J. W. Tolton and A. O. Woozley, 2 vols. New York: Dutton, 1973.

Malcolm, Norman. *Dreaming*. London: Routledge and Kegan Paul, 1959.

————. *Knowledge and Certainty*. Englewood Cliffs, N.J.: Prentice-Hall, 1963.

Moore, G. E. *Philosophical Studies*. London: Routledge and Kegan Paul, 1922.

————. *Philosophical Papers*. New York: Collier, 1962, Chaps. 2 and 7.

————. *Some Main Problems of Philosophy*. New York: Collier, 1962.

Nagel, Ernest, and Richard B. Brandt, eds. *Meaning and Knowledge*. New York: Harcourt, 1965, Chaps. 8 and 9.

Price, H. H. *Perception*. London: Metheun, 1933.

————. *Hume's Theory of the External World*. London: Oxford University Press, 1940.

Prichard, H. A. *Knowledge and Perception*. London: Oxford University Press, 1950.

Reichenbach, Hans. *Experience and Prediction*. Chicago: University of Chicago Press, 1938.

Russell, Bertrand. *The Problems of Philosophy*. London: Oxford University Press, 1912, Chaps. 1–5.

————. *Our Knowledge of the External World*. New York: Mentor, 1960.

Sellers, Wilfred. *Science, Perception, and Reality*. New York: Humanities Press, 1963.

Swartz, Robert J., ed. *Perceiving, Sensing, and Knowing: A Book of Readings from Twentieth-Century Sources in the Philosophy of Perception*. Garden City, N.Y.: Anchor, 1965.

Urban, Wilbur M. *Beyond Realism and Idealism*. London: Allen and Unwin, 1949.

Warnock, G. J., ed. *The Philosophy of Perception*. London: Oxford University Press, 1967.

6

Personal Philosophy

CHAPTER 16

Establishing a Personal Philosophy and World View

This chapter, unlike previous ones, is designed specifically to help you to systematically apply what you have studied and learned in the other parts and chapters of this book and also in other areas of your education (the sciences, social sciences, the arts, and religion) and experience, to establish your own personal philosophy and world view. Two things should be kept in mind in thinking about and actually working toward establishing your philosophy and world view: (1) there is a wide diversity of alternatives and possibilities to choose from and (2) your personal philosophy is not a static thing, carved in stone, but something that should be vital, creative, growing, and livable.

Alternatives

Students are not limited to their own societal or particular family traditions in deciding what view of any aspect of their lives and the world makes the most sense and is the most workable for them. There is a wide number of alternatives from which to choose, to combine, or to reject (after having investigated them) in all the major areas we have studied.

METAPHYSICS: THEORIES OF REALITY

First, there are many theories of what reality is: materialism, realism, idealism, phenomenalism, and dualism. Second, these theories are all related to the crucial metaphysical questions dealing with the existence and relationships of body, brain, mind, self, emotions, and will.

ETHICS: THEORIES OF MORALITY

In the area of ethics, the study of morality, one needs to consider and investigate self-interest versus other interestedness, the act versus rule approach to morality, reason versus emotions, religious versus secular morality, and his positions on various important moral issues, such as killing, stealing, and lying.

EPISTEMOLOGY: THEORIES OF KNOWLEDGE

In this area of investigation, one should first examine the various sources of knowledge and determine their reliability as far as gaining significant knowledge is concerned. Second, one should examine the theories of what truth is to determine which one or ones are most valid in determining truth and falsity. Third, one needs to determine what constitutes knowledge and how it differs from belief and opinion and also whether or not there is any possibility of attaining certain knowledge. Last, there are several theories of perception, including realism, idealism, and phenomenalism, that should be examined and critically evaluated.

PHILOSOPHY OF RELIGION

In the area of religion, one needs to know what the sources of religion are, what the nature of religion is, and what the various religious and nonreligious alternatives are. Also, one needs to come to grips with the question of whether or not there is an Ultimate Reality and what its nature is.

OTHER AREAS OF INVESTIGATION

There are also other areas such as political science, the natural and physical sciences, the arts, and social relationships that are related directly or indirectly to most of the major areas cited but will often require special investigation and evaluation.

How to Organize Your Personal Philosophy Systematically

HOW TO BEGIN

You have been exposed to a lot, so you must take things piece by piece and step by step and put them together. In approaching the setting up of your personal philosophy and world view, you should refer back to Chapters 1 and 2 to refresh yourselves on what philosophy is and does and also on how to read it, write it, and use your reasoning logically and effectively. In addition,

1. Examine every area of your life affected by a particular aspect of philosophy (metaphysics, epistemology, ethics, and philosophy of religion).
2. Apply good investigative techniques.
3. Use good rules of logic and avoid fallacies.
4. Organize your data and classify it carefully (evidence, arguments, propositions).
5. Critically evaluate the various positions, avoiding both unnecessary and invalid reductionism and expansionism.
6. Synthesize alternative viewpoints wherever possible and where it is useful to do so; in this way, you can keep the best of alternative viewpoints and eliminate their weaknesses and problems.
7. At different points during this process, *write down* your deliberations and your assumptions, principles, and positions on the various issues.
8. Review what you have written periodically and update it. You should review it *at least* once each year. Do not consider what you have written as "engraved in marble"; rather, allow for valid and justified changes to your philosophy.
9. Add your comments on anything new that happens, either in your life or in society, your nation, or the world (for example, a war, crime wave, approach to poverty, and so on). Try to keep your philosophy practical and applicable to your life and the events in it.

SPECIFICS ON WHAT TO DO

You can, of course, start with any of the major areas and develop your ideas and views on them, but I would suggest that you start with epistemology since what you do in other areas of your philosophy will depend heavily on your views of knowledge, truth, and belief.

543

EPISTEMOLOGY.　In this area of your investigations, you should

1. Evaluate the various theories of truth, and decide how you can know what truth and falsity are and how you know when you have attained them. To do this, analyze and evaluate your acceptance or nonacceptance of the truth or falsity of the major propositions in your everyday life.
2. Evaluate for yourself the reliability of the various sources of knowledge.
3. Determine the extent and limitations of your own knowledge and human knowledge in general.
4. Clarify for yourself the systematic process you will use to attain knowledge. In this last respect, examine, evaluate, and decide which theory or combination of theories of perception you find most useful and valid.

METAPHYSICS.　Since you are a part of reality and since you must feel that the external world and others are also a part of it, do the following:

1. Examine the world, yourself, and others carefully.
2. Examine the theories of materialism, realism, idealism, phenomenalism, and dualism to see if and how they relate to what you have experienced as you have examined the world, others, and yourself.
3. Critically evaluate them and try to establish a tentative world view that includes
   a. A view of the external world and the objects in it, other than human beings.
   b. A definitive and workable view of the nature of a human being (body, brain, mind, self, emotions, spirit, and will).
4. Decide what your position is on the problem of determinism and freedom, especially where human moral responsibility is concerned.

ETHICS.　In working with this most important area of human relationships, do the following:

1. Decide what your basic moral principles are and why—be sure to justify them rationally and fully.
2. Decide how to work with the act versus rule approach to morality, that is, ask yourself the question, "To what extent should morality be left up to the individuals and to what extent should individual freedom be restricted and limited by rules?" Consider the implications of emphasizing either extreme of the issue.

3. Decide which of the moral theories, or combination of them, will best suit your method of dealing with and resolving specific moral issues.
4. Apply your morality systematically to important moral issues, such as lying, cheating, stealing, breaking promises; taking human life (suicide, mercy killing, war, defense of the innocent, abortion, and capital punishment); morality in human sexuality (premarital sex, adultery, homosexuality, pornography, rape, and child molestation); and racial, religious, and sexual discrimination or prejudice.
5. Decide how you will allow for tolerance of other people's value systems that conflict with yours, and yet how there can be some kind of workable stability among all moral systems.
6. Decide how you can apply your morality to other societal areas, such as politics, law, business, education, religion, medicine, family life, and child rearing.

PHILOSOPHY OF RELIGION.   In this area of investigation, whether you are religious or not, you should

1. Decide to what extent your own personal religious feeling is important to you and how it best can be expressed.
2. Examine the arguments for and against the existence of an ultimate reality and make a choice from theism (in all of its forms), atheism (religious and nonreligious), agnosticism, deism, and secular humanism or any combinations you choose.
3. Decide, in conjunction with the foregoing, what you believe the nature of the Ultimate Reality to be, as specifically as you can.
4. Examine as many organized religions, both Eastern and Western, to decide which, if any, either individually or in combination help you best express your own personal religious feeling.
5. Decide how freedom of choice in religious and nonreligious matters and how religious tolerance can be worked into your system effectively.
   a. In this respect, ask yourself how you can have a strong commitment yourself and yet still allow other people religious freedom.
   b. Also decide how you can allow tolerance both for other religious views *and* also nonreligious views.

WORK AT YOUR PHILOSOPHY.   Work at your philosophy continually and consistently and apply it every chance you get. Make it as vital, livable, and workable as you can.

Personal Philosophy Paper

In lieu of the various "Situations for Thought and Discussion" with which I have ended each previous chapter, I am including here a suggested format for writing a personal philosophy paper that may be the first step in your lifelong task of developing your own philosophy and world view. It can also provide your instructor with a means of discovering how well you are able to apply what you have learned about philosophy during his or her course of instruction.

GENERAL DIRECTIONS CONCERNING THE PAPER.   In answering the following basic question, please be as honest and sincere as you can. Also remember that beliefs not supported with evidence or reasoning are not philosophically sound, so do your best to present your philosophy rationally, giving evidence, illustrations, and examples from sense experience or supporting your beliefs through reasoning wherever possible.

THE BASIC QUESTION.   Based on the ideas you have read, heard, and discussed during this course and all your experiences to date, what is your own personal philosophy, and why, and how do you plan to live this philosophy, or how do you actually live this philosophy in everyday life? Consider seriously the following questions as suggested guidelines for answering the basic question:

1. What is your view of knowledge, belief, and truth?
   a. What do you know with some or absolute certainty?
   b. What basic "truths" can you say you know?
   c. What basic "truths" do you live by and why?
   d. What for you is real, or what is reality? Again, how do you know?
   e. What parts do reason and emotion play in your personal philosophy? Should one be emphasized over the other? Which and why? Should there be a balance of the two? Why and how?
2. What is your view of what the nature of a human being is and why?
   a. Are human beings merely bodies and brains or is there more to them? If there is more, then what is it? Be specific and explain clearly.
   b. What part or parts do mind, emotions, soul, and will play in your description of what the nature of human beings is? Why?
   c. Is there a self or not? If not, then how do you account for human personality? If there is, then what is its nature, where does it come from, and how does it develop? Answer in detail.

546

    d. What do you feel human beings' relationship to the external world is or should be, and why?

    e. What part does freedom play in your personal philosophy *and* why? To what extent do you believe human beings are free or determined? Be specific.

3. What is your ethical system and why?

    a. What basic principle or principles do you go by in dealing with moral issues, and why?

    b. How do you incorporate other people's rights and freedoms to set up and act on their own moral systems into your system? How do you propose that freedoms be limited so that people may pursue their own values without harming other people?

    c. How do you think you should treat other human beings, and how do you think they ought to treat you, and why?

    d. How would you apply your moral system to any of the following moral issues: abortion, mercy killing, lying, stealing, premarital sex, adultery, homosexuality, pornography, capital punishment, war, suicide, and race, religious, and sex discrimination?

4. What is your basic stand on religion?

    a. Do you believe there is an Ultimate Reality of some kind or not? Why or why not? On what do you base your beliefs? What is its nature, and how do you know?

    b. Do you believe there is an afterlife or not? Why or why not?

    c. How does tolerance fit with your version of religion or nonreligion? To what extent should other people be allowed to believe or disbelieve in a supernatural being, beings, or life? If you believe your religion is the one true one, then how can you be tolerant of others and those who do not believe in God, and so on?

    d. Do you believe that a person must be religious to be moral? Why or why not?

    e. If you are religious, how do you reconcile the problem of evil in the world with the fact that God is at the same time all good and all powerful?

    f. In dealing with all the foregoing, use sense experience and reasoning as much as possible to support your answers—arguments such as "the Bible says so" are not sufficient evidence *in themselves* for your views (why the Bible rather than the Koran or the Buddhist tenets, etc.?).

5. What is your main purpose or goal in life? Do you think human beings in general have a purpose for being in the world? If so, how does it coincide with your purpose? How does it differ? If not, why not?

Bibliography

It is quite difficult to establish a proper bibliography for personal philosophy, but some of the following are suggestions that may aid you in examining human nature and the nature of the world. In addition, I refer you to the bibliographies at the end of any chapter about any topic on which you are thinking and writing:

Arendt, Hannah. *The Human Condition*. Chicago: University of Chicago Press, 1958.
Bronowski, Jacob. *The Identity of Man*. New York: Natural History Press, 1971.
Buber, Martin. *I and Thou*. New York: Scribners, 1958.
Fromm, Erich, and Ramon Xirau, eds. *The Nature of Man*. New York: Macmillan, 1968.
Hesse, Hermann. *Siddhartha,* trans. Hilda Rosner. New York: New Directions, 1951.
———. *Magister Ludi (The Glass Bead Game)*. New York: Bantam, 1970.
Tillich, Paul. *The Courage to Be*. New Haven, Conn.: Yale University Press, 1952.
———. *Dynamics of Faith*. New York: Harper, 1957.

Index